T3-BPE-229

Interest Rate, Term Structure, and Valuation Modeling

THE FRANK J. FABOZZI SERIES

Fixed Income Securities, Second Edition by Frank J. Fabozzi
Focus on Value: A Corporate and Investor Guide to Wealth Creation by James L. Grant and James A. Abate
Handbook of Global Fixed Income Calculations by Dragomir Krgin
Managing a Corporate Bond Portfolio by Leland E. Crabbe and Frank J. Fabozzi
Real Options and Option-Embedded Securities by William T. Moore
Capital Budgeting: Theory and Practice by Pamela P. Peterson and Frank J. Fabozzi
The Exchange-Traded Funds Manual by Gary L. Gastineau
Professional Perspectives on Fixed Income Portfolio Management, Volume 3 edited by Frank J. Fabozzi
Investing in Emerging Fixed Income Markets edited by Frank J. Fabozzi and Efstathia Pilarinu
Handbook of Alternative Assets by Mark J. P. Anson
The Exchange-Traded Funds Manual by Gary L. Gastineau
The Global Money Markets by Frank J. Fabozzi, Steven V. Mann, and Moorad Choudhry
The Handbook of Financial Instruments edited by Frank J. Fabozzi
Collateralized Debt Obligations: Structures and Analysis by Laurie S. Goodman and Frank J. Fabozzi

Interest Rate, Term Structure, and Valuation Modeling

FRANK J. FABOZZI

EDITOR

John Wiley & Sons, Inc.

Published by John Wiley & Sons, Inc., Hoboken, New Jersey
Published simultaneously in Canada

For general information on our other products and services, or technical support, please contact our Customer Care Department within the United States at 800-762-2974, outside the United States at 317-572-3993 or fax 317-572-4002.

Wiley also publishes its books in a variety of electronic formats. Some content that appears in print may not be available in electronic books.

ISBN: 0-471-22094-9

Printed in the United States of America

10 9 8 7 6 5 4 3 2 1

contents

preface

The valuation of fixed-income securities and interest rate derivatives, from the most simple structures to the complex structures found in the structured finance and interest rate derivatives markets, depends on the interest rate model and term structure model used by the investor. *Interest Rate, Term Structure, and Valuation Modeling* provides a comprehensive practitioner-oriented treatment of the various interest rate models, term structure models, and valuation models.

The book is divided into three sections. Section One covers interest rate and term structure modeling. In Chapter 1, Oren Cheyette provides an overview of the principles of valuation algorithms and the characteristics that distinguish the various interest rate models. He then describes the empirical evidence on interest rate dynamics, comparing a family of interest rate models that closely match those in common use. The coverage emphasizes those issues that are of principal interest to practitioners in applying interest rate models. As Cheyette states: "There is little point in having the theoretically ideal model if it can't actually be implemented as part of a valuation algorithm."

In Chapter 2, Peter Fitton and James McNatt clarify some of the commonly misunderstood issues associated with interest rate models. Specifically, they focus on (1) the choice between an arbitrage-free and an equilibrium model and (2) the choice between risk neutral and realistic parameterizations of a model. Based on these choices, they classify interest rate models into four categories and then explain the proper use of each category of interest rate model.

Stochastic differential equations (SDE) are typically used to model interest rates. In a one-factor model, an SDE is used to represent the short rate; in two-factor models an SDE is used for both the short rate and the long rate. In Chapter 3 Gerald Buetow, James Sochacki, and I review no-arbitrage interest rate models highlighting some significant differences across models. The most significant differences are those due to the underlying distribution and, as we stress in the chapter, indicates the need to calibrate models to the market prior to their use. The models covered are the Ho-Lee model, the Hull-White model, the Kalotay-

Williams-Fabozzi model, and the Black-Derman-Toy model. The binomial and trinomial formulations of these models are presented.

Moorad Choudhry presents in Chapter 4 an accessible account of the various term structure theories that have been advanced to explain the shape of the yield curve at any time. While no one theory explains the term structure at all times, a combination of two of these serve to explain the yield curve for most applications.

In Chapter 5, David Audley, Richard Chin, and Shrikant Ramamurthy review the approaches to term structure modeling and then present an eclectic mixture of ideas for term structure modeling. After describing some fundamental concepts of the term structure of interest rates and developing a useful set of static term structure models, they describe the approaches to extending these into dynamic models. They begin with the discrete-time modeling approach and then build on the discussion by introducing the continuous-time analogies to the concepts developed for discrete-time modeling. Finally, Audley, Chin, and Ramamurthy describe the dynamic term structure model.

The swap term structure is a key benchmark for pricing and hedging purposes. In Chapter 6, Uri Ron details all the issues associated with the swap term structure derivation procedure. The approach presented by Ron leaves the user with enough flexibility to adjust the constructed term structure to the specific micro requirements and constraints of each primary swap market.

There have been several techniques proposed for fitting the term structure with the technique selected being determined by the requirements specified by the user. In general, curve fitting techniques can be classified into two types. The first type models the yield curve using a parametric function and is therefore referred to as a parametric technique. The second type uses a spline technique, a technique for approximating the market discount function. In Chapter 7, Rod Pienaar and Moorad Choudhry discuss the spline technique, focussing on cubic splines and how to implement the technique in practice.

Critical to an interest rate model is the assumed yield volatility or term structure of yield volatility. Volatility is measured in terms of the standard deviation or variance. In Chapter 8, Wai Lee and I look at how to measure and forecast yield volatility and the implementation issues related to estimating yield volatility using observed daily percentage changes in yield. We then turn to models for forecasting volatility, reviewing the latest statistical techniques that can be employed.

The three chapters in Section Two explain how to quantify fixed-income risk. Factor models are used for this purpose. Empirical evidence indicates that the change in the level and shape of the yield curve are the major source of risk for a fixed-income portfolio. The risk associated with changes in the level and shape of the yield curve are referred to as term structure risk. In Chapter 9, Robert Kuberek reviews some of the leading approaches to term structure factor modeling (arbitrage models, principal component models, and spot rate and functional models), provides the examples of each type of term structure factor model, and explains the advantages and disadvantages of each.

While the major source of risk for a fixed-income portfolio is term structure risk, there are other sources of risk that must be accounted for in order to assess a portfolio's risk profile relative to a benchmark index. These non-term structure risks include sector risk, optionality risk, prepayment risk, quality risk, and volatility risk. Moreover, the risk of a portfolio relative to a benchmark index is measured in terms of tracking risk. In Chapter 10, Lev Dynkin and Jay Hyman present a multi-factor risk model that includes all of these risks and demonstrates how the model can be used to construct a portfolio, rebalance a portfolio, and control a portfolio's risk profile relative to a benchmark.

A common procedure used by portfolio and risk managers to assess the risk of a portfolio is to shift or "shock" the yield curve. The outcome of this analysis is an assessment of a portfolio's exposure to term structure risk. However, there is a wide range of potential yield curve shocks that a manager can analyze. In Chapter 11, Bennet Golub and Leo Tilman provide a framework for defining and measuring the historical plausibility of a given yield curve shock.

Section Three covers the approaches to valuation and the measurement of option-adjusted spread (OAS). Valuation models are often referred to as OAS models. In the first chapter of Section III, Chapter 12, Philip Obazee explains the basic building blocks for a valuation model.

In Chapter 13, Andrew Kalotay, Michael Dorigan, and I demonstrate how an arbitrage-free interest rate lattice is constructed and how the lattice can be used to value an option-free bond. In Chapter 14, we apply the lattice-based valuation approach to the valuation of bonds with embedded options (callable bonds and putable bonds), floaters, options, and caps/floors. In Chapter 15, Gerald Buetow and I apply the lattice-based valuation approach to value forward start swaps and swaptions. A methodology for applying the lattice-based valuation approach to value path-dependent securities is provided by Douglas Howard in Chapter 16.

The Monte Carlo simulation approach to valuing residential mortgage-backed securities—agency products (passthroughs, collateralized mortgage obligations, and mortgage strips), nonagency products, and real-estate backed asset-backed securities (home equity loan and manufactured housing loan-backed deals) is demonstrated by Scott Richard, David Horowitz, and me in Chapter 17. An alternative to the Monte Carlo simulation approach for valuing mortgage products is presented in Chapter 18 by Alexander Levin. The approach he suggests uses low-dimensional grids.

In the last chapter, Chapter 19, the effect of mean reversion on the value of a security and the option-adjusted spread is discussed by David Audley and Richard Chin.

I believe this book will be a valuable reference source for practitioners who need to understand the critical elements in the valuation of fixed-income securities and interest rate derivatives and the measurement of interest rate risk.

I wish to thank the authors of the chapters for their contributions. A book of this type by its very nature requires the input of specialists in a wide range of technical topics and I believe that I have assembled some of the finest in the industry.

Frank J. Fabozzi

contributing authors

David Audley	Consultant
Gerald W. Buetow, Jr.	BFRC Services, LLC
Oren Cheyette	BARRA, Inc.
Richard Chin	Consultant
Moorad Choudhry	City University Business School
Michael Dorigan	Andrew Kalotay Associates
Lev Dynkin	Lehman Brothers
Frank J. Fabozzi	Yale University
Peter Fitton	Neuristics Consulting, a Division of Trade, Inc.
Bennett W. Golub	BlackRock Financial Management, Inc.
David S. Horowitz	Miller, Anderson & Sherrerd
C. Douglas Howard	Baruch College, CUNY
Jay Hyman	Lehman Brothers
Andrew Kalotay	Andrew Kalotay Associates
Robert C. Kuberek	Wilshire Associates Incorporated
Wai Lee	J.P. Morgan Investment Management Inc.
Alexander Levin	Andrew Davidson and Co.
James F. McNatt	InCap Group, Inc.
Philip O. Obazee	Delaware Investments
Rod Pienaar	Deutsche Bank AG, London
Shrikant Ramamurthy	Greenwich Capital
Scott F. Richard	Miller, Anderson & Sherrerd
Uri Ron	Bank of Canada
James Sochacki	James Madison University
Leo M. Tilman	Bear, Stearns & Co., Inc.

SECTION
one

Interest Rate and Term Structure Modeling

CHAPTER 1

Interest Rate Models

Oren Cheyette, Ph.D.
Vice President
Fixed Income Research
BARRA, Inc.

An interest rate model is a probabilistic description of the future evolution of interest rates. Based on today's information, future interest rates are uncertain: An interest rate model is a characterization of that uncertainty. Quantitative analysis of securities with rate dependent cash flows requires application of such a model in order to find the present value of the uncertainty. Since virtually all financial instruments other than default- and option-free bonds have interest rate sensitive cash flows, this matters to most fixed-income portfolio managers and actuaries, as well as to traders and users of interest rate derivatives.

For financial instrument valuation and risk estimation one wants to use only models that are arbitrage free and matched to the currently observed term structure of interest rates. "Arbitrage free" means just that if one values the same cash flows in two different ways, one should get the same result. For example, a 10-year bond putable at par by the holder in 5 years can also be viewed as a 5-year bond with an option of the holder to extend the maturity for another 5 years. An arbitrage-free model will produce the same value for the structure viewed either way. This is also known as the *law of one price*. The term structure matching condition means that when a default-free straight bond is valued according to the model, the result should be the same as if the bond's cash flows are simply discounted according to the current default-free term structure. A model that fails to satisfy either of these conditions cannot be trusted for general problems, though it may be usable in some limited context.

For equity derivatives, lognormality of prices (leading to the Black-Scholes formula for calls and puts) is the standard starting point for option calculations. In the fixed-income market, unfortunately, there is no equally natural and simple assumption. Wall Street dealers routinely use a multiplicity of models based on widely varying assumptions in different markets. For example, an options desk most likely uses a version of the Black formula to value interest rate caps and floors, implying an approximately lognormal distribution of interest rates. A few feet away, the mortgage desk may use a normal interest rate model to evaluate their passthrough and CMO durations. And on the next floor, actuaries may use variants of both types of models to analyze their annuities and insurance policies.

It may seem that one's major concern in choosing an interest rate model should be the accuracy with which it represents the empirical volatility of the term structure of rates, and its ability to fit market prices of vanilla derivatives such as at-the-money caps and swaptions. These are clearly important criteria, but they are not decisive. The first criterion is hard to pin down, depending strongly on what historical period one chooses to examine. The second criterion is easy to satisfy for most commonly used models, by the simple (though unappealing) expedient of permitting predicted future volatility to be time dependent. So, while important, this concern doesn't really do much to narrow the choices.

A critical issue in selecting an interest rate model is, instead, ease of application. For some models it is difficult or impossible to provide efficient valuation algorithms for all financial instruments of interest to a typical investor. Given that one would like to analyze all financial instruments using the same underlying assumptions, this is a significant problem. At the same time, one would prefer not to stray too far from economic reasonableness—such as by using the Black-Scholes formula to value callable bonds. These considerations lead to a fairly narrow menu of choices among the known interest rate models.

The organization of this chapter is as follows. In the next section I provide a (brief) discussion of the principles of valuation algorithms. This will give a context for many of the points made in the third section, which provides an overview of the various characteristics that differentiate interest rate models. Finally, in the fourth section I describe the empirical evidence on interest rate dynamics and provide a quantitative comparison of a family of models that closely match those in common use. I have tried to emphasize those issues that are primarily of interest for application of the models in practical settings. There is little point in having the theoretically ideal model if it can't actually be implemented as part of a valuation algorithm.

VALUATION

Valuation algorithms for rate dependent contingent claims are usually based on a risk neutral formula, which states that the present value of an uncertain cash flow at time T is given by the average over all interest rate scenarios of the scenario cash flow divided by the scenario value at time T of a money market investment of \$1 today.[1] More formally, the value of a security is given by the expectation (average) over interest rate scenarios

$$P = E\left[\sum_i \frac{C_i}{M_i}\right] \tag{1}$$

where C_i is the security's cash flows and M_i is the money market account value at time t_i in each scenario, calculated by assuming continual reinvestment at the prevailing short rate.

The probability weights used in the average are chosen so that the expected rate of return on any security over the next instant is the same, namely the short rate. These are the so-called "risk neutral" probability weights: They would be the true weights if investors were indifferent to bearing interest rate risk. In that case, investors would demand no excess return relative to a (riskless) money market account in order to hold risky positions—hence equation (1).

It is important to emphasize that the valuation formula is not dependent on any *assumption* of risk neutrality. Financial instruments are valued by equation (1) *as if* the market were indifferent to interest rate risk *and* the correct discount factor for a future cash flow were the inverse of the money market return. Both statements are false for the real world, but the errors are offsetting: A valuation formula based on probabilities implying a nonzero market price of interest rate risk and the corresponding scenario discount factors would give the same value.

There are two approaches to computing the average in equation (1): by direct brute force evaluation, or indirectly by solving a related differential equation. The brute force method is usually called the Monte Carlo method. It consists of generating a large number of possible interest rate scenarios based on the interest rate model, computing the cash flows and money market values in each one, and averaging. Properly speaking, only path generation based on random numbers is a Monte Carlo method. There are other scenario methods—e.g., complete sampling of a tree—that do not depend on the use of random numbers.

[1] The money market account is the *numeraire*.

Given sufficient computer resources, the scenario method can tackle essentially any type of financial instrument.[2]

A variety of schemes are known for choosing scenario sample paths efficiently, but none of them are even remotely as fast and accurate as the second technique. In certain cases (discussed in more detail in the next section) the average in equation (1) obeys a partial differential equation—like the one derived by Black and Scholes for equity options—for which there exist fast and accurate numerical solution methods, or in special cases even analytical solutions. This happens only for interest rate models of a particular type, and then only for certain security types, such as caps, floors, swaptions, and options on bonds. For securities such as mortgage passthroughs, CMOs, index amortizing swaps, and for some insurance policies and annuities, simulation methods are the only alternative.

MODEL TAXONOMY

The last two decades have seen the development of a tremendous profusion of models for valuation of interest rate sensitive financial instruments. In order to better understand these models, it is helpful to recognize a number of features that characterize and distinguish them. These are features of particular relevance to practitioners wishing to implement valuation algorithms, as they render some models completely unsuitable for certain types of financial instruments.[3] The following subsections enumerate some of the major dimensions of variation among the different models.

One- versus Multi-Factor

In many cases, the value of an interest rate contingent claim depends, effectively, on the prices of many underlying assets. For example, while the payoff of a caplet depends only on the reset date value of a zero coupon bond maturing at the payment date (valued based on, say, 3-month LIBOR), the payoff to an option on a coupon bond depends on the exercise date values of all of the bond's remaining interest and principal payments. Valuation of such an option is in principle an inherently multidimensional problem.

Fortunately, in practice these values are highly correlated. The degree of correlation can be quantified by examining the covariance matrix of

[2] This is true even for American options. For a review see P. Boyle, M. Broadie, and P. Glasserman, "Monte Carlo Methods for Security Pricing," *Journal of Economic Dynamics and Control* (1997), pp. 1267–1322.

[3] There is, unfortunately, a version of Murphy's law applicable to interest rate models, which states that the computational tractability of a model is inversely proportional to its economic realism.

changes in spot rates of different maturities. A principal component analysis of the covariance matrix decomposes the motion of the spot curve into independent (uncorrelated) components. The largest principal component describes a common shift of all interest rates in the same direction. The next leading components are a twist, with short rates moving one way and long rates the other, and a "butterfly" motion, with short and long rates moving one way, and intermediate rates the other. Based on analysis of weekly data from the Federal Reserve H15 series of benchmark Treasury yields from 1983 through 1995, the shift component accounts for 84% of the total variance of spot rates, while twist and butterfly account for 11% and 4%, leaving about 1% for all remaining principal components.

The shift factor alone explains a large fraction of the overall movement of spot rates. As a result, valuation can be reduced to a one factor problem in many instances with little loss of accuracy. Only securities whose payoffs are primarily sensitive to the shape of the spot curve rather than its overall level (such as dual index floaters, which depend on the difference between a long and a short rate) will not be modeled well with this approach.

In principle it is straightforward to move from a one-factor model to a multi-factor one. In practice, though, implementations of multi-factor valuation models can be complicated and slow, and require estimation of many more volatility and correlation parameters than are needed for one-factor models, so there may be some benefit to using a one-factor model when possible. The remainder of this chapter will focus on one-factor models.[4]

Exogenous versus Endogenous Term Structure

The first interest rate models were not constructed so as to fit an arbitrary initial term structure. Instead, with a view towards analytical simplicity, the Vasicek[5] and Cox-Ingersoll-Ross[6] (CIR) models contain a few constant parameters that define an endogenously specified term structure. That is, the initial spot curve is given by an analytical formula in terms of the model parameters. These are sometimes also called "equilibrium" models, as they posit yield curves derived from an assumption of

---

[4] For an exposition of two-factor models, see D.F. Babbel and C.B. Merrill, *Valuation of Interest Sensitive Financial Instruments* (New Hope, PA: Frank J. Fabozzi Associates and Society of Actuaries, 1996).

[5] O. Vasicek, "An Equilibrium Characterization of the Term Structure," *Journal of Financial Economics* (November 1977).

[6] J.C. Cox, J.E. Ingersoll Jr., and S.A. Ross, "A Theory of the Term Structure of Interest Rates," *Econometrica* (March 1985).

economic equilibrium based on a given market price of risk and other parameters governing collective expectations.

For *dynamically* reasonable choices of the parameters—values that give plausible long-run interest rate distributions and option prices—the term structures achievable in these models have far too little curvature to accurately represent typical empirical spot rate curves. This is because the mean reversion parameter, governing the rate at which the short rate reverts towards the long-run mean, also governs the volatility of long-term rates relative to the volatility of the short rate—the "term structure of volatility." To achieve the observed level of long-rate volatility (or to price options on long-term securities well) requires that there be relatively little mean reversion, but this implies low curvature yield curves. This problem can be partially solved by moving to a multi-factor framework—but at a significant cost as discussed earlier. These models are therefore not particularly useful as the basis for valuation algorithms—they simply have too few degrees of freedom to faithfully represent real markets.

To be used for valuation, a model must be calibrated to the initial spot rate curve. That is, the model structure must accommodate an exogenously determined spot rate curve, typically given by fitting to bond prices, or sometimes to futures prices and swap rates. All models in common use are of this type.

There is a "trick" invented by Dybvig that converts an endogenous model to a calibrated exogenous one.[7] The trick can be viewed as splitting the nominal interest rate into two parts: the stochastic part modeled endogenously, and a non-stochastic drift term, which compensates for the mismatch of the endogenous term structure and the observed one. (BARRA has used this technique to calibrate the CIR model in its older fixed-income analytics.) The price of this method is that the volatility function is no longer a simple function of the nominal interest rate.

Short Rate versus Yield Curve

The risk neutral valuation formula requires that one know the sequence of short rates for each scenario, so an interest rate model must provide this information. For this reason, many interest rate models are simply models of the stochastic evolution of the short rate. A second reason for the desirability of such models is that they have the *Markov property*, meaning that the evolution of the short rate at each instant depends only on its current value—not on how it got there. The practical significance of this is that, as alluded to in the previous section, the valuation prob-

[7] P. Dybvig, "Bond and Bond Option Pricing Based on the Current Term Structure," in M. A. H. Dempster and S. Pliska (eds.), *Mathematics of Derivative Securities* (Cambridge, U.K.: Cambridge University Press, 1997).

lem for many types of financial instruments can be reduced to solving a partial differential equation, for which there exist efficient analytical and numerical techniques. To be amenable to this calculation technique, a financial instrument's cash flow at time t must depend only on the state of affairs at that time, not on how the evolution occurred prior to t, or it must be equivalent to a portfolio of such securities (for example, a callable bond is a position long a straight bond and short a call option).

Short-rate models have two parts. One specifies the average rate of change ("drift") of the short rate at each instant; the other specifies the instantaneous volatility of the short rate. The conventional notation for this is

$$dr(t) = \mu(r, t)dt + \sigma(r, t)dz(t) \tag{2}$$

The left-hand side of this equation is the change in the short rate over the next instant. The first term on the right is the drift multiplied by the size of the time step. The second is the volatility multiplied by a normally distributed random increment. For most models, the drift component must be determined through a numerical technique to match the initial spot rate curve, while for a small number of models there exists an analytical relationship. In general, there exists a no-arbitrage relationship linking the initial forward rate curve, the volatility $\sigma(r,t)$, the market price of interest rate risk, and the drift term $\mu(r,t)$. However, since typically one must solve for the drift numerically, this relationship plays no role in model construction. Differences between models arise from different dependences of the drift and volatility terms on the short rate.

For financial instruments whose cash flows don't depend on the interest rate history, the expectation formula (1) for present value obeys the Feynman-Kac equation

$$\frac{1}{2}\sigma^2 P_{rr} + (\mu - \lambda)P_r + P_t - rP + c = 0 \tag{3}$$

where, for example, P_r denotes the partial derivative of P with respect to r, c is the payment rate of the financial instrument, and λ, which can be time and rate dependent, is the market price of interest rate risk.

The terms in this equation can be understood as follows. In the absence of uncertainty ($\sigma = 0$), the equation involves four terms. The last three assert that the value of the security increases at the risk-free rate (rP), and decreases by the amount of any payments (c). The term $(\mu - \lambda)P_r$ accounts for change in value due to the change in the term structure with time, as rates move up the forward curve. In the absence of uncertainty it is easy to express $(\mu - \lambda)$ in terms of the initial forward rates. In the presence of uncertainty this term depends on the volatility as well, and we also have the first term, which is the main source of the complexity of valuation models.

The Vasicek and CIR models are models of the short rate. Both have the same form for the drift term, namely a tendency for the short rate to rise when it is below the long-term mean, and fall when it is above. That is, the short-rate drift has the form $\mu = \kappa(\theta - r)$, where r is the short rate and κ and θ are the mean reversion and long-term rate constants. The two models differ in the rate dependence of the volatility: it is constant (when expressed as points per year) in the Vasicek model, and proportional to the square root of the short rate in the CIR model.

The Dybvig-adjusted Vasicek model is the mean reverting generalization of the Ho-Lee model,[8] also known as the mean reverting Gaussian (MRG) model or the Hull-White model.[9] The MRG model has particularly simple analytical expressions for values of many assets—in particular, bonds and European options on bonds. Like the original Vasicek model, it permits the occurrence of negative interest rates with positive probability. However, for typical initial spot curves and volatility parameters, the probability of negative rates is quite small.

Other popular models of this type are the Black-Derman-Toy (BDT)[10] and Black-Karasinski[11] (BK) models, in which the volatility is proportional to the short rate, so that the ratio of volatility to rate level is constant. For these models, unlike the MRG and Dybvig-adjusted CIR models, the drift term is not simple. These models require numerical fitting to the initial interest rate and volatility term structures. The drift term is therefore not known analytically. In the BDT model, the short-rate volatility is also linked to the mean reversion strength (which is also generally time dependent) in such a way that—in the usual situation where long rates are less volatile than the short rate—the short-rate volatility decreases in the future. This feature is undesirable: One doesn't want to link the observation that the long end of the curve has relatively low volatility to a forecast that in the future the short rate will

[8] T.S.Y. Ho and S.B. Lee, "Term Structure Movements and Pricing Interest Rate Contingent Claims," *Journal of Finance* (December 1986); and, J. Hull and A. White, "Pricing Interest Rate Derivative Securities," *The Review of Financial Studies*, 3:4 (1990).

[9] This model was also derived in F. Jamshidian, "The One-Factor Gaussian Interest Rate Model: Theory and Implementation," Merrill Lynch working paper, 1988.

[10] F. Black, E. Derman and W. Toy, "A One Factor Model of Interest Rates and its Application to Treasury Bond Options," *Financial Analysts Journal* (January/February 1990).

[11] F. Black and P. Karasinski, "Bond and Option Prices when Short Rates are Lognormal," *Financial Analysts Journal* (July/August 1992).

become less volatile. This problem motivated the development of the BK model in which mean reversion and volatility are delinked.

All of these models are explicit models of the short rate alone. It happens that in the Vasicek and CIR models (with or without the Dybvig adjustment) it is possible to express the entire forward curve as a function of the current short rate through fairly simple analytical formulas. This is not possible in the BDT and BK models, or generally in other models of short-rate dynamics, other than by highly inefficient numerical techniques. Indeed, it is possible to show that the only short-rate models consistent with an arbitrary initial term structure for which one can find the whole forward curve analytically are in a class that includes the MRG and Dybvig-adjusted CIR models as special cases, namely where the short-rate volatility has the form[12]

$$\sigma(r, t) = \sqrt{\sigma_1(t) + \sigma_2(t) r}\,.$$

While valuation of certain assets (e.g., callable bonds) does not require knowledge of longer rates, there are broad asset classes that do. For example, mortgage prepayment models are typically driven off a long-term Treasury par yield, such as the 10-year rate. Therefore a generic short-rate model such as BDT or BK is unsuitable if one seeks to analyze a variety of assets in a common interest rate framework.

An alternative approach to interest rate modeling is to specify the dynamics of the entire term structure. The volatility of the term structure is then given by some specified function, which most generally could be a function of time, maturity, and spot rates. A special case of this approach (in a discrete time framework) is the Ho-Lee model mentioned earlier, for which the term structure of volatility is a parallel shift of the spot rate curve, whose magnitude is independent of time and the level of rates. A completely general continuous time, multi-factor framework for constructing such models was given by Heath, Jarrow, and Morton (HJM).[13]

It is sometimes said that all interest rate models are HJM models. This is technically true: In principle, every arbitrage-free model of the term structure can be described in their framework. In practice, however, it is impossible to do this analytically for most short-rate Markov models. The only ones for which it is possible are those in the MRG-CIR family described

[12] A. Jeffrey, "Single Factor Heath-Jarrow-Morton Term Structure Models Based on Markov Spot Interest Rate Dynamics," *Journal of Financial and Quantitative Analysis*, 30:4 (December 1995).

[13] D. Heath, R. Jarrow, and A. Morton, "Bond Pricing and the Term Structure of Interest Rates: A New Methodology for Contingent Claims Valuation," *Econometrica*, 60:1 (January 1992).

earlier. The BDT and BK models, for instance, cannot be translated to the HJM framework other than by impracticable numerical means. To put a model in HJM form, one must know the term structure of volatility at all times, and this is generally not possible for short-rate Markov models.

If feasible, the HJM approach is clearly very attractive, since one knows now not just the short rate but also all longer rates as well. In addition, HJM models are very "natural," in the sense that the basic inputs to the model are the initial term structure of interest rates and a term structure of interest rate volatility for each independent motion of the yield curve.

The reason for the qualification in the last paragraph is that a generic HJM model requires keeping track of a potentially enormous amount of information. The HJM framework imposes no structure other than the requirement of no-arbitrage on the dynamics of the term structure. Each forward rate of fixed maturity evolves separately, so that one must keep track of each one separately. Since there are an infinite number of distinct forward rates, this can be difficult. This difficulty occurs even in a one factor HJM model, for which there is only one source of random movement of the term structure. A general HJM model does not have the Markov property that leads to valuation formulas expressed as solutions to partial differential equations. This makes it impossible to accurately value interest rate options without using huge amounts of computer time, since one is forced to use simulation methods.

In practice, a simulation algorithm breaks the evolution of the term structure up into discrete time steps, so one need keep track of and simulate only forward rates for the finite set of simulation times. Still, this can be a large number (e.g., 360 or more for a mortgage passthrough), and this computational burden, combined with the inefficiency of simulation methods, has prevented general HJM models from coming into more widespread use.

Some applications require simulation methods because the assets' structures (e.g., mortgage-backed securities) are not compatible with differential equation methods. For applications where one is solely interested in modeling such assets, there exists a class of HJM models that significantly simplify the forward rate calculations.[14] The simplest version of such models, the "two state Markov model," permits an arbitrary dependence of short-rate volatility on both time and the level of interest rates, while the ratio of forward-rate volatility to short-rate volatility is solely a function of term. That is, the volatility of $f(t,T)$, the term T forward rate at time t takes the form

[14] O. Cheyette, "Term Structure Dynamics and Mortgage Valuation," *Journal of Fixed Income* (March 1992). The two state Markov model was also described in P. Ritchken and L. Sankarasubramanian, "Volatility Structure of Forward Rates and the Dynamics of the Term Structure," *Mathematical Finance*, 5(1) (1995), pp. 55–72.

$$\sigma_f(r, t, T) = \sigma(r, t)e^{-\int_t^T k(u)du} \tag{4}$$

where $\sigma(r,t) = \sigma_f(r,t,t)$ is the short-rate volatility and $k(t)$ determines the mean reversion rate or equivalently, the rate of decrease of forward rate volatility with term. The evolution of all forward rates in this model can be described in terms of two state variables: the short rate (or any other forward or spot rate), and the slope of the forward curve at the origin. The second variable can be expressed in terms of the total variance experienced by a forward rate of fixed maturity by the time it has become the short rate. The stochastic evolution equations for the two state variables can be written as

$$\begin{aligned} d\tilde{r}(t) &= (V(t) - k(t)\tilde{r})dt + \sigma(r, t)dz(t) \\ \frac{\partial V}{\partial t} &= \sigma^2(r, t) - 2k(t)V(t) \end{aligned} \tag{5}$$

where $\tilde{r}(t) \equiv r(t) - f(0, t)$ is the deviation of the short rate from the initial forward rate curve. The state variable $V(t)$ has initial value $V(0)=0$; its evolution equation is non-stochastic and can be integrated to give

$$V(t) = \int_0^t \sigma_f^2(r, s, t)ds = \int_0^t \sigma^2(r, s)e^{-2\int_s^t k(u)du} ds \tag{6}$$

In terms of these state variables, the forward curve is given by

$$f(t, T) = f(0, T) + \phi(t, T)\left(\tilde{r} + V(t)\int_t^T \phi(t, s)ds\right) \tag{7}$$

where

$$\phi(t, T) = \sigma_f(r, t, T)/\sigma_f(r, t, t) = e^{-\int_t^T k(s)ds}$$

is a deterministic function.

Instead of having to keep track of hundreds of forward rates, one need only model the evolution of the two state variables. Path independent asset prices also obey a partial differential equation in this model, so it appears possible, at least in principle, to use more efficient numerical methods. The equation, analogous to equation (3), is

$$\frac{1}{2}\sigma^2 P_{\tilde{r}\tilde{r}} + (V - k\tilde{r})P_{\tilde{r}} + (\sigma^2 - 2kV)P_V + P_t - rP + c = 0. \tag{8}$$

Unlike equation (3), for which one must use the equation itself applied to bonds to solve for the coefficient μ–λ, here the coefficient functions are all known in terms of the initial data: the short-rate volatility and the initial forward curve. This simplification has come at the price of adding a dimension, as we now have to contend also with a term involving the first derivative with respect to V, and so the equation is much more difficult to solve efficiently by standard techniques.

In the special case where $\sigma(r,t)$ is independent of r, this model is the MRG model mentioned earlier. In this case, V is a deterministic function of t, so the P_V term disappears from equation (8), leaving a two-dimensional equation that has analytical solutions for European options on bonds, and straightforward numerical techniques for valuing American bond options. Since bond prices are lognormally distributed in this model, it should be no surprise that the formula for options on pure discount bounds (PDB's) looks much like the Black-Scholes formula. The value of a call with strike price K, exercise date t on a PDB maturing at time T is given by

$$C = P(T)N(h_1) - KP(t)N(h_2), \tag{9}$$

where

$$h_1 = \frac{k}{(1 - e^{-k(T-t)})\sqrt{V(t)}} \ln\frac{P(T)}{KP(t)} + \frac{\sqrt{V(t)}(1 - e^{-k(T-t)})}{2k},$$

$$h_2 = h_1 - \frac{\sqrt{V(t)}(1 - e^{-k(T-t)})}{k},$$

$N(x)$ is the Gaussian distribution, and $P(t)$ and $P(T)$ are prices of PDB's maturing at t and T. (The put value can be obtained by put-call parity.) Options on coupon bonds can be valued by adding up a portfolio of options on PDBs, one for each coupon or principal payment after the exercise date, with strike prices such that they are all at-the-money at the same value of the short rate. The Dybvig-adjusted CIR model has similar formulas for bond options, involving the non-central χ^2 distribution instead of the Gaussian one.

If $\sigma(r,t)$ depends on r, the model becomes similar to some other standard models. For example, $\sigma(r,t)=a\sqrt{r}$ has the same rate dependence as the CIR model, while choosing $\sigma(r,t)=br$ gives a model similar to BK, though in each case the drift and term structure of volatility are different.

Unless one has some short- or long-term view on trends in short-rate volatility, it is most natural to choose $\sigma(r,t)$ to be time independent, and similarly $k(u)$ to be constant. This is equivalent to saying that the shape of the volatility term structure—though not necessarily its magnitude—should be constant over time. (Otherwise, as in the BDT model, one is imposing an undesirable linkage between today's shape of the forward rate volatility curve and future volatility curves.) In that case, the term structure of forward-rate volatility is exponentially decreasing with maturity, and the integrals in equations (6) and (7) can be computed, giving for the forward curve

$$f(t, T) = f(0, T) + e^{-k(T-t)}\left(\tilde{r} + V(t)\,\frac{1 - e^{-k(T-t)}}{k}\right). \tag{10}$$

Finally, if the volatility is assumed rate independent as well, the integral expression for $V(t)$ can be evaluated to give

$$V(t) = \sigma^2\,\frac{1 - e^{-2kt}}{2k}\ , \tag{11}$$

and we obtain the forward curves of the MRG model.

Empirically, neither the historical volatility nor the implied volatility falls off so neatly. Instead, volatility typically increases with term out to between 1 and 3 years, then drops off. The two state Markov model cannot accommodate this behavior, except by imposing a forecast of increasing then decreasing short-rate volatility, or a short run of negative mean reversion. There is, however, an extension of the model that permits modeling of humped or other more complicated volatility curves, at the cost of introducing additional state variables.[15] With five state variables, for example, it is possible to model the dominant volatility term structure of the U.S. Treasury spot curve very accurately.

[15] O. Cheyette, "Markov Representation of the HJM Model," working paper, 1995.

EMPIRICAL AND NUMERICAL CONSIDERATIONS

Given the profusion of models, it is reasonable to ask whether there are empirical or other considerations that can help motivate a choice of one model for applications. One might take the view that one should use whichever model is most convenient for the particular problem at hand—e.g., BDT or BK for bonds with embedded options, Black model for caps and floors, a two-state Markov model for mortgages, and a ten-state, two-factor Markov-HJM model for dual index amortizing floaters. The obvious problem with this approach is that it can't be used to find hedging relationships or relative value between financial instruments valued according to the different models. I take as a given, then, that we seek models that can be used effectively for valuation of most types of financial instruments with minimum compromise of financial reasonableness. The choice will likely depend on how many and what kinds of assets one needs to value. A trader of vanilla options may be less concerned about cross-market consistency issues than a manager of portfolios of callable bonds and mortgage-backed securities.

The major empirical consideration—and one that has produced a large amount of inconclusive research—is the assumed dependence of volatility on the level of interest rates. Different researchers have reported various evidence that volatility is best explained (1) as a power of the short rate[16] ($\sigma \propto r^{\gamma}$)—with γ so large that models with this volatility have rates running off to infinity with high probability ("explosions"), (2) by a GARCH model with very long (possibly infinite) persistence,[17] (3) by some combination of GARCH with a power law dependence on rates,[18] (4) by none of the above.[19] All of this work has been in the context of short-rate Markov models.

Here I will present some fairly straightforward evidence in favor of choice (4) based on analysis of movements of the whole term structure of spot rates, rather than just short rates, from U.S. Treasury yields over the period 1977 to early 1996.

The result is that the market appears to be well described by "eras" with very different rate dependences of volatility, possibly coinciding with periods of different Federal Reserve policies. Since all the models in

---

[16] K.C. Chan, G.A. Karolyi, F.A. Longstaff, and A.B. Sanders, "An Empirical Comparson of Alternative Models of the Short Rate," *Journal of Finance* 47:3 (1992).

[17] See R.J. Brenner, R.H. Harjes, and K.F. Kroner, "Another Look at Alternative Models of the Short-Term Interest Rate," University of Arizona working paper (1993), and references therein.

[18] Ibid.

[19] Y.Aït-Sahalia, "Testing Continuous Time Models of the Spot Interest Rate," *Review of Financial Studies*, 9:2 (1996).

common use have a power law dependence of volatility on rates, I attempted to determine the best fit to the exponent (γ) relating the two. My purpose here is not so much to provide another entrant in this already crowded field, but rather to suggest that there may be no simple answer to the empirical question. No model with constant parameters seems to do a very good job. A surprising result, given the degree to which the market for interest rate derivatives has exploded and the widespread use of lognormal models, is that the period since 1987 is best modeled by a nearly *normal* model of interest rate volatility.

The data used in the analysis consisted of spot rate curves derived from the Federal Reserve H15 series of weekly average benchmark yields. The benchmark yields are given as semiannually compounded yields of hypothetical par bonds with fixed maturities ranging from 3 months to 30 years, derived by interpolation from actively traded issues. The data cover the period from early 1977, when a 30-year bond was first issued, through March of 1996. The spot curves are represented as continuous, piecewise linear functions, constructed by a root finding procedure to exactly match the given yields, assumed to be yields of par bonds. (This is similar to the conventional bootstrapping method.) The two data points surrounding the 1987 crash were excluded: The short and intermediate markets moved by around ten standard deviations during the crash, and this extreme event would have had a significant skewing effect on the analysis.

A parsimonious representation of the spot curve dynamics is given by the two-state Markov model with constant mean reversion k and volatility that is time independent and proportional to a power of the short rate: $\sigma = \beta r^{\gamma}$. In this case, the term structure of spot rate volatility, given by integrating equation (4), is

$$\sigma(r_t)v(T) = \beta r_t^{\gamma} \frac{1 - e^{-kT}}{kT} \tag{12}$$

where T is the maturity and r_t is the time t short rate. The time t weekly change in the spot rate curve is then given by the change due to the passage of time ("rolling up the forward curve") plus a random change of the form $v(T)x_t$, where for each t, x_t, is an independent normal random variable with distribution $N(\mu, \sigma(r_t)\sqrt{52})$. (The systematic drift μ of x_t, over time was assumed to be independent of time and the rate level.) The parameters β, γ, and k are estimated as follows. First, using an initial guess for γ, k is estimated by a maximum likelihood fit of the maturity dependence of $v(T)$ to the spot curve changes. Then, using this value of k, another maximum likelihood fit is applied to fit the variance of x_t to the power law model of $\sigma(r_t)$.

The procedure is then iterated to improve the estimates of k and γ (although it turns out that the best fit of k is quite insensitive to the value of γ, and vice versa).

One advantage of looking at the entire term structure is that we avoid modeling just idiosyncratic behavior of the short end, e.g., that it is largely determined by the Federal Reserve. An additional feature of this analysis is proper accounting for the effect of the "arbitrage-free drift"—namely, the systematic change of interest rates due purely to the shape of the forward curve at the start of each period. Prior analyses have typically involved fitting to endogenous short-rate models with constant parameters not calibrated to each period's term structure. The present approach mitigates a fundamental problem of prior research in the context of one-factor models, namely that interest rate dynamics are poorly described by a single factor. By reinitializing the drift parameters at the start of each sample period and studying the volatility of changes to a well-defined term structure factor, the effects of additional factors are excluded from the analysis.

The results for the different time periods are shown in Exhibit 1.1. (The exhibit doesn't include the best fit values of β, which are not relevant to the empirical issue at hand.) The error estimates reported in the exhibit are derived by a bootstrap Monte Carlo procedure that constructs artificial data sets by random sampling of the original set with replacement and applies the same analysis to them.[20] It is apparent that the different subperiods are well described by very different exponents and mean reversion. The different periods were chosen to include or exclude the monetarist policy "experiment" under Volcker of the late 1970s and early 1980s, and also to sample just the Greenspan era. For the period since 1987, the best fit exponent of 0.19 is significantly different from zero at the 95% confidence level, but not at the 99% level. However, the best fit value is well below the threshold of 0.5 required to guarantee positivity of interest rates, with 99% confidence. There appears to be weak sensitivity of volatility to the rate level, but much less than is implied by a number of models in widespread use—in particular, BDT, BK, and CIR.

The estimates for the mean reversion parameter k can be understood through the connection of mean reversion to the term structure of volatility. Large values of k imply large fluctuations in short rates compared to long rates, since longer rates reflect the expectation that changes in short rates will not persist forever. The early 1980s saw just such a phenomenon, with the yield curve becoming very steeply inverted for a brief period. Since then, the volatility of the short rate (in absolute terms of points per year) has been only slightly higher than that of long-term rates.

[20] B.J. Efron and R.J. Tibshirani, *An Introduction to the Bootstrap* (New York: Chapman & Hall, 1993).

EXHIBIT 1.1 Parameter Estimates for the Two-State Markov Model with Power Law Volatility over Various Sample Periods*

Sample Period	Exponent (γ)	Mean Reversion (k)	Comments
3/1/77–3/29/96	1.04 ± 0.07	0.054 ± 0.007	Full data set
3/1/77–1/1/87	1.6 ± 0.10	0.10 ± 0.020	Pre-Greenspan
3/1/77–1/1/83	1.72 ± 0.15	0.22 ± 0.040	"Monetarist"policy
1/1/83–3/29/96	0.45 ± 0.07	0.019 ± 0.005	Post high-rate period
1/1/87–3/29/96	0.19 ± 0.09	0.016 ± 0.004	Greenspan

* The uncertainties are one standard deviation estimates based on bootstrap Monte Carlo resampling.

EXHIBIT 1.2 52-Week Volatility of Term Structure Changes Plotted Against the 3-Month Spot Rate at the Start of the Period

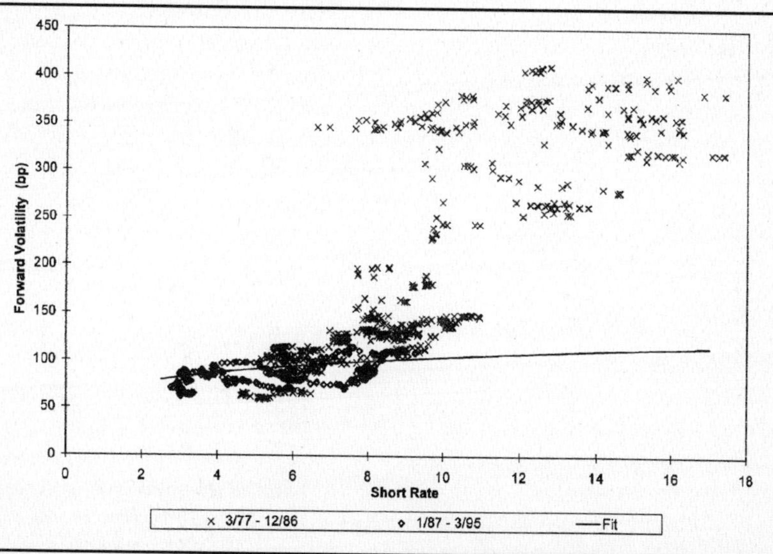

The x's are periods starting 3/77 through 12/86. The diamonds are periods starting 1/87 through 3/95. The data points are based on the best fit k for the period 1/87–3/96, as described in the text. The solid curve shows the best fit to a power law model. The best fit parameters are β=91 bp, γ=0.19. (This is *not* a fit to the points shown here, which are provided solely to give a visual feel for the data.)

Exhibit 1.2 gives a graphical representation of the data. There is clear evidence that the simple power law model is not a good fit and that the data display regime shifts. The exhibit shows the volatility of the factor in equation (12) using the value of k appropriate to the period January 1987–March 1996 (the "Greenspan era"). The vertical coordinate of each dot represents the volatility of the factor over a 52-week period; the horizontal coordinate shows the 3-month spot rate (a proxy for the short rate) at the start of the 52-week period. (Note that the maximum likelihood estimation is not based on the data points shown, but on the individual weekly changes.) The dots are broken into two sets: The x's are for start dates prior to January 1987, the diamonds for later dates. Divided in this way, the data suggest fairly strongly that volatility has been nearly independent of interest rates since 1987—a time during which the short rate has ranged from around 3% to over 9%.

From an empirical perspective, then, no simple choice of model works well. Among the simple models of volatility, the MRG model most closely matches the recent behavior of U.S. Treasury term structure.

There is an issue of financial plausibility here, as well as an empirical one. Some models permit interest rates to become negative, which is undesirable, though how big a problem this is isn't obvious. The class of simple models that provably have positive interest rates without suffering from explosions and match the initial term structure is quite small. The BDT and BK models satisfy these conditions, but don't provide information about future yield curves as needed for the mortgage problem. The Dybvig-adjusted CIR model also satisfies the conditions, but is somewhat hard to work with. There is a lognormal HJM model that avoids negative rates, but it is analytically intractable and suffers from explosions.[21] The lognormal version of the two-state Markov model also suffers from explosions, though, as with the lognormal HJM model, these can be eliminated by capping the volatility at some large value.

It is therefore worth asking whether the empirical question is important. It might turn out to be unimportant in the sense that, properly compared, models that differ only in their assumed dependence of volatility on rates actually give similar answers for option values.

The trick in comparing models is to be sure that the comparisons are truly "apples to apples," by matching term structures of volatility. It is easy to imagine getting different results valuing the same option using the MRG, CIR, and BK models, even though the initial volatilities are set equal—not because of different assumptions about the dependence of volatility on rates, but because the long-term volatilities are different in the three models even when the short-rate volatilities are the same. There are a number of published papers claiming to demonstrate dramatic differences between models, but which actually demonstrate just that the models have been calibrated differently.[22]

---

[21] Heath, Jarrow, and Morton, "Bond Pricing and the Term Structure of Interest Rates: A New Methodology for Contingent Claims Valuation."

[22] For a recent example, see M. Uhrig and U. Walter, "A New Numerical Approach to Fitting the Initial Yield Curve," *Journal of Fixed Income* (March 1996).

The two-state Markov framework provides a convenient means to compare different choices for the dependence of volatility on rates while holding the initial term structure of volatility fixed. Choosing different forms for $\sigma(r)$ while setting k to a constant in expression (4) gives exactly this comparison. We can value options using these different assumptions and compare time values. (Intrinsic value—the value of the option when the volatility is zero—is of course the same in all models.) To be precise, we set $\sigma(r, t) = \sigma_0(r/r_0)^\gamma$, where σ_0 is the initial annualized volatility of the short rate in absolute terms (e.g., 100 bp/year) and r_0 is the initial short rate. Choosing the exponent $\gamma = \{0, 0.5, 1\}$ then gives the MRG model, a square root volatility model (not CIR), and a lognormal model (not BK), respectively.

The results can be summarized by saying that a derivatives trader probably cares about the choice of exponent γ, but a fixed-income portfolio manager probably doesn't. The reason is that the differences in time value are small, except when the time value itself is small—for deep in- or out-of-the-money options. A derivatives trader may be required to price a deep out-of-the-money option, and would get very different results across models, having calibrated them using at-the-money options. A portfolio manager, on the other hand, has option positions embedded in bonds, mortgage-backed securities, etc., whose time value is a small fraction of total portfolio value. So differences that show up only for deep in- or out-of-the-money options are of little consequence. Moreover, a deep out-of-the-money option has small option delta, so small differences in valuation have little effect on measures of portfolio interest rate risk. An in-the-money option can be viewed as a position in the underlying asset plus an out-of-the-money option, so the same reasoning applies.

Exhibit 1.3 shows the results of one such comparison for a 5-year quarterly pay cap, with a flat initial term structure and modestly decreasing term structure of volatility. The time value for all three values of γ peaks at the same value for an at-the-money cap. Caps with higher strike rates have the largest time value in the lognormal model, because the volatility is increasing for rate moves in the direction that make them valuable. Understanding the behavior for lower strike caps requires using put-call parity: An in-the-money cap can be viewed as paying fixed in a rate swap and owning a floor. The swap has no time value, and the floor has only time value (since it is out-of-the money). The floor's time value is greatest for the MRG model, because it gives the largest volatility for rate moves in the direction that make it valuable. In each case, the square root model gives values intermediate between the MRG and lognormal models, for obvious reasons. At the extremes, 250 bp in or out of the money, time values differ by as much as a factor of 2 between the MRG and lognormal models. At these extremes, though, the time value is only a tenth of its value for the at-the-money cap.

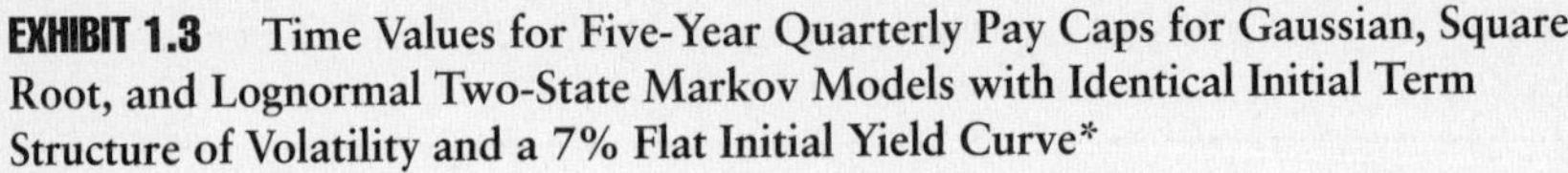

EXHIBIT 1.3 Time Values for Five-Year Quarterly Pay Caps for Gaussian, Square Root, and Lognormal Two-State Markov Models with Identical Initial Term Structure of Volatility and a 7% Flat Initial Yield Curve*

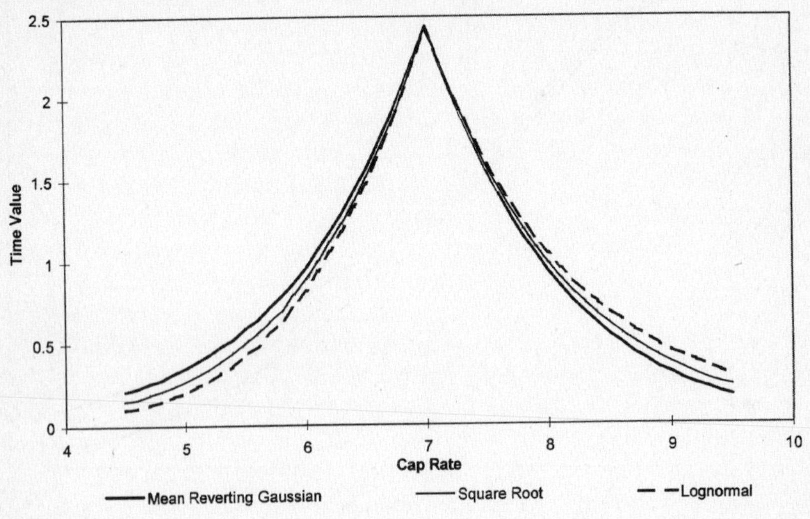

* The model parameters (described in the text) are σ_0=100 bp/yr., k=0.02/yr., equivalent to an initial short-rate volatility of 14.8%, and a 10-year yield volatility of 13.6%.

If the initial term structure is not flat, the model differences can be larger. For example, if the term structure is positively sloped, then the model prices match up for an in-the-money rather than at-the-money cap. Using the same parameters as for Exhibit 1.3, but using the actual Treasury term structure as of 5/13/96 instead of a flat 7% curve, the time values differ at the peak by about 20%—about half a point—between the MRG and lognormal models. Interestingly, as shown in Exhibit 1.4, even though the time values can be rather different, the option deltas are rather close for the three models. (The deltas are even closer in the flat term structure case.) In this example, if a 9.5% cap were embedded in a floating-rate note priced around par, the effective duration attributable to the cap according to the lognormal model would be 0.49 year, while according to the MRG model it would be 0.17 year. The difference shrinks as the rate gets closer to the cap. This ⅓ year difference isn't trivial, but it's also not large compared to the effect of other modeling assumptions, such as the overall level of volatility or, if mortgages are involved, prepayment expectations.

EXHIBIT 1.4 Sensitivity of Cap Value to Change in Rate Level as a Function of Cap Rate*

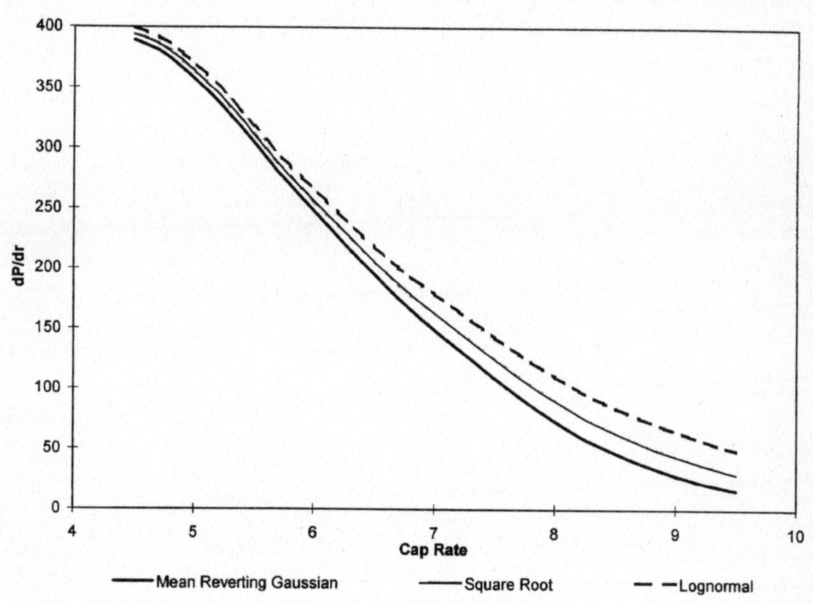

* The cap structure and model parameters are the same as used for Exhibit 1.3, except that the initial term structure is the (positively sloped) U.S. Treasury curve as of 5/13/96. The short rate volatility is 19.9% and the ten-year yield volatility is 14.9%.

These are just two numerical examples, but it is easy to see how different variations would affect these results. An inverted term structure would make the MRG model time value largest at the peak and the lognormal model value the smallest. Holding σ_0 constant, higher initial interest rates would yield smaller valuation differences across models since there would be less variation of volatility around the mean. Larger values of the mean reversion k would also produce smaller differences between models, since the short-rate distribution would be tighter around the mean.

Finally, there is the question raised earlier as to whether one should be concerned about the possibility of negative interest rates in some models. From a practical standpoint, this is an issue only if it leads to a significant contribution to pricing from negative rates. One simple way to test this is to look at pricing of a call struck at par for a zero coupon bond. Exhibit 1.5 shows such a test for the MRG model. For reasonable parameter choices (here taken to be σ_0=100 bp/year, k = 0.02/year, or

20% volatility of a 5% short rate), the call values are quite modest, especially compared to those of a call on a par bond, which gives a feel for the time value of at-the-money options over the same period. The worst case is a call on the longest maturity zero-coupon bond which, with a flat 5% yield curve, is priced at 0.60. This is just 5% of the value of a par call on a 30-year par bond. Using the actual May 1996 yield curve, all the option values—other than on the 30-year zero—are negligible. For the 30-year zero the call is worth just 1% of the value of the call on a 30-year par bond. In October 1993, the U.S. Treasury market had the lowest short rate since 1963, and the lowest 10-year rate since 1967. Using that yield curve as a worst case, the zero coupon bond call values are only very slightly higher than the May 1996 values, and still effectively negligible for practical purposes.

Again, it is easy to see how these results change with different assumptions. An inverted curve makes negative rates likelier, so increases the value of a par call on a zero-coupon bond. (On the other hand, inverted curves at low interest rate levels are rare.) Conversely, a positive slope to the curve makes negative rates less likely, decreasing the call value. Holding σ_0 constant, lower interest rates produce larger call values. Increasing k produces smaller call values. The only circumstances that are really problematic for the MRG model are flat or inverted yield curves at very low rate levels, with relatively high volatility.

EXHIBIT 1.5 **Valuation of a Continuous Par Call on Zero Coupon and Par Bonds of Various Maturities in the MRG Model**

Model parameters are:

$$\sigma_0 = 100 \text{ bp/year}$$
$$k = 0.02/\text{year}$$

The value of the call on the zero coupon bond should be zero in every case, assuming non-negative interest rates.

	5% Flat Curve		7% Flat Curve		5/96 U.S. Tsy. Yields		10/93 U.S. Tsy. Yields	
Term	Zero Cpn.	Par Bond	Zero Cpn.	Par Bond	Zero Cpn.	Par Bond	Zero Cpn.	Par Bond
3-year	<0.01	0.96	<0.01	0.93	<0.01	0.65	<0.01	0.62
5-year	<0.01	1.93	<0.01	1.83	<0.01	1.43	<0.01	1.27
10-year	0.06	4.54	<0.01	4.07	<0.01	3.47	0.02	3.06
30-year	0.60	11.55	0.10	8.85	0.08	7.86	0.09	7.26

CONCLUSIONS

For portfolio analysis applications, the mean reverting Gaussian model has much to recommend it. For this model, it is easy to implement valuation algorithms for both path independent financial instruments such as bond options, and path dependent financial instruments such as CMOs and annuities. It is one of the simplest models in which it is possible to follow the evolution of the entire yield curve (à la HJM), making it especially useful for valuing assets like mortgage-backed securities whose cash flows depend on longer term rates. The oft raised bogeyman of negative interest rates proves to have little consequence for option pricing, since negative rates occur with very low probability for reasonable values of the model parameters and initial term structure.

Option values are somewhat (though not very) sensitive to the assumed dependence of volatility on the level of rates. The empirical evidence on this relationship is far from clear, with the data (at least in the United States) showing evidence of eras, possibly associated with central bank policy. The numerical evidence shows that, for a sloped term structure, different power law relationships give modestly different at-the-money option time values, and larger relative differences for deep in- or out-of-the-money options. These differences are unlikely to be significant to fixed-income portfolio managers, but are probably a concern for derivatives traders.

CHAPTER 2

The Four Faces of an Interest Rate Model*

Peter Fitton
Chief Scientist
Neuristics Consulting, a Division of Trade, Inc.

James F. McNatt, CFA
Managing Director, Investment Banking
InCap Group, Inc.

Models of the term structure of interest rates are becoming increasingly important in the practice of finance and actuarial science. However, practitioner understanding of these models has not always kept pace with the breadth of their application. In particular, misinterpretation of the proper uses of a particular model can lead to significant errors. In this chapter, we attempt to clear up some of the most commonly misconstrued aspects of interest rate models: the choice between an arbitrage-free or equilibrium model, and the choice between risk neutral or realistic parameterizations of a model. These two dimensions define four classes of model forms, each of which has its own proper use.

Much of the confusion has arisen from overuse and misuse of the term "arbitrage-free." Virtually all finance practitioners believe that market participants quickly take advantage of any opportunities for risk-free arbitrage among financial assets, so that these opportunities do not exist

* The authors would like to thank David Becker of Lincoln National Life for asking the questions that motivated this chapter, and for the many helpful comments that were applied herein. Any remaining errors are the authors' alone.

for long; thus, the term "arbitrage-free" sounds as if it would be a good characteristic for any model to have. Simply based on these positive connotations, it almost seems hard to believe that anyone would not want their model to be arbitrage-free. Briefly, in the world of finance this expression has the associations of motherhood and apple pie.

Unfortunately, this has led some users (and even builders) of interest rate models to link uncritically the expression "arbitrage-free" with the adjective "good." One objective of this chapter is to show that arbitrage-free models are not appropriate for all purposes. Further, we show that just because a model uses the arbitrage-free approach does not mean that it is necessarily good, even for the purposes for which arbitrage-free models are appropriately used.

Another common confusion ensues from implicitly equating the terms "arbitrage-free" and "risk neutral." This arises partly from the fact that, in the academic and practitioner literature, there have been very few papers which have applied the arbitrage-free technique to a model that was not in risk neutral form. We explain the reason for this below. The natural result is that the terms have sometimes been used interchangeably. In addition, since quantitative risk management is a relatively new concept to the finance community, most well-known papers have focused only on the application of interest rate models to simple valuation and hedging problems. These have not required either the realistic or equilibrium approaches to modeling. This lack of published work has led to a mistaken belief that an arbitrage-free, risk neutral model is the only valid kind of term structure model. In this chapter, we intend to dispel that notion.

CATEGORIZATION OF APPROACHES TO TERM STRUCTURE MODELING

Arbitrage-Free Modeling

Arbitrage-free models take certain market prices as given, and adjust model parameters in order to fit the prices exactly. Despite being called "term structure" models, they do not in reality attempt to emulate the dynamics of the term structure. Instead, they assume some computationally convenient, but essentially arbitrary, random process underlying the yield curve, and then add time dependent constants to the drift (mean) and volatility (standard deviation) of the process until all market prices are matched. To achieve this exact fit, they require at least one parameter for every market price used as an input to the model.

For valuation, it is possible to produce reasonable current prices for many assets without having a realistic term structure model, by using arbitrage-free models for interpolation among existing prices. To this end, the trading models used by most dealers in the over-the-counter derivatives market employ enormous numbers of time dependent parameters. These achieve an exact fit to prices of assets in particular classes, without regard to any differences between the behaviors of the models and the actual behavior of the term structure over time. Placed in terms of a physical analogy, the distinction here is between creating a robot based on a photograph of an animal, and creating a robot based on multiple observations of the animal through time. While the robot produced using only the photograph may *look* like the animal, only the robot built based on behavioral observations will *act* like the animal. An arbitrage-free model is like the former robot, constructed with reference to only a single point in time; that is, a snapshot of the fixed-income marketplace.

As an example of an arbitrage-free model, at *RISK Magazine's* "Advanced Mathematics for Derivatives" conference in New York on October 26 and 27, 1995, Merrill Lynch's Greg Merchant presented a linear normal model that used time dependent drifts, volatilities, and correlations to reproduce prices in the Eurodollar, cap, and swaption markets, respectively. It is important to realize that an arbitrage-free model such as this one is just an interpolation system, which reads prices off some complicated hypersurface that passes through each of the points at which prices are known.

Equilibrium Modeling

In contrast to arbitrage-free models, equilibrium term structure models are truly models of the term structure process. Rather than interpolating among prices at one particular point in time, they attempt to capture the behaviors of the term structure over time. An equilibrium model employs a statistical approach, assuming that market prices are observed with some statistical error, so that the term structure must be *estimated*, rather than taken as given. Equilibrium models do not exactly match market prices at the time of estimation, because they use a small set of state variables (fundamental components of the interest rate process) to describe the term structure. Extant equilibrium models do not contain time dependent parameters; instead they contain a small number of statistically estimated constant parameters, drawn from the historical time series of the yield curve.

Risk Neutral Probabilities: The Derivative Pricing Probability Measure

When we create a model for pricing interest rate derivatives, the "underlying" is not the price of a traded security, as it would be in a model for equity options. Instead, we specify a random process for the instantaneous, risk-free spot interest rate, the rate payable on an investment in default-free government bonds for a very short period of time. For convenience, we call this interest rate "the short rate." Financial analysts have chosen to create models around the short rate because it is the only truly riskless interest rate in financial markets. An investment in default-free bonds for any non-instantaneous period of time carries *market risk*, the chance that the short rate will rise during the term of the investment, leading to a decline in the investment's value.

As with any risky investment, an investor in bonds subject to market risk expects to earn a risk-free return (that is, the return from continuously investing at the short rate, whatever that may be) plus a risk premium, which could increase or decrease as the term of the investment increases. Thus, the spot rate for a particular term is composed of the return expected under the random process for the short rate up to the end of that term, plus a *term premium*, an additional return to compensate the investor for the interest rate risk of the investment. The term premium offered in the market depends on the aggregate risk preference of market participants, taking into account their natural preferences for securities that conform to their investment (term) needs.

Let r_t be the short rate at time t. Let $D(t, T)$ be the price, at time t, of a discount bond paying one dollar at time T. Let $s(t, T)$ be the spot rate at time t for the term $(T–t)$. Finally, let $\phi(T–t)$ be the term premium (expressed as an annual excess rate of return) required by investors for a term of $(T–t)$. All rates are continuously compounded. We can then write,

$$D(t, T) = \frac{1}{e^{s(t,T) \times (T-t)}} = \frac{1}{e^{\phi(T-t) \times (T-t)}} E\left[\frac{1}{e^{\int_t^T r_s ds}}\right] \tag{1}$$

The second term in the two-term expression above is a discount factor that reflects the expected return from investing continuously at the short rate for the term $(T–t)$. The first term is the additional discount factor that accounts for the return premium that investors require to compensate them for the market risk of investing for a term of $(T–t)$. The use of an integral in the expression for the expected short rate discount factor is necessary because the short rate is continuously changing over the bond's term.

From this description and formula, it may seem necessary to know the term premium for every possible term, in addition to knowing the random process for the short rate, in order to value a default-free discount bond. This is not the case, however. As in the pricing of a forward contract or option on a stock, we can use the mathematical sleight-of-hand known as *risk neutral valuation* to find the relative value of a security that is derivative of the short rate.

The principle of risk neutral valuation as it applies to bonds and other interest rate derivatives is that, regardless of how risk averse investors are, we can identify a set of spot rates that value discount bonds correctly relative to the rest of the market. We do not have to identify separately the term premium embedded in each spot rate in order to use it to discount future cash flows. This fact can be used to make the valuation of all interest rate derivatives easier by *risk adjusting* the term structure model; that is, by changing the probability distribution of the short rate so that the spot rate of every term is, under the new model, equal to the expected return from investing at the short rate over the same term. This is accomplished by redefining the model so that, instead of being a random process for the short rate, it is a random process for the short rate plus a function of the term premium. If we specify the process for r_t^* in such a way that

$$r_s^* = r_s + \phi(s-t) + \phi'(s-t) \times (s-t) \tag{2}$$

at every future point in time s (accomplished by adjusting the rate of increase of r_t upward) then we can write,

$$D(t,T) = \frac{1}{e^{s(t,T)\times(T-t)}} = E\left[\frac{1}{e^{\int_t^T (r_s + \phi(T-t))ds}}\right] = E\left[\frac{1}{e^{\int_t^T r_s^* ds}}\right] \tag{3}$$

By transforming the short rate process in this manner, we have created a process for a random variable which, when used to discount a certain future cash flow, gives an expected present value equal to the present value obtained by discounting that cash flow at the appropriate spot rate. It is important to note that this random variable is no longer the short rate, but something artificial that we might refer to as the *risk adjusted short rate*.[1]

[1] This is not the way that risk neutrality is usually presented. Typically, writers have focused on the stochastic calculus, using Girsanov's Theorem to justify a change of probability measure to an *equivalent* (i.e., an event has zero probability under one measure if and only if it has zero probability under the other measure) *martingale measure*. This complexity and terminology can obscure the simple intuition that we are making a change of variables in order to restate the problem in a more easily solvable form. For this approach to explaining risk neutral valuation, see G. Courtadon, "The Pricing of Options on Default-free Bonds," *Journal of Financial and Quantitative Analysis* (March 1982), pp. 301–329, or J. Harrison and S. Pliska, "Martingales and Stochastic Integrals in the Theory of Continuous Trading," *Stochastic Processes and their Applications* (1981), pp. 215–260.

The resulting *risk neutral model* might be construed as a model for the true behavior of the short rate in an imaginary world of risk neutral market participants, where there is no extra expected return to compensate investors for the extra price risk in bonds of longer maturity. This impression, while accurate, is not very informative. The important aspect of the risk neutral model is that the term premia, whatever their values, that exist in the marketplace are embedded in the interest rate process itself, so that the expected discounted value of a cash flow at the risk adjusted short rate is equal to the discounted value of the cash flow at the spot rate.[2]

The value of the *risk neutral probability measure* is that, under this parameterization, an interest-sensitive instrument's price can be estimated by averaging the present values of its cash flows, discounted at the short term interest rates along each path of the short rate under which those cash flows occur. In contrast, valuing assets under the model before it was risk adjusted would require a more complicated discounting procedure which applied additional discount factors to the short rate paths to compensate for market risk; however, the price obtained under both approaches would be the same. For this reason, we use randomly generated scenarios from risk neutral interest rate models for pricing.

To sum up, there is nothing magical about risk neutrality. There are any number of changes of variables we could make to a short rate process that would retain the structure of the model, but have a different (but equivalent) probability distribution for the new variable. We could change the measure to represent imaginary worlds in which market participants were risk seeking (negative term premia), or more risk averse than in the real world; regardless, as long as we structured the discounting procedure properly we would always determine the same model price for an interest rate derivative. The specific change of variables that produces a risk neutral model simply makes the algebra easier than the others, because one can ignore risk preferences.

Realistic Probabilities: The Estimated Market Probability Measure

We have described why risk neutral interest rate scenarios are preferred for pricing bonds and interest rate derivatives. However, it is important to note

[2] Note that this is *not* the same as the expectations hypothesis of the term structure, which holds that the term structure's shape is determined solely by the market's expectations about future rates. The expectations hypothesis is a theory of the real term structure process, whereas the risk neutral approach is an analytical convenience which takes no position about the truth or falsity of any term structure theory. For a brief, cogent discussion of the expectations hypothesis in contrast to risk neutral pricing, see Don Chance, "Theories of the Term Structure: Part I," *Essays in Derivatives* (New Hope, PA: Frank J. Fabozzi Associates, 1998).

that risk neutral scenarios are not appropriate for all purposes. For example, for scenario-based evaluation of portfolio strategies, realistic simulation is needed. And a computerized system for stress testing asset/liability strategies under adverse movements in interest rates is to actuaries what a wind tunnel is to aerospace engineers. The relevance of the information provided by the testing depends completely on the realism of the simulated environment. Stated differently, the test environment must be like the real environment; if not, the test results are not useful.

The realistic term structure process desired for this kind of stress testing must be distinguished from the risk neutral term structure process used for pricing. The risk neutral process generates scenarios in which all term premia are zero. This process lacks realism; in the real world, term premia are clearly not zero, as evidenced by the fact that the implied spot curve from Treasuries has been upward sloping 85% of the time in the 1955–1994 period.[3] This predominantly upward slope reflects an expected return premium for bonds of longer maturity, although approximately 15% of the time some other configuration of buyer preferences can be inferred; for example, an inverted curve suggests that buyers demand an increasing premium for decreasing the term of their positions.

Thus, the user of an interest rate model must be careful. When generating scenarios for reserve adequacy testing, where the purpose is to examine the effect on a company's balance sheet of changes in the real (risk averse) world, he must not use the scenarios from a risk neutral interest rate model.

WHEN DO I USE EACH OF THE MODELING APPROACHES?

The two dimensions, risk neutral versus realistic and arbitrage-free versus equilibrium, define four classes of modeling approaches. Each has its appropriate use.

Risk Neutral and Arbitrage-Free

The risk neutral and arbitrage-free model is the most familiar form of an interest rate model for most analysts. The model has been risk adjusted to use for pricing interest rate derivatives, and its parameters have been inter-

[3] This fact is one of the many useful observations about the realistic term structure process appearing in David Becker, *Stylized Historical Facts Regarding Treasury Interest Rates from 1955 to 1994* (Fort Wayne, IN: Technical report, Lincoln National Life, 1995). See also David Becker, "The Frequency of Inversions of the Yield Curve, and Historical Data on the Volatility and Level of Interest Rates," *Risks and Rewards* (October 1991), pp. 3–5.

polated from a set of current market prices rather than being statistically estimated from historical data. It is appropriately used for current pricing when the set of market prices is complete and reliable.

It is worth noting that, just because two models are each both risk neutral and arbitrage-free, we cannot conclude that they will give the same price for a particular interest rate derivative. Two arbitrage-free models will produce the same prices only for the instruments in a subset common to both sets of input data. The form of the model, and particularly the number of random factors underlying the term structure process, can make a large difference to valuations of the other instruments.

When the market data are sparse, the behavior of the model becomes important. For example, the value of a Bermudan or American swaption depends on the correlations among rates of different maturities. The swaption market is not liquid, nor are its prices widely disseminated, so there is no way to estimate a "term structure of correlations" that would allow a simple arbitrage-free model to interpolate reasonable swaption prices. In this case, a multi-factor model which captures the nature of correlations among rates of different maturities, including the way that those correlations are influenced by the shape of the term structure, will perform better for pricing swaptions than will a one-factor model. Models with good statistical fit to historical correlation series are needed for Bermudan or American options on floating-rate notes, caps, and floors for the same reason. Model behavior is also important for long-dated caps and floors, where there is a lack of reliable data for estimating the "term structure of volatilities" beyond the 5-year tenor.

Risk Neutral and Equilibrium

There are a number of sources of "error" in quotations of the market prices of bonds, so that the discount rates that exactly match a set of price quotations may contain bond-specific effects, corrupting the pricing of other instruments. These sources, defined as any effects on a bond's market price apart from the discount rates applying to all market instruments, include differences in liquidity, differential tax effects, bid-ask spreads (the bid-ask spread defines a range of possible market prices, implying a range of possible discount rates), quotation stickiness, timeliness of data, the human element of the data collection and reporting process, and market imperfections.

Since arbitrage-free models accept all input prices as given, without reference to their reasonability or comparability to other prices in the input data, they impound in the pricing model any bond-specific effects. In contrast, equilibrium models capture the global behavior of the term structure over time, so security-specific effects are treated in the appropriate way, as noise. For this reason, risk neutral equilibrium models can have an advantage over arbitrage-free models in that equilibrium models are not overly sensitive to outliers. Also, for current pricing (as distinguished from horizon pricing, described below), equilibrium models can be estimated from historical data when current market prices are sparse. Thus, a risk neutral and equilibrium model can be used for pricing when the current market prices are unreliable or unavailable.

For most standard instruments, circumstances rarely prevail such that the current market prices needed for estimating an arbitrage-free model are not available. However, such circumstances always prevail for horizon pricing, where the analyst calculates a price for an instrument in some assumed future state of the market. Since arbitrage-free models require a full set of market prices as input, arbitrage-free models are useless for horizon pricing, the future prices being unknown. Thus, the horizon prices obtained under the different values of the state variables in an equilibrium model provide an analytical capability that arbitrage-free models lack.

USING MODELS OF BORROWER BEHAVIOR WITH A RISK NEUTRAL INTEREST RATE MODEL

Often, an interest rate model is not enough to determine the value of a fixed-income security or interest rate derivative. To value mortgage-backed securities or collateralized mortgage obligations, one also needs a prepayment model. To value bonds or interest rate derivatives with significant credit risk, one needs a model of default and recovery. To value interest-sensitive annuities and insurance liabilities, one needs models of lapse and other policyholder behaviors. In all of these behavioral models, the levels of certain interest rates are important explanatory variates, meaning that, for example, the prepayment speeds in a CMO valuation system are driven primarily by the interest rate scenarios.

Common practice has been to estimate parameters for prepayment, default, and lapse models using regression on historical data about interest rates and other variables. Then, in the valuation process, the analyst uses the interest rates from a set of risk neutral scenarios to derive estimates for the rates of prepayment, default, or lapse along those scenarios. This borrower behavior information is combined with the interest rates to produce cash flows and, ultimately, prices. Unfortunately, this practice leads to highly misleading results.

The primary problem here is that the regressions have been estimated using historical data, reflecting the *real* probability distributions of borrower behavior, and then used with scenarios from a risk neutral model, with an *artificial* probability distribution. The risk neutral model is not a process for the short rate; rather, it is a process for the risk adjusted short rate. Since the real world is risk averse, the risk adjusted short rate usually has an expected value much higher than the market's forecast of the short rate; the extra premium for interest rate risk permits one to value optionable default-free bonds by reference to the forward rate curve.

The same procedure can be applied to corporate bonds. Corporate bonds are exposed to default risk in addition to interest rate risk. One may construct a behavioral model of failure to pay based on historical data about default rates and recovery, perhaps using bond ratings as explanatory variates in addition to interest rates. One can then attempt to compute the present value of a corporate bond by finding the expected value of the discounted cash flows from the two models in combination: a risk neutral model of the Treasury curve, and a realistic model of default behavior as a function of interest rates and other variables. Because the cash flows of the bond, adjusted for default, will be less than the cash flows for a default-free bond, the model will price the corporate bond at a positive spread over the Treasury curve.

This spread will almost certainly be substantially too low in comparison to the corporate's market price. The reason for this is that, just as investors demand a return premium for interest rate risk, they demand an additional return for default risk. The application of an econometrically estimated model of default to pricing has ignored the default risk premium encapsulated in the prices of corporate bonds. Market practice has evolved a simple solution to this; one adjusts the default model to fit (statistically, in the equilibrium case; exactly, in the arbitrage-free case) the current prices of active corporates in the appropriate rating class. By using the market prices of active corporates to imbed the default risk premium in the model, the analyst is really applying the principle of risk neutral valuation to the default rate. The combined model of risk adjusted interest rates and risk adjusted default rates now discounts using the corporate bond spot rate curve instead of the Treasury spot curve.

The same technique of risk neutralizing a model by embedding information about risk premia derived from current market prices can be applied to prepayment models as well. The results of a prepayment model can be risk adjusted by examining the prices of active mortgage-backed securities. Unfortunately, one can only guess at the appropriate expected return premium for insurance policy lapse risk or mortality risk. Nevertheless, these quantities should be used to "risk neutralize" these models of behavior to the extent practical. The integrity of risk neutral valuation depends on risk adjusting all variables modeled; otherwise, model prices will be consistently overstated.

A final note can be made in this regard about option adjusted spread (OAS). OAS can be understood in this context as a crude method to risk adjust the pricing system to reflect all risk factors not explicitly modeled.

Realistic and Arbitrage-Free

A realistic, arbitrage-free model starts by exactly matching the term structure of interest rates implied by a set of market prices on an initial date, then evolves that curve into the future according to the realistic probability measure. This form of a model is useful for producing scenarios for evaluation of hedges or portfolio strategies, where it is important that the initial curve in each scenario exactly matches current market prices. The difficulty with such an approach lies in the estimation; realistic, arbitrage-free models are affected by *confounding*, where it is impossible to discriminate between model misspecification error and the term premia. Since the model parameters have been set to match market prices exactly, without regard to historical behavior, too few degrees of freedom remain to estimate both the term premia and an error term. Unless the model perfectly describes the true term structure process (that is, the time dependent parameters make the residual pricing error zero at all past and future dates, not just on the date of estimation), the term premia cannot be determined. The result is that realistic, arbitrage-free models are not of practical use.

Realistic and Equilibrium

Since the arbitrage-free form of a realistic model is not available, the equilibrium form must be used for stress testing, Value at Risk (VAR) calculations, reserve and asset adequacy testing, and other uses of realistic scenarios.

Some analysts express concern that, because the *predicted* initial curve under the equilibrium model does not perfectly match observed market prices, then the results of scenario testing will be invalid. However, the use of an equilibrium form does not require that the predictions be used instead of the current market prices as the first point in a scenario. The scenarios can contain the observed curve at the initial date and the conditional predictions at future dates. This does not introduce inconsistency, because the equilibrium model is a statistical model of term structure behavior; by taking this approach we explicitly recognize that its predictions will deviate from observed values by some error. In contrast, the use of an arbitrage-free, realistic model implicitly assumes that the model used for the term structure process is absolutely correct.

EXHIBIT 2.1 When to Use Each of the Model Types

Model Classification	Risk Neutral	Realistic
Arbitrage-free	• Current pricing, where input data (market prices) are reliable	• Unusable, since term premium cannot be reliably estimated
Equilibrium	• Current pricing, where inputs (market prices) are unreliable or unavailable • Horizon pricing	• Stress testing • Reserve and asset adequacy testing

EXHIBIT 2.2 Four Forms of the Black-Karasinski Model

Model Classification	Risk Neutral	Realistic
Arbitrage-free	$du = \kappa(t)\,(\theta(t) - u)\,dt + \sigma(t)\,dz$ • u_0 and $\theta(t)$ matched to bond prices • $\kappa(t)$ and $\sigma(t)$ matched to cap or option prices	$du = \kappa(t)\,(\theta(t) - \lambda(u,t) - u)\,dt + \sigma(t)\,dz$ • u_0 and $\theta(t)$ matched to bond prices • $\kappa(t)$ and $\sigma(t)$ matched to cap or option prices • $\lambda(u,t)$ cannot be reliably estimated
Equilibrium	$du = \kappa(\theta - u)\,dt + \sigma\,dz$ • u_0 statistically fit to bond prices • κ, θ, σ historically estimated	$du = \kappa(\theta - \lambda(u) - u)\,dt + \sigma\,dz$ • u_0 statistically fit to bond prices • κ, θ, σ, $\lambda(u)$ historically estimated

Summary of the Four Faces

Exhibit 2.1 summarizes the uses of the four faces of an interest rate model. Exhibit 2.2 shows the mathematical form of a commonly used interest rate model, disseminated by Black and Karasinski,[4] under each of the modeling approaches and probability measures. In each equation, u is the natural logarithm of the short rate.

In the above models, σ is the instantaneous volatility of the short rate process, κ is the rate of mean reversion, θ is the mean level to which the natural logarithm of the short rate is reverting, and λ represents the term premium demanded by the market for holding bonds of longer maturity. The value of the state variable u at the time of estimation is represented by u_0.

The realistic model forms can be distinguished from the risk neutral forms by the presence of the term premium function λ. The difference between the arbitrage-free forms and the equilibrium forms can be discerned in that the parameters of the arbitrage-free forms are functions of time.

[4] Fischer Black and Piotr Karasinski, "Bond and Option Pricing when Short Rates are Lognormal," *Financial Analysts Journal* (July–August 1991), pp. 52–59.

CHAPTER 3

A Review of No Arbitrage Interest Rate Models

Gerald W. Buetow, Jr., Ph.D., CFA
President
BFRC Services, LLC

Frank J. Fabozzi, Ph.D., CFA
Adjunct Professor of Finance
School of Management
Yale University

James Sochacki, Ph.D.
Associate Professor of Applied Mathematics
Department of Mathematics and Statistics
James Madison University

Interest rates are commonly modeled using stochastic differential equations (SDEs). One-factor models use an SDE to represent the short rate and two-factor models use an SDE for both the short rate and the long rate. The SDEs used to model interest rates must capture some of the market properties of interest rates such as mean reversion and/or a volatility that depends on the level of interest rates. There are two distinct approaches used to implement the SDEs into a term structure model: equilibrium and no arbitrage. Each can be used to value bonds and interest rate contingent claims. Both approaches start with the same SDEs but apply the SDE under a different framework to price securities.

Equilibrium models such as those developed by Vasicek,[1] Cox, Ingersoll, and Ross,[2] Longstaff,[3] Longstaff and Schwartz,[4] and Brennan and Schwartz[5] all start with an SDE model and develop pricing mechanisms for bonds under an equilibrium framework. The actual implementation may vary depending on the model. Vasicek and CIR develop analytic pricing expressions while Backus, Foresi, and Telmer[6] present econometric and recursive approaches to implement the equilibrium models. Brennan and Schwartz use a finite difference scheme that approximates a partial differential equation.

No arbitrage models such as Black and Karasinski,[7] Black, Derman, and Toy,[8] Ho and Lee,[9] Heath, Jarrow, and Morton,[10] and Hull and White[11] begin with the same or similar SDE models as the equilibrium approach but use market prices to generate an interest rate lattice. The lattice represents the short rate in such a way as to ensure there is a no arbitrage relationship between the market and the model. The numerical

---

[1] O. Vasicek, "An Equilibrium Characterization of the Term Structure," *Journal of Financial Economics* (1977), pp. 177–188.

[2] J. Cox, J. Ingersoll, and S. Ross, "A Theory of the Term Structure of Interest Rates," *Econometrica* (1985), pp. 385–408.

[3] F. Longstaff, "A Non-linear General Equilibrium Model of the Term Structure of Interest Rates," *Journal of Financial Economics* (1989), 23, pp. 195–224 and "Multiple Equilibria and Term Structure Models," *Journal of Financial Economics* (1992), pp. 333–344.

[4] F. Longstaff and E. Schwartz, "Interest Rate Volatility and the Term Structure: A Two-Factor General Equilibrium Model," *Journal of Finance* (1992), pp. 1259–1282.

[5] M. Brennan and E. Schwartz, "A Continuous Time Approach to the Pricing of Bonds," *Journal of Banking and Finance* (1979), pp. 133–155, and, "An Equilibrium Model of Bond Pricing and a Test of Market Efficiency," *Journal of Financial and Quantitative Analysis* (1982), pp. 301–329.

[6] D. Backus, S. Foresi, and C. Telmer, "Affine Term Structure Models and the Forward Premium Anomaly," *Journal of Finance* (2001), pp. 279–304.

[7] F. Black and P. Karasinski, "Bond and Option Pricing when Short Rates are Lognormal," *Financial Analyst Journal* (July–August 1991), pp. 52–59.

[8] F. Black, E. Derman, and W. Toy, "A One Factor Model of Interest Rates and Its Application to the Treasury Bond Options," *Financial Analyst Journal* (January–February 1990), pp. 33–39.

[9] T. Ho and S. Lee, "Term Structure Movements and Pricing Interest Rate Contingent Claims," *Journal of Finance* (1986), pp. 1011–1029.

[10] D. Heath, R. Jarrow, and A. Morton, "Bond Pricing and the Term Structure of Interest Rates: A New Methodology," *Econometrica* (1992), pp. 77–105.

[11] J. Hull and A. White, "Pricing Interest Rate Derivative Securities," *Review of Financial Studies* (1990), 3, pp. 573–592, and, "One Factor Interest Rate Models and the Valuation of Interest Rate Derivative Securities," *Journal of Financial and Quantitative Analysis* (1993), pp. 235–254.

approach used to generate the lattice will depend on the SDE model(s) being used to represent interest rates.

No arbitrage models are the preferred framework to value interest rate derivatives. This is because they minimally ensure that the market prices for bonds are exact. Equilibrium models will not price bonds exactly and this can have tremendous effects on the corresponding contingent claims. No arbitrage lattices also allow for a systematic valuation approach to almost all interest rate securities.

Three general SDE functional forms are considered in this work. The first is the Hull-White (HW) model. The HW model is a more general version of the Ho and Lee (HL)[12] approach except that it allows for mean reversion. Implementing the HW in a binomial framework removes a degree of freedom and in this case the HW model collapses to the HL model if a constant time step is retained. The second model we consider is the Black-Karasinski (BK) model. The BK model is a more general form of the Kalotay, Williams, and Fabozzi (KWF) model.[13] The BK model (like the HW model) in the binomial setting does not have enough degrees of freedom to be properly modeled and so the time step must be allowed to vary. The third is the Black, Derman, and Toy model.

We implement the HW and BK trinomial models using the Hull and White approach. Within the trinomial setting the time step remains constant and mean reversion can be explicitly incorporated. We discuss the SDEs, the properties of the SDEs, the numerical solutions to the SDEs, and the binomial and trinomial interest rate lattices for these models.

The focus of our presentation is on the end user and developer of interest rate models. We will highlight some significant differences across models. Most of these are due to the different distributions that underlie the models. This is done to emphasize the need to calibrate all models to the market prior to their use. By calibrating the models to the market we reduce the effects of the distributional differences and ensure a higher level of consistency in the metrics produced by the models.

The outline of this chapter is as follows. In the next section we present the SDEs and some of their mathematical properties. We also use the mathematics to highlight properties of the short rate. We then develop the methodology used to implement our approach in both the binomial and trinomial frameworks. A comparison of some numerical results across the different models including some interest rate risk and valuation metrics is then presented.

---

[12] T. Ho and S. Lee, "Term Structure Movements and Pricing Interest Rate Contingent Claims."

[13] A. Kalotay, G. Williams, and F.J. Fabozzi, "A Model for the Valuation of Bonds and Embedded Options," *Financial Analyst Journal* (May–June 1993), pp. 35–46.

THE GENERAL MODELS FOR THE SHORT RATE

The models considered in this chapter take the form of the following one-factor SDE:

$$df(r(t)) = [\theta(t) + \rho(t)g(r(t))]dt + \sigma(r(t), t)dz \tag{1}$$

where f and g are suitably chosen functions, θ is determined by the market, and ρ can be chosen by the user of the model or dictated by the market. We will show that θ is the drift of the short rate and ρ is the tendency to an equilibrium short rate. The term σ is the local volatility of the short rate. The term $dz = \varepsilon\sqrt{dt}$ arises from a normally distributed Wiener process, since $\varepsilon \sim N(0,1)$, where $N(0,1)$ is the normal distribution with mean 0 and standard deviation of 1. This means that the term $\sigma(r(t),t)dz$ has an average or expected value of 0.

Equation (1) has two components. The first component is the expected or average change in rates over a small period of time, *dt*. This is the component where certain characteristics of interest rates, such as mean reversion, are incorporated. The second component is the unknown or the risk term since it contains the random term. This term dictates the distribution characteristics of interest rates. Depending on the model, interest rates are either normally or lognormally distributed.

The Ho-Lee Model

In the HL model or process $f(r) = r$, $g(r) = 0$, and $\rho = 0$ in equation (1). The HL process is, therefore, given by

$$dr = \theta dt + \sigma dz \tag{2}$$

Since z is a normally distributed Wiener process, we say the HL process is a normal process for the short rate. The solution to equation (2), assuming $r(0) = r_0$ is given by

$$r(t) = r_0 + \int_0^t \theta ds + \int_0^t \sigma dz \tag{3a}$$

where the integral involving σ is a stochastic integral. If θ is constant this can be expressed as

$$r(t) = r_0 + \theta t + \int_0^t \sigma dz \tag{3b}$$

Equation (3b) shows that the HL process models an interest rate that can change proportionally with time t through the constant of proportionality, θ, and a random disturbance determined by σ. That is, the larger θ is in magnitude the larger the average change in the short rate over time. This is why θ is called the "drift in the short rate." Also, the smaller θ is the larger the influence of the random disturbance. The short rate can be negative in the HL process. This is a shortcoming of the model. Hull shows that θ is related to the slope of the term structure.[14]

To obtain a numerical approximation for equation (2) we approximate equation (2) by using equations (3a) and (3b). Letting $t_k = k\tau$ and $r_k \approx r(k\tau)$ gives

$$r_{k+1} - r_k = \theta_k\tau + \sigma_k\Delta z_k$$

or

$$r_{k+1} = r_k + \theta_k\tau + \sigma_k\Delta z_k \tag{4}$$

where Δz_k is a numerical (discrete) approximation to dz. Since $dz = \varepsilon\sqrt{dt}$, we can further approximate equation (4) by

$$r_{k+1} = r_k + \theta_k\tau + \sigma_k\varepsilon_k\sqrt{\tau} \tag{5}$$

where ε_k is a random number given by a normal distribution $N(0,1)$. Equation (5) is the form of the expression that is used for r_{k+1} to build the HL binomial tree.

We first consider the solution to equation (5) without the stochastic term when θ is constant. Equation (5) under these requirements is

$$r_{k+1} = r_k + \tau\theta \tag{6a}$$

and the solution is given by

$$r_k = c + k\delta \tag{6b}$$

where c and δ are constants. In particular, $c = r_0$ and $\delta = \theta\tau$. It is seen from this last equation that the mean short rate in the HL process increases or decreases at a constant rate θ over time depending on the sign of θ. As a matter of fact, equation (6b) shows that the short rate grows without bound if $\theta > 0$ and decreases without bound (i.e. becomes very negative) if $\theta < 0$.

[14] J. Hull, *Options, Futures, and Other Derivatives, Fourth Edition* (Saddle River, NJ: Prentice Hall, 2000).

The Hull-White Model

In the HW model or process $f(r) = r$, $g(r) = r$, and $\rho = -\phi$. Therefore, the stochastic process for the HW model for the short rate is

$$dr = (\theta - \phi r)dt + \sigma dz \tag{7}$$

The short rate process in the HW model is seen to be normal as in the HL process. We consider the case where the parameters θ and ϕ are constant over time. Note that if $\phi = 0$ the HL process reduces to the HW process. (The HW process will, therefore, be similar to the HL process if ϕ is close to 0.) We will see that the introduction of ϕ in the HW model is an attempt to incorporate mean reversion and to correct for the uncontrolled growth (or decline) in the HL model shown later in this chapter.

Eliminating the stochastic term in equation (7) gives the ordinary differential equation

$$dr = (\theta - \phi r)dt \tag{8}$$

whose solution is given by

$$r(t) = \frac{\theta}{\phi} + ce^{-\phi t} \tag{9}$$

where

$$c = r_0 - \frac{\theta}{\phi} \tag{10}$$

If $\phi > 0$ we see from equation (9) that

$$\lim_{t \to \infty} r(t) = \frac{\theta}{\phi} = \mu$$

Therefore, for positive mean reversion ($\phi > 0$) the HW process will converge to the short rate, μ. Due to this, the term μ is called the "target" or "long run mean rate." For negative mean reversion ($\phi < 0$), the short rate grows exponentially over time.

Factoring ϕ in equation (7) leads to

$$dr = \phi(\mu - r)dt + \sigma dz$$

and eliminating the stocastic term leads to

$$dr = \phi(\mu - r)dt$$

We see that if $r > \mu$ then dr is negative and r will decrease and if $r < \mu$ then dr is positive and r will increase. That is, r will approach the target rate μ. The larger ϕ is the faster this approach to the target rate μ. This is why ϕ is called the "mean reversion" or "mean reversion rate." It regulates how fast the target rate is reached. However, it does not eliminate the negative rates that can occur in the HL process.

Since the target rate μ is equal to θ/ϕ, we can solve for the drift, θ, or the mean reversion, ϕ. That is,

$$\theta = \mu\phi \tag{11}$$

or

$$\phi = \frac{\theta}{\mu} \tag{12}$$

It is seen from equations (11) and (12) that there is a strong relationship between the drift and mean reversion that can be used to reach any desired target rate. How large the mean reversion should be is an important financial question. Equations (11) and (12) can be used to set target rates. Equations (9) and (10) allow one to determine how long it takes to reach the target rate.

Approximating equation (7) gives us

$$r_{k+1} = r_k + (\theta_k - \phi_k r_k)\tau + \sigma_k \varepsilon_k \sqrt{\tau} \tag{13}$$

If θ and ϕ are constant and we eliminate the stochastic term then the solution to equation (13) has the form

$$r_k = \alpha\beta^k + \gamma$$

To determine α, β, and γ we substitute this form for r_k into equation (13) under these conditions and obtain that $\beta = (1 - \phi\tau)$, $\gamma = \theta/\phi = \mu$, and $\alpha = r_0 - \mu$. Therefore,

$$r_k = \alpha(1 - \phi\tau)^k + \frac{\theta}{\phi} \tag{14}$$

Note that if $0 < \phi\tau < 2$ then $-1 < 1 - \phi\tau < 1$ and

$$\lim_{k \to \infty} r_k = \frac{\theta}{\phi} = \mu$$

which is the same result we obtained from equation (9) for the HW SDE. The condition $0 < \phi\tau < 2$ is easily maintained in modeling the short rate.

The Kalotay-Williams-Fabozzi Model

For the KWF process $f(r) = \ln(r)$, $g(r) = 0$, and $\rho = 0$ in equation (1). This leads to the differential process

$$d\ln(r) = \theta dt + \sigma dz \tag{15a}$$

This model is directly analogous to the HL model. If $u = \ln r$ then we obtain the HL process (equation(2)) for u

$$du = \theta dt + \sigma dz \tag{15b}$$

Because u follows a normal process, $\ln(r)$ follows a normal process and so r follows a lognormal process. Since u follows the same process as the HL and HW models, u can become negative, but $u = \ln(r)$ and $r = e^u$ ensuring r is always positive. Therefore, the KWF model eliminates the problems of negative short rates that occurred in the HL and HW models.

Eliminating the stochastic term in equation (15) we obtain

$$d\ln(r) = \theta(t)dt$$

and

$$du = \theta(t)dt$$

From equation (3a) we have

$$\ln r(t) = u = u(0) + \int_0^t \theta(s)ds$$

since $u(0) = \ln r(0) = \ln r_0$,

$$\ln r(t) = \ln r(0) + \int_0^t \theta(s)ds$$

Taking the exponential of both sides gives us

$$r(t) = r_0 e^{\int_0^t \theta(s)ds} \tag{16}$$

showing that $r(t) > 0$ since $r(0) > 0$. Therefore, if $\theta(t) > 0$ the short rate in the KWF process grows without bound and if $\theta(t) < 0$ the short rate in the KWF process decays to 0.

From equation (5) for the HL process the discrete approximation to equation (15b) is

$$u_{k+1} = u_k + \theta_k \tau + \sigma_k \varepsilon_k \sqrt{\tau} \tag{17a}$$

and the exponential of this equation gives the discrete approximation to equation (15a):

$$r_{k+1} = r_k e^{\theta_k \tau + \sigma_k \varepsilon_k \sqrt{\tau}} \tag{17b}$$

From equation (17b) and equation (16) we see that the numerical approximation to equation (15a) has similar properties to the solution to the HL SDE. That is, if $\theta(t) > 0$ the short rate grows without bound and if $\theta(t) < 0$ the short rate decays to 0.

The Black-Karasinski Model

In the BK model we set $f(r) = \ln r$, $\rho = -\phi$, and $g(r) = \ln r$ in equation (1) to obtain the SDE

$$d \ln r = (\theta - \phi \ln r)dt + \sigma dz \tag{18a}$$

We now work with equation (18a) using equation (7) for the HW process in a manner similar to how we used results from the HL process to develop the KWF process. If we let $u = \ln r$ in equation (18a) we obtain

$$du = (\theta - \phi u)dt + \sigma dz \tag{18b}$$

which is the HW process for u. Again, note that u has all the same properties as r in the HW model. Since $r = e^u$ in the BK process, $r > 0$. This is the advantage the BK model has over the HW model. Therefore, we see that the BK process is an extension of the KWF process as the HW process is an extension of the HL process. The main difference is the BK is a lognormal extension of the lognormal KWF process. As a matter of fact, if $\phi = 0$ the BK process reduces to the KWF process. Black and Karasinski introduced ϕ to control the growth of the short rate in the KWF process.

From equation (9) we have

$$u(t) = \frac{\theta}{\phi} + ce^{-\phi t}$$

and after taking exponentials

$$r(t) = e^{u(t)} = e^{\frac{\theta}{\phi} + ce^{-\phi t}} \tag{19}$$

For $\phi < 0$ we see that r grows without bound and that for $\phi > 0$

$$\lim_{t \to \infty} r(t) = e^{\frac{\theta}{\phi}} = \mu$$

The target rate for the BK process is the exponential of the target rate for the HW process.

As in the HW process, from equation (19) (or equations (9) and (10)) we see that

$$c = \ln r_0 - \frac{\theta}{\phi} \tag{20}$$

in the BK process. The closer the initial rate is to the target rate the faster the BK process converges to the target rate. From equations (19) and (20) we see that if the initial short rate is the target rate then $r(t) = \mu$ for all t in the BK process which is analogous to the HW process.

Given the target rate μ we can solve for the drift or the mean reversion similarly to equations (11) and (12) in the HW model. We have

$$\theta = \phi \ln \mu \tag{21}$$

and

$$\phi = \frac{\theta}{\ln \mu} \tag{22}$$

We discretize $u = \ln r$ in equation (18b) just as we did for the HW SDEs and then let $r = e^u$. This is analogous to how we used the HL discrete process to get the KWF discrete process. The equations corresponding to equation (13) are

$$u_{k+1} = u_k + (\theta_k - \phi_k u_k)\tau + \sigma_k \varepsilon_k \sqrt{\tau} \tag{23a}$$

or after taking the exponential of both sides of equation (23a)

$$r_{k+1} = r_k e^{(\theta_k - \varphi_k \ln r_k)\tau + \sigma_k \varepsilon_k \sqrt{\tau}} \tag{23b}$$

For constant θ and ϕ (similarly to equation (14)), the solution to equation (23b) after eliminating the stochastic term is

$$r_k = e^{\alpha(1-\phi r)^k + \frac{\theta}{\phi}} \tag{24}$$

Note from equation (24) that

$$\lim_{k \to \infty} r_k = e^{\frac{\theta}{\phi}} = \mu$$

for $0 < \phi\tau < 2$. This is similar to the result we obtained from equation (14) for the HW SDEs.

The Black-Derman-Toy Model

The Black-Derman-Toy (BDT) model is a lognormal model with mean reversion, but the mean reversion is endogenous to the model. The mean reversion in the BDT model is determined by market conditions.

The equation describing the interest rate dynamics in the BDT model has $f(r) = \ln r$ and $g(r) = \ln r$ in equation (1) as in the BK model. Therefore, the short rate in the BDT model follows the lognormal process

$$d \ln r + [\theta(t) + \rho(t) \ln r]dt + \sigma(t)dz$$

However, in the BDT model $\rho(t) = \frac{d}{dt}\ln\sigma(t) = \frac{\sigma'(t)}{\sigma(t)}$ giving us

$$d\ln r = \left(\theta(t) + \frac{\sigma'(t)}{\sigma(t)}\ln r\right)dt + \sigma(t)dz \tag{25a}$$

Making the substitution $u = \ln r$ leads to

$$du = \left(\theta(t) + \frac{\sigma'(t)}{\sigma(t)}u\right)dt + \sigma(t)dz \tag{25b}$$

Notice the similarity in equations (25) and the equations (18) of the BK model. We expect

$$\frac{\sigma'(t)}{\sigma(t)}$$

to behave similarly to $-\phi(t)$ in the BK model. This expression should give mean reversion in the short rate when it is negative. That is, we expect that if $\sigma'(t) < 0$ (implying $\sigma(t)$ is decreasing) then the BDT model will give mean reversion. On the other hand, when $\sigma'(t) > 0$ (implying $\sigma(t)$ is increasing) the short rates in the BDT model will grow with no mean reversion. If $\sigma(t)$ is constant in the BDT model, then $\sigma'(t) = 0$ so $\rho = 0$ and equation (25a) becomes the KWF model (equation (15)). Therefore, we will only study the case of varying local volatility for the BDT model.

Eliminating the stochastic term in equation (25) leads to

$$d\ln r = du = \left(\theta(t) + \frac{\sigma'(t)}{\sigma(t)}u\right)dt = \left(\theta(t) + \frac{\sigma'(t)}{\sigma(t)}\ln r\right)dt \tag{26}$$

Solving this equation for u as we did in the KF and BK models, gives us

$$u(t) = \left[\frac{u(0)}{\sigma(0)} + \int_0^t \frac{\theta(s)}{\sigma(s)}ds\right]\sigma(t)$$

or

$$r(t) = e^{\left(\frac{\log(r_0)}{\sigma_0} + \int_0^t \frac{\theta(s)}{\sigma(s)}ds\right)\sigma(t)} = e^{\frac{\sigma(t)\log(r_0)}{\sigma_0}} e^{\sigma(t)\int_0^t \frac{\theta(s)}{\sigma(s)}ds}$$

or

$$r(t) = r_0 e^{\frac{\sigma(t) - \sigma_0}{\sigma_0}\log(r_0)} e^{\sigma(t)\int_0^t \frac{\theta(s)}{\sigma(s)}ds} \tag{27}$$

Note that the BDT mean short rate depends on the local volatility. If the local volatility has a decreasing structure, then the first exponential term in equation (27) has a negative exponent and will cause a decrease in the short rate and vice versa if the local volatility has an increasing structure. It is important to note that mean reversion in the BDT model comes from the local volatility structure (i.e., it is endogenous).

We now consider numerical solutions to the BDT process. To discretize equation (25a) for the BDT model we start off again by approximating *du* in equation (25b) by *u* to get

$$u_{k+1} = u_k + (\theta_k + \rho_k u_k)\tau + \sigma_k \varepsilon_k \sqrt{\tau} \tag{28}$$

The exponential of equation (28) gives us

$$r_{k+1} = r_k e^{[(\theta_k + \rho_k \ln r_k)\tau + \sigma_k \varepsilon_k \sqrt{\tau}]} \tag{29}$$

where

$$\rho_k = \frac{\sigma_k'}{\sigma_k}$$

We approximate this term by

$$\frac{\frac{\sigma_{k+1} - \sigma_k}{\tau}}{\sigma_k}$$

That is, we approximate σ_k' by a discrete approximation to the derivative. We now have

$$u_{k+1} = u_k + \left(\theta_k + \frac{\frac{\sigma_{k+1} - \sigma_k}{\tau}}{\sigma_k} u_k\right)\tau + \sigma_k \varepsilon_k \sqrt{\tau}$$

or

$$u_{k+1} = \frac{\sigma_{k+1}}{\sigma_k} u_k + \theta_k \tau + \sigma_k \varepsilon_k \sqrt{\tau} \tag{30}$$

If the random term is 0 equation (30) becomes

$$u_{k+1} = \frac{\sigma_{k+1}}{\sigma_k} u_k + \theta_k \tau \tag{31}$$

In particular, if

$$\frac{\sigma_{k+1}}{\sigma_k} = \alpha$$

where α is a constant then

$$u_k = \alpha^k u_0 + \sum_{j=0}^{k-1} \alpha^j \theta_{k-j-1} \tau$$

The exponential of this gives

$$r_k = r_0 e^{(\alpha^k - 1)\ln r_0} e^{\sum_{j=0}^{k-1} \alpha^j \theta_{k-j-1} \tau}$$

This equation is interesting because $\ln r_0 < 0$. If $\alpha > 1$ then the first exponential term decreases. When $\theta < 0$ the second exponential term also decreases and the BDT short rate should approach a target rate. Conversely, when $\theta > 0$ the second exponential term increases. In this case we can approach a target rate or the second term can dominate. If $\alpha < 1$ then a similar situation arises. Therefore, in order to get meaningful numerical results for the BDT short rates we strongly recommend that α be close to 1 and that the term structure of spot rates not have too large a slope.

The analysis of the equations without the stochastic term presented in this section is important. Recall that the characteristics of the random term are such that average influence of this term will be much smaller than the mean term in the SDEs. Consequently, the properties presented within this section will also hold under more general circumstances. The discrete approximations we developed for the models will be used to build the binomial and trinomial models in the next section. Note that we are highlighting the difference across the models and do not calibrate the models to market information.

For numerical reasons, the BK and HW models are best implemented in the trinomial framework. The HL, KWF, and BDT models are more easily implemented in the binomial framework.[15] We will discuss

[15] See G.W. Buetow and J. Sochacki, *Binomial Interest Rate Models*, AIMR Research Foundation, 2001.

the specifics of this in the next section. For the trinomial framework we use the approach of Hull and White.[16]

BINOMIAL AND TRINOMIAL SOLUTIONS TO THE STOCHASTIC DIFFERENTIAL EQUATIONS

In this section we present the binomial and trinomial lattice models that are obtained for the discretized versions of SDEs given in the previous section. The binomial method models the short rate in a geometrically analogous manner as equities.[17] The up move has a probability q and so the down move has a probability of $1 - q$. We use $q = 0.5$ within the framework of risk neutrality. This binomial process of two possible moves for the short rate in the next time period is then continued at each time to produce a binomial lattice of interest rates.

The trinomial model is similar in spirit to the binomial except there are three possible states emanating from each node. From each point in time we call the upward-most move the "up move," the downward-most move the "down move," and the center move the "middle move." The probabilities for an up move, middle move and down move are given by q_1, q_2, and q_3 with $q_1 + q_2 + q_3 = 1$.

Interest rate lattices should possess the property of recombination for them to be computationally tractable. That is, from any given node in the binomial model we will require an up move followed by a down move to get to the same point as a down move followed by an up move. This ensures that the number of nodes in the binomial lattice increase by only one at each time step. In the trinomial case recombination is a little more complicated. From any node in the trinomial lattice an up move followed by a down move will get to the same node as two successive middle moves and as a down move followed by an up move. This ensures that the number of nodes in the trinomial lattice increase by only two at each time step.

Exhibit 3.1 represents a binomial short rate lattice and Exhibit 3.2 represents a trinomial short rate lattice. The notation $r_{j,k}$ is used to denote the short rate value at level j at time t_k. In the binomial lattice, an up move from $r_{j,k}$ is given by $r_{j,k+1}$ and a down move is given by $r_{j+1,k+1}$. At time t_k there are $k + 1$ possible values for the short rate in the bino-

[16] J. Hull and A. White, "Pricing Interest Rate Derivative Securities," "One Factor Interest Rate Models and the Valuation of Interest Rate Derivative Securities," and "Numerical Procedures for Implementing Term Structure Models I: Single-Factor Models," *Journal of Derivatives* (Fall 1994), pp. 7–16.

[17] See J. Cox, S. Ross, and M. Rubinstein, "Option Pricing a Simplified Approach," *Journal of Financial Economics* (1979), pp. 229–264.

mial lattice. That is, j ranges from 1 to $k + 1$. In the trinomial model, an up move, middle move, and down move from the short rate $r_{j,k}$ is given by $r_{j,k+1}$, $r_{j+1,k+1}$, and $r_{j+2,k+1}$, respectively. In the trinomial model there are $2k + 1$ possible values for the short rate at time t_k. That is, j ranges from 1 to $2k + 1$. The short rates forming the top of the lattice will be called the up state for the short rates and the short rates forming the bottom of the lattice will be called the down state for the short rates. For the binomial and trinomial model, the up state is the set of short rates $r_{1,k}$ for $0 \leq k \leq n$ and the down state for the binomial case is the set of short rates $r_{k,k}$ for $0 \leq k \leq n$; within the trinomial tree the down state is the set of short rates $r_{2k+1,k}$ for $0 \leq k \leq n$.

Hull-White Binomial Lattice

Since the HW model is a more general version of the HL model we present the binomial version only for the HW. In the HW binomial lattice the expressions for $r_{j,k}$ that correspond to equation (13) are

$$r_{j,\,k+1} = r_{j,\,k} + \theta_k \tau_k - \phi_k r_{j,\,k} \tau_k + \sigma_k \sqrt{\tau_k} \tag{32}$$

EXHIBIT 3.1 Binomial Lattice

			$r_{1,3}$
		$r_{1,2}$	
	$r_{1,1}$		$r_{2,3}$
$r_{1,0}$		$r_{2,2}$	
	$r_{2,1}$		$r_{3,3}$
		$r_{3,2}$	
			$r_{4,3}$
t_0	t_1	t_2	t_3

EXHIBIT 3.2 Trinomial Lattice

			$r_{1,4}$
		$r_{1,2}$	$r_{2,4}$
	$r_{1,1}$	$r_{2,2}$	$r_{3,4}$
$r_{1,0}$	$r_{2,1}$	$r_{3,2}$	$r_{4,4}$
	$r_{3,1}$	$r_{4,2}$	$r_{5,4}$
		$r_{5,2}$	$r_{6,4}$
			$r_{7,4}$
t_0	t_1	t_2	t_3

for an up move and

$$r_{j+1,k+1} = r_{j,k} + \theta_k \tau_k - \phi_k r_{j,k} \tau_k - \sigma_k \sqrt{\tau_k} \tag{33}$$

for a down move. (We are using τ_k for Δt_k.)

These equations suggest that in order to have recombination the following must be true:

$$\tau_{k+1} = \tau_k \frac{4\left(\frac{\sigma_k}{\sigma_{k+1}}\right)^2}{\left[1 + \sqrt{1 + 4\left(\frac{\sigma_k}{\sigma_{k+1}}\right)^2 \tau_k \phi_{k+1}}\right]^2} \tag{34}$$

Equation (34) illustrates that if you want a constant time step when the local volatility is constant, the mean reversion must be 0. The recombination requirement has put the stringent condition on the HW binomial lattice that the mean reversion is determined by the local volatility. To avoid this problem within the binomial framework we must allow the time step to vary with k in equations (32) through (34). As a matter of fact, for a constant time step,

$$\phi_{k+1} = \frac{\sigma_k - \sigma_{k+1}}{\sigma_k \tau} \tag{35}$$

which can also be solved for σ_{k+1} to give

$$\sigma_{k+1} = \sigma_k(1 - \phi_{k+1}\tau) \tag{36}$$

Equation (36) shows that the mean reversion can be used to match any given local volatility for a constant time step. If the local volatility is decreasing the mean reversion will be positive, and if the local volatility is increasing the mean reversion will be negative. We point out that if a variable time step is used, one does not have to have mean reversion match local volatility.

Black-Karasinski Binomial Lattice

Since the BK model is a more general form of the KWF model, we only present the binomial version for the BK model. The expressions corresponding to equations (32) and (33) of the HW model and from equation (23b) are

$$r_{j,k+1} = r_{j,k}e^{(\theta_k - \phi_k \ln(r_{j,k}))\tau_k + \sigma_k\sqrt{\tau_k}} \quad (37)$$

for an up move and

$$r_{j+1,k+1} = r_{j,k}e^{(\theta_k - \phi_k \ln(r_{j,k}))\tau_k - \sigma_k\sqrt{\tau_k}} \quad (38)$$

for a down move.

Using equations (37) and (38) we can develop equations for the BK binomial lattice that are identical to equations (34) and (36) for the HW binomial lattice. This should be expected since the BK SDE is just a lognormal version of the HW SDE. A crucial point here is that we can use the HW and BK models to match local volatility and to compare results. It is important to point out that the HW and BK binomial lattices have a variable time step. If a variable time step is used then interpolation is required to give the short rates at the fixed time steps. We do not offer this framework. Instead we present the HW and the BK models in the trinomial framework.

Within the binomial framework, the HW and BK models only approximate the distributional properties of their respective SDE's. The accuracy of the approximation is a function of the mean reversion. As the mean reversion increases, the accuracy decreases. Note that since the HL and KWF models have a zero mean reversion the distributional characteristics of their SDE's are perfectly matched within the binomial framework. This is the reason for using the trinomial method for the HW and BK models.

The Trinomial Lattices

A better way to keep a constant time step and to match the appropriate distributional properties is to use a trinomial lattice instead of a binomial lattice. If we use a trinomial lattice for the HW SDEs, then from equation (13) we use

$$r_{j,k+1} = r_{j,k} + \theta_k\tau - \phi_k r_{j,k}\tau + \alpha_k\sigma_k\sqrt{\tau} \quad (39a)$$

for an up move,

$$r_{j+2,k+1} = r_{j,k} + \theta_k\tau - \phi_k r_{j,k}\tau - \alpha_k\sigma_k\sqrt{\tau} \quad (39b)$$

for a down move, and

$$r_{j+1,\,k+1} = r_{j,\,k} + \theta_k \tau - \phi_k r_{j,\,k} \tau \tag{39c}$$

for a middle move. Similarly, if we use a trinomial lattice for the BK SDEs then from equation (23b) we use

$$r_{j,\,k+1} = r_{j,\,k} e^{(\theta_k - \phi_k \ln(r_{j,\,k}))\tau + \alpha_k \sigma_k \sqrt{\tau}} \tag{40a}$$

for an up move,

$$r_{j+2,\,k+1} = r_{j,\,k} e^{(\theta_k - \phi_k \ln(r_{j,\,k}))\tau - \alpha_k \sigma_k \sqrt{\tau}} \tag{40b}$$

for a down move, and

$$r_{j+1,\,k+1} = r_{j,\,k} e^{(\theta_k - \phi_k \ln(r_{j,\,k}))\tau} \tag{40c}$$

for a middle move.

Note that a constant time step is now used. The expression α_k is used to guarantee recombination. The probabilities of an up, middle, and down move are chosen to give the correct variance.

The No Arbitrage Equations

The procedure to generate the no arbitrage equations for the binomial and trinomial lattices is outlined in the appendix. The no arbitrage polynomial for the short rates in the binomial tree is given by,

$$f_i = c_{1,\,i} \prod_{j=1}^{i} (1 + r_{j,\,i}\tau) + \sum_{m=1}^{i} c_{m+1,\,i} \prod_{n \neq m}^{i} (1 + r_{n,\,i}\tau) \tag{41}$$

where, for $i \geq 3$

$$a_{1,\,i} = \prod_{n=0}^{i-1} \prod_{m=1}^{i} (1 + r_{m,\,n}\tau)$$

$a_{2,i} = b_{1,i-1}$, $a_{j,i} = b_{j-2,i-1} + b_{j-1,i-1}$, for $j = 3, \ldots, i$, $a_{i+1,j} = b_{i-1,i-1}$, and $c_{1,i} = P_{i+1} a_{1,i}$, $c_{j+1,i} = q^{i-j}(1-q)^{j-1} a_{j+1,i}$ for $j = 1, \ldots, i$.

We solve equation (41) for θ_i by setting $f_i = 0$. We then use θ_i to compute $r_{j,i}$ for $j = 1, ..., i$ at the ith period. The bisection method will converge quickly because there is only one root between –1 and 1 for the HW binomial lattice and one root between 0 and 1 for the BK binomial lattice.[18]

After generating the new rates we let

$$b_{j,i} = a_{j+1,i} \prod_{\substack{m=1 \\ m \neq j}}^{i} (1 + r_{m,i}\tau)$$

For the variable time step, τ_i we replace the terms $(1 + r_{j,i}\tau)$ by $(1 + r_{j,i}\tau)^{\tau_i/\tau}$ and the terms $(1 + r_{n,i}\tau)$ by

$$(1 + r_{n,i}\tau)^{\tau_i/\tau}$$

in equation (41).

Similarly, the no arbitrage polynomial for the trinomial trees is given by,

$$f_i = c_{1,i} \prod_{j=1}^{2i-1} (1 + r_{j,i}\tau) + \sum_{m=1}^{2i-1} c_{m+1,i} \prod_{\substack{n=1 \\ n \neq m}}^{2i-1} (1 + r_{n,i}\tau) \tag{42}$$

where we first let

$$a_{1,i} = \prod_{j=1}^{2i-3} (1 + r_{j,i}\tau)$$

$$a_{2,i} = q_1 b_{1,i-1} a_{2,i-1},\ a_{3,i} = q_2 b_{1,i-1} a_{2,i-1} + q_1 b_{2,i-1} a_{3,i-1}$$

$$a_{j,i} = q_3 b_{j-3,i-1} a_{j-2,i-1} + q_2 b_{j-2,i-1} a_{j-1} + q_1 b_{j-1,i-1} a_{j,i-1}, \text{ for } j = 4, ..., 2i-2,$$

$$a_{2i-1,i} = q_3 b_{2i-4,i-1} a_{2i-3,i-1} + q_2 b_{2i-3,i-1} a_{2i-2,i-1},\ a_{2i,i} = q_3 b_{2i-3,i-1} a_{2i-2,i-1}$$

and then let

$$c_{1,i} = P_{i+1} a_{1,i},\ c_{j,i} = a_{j,i} \text{ for } j = 2, ..., 2i+1$$

[18] See Richard L. Burden and Douglas Faires, *Numerical Methods, Second Edition* (Pacific Grove, CA: Brooks/Cole Publishing Company, 1998).

We solve equation (42) for θ_i by setting $f_i = 0$ using the bisection method. From this the short rates for either the HW or BK trinomial lattices are determined at step i. We then let

$$b_n = \prod_{\substack{j=1 \\ j \neq n}}^{2i-1} (1 + r_{j,i}\tau)$$

for $n = 1, \ldots, 2i - 1$ and then repeat the process. In these derivations $P_i = 1/(1 + R_i\tau)^i$ is the discount factor given by the spot rates (zero curve).

The Hull and White Lattice

We now briefly outline the Hull and White methodology for generating HW and BK trinomial lattices.[19] The Hull and White methodology uses

$$r_{j,k} = x + (j_k)\Delta\rho \tag{43}$$

for the HW trinomial lattice short rates and

$$r_{j,k} = e^{[x + (j_k)\Delta\rho]} \tag{44}$$

for the BK trinomial lattice short rates.

They choose $\Delta\rho = \sigma\sqrt{3\tau}$ to minimize numerical error and introduce the mean reversion through the probabilities q_1, q_2, and q_3. Specifically, they use

$$q_1 = \frac{1}{6} + \frac{(j_k)^2\phi^2\tau^2 + (j_k)\phi\tau}{2}$$

$$q_2 = \frac{2}{3} - (j_k)^2\phi^2\tau^2$$

and

$$q_3 = \frac{1}{6} + \frac{(j_k)^2\phi^2\tau^2 - (j_k)\phi\tau}{2}$$

[19] For complete details we refer the reader to Hull and White, "Numerical Procedures for Implementing Term Structure Models I: Single-Factor Models."

for the up, middle, and down moves at $r_{j,k}$, respectively, since this matches the expected change and variance of the short rate over the next time period. However, as they point out, these probabilities must remain positive. In order to do this they "prune" the upper and lower branches of their lattice at the level j that keeps these probabilities positive. Since q_2 is the only one that can become negative they require the following,

$$j < \frac{\sqrt{6}}{3\phi\tau} \approx \frac{0.816}{\phi\tau}$$

At this maximum value of j, Hull and White apply a different branching procedure with different probabilities in order to "prune" the lattice. However, as they point out, using this value of j can lead to computational problems so they actually use the first j satisfying

$$j_k > \frac{3-\sqrt{6}}{3\phi\tau} \approx \frac{0.184}{\phi\tau}$$

This leads to a reduction in the spread of the rates.

COMPARATIVE STUDY OF THE NUMERICAL SOLUTIONS

In this section a comparison between the methodologies is presented. In particular, we look at the effects of mean reversion and local volatility on the drift and the spread in the short rates. We present numerical results for the term structures, volatility, and mean reversion in Exhibit 3.3. The exhibit also includes the bond information for use later.

Original Term Structure with No Mean Reversion

We first consider the original term structure with no mean reversion for the HL and HW models. In Exhibit 3.4 we present the binomial tree for the HL model and the trinomial for the HW model using the HW trinomial methodology. We use a 10% volatility throughout the trees. We see that the spread in the short rates increases over time in the models as expected. We also see that the HL model can give negative short rates.

In Exhibit 3.5 we present the binomial tree for the KWF model, the trinomial for the BK model using the HW trinomial methodology, and the BDT binomial model. The KWF and BK models use the 10% volatility throughout the tree and no mean reversion. Note the volatile nature of the BDT model. This is due to the time varying volatility structure and the way mean reversion is incorporated into the BDT model through this decreasing volatility structure. Note that all the short rates are positive and that the spread in the rates is significantly less than in Exhibit 3.4.

Exhibit 3.6 presents the trinomial lattices for the HW and BK models using the information in Exhibit 3.3 and a mean reversion of 5%. The volatility is 10%. Notice the pruning that takes place within the lattice when we have mean reversion. This produces lattices that are significantly different than those shown in Exhibits 3.4 and 3.5. This is a peculiarity of the Hull and White methodology. The pruning is a result of incorporating mean reversion into the model and ensuring that the distributional characteristics of the SDE's are retained.

Comparison of the Models Using Common Risk and Value Metrics

Here we contrast the effective duration, effective convexity, and the option-adjusted spread (OAS) for 10-year callable and putable bonds each with a one-year delay on the embedded option. The information in Exhibit 3.3 is used for the analysis. We computed the effective duration for the original term structures shown in Exhibit 3.3 using a yield change of 25 basis points. The original term structure is then shifted up and down in a parallel manner by ±250 basis points and by ±500 basis points, respectively. In other words, we computed the effective duration at five different term structure levels using a yield change of 25 basis points.

EXHIBIT 3.3 Input Information

Original TS	Volatility	Mean Reversion
6.20%	10.00%	5%
6.16%	10.00%	
6.15%	9.00%	
6.09%	9.00%	
6.02%	8.00%	
6.02%	8.00%	
6.01%	7.00%	
6.01%	7.00%	
6.00%	7.00%	
6.01%	7.00%	

Bond Information for ED, EC, and OAS	
Call Price (Regular Callable)	$102.50
Put Price (Regular Putable)	$95.00
Annual Coupon ($ per $100)	$6.00
Time Option Starts (years from now)	1

EXHIBIT 3.4 The HL Binomial and HW Trinomial Trees for the Original Term Structure with No Mean Reversion

a. The Ho-Lee Interest Rate Lattice

										136.31%
									118.42%	
								101.50%		116.31%
							85.20%		98.42%	
						69.85%		81.50%		96.31%
					54.99%		65.20%		78.42%	
				41.49%		49.85%		61.50%		76.31%
			28.93%		34.99%		45.20%		58.42%	
		17.05%		21.49%		29.85%		41.50%		56.31%
	6.20%		8.93%		14.99%		25.20%		38.42%	
		–2.95%		1.49%		9.85%		21.50%		36.31%
			–11.07%		–5.01%		5.20%		18.42%	
				–18.51%		–10.15%		1.50%		16.31%
					–25.01%		–14.80%		–1.58%	
						–30.15%		–18.50%		–3.69%
							–34.80%		–21.58%	
								–38.50%		–23.69%
									–41.58%	
										–43.69%
Time in Years	0.0	1.0	2.0	3.0	4.0	5.0	6.0	7.0	8.0	9.0

EXHIBIT 3.4 (Continued)

b. The Hull-White Trinomial Interest Rate Lattice Using the HW Method with No Mean Reversion

										203.31%
									172.58%	185.99%
								142.30%	155.26%	168.67%
							131.70%	124.98%	137.94%	151.35%
						107.78%	114.38%	107.66%	120.62%	134.03%
					84.92%	90.46%	97.06%	90.34%	103.30%	116.71%
				63.71%	67.60%	73.14%	79.74%	73.02%	85.98%	99.39%
			43.65%	46.38%	50.28%	55.82%	62.42%	55.70%	68.66%	82.07%
		24.39%	26.33%	29.06%	32.96%	38.50%	45.10%	38.38%	51.34%	64.75%
	6.20%	7.07%	9.01%	11.74%	15.64%	21.18%	27.78%	21.06%	34.02%	47.43%
		−10.25%	−8.31%	−5.58%	−1.68%	3.86%	10.46%	3.74%	16.70%	30.11%
			−25.63%	−22.90%	−19.00%	−13.46%	−6.86%	−13.58%	−0.62%	12.79%
				−40.22%	−36.32%	−30.78%	−24.18%	−30.90%	−17.94%	−4.53%
					−53.64%	−48.10%	−41.50%	−48.22%	−35.26%	−21.85%
						−65.42%	−58.83%	−65.54%	−52.58%	−39.18%
							−76.15%	−82.86%	−69.90%	−56.50%
								−100.18%	−87.22%	−73.82%
									−104.54%	−91.14%
										−108.46%
Time in Years	0.0	1.0	2.0	3.0	4.0	5.0	6.0	7.0	8.0	9.0

EXHIBIT 3.5 The BDT and KWF Binomial and the BK Trinomial Trees for the Original Term Structure with No Mean Reversion

a. The Kalotay, Williams, and Fabozzi Interest Rate Lattice

Time in Years	0.0	1.0	2.0	3.0	4.0	5.0	6.0	7.0	8.0	9.0
										14.72%
									12.92%	
								11.87%		12.05%
							10.65%		10.58%	
						9.76%		9.72%		9.87%
					8.43%		8.72%		8.66%	
				7.89%		7.99%		7.96%		8.08%
			7.44%		6.90%		7.14%		7.09%	
		6.73%		6.46%		6.54%		6.52%		6.61%
	6.20%		6.09%		5.65%		5.84%		5.81%	
		5.51%		5.29%		5.36%		5.34%		5.41%
			4.98%		4.62%		4.78%		4.75%	
				4.33%		4.39%		4.37%		4.43%
					3.79%		3.92%		3.89%	
						3.59%		3.58%		3.63%
							3.21%		3.19%	
								2.93%		2.97%
									2.61%	
										2.43%

EXHIBIT 3.5 (Continued)

b. The Black-Karasinski Trinomial Interest Rate Lattice Using the HW Method with No Mean Reversion

										28.45%
									23.21%	23.92%
								19.82%	19.52%	20.12%
							16.52%	16.67%	16.41%	16.92%
						14.08%	13.89%	14.02%	13.80%	14.23%
					11.31%	11.84%	11.68%	11.79%	11.61%	11.97%
				9.82%	9.51%	9.96%	9.83%	9.92%	9.76%	10.06%
			8.60%	8.26%	8.00%	8.37%	8.26%	8.34%	8.21%	8.46%
		7.25%	7.23%	6.95%	6.73%	7.04%	6.95%	7.01%	6.90%	7.12%
	6.20%	6.09%	6.08%	5.75%	5.66%	5.92%	5.84%	5.90%	5.81%	5.98%
		5.12%	5.11%	4.91%	4.76%	4.98%	4.91%	4.96%	4.88%	5.03%
			4.30%	4.13%	4.00%	4.19%	4.13%	4.17%	4.11%	4.23%
				3.47%	3.37%	3.52%	3.48%	3.51%	3.45%	3.56%
					2.83%	2.96%	2.92%	2.95%	2.90%	2.99%
						2.49%	2.46%	2.48%	2.44%	2.52%
							2.07%	2.09%	2.05%	2.12%
								1.75%	1.73%	1.78%
									1.45%	1.50%
										1.26%
Time in Years	0.0	1.0	2.0	3.0	4.0	5.0	6.0	7.0	8.0	9.0

EXHIBIT 3.5 (Continued)

c. The Black, Derman, and Toy Interest Rate Model

									11.39%
								10.29%	
							6.47%		9.89%
						9.52%		8.93%	
					7.36%		6.34%		8.59%
				8.12%		8.10%		7.76%	
			7.24%		6.79%		6.21%		7.46%
		7.44%		6.78%		6.90%		6.74%	
	6.73%		6.30%		6.26%		6.08%		6.47%
6.20%		6.09%		5.66%		5.88%		5.85%	
	5.51%		5.49%		5.77%		5.95%		5.62%
		4.98%		4.73%		5.00%		5.09%	
			4.78%		5.32%		5.83%		4.88%
				3.95%		4.26%		4.42%	
					4.91%		5.71%		4.24%
						3.63%		3.84%	
							5.59%		3.68%
								3.33%	
									3.20%
Time in Years	1	2	3	4	5	6	7	8	9

EXHIBIT 3.6 Trinomial Model

a. The Hull-White Trinomial Interest Rate Lattice Using the HW Method with Mean Reversion of 5%

				83.50%	87.60%	91.92%	96.84%	101.89%	107.24%
			63.14%	66.18%	70.28%	74.60%	79.52%	84.57%	89.91%
		43.51%	45.82%	48.86%	52.96%	57.28%	62.20%	67.25%	72.59%
	24.39%	26.18%	28.50%	31.54%	35.64%	39.96%	44.88%	49.93%	55.27%
6.20%	7.07%	8.86%	11.17%	14.22%	18.32%	22.64%	27.56%	32.61%	37.95%
	−10.25%	−8.46%	−6.15%	−3.10%	1.00%	5.32%	10.24%	15.29%	20.63%
		−25.78%	−23.47%	−20.42%	−16.32%	−12.00%	−7.09%	−2.03%	3.31%
			−40.79%	−37.75%	−33.64%	−29.32%	−24.41%	−19.35%	−14.01%
				−55.07%	−50.96%	−46.64%	−41.73%	−36.67%	−31.33%
Time in Years	1	2	3	4	5	6	7	8	9

b. The Black-Karasinski Trinomial Interest Rate Lattice Using the HW Method with Mean Reversion of 5%

				11.34%	11.87%	11.73%	11.84%	11.67%	12.03%
			9.83%	9.53%	9.99%	9.86%	9.96%	9.81%	10.12%
		8.60%	8.27%	8.02%	8.40%	8.29%	8.38%	8.25%	8.51%
	7.25%	7.26%	6.95%	6.74%	7.06%	6.98%	7.04%	6.94%	7.16%
6.20%	6.09%	6.08%	5.85%	5.67%	5.94%	5.87%	5.92%	5.84%	6.02%
	5.12%	5.11%	4.92%	4.77%	4.99%	4.93%	4.98%	4.91%	5.06%
		4.30%	4.14%	4.01%	4.20%	4.15%	4.19%	4.13%	4.26%
			3.48%	3.37%	3.53%	3.49%	3.52%	3.47%	3.58%
				2.84%	2.97%	2.93%	2.96%	2.92%	3.01%
Time in Years	1	2	3	4	5	6	7	8	9

Exhibit 3.7 presents the effective duration and convexity results for the two securities for each model. The results are interesting. It is clear that the normal models do not agree with the lognormal models. Specifically, the normal models do not match the characteristics of the price yield relationship at extreme interest rate levels.[20] Furthermore, each model gives slightly different results. This is an important finding and must be appreciated by any user of these models.

Exhibit 3.8 presents the OAS results. We used a market price that is 3% below the model price for the OAS computation. They are consistent with the results in Exhibit 3.7. Note that the normal models produce OAS values larger than any of the lognormal models. This is due to the distributional differences and the property of allowing very low and negative interest rates. Clearly, normal models are not desirable when evaluating securities with embedded options.[21]

CONCLUSION

This chapter summarized five different term structure models that evolve from three general stochastic differential equations. We contrasted the salient characteristics across the different models including the distributional differences. The differences were highlighted both mathematically and numerically. Without market calibration the models produce very different results. Both the end user and the developer must be aware of these properties in order to properly implement and interpret any results from the models. Even with calibration the models will produce different results due to the reasons presented here. Calibration reduces the differences across the models but does not eliminate them. The methods presented here can also be used to calibrate the models.

[20] See G.W. Buetow and R. Johnson, "Primer on Effective Duration and Effective Convexity," *Professional Perspectives on Fixed Income Portfolio Management, Volume 1*, Frank J. Fabozzi (Ed.) (New Hope, PA: Frank J. Fabozzi Associates, 2000) and Frank J. Fabozzi, G. W. Buetow, and R. Johnson, "Measuring Interest Rate Risk," *The Handbook of Fixed Income Securities, 6th Edition*, Frank J. Fabozzi (Ed.) (New York: McGraw Hill, 2001) for more details on the behavior of putable and callable bonds.

[21] Details of these phenomena are provided in G.W. Buetow, B. Hanke, and Frank J. Fabozzi, "The Impact of Different Interest Rate Models on Effective Duration, Effective Convexity and Option-Adjusted Spreads," *Journal of Fixed Income* (Winter 2001), pp. 41–53.

EXHIBIT 3.7 Effective Duration and Effective Convexity Results

Shift==>	−500 bp		−250 bp		Current		250 bp		500 bp	
Model/ Structure	Eff. Duration	Eff. Convexity	Eff. Duration	Eff. Convexity	Eff. Duration	Eff. Convexity	Eff. Duration	Eff. Convexity	Eff. Duration	Eff. Convexity
Ho Lee										
Callable Bond	3.72119	−31.15230	3.62427	10.51371	3.43354	9.58153	4.19081	−6.18888	4.18588	12.92063
Putable Bond	6.48070	55.51213	5.96968	26.45835	4.82856	41.73014	4.33750	17.68955	3.52379	15.98202
BDT										
Callable Bond	0.98815	0.97643	0.96433	0.92992	5.72746	−100.52077	6.97619	31.91884	6.59872	29.24115
Putable Bond	8.15290	41.20380	7.75444	37.88876	6.94320	136.25219	0.91997	0.84634	0.89929	0.80871
KWF										
Callable Bond	0.98815	0.97643	0.96433	0.92992	5.48099	−8.70115	6.90354	18.94888	6.59875	29.22747
Putable Bond	8.15311	41.26110	7.75438	37.97492	6.02987	132.82680	0.91997	0.84634	0.89929	0.80871
HW-HW										
Callable Bond	3.35706	5.81085	3.24446	8.80890	3.33140	9.55382	3.46677	−9.19552	4.65946	14.99510
Putable Bond	5.82483	23.71025	5.33913	20.81987	4.79375	17.78372	4.14647	14.50538	3.30034	10.76225
BK-HW										
Callable Bond	0.98815	0.97643	0.96433	0.92992	5.21624	−77.28716	6.93694	31.17366	6.56855	28.88729
Putable Bond	8.09134	40.58931	7.70100	37.39723	6.79269	72.05773	0.91997	0.84634	0.89929	0.80871

EXHIBIT 3.8 Option-Adjusted Spread Results

	Ho-Lee	BDT	KWF	HW-HW	BK-HW
Callable Bond	0.8454%	0.4785%	0.5449%	0.8350%	0.5063%
Putable Bond	0.5884%	0.4732%	0.5249%	0.5688%	0.4774%

APPENDIX

In this appendix we outline how to obtain equations (41) and (42). For equation (41) we use Exhibit 3.1. For equation (42) we use Exhibit 3.2.

We first solve for $r_{1,1}$ and $r_{2,1}$ in Exhibit 3.1. Equating the price from the spot rate term structure with the price from the binomial lattice gives us

$$P_2 = \frac{1}{(1+R_2\tau)^2} = \frac{qp_{1,1} + (1-q)p_{2,1}}{1+r_{1,0}\tau} \tag{A1}$$

Substituting in the discount factors $p_{j,1} = 1/(1 + r_{j,1}\tau)$ for $j = 1, 2$ and clearing fractions we obtain

$$\begin{aligned} P_2(1 + r_{1,0}\tau)(1 + r_{1,1}\tau)(1 + r_{2,1}\tau) - q(1 + r_{2,1}\tau) \\ - (1 - q)(1 + r_{1,1}\tau) = 0 \end{aligned} \tag{A2}$$

We let $r_{1,0} = R_1$. This equation can now be solved for θ_1.

For the next period in the binomial lattice we have from Exhibit 3.1 that

$$\begin{aligned} P_3 &= \frac{1}{(1+R_3\tau)^3} = \frac{qp_{1,1} + (1-q)p_{2,1}}{1+r_{1,0}\tau} \\ &= \frac{q\left(\frac{qp_{1,2} + (1-q)p_{2,2}}{1+r_{1,1}\tau}\right) + (1-q)\left(\frac{qp_{2,2} + (1-q)p_{3,2}}{1+r_{2,1}\tau}\right)}{1+r_{1,0}\tau} \end{aligned}$$

which reduces to

$$\begin{aligned} P_3(1 + r_{1,0}\tau)(1 + r_{1,1}\tau)(1 + r_{2,1}\tau)(1 + r_{1,2}\tau)(1 + r_{2,2}\tau)(1 + r_{3,2}\tau) \\ - q^2(1 + r_{2,1}\tau)(1 + r_{2,2}\tau)(1 + r_{3,2}\tau) - q(1 - q)[(1 + r_{1,1}\tau) + (1 + r_{2,1}\tau)] \\ (1 + r_{1,2}\tau)(1 + r_{3,2}\tau) - (1 - q)^2(1 + r_{1,1}\tau)(1 + r_{1,2}\tau)(1 + r_{2,2}\tau) = 0 \end{aligned} \tag{A3}$$

We now solve equation (A3) for θ_2 using the bisection method.

From equation (A2) and equation (A3) we can generate the remainder of the no arbitrage equations that give the short rates in the binomial lattice. Note that equation (A2) can be written as

$$c_{1,1}(1 + r_{1,1}\tau)(1 + r_{2,1}\tau) + c_{2,1}(1 + r_{2,1}\tau) + c_{3,1}(1 + r_{1,1}\tau) = 0 \tag{A4}$$

and that equation (A3) can be written as

$$c_{1,2}(1 + r_{1,2}\tau)(1 + r_{2,2}\tau)(1 + r_{3,2}\tau) + c_{2,2}(1 + r_{2,2}\tau)(1 + r_{3,2}\tau) + c_{3,2}(1 + r_{1,2}\tau)(1 + r_{3,2}\tau) + c_{4,2}(1 + r_{1,2}\tau)(1 + r_{2,2}\tau) = 0 \tag{A5}$$

We now introduce some variables that will help to generate the coefficients $c_{i,k}$ for the polynomials that determine the interest rates at time period k. We start by doing it for the polynomials in equations (A4) and (A5). This is done in two steps. The first step is to notice how the coefficients are related to the interest rates at the previous time periods. Note that if we let $a_{1,1} = 1 + r_{1,0}\tau$, $a_{2,1} = -1$, and $a_{3,1} = -1$ then $c_{1,1} = P_2 a_{1,1}$, $c_{2,1} = qa_{2,1}$, and $c_{3,1} = (1 - q)a_{3,1}$ in equation (A4). In order to generate equation (A5) we first let $b_{1,1} = a_{2,1}(1 + r_{2,1}\tau)$, $b_{2,1} = a_{3,1}(1 + r_{1,1}\tau)$. We can then generate $a_{1,2} = (1 + r_{1,0}\tau)(1 + r_{1,1}\tau)(1 + r_{2,1}\tau)$, $a_{2,2} = b_{1,1}$, $a_{3,2} = b_{1,1} + b_{2,1}$, and $a_{4,2} = b_{2,1}$. It is now seen that $c_{1,2} = P_3 a_{1,2}$, $c_{2,2} = q^2 a_{2,2}$, $c_{3,2} = q(1 - q)a_{3,3}$, and $c_{4,2} = (1 - q)^2 a_{4,2}$. We now let $b_{1,2} = a_{3,1}(1 + r_{2,2}\tau)(1 + r_{3,2}\tau)$, $b_{2,2} = a_{3,2}(1 + r_{1,2}\tau)(1 + r_{3,2}\tau)$, and $b_{3,2} = a_{4,2}(1 + r_{1,2}\tau)(1 + r_{2,2}\tau)$ and continue the process to obtain equation (41).

For the trinomial lattice no arbitrage polynomial we first solve for $r_{1,1}$, $r_{2,1}$, and $r_{3,1}$ in Exhibit 3.2. Equating the price from the spot rate term structure with the price from the trinomial lattice gives us

$$P_2 = \frac{1}{(1 + R_2\tau)^2} = \frac{q_1 p_{1,1} + q_2 p_{2,1} + q_3 p_{3,1}}{1 + r_{1,0}\tau}$$

which is similar to equation (A1). Proceeding as in the binomial lattice we find that

$$P_2(1 + r_{1,0}\tau)(1 + r_{1,1}\tau)(1 + r_{2,1}\tau)(1 + r_{3,1}\tau) - q_1(1 + r_{2,1}\tau)(1 + r_{3,1}\tau) - q_2(1 + r_{1,1}\tau)(1 + r_{3,1}\tau) - q_3(1 + r_{1,1}\tau)(1 + r_{2,1}\tau) = 0 \tag{A6}$$

As in the binomial case, $r_{1,0} = R_1$ and equation (A6) is solved for θ_1 using the bisection method.

For the next period in the trinomial lattice (Exhibit 3.2) gives us

$$P_3 = \frac{1}{(1 + R_3\tau)^3} = \frac{qp_{1,1} + q_2 p_{2,1} + q_3 p_{3,1}}{1 + r_{1,0}\tau}$$

$$= \frac{q_1\left(\dfrac{q_1 p_{1,2} + q_2 p_{2,2} + q_3 p_{3,2}}{1 + r_{1,1}\tau}\right) + q_2\left(\dfrac{q_1 p_{2,2} + q_2 p_{3,2} + q_3 p_{3,3}}{1 + r_{2,1}\tau}\right) + q_3\left(\dfrac{q_1 p_{3,3} + q_2 p_{3,4} + q_3 p_{3,5}}{1 + r_{3,1}\tau}\right)}{1 + r_{1,0}\tau}$$

which simplifies to the following equation similar to equation (A3)

$$\begin{aligned}
&P_3(1+r_{1,0}\tau)\prod_{j=1}^{3}(1+r_{j,1}\tau)\prod_{j=1}^{5}(1+r_{j,2}\tau) \\
&-q_1^2(1+r_{2,1}\tau)(1+r_{3,1}\tau)\prod_{j=2}^{5}(1+r_{j,2}\tau) \\
&-[q_1q_2(1+r_{2,1}\tau)(1+r_{3,1}\tau)+q_1q_2(1+r_{1,1}\tau)(1+r_{3,1}\tau)]\prod_{\substack{j=1\\j\neq 2}}^{5}(1+r_{j,2}\tau) \\
&-[q_1q_3(1+r_{2,1}\tau)(1+r_{3,1}\tau)+q_2^2(1+r_{1,1}\tau)(1+r_{3,1}\tau)+q_3q_1(1+r_{1,1}\tau)(1+r_{2,1}\tau)] \\
&\prod_{\substack{j=1\\j\neq 3}}^{5}(1+r_{j,2}\tau) \\
&-[q_2q_3(1+r_{1,1}\tau)(1+r_{3,1}\tau)+q_3q_2(1+r_{1,1}\tau)(1+r_{2,1}\tau)]\prod_{\substack{j=1\\j\neq 4}}^{5}(1+r_{j,2}\tau) \\
&-q_3^2(1+r_{1,1}\tau)(1+r_{2,1}\tau)\prod_{j=1}^{4}(1+r_{j,2}\tau) = 0
\end{aligned} \tag{A7}$$

Equation (A7) is also solved for θ_2 using the bisection method. We now proceed as in the binomial lattice case to generate the no arbitrage equation for θ_i given in equation (42).

CHAPTER 4

An Introductory Guide to Analyzing and Interpreting the Yield Curve

Moorad Choudhry
Senior Fellow
Centre for Mathematical Trading and Finance
City University Business School

Considerable effort is expended by bond analysts and economists in analyzing and interpreting the shape of the yield curve. This is because the market perceives that there is a considerable information content associated with any yield curve at any time. In this chapter we review the main theories that have been put forward to explain the shape of the yield curve, all of which have fairly long antecedents. None of the theories can adequately explain everything about yield curves and the shapes they assume at any time; so, generally, observers seek to explain specific curves using a combination of the accepted theories. This subject is a large one, and it is possible to devote several books to it, so here we seek to introduce the main ideas, with readers directed to the various articles referenced herein. We assume we are looking at yield curves plotted using risk-free interest rates.

SHAPES OBSERVED FOR THE YIELD CURVE

The existence of a yield curve itself indicates that there is a cost associated with funds of different maturities, otherwise we would observe a flat yield curve. The fact that we very rarely observe anything approaching a flat yield curve suggests that investors require different rates of return depending on the maturity of the instrument they are holding.

From observing yield curves in different markets at any time, we notice that a yield curve can adopt one of four basic shapes, which are:

1. *Normal or conventional* in which yields are at "average" levels and the curve slopes gently upwards as maturity increases, all the way to the longest maturity;
2. *Upward-sloping or positive or rising* in which yields are at historically low levels, with long rates substantially greater than short rates;
3. *Downward-sloping or inverted or negative* in which yield levels are very high by historical standards, but long-term yields are significantly lower than short rates;
4. *Humped* where yields are high with the curve rising to a peak in the medium-term maturity area, and then sloping downwards at longer maturities.

Occasionally yield curves will incorporate a mixture of the above features. For instance, a commonly observed curve in developed economies exhibits a positive sloping shape up to the penultimate maturity bond, and then a declining yield for the longest maturity. A diagrammatic representation of each type of curve is given in Exhibit 4.1.

EXHIBIT 4.1 Observed Yield Curve Shapes

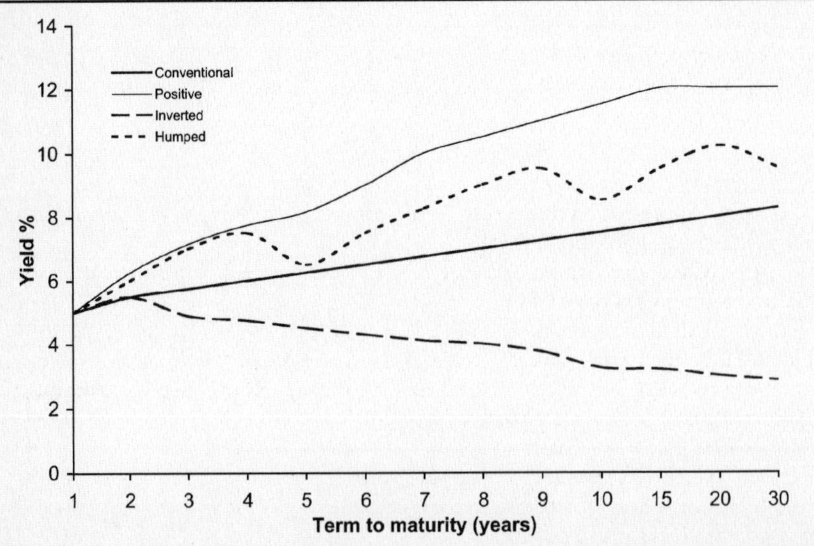

THE EXPECTATIONS HYPOTHESIS

Simply put, the *expectations hypothesis* states that the slope of the yield curve reflects the market's expectations about future interest rates. There are in fact four main versions of the hypothesis, each distinct from the other—and mutually incompatible.

The *expectations hypothesis* has a long history, first being described in Fisher[1] and later developed by Hicks[2] among others.[3] As Shiller[4] describes, the thinking behind it probably stems from the way market participants discuss their view on future interest rates when assessing whether to purchase long-dated or short-dated bonds. For instance, if interest rates are expected to fall, investors will purchase long-dated bonds in order to "lock in" the current high long-dated yield. If all investors act in the same way, the yield on long-dated bonds will, of course, decline as prices rise in response to demand; this yield will remain low as long as short-dated rates are expected to fall, and will only revert to a higher level once the demand for long-term rates is reduced. Therefore, downward-sloping yield curves are an indication that interest rates are expected to fall, while an upward-sloping curve reflects market expectations of a rise in short-term interest rates.

The expectations hypothesis suggests that bondholders' expectations determine the course of future interest rates. The two main versions of the hypothesis are the *local expectations hypothesis* and the *unbiased expectations hypothesis*. The *return-to-maturity expectations hypothesis* and *yield-to-maturity expectations hypothesis* are the other two versions.[5]

The *unbiased expectations hypothesis* states that current forward rates are unbiased predictors of future spot rates. Let $f_t(T,T+1)$ be the forward rate at time t for the period from T to $T + 1$. If the one-period spot rate at time T is r_T, then according to the unbiased expectations hypothesis,

$$f_t(T,T+1) = E_t(r_T) \tag{1}$$

[1] I. Fisher, "Appreciation of Interest," *Publications of the American Economic Association* (August 1986), pp. 23–39.

[2] J. Hicks, *Value and Capital* (Oxford, UK: Oxford University Press, 1946).

[3] See the footnote on page 644 of R. Shiller, "The Term Structure of Interest Rates," Chapter 13 in B. Friedman, F. Hahn (eds.), *Handbook of Monetary Economics* (North-Holland: 1990) for a fascinating historical note on the origins of the expectations hypothesis. An excellent overview of the hypothesis itself is contained in Chapter 18 in J. Ingersoll, *Theory of Financial Decision Making*, (Rowman & Littlefield: 1987), pp. 389–392.

[4] Shiller, "The Term Structure of Interest Rates."

[5] See Ingersoll, *Theory of Financial Decision Making*. This is an excellent account, both comprehensive and accessible.

which states that the forward rate $f_t(T,T+1)$ is the expected value of the future one-period spot rate given by r_T at time T.

The local expectations hypothesis states that all bonds will generate the same expected rate of return if held over a small term. It is given by

$$\frac{E_t[P(t+1, T)]}{P(t, T)} = 1 + r_t \tag{2}$$

where P is the zero-coupon bond price.

This version of the hypothesis is the only one that is consistent with no-arbitrage because the expected rates of return on all bonds are equal to the risk-free interest rate. For this reason the local expectations hypothesis is sometimes referred to as the *risk-neutral expectations hypothesis*.

The local expectations hypothesis states that all bonds of the same class, but differing in term to maturity, will have the same expected holding period rate of return. This suggests that a 6-month bond and a 20-year bond will produce the same rate of return, on average, over the stated holding period. So if we intend to hold a bond for six months we will receive the same return no matter which specific bond we buy. In general, holding period returns from longer-dated bonds are, on average, higher than those from short-dated bonds. Intuitively we would expect this, with longer-dated bonds offering higher returns to compensate for their higher price volatility (risk). The local expectations hypothesis would not agree with the conventional belief that investors, being risk averse, require higher returns as a reward for taking on higher risk; in addition, it does not provide any insight about the shape of the yield curve.

Cox, Ingersoll, and Ross showed that the local expectations hypothesis best reflected equilibrium between spot and forward yields.[6] This was demonstrated using a feature known as Jensen's inequality. Jarrow states:

> ... in an economic equilibrium, the returns on ... similar maturity zero-coupon bonds cannot be too different. If they were too different, no investor would hold the bond with the smaller return. This difference could not persist in an economic equilibrium.[7]

---

[6] J. Cox, J.E. Ingersoll, and S.A. Ross, "A Re-examination of Traditional Hypotheses About the Term Structure of Interest Rates," *Journal of Finance* (September 1981), pp. 769–799.

[7] R. Jarrow, *Modelling Fixed Income Securities and Interest Rate Options* (New York: McGraw-Hill: 1996), p. 50.

This reflects economic logic, but in practice other factors can impact on holding period returns between bonds that do not have similar maturities. For instance, investors will have restrictions as to which bonds they can hold—depository institutions are required to hold short-dated bonds for liquidity purposes. In an environment of economic disequilibrium, these investors would still have to hold shorter-dated bonds—even if the holding period return was lower.

So although it is economically neat to expect that the return on a long-dated bond is equivalent to rolling over a series of shorter-dated bonds, it is often observed that longer-term (default-free) returns exceed annualized short-term default-free returns. So an investor who continually rolled over a series of short-dated zero-coupon bonds would most likely receive a lower return than if they had invested in a long-dated zero-coupon bond.

Rubinstein gives an excellent, accessible explanation of why this should be so.[8] The reason is that compared to the theoretical model, future spot rates are not, in reality, known with certainty. This means that short-dated zero-coupon bonds are more attractive to investors for two reasons. First, they are more appropriate instruments to use for hedging purposes. Secondly, they are more liquid instruments, in that they may be more readily converted back into cash than long-dated instruments. With regard to hedging, consider an exposure to rising interest rates; if the yield curve shifts upwards at some point in the future, the price of long-dated bonds will fall by a greater amount. This is a negative result for holders of such bonds, whereas the investor in short-dated bonds will benefit from rolling over his funds at the (new) higher rates. With regard to the second issue, Rubinstein states:

> ... it can be shown that in an economy with risk-averse individuals, uncertainty concerning the timing of aggregate consumption, the partial irreversibility of real investments (longer-term physical investments cannot be converted into investments with earlier payouts without sacrifice), [and] ... real assets with shorter-term payouts will tend to have a "liquidity" advantage.

Therefore the demand for short-term instruments is frequently higher, and hence short-term returns are often lower than long-term returns.

The *pure* or *unbiased expectations hypothesis* is more commonly encountered and states that current implied forward rates are unbiased estimators of future spot interest rates.[9] It assumes that investors act in a

---

[8] M. Rubinstein, *Rubinstein on Derivatives* (London: RISK Publishing, 1999), pp. 84–85.

[9] For original discussion, see F. Lutz, "The Structure of Interest Rates," *Quarterly Journal of Economics* (November 1940), pp. 36–63; and Fisher, "Appreciation of Interest."

way that eliminates any advantage of holding instruments of a particular maturity. Therefore if we have a positive-sloping yield curve, the unbiased expectations hypothesis states that the market expects spot interest rates to rise; equally, an inverted yield curve is an indication that spot rates are expected to fall. If short-term interest rates are expected to rise, then longer yields should be higher than shorter ones to reflect this. If this were not the case, investors would only buy the shorter-dated bonds and roll over the investment when they matured. Likewise, if rates are expected to fall then longer yields should be lower than short yields.

The unbiased expectations hypothesis states that the long-term interest rate is a geometric average of expected future short-term rates. This gives us:

$$(1 + rs_N)^N = (1 + rs_1)(1 + {}_1rf_2) \ldots (1 + {}_{N-1}rf_N) \tag{3}$$

or

$$(1 + rs_N)^N = (1 + rs_{N-1})^{N-1}(1 + {}_{N-1}rf_N) \tag{4}$$

where rs_N is the spot yield on a N-year bond and ${}_{n-1}rf_n$ is the implied 1-year rate n years ahead.

For example, if the current 1-year spot rate is $rs_1 = 5.0\%$ and the market is expecting the 1-year rate in a year's time to be ${}_1rf_2 = 5.539\%$, then the market is expecting a 100 investment in two 1-year bonds to yield

$$100(1.05)(1.05539) = 110.82$$

after two years. To be equivalent to this, an investment in a 2-year bond has to yield the same amount, implying that the current 2-year rate is $rs_2 = 5.7\%$ as shown below:

$$100(1 + rs_2)^2 = 110.82$$

which gives us $rs_2 = 5.27\%$, and provides the correct future value as shown below:

$$100(1.0527)^2 = 110.82$$

This result must be so—to ensure no arbitrage opportunities exist in the market; in fact this is illustrated in elementary texts that discuss and derive forward interest rates. According to the unbiased expectations hypothesis the forward rate ${}_0rf_2$ is an unbiased predictor of the spot rate

${}_1rs_1$ observed one period later; on average the forward rate should equal the subsequent spot rate. The hypothesis can be used to explain any shape in the yield curve.

A rising yield curve is therefore explained by investors expecting short-term interest rates to rise, that is ${}_1rf_2 > rs_2$. A falling yield curve is explained by investors expecting short-term rates to be lower in the future. A humped yield curve is explained by investors expecting short-term interest rates to rise and long-term rates to fall. Expectations, or views on the future direction of the market, are primarily a function of the expected rate of inflation. If the market expects inflationary pressures in the future, the yield curve will be positively-shaped; if inflation expectations are inclined towards disinflation, then the yield curve will be negative. However, several empirical studies including one by Fama[10] have shown that forward rates are essentially biased predictors of future spot interest rates—and often overestimate future levels of spot rates.

The unbiased hypothesis has also been criticized for suggesting that investors can forecast (or have a view on) very long-dated spot interest rates, which might be considered slightly unrealistic. As yield curves in most developed-country markets exist to a maturity of up to 30 years or longer, such criticisms have some substance. Are investors able to forecast interest rates 10, 20, or 30 years into the future? Perhaps not. Nevertheless, this is indeed the information content of, say, a 30-year bond; because the yield on the bond is set by the market, it is perfectly valid to suggest that the market has a view on inflation and future interest rates for up to 30 years forward.

The expectations hypothesis is stated in more than one way; other versions include the *return-to-maturity expectations hypothesis*, which states that the total return generated from an investment of term t to T by holding a $(T - t)$-period bond will be equal to the expected return generated by a holding a series of 1-period bonds and continually rolling them over on maturity. More formally we write

$$\frac{1}{P(t, T)} = E_t[(1 + r_t)(1 + r_{t+1})\dots(1 + r_{T-1})] \tag{5}$$

The left-hand side of equation (5) represents the return received by an investor holding a zero-coupon bond to maturity, which is equal to the expected return associated with rolling over \$1 from time t to time T by continually reinvesting one-period maturity bonds, each of which has a yield of the future spot rate r_t.

[10] E.F. Fama, "The Information in the Term Structure," *Journal of Financial Economics* (December 1984), pp. 509–528.

A related version, the *yield-to-maturity hypothesis*, described in terms of yields, states that the periodic return from holding a zero-coupon bond will be equal to the return from rolling over a series of coupon bonds, but refers to the annualized return earned each year rather than the total return earned over the life of the bond. This assumption enables a zero-coupon yield curve to be derived from the redemption yields of coupon bonds. It is given by

$$\left[\frac{1}{P(t,T)}\right]^{1/(T-t)} = E_t\{[(1+r_t)(1+r_{t+1})\ldots(1+r_{T-1})]^{1/(T-t)}\} \qquad (6)$$

where the left-hand side of equation (6) specifies the yield-to-maturity of the zero-coupon bond at time t. In this version the expected holding period *yield* on continually rolling over a series of 1-period bonds will be equal to the yield that is guaranteed by holding a long-dated bond until maturity.

The unbiased expectations hypothesis of course states that forward rates are equal to the spot rates expected by the market in the future. Cox, Ingersoll, and Ross suggest that only the local expectations hypothesis describes a model that is purely arbitrage-free, as under the other scenarios it would be possible to employ certain investment strategies that would produce returns in excess of what was implied by today's yields.[11] Although it has been suggested[12] that the differences between the local and the unbiased hypotheses are not material, a model that describes such a scenario would not reflect investors' beliefs—which is why further research is ongoing in this area.

The unbiased expectations hypothesis does not, by itself, explain all the shapes of the yield curve or the information content contained within it, so it is often tied in with other explanations, including the liquidity preference theory.

LIQUIDITY PREFERENCE THEORY

Intuitively we might feel that longer maturity investments are riskier than shorter ones. An investor lending money for a 5-year term will usually demand a higher rate of interest than if they were to lend the same cus-

[11] Cox, Ingersoll, and Ross, "A Re-examination of Traditional Hypothesis About the Term Structure of Interest Rates."

[12] For example, see J. Campbell, "A Defense of Traditional Hypotheses About the Term Structure of Interest Rates," *Journal of Finance* (March 1986), pp. 183–193; see also M. Livingstone, *Money and Capital Markets* (Prentice-Hall: 1990), pp. 254–256.

tomer money for a 5-week term. This is because the borrower may not be able to repay the loan over the longer time period as they may, for instance, have gone bankrupt in that period. For this reason longer-dated yields should be higher than short-dated yields, to compensate the lender for the higher risk exposure during the term of the loan.[13]

We can consider this theory in terms of inflation expectations as well. Where inflation is expected to remain roughly stable over time, the market would anticipate a positive yield curve. However, the expectations hypothesis cannot, by itself, explain this phenomenon—under stable inflationary conditions one would expect a flat yield curve.

The risk inherent in longer-dated investments, or the *liquidity preference theory*, seeks to explain a positively-shaped curve. Generally, borrowers prefer to borrow over as long a term as possible, while lenders will wish to lend over as short a term as possible. Therefore, as we first stated, lenders have to be compensated for lending over the longer term; this compensation is considered a premium for a loss in *liquidity* for the lender. The premium is increased the further the investor lends across the term structure, so that the longest-dated investments will, all else being equal, have the highest yield. So the liquidity preference theory states that the yield curve should almost always be upward-sloping, reflecting bondholders' preference for the liquidity and lower risk of shorter-dated bonds. An inverted yield curve could still be explained by the liquidity preference theory when it is combined with the unbiased expectations hypothesis. A *humped* yield curve might be viewed as a combination of an inverted yield curve together with a positive-sloping liquidity preference curve.

The difference between a yield curve explained by unbiased expectations and an actual observed yield curve is sometimes referred to as the *liquidity premium*. This refers to the fact that in some cases short-dated bonds are easier to transact in the market than long-term bonds. It is difficult to quantify the effect of the liquidity premium—which is not static and fluctuates over time. The liquidity premium is so called because, in order to induce investors to hold longer-dated securities, the yields on such securities must be higher than those available on short-dated securities, which are more liquid and may be converted into cash more easily. The liquidity premium is the compensation required for holding less liquid instruments.

If longer-dated securities then provide higher yields, as is suggested by the existence of the liquidity premium, they should generate, on average, higher total returns over an investment period. This is inconsistent with the local expectations hypothesis. More formally we can write:

[13] For original discussion, see Hicks, *Value and Capital.*

$$0 = L_1 < L_2 < L_3 < \ldots < L_n \text{ and } (L_2 - L_1) > (L_3 - L_2) > \ldots > (L_n - L_{n-1})$$

where L is the premium for a bond with term to maturity of n years. This states that the premium increases as the term to maturity rises and that an otherwise flat yield curve will have a positively-sloping curve, with the degree of slope steadily decreasing as we extend along the yield curve. This is consistent with observation of yield curves under "normal" conditions.

The expectations hypothesis assumes that forward rates are equal to the expected future spot rates, as shown by equation (7):

$$_{n-1}rf_n = E(_{n-1}rs_n) \tag{7}$$

where $E(\ )$ is the expectations operator for the current period. This assumption implies that the forward rate is an unbiased predictor of the future spot rate, as we suggested earlier. Liquidity preference theory, on the other hand, recognizes the possibility that the forward rate may contain an element of liquidity premium which declines over time as the starting period approaches, given by equation (8):

$$_{n-1}rf_n > E(_{n-1}rs_n) \tag{8}$$

If there was uncertainty in the market about the future direction of spot rates—and hence where the forward rate should lie—equation (8) is adjusted to give the reverse inequality.

Exhibit 4.2 is a diagrammatic representation of the liquidity premium element in an hypothetical yield curve.

EXHIBIT 4.2 Yield Curve Explained by Expectations Hypothesis and Liquidity Preference

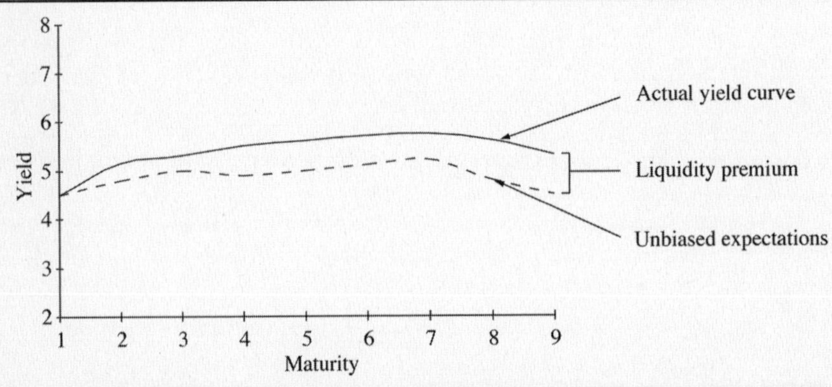

MONEY SUBSTITUTE HYPOTHESIS

A particular explanation of short-dated bond yield curves has been attempted by Kessel.[14] In the *money substitute theory,* short-dated bonds are regarded as substitutes for holding cash. Investors hold only short-dated market instruments because these are viewed as low or negligible risk. As a result, the yields of short-dated bonds are depressed due to the increased demand and lie below longer-dated bonds. Borrowers, on the other hand, prefer to issue debt for longer maturities, and on as few occasions as possible, to minimize funding costs and reduce uncertainty. Therefore, the yields of longer-dated paper are driven upwards due to a combination of increased supply and lower liquidity. In certain respects the money substitute theory is closely related to the liquidity preference theory and, by itself, does not explain inverted or humped yield curves.

SEGMENTATION HYPOTHESIS

The capital markets are made up of a wide variety of users, each with different requirements. Certain classes of investors will prefer dealing at the short-end of the yield curve, while others will concentrate on the longer-end of the market. The *segmented markets theory* suggests that activity is concentrated in certain specific areas of the market, and that there are no interrelationships between these parts of the market; the relative amounts of funds invested in each area of the maturity spectrum cause differentials in supply and demand, which results in humps in the yield curve. That is, the shape of the yield curve is determined by supply and demand for certain specific maturity investments, each of which has no reference to any other part of the curve.

The *segmented markets hypothesis* seeks to explain the shape of the yield curve by stating that different types of market participants invest in different sectors of the term structure, according to their requirements. So, for instance, the banking sector has a requirement for short-dated bonds, while pension funds will invest in the long-end of the market. This was first described in Culbertson.[15] There may also be regulatory reasons why different investors have preferences for particular maturity investments.

[14] R.A. Kessel, "The Cyclical Behaviour of the Term Structure of Interest Rates," in *Essays in Applied Price Theory* (Chicago, IL: University of Chicago, 1965).

[15] J.M. Culbertson, "The Term Structure of Interest Rates," *Quarterly Journal of Economics* (November 1957), pp. 485–517.

So, for example, banks and other types of depository institutions concentrate a large part of their activity at the short-end of the curve, as part of daily cash management (known as *asset and liability management*) and for regulatory purposes (known as *liquidity requirements*). Fund managers such as pension funds and insurance companies are active at the long-end of the market. Few institutional investors, however, have any preference for medium-dated bonds. This behavior on the part of investors will lead to high prices (low yields) at both the short- and long-ends of the yield curve and lower prices (higher yields) in the middle of the term structure.

According to the segmented markets hypothesis, a separate market exists for specific maturities along the term structure, thus interest rates for these maturities are set by supply and demand.[16] Where there is no demand for a particular maturity, the yield will lie above other segments. Market participants do not hold bonds in any other area of the curve outside their area of interest[17] so that short-dated and long-dated bond yields exist independently of each other. The segmented markets theory is usually illustrated by reference to banks and life companies. Banks and other types of depository institutions hold their funds in short-dated instruments, usually no longer than five years in maturity. This is because of the nature of retail banking operations, with a large volume of instant access funds being deposited at banks, and also for regulatory purposes. Holding short-term, liquid bonds enables banks to meet any sudden or unexpected demand for funds from customers. The classic theory suggests that as banks invest their funds in short-dated bonds, the yields on these bonds is driven down. When they subsequently liquidate part of their holding, perhaps to meet higher demand for loans, the yields are driven up and prices of the bonds fall. This affects the short-end of the yield curve but not the long-end.

The segmented markets theory can be used to cover an explanation of any particular shape of the yield curve, although it may be argued that it fits best with positive-sloping curves. However, it does not offer us any help if used to *interpret* the yield curve whatever shape it may be, and therefore offers no information content during analysis. By definition, the theory suggests that for investors, bonds with different maturities are not perfect substitutes for each other. This is because different bonds would have different holding period returns, making them imperfect substitutes of one another. As a result of bonds being imperfect substitutes, markets are segmented according to maturity.

---

[16] See Culbertson, "The Term Structure of Interest Rates."

[17] For example, retail and commercial banks hold bonds in the short dates, while life assurance companies hold long-dated bonds.

The segmentations hypothesis is a reasonable explanation of certain features of a conventional positively-sloping yield curve, but, by itself, is not sufficient. There is no doubt that banks and building societies have a requirement to hold securities at the short-end of the yield curve, as much for regulatory purposes as for yield considerations; however, other investors are probably more flexible and will place funds where value is deemed to exist. Nevertheless, the higher demand for benchmark securities does drive down yields along certain segments of the curve.

A slightly modified version of the market segmentation hypothesis is known as the *preferred habitat theory*, first described in Modigliani and Sutch,[18] which states not only that investors have a preferred maturity but also that they may move outside this sector if they receive a premium for so doing. This would explain "humped" shapes in yield curves.

This suggests that different market participants have an interest in specified areas of the yield curve, but can be induced to hold bonds from other parts of the maturity spectrum if there is sufficient incentive. Hence banks may, at certain times, hold longer-dated bonds once the price of these bonds falls to a certain level, making the return on the bonds worth the risk involved in holding them. Similar considerations may persuade long-term investors to hold short-dated debt. So higher yields will be required to make bondholders shift out of their usual area of interest. This theory essentially recognizes the flexibility that investors have, outside regulatory or legal requirements (such as the terms of an institutional fund's objectives), to invest in whatever part of the yield curve they identify value. The preferred habitat theory may be viewed as a version of the liquidity preference hypothesis, where the preferred habitat is the short-end of the yield curve, so that longer-dated bonds must offer a premium in order to entice investors to hold them.[19]

THE COMBINED THEORY

The explanation for the shape of the yield curve at any time is more likely to be described by a combination of the pure expectations hypothesis and the liquidity preference theory, and possibly one or two other theories. Market analysts often combine the unbiased expectations hypothesis with the liquidity preference theory into an "eclectic" theory. The result is fairly consistent with any shape of yield curve, and is also a predictor of rising interest rates.

[18] F. Modigliani and R. Sutch, "Innovations in Interest Rate Policy," *American Economic Review* (1966), pp. 178–197.

[19] This is described in Cox, Ingersoll, and Ross, "A Re-examination of Traditional Hypotheses About the Term Structure of Interest Rates."

EXHIBIT 4.3 Positive Yield Curve with Constant Expected Future Rates

Period n	0	1	2	3	4	5
$E(rs)$		4.5%	4.5%	4.5%	4.5%	4.5%
Forward rate ${}_0rf_n$		5.00%	5.50%	6.00%	6.50%	7.50%
Spot rate rs_n	5%	5.30%	5.80%	6.20%	6.80%	7%

In the combined theory, the forward interest rate is equal to the expected future spot rate, together with a quantified liquidity premium. This is shown by equation (9):

$$ {}_0rf_i = E({}_{i-1}rs_1) + L_i \tag{9}$$

where L_i is the liquidity premium for a term to maturity of i years. The size of the liquidity premium is expected to increase with increasing maturity[20]—an example is given below.

Consider the interest rate structure in Exhibit 4.3. The current term structure is positive-sloping since the spot rates increase with increasing maturity. However, the market expects future spot rates to be constant at 4.5%. The forward and spot rates are also shown; however, the forward rate is a function of the expected spot rate and the liquidity premium. This premium is equal to 0.50% for the first year, 1.0% in the second and so on.

The combined theory is consistent with an inverted yield curve. This will apply even when the liquidity premium is increasing with maturity; for example, where the expected future spot interest rate is declining. Typically this would be where there was a current term structure of falling yields along the term structure. The spot rates might be declining where the fall in the expected future spot rate exceeds the corresponding increase in the liquidity premium.

THE FLAT YIELD CURVE

The conventional theories do not seek to explain a flat yield curve. Although it is rare to observe flat curves in a market, certainly for any length of time, they do emerge occasionally in response to peculiar economic circumstances. Conventional thinking contends that a flat curve is not tenable because investors should, in theory, have no incentive to hold long-dated bonds over shorter-dated bonds when there is no yield pre-

[20] So that $L_i > L_{i-1}$.

mium, so that as they sell off long-dated paper the yield at the long-end should rise, producing an upward-sloping curve.

In previous circumstances of a flat curve, analysts have produced different explanations for their existence. In November 1988 the U.S. Treasury yield curve was flat relative to the recent past. Researchers contended that this was the result of the market's view that long-dated yields would fall as bond prices rallied upwards.[21] One recommendation is to buy longer maturities when the yield curve is flat, in anticipation of lower long-term interest rates, which is directly opposite to the view that a flat curve is a signal to sell long bonds. In the case of the U.S. market in 1988, long bond yields did in fact fall by approximately 2% in the following 12 months.

This would seem to indicate that one's view of future long-term rates should be behind the decision to buy or sell long bonds, rather than the shape of the yield curve itself. A flat curve may well be more heavily influenced by supply and demand factors than anything else, with the majority opinion eventually winning out and forcing a change in the curve to a more conventional shape.

FURTHER VIEWS ON THE YIELD CURVE

Throughout this discussion we assume an economist's world of the perfect market (also sometimes called the *frictionless* financial market). Such a perfect capital market is characterized by:

- Perfect information
- No taxes
- Bullet maturity bonds
- No transaction costs

Of course, in practice markets are not completely perfect. However, assuming perfect markets makes the discussion of spot and forward rates and the term structure easier to handle. When we analyze yield curves for their information content, we have to remember that the markets that they represent are not perfect, and that frequently we observe anomalies that are not explained by the conventional theories.

At any one time it is probably more realistic to suggest that a range of factors contributes to the yield curve being one particular shape. For instance, short-term interest rates are greatly influenced by the availabil-

[21] See H. Levy, *Introduction to Investments*, Second Edition (Cincinnati, Ohio: South-Western College Publishing, 1999), pp. 562–564.

ity of funds in the money market. The slope of the yield curve (usually defined as the 10-year yield minus the 3-month interest rate) is also a measure of the degree of tightness of government monetary policy. A low, upward-sloping curve is often thought to be a sign that an environment of cheap money, due to a looser monetary policy, is to be followed by a period of higher inflation and higher bond yields. Equally, a high downward-sloping curve is taken to mean that a situation of tight credit, due to a stricter monetary policy, will result in falling inflation and lower bond yields.

Inverted yield curves have often preceded recessions; for instance, *The Economist* in an article from April 1998 remarked that, with one exception, every recession in the United States since 1955 had been preceded by a negative yield curve.[22] The analysis is the same: If investors expect a recession they also expect inflation to fall, so the yields on long-term bonds will fall relative to short-term bonds. So the conventional explanation for an inverted yield curve is that the markets and the investment community expect either a slow-down of the economy, or an outright recession.[23] In this case one would expect the monetary authorities to ease the money supply by reducing the base interest rate in the near future: hence an inverted curve. At the same time, a reduction of short-term interest rates will affect short-dated bonds and these are sold off by investors, further raising their yield.

While the conventional explanation for negative yield curves is an expectation of economic slow-down, on occasion other factors will be involved. In the UK during the period July 1997–June 1999, the gilt yield curve was inverted.[24] There was no general view that the economy was heading for recession; in fact, the newly elected Labour government inherited an economy believed to be in satisfactory shape. Instead, the explanation behind the inverted shape of the gilt yield curve focused on two other factors: (1) the handing of responsibility for setting interest rates to the Monetary Policy Committee (MPC) of the Bank of England and (2) the expectation that the UK would, over the medium term, abandon sterling and join the euro currency. The yield curve at this time suggested that the market expected the MPC to be successful and keep

[22] The exception was the one precipitated by the 1973 oil shock.

[23] A recession is formally defined as two successive quarters of falling output in the domestic economy.

[24] Although the gilt yield curve changed to being positively-sloped out to the 7–8 year maturity area, for a brief period in June–July 1999, it very quickly reverted to being inverted throughout the term structure, and remained so until May–June 2001, when it changed once again to being slightly positive-sloping up to the 4-year term, and inverting from that point onwards. This shape at least is more logical and explainable.

inflation at a level of around 2.5% over the long term (its target is actually a 1% range either side of 2.5%), and also that sterling interest rates would need to come down over the medium term as part of *convergence* with interest rates in euroland. These are both medium-term expectations however, and, in the author's view, are not logical at the short-end of the yield curve. In fact the term structure moved to a positive-sloped shape up to the 6–7 year area, before inverting out to the long-end of the curve, in June 1999. This is a more logical shape for the curve to assume, but it was short-lived and returned to being inverted after the two-year term.

There is, therefore, significant information content in the yield curve, and economists and bond analysts will consider the shape of the curve as part of their policy-making and investment advice. The shape of parts of the curve, whether the short-end or long-end, as well that of the entire curve, can serve as useful predictors of future market conditions. As part of an analysis it is also worthwhile considering the yield curves across several different markets and currencies. For instance, the interest-rate swap curve, and its position relative to that of the government bond yield curve, is also regularly analyzed for its information content. In developed-country economies, the swap market is invariably as liquid as the government bond market, if not more liquid, and so it is common to see the swap curve analyzed when making predictions about, say, the future level of short-term interest rates.

Government policy will influence the shape and level of the yield curve, including policy on public sector borrowing, debt management and open-market operations.[25] The market's perception of the size of public sector debt will influence bond yields; for instance, an increase in the level of debt can lead to an increase in bond yields across the maturity range. Open-market operations can have a number of effects. In the short-term it can tilt the yield curve both upwards and downwards; longer term, changes in the level of the base rate will affect yield levels. An anticipated rise in base rates can lead to a drop in prices for short-term bonds, whose yields will be expected to rise; this can lead to a (temporary) inverted curve. Finally, debt management policy[26] will influence the yield curve. Much government debt is rolled over as it matures, but the maturity of the replacement debt can have a significant influence on the yield curve in the form of humps in the market segment in which the debt is placed, if the debt is priced by the market at a relatively low price and hence high yield.

[25] "Open-market operations" refers to the daily operation by the Bank of England to control the level of the money supply (to which end the Bank purchases short-term bills and also engages in repo dealing).

[26] In the United Kingdom this is now the responsibility of the Debt Management Office.

The Information Content of the UK Gilt Curve: A Special Case

In the first half of 1999 various factors combined to increase the demand for gilts, especially at the long-end of the yield curve, at a time of a reduction in the supply of gilts as the government's borrowing requirement was falling. This increased demand led to a lowering in market liquidity as prices rose and gilts became more expensive (that is, lower-yielding) than government securities in most European countries. This is a relatively new phenomenon, witness 10-year UK government yields at 5.07% compared to U.S. and Germany at 6.08% and 5.10%, respectively, at one point in August 1999.[27] At the long-end of the yield curve, UK rates were, for the first time in over 30 years, below both German and U.S. yields, reflecting the market's positive long-term view of the UK economy. At the end of September 1999, the German 30-year bond (the 4¾% July 2028) was yielding 5.73% and the U.S. 6.125% 2027 was at 6.29%, compared to the UK 6% 2028, which was trading at a yield of 4.81%.

The relatively high price of UK gilts was reflected in the yield spread of interest-rate swaps versus gilts. For example, in March 1999, 10-year swap spreads over government bonds were over 80 basis points in the UK compared to 40 basis points in Germany. This was historically large and was more than what might be required to account purely for the credit risk of swaps. It appears that this reflected the high demand for gilts, which had depressed the long-end of the yield curve. At this point the market contended that the gilt yield curve no longer provided an accurate guide to expectations about future short-term interest rates. The sterling swap market, where liquidity is always as high as the government market and (as on this occasion) often higher, was viewed as being a more accurate prediction of future short-term interest rates. In hindsight this view turned out to be correct; swap rates fell in the UK in January and February 1999, and by the end of the following month the swap yield curve had become slightly upward-sloping, whereas the gilt yield curve was still inverted. This does indeed suggest that the market foresaw higher future short-term interest rates and that the swap curve predicted this, while the gilt curve did not. Exhibit 4.4 shows the change in the swap yield curve to a more positive slope from December 1998 to March 1999, while the gilt curve remained inverted. This is an occasion when the gilt yield curve's information content was less relevant than that in another market yield curve, due to the peculiar circumstances resulting from lack of supply to meet increased demand.

---

[27] Yields obtained from Bloomberg.

EXHIBIT 4.4 UK Gilt and Swap Yield Curves

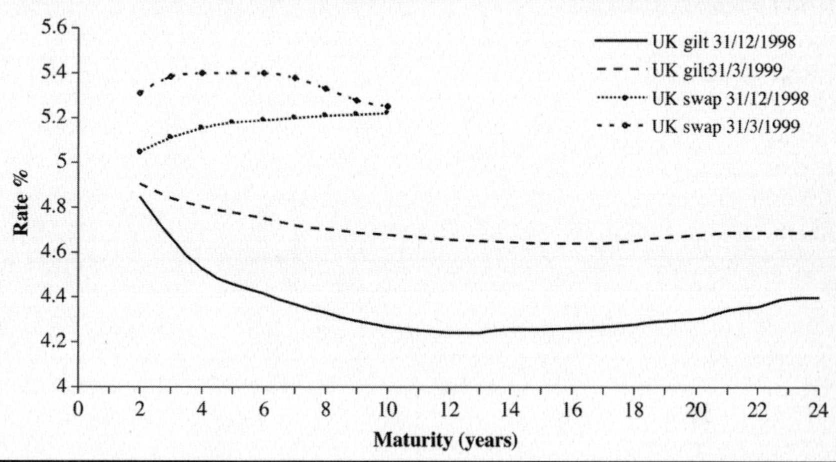

Source: Bank of England.

CHAPTER 5

Term Structure Modeling*

David Audley
Consultant

Richard Chin
Consultant

Shrikant Ramamurthy
Senior Vice President
Greenwich Capital

It is the objective of this chapter is to describe the principles and approaches to term structure modeling. Readers familiar with the academic literature addressing the term structure will see that we have adopted an eclectic mixture of ideas from this area (we indicate the sources of these ideas, where appropriate). However, such readers also will note some marked departures from the usual academic assumptions, necessitating unusual implementations. These are driven by the reality of the markets, often overlooked for the sake of analytic cleanliness. We will highlight these and their implications as well.

Computational implementation of anything as complex as the dynamic term structure model described in this chapter naturally engenders the rigorous adherence to, yet clever application of, some arcane ideas from software/system engineering. This is beyond the scope of this introduction, but such topics include numerical recipes; mechanisms to ensure internal consistencies during development and build-up; tests for

* This chapter is based on a research paper written by the authors while employed by Prudential Securities.

internal consistency, verification and validation of completed applications (e.g., put-call parity, cash and carry arbitrage, and others); parameterization of models and applications from the markets; and the utility of advanced computer architectures.

The following division of topics as well as the section flow address theoretical aspects of the term structure and term structure models, followed by the application of the theory to financial instruments and markets. This is meant to serve only as a "sampler" of how term structure models can be used as strategic tools.

In what follows, we will describe some fundamental concepts of the term structure of interest rates, develop a useful set of static term structure models and describe the usual approaches to extending these into dynamic models. We begin with the familiar, *discrete-time* modeling approach. That is, units of time quanta are defined (usually in terms of compounding frequency) and financial manipulations are indexed with integer, multiple periods.

We then build on the discussion by introducing the *continuous-time* analogies to the concepts developed for discrete-time modeling. Continuous-time modeling allows financial manipulations to be freed from discretization artifacts (such as compounding frequency) and provides an algebraic framework that more naturally and rigorously accommodates "rate" as a concept of change. In addition, this approach opens up a huge field of applicable mathematics with the attendant opportunity for abstraction. For example, continuous-time models free the analyst from artificial *a priori* assumptions about interest-rate lattices; allowing concentration on the financial analyses at hand; deferring time-step issues to final implementation of an algorithm; and choosing an approach based on convenience, speed, and accuracy.

We next describe the *dynamic* term-structure model. The assumptions, derivation, and parameterizations of the general model are described. In the last section we apply the dynamic term structure model to zero-coupon bonds, coupon-paying bonds, and the determination of par-coupon and horizon yield curves. Applications to other fixed-income products are presented in other chapters of this book.

INTRODUCTION TO TERM STRUCTURE MODELING

The term structure of interest rates (or term structure) is simply a price or yield relationship among a set of securities that differ only in the timing of their cash flows or their term until maturity. These securities invariably have a specified set of other attributes in common so that the study of the term relationship is meaningful.

It is common to think of the term structure as consisting of the current-coupon U.S. Treasury issues only. This restriction is not necessary since it is possible to define other term structures derived from other securities. For example, it is meaningful to define the term structure of sets of coupon or principal Treasury strips. Other examples include off-the-run Treasury issues, agency debentures, interest-rate swaps or the notes of single-A rated banks and finance companies. The set of securities used to *define* a term structure is called the *reference set*. A *market sector* (sometimes referred to as a *market* or a *sector*) consists of all those instruments described by a specific term structure. There is the market sector of coupon or principal Treasury strips, off-the-run Treasuries, agency debentures, interest-rate swaps, and single-A rated banks and finance companies, and so forth. Very often, the reference set for a market sector may have restrictions on the structure (non-callables only), liquidity (recent issues only), or price (close to par only) of the securities that make up the set.

The relationship expressed by the term structure is traditionally the par-coupon yield relationship, hence the terminology: *yield curve*. This also is not a necessary restriction. In general, the term structure could be the *discount function*, the *spot-yield curve*, or some other expression of the price or yield relationship between the securities. Given the widespread usage of the (par) yield curve for the Treasury market, it is not surprising that many market sectors are defined from a reference set derived from the Treasury market. For example, the reference set that defines the agency debenture market is a set of yield *spreads* to the on-the-run Treasuries, so that a 5-year debenture issued by an agency may be priced at par to yield 15 basis points more than the current 5-year Treasury issue. If the Treasury issue is trading at a 6.60% yield to maturity, the par priced agency issue has a 6.75% coupon. By inference, from the *spread* quote of 15 basis points, the *reference yield* for the 5-year term is 6.75%. Similar statements can be made for the interest-rate swap and the corporate-bond markets.

It needs to be emphasized that the reference set of bonds used to define the term structure of interest rates and the resulting term structure itself are not one and the same. Indeed, the term structure, as a complete description of the entire yield curve, ultimately can be used to analyze all manner of option laden, index amortizing swaps or debentures that are in the same market sector. The "vanilla" *reference set* consists of individual bonds that are used mainly to define the term structure or to derive its defining relationships—spot-yield curve, spot-rate process, discount function, and the like.

Theories about the term structure of interest rates fall into two categories:

- *Qualitative theories* seek to explain the shape of the yield curve based on economic principles. Three theories attract the widest attention: the expectations, liquidity-preference, and preferred-habitat (or hedging pressure) theories.
- *Quantitative theories* seek to *mathematically* characterize the term structure (often in harmony with one of the qualitative theories).

Usually, a quantitative theory about the term structure of interest rates culminates in a mathematical model, a *term structure model*, that exhibits useful properties. Specifically, a term structure model is the mathematical representation of the relationship among the securities in a market sector. This formalizes the distinction between the reference set used to define a market sector and a term structure model.

Term Structure Models

The simplest and most familiar term structure model is the (semi-logarithmic) graph of the U.S. Treasury yield curve found daily in the *Wall Street Journal* and in the business section of many newspapers. This model is useful mainly as a visualization of the yield relationship between the most recently issued shorter-term Treasury instruments and bonds. The graph can be characterized by a mathematical equation and is one example of the set of interpolation models of the term structure. These "connect-the-dots" models can be useful in providing a quantitative way to price bonds outside the current-coupon Treasury issues, but their utility is rather limited. Bonds that are valued through a linear-interpolation technique may not be "fairly" valued in the sense that an average yield may not be equal to the "par-coupon" yield corresponding to the same date. Later in this chapter we provide a discussion of how the par-coupon curve is constructed to be fairly valued in comparison to the set of reference Treasury issues.

The term structure model as described above simply provides a snapshot of the relationship between the yields for selected Treasury maturities on a given day. It is often required that term structure models exhibit additional "analytic" properties. One such property is the consistency associated with the preclusion of riskless arbitrage when the term structure model is used for pricing. More will be said about this later in the chapter. For now, it is intended merely to indicate that the "visualization" of the yield relationship to term may be neither completely useful nor adequate.

More generally, term structure models are called on to describe the evolution of a set of interest rates over time. This motivates the following distinction in classifying term structure models:

- *Static models* of the term structure offer a mechanism to establish the "present value of a future dollar" in a deterministic economy. That is, no allowance for uncertainty or interest-rate volatility is explicitly incorporated into the model.
- *Dynamic models* of the term structure, in contrast to static models, explicitly allow for uncertainty in the future course of interest rates.

Ideally, a dynamic model of the term structure should have useful static models embedded within. That is, with no contingency on the receipt of a future cash payment or when there is an assumption of negligible volatility, a dynamic model should correspond to a consistent static model.

The essence of term structure modeling is the process of converting the market description of a sector's reference set (the data) into a mathematical set of relationships that characterizes all issues in a sector. This is by no means trivial to do correctly. For example, the same model that correctly values a note in the Treasury market should also correctly value an option on that note, the futures contract into which that note may be deliverable, and an option on that futures contract. It should also reveal if the traded basis on that note is rich or cheap relative to the cash, futures, and options markets. It should also be able to describe any stripping or reconstitution opportunities between coupon and principal strips and the cash market. These analyses should not be the result of several models, but of a single term structure model.

A key element of the modeling process is to eliminate distinguishing characteristics associated with each constituent of the reference set. For example, in the on-the-run set of Treasury issues, there are bills as well as notes and bonds. The bills have different conventions for day counting, pricing, and yield expression from those of the coupon paying issues of the sector. These characteristics need to be removed prior to developing the mathematical relation of the term structure model (as do the distinguishing characteristics for notes and bonds). In this simple example, a model of the Treasury term structure might be the spot curve or the discount function, as opposed to a "connect-the-dots" model to which no yield adjustments have been made.

The mathematical relationship of a term structure model can be used to characterize all issues in a sector. As is the case for the Treasury sector, every instrument can be considered a collection of zero-coupon bonds (the maturities of which correspond to the coupon/principal payment dates, the denominations of which correspond to the amount of coupon/principal paid). Accordingly, the discount function or equivalently, its corresponding spot-yield curve, furnishes a pricing technique for each zero-coupon bond and, therefore, for each of the instruments. With this insight, the utility of an equivalence between the spot-yield curve and discount function, which are derived from the original reference set, is readily apparent.

It will be seen later that a technical discussion of term structure models is really equivalent to a discussion of the (zero-coupon) spot-yield curve. The *theory* of the term structure of interest rates focuses on a term structure model that models the movement of the spot (zero-coupon) yield over time. Once such a term structure model is developed, any coupon paying bond may be viewed in terms of its constituent zero-coupon bonds and analyzed in the context of this term structure model.

Dynamic Term Structure Models

Modern financial markets are predicated on the notions of contingency and uncertainty. Many recent financial innovations are directed at coping with the uncertainty of markets and the contingency of obligations. As part of this evolutionary process, dynamic models of securities and their behavior in the markets are at the forefront of financial economic research and application. In the fixed-income markets, this condition dominates and drives the need for dynamic term structure models.

The dynamic term structure model of a market sector, as defined by a reference set of securities, is a mathematical set of relationships that can be used to characterize any security in that market sector in which market uncertainty dominates the expected timing and receipt of cash flows. There are several qualitative essentials that need to be accommodated by a useful modeling approach. The ability to value fixed-income securities at any point in time (present or future) for conventional or forward settlement is a necessary first step. This is especially true in the valuation of compound or derivative instruments. Indeed, before the value of a bond option may be determined, the ability to calculate the (probabilistic) expected value of the bond on the future exercise date (conditioned on current market condition) is needed. Complementing this, reasonable variations from this expectation also need to be determined and weighed relative to the expected outcome. It is essentially this same idea that allows for the analysis of a futures contract, an interest-rate cap, or an option on a swap. In addition, to determine the performance risk that results from market moves, a rationale for incorporating market changes needs to be embedded into the modeling process.

With these premises in mind, the following assertions regarding dynamic models for the term structure of interest rates are postulated:

- The model must have the capability to extrapolate into the future an *equilibrium* evolution of the term structure of interest rates, given its form on a specified day, and must preclude riskless arbitrage.
- The model must allow a probabilistic description of how the term structure may deviate from its expected extrapolation while maintaining the model's equilibrium assumption.
- The model must embody a rationale to incorporate *perturbations* from the equilibrium that correspond to the economic fundamentals that drive the financial markets.

This treatise is focused on a dynamic term structure model that responds to the imperatives outlined.

TERM STRUCTURE MODELING IN DISCRETE TIME

In this section we present some fundamental concepts in term structure theory, such as the discount function, the spot rate and spot yield, and the forward rate. While these initially may appear to be esoteric in nature, they are in fact closely interrelated quantities that directly represent the term structure, or act to influence the course of future interest rates in an arbitrage-free environment. In this section these concepts are shown to be incorporated into the different expressions that describe the various qualitative term structure theories, such as the expectation, preferred-habitat, and liquidity-preference hypotheses. The continuous-time term structure model discussed later in this chapter evolved from the eclectic compilation of earlier theories.

Discount Function

The discount function incorporates market yield-curve information to express the present value of a future dollar as a function of the term to its receipt. As such, the discount function is a valid expression of the term structure of interest rates by virtue of the price/yield relationship. Since the discount function is used to quantify the value of a future dollar, the discount function also provides a direct means to value a coupon paying bond since the coupon and principal payments are simply scalar multiples of a single dollar. As a result, the discount function can be used as a reference check for other quantitative term structure models.

Quantitative term-structure models ultimately deal with the analysis of pure discount bonds. (Discount bonds, or zero-coupon bonds, are the simplest types of bonds to analyze as there is only the repayment of par at maturity. Further, all other bonds can be built from a series of discount bonds and options on discount bonds.) As a consequence of modeling the yield movements of discount bonds, term structure models describe their price movements since the price/yield relationship allows the term structure to be analyzed in terms of either price or yield.

This relationship is addressed further later in this chapter, in which the term structure model is expressed in terms of price as a function of rate and time.

If it is assumed that the discount bond pays one dollar at maturity, then the present value of the bond is some decimal fraction less than one. For a set of discount bonds of increasing maturities, there is the corresponding set of present values starting from approximately 0.999 and decreasing thereafter. This set of present values is called the "*discount function*," and is shown in Exhibit 5.1.

The discount function is the term-to-maturity relationship of the present value of a future unit of cash flow. More formally, for a cash flow, *CF*, received after a term, *T*, from today, *t*, the present value, *PV*, of that cash flow is discounted, *d*, from the future value *CF* as expressed by the relation

$$PV(t, T) = d(t, T) \times CF(t, T) \tag{1}$$

where

$PV(t,T)$ = present value of the cash flow at t
$d(t,T)$ = discount at t for a cash flow received T after t
$CF(t,T)$ = cash flow received at $t + T$

EXHIBIT 5.1 Discount Function

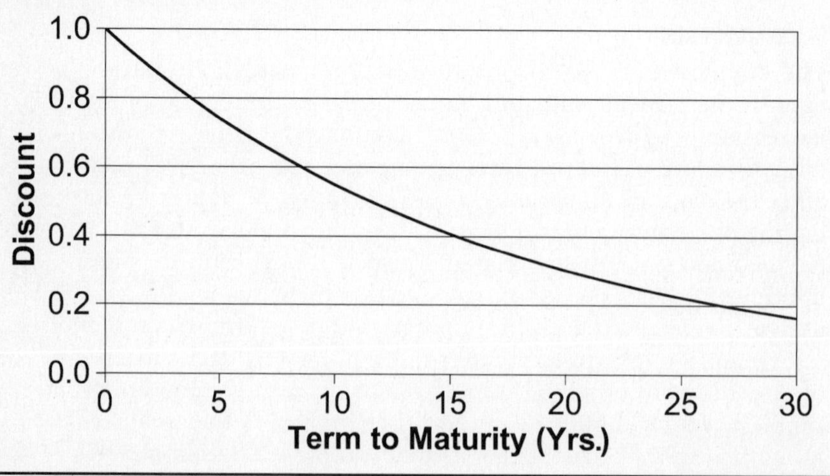

As we are able to generate the discount function, *d*, for all terms-to-maturity, *T*, this can be a valid representation of the term structure of interest rates. Indeed, the discount function reflects the Treasury term structure when the discount function exactly reprices the current-coupon Treasury issues.

Deriving the Discount Function for On-the-Run Treasuries

More generally, let $P(t,i)$ be the set of closing prices on (date) t for the set of current-coupon Treasury bonds (where the index, i, associates a specific issue)

$P(t,$3-month):	price of the 3-month (13-week) bill, at time t
$P(t,$6-month):	price of the 6-month (26-week) bill, at time t
$P(t,$2-year):	price of the 2-year note, at time t
. . .	. . .
$P(t,$30-year):	price of the 30-year bond, at time t

Each of these instruments has its own time series of cash flows, each with its own individual term-to-maturity. For the Treasury bills, the cash flows and associated terms-to-maturity are

3-month bill: $CF(t,T(\text{3-month},1))$
6-month bill: $CF(t,T(\text{6-month},1))$

and for the periodic instruments,

2-year note:	$CF(t,T(\text{2-year},1))$, $CF(t,T(\text{2-year},2))$, $CF(t,T(\text{2-year},3))$, $CF(t,T(\text{2-year},4))$
. . .	. . .
30-year bond:	$CF(t,T(\text{30-year},1))$, $CF(t,T(\text{30-year},2))$, . . ., $CF(t,T(\text{30-year},60))$,

where the term to each of the cash flows, $T(i,j)$, is specific to the instrument. The index j is the sequence of the cash flow in the time series for security i.

The present value of a coupon paying instrument is simply the sum of the discounted present values of the cash flows that make up the coupon payments and the payment of principal. Accordingly, for the discount function to model the Treasury term structure (i.e., the market sector defined by the on-the-run Treasury reference set), the following equations must be simultaneously satisfied. In this way, the discount function will reprice the current-coupon Treasury issues.

$$P(t,\text{3-month}) = d(t,T(\text{3-month},1)) \times CF(t,T(\text{3-month},1))$$
$$P(t,\text{6-month}) = d(t,T(\text{6-month},1)) \times \mathrm{CF}(t,T(\text{6-month},1))$$

$$
\begin{aligned}
P(t,\text{2-year}) \quad &= d(t,T(\text{2-year},1)) \times CF(t,T(\text{2-year},1)) \\
&+ d(t,T(\text{2-year},2)) \times CF(t,T(\text{2-year},2)) \\
&+ d(t,T(\text{2-year},3)) \times CF(t,T(\text{2-year},3)) \\
&+ d(t,T(\text{2-year},4)) \times CF(t,T(\text{2-year},4)) \\
\ldots \quad & \quad \ldots \\
P(t,\text{30-year})) \quad &= d(t,T(\text{30-year},1)) \times CF(t,T(\text{30-year},1)) \\
&+ d(t,T(\text{30-year},2)) \times CF(t,T(\text{30-year},2)) \\
& \quad \ldots \\
&+ d(t,T(\text{30-year},60)) \times CF(t,T(\text{30-year},60))
\end{aligned}
$$

The last cash flow of each series consists of the principal payment and, for the notes and bond, one coupon payment. The solution to these simultaneous equations furnishes many distinct points of term in which the discount function is defined; the long bond alone may have as many as 60 term points. Depending on the circumstances surrounding each auction, there may be as many as over 90 distinct points of term defining the discount function.

As with the earlier "connect-the-dots" model for the yield curve, in which the yield points were connected to generate intermediate values for the term structure, similar ideas can be used to accommodate the cash flows that do not fall on one of the terms, $T(i,j)$, enumerated above. In fact, interpolation techniques using spline functions may be applied to create a continuous discount-function curve.[1]

The discount function forms the basis for the development of a term structure model, as will be developed further in later sections. As the discount function is an expression of the term structure based on price, there is no ambiguity of compounding periodicity, as with yield based term structure models. The discount function simply expresses the non-dimensional, fractional, present value of a unit cash flow to be received after some term. The term may be specified in a unit of time (e.g., years, months, or days) or in periods, in which the period length is a unit of time.

Spot-Yield Curve

With the assumption of a compounding convention (usually semiannual), the discount function can be used to derive the equivalent Treasury zero-coupon structure—sometimes referred to as the *spot-yield curve*. In this case, the spot-yield curve is an equivalent term structure representation based on yield that provides a view of the term structure

[1] See Oldrich A. Vasicek and H. Gifford Fong, "Term Structure Modeling Exponential Spline," *Journal of Finance* (May 1982), pp. 339–348.

that is more familiar to readers. The equivalence between these two forms of the term structure is used later in this chapter.

The *spot yield*, R, is related to the discount function, d, through the price/yield relation. By definition of the internal rate of return (IRR), the present value at t, $PV(t,n)$, of a cash flow received n periods in the future, $CF(t,n)$, has the IRR (or spot yield), $R(t,n)$, through the relation

$$PV(t, n) = \frac{CF(t, n)}{[1 + R(t, n)]^n} \tag{2}$$

We use the discrete notion of integer periods, with each period of length P, to keep the math simple at this point.

Comparing equations (2) and (1) provides the relation between the spot yield and the discount function

$$d(t, n) = \frac{1}{[1 + R(t, n)]^n} \tag{3}$$

where

$d(t,n)$ = discount of a cash flow received n periods after t
$R(t,n)$ = n-period spot yield on t

The spot-yield curve is just the set of spot yields for all terms-to-maturity. In contrast, the *spot rate* is simply the one-period rate prevailing on t for repayment one period later. In the above notation, the spot rate is denoted $R(t,1)$.

We can generalize the earlier comment about coupon paying bonds in terms of the set of spot yields. The present value of a coupon paying instrument is simply the sum of the discounted (present value) of the cash flows that make up the coupon payments and the payment of principal. The analogy to equation (2) for a coupon paying bond using spot yields is

$$PV(t, n) = \frac{CF(t, 1)}{[1 + R(t, 1)]} + \frac{CF(t, 2)}{[1 + R(t, 2)]^2} + \ldots + \frac{CF(t, n)}{[1 + R(t, n)]^n} \tag{2a}$$

Similarly, the analogy to equation (1) for a coupon paying bond using the discount function is given by

$$PV(t,n) = d(t,1) \times CF(t,1) + d(t,2) \times CF(t,2) + \ldots + d(t,n) \times CF(t,n) \tag{1a}$$

Implied Forward Rate

A consequence of the discount function, spot yield, and spot rate is the immediate relation to the (implied) forward rates. The *implied forward rate* is the spot rate embodied in today's yield curve for some period in the future. The forward rate generally is regarded as an indication of future spot rates in an arbitrage-free economy. In the absence of arbitrage and uncertainty, the future spot rate, by definition, is equal to the forward rate. In the arbitrage-free term structure model discussed later in this chapter, it can be shown that the future spot rate continuously converges toward the forward rate as the spot rate evolves over time.

Specifically, the one-period forward rate, F, can be determined from the spot yields as follows. Consider the one-period and two-period spot yields; the forward rate, F, may be found from

$$(1 + R(t,2))^2 = (1 + R(t,1)) \times (1 + F(t,1,1)) \tag{4}$$

where

$R(t,2)$ = two-period spot yield on t
$R(t,1)$ = one-period spot rate on t
$F(t,1,1)$ = one-period forward rate one-period from t

This relation follows from the no-arbitrage assumption intrinsic in the concept of forward rates. The calculation of the forward rate presumes that an investment today for two periods provides the same return as a one-period investment today immediately rolled into another one-period investment one period from now. That is

$$PV(t) = \frac{CF(t,2)}{[1 + R(t,2)]^2} \tag{5}$$

$$= \frac{CF(t,2)}{[1 + R(t,1)] \times [1 + F(t,1,1)]} \tag{6}$$

By equating equations (5) and (6), equation (4) results.

Deriving Forward Rates from Spot Yields

Implied from the term structure, through the spot-yield curve, is a set of forward rates. These forward rates may be iteratively defined from the above and written as follows

$$(1 + R(t,n))^n = (1 + R(t,n-1))^{n-1} \times (1 + F(t,1,n-1))$$

where in addition to the earlier notation, $F(t,1,n{-}1)$ = one-period forward rate $n{-}1$ periods from t, and noting, through substitution, that

$$\begin{aligned}&(1+R(t,n))^n \\ &=(1+R(t,1))\times(1+F(t,1,1))\times(1+F(t,1,2))\times\ldots\times(1+F(t,1,n{-}1))\end{aligned} \tag{7}$$

which furnishes the first $n - 1$ one-period forward rates.

The relation between spot yield, spot rate and forward rates, equation (7), can be combined with equation (2) to furnish a method for calculating the present value, at t, of a single n-period future cash flow based on a series of one-period forward rates

$$PV(t,n) = \frac{CF(t,n)}{[1+R(t,1)]\times\ldots\times[1+F(t,1,n-1)]} \tag{8}$$

Since the present value of a coupon paying security is simply the sum of the discounted present value of the cash flows that make up the coupon payments and the payment of principal [see equations (la) and (2a)], the analogy to equation (8) for determining the present value of a coupon paying bond is

$$\begin{aligned}PV(t,n) = {} & \frac{CF(t,1)}{[1+R(t,1)]} \\ & + \frac{CF(t,2)}{[1+R(t,1)]\times[1+F(t,1,1)]} \\ & + \ldots \\ & + \frac{CF(t,n)}{[1+R(t,1)]\times\ldots\times[1+F(t,1,n-1)]}\end{aligned} \tag{8a}$$

Equation (8a) may be used to define multi-period forward rates.

Deriving Forward Rates from the Discount Function

The discount function provides a direct method for generating forward rates. The one-period forward return $n - 1$ periods from t is obtained through the following

$$1 + F(t,1,n-1) = \frac{d(t,n-1)}{d(t,n)} \tag{9}$$

Equation (9) may be derived from earlier equations, or from the following argument that creates a synthetic forward position. For each unit of cash delivered n periods from today, t, we pay $d(t,n)$. We take a long position in this zero. We also short $d(t,n)/d(t,n-1)$ units of cash to be delivered $n - 1$ periods from t. For this we receive $d(t,n-1)$ times $d(t,n)/d(t,n-1)$, or simply $d(t,n)$, units. There is no net change in our cash position today. After $n - 1$ periods we pay out $d(t,n)/d(t,n-1)$ and after n periods receive one unit of cash. Thus the forward price per unit, FP, to be paid $n - 1$ periods from now is

$$FP(t, 1, n-1) = \frac{d(t, n)}{d(t, n-1)} \tag{9a}$$

where

$FP(t,1,n-1)$ = forward price of a one-period unit of cash $n - 1$ periods from now

The forward price then gives the forward one-period rate, $n - 1$ periods from t as

$$FP(t, 1, n-1) = \frac{1}{1 + F(t, 1, n-1)} \tag{9b}$$

Equating (9a) to (9b) results in Equation (9).

Term Structure in a Certain Economy

As discussed earlier, term structure models describe the evolution of interest rates over time. Often, future interest rates are expressed in terms of the future spot rate. If the future spot rate (or equivalently, the future rate of return on a bond) is known, the future term structure of interest rates may be found from the previously established inter-relationships between the spot rate and the discount function or spot yield. In fact, it is this relationship between the spot rate and the discount function that is used to motivate the formulation of the term structure model described later in this chapter as a function of the spot rate. As a precursor to a generalized term structure theory, we first discuss the ramifications for a term structure in a certain economy.[2]

If the future course of interest rates is known with certainty, then arbitrage arguments demand that future spot rates be identical to future

[2] In this context, "certain" refers to an economy with a lack of randomness, in other words, a lack of uncertainty.

forward rates. In the notation presented in equation (7), this is equivalent to noting that

$$R(t + nP,1) = F(t,1,n) \tag{10}$$

for $n = 1, 2, 3, \ldots$ and where P is the term of the period. If this condition were violated, say, for example,

$$F(t,1,n) > R(t + nP,1)$$

then the same arbitrage argument may be made as before: If we buy the synthetic forward (this is a long position in a unit zero to be delivered $n + 1$ periods from today, t); and short $d(t,n + 1)/d(t,n)$ units of cash to be delivered n periods from today, t, no cash changes hands today. However, after n periods, we pay the forward price, FP,

$$FP(t, 1, n) = \frac{1}{1 + F(t, 1, n)}$$

to receive one unit of cash after $n + 1$ periods. Also, after n periods, at $t + nP$, we sell the one-period unit zero for a price of

$$\frac{1}{1 + R(t + nP, 1)}$$

We know we can do this since there is no uncertainty in the economy. If, as assumed, $F(t,1,n) > R(t + nP,1)$, then after n periods the long and short positions yield a positive net cash flow, or a riskless arbitrage, of

$$\frac{1}{1 + R(t + nP, 1)} - \frac{1}{1 + F(t, 1, n)} > 0$$

after n periods with no uncertainty and with no net investment. Arbitrageurs will exploit the imbalance of the n-period forward rate with the spot rate n periods from now by continuing to buy the synthetic forward until demand outstrips supply. In this scenario, the synthetic forward price goes up, and the forward rate, $F(t,1,n)$, goes down to $R(t + nP,1)$—with predictable effect on $d(t,n+1)$ and/or $d(t,n)$. On the other hand, if $F(t,1,n) < R(t + nP,1)$, we may reverse our positions and the same argument carries through to show $F(t,1,n)$ will increase to $R(t + nP,1)$.

Using the no-arbitrage condition in a certain economy, equation (10), in the present value expression from the implied forward-rate expression, equation (8) (which always holds irrespective of assumptions about the economy), we have,

$$
\begin{aligned}
PV(t, n) &= \frac{CF(t, n+1)}{[1+R(t, 1)] \times [1+R(t+P, 1)] \times \ldots \times [1+R(t+nP, 1)]} \\
&= \frac{CF(t, n+1)}{[1+R(t, n+1)]^{n+1}}
\end{aligned}
\tag{11}
$$

This means that the certain return of holding an $n + 1$ period zero until maturity is the same as the total return on a series of one-period bonds over the same period. Later we will discuss the various forms of equation (11) from various qualitative term structure theories.

Given equation (11), we have, at time P (one period) later,

$$PV(t+P, n) = \frac{CF(t, n+1)}{[1+R(t+P, 1)] \times \ldots \times [1+R(t+nP, 1)]}$$

so we find that the single-period return on a long-term zero is

$$\frac{PV(t+P)}{PV(t)} = 1 + R(t, 1) \tag{12}$$

Since the term-to-maturity was not specified, equation (12) must be true for zeros of any maturity. That is, the return realized on every discount bond over any period is equal to one plus the prevailing spot rate over that period. This will be expanded upon later in this chapter.

Alternatively, we can use our relation for the discount function in Equation (1), noting

$$PV(t+P, n) = d(t+P, n) \times CF(t, n+1)$$

and

$$PV(t, n) = d(t, n+1) \times CF(t, n+1)$$

and restate equation (12) in terms of the discount function

$$\frac{d(t+P, n)}{d(t, n+1)} = 1 + R(t, 1) \tag{12a}$$

While these developments for the certain economy may appear trivial and obvious, they serve as a guide for modeling the term structure under uncertainty as well.

Term Structure in the Real World—Nothing Is Certain

In the real-world economy, the future course of interest rates contains uncertainty. In attempting to deal with uncertainty, however, it would not be inconceivable that a belief in the efficiency of the market would prompt one to use the term structure and the relation between forward rates and spot rates as indicators of expectation about the future. Indeed, market efficiency states that prices reflect all available information bearing on the valuation of the instrument. Equilibrium supply and demand for fixed-income instruments reflect a market cleared consensus of the economic future. As uncertainty represents a departure from this consensus, the expected equilibrium offers a natural starting point for analysis.

Expectations Hypothesis

The expectations theory of the term structure of interest rates offers a good starting point for dealing with an uncertain future. Actually, there is a whole family of expectations theories. Broadly, the expectations theory states that the expected one-period rate of return on an investment is the same, regardless of the maturity of the investment. That is, if the investment horizon is one year, it would make no difference to invest in a one-year instrument, a two-year instrument sold after one year, or two sequential six-month instruments.

The most common form of this statement uses equation (10) as the basis for the theory. This is referred to as the *unbiased expectations hypothesis*, which states that the expected future spot rate is equal to the forward rate, or

$$E[R(t+nP,1)] = F(t+kP,1,n-k)$$

for $k = 0, 1, \ldots, n - 1$, and where $E[\cdot]$ is the expectation operator.

Using this relation, we find from equation (8) that the present value in an economy characterized by unbiased expectations is

$$PV(t,n) = \frac{CF(t,n+1)}{[1+R(t,1)]\times\{1+E[R(t+P,1)]\}\times\ldots\times\{1+E[R(t+nP,1)]\}} \tag{13}$$

Therefore, the unbiased expectations hypothesis concludes that the guaranteed return from buying a $(n + 1)$ period bond and holding it to maturity is equivalent to the product of the expected returns from holding one-period bonds using a strategy of rolling over a series of one-period bonds until maturity.

Alternatively, the *return-to-maturity expectations hypothesis* is based on equation (11). Here we find that present value in such an economy is

$$PV(t,n) = \frac{CF(t,n+1)}{E\{[1+R(t,1)]\times[1+R(t+P,1)]\times\ldots\times[1+R(t+nP,1)]\}} \tag{14}$$

The return-to-maturity expectations hypothesis assumes that an investor would expect to earn the same return by rolling over a series of one-period bonds as buying an $(n + 1)$-period bond and holding it to maturity.

The last version of the expectations hypothesis that we will mention (there are others) is the *local-expectations hypothesis* (or risk-neutral hypothesis). This hypothesis is based on equation (12), or equivalently, the discount-function based equation (12a). Under this hypothesis, the expected rate of return over a single period is equal to the prevailing spot rate of interest. Applying these expressions recursively gives

$$\begin{aligned} PV(t) &= \frac{E[PV(t+P)]}{[1+R(t,1)]} \\ &= E\left\{\frac{PV(t+2P)}{[1+R(t+P,1)]\times[1+R(t,1)]}\right\} \\ &= CF(t,n+1) \\ &\quad \times E\left\{\frac{1}{[1+R(t,1)]\times[1+R(t+P,1)]\times\ldots\times[1+R(t+nP,1)]}\right\} \end{aligned} \tag{15}$$

Equations (13), (14), and (15) are clearly different in that the coefficient of the cash flow, $CF(t,n+1)$, received $n + 1$ periods in the future is a different expression in each case. Furthermore, by the principle from mathematical analysis known as Jensen's inequality, only one of the expressions can be true if the future course of interest rates is uncertain.

In fact, in discrete time, we find that bond prices given by the unbiased and return-to-maturity hypotheses are equal but less than that given by the expectations hypothesis. Although the three hypotheses are different, in discrete time, any of these hypotheses is an acceptable description of equilibrium.

In the next section, term structure modeling in continuous time is developed. Equations (13), (14), and (15) have continuous-time analogs, which (as in discrete time) are different from one another. This is again due to Jensen's inequality. Unlike in discrete time, however, only the local expectations hypothesis is acceptable as a statement of equilibrium because the expected returns under each of these hypotheses are not consistent with those implied in a general equilibrium.[3]

Preferred Habitat Hypothesis

Crucial alternatives to the expectations theory of the term structure of interest rates are theories that add an element of risk when conferring the expected rate of return for bonds of different maturities; that is, the indifference assumption that was stated earlier no longer holds. If the investment horizon is one year, it does make a difference whether to invest in a one-year instrument, a two-year instrument sold after one year, or two sequential six-month instruments. The *preferred habitat theory* argues that we first must know the investment horizon to determine relative risk among bonds. In the simple example, the horizon is one year. The one-year instrument is safest for this horizon. Under the preferred habitat theory, the investor would require a higher rate of return on both the two-year and six-month instrument.

Liquidity Preference Hypothesis

The *liquidity preference theory* can be considered a special case of the preferred habitat theory. Here, it is held that investors demand a risk premium as compensation for holding longer-term bonds. In addition, since the variability of price increases with maturity, the risk premium demanded by investors increases. As a special instance of the preferred-habitat theory, the liquidity preference theory says that as all investors have a habitat of a single period, the shortest-term bond is judged safest.

With each of these theories, one can assess their efficacy only in the context of the general economy. Specifically, we assume that the economy is one in which investors have an inclination to consume, as well as to invest (in fact, even in a diverse set of risky investments). With a specification of utility of consumption and wealth, as well as a formal expression for risk aversion, the risk-based term structure theories can be viewed in the context of markets. Given that risk-based term structure theories can be viewed in the context of a defined market, the following conclusions can be made.

[3] See John C. Cox, Jonathan E. Ingersoll, Jr., and Stephen A. Ross, "Re-examination of Traditional Hypotheses About the Term Structure of Interest Rates," *Journal of Finance* (September 1981), pp. 769–799.

Term premiums are monotonic in maturity (or term). Interest-rate risk is inherently intertemporal. That is, it is a multi-period phenomena, in which an unexpected interest-rate change at any period affects all future returns and risk compounds over time. The traditional notion of preferred habitat seems difficult to reconcile with real markets. As it turns out, the traditional notion omits the importance of risk aversion. As we incorporate a varying need to hedge against interest-rate changes, the theory converges to a more acceptable view of markets. The generalization of these economic analyses has led to what has been called an *eclectic theory* of the term structure that recognizes and accommodates the many factors that play a role in shaping the term structure. Expectations of future events, risk preferences, and the characteristics of a variety of investment alternatives are all important, as are the individual preferences (habitats) of market participants about the timing of their consumption. It is this eclectic theory that we embrace in the following development of the dynamic term structure discussed later in this chapter.

CONCEPTS IN TERM STRUCTURE MODELING IN CONTINUOUS TIME

In this section we discuss how the earlier concepts of discount function, spot rate, spot yield, and forward rate have their analogies in the continuous-time domain. It will be seen that while the mathematics are slightly more complex, the roles that each of these quantities play in the term structure of interest rates remain unchanged.

In summary, the priced-based representation of the term structure, or the discount function, facilitates both the mathematical formulation of the problem and its subsequent solution. Once the term structure equation is solved explicitly in terms of price, the price/yield equation (in continuous time) is used to convert the term structure to its equivalent representation in terms of yield.

Given the intertemporal nature of the term structure and the apparent efficiency of the market to incorporate information, it is assumed that the market acts instantaneously, and that a period in time is but an instant. This is the underlying premise for continuous-time models in economics and finance.

Traditional fixed-income analysis assumes that compounding occurs at discrete points or over finite intervals, typically on a semiannual basis. However, as the compounding period grows ever shorter, discrete compounding is replaced by continuous compounding. We expand our original equation (2) for the present value (at t), $PV(t,T)$, of a cash flow received T years from today, $CF(t,T)$, which is invested *at the spot yield*, $R(t,T)$, to be

$$PV(t, T) = CF(t, T)e^{-TR(t, T)} \tag{16}$$

Equation (16) is the fundamental price/yield relationship for the case of continuous compounding of a discount bond and is the direct analog of the price/yield relationship shown in equation (2) for discrete compounding.

Discount Function

For a pure discount bond that pays one dollar at maturity, $CF(t,T) = 1$. Let P be the price of the pure discount bond. Thus equation (16) becomes

$$P(t, T) = e^{-TR(t, T)} \tag{17}$$

Combining the above with equation (1), which equates the price of a discount bond to the discount function, we obtain

$$P(t, T) = e^{-TR(t, T)} = d(t, T) \tag{18}$$

Equation (18) provides an expression for the relationship between the *discount function d* and the spot yield R, and is the continuous-time analogy to equation (3).

Spot Rate

In the previous section, the spot rate was defined as the one-period rate of return. Under continuous compounding, the *spot rate r* is defined as the continuously compounded *instantaneous rate of return.* Stated another way, the spot rate is the return on a discount bond that matures in the next instant. The spot rate is really an expression of the concept that a discount bond with a specified term-to-maturity and yield is equivalent to a series of instantaneously maturing discount bonds that are continuously reinvested at a rate r until the final term T. This is discussed in the following section.

Spot Yield

If the spot rate is a known function of time, then a loan amount W that is invested at the spot rate r will grow by an increment dW that is given by

$$dW(t) = W(t)r(t)dt \tag{19}$$

where

$dW(t)$ = incremental increase in the value of the loan from time t to time $t + dt$
$W(t)$ = value of loan at time t
$r(t)$ = spot rate at time t

To find the value of the loan W at maturity, integrate equation (19)

$$\int_t^{t+T} \frac{dW(\tau)}{W(\tau)} = \int_t^{t+T} r(\tau)d\tau$$

$$W(t) = W(t+T)\exp\left(-\int_t^{t+T} r(\tau)d\tau\right) \tag{20}$$

If W is a discount bond, $W(t)$ is equal to the present value $P(t, T)$ and $W(t + T)$ is one. Equation (20) is rewritten as

$$P(t, T) = \exp\left(-\int_t^{t+T} r(\tau)d\tau\right) \tag{21}$$

From equation (17), the price P is expressed in terms of its spot yield R. By equating (17) and (21), we obtain the following expression for the *spot yield* in terms of the spot rate

$$R(t, T) = \frac{1}{T}\int_t^{t+T} r(\tau)d\tau \tag{22}$$

Equation (22) is a general expression that always holds.

Another view of the relationship between the spot yield and the spot rate is that instead of continuously reinvesting at the spot rate r for a fixed maturity T to obtain the spot yield R, if the term-to-maturity grows ever shorter, the spot yield R approaches the spot rate r "in the limit." r may be stated as

$$r(t) = R(t, T = 0) = \lim_{T \to 0} R(t, T) \tag{23}$$

Graphically, the spot rate at $t = 0$ may be visualized as the yield corresponding to the point at which the spot-yield curve intercepts the yield axis.

Forward Rate

The forward rate, $F(t_0,t)$ is the marginal rate of return for extending an investment to an additional increment of term at $t > t_0$. The forward rate is defined by

$$R(t, T) = \frac{1}{T}\int_{t}^{t+T} F(t, \tau)d\tau \tag{24}$$

Comparing the above notations for the forward rate with that in equation (4), note that the parameter "1" from the previous parameter set (denoting one time period) is no longer present. In the continuous-time domain, one time period collapses to just an instant.

Rearranging and applying Leibniz's Rule, the above becomes

$$\begin{aligned}\frac{d}{dT}[TR(t, T)] &= \frac{d}{dT}\int_{t}^{t+T} F(t, \tau)d\tau \\ &= F(t, t+T) \\ &= F(t, s)\end{aligned} \tag{25}$$

where s is the maturity date. The above equations relate the forward rate to the spot yield R. As with the case of discrete compounding, the forward rate may be expressed similarly in terms of the discount function $d(t,T)$ or the spot rate $r(t)$.

From equations (17), (18), and (25),

$$F(t, t+T) = \frac{-d}{dT}ln[d(t, T)] \tag{26}$$

where $ln[\ ]$ is the natural logarithm.

Separately, from equations (22) and (24),

$$\begin{aligned}r(t) &= \lim_{T\to 0} R(t, T) \\ r(t) &= \lim_{T\to 0}\frac{1}{T}\int_{t}^{t+T} F(t, \tau)d\tau \\ &= \lim_{T\to 0}\frac{1}{T} F(t, t_*)T \qquad (t < t_* < t+T) \\ &= F(t, t)\end{aligned} \tag{27}$$

Under a certain economy, equations (22) and (27) show that the spot rate needs to be equal to the forward rate to preclude arbitrage. In the case in which the spot-yield curve $R(t,T)$ (and consequently the term structure) is defined, it follows that the spot rate needs to be equal to the instantaneous forward rate over the term of the discount bond for equation (27) to hold true (see equation (7) for the analogy in the case of discrete compounding).

Since R is the yield of a discount bond and the term structure of interest rates is the set of spot yields as a function of maturity, equation (22) defines the term structure when the evolution of the spot rate is a known function of time. However, in general, the spot rate is not known; only the current spot rate is known from the current spot-yield curve. Nevertheless, term structure theory expands the basic relationship that is shown in equation (22), namely that the yield of a discount bond is a function of the spot rate. This is discussed in more detail in the next section when the spot rate assumes the form of a stochastic differential equation.

Term Structure in Continuous Time

As stated in the previous section, the term structure of interest rates describes the relationship between the yields of default-free, zero-coupon securities as a function of maturity. Consequently, the term structure may be envisioned as a continuous set of yields for zero-coupon securities over a range of maturities.

Equation (18) describes the price/yield relationship for a single zero-coupon bond of a given maturity. As the term-to-maturity T spans the range of possible maturities within the term structure, the associated spot yields are generated for each maturity point, i.e., R is a function of the term T. Furthermore, for any one value of T, the spot yield will vary as a function of the time t. In general, the spot yield R is a function of the term-to-maturity T, the time t and the spot rate r [as shown by equation (22)]. R may be expressed as

$$R = R(r, t, T) \tag{28}$$

Equation (28) describes the functional form of the term structure in terms of the spot yield R. In order to describe the term structure completely, an equation is needed that mathematically specifies the form of the relationship between the spot yield R and the term T over time t.

Such an equation for the term structure may be found by considering that the term structure may be expressed equivalently in terms of the prices of discount bonds (i.e., through the discount function). Thus equation (17) may be rewritten as

$$R(r, t, T) = -\frac{1}{T}ln[P(r, t, T)] \tag{29}$$

where *ln*[ ] is the natural logarithm.

If an expression for $P(r,t,T)$ can be found that defines the value of a zero-coupon bond at different points in time and for varying terms T, then the term structure of interest rates has been defined fully. Alternatively, equation (29) provides an equivalent description of the evolution of the term structure over time in terms of the spot yield.

Next, a methodology is described that allows for the derivation of a formula for $P(r,t,T)$, hence arriving at a model of the term structure of interest rates.

TERM STRUCTURE MODEL

In this section we review four fundamental principles that guided the development of the term structure model:

- "General"-equilibrium model
- Arbitrage-free term structure
- Continuous-time/continuous-state approach
- Generality of the model

These four principles not only provide an elegant mathematical formulation of the term structure of interest rates, but also one that is applicable to a number of different market sectors.

"General" Equilibrium Model

General equilibrium models of the economy describe the basic workings of the macro economy as a function of a given "state variable." This implies that the production processes and assets that constitute the economy are determined by the value of the state variable. As one of the definitive works on term structure theory, Cox-Ingersoll-Ross (CIR) showed that this general equilibrium model of the economy may be used to derive a model for the term structure of interest rates in terms of this state variable.[4] Such an approach is considered to be a general equilibrium model of interest rates in that the interest-rate model is a consequence of a general economic model.

[4] John C. Cox, Jonathan E. Ingersoll, Jr., and Stephen A. Ross, "A Theory of the Term Structure of Interest Rates," *Econometrica* (March 1985), pp. 385–407.

In contrast to general equilibrium models, "partial equilibrium" models assume a particular form of the interest-rate process as a given. This type of approach does not require the particular interest-rate process to be a result of some greater underlying theory. Examples of partial equilibrium models are those of Vasicek,[5] Ho and Lee,[6] and Black-Derman-Toy,[7] among others. In addition, partial equilibrium models are calibrated exogenously to the current term structure of interest rates. Without this exogenous information, partial equilibrium models cannot quantify the term structure.

On the other hand, general equilibrium models theoretically can specify a term structure independently of any bond-market information. It has been observed though that such a term structure (as provided by earlier general equilibrium models) may not be consistent with the entire market term structure. For this reason and due to the difficulty that some term structure practitioners have had in quantifying the parameters in the CIR model, many implementers of term structure models have pursued the development of partial equilibrium models.

We approached these issues in the development of this term structure model in a variety of ways. While the model described herein is not purely a general equilibrium model, we began with the basic CIR model as a starting point, and then further generalized that model's stochastic interest-rate process. Furthermore, we developed an approach for the specification of CIR-type model parameters such that the derived term structure was consistent with the observed market term structure. Thus drawing upon a cornerstone in term structure theory, we developed an extension to the CIR model that can be readily applied to the financial marketplace.

Arbitrage-Free Term Structure

One underlying principle that the term structure model under discussion shares with many of the above mentioned references is that the term structure is "arbitrage free." This concept is an extension of the arbitrage-free principles found in the Black-Scholes' options theory for commodity and equity markets, and states that the term structure observes a given relationship among its constituent parts and that purely arbitrary yield-curve shapes do not occur. Given today's yield curve, subsequent yield

[5] Oldrich Vasicek, "An Equilibrium Characterization of the Term Structure," *Journal of Financial Economics* (1977), pp. 177–188.

[6] Thomas S.Y. Ho and Sang B. Lee, "Term Structure Movements and Pricing Interest Rate Contingent Claims," *Journal of Finance* (December 1986), pp. 1011–1029.

[7] Fischer Black, Emanuel Derman and William Toy, "A One Factor Model of Interest Rates and its Application to Treasury Bond Options," *Financial Analysts Journal* (January/February 1990), pp. 33–39.

curves are assumed to evolve in a "rational" manner that precludes riskless arbitrage. This indicates that the prices of bonds defining the yield curve move in such a way that it is not possible to create a portfolio of securities that always will outperform another portfolio without entailing any risk or net investment; in other words, there is no "free lunch." Appendix B shows that the arbitrage-free principle plays an important role in the mathematical pricing of fixed-income securities.

Continuous-Time/Continuous-State Approach

Another distinguishing feature of this term structure model is the strict adherence to the "continuous-time/continuous-state" approach to the modeling of stochastic processes. This assumes that interest rates and bond prices move in a continuous fashion over time, rather than in discrete jumps. Thus a spot-yield curve may be found for any point in time during the life of a bond, rather than only at specific points (such as a coupon payment date). This concept is consistent with the notion of a continuous yield curve and allows for the use of continuous stochastic calculus.

Continuous Probability Distributions

Furthermore, the generality of the transitional probability density function, as a complete specification of the statistical properties of the rate process, is maintained throughout the term of the bond. This is in contrast to the common approach of describing individual sample paths or scenarios, as found in Monte Carlo approaches to security analysis. The ability to extend the analyses to compound, derivative instruments is unimpaired through the use of this transitional probability density function. Moreover, the continuous-time/continuous-state approach avoids the computational issues associated with the number of sample paths analyzed. Since the complete specification of the statistical properties is maintained, it is as if an infinite number of sample paths are run.

Numerical Solution Technique

The computer numerical solution technique that accompanies the continuous-time formulation is one that is well known in the engineering and physical sciences as the "Crank-Nicholson" finite-difference method for the solution of partial differential equations (PDEs). This solution technique has been used extensively in the study of aerodynamics and fluid flow, and has the flexibility to focus its computational efforts in areas that require greater numerical precision, such as the time period surrounding an option exercise period. This is in contrast to binomial interest-rate lattices, which are constrained to jump, for example, in six-month intervals, such as in some commercially available applications.

Generality of the Model

The formulation and implementation of the term structure model needs to be completely general so as to be applicable across a broad range of fixed-income markets in a straightforward and consistent manner. For example, once the value of the fixed-income instrument is found, the value of its derivative (such as its futures contract) also may be found. Furthermore, it is possible to value the quality and delivery options within the bond futures contract. These effects also can be incorporated when valuing an option on the bond futures contract.

General Assumptions

The analytical model that describes spot-rate movement is a one-factor, mean reverting, diffusion process model. The model assumes:

1. The evolution of interest rates is a continuous process and may be described by a single variable, i.e., by the instantaneous spot rate, which is the return on an investment over an infinitesimally short period of time. This allows for the use of continuous-time mathematics, which requires greater technical sophistication, but which increases the flexibility of the mathematical modeling process.
2. The model assumes that interest rates move in a random fashion, which is known as Brownian motion or a Wiener process. The Weiner process has been used in the physical sciences to describe the motion of molecular particles as they diffuse (or spread) over time and space.
3. The term structure of interest rates is assumed to be represented by a Markov process, which states that the future movement in interest rates depends only on the current term structure and that all past information is embodied in the current term structure.
4. The term structure is arbitrage free in that a portfolio of securities derived from the term structure is constrained to have an instantaneous rate of return that is equal to the risk-free rate. Future movements in interest rates are similarly constrained so that the possibility of riskless profits are precluded. This implies that there are a sufficient number of sophisticated investors who will take advantage of any temporary mispricings in the marketplace, thus quickly diluting any arbitrage opportunities that exist.

   Technically, an arbitrage-free term structure indicates that a portfolio of securities derived from the term structure may be constructed such that the portfolio instantaneously returns the risk-free rate (see Appendix B). Since the above holds true for any arbitrary set of maturities in this portfolio of securities, it is said to be true for all maturities. This indicates that all securities that comprise the term structure are related in a common fashion. This commonality is expressed through the concept of the *market price of risk,* which is the incremental return over the risk-free rate that is required for incurring a given amount of additional risk. In this context, risk is measured by the variance of a bond's rate of return. A result of the arbitrage-free nature of the term structure is that all securities share the same market price of risk. As we demonstrate in Appendix B at the end of the chapter, the risk premium is one component of the market price of risk.

5. The price of a default-free, zero-coupon (discount) bond at any point in time continuously depends on the spot rate, time, and maturity of the bond. This models the interaction between the bond's price and the probabilistic movement in the spot rate. This is an extension of the point discussed earlier in this chapter that stated the yield of a discount bond is a function of the spot rate.
6. The market is efficient in that all investors have the same timely access to relevant market information. Furthermore, investors are rational and there are no transaction costs.

Spot-Rate Model

As a result of assumptions 1 through 3 above, the equation that describes the diffusion process for the movement in the spot rate is given by equation (30)

$$dr = k(\theta - r)dt + \sigma\sqrt{r}dz \tag{30}$$

where

r = spot rate, the instantaneous rate of return
dr = infinitesimal change in the spot rate
k = mean reversion constant
θ = "target" spot rate as a function of time
dt = infinitesimal change in time
σ = volatility of r
dz = infinitesimal change in the normal random variable z

Mean Reversion

Equation (30) states that the rate r changes with respect to time and the degree of randomness. The first term on the right-hand side of equation (30) states that the "drift" in the spot rate over time is proportional to the difference between the rate r and θ. As r deviates from θ, the change in r is such that r has a tendency to revert back to θ, a feature that is known as "mean reversion." The presence of mean reversion imposes a centralizing tendency such that rates are not expected to go to extremely high or low levels. In addition, mean reversion precludes the existence of negative interest rates in our interest-rate model, given that the initial interest rates are positive.

Appendix B presents a closed-form expression for θ as a function of time. Note that θ is not assumed to be constant, which is usually the case for the traditional CIR approach.

Effect of Randomness

The second term on the right-hand side of equation (30) states that the contribution to the change in r due to randomness is driven by movements in the random variable z. The variable z is normally distributed with a mean of zero and a variance that is proportional to time. This indicates that the amount of random "noise," as represented by the variable z, may be any positive or negative value, but that its expected value is zero. In addition, as time passes, the variance increases so that the "amplitude" of the noise also increases (see Appendix A).

The variables σ and r, which are coefficients of dz in equation (30), show that the change in r also depends on the level of volatility and interest rates. The variable z has its own defined level of uncertainty so that as volatility and rate change, the overall degree of uncertainty is influenced by the level of these variables.

Endogenous Parameterization (Tuning the Model)

Equation (30) describes the rate in terms of the parameters k, σ, and θ. The volatility parameter σ is specified externally so that it reflects either the historical level of volatility or the volatility that is currently present in the market. Secondly, θ reflects the current term structure (see Appendix B) such that the future movements in r are influenced by today's term structure. Finally, the mean reversion constant k determines the speed of adjustment of r back to θ. In order for the interest-rate model to be of any utility, the parameter k is chosen to be consistent with the observed market prices of bonds comprising the current yield curve, while θ is derived directly from the current yield curve. This process of determining k and θ "parameterizes" the model to the observed yield curve.

There are several variations of equation (30) existing within the academic literature that appear to be similar to equation (30).[8] However, the details surrounding the functional form of each term in equation

[8] See K.C. Chan, G.A. Karolyi, F.A. Longstaff, and A.B. Sanders, "An Empirical Comparison of Alternative Models of the Short-Term Interest Rate," *Journal of Finance* (July 1992), pp. 1209–1227.

(30) and the associated parameterization process can result in very different models. The specification of parameters for this term structure model is driven by the requirement to be able to precisely reprice the set of securities that constitute the reference yield curve. A properly calibrated term structure model needs to be able to define a bond whose cash flow characteristics match those of an on-the-run issue exactly and then have the price of that constructed bond match exactly the market price of the Treasury issue. By repeating this process for each of the on-the-run issues, the mean reversion constant and the risk premium that are appropriate over the range of reference issues may be quantified.

As a technical side note, the term structure model needs to satisfy internal consistency checks, and the parameter specification process plays a part in the internal system for checks and balances. For the set of chosen parameters, the price furnished by the term structure model—as the solution to a PDE—needs to be equal to that provided by applying the discount function to the cash flows of the specific on-the-run issue, as explained earlier in this chapter. Thus the discount function is a direct means of verifying the results of the term structure model. In fact, the PDE may be decomposed into two coupled ordinary differential equations (ODE) in the absence of any embedded options. Thus prices obtained from the PDE, ODE, and discount-function approaches all need to be identical.

Calculation of the Spot Rate

The solution to equation (30) is obtained through computer numerical solution techniques and accounts for the current value of the spot rate (as an initial condition) and its level of volatility. As time moves forward, the solution expresses the probable distribution of the spot rate as the spot rate propagates through time. Thus, at any point in time, it is possible to calculate the probability distribution of the spot rate. It was discussed previously that the price of a bond depends on the spot rate so that the spot-rate probability distribution is also the probability distribution for the bond price. This is useful in calculating the probability that an embedded call or put option will be exercised, which is the probability that the price of a particular bond is greater than or less than, respectively, the specified strike price at exercise.

The calculation of the probabilities is made possible by assuming a specific mathematical form for the random variable z, or a Wiener process. Generally, a probability distribution function is described by its mean and variance as functions of time. If these quantities are known, then the probability of different spot rates is known. The Wiener process assumption states that the statistical variance for the random variable z varies with the length of time under consideration. As time increases, the variance of z also increases. The known change in the variance of z is subsequently translated (in a known fashion) to the change in the variance of the rate r, which may be used to obtain the desired probability in terms of r.

Bond-Price Valuation Model

As a consequence of assumptions 4 and 5 (the price of a default-free discount bond depends continuously on the spot rate), it can be shown that the price of a discount bond of term T is expressed as (see Appendix B)

$$\frac{\partial P}{\partial t} = rP - [k(\theta - r) + \lambda \sigma r]\frac{\partial P}{\partial r} - \frac{1}{2}\sigma^2 r \frac{\partial^2 P}{\partial r^2} \tag{31}$$

where

P	=	price of zero-coupon bond for time t and rate r
$\partial P/\partial t$	=	partial derivative of price with respect to time
$\partial P/\partial r$	=	partial derivative of price with respect to rate
$\partial^2 P/\partial r^2$	=	second partial derivative of price with respect to rate
λ	=	"risk premium," or the variable that represents the additional return over the risk-free rate for holding a longer-term instrument. This is determined from the current term structure.

Calculation of the Term Structure

Equation (31) is a PDE whose solution is obtained through a numerical finite-difference technique. The solution gives the price P of the bond for different times and spot rates, and can be visualized as a three-dimensional surface, for which the height of the surface is the price of the bond and the location of the point (i.e., longitude and latitude) is given by the time and spot rate. The solution takes into account that the bond's price is par at maturity, regardless of the level of interest rates. As the solution steps back from the maturity date, the price of the bond may be calculated for varying levels of the spot rate and the familiar price/rate graph may be drawn for this time-step.[9]

As the solution process continues backward from maturity to the present day, the theoretical price corresponding to today's spot rate can

[9] Not all bond prices are equally likely to occur since interest-rate movements and the probabilities associated with these movements are described by equation (30).

be calculated. Once the price behavior of a bond is known, the value of an option on that bond may also be calculated.

Since the solution to equation (31) furnishes the price as a function of time and rate, equation (29) of the previous section may be solved to provide the zero-coupon yield for a bond with the term-to-maturity T. As the term T is varied, the entire term structure may be obtained.[10]

MODEL APPLICATIONS

We conclude this chapter with a description of the application of the term structure model developed in the previous section in the valuation of fixed-income securities. For the simple case of non-callable bonds, many term structure models can be used to determine value. In fact, the spline-fit discount function is a very straightforward method of calculating the value of such a bond. However, when option embedded bonds or compound instruments are considered, the PDE approach is required to reflect the specific nature of the option features. As this chapter demonstrates, the PDE based term structure model is but the first step that leads to a greater assortment of analytical financial tools. Applications to bonds with embedded options and interest rate derivatives are provided in other chapters.

Zero-Coupon Bonds

Most yield curves, such as the U.S. Treasury curve, are expressed in terms of the yields of coupon bearing bonds, not zero-coupon bonds. Thus a procedure is required to translate the current-coupon yield curve to an initial zero curve (i.e., the current term structure) expressed in terms of a spot-yield curve. One of several methods may be employed.[11] In summary, a reference set of securities is chosen to represent the yield curve, and each of the cash flows from this set of securities is treated as a zero-coupon bond that is part of the term structure. Since each of the reference securities has a known market price, the price/yield relation-

[10] The obtained term structure, in general, can take a variety of shapes. If the current spot rate is below the current value of the long-term rate, θ, the obtained term structure will be upward sloping. If the current spot rate is substantially above the long-term rate, the obtained term structure will be inverted to downward sloping. For spot-rate values in between, the term structure will be humped, displaying both upward sloping and downward sloping segments. Thus an attractive feature of the term structure model is the ability to obtain term structure specifications that are consistent with those that have been observed historically.

[11] See Vasicek and Fong,"Term Structure Modeling Exponential Spline."

ship, along with a curve fitting process, is applied sequentially to each of the cash flows to derive the current term structure. This process establishes the set of initial conditions necessary to predict the evolution of the term structure.[12]

If the actual zero-coupon yields are compared to the theoretical zero-coupon yields, then the richness or cheapness of the zero-coupon market may be gauged. Since the discount function may be constructed from any reasonable set of reference bonds, if the reference bonds consisted of off-the-run Treasury issues that are commonly stripped and/or reconstituted, then the corresponding theoretical zero curve should be indicative of the shape and level of the market strip curve.

Additionally, as the Treasury curve flattens or steepens, the theoretical zero curve changes accordingly to reflect the new shape of the Treasury curve. Consequently, as the Treasury curve steepens or flattens, the degree of anticipated yield-spread widening or tightening in the zero market may be estimated.

Coupon Paying Bonds

While our discussion thus far applies mainly to the price of a zero-coupon bond, it is more common to encounter coupon paying bonds. To value coupon paying bonds, we simply sum the present values of each of the coupon payments to determine the price. As discussed earlier, each coupon is treated as an individual zero-coupon bond.

Determination of the Theoretical Fair Value

Once the term structure is defined, it may be used to value any collection of cash flows and serves as the standard of fair value. The theoretical price of a security that is calculated in this manner may be compared to its actual market price. Any difference in price that results indicates whether the security is rich or cheap relative to its fair value. If the market price is equal to the fair value, then the security is said to be fairly priced.

Generally, Treasury securities are chosen to represent the basis for fair value and most securities (such as corporate and government-agency debt obligations) are cheap to Treasuries. However, if there are a sufficient number of securities from a particular sector or issuer, these issues may be used as the reference set of securities and a new yield curve may be defined to be the standard of fair value. Thus corporate, agency, or municipal debt issues may be compared to their own family of securities or to their own sector to determine their relative value within the specified sector.

[12] See the discussion in an earlier section under discount function.

Determination of Par-Coupon and Horizon Yield Curves

A par-coupon yield curve is a theoretical yield curve comprised of par priced bonds along the maturity spectrum. Each of these par priced bonds is constructed from the same discount function, which in turn is derived from a specified set of reference bonds. Since the discount function is defined continuously at different maturity points and cash-flow dates (via a spline-fitting procedure, for example), the par-coupon bonds corresponding to these same points may be determined.

The procedure for constructing a par-coupon bond involves an iterative process in which an initial coupon is assumed. For a given maturity date and associated coupon-payment dates, the cash flows and cash-flow dates are known for the assumed coupon level. The present value of each of the cash flows is found through the discount function, and the sum of the present values is compared to a price of par. The coupon then is varied until a par priced bond is found. The process may be repeated for as many maturity points as desired to construct an entire par-coupon yield curve.

A par-coupon yield curve is helpful in pricing bonds with off-the-run maturities. Often the question arises as to what exactly is the comparable Treasury yield when pricing off-the-run bonds. Depending on the fixed-income market sector, the comparable Treasury yield may be that of a specific Treasury note, or it may be an interpolated yield. The par-coupon curve provides a more technically rigorous means of calculating the interpolated yield, as opposed to a simple straight-line interpolation scheme.

Another application of the concept of the par-coupon yield curve is the "horizon yield curve," the par-coupon yield curve for a future horizon date. Since the discount function may be determined as a function of time, the corresponding horizon yield curves at various points in time also may be found. The horizon yield curve is one way to help visualize how the present yield curve may evolve in the future in an arbitrage-free environment. (Of course, as new information is incorporated into the marketplace as time passes, the actual yield curve may deviate from the horizon yield curve. However, a horizon yield curve may still be calculated that reflects particular views about the future movements in both short-term and long-term rates.)

Yield-Curve Shocks and Shifts

The shape of the yield curve is governed by exogenous (real-world) factors. As the Federal Reserve alters its monetary policy, or as the inflation outlook changes, the yield curve responds accordingly. These perturbations to the curve can be characterized as "shocks" to short-term rates and as "shifts" to long-term rates. A shock can occur when there is a sudden and unexpected event that causes short-term rates to jump, even though the overall economic fundamentals have not changed.

The clearest example of a shock is the Crash of 1987, during which investors fled to the safety of the Treasury market. During October 19, short-term rates dropped by approximately 90 to 100 basis points as investors sought a temporary safe haven. At the same time, long-term rates fell by about 20 to 30 basis points. Since the Crash was a market phenomenon, rather than an altering of economic fundamentals, it is characterized as a shock to the system. (This is described mathematically within the term structure model as a change to the initial condition of the differential equation, where the differential equation remains the same. The solution to the differential equation shows how the entire yield curve responds to a shock in short-term rates.)

A shift in the yield curve results from a change in the economic landscape where Federal budgetary concerns or inflation outlooks can affect the view on long-term interest rates. (In contrast to a shock, the term structure model represents a shift as a re-specification of the parameters to the differential equation, while the initial condition has remained unchanged. The most general situation can consist of a combination of shocks and shifts.)

The basic premise underlying the shocked and/or shifted horizon yield curve is that the curve evolves in an arbitrage-free manner as prescribed by the term structure model despite alterations to the curve. Thus, even though a shock or a shift has occurred, the entire yield curve responds in such a way as to preclude arbitrage. As a result of different combinations of shocks and shifts of varying magnitudes, a series of horizon yield curves can be found for different yield-curve steepening and flattening scenarios.

SUMMARY

A continuous-time model of the term structure of interest rates represents a state-of-the-art approach in the valuation of fixed-income instruments. The term structure model addressed in this chapter expands upon the well known Cox-Ingersoll-Ross model, and is used to analyze a broad range of securities markets, such as futures and futures options, sinking-fund bonds and floating-rate notes, and caps and floors. In this chapter we introduced the basic framework for the analysis of debt securities, but the extension of the basic theory allows for the analysis of OTC options, floating-rate notes, delivery, and timing options within futures contracts and other derivative securities.

APPENDIX A: ITO'S LEMMA

Ito's Lemma is a powerful tool that is often used in stochastic calculus and term-structure theory. The following shows the derivation of this formula, which is based on the extension of basic concepts in calculus. Appendix B makes use of these results in the derivation of the price equation (31).

Let P be a function of the two variables r and t expressed as the following

$$P = P(r, t) \tag{A.1}$$

An application of Taylor's Theorem to P furnishes

$$\begin{aligned} dP = {} & \frac{\partial P}{\partial r}dr + \frac{\partial P}{\partial t}dt + \frac{1}{2}\frac{\partial^2 P}{\partial r^2}(dr)^2 + \frac{1}{2}\frac{\partial P^2}{\partial t^2}(dt)^2 + \frac{\partial^2 P}{\partial r \partial t}drdt \\ & + \text{higher order terms} \end{aligned} \tag{A.2}$$

Let r be a function described by the following

$$dr = a(r, t)dt + b(r, t)dz \tag{A.3}$$

where dz is a Weiner process such that

$$dz = \varepsilon\sqrt{dt} \tag{A.4}$$

and ε is normally distributed with a mean of zero and variance of one.

With substitution of equation (A.4) into (A.3) and squaring

$$(dr)^2 = b^2\varepsilon^2 dt + \text{higher order terms in } dt \tag{A.5}$$

To evaluate equation (A.5), we use Chebyshev's inequality

$$Pr\{|x - u| > \varepsilon\} \le \frac{\sigma^2}{\varepsilon^2}$$

or

$$Pr\{|dr^2 - E(dr^2)| > \varepsilon\} \le \frac{Var(dr^2)}{\varepsilon^2} \tag{A.6}$$

The expected value of $(dr)^2$ is given by

$$E[(dr^2)] = E(b^2\varepsilon^2 dt) = b^2(dt)E(\varepsilon^2) \quad \text{(A.7)}$$

The variance of ε is one. Therefore, an alternate expression for the variance yields

$$E(\varepsilon^2) - [E(\varepsilon)]^2 = 1$$

Since $E[\varepsilon] = 0$,

$$E(\varepsilon^2) = 1 \quad \text{(A.8)}$$

equation (A.7) becomes

$$E[(dr)^2] = b^2 dt \quad \text{(A.9)}$$

The variance of $(dr)^2$ is given by

$$Var[(dr)^2] = Var(b^2\varepsilon^2 dt) \quad \text{(A.10)}$$

For a variable y, the variance of cy, where c is a constant, is

$$Var(cy) = c^2 Var(y) \quad \text{(A.11)}$$

Applying equation (A.11) to (A.10),

$$Var[(dr)^2] = b^4(dt)^2 Var(\varepsilon^2) = 0(dt^2) \quad \text{(A.12)}$$

Since the variance of $(dr)^2$ is of higher order, it can be neglected so that the variance is, in effect, zero.

Substituting for the expected value and variance of $(dr)^2$ into (A.6) gives

$$Pr\{|dr^2 - E(dr^2)| > \varepsilon\} \leq \frac{0(dt^2)}{\varepsilon^2}$$

and

$$dr^2 = E(dr^2) = b^2 dt \tag{A.13}$$

Substituting Equation (A.13) into (A.2) and neglecting terms higher than first order in dt, Equation (A.2) becomes

$$dP = \frac{\partial P}{\partial r}dr + \frac{\partial P}{\partial t}dt + \frac{1}{2}\frac{\partial^2 P}{\partial r^2}b^2 dt \tag{A.14}$$

Equation (A.14) is Ito's Lemma. Substituting equation (A.3) into the above,

$$dP = \frac{\partial P}{\partial r}(adt + bdz) + \frac{\partial P}{\partial t}dt + \frac{1}{2}\frac{\partial^2 P}{\partial r^2}b^2 dt$$

which yields

$$dP = \left[a\frac{\partial P}{\partial r} + \frac{\partial P}{\partial t} + \frac{1}{2}b^2\frac{\partial^2 P}{\partial r^2}\right]dt + b\frac{\partial P}{\partial r}dz \tag{A.15}$$

Equation (A.15) may also be expressed as the following

$$dP = P\mu dt - P\rho dz \tag{A.16}$$

where

$$\mu = \frac{1}{P}\left[a\frac{\partial P}{\partial r} + \frac{\partial P}{\partial t} + \frac{1}{2}b^2\frac{\partial^2 P}{\partial r^2}\right] \tag{A.17}$$

$$\rho = -\frac{1}{P}b\frac{\partial P}{\partial r} \tag{A.18}$$

The parameters μ and ρ are the mean and standard deviation, respectively, of the instantaneous rate of return on a discount bond.

APPENDIX B: DERIVATION OF THE PRICE EQUATION

Equation (30) describes the process for the propagation of the spot rate and is given by

$$dr = k(\theta - r)dt + \sigma\sqrt{r}dz \tag{B.1}$$

Comparing the above with the general equation (A.3), it is seen that

$$a = k(\theta - r) \tag{B.2}$$

$$b = \sigma\sqrt{r} \tag{B.3}$$

Equation (A.15) becomes

$$dP = \left[k(\theta - r)\frac{\partial P}{\partial r} + \frac{\partial P}{\partial t} + \frac{1}{2}\sigma^2 r\frac{\partial^2 P}{\partial r^2}\right]dt + \sigma\sqrt{r}\frac{\partial P}{\partial r}dz \tag{B.4}$$

To apply the principal of an arbitrage-free term structure, consider equation (A.16).

$$dP = P\mu dt - P\rho dz \tag{B.5}$$

Any security W_i with maturity s_i is subject to the same relationship (B.5) such that

$$dW_i = W_i\mu_i dt - W_i\rho_i dz \tag{B.6}$$

Consider a portfolio W consisting of owning an amount of W_2 and shorting an amount W_1 such that

$$W = W_2 - W_1 \tag{B.7}$$

where

$$W_2 = \left(\frac{\rho_1}{\rho_1 - \rho_2}\right)W \tag{B.8}$$

and

$$W_1 = \left(\frac{\rho_2}{\rho_1 - \rho_2}\right) W \tag{B.9}$$

Then

$$dW = dW_2 - dW_1$$

Applying equation (B.6), the above becomes

$$\begin{aligned} dW &= \left(\frac{\mu_2 \rho_1}{\rho_1 - \rho_2}\right) W dt - \left(\frac{\rho_1 \rho_2}{\rho_1 - \rho_2}\right) W dz - \left(\frac{\mu_1 \rho_2}{\rho_1 - \rho_2}\right) W dt + \left(\frac{\rho_1 \rho_2}{\rho_1 - \rho_2}\right) W dz \\ &= \left(\frac{\mu_2 \rho_1 - \mu_1 \rho_2}{\rho_1 - \rho_2}\right) W dt \end{aligned} \tag{B.10}$$

Since the stochastic element dz is not present in equation (B.10), the rate of return on the portfolio W is equal to the riskless rate r. Therefore equation (B.10) may be written as

$$dW = rW dt$$

Thus

$$r = \frac{\mu_2 \rho_1 - \mu_1 \rho_2}{\rho_1 - \rho_2}$$

This gives the following relationship

$$r\rho_1 - r\rho_2 = \mu_2 \rho_1 - \mu_1 \rho_2$$

and

$$\frac{\mu_2 - r}{\rho_2} = \frac{\mu_1 - r}{\rho_1} \tag{B.11}$$

Since the maturities s_1 and s_2 were chosen arbitrarily, the above is true for any maturity s. Therefore, the term

$$\frac{\mu - r}{\rho}$$

is not a function of maturity and may be written as

$$\frac{\mu - r}{\rho} = q(t, r) \tag{B.12}$$

where $q(t, r)$ is the market price of risk.

Applying separation of variables, choose $q(t, r)$ to be the following

$$q(t, r) = \lambda(t)\sqrt{r} \tag{B.13}$$

where $\lambda(t)$ is the risk premium which can be shown to be

$$\lambda(t) = \frac{1}{2}\frac{\sigma}{\kappa}\{1 - \exp[-\kappa(s - t)]\} \tag{B.14}$$

(As the time, t, approaches the maturity, s, the risk premium decreases toward zero, which reflects the decreasing risk associated with shorter-term instruments.) Equation (B.12) is rewritten as

$$\mu = r + \lambda\sqrt{r}\rho \tag{B.15}$$

This states that the expected return of a bond is equal to the riskless rate plus another term related to the risk premium.

With equations (A.18) and (B.3), the above becomes

$$\mu = r + \lambda\sqrt{r}\left(-\sigma\sqrt{r}\frac{\partial P}{\partial r}\frac{1}{P}\right) \tag{B.16}$$

Substituting the above into equation (B.5), (B.5) becomes

$$dP = P\left(r - \lambda\sigma r\frac{\partial P}{\partial r}\frac{1}{P}\right)dt - P\rho dz$$

Equating the coefficients of dt between the above and equation (B.4),

$$\frac{\partial P}{\partial t} = rP - [k(\theta - r) + \lambda\sigma r]\frac{\partial P}{\partial r} - \frac{1}{2}\sigma^2 r\frac{\partial^2 P}{\partial r^2} \tag{B.17}$$

subject to the boundary condition

$$P(r, s) = 1 \tag{B.18}$$

This completes the derivation of equation (31).

Finally, if we assume a separation of variables for $P(r,t)$ of the form

$$P(r, t) = \exp[C(t) - B(t)r] \tag{B.19}$$

it can be derived that the "target" spot rate, θ, of the form

$$\theta(t_0 + T) = -\frac{d}{dT}\ln d(t_0, T) - \frac{1}{k}\frac{d^2}{dT^2}\ln d(t_0, T) \tag{B.20}$$

$$\theta(t_0 + T) = F(t_0, t_0 + T) + \frac{1}{k}\frac{d}{dT}F(t_0, t_0 + T) \tag{B.21}$$

will provide a solution to equation (31) that will exactly reprice the reference set where the discount function $d(t_0,T)$ and the forward rates $F(t_0, t_0 + T)$ are derived from the reference set as described in the body of this chapter using spline functions. Furthermore, this property is true for all volatilities when the risk premium of equation (B.14) is used.

CHAPTER 6

A Practical Guide to Swap Curve Construction

Uri Ron
Senior Trader
Bank of Canada

Swaps are increasingly used by governments, financial intermediaries, corporations, and investors for hedging, arbitrage, and to a lesser extent, speculation. Swaps are also used as benchmarks for evaluating the performance of other fixed-income markets, and as reference rates for forecasting.

Swaps offer an operationally efficient and flexible means of transforming cash flow streams. The swap market has little or no government regulation, and provides a high degree of privacy. The swap market's liquidity, depth, and high correlation with fixed-income products, other than plain vanilla government bonds, render its derived term structure a fundamental pricing mechanism for these products and a relevant benchmark for measuring the relative value of different fixed-income products.[1]

The role of the swap term structure as a relevant benchmark for pricing and hedging purposes is expected to increase as government fiscal situations improve. An improved fiscal situation reduces the size of government debt programs, in effect decreasing the liquidity and efficiency of government debt markets. Furthermore, the financial markets

[1] For correlations of swap rates and other fixed-income rates for the U.S. market, see M. Fleming, "The Benchmark U.S. Treasury Market: Recent Performance and Possible Alternatives," *FRBNY Economic Policy Review* (April 2000).

crisis in the fall of 1998 reinforced the "flight to quality" phenomenon, where spreads between governments' issues and other fixed-income securities widened substantially under adverse market conditions, thereby calling into question the role of the government market as a relevant benchmark for nongovernment issues. The swap term structure again emerges as a potential substitute.

With the increased importance of the swap market, practitioners recognize the importance of a consistent and computationally efficient swap term structure for marking to market financial transactions; marking to market is the practice of valuing an instrument to reflect current market conditions. While the general framework for the construction of the swap term structure is widely known, the derivation details are vague and not well documented. This chapter attempts to bridge this gap by carefully covering all angles of the swap term-structure derivation procedure while leaving enough flexibility to adjust the constructed term structure to the specific micro requirements and constraints of each primary swap market.

Marking to market fixed-income portfolios is instrumental for trading, accounting, performance valuation, and satisfying inter-institution collateralization requirements. The current methodology in capital markets for marking to market fixed-income securities is to estimate and discount future cash flows using rates derived from the appropriate term structure. The swap term structure is increasingly used as the foundation for deriving relative term structures and as a benchmark for pricing and hedging.

The first section describes the motivation for using the swap term structure as a benchmark for pricing and hedging fixed-income securities. A swap term-structure derivation technique designed to mark to market fixed-income products is then described in detail. Finally, different aspects of the derived swap term structure are discussed.

THE SWAP CURVE ADVANTAGE

The swap market offers a variety of advantages. It has almost no government regulations, making it more comparable across different markets; some sovereign issues offer a variety of tax benefits to domestic and/or foreign investors, making government curve comparative analysis across countries latently inconsistent. The swap market is an increasingly liquid market, with narrow bid-ask spreads and a wide spectrum of maturities. The supply of swaps is solely dependent on the number of counterparties wishing to transact at any given time. No position in an underlying asset is required, avoiding any potential repo "specials" effects.[2] Given the liquidity and large size of the swap market, new swaps with standard maturities are issued daily, keeping a constant forecast horizon, mitigating any potential coupon effects; bonds with high coupons tend to have lower yields to maturity than bonds with low coupons.[3] The fungibility of swaps also prevents swaps with similar cash flows from trading at substantially different rates, contributing to market efficiency.

Swaps have similar credit-risk properties across countries, making them more comparable than the government term structure. Government debt is considered risk-free; however, governments entail different credit-risk qualities across countries. Credit risk is embedded in the swap curve as swaps are based on the balance sheet of the banking sector (see Exhibit 6.1 for inputs). In addition, swap rates are highly correlated with yields on other fixed-income securities, even under adverse market conditions, making swaps latently a better hedging vehicle than government issues. Other fixed-income securities include agency debt, corporate debt, and mortgage-backed securities.

Swap prices are frequently quoted as a spread over government issues, therefore serving as a rough indicator of credit risk of the banking sector. A swap spread is the difference between the fixed rate on an interest rate swap contract and the yield on a government bond with an equivalent tenor. The fixed swap rate is the rate that equates the present value of the swap to zero. Quoting the swap curve as a spread over the government curve can be unreliable, as there is a maturity mismatch and coupon effect between the different quoted government notes and their corresponding swap issues. Swap rates should be quoted directly off the swap market. Quoting the swap rate as a spread over government issues is common mainly in Anglo-Saxon swap markets.

The most prominent impediment to swap market liquidity is swap counterparty credit exposure, which is balance-sheet intensive, in that it is a bilateral contract. The risk is the potential loss to a counterparty of the present value of a swap position if a swap party defaults. Therefore, parties to a swap transaction must be confident in the credit quality of their swap counterparty. A variety of credit-enhancement mechanisms have been developed to somewhat reduce this potential credit exposure.

[2] A repo transaction is the borrowing of money by selling securities to a counterparty and buying them back at a later date at a pre-agreed price. The repo rate is the interest rate embedded in a repurchase agreement. Repo "specials" carry different rates, thereby introducing inconsistencies to the derived term structure, such as the government term structure.

[3] A.M. Malz, "Interbank Interest Rates as Term Structure Indicators," Federal Reserve Bank of New York (March 1998).

Some of the mechanisms include the use of credit-enhanced subsidiaries, credit derivatives, posting of collateral, recouponing, and an automatic swap unwind clause triggered by a credit event.

EXHIBIT 6.1 Swap Inputs

Canadian Dollar (CAD)

- Interbank overnight financing rate
- Banker's acceptance out to three months
- BAX futures out to two years
- Swap rates

European Dollar (EUR)

- Interbank overnight financing rate
- Interbank deposit rates out to three months
- LIFFE three-month EURIBOR futures out to three years
- Swap rates

Japanese Yen (JPY)

- Interbank overnight financing rate
- Interbank deposit rates out to three months
- CME three-month Yen LIBOR futures out to two years
- Swap rates

United Kingdom Sterling (GBP)

- Interbank overnight financing rate
- Interbank deposit rates out to three months
- LIFFE three-month Sterling LIBOR futures out to two years
- Swap rates

US Dollar (USD)

- Interbank overnight financing rate
- LIBOR fixings out to three months
- Eurodollar futures or FRAs out to five years
- Swap rates (frequently quoted as government bond yield for chosen benchmark adjusted for swap spreads)

In summary, the swap term structure offers several advantages over government curves, and is a robust tool for pricing and hedging fixed-income products. Correlations among governments and other fixed-income products have declined, making the swap term structure a more efficient hedging and pricing vehicle.[4] With the supply of government issues declining and high correlations of credit spreads to swap spreads, the swap term structure is a potential alternative to the government term structure as a benchmark for measuring the relative value of different debt classes. The next section presents a methodology for deriving the swap term structure.

SWAP CURVE CONSTRUCTION

The swap curve depicts the relationship between the term structure and swap rates. The swap curve consists of observed market interest rates, derived from market instruments that represent the most liquid and dominant instruments for their respective time horizons, bootstrapped and combined using an interpolation algorithm. This section describes a complete methodology for the construction of the swap term structure.

Curve Inputs

In deriving the swap curve, the inputs should cover the complete term structure (i.e., short-, middle-, and long-term parts). The inputs should be observable, liquid, and with similar credit properties. Using an interpolation methodology, the inputs should form a complete, consistent, and smooth yield curve that closely tracks observed market data. Once the complete swap term structure is derived, an instrument is marked to market by extracting the appropriate rates off the derived curve.

The technique for constructing the swap term structure, as constructed by market participants for marking to market purposes, divides the curve into three term buckets. The short end of the swap term structure is derived using interbank deposit rates. The middle area of the swap curve is derived from either forward rate agreements (FRAs) or interest rate futures contracts. The latter requires a convexity adjustment[5] to render it equivalent to FRAs. The long end of the term structure is constructed using swap par rates derived from the swap market.

A combination of the different interest rates forms the basis for the swap curve term structure. For currencies where the future or forward

[4] D. Theobald and G. Singh, "The Outlook for Swaps as a Hedge Vehicle," JP Morgan (2000).

[5] The adjustment required to convert a futures interest rate to a forward interest rate.

market is illiquid, inefficient, or non-existent for certain tenors,[6] it is customary to use longer-term interbank deposit rates and rely more heavily on interpolation. On the other hand, for currencies such as the U.S. dollar, where an efficient liquid futures market exists, for longer-term maturities it is customary to use futures contracts with longer maturities (i.e., beyond two years out to five years).

The inputs used to construct the term structure are currency-dependent. Some currencies offer more liquid and deeper markets than others (see Exhibit 6.1). A swap term structure should be constructed given these micro constraints.

Deriving the Swap Curve

To derive the swap term structure, observed market interest rates combined with interpolation techniques are used; also, dates are constructed using the applicable business-day convention. Swaps are frequently constructed using the modified following business-day convention, where the cash flow occurs on the next business day unless that day falls in a different month. In that case, the cash flow occurs on the immediately preceding business day to keep payment dates in the same month.[7] The swap curve yield calculation convention frequently differs by currency. Exhibit 6.2 lists the different payment frequencies, compounding frequencies, and day count conventions, as applicable to each currency-specific interest rate type.

EXHIBIT 6.2 Yield Calculation Conventions by Currency

Currency/Rate	Payment Freq.	Compounding Freq.	Day Count Convention
CAD cash rates			ACT/365
CAD swap rates	S/A	S/A	ACT/365
EUR cash rates			ACT/360
EUR swap rates	A	A	30/360
JPY cash rates			ACT/360
JPY swap rates	S/A	S/A	ACT/365
GBP cash rates			ACT/365
GBP swap rates	S/A	S/A	ACT/365
USD cash rates			ACT/360
USD swap rates	S/A	S/A	30/360

[6] Time to maturity of financial instrument.

[7] *ISDA Credit Derivatives Definitions*. International Swaps and Derivatives Association (ISDA) (1999).

The Short End of the Swap Curve

The short end of the swap curve, out to three months, is based on the overnight, 1-month, 2-month, and 3-month deposit rates. The short-end deposit rates are inherently zero-coupon rates and need only be converted to the base currency swap rate compounding frequency and day count convention. The following equation is solved to compute the continuously compounded zero swap rate (r_c):

$$r_c = \frac{t_y}{t_m} \times \ln\left(1 + \frac{r_d}{\frac{t_y}{t_m}}\right) \tag{1}$$

where r_d represents the observed market deposit rate, t_m represents the number of days to maturity, and t_y represents the number of days in a year as specified according to the day count convention used. Continuously compounded interest rates are used for consistency with other parts of this chapter.

The Middle Area of the Swap Curve

The middle area of the swap curve up to two years is derived from either FRA rates or interest rate futures contracts. FRAs are preferable, as they carry a fixed time horizon to settlement and settle at maturity, whereas futures contracts have a fixed settlement date and are marked to market daily. FRAs for most currencies, however, are not observable or suffer from lack of liquidity. On the other hand, futures contracts are exchange traded, rendering them more uniform, liquid, and transparent. Extracting forward rates from futures rates requires a convexity adjustment. It is an adjustment for the difference in convexity characteristics of futures contracts and forward rates. Most interest rate futures have zero convexity, a fixed payoff per basis point change, regardless of the level of underlying interest rates, whereas FRAs are convex instruments. The convexity bias is positively correlated to the futures contract maturity, and is of the magnitude of one to two basis points for maturities around one year, gradually increasing with term to maturity.

A long position in FRAs or swaps and a short position in futures has net positive convexity. The short futures position has a positive payoff when interest rates rise and lower losses when interest rates fall, as they can be refinanced at a lower rate. This mark to market positive effect of futures contracts creates a bias in favor of short sellers of futures contracts. This bias must be removed from futures contracts prices to derive an unbiased estimator of the equivalent forward rates.

Convexity Adjustment Estimation Estimating the convexity adjustment requires an estimation of the future path of interest rates up to the future contract maturity. Convexity adjustments for several futures markets are provided by brokers or from market data vendors. An alternative methodology is to use the Hull-White term structure model to estimate the convexity bias.[8] In the Hull-White model, the continuously compounded forward rate, lasting between times t_1 and t_2 (denominated in years from current date), equals the continuously compounded future rate less the following convexity adjustment:

$$\left(\frac{\frac{1-e^{-a(t_2-t_1)}}{a}}{t_2-t_1}\right)\left[\left(\frac{\frac{1-e^{-a(t_2-t_1)}}{a}}{t_2-t_1}\right)(1-e^{-2at_1})+2a\frac{\frac{1-e^{-a(t_1)}}{a}}{t_1}\right]\frac{\sigma^2}{4a} \tag{2}$$

where σ is the standard deviation of the change in short-term interest rates expressed annually, and a is the mean reversion rate.

Mean Reversion Rate Estimation Convexity bias estimation requires an estimate of the mean reversion rate (a) and the standard deviation (σ) of the change in short-term interest rates expressed annually. Historical data can be used to estimate the mean reversion rate. A typical range of values for the mean reversion rate is 0.001 for negligible effects to 0.1, which could have material effects. For simplicity, a constant default value for mean reversion speed could be assumed. For example, Bloomberg assumes a constant mean reversion rate of 0.03.

We assume that the short-term interest rates follow the following Vasicek discount bond prices stochastic process:[9]

$$dr_t = a(\theta - r_t)dt + \sigma dz_t \tag{3}$$

where r_t is the short-term interest rate at time t, and dz_t is the increment of a standard Wiener process. Parameter θ specifies the long run value of r_t.

[8] J.C. Hull and A. White, "Pricing Interest Rate Derivative Securities," *The Review of Financial Studies* 3 (1990).

[9] O. Vasicek, "An Equilibrium Characterization of the Term Structure," *Journal of Financial Economics* 5 (1977).

To estimate the Vasicek continuous stochastic time model, the model must be discretized. We discretized and estimated the continuous time model as follows:

$$\Delta r_t = \varphi + \delta r_{t-1} + \varepsilon_t \tag{4}$$

where

$$\varepsilon_t | I_{t-1} \sim N(0, \sigma_t^2) \tag{5}$$

The parameter δ is used to estimate the negative of the mean reversion rate, $-a$, where I_{t-1} is the information set at time $t - 1$.

Interest Rates Volatility Estimation There are several alternative methodologies for estimating the standard deviation (σ) of the change in short-term interest rates. Two derivation methodologies are explored next.

The first methodology flows from the mean reversion estimation process. It estimates the conditional standard deviation of short-term interest rates using the $GARCH(1, 1)$ model:

$$\sigma_t^2 = \alpha + \beta\varepsilon_{t-1}^2 + \gamma\sigma_{t-1}^2 \tag{6}$$

The conditional density of Δr_t is:

$$f(r_t | I_{t-1}) = \frac{1}{\sqrt{2\pi\sigma_t^2}} \exp\left(\frac{-\varepsilon_t^2}{2\sigma_t^2}\right) \tag{7}$$

The log-likelihood function, where N represents the total number of observations,

$$L = \sum_{t=1}^{N} \log f(r_t | I_{t-1}) \tag{8}$$

is then maximized numerically with respect to the population parameters. Maximizing the log-likelihood function gives estimates of α, β, and γ. The annualized standard deviation equals $\sigma_t\sqrt{252}$, assuming there are 252 trading days in a year.

The second methodology uses the implied volatility from interest rate caps that correspond to the appropriate time horizon. An interest rate cap comprises q caplets, where q *is* the number of reset dates. Each caplet corresponds to the rate at time t_k and provides payoff at time t_{k+1}. An interest rate cap provides insurance against adverse upward movements in floating rate obligations during a future period. An interest rate caplet provides the cap holder with the following payoff:

$$n\delta_k \max(R_k - R_x, 0) \tag{9}$$

where n denotes caplet notional, R_x denotes the cap rate, R_k is the reset rate at time t, and $\delta_k = t_{k+1} - t_k$. As an interest rate caplet market value is observable, assuming R_k is lognormal, the implied interest rate caplet volatility σ_k can be computed using the following extension to the Black-Scholes model:[10]

$$n\delta_k P(0, t_{k+1})[F_k N(d_1) - R_x N(d_2)] \tag{10}$$

where

$$d_1 = \frac{\ln(F_k/R_x) + \sigma_k^2 t_k/2}{\sigma_k\sqrt{t_k}}$$

$$d_2 = d_1 - \sigma_k\sqrt{t_k}$$

$P(0, t)$ is the spot price of a zero-coupon bond paying \$1 at time T. F_k denotes the forward rate for the period between t_k and t_{k+1}. $N(x)$ is the cumulative probability distribution function, where $x \sim N(0, 1)$. The volatility σ_k is solved for the period between t_k and t_{k+1}.

The estimated conditional standard deviation or the implied volatility, for the period between t_k and t_{k+1}, and the mean reversion rate are used in combination with the Hull-White model to adjust for the interest rates futures convexity bias. Futures rates with maturities from the six-month to the two-year time horizon are frequently used. For currencies with highly liquid interest rates futures markets, interest rate futures could be used out to five years.

[10] J.C. Hull, *Options Futures and Other Derivatives, 4th edition* (Upper Saddle River, NJ: Prentice-Hall, Inc., 1999).

Futures Prices Futures prices are quoted as (100 – future interest rate × 100). The quarterly compounded future interest rates adjusted for convexity are converted to continuously compounded zero rates as follows.

Convert the quarterly compounded future rate to the continuously compounded future rate using equation (1), where t_m equals the future's accrual period (difference in days between two consecutive futures contracts).

The continuously compounded future rate is then converted to a continuously compounded zero rate using the following transformation:

$$r_2 = \frac{r_f(t_2 - t_1) + r_1 t_1}{t_2} \tag{11}$$

where r_f is the continuously compounded future rate for the period between t_1 and t_2, and r_1 and r_2 are the continuously compounded zero rates for maturities t_1 and t_2, respectively.

The Long End of the Swap Curve

The long end of the swap curve is derived directly from observable coupon swap rates. These are generic plain vanilla interest rate swaps with fixed rates exchanged for floating interest rates. The fixed swap rates are quoted as par rates and are usually compounded semiannually (see Exhibit 6.2). The bootstrap method is used to derive zero-coupon interest rates from the swap par rates. Starting from the first swap rate, given all the continuously compounded zero rates for the coupon cash flows prior to maturity, the continuously compounded zero rate for the term of the swap is bootstrapped as follows:

$$r_T = -\frac{\ln\left[\dfrac{100 - \sum_{i=m}^{T-m}\left(\dfrac{c}{m}e^{-r_i \times t_i}\right)}{100 + \dfrac{c}{m}}\right]}{T} \tag{12}$$

where m is the swap payment frequency per annum, c is the coupon per annum, which is equal to the observed swap rate times the swap notional, and r_i represents the continuously compounded zero rate for time t_i. The bootstrapped interest rate, r_T, is the continuously compounded zero rate for time T.

Progressing recursively along the observed swap rates interpolating between market observations as required forms the complete long end of the swap curve.

Interpolation Algorithm

There is no single correct way to link deposit, futures, and swap interest rates to construct the complete swap term structure; however, several fundamental characteristics and conventions should be followed, to ensure yield curve validity. The derived yield curve should be consistent and smooth, and should closely track observed market data points. However, over-smoothing the yield curve might cause the elimination of valuable market pricing information. This is the main criticism against the use of more advanced interpolation yield curve modeling techniques for pricing derivatives, such as the Nelson and Siegel[11] and Svensson[12] functions. These functions fit the market data very loosely, which is appropriate for extracting expectations or comparative analysis across countries, but is not appropriate for market pricing. The market convention has been to use several interpolation techniques to generate a complete term structure that closely mimics the observed market data for marking to market purposes. The most prevalent algorithms of interpolation used in practice to create a swap term structure include linear interpolation and cubic splines.[13]

Piecewise Linear Interpolation

All observed market data points are connected by a straight line to form a complete term structure. The value of a new data point is assigned according to its position along a straight line between observed market data points. Linear interpolation is simple to implement and closely tracks observed market interest rates. However, it tends to produce kinks around transition areas where the yield curve is changing slope. Therefore, linear interpolation is inappropriate for modeling yield curves that change slope frequently and exhibit significant term structure curvature. As illustrated in Exhibits 6.3 through 6.7, the swap term structure is not characterized by a continuously changing slope nor does it exhibit significant curvature.

[11] C.R. Nelson and A.F. Siegel, "Parsimonious Modelling of Yield Curves," *Journal of Business* 60 (1987).
[12] L.E. Svensson, "Estimating and Interpreting Forward Interest Rates: Sweden 1992–94," CEPR Discussion Paper 1051 (October 1994).
[13] For other non-linear curve modelling techniques see D. Satyajit, *Risk Management and Financial Derivatives,* (NY: McGraw-Hill, Inc., 1998).

EXHIBIT 6.3 USD Swap Zero Curve (Continuously Compounded) as of 14 April 2000

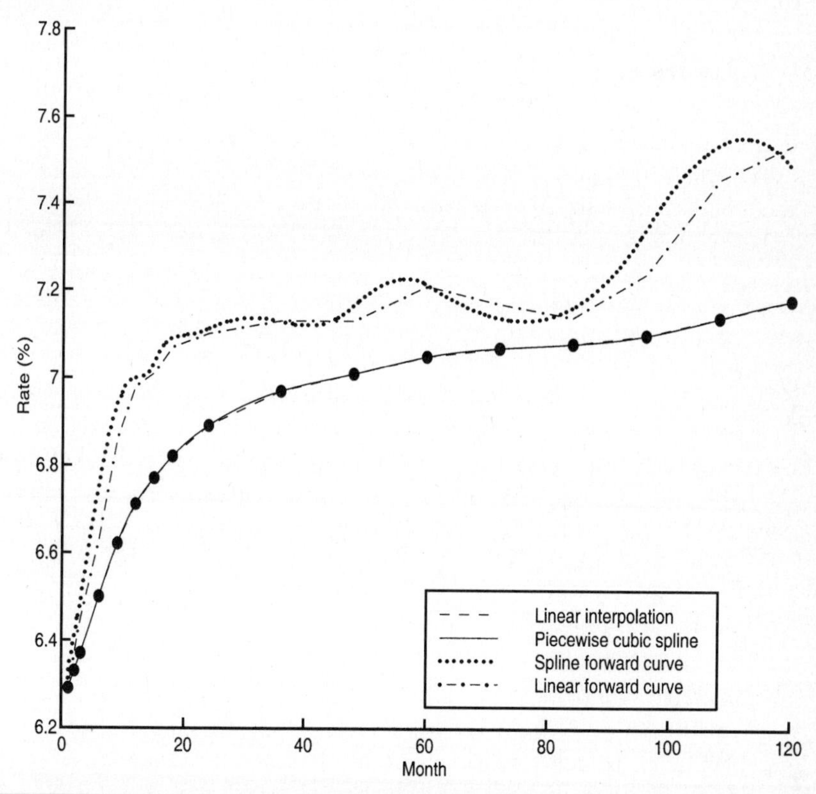

Constructing Piecewise Linear Interpolation Piecewise linear interpolation can be presented in a closed form, which simplifies the interpolation process.

$$R(t) = R(t_i) + \left[\frac{(t-t_i)}{(t_{i+1}-t_i)}\right] \times [R(t_{i+1}) - R(t_i)] \quad (13)$$

Here, i is the market observation index with time to maturity of t_i, and $R(t)$ represents the interest rate corresponding to maturity t, where $t_i \le t \le t_{i+1}$. The formula can be used to derive any swap rate between two market observations $R(t_i)$ and $R(t_{i+1})$.

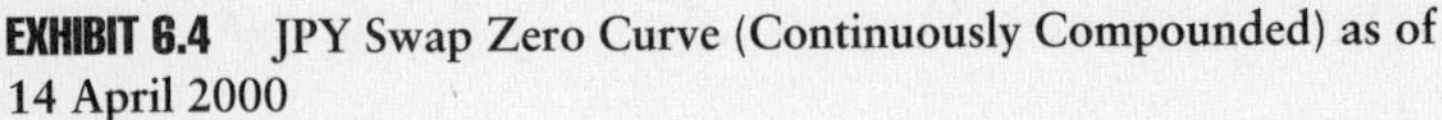

EXHIBIT 6.4 JPY Swap Zero Curve (Continuously Compounded) as of 14 April 2000

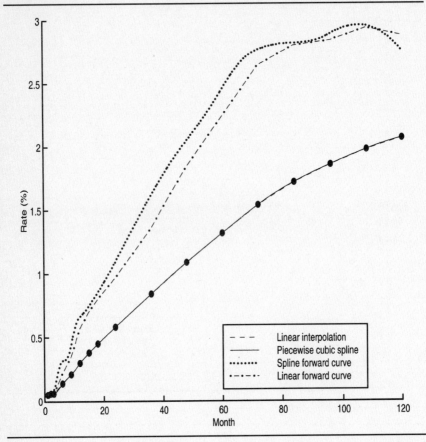

Piecewise Cubic Spline Interpolation

Use of polynomial functions that pass through the observed market data points create a fitted smooth yield curve that does not oscillate wildly between observations. It is possible to either use a single high-order polynomial of degree $n - 1$ (n is the number of observations), or piece together low-order polynomials (e.g., quadratic, cubic). The advantage of using a number of lower-order polynomials (splines) is that the extra degrees of freedom can be used to impose additional constraints to ensure smoothness and prevent wild oscillatory patterns between observations. The piecewise cubic spline technique goes through all observed data points and creates by definition the smoothest curve that fits the observations and avoids kinks.

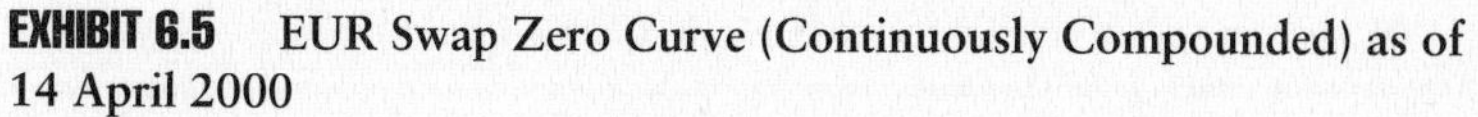

EXHIBIT 6.5 EUR Swap Zero Curve (Continuously Compounded) as of 14 April 2000

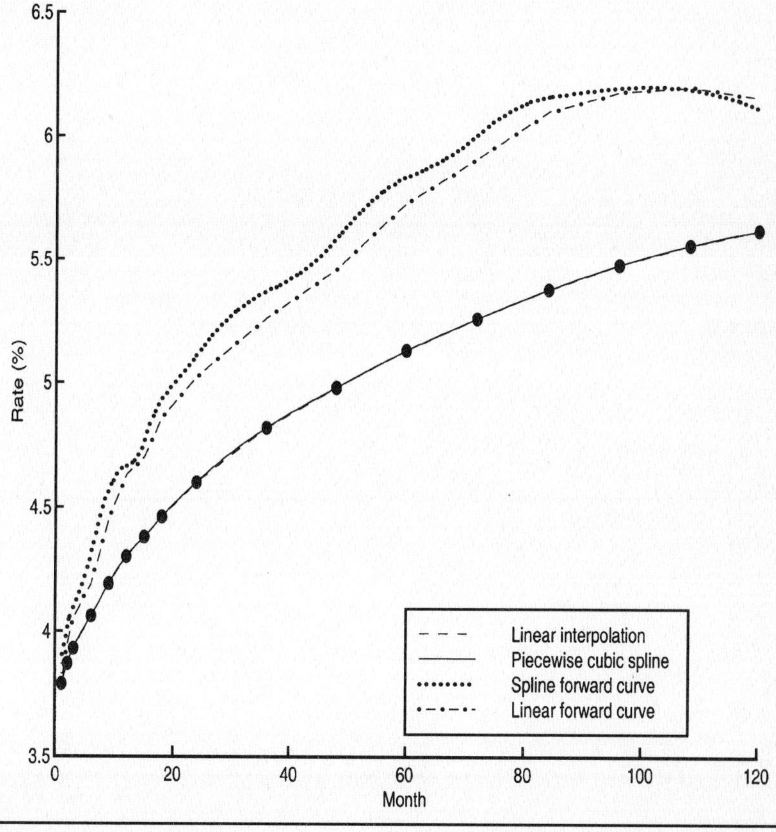

Constructing a Piecewise Cubic Spline To construct a set of cubic splines, let the function $R_i(t)$ denote the cubic polynomial associated with the t segment $[t_i, t_{i+1}]$:

$$R_i(t) = a_i(t-t_i)^3 + b_i(t-t_i)^2 + c_i(t-t_i) + r_i \tag{14}$$

where n is the number of market observations, r_i represents market observation (knot point) i, and t_i represents time to maturity of market observation i.

There are n market observations, $n - 1$ splines, and three coefficients per spline. Overall, there are $3n - 3$ unknown coefficients. The coefficients of the cubic spline function defined over the interval $[t, T]$ can be obtained by imposing the following constraints:

$$a_i(t_{i+1}-t_i)^3 + b_i(t_{i+1}-t_i)^2 + c_i(t_{i+1}-t_i) = r_{i+1}-r_i$$

$$3a_{i-1}(t_i-t_{i-1})^2 + 2b_{i-1}(t_i-t_{i-1}) + c_{i-1}-c_i = 0$$

$$6a_{i-1}(t_i-t_{i-1}) + 2b_{i-1}-2b_i = 0$$

$$b_1 = 0$$

$$6a_{n-1}(t_n-t_{n-1}) + 2b_{n-1} = 0$$

EXHIBIT 6.6 CAD Swap Zero Curve (Continuously Compounded) as of 14 April 2000

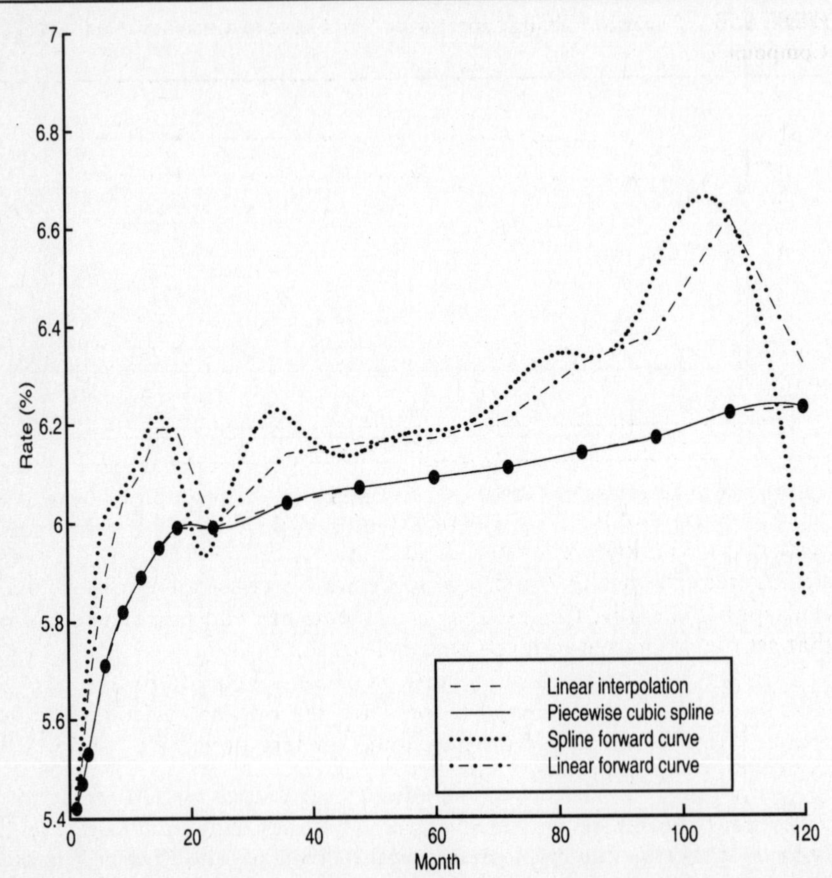

EXHIBIT 6.7A Linear Interpolation: Swap Zero Curve by Currency (Continuously Compounded)

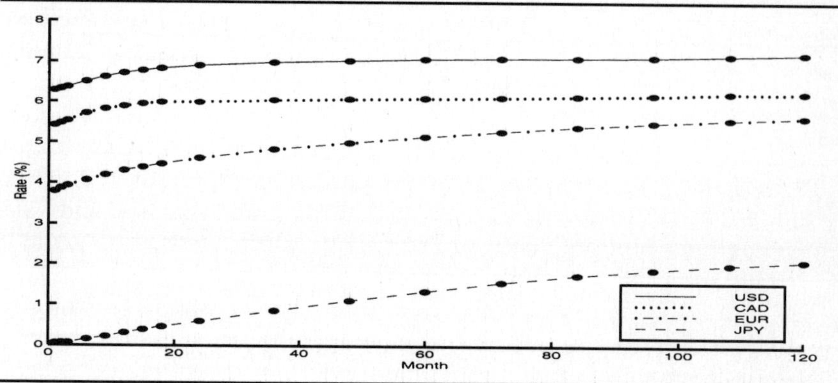

EXHIBIT 6.7B Piecewise Cubic Spline: Swap Zero Curve by Currency (Continuously Compounded)

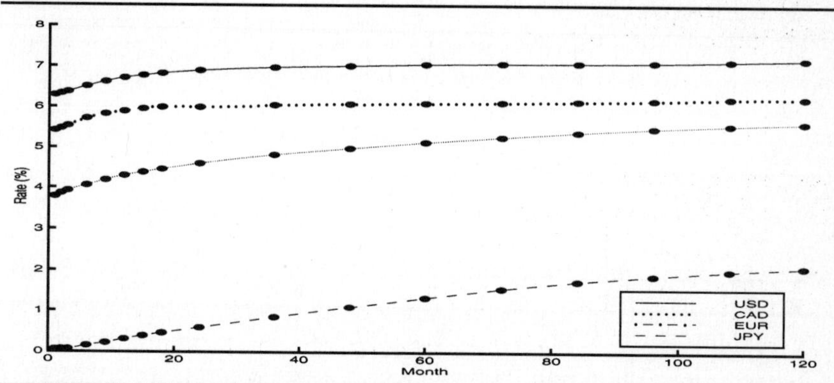

The first set of $n - 1$ constraints require that the spline function join perfectly at the knot points. The second and third set of $2n - 2$ constraints require that first and second derivative constraints match adjacent splines. Finally, the last two constraints are end point constraints that set the derivative equal to zero at both ends.

The linear algebraic system consists of $3n - 3$ equations and $3n - 3$ unknowns that can be solved to produce the optimal piecewise cubic spline. Press, Teukolsky, Vetterling, and Flannery describe a routine for cubic spline interpolation.[14]

---

[14] W. Press, S. Teukolsky, W. Vetterling, and B. Flannery, *Numerical Recipes in C*, 2nd edition (NY: Cambridge University Press, 1998). See also Chapter 7 in this book.

Consolidation

The complete term structure is formed by joining the different parts of the swap term structure together using the chosen interpolation methodology. The end result is a complete swap term structure that is a fundamental tool in marking to market fixed-income securities.

The construction of the swap term structure is not a uniform practice. The substitutable inputs, overlapping instrument maturity dates, inconsistencies between different inputs, different alternatives for transition points between different sections of the term structure, and variety of instruments and derivation techniques all combine to form a variety of plausible swap term structures. The most prominent problems arise around the transition areas between inputs as especially exhibited in Exhibit 6.6. The transition areas, especially around the two-year mark, lack smoothness and an oscillatory pattern is observable. Several possible solutions include using different term structures for different applications and adjustments to the set of rates utilized. In general, institutions tend to adopt their own approaches to these issues. However, over-adjustment and over-smoothing of the term structure can be counterproductive. By eliminating variation, valuable pricing information embedded in the term structure might be "smoothed" away.

The swap term structures for major currencies are presented in Exhibits 6.3 through 6.7. In general, both linear interpolation and piecewise cubic spline derivation techniques generate similar zero and forward swap term structures. However, after zooming in on relatively unstable areas of the term structure, one can detect the better fit of piecewise cubic spline over linear interpolation in preserving a term structure curvature and smoothness. Nevertheless, cubic splines may produce inconsistent or implausible forward term structures such as exhibited at the long end of Exhibit 6.6. As these are estimates of the swap term structure, it is impossible to determine precisely which estimate serves as a better benchmark. The swap zero and forward term structures for major currencies are much smoother and consistent than those for the less-prevalent currencies. This attribute characterizes more liquid, developed, and deeper markets.

CONCLUSIONS

The swap term structure is a pivotal element in pricing fixed-income products, measuring the relative value of debt classes, and measuring interest rate expectations. The swap term structure also offers many advantages over the government term structure. This chapter has outlined a methodology for deriving the swap term structure. The derived zero term structure is used to mark to market financial instruments by estimating and discounting their future cash flows to derive their present value. The different time buckets of the swap term structure are extracted from different market rates and instruments. The variety of plausible extraction and interpolation techniques and data availability problems prevent the derivation of a completely uniform efficient yield curve.

The outlined model carefully preserves variations in market observations, thereby maintaining important pricing information. However, linear interpolation can introduce inaccuracies when there is significant curvature in the term structure, or sparse or noisy data. Cubic spline interpolation, on the other hand, may produce inconsistent or implausible forward term structures.

The most problematic area of the term structure tends to be the transition area between time buckets. Nevertheless, linear interpolation and cubic splines are the most prevalent yield curve generation techniques used in the marketplace for marking to market purposes. To get mark-to-market prices that are consistent with the marketplace, institutions use the specified inputs and derivation techniques. However, an institution may develop more robust term structure derivation techniques for identifying mispriced securities, such as a multiple factor model.

The importance of the swap term structure as a benchmark for pricing fixed-income products and for comparative equity valuation is expected to increase.[15]

[15] Equities are valued against bonds through the reverse price to earnings ratio to government yield. With the decreasing role of government bonds as a benchmark for fixed-income debt and their increased price volatility and scarcity, the swap term structure, which shows greater stability, is an ideal substitute.

CHAPTER 7

Fitting the Term Structure of Interest Rates Using the Cubic Spline Methodology

Rod Pienaar
Corporate & Investment Banking Division
Deutsche Bank AG, London

Moorad Choudhry
Senior Fellow
Centre for Mathematical Trading and Finance
City University Business School

The term structure of interest rates defines the set of spot or zero-coupon rates that exist in a debt capital market of default-free bonds, distinguished only by their term to maturity. In practice the term structure is defined as the array of discount factors on the same maturity term. Extracting the term structure from market interest rates has been the focus of extensive research, reflecting its importance in the field of finance.

The term structure is used by market practitioners for valuation purposes and by central banks for forecasting purposes. The accurate fitting of the term structure is vital to the smooth functioning of the market. A number of approaches with which to undertake this have been proposed, and the method chosen is governed by the user's requirements. Practitioners desire an approach that is accessible, straightforward to implement, and as accurate as possible. In general there are two classes of curve fitting techniques—the *parametric* methods (so-called because they attempt to model the yield curve using a parametric function) and the *spline* methods.[1] Parametric methods include the Nelson-Siegel model and a modification of this proposed by Svensson, as well as models described by Wiseman and Bjork and Christensen.[2] James and Webber suggest that these methods produce a satisfactory overall shape for the term structure but are suitable only where good accuracy is not required.[3] Market practitioners instead generally prefer an approach that gives a reasonable tradeoff between accuracy and ease of implementation, an issue we explore in this chapter.

The cubic spline process presents no conceptual problems, and is an approximation of the market discount function. McCulloch uses cubic splines and Beim states that this approach performs at least as satisfactorily as other methods.[4] Although the basic approach can lead to unrealistic shapes for the forward curve (for example, see Vasicek and Fong[5] and their suggested improvement on the approach using exponential splines), it is an accessible method and one that gives reasonable accuracy for the spot rate curve. Adams and Van Deventer[6] illustrate how one can use the technique to obtain maximum smoothness for forward curves (and an extension to *quartic* splines), while the basic technique has been improved as described by Fisher, Nychka, and Zervos,[7] Waggoner,[8] and Anderson and Sleath.[9] These references are considered later.

---

[1] Parametric models are also known as *parsimonious* models.

[2] C. Nelson and A. Siegel, "Parsimonious modeling of the Yield Curve," *Journal of Business* 60, no 4 (1987), pp.473–489. L. Svensson, "Estimating Forward Interest Rates with the Extended Nelson and Siegel Method," *Sveriges Riksbank Quarterly Review* 3, (1995). J. Wiseman, "The Exponential Yield Curve Model," *JPMorgan European Fixed Income Research*, 1994. T. Bjork and B. Christensen, "Interest Rate Dynamics and Consistent Forward Rate Curves," *University of Aarhus Working Paper*, 1997, pp. 1–38.

[3] J. James and N. Webber, *Interest Rate Modelling*, Wiley 2000, p. 444

[4] J. McCulloch, "The Tax-Adjusted Yield Curve," *Journal of Finance* 30, 1975, pp. 811–830. D. Beim, "Term Structure and the Non-Cash Value in Bonds," *First Boston Working Paper series*, 1992.

[5] O. Vasicek and H. Fong, "Term Structure Modelling Using Exponential Splines," *Journal of Finance* 37, 1982, pp. 339–361.

[6] K. J. Adams and D. Van Deventer, "Fitting Yield Curves and Forward Curves with Maximum Smoothness," *Journal of Fixed Income* 6, 1994, pp. 52–62.

[7] M. Fisher, D. Nychka, and D. Zervos, "Fitting the Term Structure of Interest Rates with Smoothing Splines," Working Paper No. 95-1, *Finance and Economics Discussion Series*, Federal Reserve Board 1995.

[8] D. Waggoner, "Spline Methods for Extracting Interest Rate Curves from Coupon Bond Prices," *Working Paper No. 97-10*, Federal Reserve Bank of Atlanta 1997.

[9] N. Anderson and J. Sleath, "New Estimates of the UK Real and Nominal Yield Cuirves," *Bank of England Quarterly Bulletin*, November 1999, pp. 384–392.

CUBIC SPLINES

Splines are a non-parametric polynomial interpolation method.[10] There is more than one way of fitting them. The simplest method is an ordinary least squares regression spline, but this approach produces wildly oscillating curves. The more satisfactory manner is a smoothing splines method. We consider the basic approach and how to implement it in this chapter.

Fitting a Discount Function

In mathematics a "spline" is a piecewise polynomial function, made up of individual polynomial sections or segments that are joined together at (user-selected) points known as *knot points*. Splines used in term structure modelling are generally made up with cubic polynomials, and the reason for cubic polynomials, as opposed to polynomials of order say, two or five, is explained in straightforward fashion by de la Grandville.[11] A cubic spline is a function of order three, and a piecewise cubic polynomial that is twice differentiable at each knot point. At each knot point the slope and curvature of the curve on either side must match. We employ the cubic spline approach to fit a smooth curve to bond prices (yields) given by the term discount factors.

A polynomial of sufficiently high order may be used to approximate to varying degrees of accuracy any continuous function, which is why a polynomial approximation of a yield curve may be attempted. For example James and Webber state that given a set of m points with distinct values, a Lagrange polynomial of degree m will pass through every point.[12] However, the fit can be very wild with extreme behavior at the long end. We will demonstrate how a cubic spline approximation can be used to obtain better results.

This chapter provides a discussion of piecewise cubic spline interpolation methodology and its application to the term structure. Our intent is to provide a comprehensive and accessible approach to cubic spline interpolation for implementation by practitioners so that the reader will have a full understanding of how cubic splines are calculated and the implications of using piecewise cubic spline interpolation methods. In addition, the reader can employ the approach shown to implement the methodology for their own applications, including constructing spot and forward yield curves from market-determined interest rates. We recommend a

---

[10] A spline originally referred to a tool used by draughtsmen or carpenters for drawing smooth curves.

[11] O. De la Grandville, *Bond Pricing and Portfolio Analysis*, MIT Press 2001, pp. 248–252.

[12] James and Webber, *Interest Rate Modeling*, pp. 430–432.

cubic spline technique because this ensures that the curve passes through all the selected (market determined) node points. This enables practitioners to fit a yield curve to observed market rates (LIBOR or bond yields) reasonably accurately and produces a satisfactory zero-coupon curve under most circumstances.

Our starting point is a set of zero curve tenors (or discount factors) obtained from a collection of market instruments such as cash deposits, futures, swaps, or coupon bonds. We therefore have a set of tenor points and their respective zero rates (or discount factors). The mathematics of cubic splines is straightforward but we assume a basic understanding of calculus and a familiarity with solving simultaneous linear equations by substitution. An account of the methods analyzed in this chapter is given in Burden and Faires, which has very accessible text on cubic spline interpolation.[13]

Background on Cubic Splines

When fitting a curve by interpolating between nodes or tenor points, the user must consider conflicting issues. There is a need to balance between simplicity and correctness, and hence a tradeoff between ease of use and the accuracy of the result. In certain cases practitioners will accept a lower degree of accuracy at the nodes, in favor of smoothness across the curve. In the cubic spline approach the primary aim is smoothness. In an attempt to create a smooth and accurate measurement at the nodes however, we may be confronted by oscillation in the curve. Although linear interpolation is a reasonable calculation method, interest rate markets are not linear environments made up of coupled straight lines. The point between two tenors cannot be accurately estimated using a straight line.

Although there are a number of alternative methods available to the practitioner, a reasonable approach is to retain the concept of piecewise interpolation but to abandon the use of straight lines. The reason that we do not depart from piecewise interpolation is because this method of curve smoothing provides accuracy at the nodes, since each piecewise function touches a node. Accuracy at the nodes can be an important consideration when a pricing methodology based on the elimination of arbitrage is employed. Thus we continue with piecewise fitting, but instead of applying a linear fitting technique, we apply a cubic polynomial to each piece of the interpolation. Cubic splines provide a great deal of flexibility in creating a continuous smooth curve both between and at tenor points.[14]

---

[13] R. Burden and D. Faires, *Numerical Analysis*, Brooks/Cole 1997.

[14] See footnote 10 for a word on the origin of the use of the term "spline."

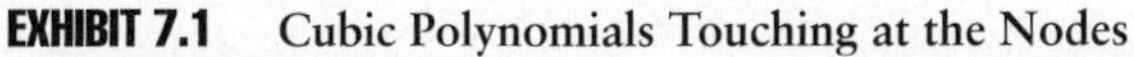

EXHIBIT 7.1 Cubic Polynomials Touching at the Nodes

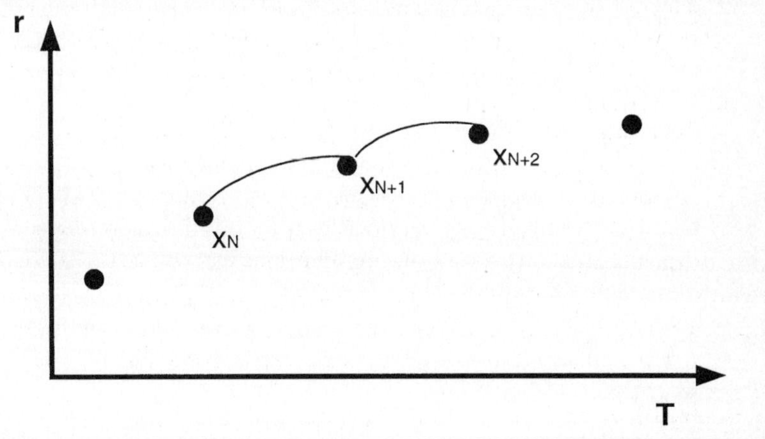

CUBIC SPLINE METHODOLOGY

We assume that the practitioner has already calculated a set of nodes using a yield curve construction technique such as bootstrapping. A zero curve is then fitted using the cubic spline methodology by interpolating between nodes using individual cubic polynomials. Each polynomial has its own parameters but are constructed in such a way that their ends touch each node at the start and end of the polynomial. The set of splines, which touch at the nodes, therefore form a continuous curve. Our objective is to produce a continuous curve, joining market observed rates as smoothly as possible, which is the most straightforward means by which we can deduce meaningful data on the correct interest rate term structure in the market.

In Exhibit 7.1 we can see that two cubic polynomials which join at point x_{N+1} are used to form a continuous curve. However, it is also clear from the curves in the exhibit that the two polynomials do not result in a smooth curve. In order to have a smooth curve we need to establish "smoothing" criteria for each spline. To do this we must first ensure that the polynomials touch or join together at the nodes. Secondly we must ensure that where the polynomials touch, the curve is smooth. Finally we ensure that the curve is continuously differentiable, or in other words, the curve has a smooth rate of change at and between tenor points. The required criteria to meet these conditions are:

Requirement 1: The value of each polynomial is equal at tenor points.
Requirement 2: The first differential of each polynomial is equal at tenor points.

Requirement 3: The second differential of each polynomial is equal at tenor points.
Requirement 4: The second differential of each polynomial is continuous between tenor points.

Consider a polynomial of the form $y = ax^3 + bx^2 + cx + d$, the second differential $y'' = 6ax + 2b$ is a linear function and by its very definition is continuous between tenor points. The fourth requirement is therefore always met and in this chapter we will not deal with this requirement in any further detail. In the rest of this chapter we will refer to the first three requirements and how they are met at the nodes.

THE HYPOTHESIS

Assuming the final solution is unknown at this stage, it seems plausible that an almost infinite set of parameters a, b, and c can be found which will result in all of our cubic spline requirements being met.

We observe in Exhibit 7.2 three imaginary curves, all of which would meet our requirements that the:

- first differential of each spline is equal at tenor points; and the
- second differential of each spline is equal at tenor points.

Admittedly we have considered nodes that are sitting in a straight line but even where the nodes do not line up it may be possible to find a range of possible solutions. Taking this further, spline A and spline B as shown in Exhibit 7.3 are valid solutions yet it is intuitive, given our knowledge of interest rate markets, that A is likely to be more suitable for our purposes of yield curve interpolation.

EXHIBIT 7.2 Hypothetical Solutions

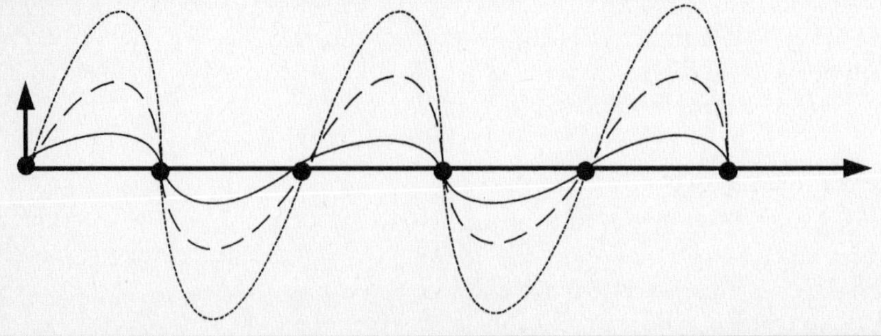

EXHIBIT 7.3 Hypothetical Splines

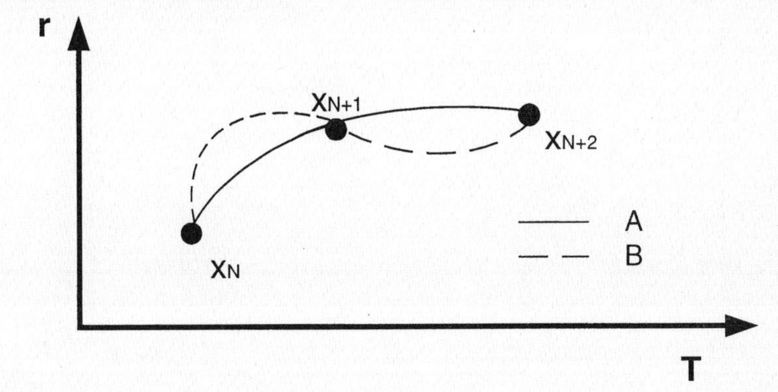

The issue to determine therefore, is: Is there an infinite set of parameters, each of which would meet our requirements for fitting the curve; or is it possible to determine a single solution? Of course, our requirement is in a single solution; moreover, a solution that can be found quickly from any set of market rates.

PRACTICAL APPROACH

By splitting the yield curve into individual node/tenor pairs, we may work with individual lines within each tenor. A cubic polynomial can then be added to each line to provide the cubic spline. For ease of illustration, we take this one step further and imagine an alternative horizontal axis. This is referred to as X as shown in Exhibit 7.4. Assume that between each node pair that this horizontal axis X runs from 0 (at x_N) to $x_{N+1} - x_N$ (at x_{N+1}).

In Exhibit 7.4 the X axis is a calculated value determined from the x axis. The points x_N and x_{N+1} are isolated for spline S_N. It is then assumed that X_0 equals zero at x_N and stretches to X_N which equals $(x_{N+1} - x_N)$ on the X axis. If these lines are fully isolated then a cubic polynomial, of the form $y = aX^3 + bX^2 + cX + d$, can be constructed to touch the points x_N and x_{N+1}.

The First Requirement

In order for the polynomial to touch the nodes, a cubic polynomial must be constructed so that at point X_0 the polynomial provides a result that is equal to y_N. This is very easy to achieve. Since X is equal to zero at its starting point, the polynomial takes the following form:

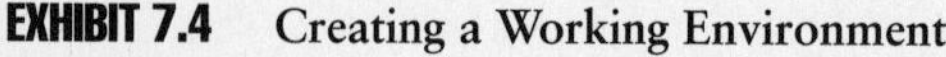

EXHIBIT 7.4 Creating a Working Environment

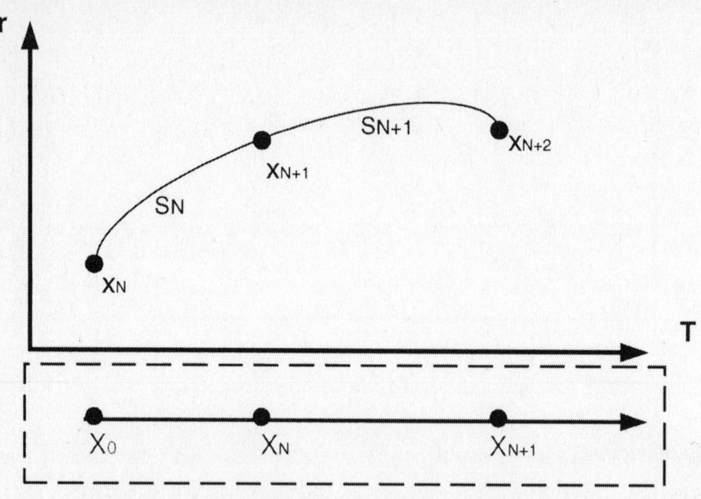

$$y_N = a_N 0^3 + b_N 0^2 + c_N 0 + d_N$$
$$y_N = d_N$$

So as long as d_N is equal to y_N, then our polynomial will touch the node at X_0.

In order for the polynomial to touch the second node, the node at point x_{N+1}, then the polynomial must take the following form at point X_N:

$$y_{N+1} = a_N(x_{N+1} - x_N)^3 + b_N(x_{N+1} - x_N)^2 + c_N(x_{N+1} - x_N) + d_N$$

or

$$d_{N+1} = a_N X_N^3 + b_N X_N^2 + c_N X_N + d_N \tag{1}$$

where $X_N = x_{N+1} - x_N$.

It is worth noting that at this point in our process we do not know what the values of a, b, or c are. These will be derived below from our other requirements.

The Second Requirement

To meet the second requirement of a cubic spline, the first differential $y_N{}'$ must equal the first differential $y_{N+1}{}'$ at the tenor point x_{N+1}. In other words at node x_{N+1}:

$$3a_N X_N^2 + 2b_N X_N + c_N = 3a_{N+1} X_{N+1}^2 + 2b_{N+1} X_{N+1} + c_{N+1} \quad (2)$$

We know from our conditional working environment that at node x_{N+1} for function y_N' that $X = (x_{N+1} - x_N)$. We also know from the same assumption that $X = 0$ at the start of the next polynomial, i.e., for function y_{N+1}'. Therefore:

$$3a_{N+1}0^2 + 2b_{N+1}0 + c_{N+1} = 3a_N X_N^2 + 2b_N X_N + c_N$$

so that

$$c_{N+1} = 3a_N X_N^2 + 2b_N X_N + c_N \quad (3)$$

Third Requirement

To meet the third requirement of a cubic spline, the second differential y_N'' assessed at the point x_{N+1} should equal the second differential y_{N+1}''. In other words at node x_{N+1}:

$$6a_N X_N + 2b_N = 6a_{N+1} X_{N+1} + 2b_{N+1}$$

We know from our conditions that at node x_{N+1} for function y_N'' that $X = (x_{N+1} - x_N)$. We also know from the same assumption that $X = 0$ for function y_{N+1}''. Therefore:

$$6a_N X_N + 2b_N = 6a_{N+1}0 + 2b_{N+1}$$

$$6a_N X_N = 2b_{N+1} - 2b_N$$

$$a_N = \frac{b_{N+1} - b_N}{3X_N} \quad (4)$$

Meeting All Requirements Simultaneously

We now have equations which ensure that each of the three requirements can be met. We now need a solution that will ensure that all requirements are met at the same time. By substitution, a set of calculations can be performed which meet both requirements and reduce these equations down to a factor of parameter b only.

Using equation (4) as a substitute for a in equation (3) we obtain:

$$c_{N+1} = 3a_N X_N^2 + 2b_N X_N + c_N$$

$$c_{N+1} = \frac{3X_N^2(b_{N+1} - b_N)}{3X_N} + 2b_N X_N + c_N$$

$$c_{N+1} = X_N(b_{N+1} - b_N) + 2b_N X_N + c_N$$

$$c_{N+1} = X_N(b_{N+1} + b_N) + c_N \tag{5}$$

Using equation (4) as a substitute for *a* in equation (1) we get:

$$d_{N+1} = \frac{(b_{N+1} - b_N)}{3X_N} X_N^3 + b_N X_N^2 + c_N X_N + d_N$$

$$d_{N+1} = \frac{(b_{N+1} - b_N)}{3} X_N^2 + b_N X_N^2 + c_N X_N + d_N$$

$$c_N X_N = -\frac{(b_{N+1} - b_N)}{3} X_N^2 - b_N X_N^2 + d_{N+1} - d_N$$

$$c_N = -X_N \frac{(b_{N+1} + 2b_N)}{3} + \frac{(d_{N+1} - d_N)}{X_N} \tag{6}$$

Taking this solution one step further we can substitute equation (6) into equation (5) as follows:

$$\frac{(d_{N+2} - d_{N+1})}{X_{N+1}} - X_{N+1}\frac{(b_{N+2} + 2b_{N+1})}{3} = X_N(b_{N+1} + b_N) - X_N\frac{(b_{N+1} + 2b_N)}{3} + \frac{(d_{N+1} - d_N)}{X_N}$$

$$-X_{N+1}(b_{N+2} + 2b_{N+1}) = 3X_N(b_{N+1} + b_N) - X_N(b_{N+1} + 2b_N) + 3\frac{(d_{N+1} - d_N)}{X_N} - 3\frac{(d_{N+2} - d_{N+1})}{X_{N+1}}$$

$$-X_{N+1}(b_{N+2} + 2b_{N+1}) = X_N(2b_{N+1} + b_N) + 3\frac{(d_{N+1} - d_N)}{X_N} - 3\frac{(d_{N+2} - d_{N+1})}{X_{N+1}}$$

$$X_{N+1}b_{N+2} = -X_N(2b_{N+1} + b_N) - 3\frac{(d_{N+1} - d_N)}{X_N} + 3\frac{(d_{N+2} - d_{N+1})}{X_{N+1}} - 2X_{N+1}b_{N+1}$$

$$b_{N+2} = \frac{-2X_N b_{N+1} - X_N b_N - 2X_{N+1}b_{N+1} - 3\dfrac{(d_{N+1} - d_N)}{X_N} + 3\dfrac{(d_{N+2} - d_{N+1})}{X_{N+1}}}{X_{N+1}} \tag{7}$$

A Unique Solution

For clarity and ease of illustration, the results of these equations are set out as a table of related formulas shown in Exhibit 7.5.

It is a simple matter to determine the values of parameters a, b, c, and d at each node n by using the formulas set out in Exhibit 7.5. Each node (from $n > 2$) is directly or indirectly dependent on the values of previous parameters and can be determined from those previous parameters. This is an important result, and means that any errors in the calculation early on are replicated and magnified throughout the analysis. However, the first two occurrences of b (b_1 and b_2) do not have previous nodes from which to determine their values. In other words the only values for which we do not have solutions are those for b_1 and b_2.

Depending on the values assumed for b_1 and b_2, the result is *usually* an oscillating b and ever increasing $|b|$. This means that the slope of the spline gets steeper at each tenor as the absolute value of the first differential increases, so the slope of the curve oscillates.

This systematic wave, shown in Exhibit 7.6, is clearly not the kind of behavior that is commonly observed in a yield curve and should therefore not be modeled into the curve. Furthermore, we have no unique solution at this stage. An infinite number of values can be assigned to b_1 and b_2 and therefore an infinite number of solutions can be obtained (most of which exhibit the depicted oscillation effect). So this is still not what we seek.

We need an additional restriction that allows us to find a single solution and which eliminates the oscillation of the output. The restriction that we put in place is to set the second differential of the first spline y_0'' and last spline y_N'' equal to a constant. We will use a constant of zero for now, but we come back to this constant at a later stage. Creating this additional restriction means that we are left with only one unknown, parameter b_2. This is demonstrated, using the constant zero, in Exhibit 7.7.

If we find a value for b_2 that results in a final value of zero for b_N then we have a single solution and this solution should eliminate the oscillation shown above. We can determine this solution using two different methods: (1) iteration or (2) Gaussian Elimination of a tri-diagonal matrix.

Before we consider each of these solution techniques, we consider first the requirement of a boundary condition in order to obtain a unique solution for a cubic spline. In our discussion above we ordained a boundary condition of $b_1 = b_N = 0$. In practice two boundary conditions have become widely accepted:

Condition 1. Natural spline
In a natural spline the second differential at x_0 and x_N is set to zero. In other words $y_0'' = y_N'' = 0$.

EXHIBIT 7.5 Formula Matrix

X	y(d)	Using Equation 4 We Can Derive *a*	Using Equation 7 We Can Derive *b*	Using Equation 6 We Can Derive *c*
X_1	d_1	$\frac{b_2 - b_1}{3X_1}$	b_1	$-X_1\frac{(b_2 + 2b_1)}{3} + \frac{(d_2 - d_1)}{X_1}$
X_2	d_2	$\frac{b_3 - b_2}{3X_2}$	b_2	$-X_2\frac{(b_3 + 2b_2)}{3} + \frac{(d_3 - d_2)}{X_2}$
X_3	d_3	$\frac{b_4 - b_3}{3X_3}$	$\frac{-2X_1b_2 - X_1b_1 - 2X_2b_2 - 3\frac{d_2 - d_1}{X_1} + 3\frac{d_3 - d_2}{X_2}}{X_2}$	$-X_3\frac{(b_4 + 2b_3)}{3} + \frac{(d_4 - d_3)}{X_3}$
...	...	...	...	...
X_{N-1}	d_{N-1}	$\frac{b_N - b_{N-1}}{3X_{N-1}}$	$\frac{-2X_{N-3}b_{N-2} - X_{N-3}b_{N-3} - 2X_{N-2}b_{N-2} - 3\frac{d_{N-2} - d_{N-3}}{X_{N-3}} + 3\frac{d_{N-1} - d_{N-2}}{X_{N-2}}}{X_{N-2}}$	$-X_{N-1}\frac{(b_N + 2b_{N-1})}{3} + \frac{(d_N - d_{N-1})}{X_{N-1}}$
X_N	d_N	N/A	$\frac{-2X_{N-2}b_{N-1} - X_{N-2}b_{N-2} - 2X_{N-1}b_{N-1} - 3\frac{d_{N-1} - d_{N-2}}{X_{N-2}} + 3\frac{d_N - d_{N-1}}{X_{N-1}}}{X_{N-1}}$	N/A

EXHIBIT 7.6 Typical Spline with No Boundary Conditions

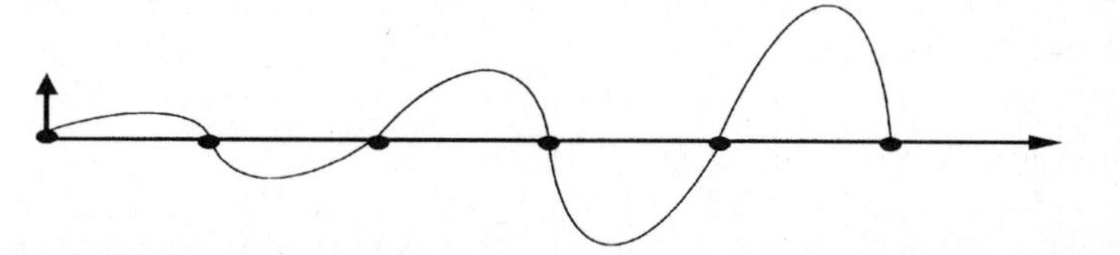

Condition 2. Clamped spline

In a clamped spline the first differential of the function that produced the nodes and the first differential of the spline are set equal. In other words $y_0{}' = f(x_0)'$ and $y_N{}' = f(x_N)'$. It is immediately apparent when we construct a yield curve that we do not have a function that can be used to replicate the nodes. The first differential of this function is therefore not available. A reasonable approximation can be used based on the slope of the linear interpolation function between the first two and the last two nodes. Although this provides a reasonable approximation in most circumstances, it is not always an appropriate measure. An incorrect choice of boundary values could result in spurious and oscillating results at the short and/or long end of the curve.

An example using the same input data but different (albeit rather extreme) boundary values is shown in Exhibit 7.8. The natural boundary uses values zero and zero. In the clamped boundary we have used –50 and –50 as boundary values. Although these boundary values are extreme, they do illustrate the effect that inappropriate boundary values can have on spline results.

These results are not unexpected. Readers may question the practical difference between having a natural boundary condition against having a boundary condition that is obviously inappropriate. Both approaches may lead to oscillation and an incorrect result. The sole practical difference is that where we set our own boundary value, however inappropriate, the extent of the error is under our own control. For this reason users may prefer this approach.

The Solution

We now consider each approach to obtaining the solution.

Iterative Solution

A solution for b_2 can be obtained by iteration. This "trial-and-error" style approach is straightforward to understand but is not without its limitations.

EXHIBIT 7.7 Formula Matrix with Natural Boundary Values of Zero

X	y (d)	Using Equation 4 We Can Derive a	Using Equation 7 We Can Derive b	Using Equation 6 We Can Derive c
X_1	d_1	$\frac{b_2 - b_1}{3X_1}$	0	$-X_1\frac{(b_2 + 2b_1)}{3} + \frac{(d_2 - d_1)}{X_1}$
X_2	d_2	$\frac{b_3 - b_2}{3X_2}$	The only parameter left to solve for is b_2.	$-X_2\frac{(b_3 + 2b_2)}{3} + \frac{(d_3 - d_2)}{X_2}$
X_3	d_3	$\frac{b_4 - b_3}{3X_3}$	$\frac{-2X_1b_2 - X_1b_1 - 2X_2b_2 - 3\frac{d_2 - d_1}{X_1} + 3\frac{d_3 - d_2}{X_2}}{X_2}$	$-X_3\frac{(b_4 + 2b_3)}{3} + \frac{(d_4 - d_3)}{X_3}$
…	…	…	…	…
X_{N-1}	d_{N-1}	$\frac{b_N - b_{N-1}}{3X_{N-1}}$	$\frac{-2X_{N-3}b_{N-2} - X_{N-3}b_{N-3} - 2X_{N-2}b_{N-2} - 3\frac{d_{N-2} - d_{N-3}}{X_{N-3}} + 3\frac{d_{N-1} - d_{N-2}}{X_{N-2}}}{X_{N-2}}$	$-X_{N-1}\frac{(b_N + 2b_{N-1})}{3} + \frac{(d_N - d_{N-1})}{X_{N-1}}$
X_N	d_N	N/A	0	N/A

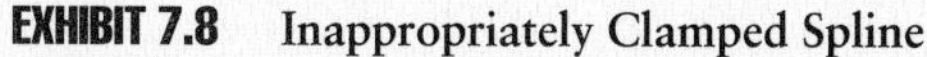

EXHIBIT 7.8 Inappropriately Clamped Spline

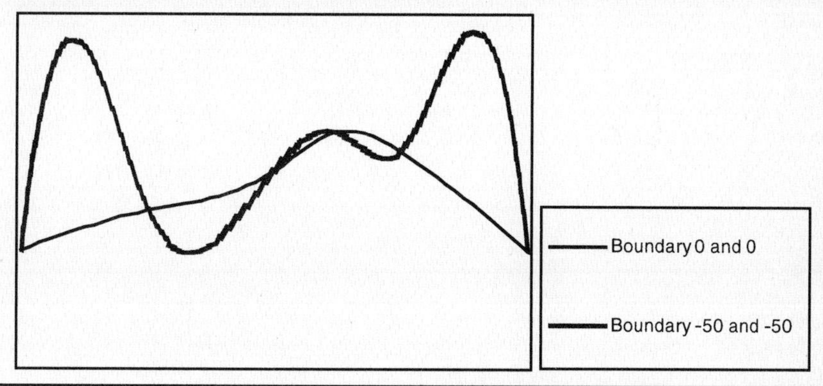

When a cubic spline solution is solved by iteration for a single parameter, the degree of accuracy required is very high. In test solutions we found that a higher degree of accuracy was required for a higher number of nodes. A calculation for 15 nodes or more required the solution to be accurate to at least eight decimal places. Even apparently negligible differences in decimal accuracy can result in strange spline parameters and in turn produce the same oscillation observed above when no boundary values were set. This is particularly evident at the long end of the curve as the error becomes compounded by previous inaccuracies, thus leading to yield curves of limited practical application when anything longer than the medium-term maturity range is modeled.

A fictional set of numbers has been used to demonstrate this point in Exhibit 7.9. The "Date" column holds the maturity dates for each rate, while the "Rate" column is of course the set of interest rates for each particular term to maturity. This data is illustrated graphically in Exhibit 7.10.

In Exhibit 7.9, an accuracy of eight decimal places is shown but in fact a much higher level (over 15 decimal places) of accuracy was required to calculate the results. When we adjust the level of accuracy, just on parameter b_2, to seven decimal places, the results are significantly flawed, as shown in Exhibit 7.11.[15]

It can be seen that within the long dates, parameter b starts to oscillate and grow in an exponential manner. A graphical representation of the rates as a result of this flawed data is shown at Exhibit 7.12. Note that the oscillation error is highly pronounced.

[15] The results were calculated using the "Goal Seek" function on Microsoft Excel.

EXHIBIT 7.9 Iterative Solution to 15 Decimal Places

Date	Rate (d)	Parameter a	Parameter b	Parameter c
1-Jan-00	6.000	−0.00001228	0.00000000	0.00544212
7-Jan-00	6.030	0.00000351	−0.00022106	0.00411577
31-Jan-00	6.050	−0.00000019	0.00003181	−0.00042615
1-Apr-00	6.100	−0.00000001	−0.00000235	0.00137086
1-Jul-00	6.200	0.00000002	−0.00000426	0.00076898
1-Oct-00	6.250	−0.00000001	0.00000117	0.00048462
1-Jan-01	6.300	0.00000000	−0.00000042	0.00055340
1-Jul-01	6.400	−0.00000000	0.00000083	0.00062739
1-Jan-02	6.520	0.00000000	−0.00000126	0.00054853
1-Jan-03	6.610	−0.00000000	0.00000004	0.00010301
1-Jan-05	6.700	0.00000000	0.00000000	0.00013362
1-Jan-06	6.750	−0.00000000	0.00000003	0.00014328
1-Jan-07	6.800	0.00000000	−0.00000010	0.00011518
1-Jan-10	6.900	−0.00000000	0.00000014	0.00015545
1-Jan-11	6.960	0.00000000	−0.00000020	0.00013152
1-Jan-12	7.000	−0.00000000	0.00000023	0.00014041
1-Jan-14	7.100	0.00000000	−0.00000047	−0.00003778
1-Jan-15	7.050	−0.00000000	0.00000013	−0.00016286
1-Jan-20	7.000	0.00000000	−0.00000004	0.00000616
1-Jan-25	6.950	−0.00000000	0.00000002	−0.00002600
1-Jan-30	6.950		0.00000000	

EXHIBIT 7.10 Appropriate Solution Using 15 Decimal Places

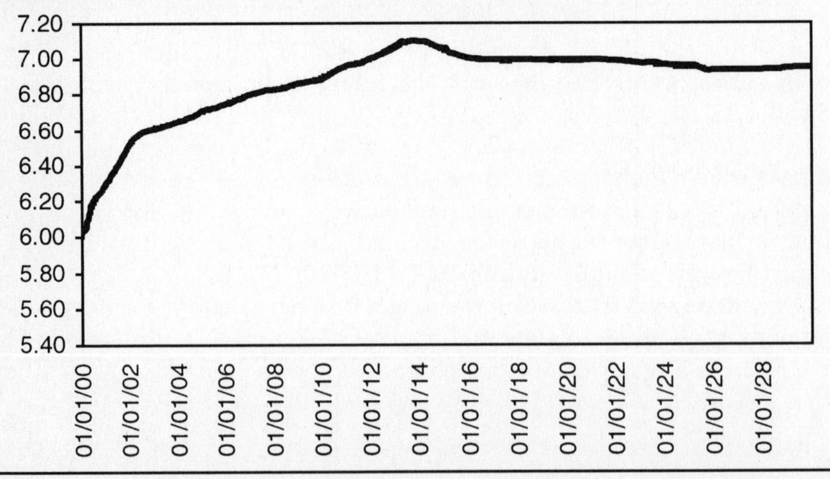

EXHIBIT 7.11 Iterative Solution to 7 Decimal Places

Date	Rate (d)	Parameter a	Parameter b	Parameter c
1-Jan-00	6.000	–0.00001228	0.00000000	0.00544210
7-Jan-00	6.030	0.00000351	–0.00022105	0.00411580
31-Jan-00	6.050	–0.00000019	0.00003179	–0.00042640
1-Apr-00	6.100	–0.00000001	–0.00000230	0.00137252
1-Jul-00	6.200	0.00000002	–0.00000442	0.00076105
1-Oct-00	6.250	–0.00000002	0.00000174	0.00051482
1-Jan-01	6.300	0.00000002	–0.00000255	0.00044055
1-Jul-01	6.400	–0.00000006	0.00000695	0.00123776
1-Jan-02	6.520	0.00000008	–0.00002345	–0.00179846
1-Jan-03	6.610	–0.00000011	0.00006372	0.01289764
1-Jan-05	6.700	0.00000103	–0.00017986	–0.07200383
1-Jan-06	6.750	–0.00000419	0.00095266	0.21006837
1-Jan-07	6.800	0.00000395	–0.00363079	–0.76744773
1-Jan-10	6.900	–0.00006704	0.00936251	5.51451411
1-Jan-11	6.960	0.00028391	–0.06404843	–14.44584982
1-Jan-12	7.000	–0.00043548	0.24683078	52.26970709
1-Jan-14	7.100	0.00407923	–0.70817417	–284.97230573
1-Jan-15	7.050	–0.00230683	3.75858533	828.42777079
1-Jan-20	7.000	0.00741195	–8.87822401	–8,520.0324431
1-Jan-25	6.950	–0.02736125	31.74664902	33,260.580061
1-Jan-30	6.950		–118.13828171	

EXHIBIT 7.12 Incorrect Solution Using 7 Decimal Places

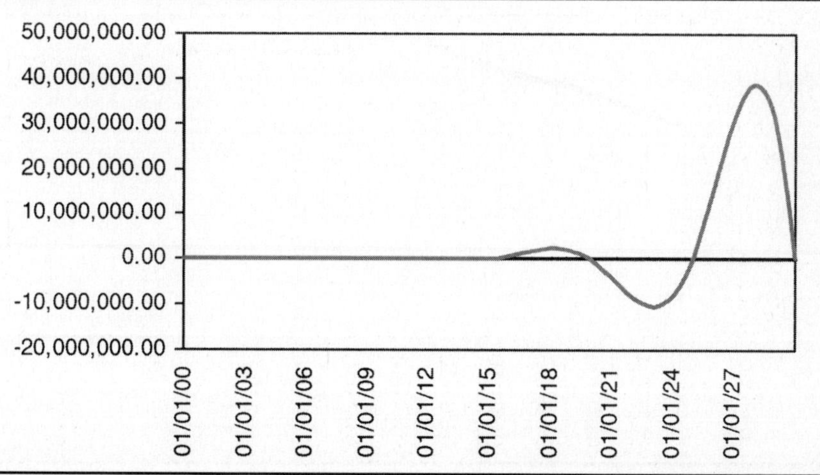

The degree of accuracy obtained through iteration is dependent on the starting point for the first calculation and the number of iterations allowed as a maximum. There is no way of ensuring that the required degree of accuracy will be obtained without undertaking very high magnitude (and process intensive) calculations in the iterative algorithm. Without the comfort of extensive manual review of the results by a person with a clear understanding of the calculation and its implications, we do not recommend the use of the iteration approach to derive a solution.

Solving for a System of Linear Equations by Elimination

We now consider again equation (7) derived above, and rearrange it slightly as equation (8).

$$
\begin{aligned}
&X_{N+1}b_{N+2} + 2(X_N + X_{N+1})b_{N+1} + X_N b_N \\
&= -3\frac{(d_{N+1} - d_N)}{X_N} + 3\frac{(d_{N+2} - d_{N+1})}{X_{N+1}}
\end{aligned} \tag{8}
$$

It can be seen that all parameters X and d can be obtained by reference to values that are already known at the nodes. These are in fact node (or time-to-maturity) dependent constants. In other words, we have a system of linear equations from node 1 to N. Simultaneous linear equations can be solved by substitution. This method of solving linear equations can be applied to larger sets of linear equations, although we require increased processing power.

The system of equations can be represented in a N–2 by N+1 matrix as follows:

$$
\left[\begin{array}{ccccc|c}
X_0 & 2(X_0 + X_1) & X_1 & & & -3\frac{(d_1 - d_0)}{X_0} + 3\frac{(d_2 - d_1)}{X_1} \\
X_1 & 2(X_1 + X_2) & X_2 & & & -3\frac{(d_2 - d_1)}{X_1} + 3\frac{(d_3 - d_2)}{X_2} \\
 & \cdots & \cdots & \cdots & & \cdots \\
 & & \cdots & \cdots & \cdots & \cdots \\
 & & X_{N-2} & 2(X_{N-2} + X_{N-1}) & X_{N-1} & -3\frac{(d_{N-1} - d_{N-2})}{X_{N-2}} + 3\frac{(d_N - d_{N-1})}{X_{N-1}}
\end{array}\right]
$$

In essence, if you look at the parameters b for which we are attempting to solve, this can be laid over the above matrix as follows:

$$
\begin{array}{ccccccc}
b_0 & b_1 & b_2 & & & & \\
 & b_1 & b_2 & b_3 & & & \\
 & & \cdots & \cdots & \cdots & & \\
 & & & \cdots & \cdots & \cdots & \\
 & & & & b_{N\text{-}2} & b_{N\text{-}1} & b_N
\end{array}
$$

In other words we are looking for a set of values for b_0 to b_N that will solve the linear system for each and every node N.

Our basic limitation imposed above is not lifted. We set b_0 and b_N equal to 0 in order to apply the natural boundary condition. We can then substitute our solution for equation/row 1 into equation/row 2. We perform a similar continuous set of substitutions until we have a solution for b_{N-1}. This solution can then be substituted backward through the solved equations to obtain a solution for b_1.

A matrix of this form, that is, an upper and lower triangular quadrant for which no value is required (observed by the grey shaded area) is also known as a *tri-diagonal matrix*. More advanced methods of solving matrices (and in particular tri-diagonal types) are available. It is outside the scope of this chapter to cover these methods in detail.[16] For the purposes of illustration however, we have prepared a simple example solution for a small matrix of values, and this appears as an Appendix to this chapter.

The same values used for the iterative solution were processed using the elimination solution. The results and their illustrative chart are set out in Exhibits 7.13 and 7.14, respectively.

On first observation these values appear to be identical to those obtained using the iterative solution. In fact even at the highest level of accuracy possible in our iterative solution, we notice a difference in the values for parameter c when we look at the dates January 1, 2014, onwards (which appear in the gray boxes in Exhibit 7.13). Although this is not apparent in the exhibit, the results in the table where numbers appear with greater accuracy show these and other small differences not shown in Exhibit 7.14.

Based on these results, we conclude that the technique of solving for a system of linear equations is superior to an iterative solution. This is because:

[16] Interested readers may wish to consult Burden and Faires, *Numerical Analysis*.

EXHIBIT 7.13 Tri-Diagonal Solution

Date	Rate (d)	Parameter a	Parameter b	Parameter c
1-Jan-00	6.000	−0.00001228	0.00000000	0.00544212
7-Jan-00	6.030	0.00000351	−0.00022106	0.00411577
31-Jan-00	6.050	−0.00000019	0.00003181	−0.00042615
1-Apr-00	6.100	−0.00000001	−0.00000235	0.00137086
1-Jul-00	6.200	0.00000002	−0.00000426	0.00076898
1-Oct-00	6.250	−0.00000001	0.00000117	0.00048462
1-Jan-01	6.300	0.00000000	−0.00000042	0.00055340
1-Jul-01	6.400	−0.00000000	0.00000083	0.00062739
1-Jan-02	6.520	0.00000000	−0.00000126	0.00054853
1-Jan-03	6.610	−0.00000000	0.00000004	0.00010301
1-Jan-05	6.700	0.00000000	0.00000000	0.00013362
1-Jan-06	6.750	−0.00000000	0.00000003	0.00014328
1-Jan-07	6.800	0.00000000	−0.00000010	0.00011518
1-Jan-10	6.900	−0.00000000	0.00000014	0.00015545
1-Jan-11	6.960	0.00000000	−0.00000020	0.00013151
1-Jan-12	7.000	−0.00000000	0.00000023	0.00014041
1-Jan-14	7.100	0.00000000	−0.00000047	−0.00003779
1-Jan-15	7.050	−0.00000000	0.00000013	−0.00016284
1-Jan-20	7.000	0.00000000	−0.00000004	0.00000594
1-Jan-25	6.950	−0.00000000	0.00000002	−0.00002515
1-Jan-30	6.950		0.00000000	

EXHIBIT 7.14 Solution Using Tri-Diagonal Method

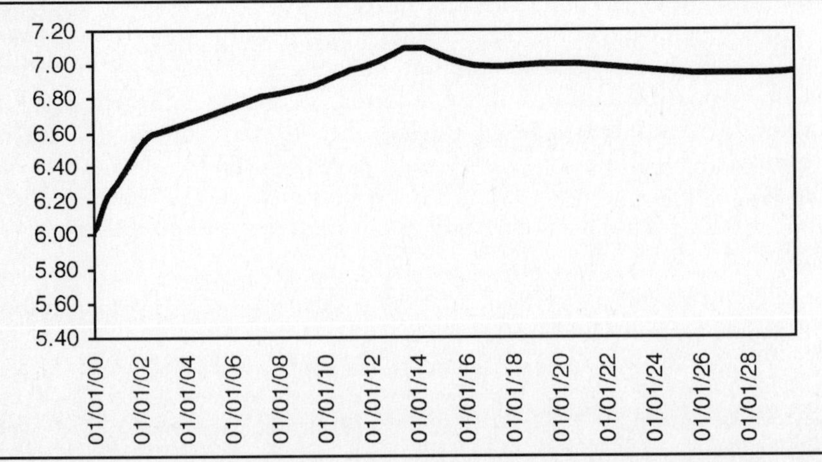

- No starting point for the calculation needs to be determined by the user or the system;
- The accuracy of the solution is not dependent on the number of iterative calculations performed; and
- The results do not need the same degree of review to assess their accuracy.

This is not to say that this method is flawless. Even a tri-diagonal methodology is reliant on the degree of precision applied in its calculation. Modern computing hardware and software have limitations in the size or length of the floating point numbers that it can process. However if programmed with care, a typical application can deal with significantly large numbers.

EMPIRICAL PROOF OF PRECISION

In our cubic spline application (CUBED^3) we have chosen C++ as the programming language and we have used the C++ 'long double' variable type to store and process our values. A long double is usually anything between a 74- and 128-bit place holder, depending on the compiler and the system on which the calculations are performed. Applying some basic binary mathematics and allowing 1 bit for sign storage we can calculate:

$$2^{71} = 2{,}361{,}183{,}241{,}434{,}820{,}000{,}000$$

This should be sufficient to provide an adequate level of accuracy for most cubic spline calculations required of a zero curve application.[17]

To test this we have performed empirical testing to corroborate our conclusion using a completely fictitious set of data that was designed to provide an extreme testing environment and data that is more sensitive to calculation anomalies than any likely to occur in real life.[18] Our fake input values were chosen to include:

- a large number of nodes (over 100);
- high oscillations at various points in the curve; and
- various points of flat data.

[17] This assurance is based on the fact that a typical yield curve application very, very rarely has more than 30 nodes. Any application where there are large node numbers may require higher levels of accuracy.

[18] In other words, we use interest rate values that are extreme and unlikely to be observed in a yield curve in practice. Bond traders would be amused if one morning they discovered that the bond redemption yield curve looked anything like Exhibit 7.15.

EXHIBIT 7.15 Test Data

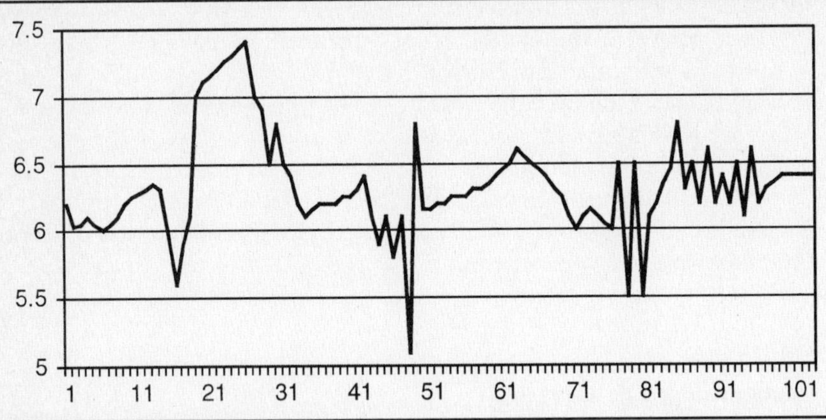

EXHIBIT 7.16 Cubic Spline Test Results

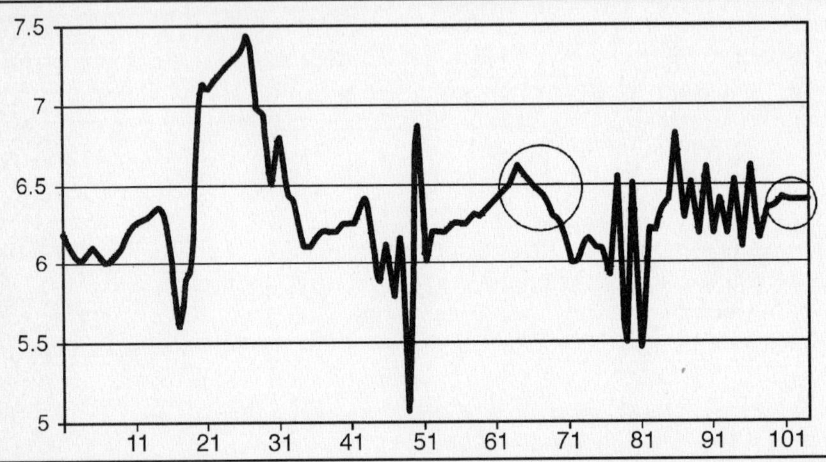

A large number of tenors was chosen to compound any rounding errors that might occur as part of the elimination multiplier. Oscillation at various points in the curve is used to set up waves that can continue when they subsequently flow into areas of flat data and which would highlight errors, if they occur. Flat sections of the curve are used so that any errors become highly visible.

A graph of this extreme test data is set out in Exhibit 7.15. The resulting smooth graph after the cubic spline parameter has been calculated and applied is shown in Exhibit 7.16. Two areas on the graph with relatively flat or consistent data values have been highlighted in Exhibit

7.16 as potential areas where calculation error may be observed. These areas of the graph are isolated and shown in Exhibits 7.17 and 7.18.

In the first area we observe some oscillation. However, this is not oscillation as a result of calculation errors. This is a smoothing effect that is required to meet the requirements of a cubic spline and to ensure a smooth curve. The data between points 63 and 71 is consistently downward sloping but the data then slopes upward again at point 72. The curve starts to "adapt" at an earlier stage in order to facilitate this change in direction. Therefore this behavior is unavoidable, but under most applications for the spot curve does not present a material problem.

EXHIBIT 7.17 Extract 1 (X-Axis Values of Points 63 to 71)

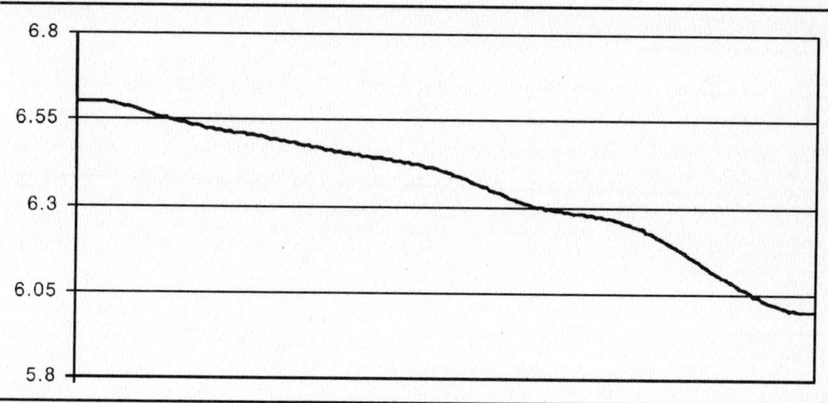

EXHIBIT 7.18 Extract 2 (X-Axis Values of Points 98 to 101)

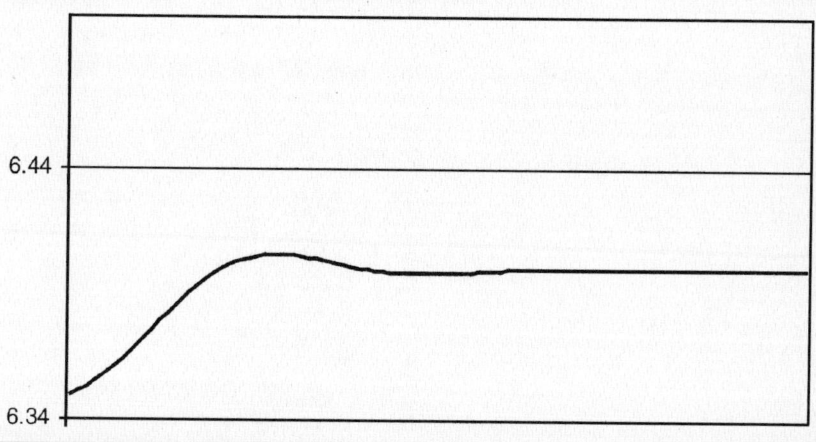

The second area of the curve provides another typical cubic spline example as the curve "adapts" to its new parameters. Once again this is a natural spline phenomenon and not an error in the calculated values.

Empirical data does not prove beyond a doubt that a cubic spline method, applied using an appropriate solution technique and precise software, will always produce accurate results. Nonetheless we believe that it is reasonable to assume from the test data set out above that the cubic spline methodology, used in conjunction with appropriate calculation tools, provides accurate zero curve results in most fixed-income market conditions.

A LOOK AT FORWARD RATES

Previous literature has highlighted the use of the cubic spline approach to model forward curves and its limitations. Certainly a cubic spline discussion would be incomplete without a look at its application to forward rates. We will use our empirical data to highlight typical forward rate behavior under the cubic spline technique. Our sample data do not reflect actual market conditions and represent an extreme data set, to say the least. However, it does highlight a point with regards to forward rates that can often be observed sometimes under normal market conditions. To this end we isolate the last sub-set of the data, as shown in Exhibit 7.16, and plot the forward rates for that data set.

From data that was interpolated using the linear method versus data interpolated using the cubic spline, a comparison of forwards shows how the forwards in a cubic spline environment can oscillate. As expected, the relatively minor oscillations observed first in the zero rates curve are compounded excessively in the forward rate calculation. The linear interpolation approach, shown for comparison purposes at Exhibit 7.19, eliminates much of the oscillation but of course is not a smooth curve, which is as undesirable. The user is confronted with the need to balance the conflicting requirements—a tradeoff is called for and for most practical applications the cubic spline approach and its smoothing results is preferred. It remains important however that the user reviews cubic spline data by looking at both the zero and forward rates.

Using the actual United Kingdom 10-year zero curve for January 2, 2000, the forward rates have been calculated using cubic spline and linear interpolation and compared in Exhibits 7.20 and 7.21, respectively. There is no observed reason to favor the latter approach over the former.

EXHIBIT 7.19 Forward Rate Comparison (Linear versus Cubic)

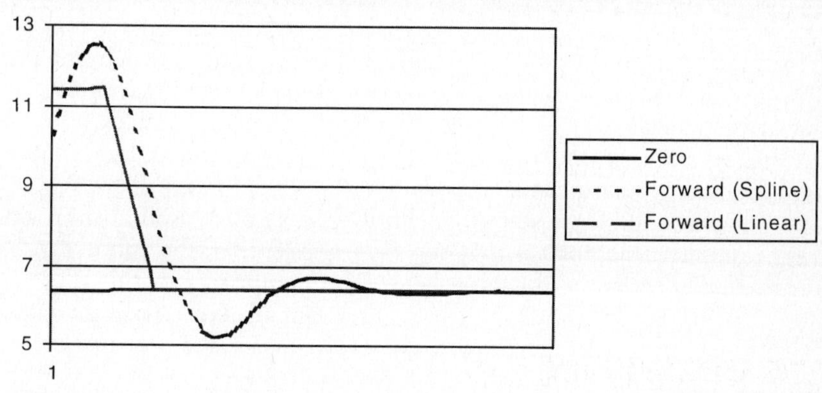

EXHIBIT 7.20 Actual United Kingdom 10-Year Zero and Forward Rates—Cubic Spline

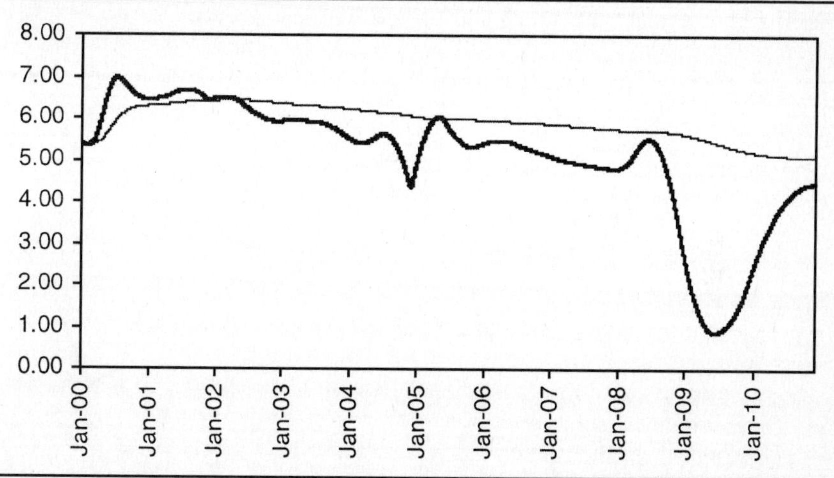

Improvements to the Basic Approach

As a result of the drawback when fitting the forward curve, the basic technique has been improved to remove the oscillation effect at longer maturities. As we saw from the test results presented earlier, the oscillation of a spline is partly a function of the number of nodes used. The paradox with this factor is that in practice, at very long maturities the forward (and also the spot) curve would be expected to be reasonably flat. To remove the oscillation, as described first by Fisher, Nychka, and Zervos, this involves the addition of a *roughness penalty* when minimizing the sums of squares.[19]

Waggoner introduced a *variable roughness penalty*, which enabled the approach to retain the flexibility at the short end and reduce oscillation at the long end.[20] Using the Waggoner approach enables users to retain the flexibility and ease of the cubic spline approach as well as a more realistic forward curve.

Anderson and Sleath state that the advantage of the spline approach over parametric methods is that separate segments of the spline can be adjusted independently of each other.[21] The significance of this is that a change in market levels at one end of the term structure will not affect significantly any other parts of the curve. This is a drawback of the parametric methods. Ironically Anderson and Sleath modify the Waggoner model in a way that would appear to incorporate elements of the parametric approach, and their results appear to improve on the earlier works.

EXHIBIT 7.21 Actual United Kingdom 10-Year Zero and Forward Rates—Linear Interpolation

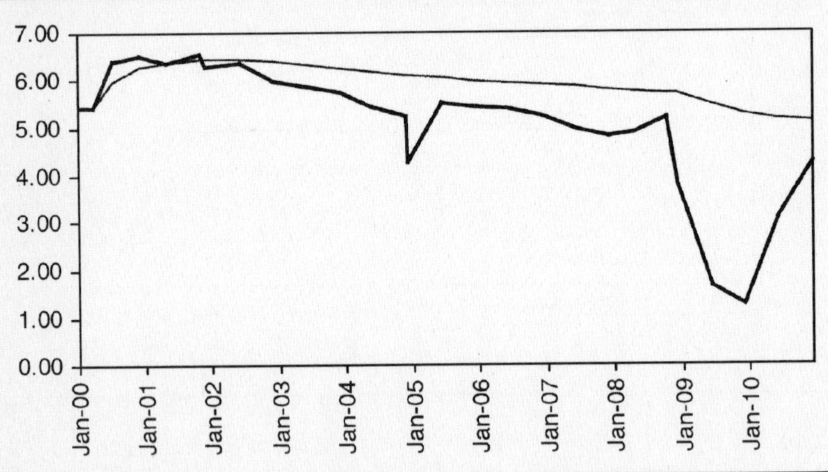

[19] Fisher, Nychka, and Zervos, "Fitting the Term Structure of Interest Rates with Smoothing Splines."

[20] Waggoner, "Spline Methods for Extracting Interest Rate Curves from Coupon Bond Prices."

[21] Anderson and Sleath, "New Estimates of the UK Real and Nominal Yield Cuirves."

CONCLUSION

The purpose of this chapter has been to present an accessible account of how the cubic spline methodology of term structure estimation could be implemented by users involved in any area of the debt capital markets. The technique is straightforward and quick, and is valid for a number of applications, most of which are "normal" or conventional yield curves. For example, users are recommended to use it when curves are positively sloping, or when there are relatively few humps in the curve. The existence of humps along the short or medium terms of the curve can cause excessive oscillation in the forward curve but the zero curve may still be used for valuation or relative value purposes.

Oscillation is a natural effect of the cubic spline methodology and its existence does not impair its effectiveness under many conditions. If observed rates produce very humped curves, the fitted zero-curve using cubic spline does not produce usable results. For policy-making purposes, for example as used in central banks, and also for certain market valuation purposes, users require forward rates with minimal oscillation. In such cases however, the Waggoner or Anderson-Sleath models will overcome this problem. We therefore recommend the cubic spline approach under most market conditions.

APPENDIX

Example matrix solution based on Gaussian elimination.

We will solve for the following values (where the values of X have already been calculated).

x	X	y
0.90	0.40	1.30
1.30	0.60	1.50
1.90	0.20	1.85
2.10	0.90	2.10
3.00	0.80	1.95
3.80	0.50	0.40
4.30		0.25

First we construct our matrix as follows.

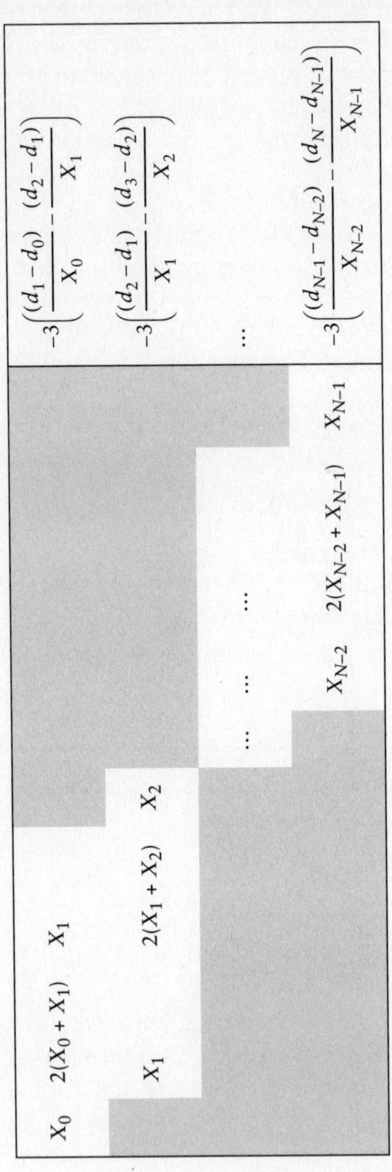

$$
\left[\begin{array}{cccccc|c}
X_0 & 2(X_0 + X_1) & X_1 & & & & -3\left(\frac{(d_1 - d_0)}{X_0} - \frac{(d_2 - d_1)}{X_1}\right) \\
& X_1 & 2(X_1 + X_2) & X_2 & & & -3\left(\frac{(d_2 - d_1)}{X_1} - \frac{(d_3 - d_2)}{X_2}\right) \\
& & \cdots & \cdots & \cdots & & \cdots \\
& & & X_{N-2} & 2(X_{N-2} + X_{N-1}) & X_{N-1} & -3\left(\frac{(d_{N-1} - d_{N-2})}{X_{N-2}} - \frac{(d_N - d_{N-1})}{X_{N-1}}\right)
\end{array}\right]
$$

Where b_1 is set to zero this provides the following values.

b1	b2	b3	b4	b5	b6	b7	
0.0	2.0	0.6					0.3
	0.6	1.6	0.2				2.0
		0.2	2.2	0.9			–4.3
			0.9	3.4	0.8		–5.3
				0.8	2.6	0.5	4.9

In turn we can substitute row 1 into row 2 to obtain:

b1	b2	b3	b4	b5	b6	b7	
0.0	2.0	0.6					0.3
	0.0	4.7	0.7				6.4
		0.2	2.2	0.9			–4.3
			0.9	3.4	0.8		–5.3
				0.8	2.6	0.5	4.9

Similar substitutions, and the fact that b_7 is constrained as zero, yield the matrix below.

b1	b2	b3	b4	b5	b6	b7	
0.0	2.0	0.6					0.3
	0.0	4.7	0.7				6.4
		0.0	51.4	21.3			–107.0
			0.0	172.9	45.7		–196.4
				0.0	516.2	0.0	1,258.0

This means that we can solve for b_6. Once we have a solution for b_6, we can solve for b_5 and so on. As a final result, we get the following values for parameter b.

b1	b2	b3	b4	b5	b6	b7
0.0	–0.338	1.544	–1.344	–1.780	2.437	0.0

Parameters a and c can be determined directly from the values of b above.

CHAPTER 8

Measuring and Forecasting Yield Volatility*

Frank J. Fabozzi, Ph.D., CFA
Adjunct Professor of Finance
School of Management
Yale University

Wai Lee
Assistant Vice President
J.P. Morgan Investment Management Inc.

There are two critical components to an interest rate risk management system. The first component is an estimate of the price sensitivity of each fixed income security and derivative position to changes in interest rates. This estimate is typically obtained by changing rates by a small number of basis points and calculating based on a valuation model how the price changes. The result is an effective or option-adjusted duration measure. If the valuation model employed is poor, the resulting duration measure will not be a good estimate of the price sensitivity of an instrument to rate changes. A critical input to valuation models for cash market instruments with embedded options and option-like derivatives is the estimated yield volatility. The second component of an interest rate risk management system is the estimated yield volatility to assess the

* We are grateful for the many constructive comments of George Chacko of the Harvard Business School.

potential loss exposure. Consequently, yield volatility estimates play a dual role in an interest rate risk management system.

The previous chapters in this book discussed the measurement of interest rate exposure and the implementation of interest rate risk control strategies based on some expected yield volatility. The focus of the earlier chapters was not on the measurement of yield volatility. In this chapter, we look at how to measure and forecast yield volatility. Volatility is measured in terms of the standard deviation or variance. We begin this chapter with an explanation of how yield volatility as measured by the daily percentage change in yields is calculated from historical yields. We will see that there are several issues confronting a trader or investor in measuring historical yield volatility. Next we turn to modeling and forecasting yield volatility, looking at the state-of-the-art statistical techniques that can be employed.

CALCULATING THE STANDARD DEVIATION FROM HISTORICAL DATA

The variance of a random variable using historical data is calculated using the following formula:

$$\text{Variance} = \sum_{t=1}^{T} \frac{(X_t - \overline{X})^2}{T-1} \tag{1}$$

and then

$$\text{Standard deviation} = \sqrt{\text{Variance}}$$

where

X_t = observation t on variable X
$\overline{X}$ = the sample mean for variable X
T = the number of observations in the sample

Our focus in this chapter is on yield volatility. More specifically, we are interested in the percentage change in daily yields. So, X_t will denote the percentage change in yield from day t and the prior day, t–1. If we let y_t denote the yield on day t and y_{t-1} denote the yield on day t–1, then X_t which is the natural logarithm of percentage change in yield between two days, can be expressed as:

$$X_t = 100[\text{Ln}(y_t/y_{t-1})]$$

For example, on 10/18/95 the Treasury 30-year zero rate was 6.56% and on 10/19/95 it was 6.59%. Therefore, the natural logarithm of X for 10/19/95 is:

$$X = 100[\text{Ln}(6.593/6.555)] = 0.5780$$

To illustrate how to calculate a daily standard deviation from historical data, consider the data in Exhibit 8.1 which show the yield on Treasury 30-year zeros from 10/8/95 to 11/12/95 in the second column. From the 26 observations, 25 days of daily percentage yield changes are calculated in the third column. The fourth column shows the square of the deviations of the observations from the mean. The bottom of Exhibit 8.1 shows the calculation of the daily mean for the 25 observations, the variance, and the standard deviation. The daily standard deviation is 0.6360%.

The daily standard deviation will vary depending on the 25 days selected. For example, the daily yields from 8/20/95 to 9/24/95 were used to generate 25 daily percentage yield changes. The computed daily standard deviation was 0.8453%.

Determining the Number of Observations

In our illustration, we used 25 observations for the daily percentage change in yield. The appropriate number depends on the situation at hand. For example, traders concerned with overnight positions might use the 10 most recent days (i.e., two weeks). A bond portfolio manager who is concerned with longer term volatility might use 25 days (about one month).

The selection of the number of observations can have a significant effect on the calculated daily standard deviation. This can be seen in Exhibit 8.2 which shows the daily standard deviation for the Treasury 30-year zero, Treasury 10-year zero, Treasury 5-year zero, and 3-month LIBOR for 60 days, 25 days, 10 days, and 683 days ending 11/12/95.

Annualizing the Standard Deviation

If serial correlation is not significant, the daily standard deviation can be annualized by multiplying it by the square root of the number of days in a year. That is,

$$\text{Daily standard deviation} \times \sqrt{\text{Number of days in a year}}$$

EXHIBIT 8.1 Calculation of Daily Standard Deviation Based on 25 Daily Observations for 30-Year Treasury Zero (October 9, 1995 to November 12, 1995)

t	Date	y_t	$X_t = 100[\text{Ln}(y_t/y_{t-1})]$	$(X_t - \overline{X})^2$
0	08-Oct-95	6.694		
1	09-Oct-95	6.699	0.06720	0.02599
2	10-Oct-95	6.710	0.16407	0.06660
3	11-Oct-95	6.675	–0.52297	0.18401
4	12-Oct-95	6.555	–1.81311	2.95875
5	15-Oct-95	6.583	0.42625	0.27066
6	16-Oct-95	6.569	–0.21290	0.01413
7	17-Oct-95	6.583	0.21290	0.09419
8	18-Oct-95	6.555	–0.42625	0.11038
9	19-Oct-95	6.593	0.57804	0.45164
10	22-Oct-95	6.620	0.40869	0.25270
11	23-Oct-95	6.568	–0.78860	0.48246
12	24-Oct-95	6.575	0.10652	0.04021
13	25-Oct-95	6.646	1.07406	1.36438
14	26-Oct-95	6.607	–0.58855	0.24457
15	29-Oct-95	6.612	0.07565	0.02878
16	30-Oct-95	6.575	–0.56116	0.21823
17	31-Oct-95	6.552	–0.35042	0.06575
18	01-Nov-95	6.515	–0.56631	0.22307
19	02-Nov-95	6.533	0.27590	0.13684
20	05-Nov-95	6.543	0.15295	0.06099
21	06-Nov-95	6.559	0.24424	0.11441
22	07-Nov-95	6.500	–0.90360	0.65543
23	08-Nov-95	6.546	0.70520	0.63873
24	09-Nov-95	6.589	0.65474	0.56063
25	12-Nov-95	6.539	–0.76173	0.44586
		Total	–2.35020	9.7094094

$$\text{Sample mean} = \overline{X} = \frac{-2.35020}{25} = -0.09401\%$$

$$\text{Variance} = \frac{9.7094094}{25-1} = 0.4045587$$

$$\text{Std} = \sqrt{0.4045587} = 0.6360\%$$

EXHIBIT 8.2 Comparison of Daily and Annual Volatility for a Different Number of Observations (Ending Date November 12, 1995) for Various Instruments

Number. of Observations	Daily Standard Deviation (%)	Annualized Standard Deviation (%)		
		250 Days	260 Days	365 Days
Treasury 30-Year Zero				
683	0.4902	7.75	7.90	9.36
60	0.6283	9.93	10.13	12.00
25	0.6360	10.06	10.26	12.15
10	0.6242	9.87	10.06	11.93
Treasury 10-Year Zero				
683	0.7498	11.86	12.09	14.32
60	0.7408	11.71	11.95	14.15
25	0.7092	11.21	11.44	13.55
10	0.7459	11.79	12.03	14.25
Treasury 5-Year Zero				
683	1.0413	16.46	16.79	19.89
60	0.8267	13.07	13.33	15.79
25	0.7224	11.42	11.65	13.80
10	0.8346	13.20	13.46	15.94
3-Month LIBOR				
683	0.7496	11.85	12.09	14.32
60	0.2994	4.73	4.83	5.72
25	0.1465	2.32	2.36	2.80
10	0.2366	3.74	3.82	4.52

Market practice varies with respect to the number of days in the year that should be used in the annualizing formula above. Typically, either 250 days, 260 days, or 365 days are used.

Thus, in calculating an annual standard deviation, the manager must decide on:

1. The number of daily observations to use
2. The number of days in the year to use to annualize the daily standard deviation.

Exhibit 8.2 shows the difference in the annual standard deviation for the daily standard deviation based on the different number of observations and using 250 days, 260 days, and 365 days to annualize. Exhibit 8.3 compares the 25-day annual standard deviation for two different time periods for the 30-year zero, 10-year zero, 5-year zero, and 3-month LIBOR.

Reexamination of the Mean

Let's address the question of what mean should be used in the calculation of the forecasted standard deviation. Suppose at the end of 10/24/95 a trader is interested in a forecast for volatility using the 10 most recent days of trading and updating that forecast at the end of each trading day. What mean value should be used?

The trader can calculate a 10-day moving average of the daily percentage yield change. Exhibit 8.1 shows the daily percentage change in yield for the Treasury 30-year zero from 10/9/95 to 11/12/95. To calculate a moving average of the daily percentage yield change on 10/24/95, the trader would use the 10 trading days from 10/11/95 to 10/24/95. At the end of 10/25/95, the trader would calculate the 10-day average by using the percentage yield change on 11/25/95 and would exclude the percentage yield change on 10/11/95. That is, the trader would use the 10 trading days from 10/12/95 to 10/25/95.

EXHIBIT 8.3 Comparison of Daily Standard Deviation Calculated for Two 25-Day Periods for Various Instruments

Dates		Daily Standard	Annualized Standard Deviation(%)		
From	To	Deviation(%)	250 Days	260 Days	365 Days
Treasury 30-Year Zero					
10/8/95	11/12/95	0.6360	10.06	10.26	12.15
8/20/95	9/24/95	0.8453	13.36	13.63	16.15
Treasury 10-Year Zero					
10/8/95	11/12/95	0.7092	11.21	11.44	13.55
8/20/95	9/24/95	0.9045	14.30	14.58	17.28
Treasury 5-Year Zero					
10/8/95	11/12/95	0.7224	11.42	11.65	13.80
8/20/95	9/24/95	0.8145	12.88	13.13	15.56
3-Month LIBOR					
10/8/95	11/12/95	0.1465	2.32	2.36	2.80
8/20/95	9/24/95	0.2523	3.99	4.07	4.82

EXHIBIT 8.4 10-Day Moving Daily Average for Treasury 30-Year Zero

10 Trading Days Ending	Daily Average (%)
24-Oct-95	–0.203
25-Oct-95	–0.044
26-Oct-95	0.079
29-Oct-95	0.044
30-Oct-95	0.009
31-Oct-95	–0.047
01-Nov-95	–0.061
02-Nov-95	–0.091
05-Nov-95	–0.117
06-Nov-95	–0.014
07-Nov-95	–0.115
08-Nov-95	–0.152
09-Nov-95	–0.027
12-Nov-95	–0.111

Exhibit 8.4 shows the 10-day moving average calculated from 10/24/95 to 11/12/95. Notice the considerable variation over this period. The 10-day moving average ranges from –0.203% to 0.079%. For the period from 4/15/93 to 11/12/95, the 10-day moving average ranged from –0.617% to 0.603%.

Rather than using a moving average, it is more appropriate to use an expectation of the average. Longerstacey and Zangari argue that it would be more appropriate to use a mean value of zero.[1] In that case, the variance as given by equation (1) simplifies to:

$$\text{Variance} = \sum_{t=1}^{T} \frac{X_t^2}{T-1} \qquad (2)$$

Weighting of Observations

The daily standard deviation given by equations (1) and (2) assigns an equal weight to all observations. So, if a trader is calculating volatility based on the most recent 10 days of trading, each day is given a weight of 10%.

[1] Jacques Longerstacey and Peter Zangari, *Five Questions about RiskMetrics™*, JP Morgan Research Publication 1995.

EXHIBIT 8.5 Moving Daily Standard Deviation Based on 10 Days of Observations

10 Trading Days Ending	Daily Standard Deviation (%)
24-Oct-95	0.757
25-Oct-95	0.819
26-Oct-95	0.586
29-Oct-95	0.569
30-Oct-95	0.595
31-Oct-95	0.602
01-Nov-95	0.615
02-Nov-95	0.591
05-Nov-95	0.577
06-Nov-95	0.520
07-Nov-95	0.600
08-Nov-95	0.536
09-Nov-95	0.544
12-Nov-95	0.600

For example, suppose that a trader is interested in the daily volatility of the Treasury 30-year zero yield and decides to use the 10 most recent trading days. Exhibit 8.5 reports the 10-day volatility for various days using the data in Exhibit 8.1 and the formula for the variance given by equation (2). For the period 4/15/93 to 11/12/95, the 10-day volatility ranged from 0.164% to 1.330%.

In April 1995, the Basle Committee on Banking Supervision at the Bank for International Settlements proposed that volatility (as measured by the standard deviation) be calculated based on an equal weighting of daily historical observations using one year of observations.[2] Moreover, the committee proposed that volatility estimates should be updated at least quarterly.[3]

However, there is reason to suspect that market participants give greater weight to recent movements in yield when determining volatility. Moreover, what has been observed in several studies of the stock market is that high periods of volatility are followed by high periods of volatility.

[2] The proposal, entitled "The Supervisory Treatment of Market Risks," is an amendment to the *1988 Basle Capital Accord*.

[3] RiskMetrics™ has a "Special Regulatory Dataset" that incorporates the 1-year moving average proposed by the Basle Committee. Rather than updating at least quarterly as proposed by the Basle Committee, the dataset is updated daily.

To give greater importance to more recent information, observations further in the past should be given less weight. This can be done by revising the variance as given by equation (2) as follows:

$$\text{Variance} = \sum_{t=1}^{T} \frac{W_t X_t^2}{T-1} \tag{3}$$

where W_t is the weight assigned to observation t such that the sum of the weights is equal to 1 (i.e., $\sum W_t = 1$) and the further the observation from today, the lower the weight.

The weights should be assigned so that the forecasted volatility reacts faster to a recent major market movement and declines gradually as we move away from any major market movement. The approach by JP Morgan in RiskMetrics™ is to use an *exponential moving average*. The formula for the weight W_t in an exponential moving average is:

$$W_t = (1 - \beta)\beta^t$$

where β is a value between 0 and 1. The observations are arrayed so that the closest observation is $t = 1$, the second closest is $t = 2$, etc.

For example, if β is 0.90, then the weight for the closest observation ($t = 1$) is:

$$W_1 = (1 - 0.90)\,(0.90)^1 = 0.09$$

For $t = 5$ and β equal to 0.90, the weight is:

$$W_5 = (1 - 0.90)\,(0.90)^5 = 0.05905$$

The parameter β is measuring how quickly the information contained in past observations is "decaying" and hence is referred to as the "decay factor." The smaller the β, the faster the decay. What decay factor to use depends on how fast the mean value for the random variable X changes over time. A random variable whose mean value changes slowly over time will have a decay factor close to 1. A discussion of how the decay factor should be selected is beyond the scope of this chapter.[4]

[4] A technical description is provided in *RiskMetrics™—Technical Document*, pp. 77–79.

MODELING AND FORECASTING YIELD VOLATILITY

Generally speaking, there are two ways to model yield volatility. The first way is by estimating historical yield volatility by some time series model. The resulting volatility is called *historical volatility*. The second way is to estimate yield volatility based on the observed prices of interest rate derivatives. Yield volatility calculated using this approach is called *implied volatility*. In this section, we discuss these two approaches, with more emphasis on historical volatility. As will be explained later, computing implied volatility from interest rate derivatives is not as simple and straightforward as from derivatives of other asset classes such as equity. Apart from assuming that a particular option pricing model is correct, we also need to model the time evolution of the complete term structure and volatilities of yields of different maturities. This relies on state-of-the-art modeling technique as well as superior computing power.

Historical Volatility

We begin the discussion with a general stochastic process of which yield, or interest rate, is assumed to follow:

$$dy = \mu(y, t)dt + \sigma(y, t)dW \tag{4}$$

where y is the yield, μ is the expected instantaneous change (or drift) of yield, σ is the instantaneous standard deviation (volatility), and W is a standard Brownian motion such that the change in W (dW) is normally distributed with mean zero and variance of dt. Both μ and σ are functions of the current yield y and time t.

Since we focus on volatility in this chapter, we leave the drift term in its current general form. It can be shown that many of the volatility models are special cases of this general form. For example, assuming that the functional form of volatility is

$$\sigma(y, t) = \sigma_0 y \tag{5}$$

such that the yield volatility is equal to the product of a constant, σ_0, and the current yield level, we can rewrite equation (4) as[5]

$$d\ln y = \mu'(y, t)dt + \sigma_0 dW \tag{6}$$

[5] Equation (6) is obtained by application of Ito's Lemma. We omit the details here.

The discrete time version of this process will be

$$\ln y_{t+1} = \ln y_t + \mu' + \sigma_0(W_{t+1} - W_t) \quad (7)$$

Thus, when we calculate yield volatility by looking at the natural logarithm of percentage change in yield between two days as in the earlier section, we are assuming that yield follows a log-normal distribution, or, the natural logarithm of yield follows a normal distribution. σ_0, in this case, can be interpreted as the *proportional yield volatility*, as the yield volatility is obtained by multiplying σ_0 with the current yield. In this case, yield volatility is proportional to the level of the yield. We call the above model the *Constant Proportional Yield Volatility Model* (*CP*).

This simple assumption offers many advantages. Since the natural logarithm of a negative number is meaningless, a log-normal distribution assumption for yield guarantees that yield is always non-negative. Evidence also suggests that volatility of yield increases with the level of yield. A simple intuition is for scale reasons. Thus, while the volatility of changes in yield is unstable over time since the level of yield changes, the volatility of changes in natural logarithm of yield is relatively stable, as it already incorporates the changes in yield level. As a result, the natural logarithm of yield can be a more useful process to examine.[6]

A potential drawback of the CP model is that it assumes that the proportional yield volatility itself is constant, which does not depend on time nor on the yield level. In fact, there exists a rich class of yield volatility models that includes the CP model as a special case. We call this group the *Power Function Model.*[7]

Power Function Model

For simplicity of exposition, we write the yield volatility as σ_t, which is understood to be a function of time and level of yield. For example, consider the following representation of yield volatility:

$$\sigma_t = \sigma_0 y_{t-1}^{\gamma} \quad (8)$$

In this way, yield volatility is proportional to a power function of yield. The following are examples of the volatility models assumed in some

[6] See Thomas S. Coleman, Lawrence Fisher, and Roger G. Ibbotson, "A Note on Interest Rate Volatility," *Journal of Fixed Income* (March 1993), pp. 97–101, for a similar conclusion.

[7] In the finance literature, this is also known as the *Constant Elasticity of Variance Model.*

well known interest rate models, which can be represented as special cases of equation (8):

1. $\gamma = 0$: Vasicek,[8] Ho-Lee[9]
2. $\gamma = 0.5$: Cox-Ingersoll-Ross (CIR)[10]
3. $\gamma = 1$: Black,[11] Brennan-Schwartz[12]

The Vasicek model and Ho-Lee model maintain an assumption of a normally distributed interest rate process. Simply speaking, yield volatility is assumed to be constant, independent of time, and independent of yield level. Theoretically, when the interest rate is low enough while yield volatility remains constant, this model allows the interest rate to go below zero.

The CIR model assumes that yield volatility is a constant multiple of the square root of yield. Its volatility specification is thus also known as the *Square Root Model.* Since the square root of a negative number is meaningless, the CIR model does not allow yield to become negative. Strictly speaking, the functional form of equation (8) only applies to the instantaneous interest rate, but not to any yield of longer maturities within the CIR framework. To be specific, when applied to, say, the 10-year yield, yield volatility is obtained from the stochastic process of the 10-year yield, which can be derived from the closed-form solution for the bond price. To simplify the discussion, we go with the current simple form instead.

The volatility assumption in the Black model and Brennan-Schwartz model is equivalent to the previous CP model. In other words, yield is assumed to be log-normally distributed with constant proportional yield volatility.

Many of these functional forms for yield volatility are adopted primarily because they lead to closed-form solutions for pricing of bonds, bond options, and other interest rate derivatives, as well as for simplicity and convenience. There is no simple answer for which form is the best. However, it is generally thought that $\gamma = 0$, or a normal distribution with constant yield volatility, is an inappropriate description of an interest rate

[8] Oldrich Vasicek, "An Equilibrium Characterization of the Term Structure," *Journal of Financial Economics* (1977), pp. 177–188.

[9] Thomas S.Y. Ho and Sang-Bin Lee, "Term Structure Movements and Pricing Interest Rate Contingent Claims," *Journal of Finance* (1986), pp. 1011–1029.

[10] John C. Cox, Jonathan E. Ingersoll, and Stephen A. Ross, "A Theory of the Term Structure of Interest Rates," *Econometrica* (1985), pp. 385–407.

[11] Fischer Black, "The Pricing of Commodity Contracts," *Journal of Financial Economics* (1976), pp. 167–179.

[12] Michael Brennan and Eduardo Schwartz, "A Continuous Time Approach to the Pricing of Bonds," *Journal of Banking and Finance* (1979), pp. 133–155.

process, even though the occasions of observing negative interest rate in the model is found to be rare. As a result, many practitioners adopt the CP model, as it is straightforward enough, while it eliminates the drawback of the normal distribution.

One way to determine which yield volatility functional form to use is to empirically estimate the model with historical data. To illustrate, we use the 3-month, 10-year, and 30-year spot yields as examples. These yields are obtained by spline fitting the yield curve of Treasury strips every day within the sample period. We use the daily data from January 1, 1986 to July 31, 1997. To be consistent with the previous section, we assume that the average daily yield change is zero. Thus, the model to be estimated is:

$$y_t - y_{t-1} = \varepsilon_t$$

$$E[\varepsilon_t^2] = \sigma_t^2 = \sigma_0^2 y_{t-1}^{2\gamma} \tag{9}$$

where E[.] denotes the statistical expectation operator. The econometric technique employed is the Maximum Likelihood Estimation (MLE).[13] We assume a conditional normal distribution for changes in yield, after the dependence of volatility on level of yield has been incorporated. The details of this technique are beyond the scope of this chapter.[14] The results are reported in Exhibit 8.6, where an 8.00% yield is written as 0.08, for example.

Volatility of yields of all three maturities are found to increase with the level of yield, but to a different extent. As the results suggest, assuming the same value of γ for yields of all maturities can be inappropriate. For the 3-month spot yield, γ is found to be about 0.25, significantly below the 0.5 assumed in the CIR model. For the 10-year spot yield, γ is about 0.57, close to CIR's assumption. Finally, for the 30-year spot yield, γ is about

[13] The model can also be estimated by Generalized Method of Moments (GMM), which does not impose any distributional assumption. We use MLE here in order to be consistent with the estimation of GARCH models to be discussed later. See K.C. Chan, G. Andrew Karolyi, Francis A. Longstaff, and Anthony B. Sanders, "An Empirical Comparison of Alternative Models of the Short-Term Interest Rate," *Journal of Finance* (July 1992), pp. 1209–1227, for a similar treatment. Also see Timothy G. Conley, Lars Peter Hansen, Erzo G.J. Luttmer, and José A. Scheinkman, "Short-Term Interest Rates as Subordinated Diffusions," *Review of Financial Studies* (Fall 1997), pp. 525–577, for a more rigorous treatment.

[14] Readers can consult James Hamilton, *Time Series Analysis* (Princeton, NJ: Princeton University Press, 1994). Also, there is some evidence that a conditional *t*-distribution is more appropriate for interest rate data. For simplicity, we maintain the conditional normal here.

1.27, significantly above the value of 1 assumed in the CP model. Furthermore, as the previous section mentioned, using different time periods can lead to different estimates. For instance, the behavior of interest rates in the late 1970s and the early 1980s were very different from those in the last decade. As a result, one should not be surprised that the dependence of volatility on the yield level might appear to be different from the last decade.

To illustrate the use of the Power Function Model, Exhibit 8.7 plots the forecasted volatility of the 30-year spot yield based on the estimates in Exhibit 8.6. For comparison purposes, we also plot the forecasted volatility when we impose the restriction of $\gamma = 1$. In the latter case, we are actually estimating the constant proportional yield volatility, σ_0, using the whole sample period. The value denotes the yield volatility on each day, annualized by 250 days.

EXHIBIT 8.6 Estimation of Power Function Models*

	3-Month Treasury Bill	10-Year Treasury Zero	30-Year Treasury Zero
σ_0	0.0019	0.0027	0.0161
	(12.31)	(11.00)	(5.58)
γ	0.2463	0.5744	1.2708
	(8.88)	(15.71)	(18.03)

* *t*-statistics are reported in parentheses.

EXHIBIT 8.7 250-Day Annualized Yield Volatility of 30-Year Spot Yield: Power Function Model

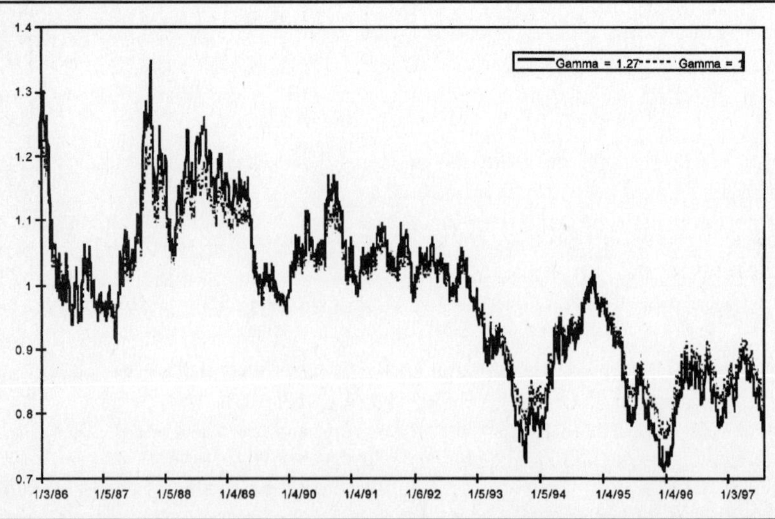

As shown in Exhibit 8.7, using the CP model with constant proportional yield volatility ($\gamma = 1$) does not significantly differ from using the estimated value of $\gamma = 1.27$.

One critique of the Power Function Model is the fact that while it allows volatility to depend on the yield level, it does not incorporate the observation that a volatile period tends to be followed by another volatile period, a phenomenon known as *volatility clustering*. Nor does it allow past yield shocks to affect current and future volatility. To tackle these problems, we introduce a very different class of volatility modeling and forecasting tool.

Generalized Autoregressive Conditional Heteroskedasticity Model

Generalized Autoregressive Conditional Heteroskedasticity (GARCH) Model is probably the most extensively applied family of volatility models in empirical finance. It is well known that statistical distributions of many financial prices and returns series exhibit fatter tails than a normal distribution. These characteristics can be captured with a GARCH model. In fact, some well-known interest rate models, such as the Longstaff-Schwartz model, adopt GARCH to model yield volatility, which is allowed to be stochastic.[15] The term "conditional" means that the value of the variance depends on or is conditional on the information available, typically by means of the realized values of other random variables. The term "heteroskedasticity" means that the variance is not the same for all values of the random variable at different time periods.

If we maintain the assumption that the average daily yield change is zero, as before, the standard GARCH(1,1) model can be written as:

$$y_t - y_{t-1} = \varepsilon_t$$

$$E[\varepsilon_t^2] = \sigma_t^2 = a_0 + a_1\varepsilon_{t-1}^2 + a_2\sigma_{t-1}^2 \qquad (10)$$

where ε_t is just the daily yield change, interpreted as yield shock, E[.] denotes the statistical expectation operator, a_0, a_1, and a_2 are parameters to be estimated. In this way, yield volatility this period depends on

[15] Francis A. Longstaff and Eduardo S. Schwartz, "Interest Rate Volatility and the Term Structure: A Two-Factor General Equilibrium Model," *Journal of Finance* (1992), pp. 1259–1282. Also see Francis A. Longstaff and Eduardo S. Schwartz, "Implementation of the Longstaff-Schwartz Interest Rate Model," *Journal of Fixed Income* (1993), pp. 7–14 for practical implementation of the model and how yield volatility is modeled by GARCH.

yield shock as well as yield volatility in the last period. The GARCH model also estimates the long-run equilibrium variance, ω, as

$$E[\varepsilon_t^2] = \overline{\omega} = \frac{a_0}{1 - a_1 - a_2} \tag{11}$$

The GARCH model is popular not only for its simplicity in specification and its parsimonious nature in capturing time series properties of volatilities, but also because it is a generalization of some other measures of volatility. For example, it has been shown that equal-weighted rolling sample measure of variance and exponential smoothing scheme of volatility measure are both special cases of GARCH, but with different restrictions on the parameters. Other technical details of GARCH are beyond the scope of this chapter.[16]

Experience has shown that a GARCH(1,1) specification generally fits the volatility of most financial time series well, and is quite robust. The unknown parameters can again be estimated using MLE. The estimated models for the yields on 3-month Treasury bills and the 10-year and 30-year Treasury zeros are reported in Exhibit 8.8. Again, we plot the forecasted yield volatility, annualized by 250 days, of the 30-year spot rate in Exhibit 8.9 as an example.

EXHIBIT 8.8 Estimation of GARCH(1,1) Models

	3-Month Treasury Bill	10-Year Treasury Zero	30-Year Treasury Zero
a_0	1.6467×10^{-8}	3.0204×10^{-8}	1.6313×10^{-8}
	(17.85)	(1.59)	(8.65)
a_1	0.0878	0.0896	0.0583
	(15.74)	(12.19)	(12.44)
a_2	0.8951	0.8441	0.9011
	(211.36)	(122.12)	(123.43)

[16] See, for example, Robert F. Engle, "Statistical Models for Financial Volatility," *Financial Analysts Journal* (1993), pp. 72–78; and Wai Lee and John Yin, "Modeling and Forecasting Interest Rate Volatility with GARCH," Chapter 20 in Frank J. Fabozzi (ed.), *Advances in Fixed Income Valuation Modeling and Risk Management* (New Hope, PA: FJF Associates, Pennsylvania, 1997), for an extensive discussion of GARCH as well as many other extensions.

EXHIBIT 8.9 250-Day Annualized Yield Volatility of 30-Year Spot Yield: GARCH(1,1) Model

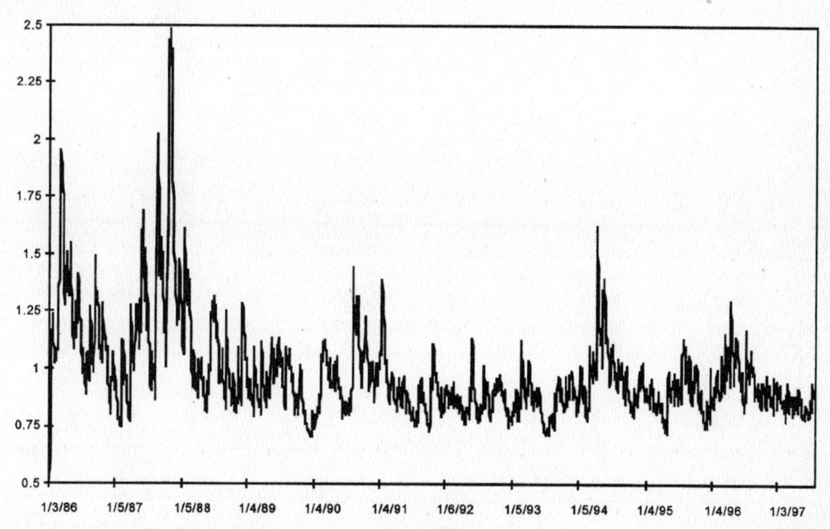

One can immediately see that GARCH volatility is very different from the previous Power Function volatility. The reason is that GARCH incorporates the random and often erratic yield shocks as well as serial dependence in yield volatility into the volatility model; in contrast, the Power Function model only allows yield volatility to depend on the *level* of yield, without considering how past yield shocks and volatilities may affect the future volatility. The phenomenon of volatility clustering is well captured by GARCH, as revealed in Exhibit 8.9. On the other hand, the above GARCH(1,1) model does not consider the possible dependence of yield volatility on the level of yield. Thus, theoretically, GARCH volatilities do allow yields to become negative, which is an undesirable feature.

Power Function—GARCH Models

To capture the strength of both classes of models, one may consider combining the two into a more general form, at the expense of more complicated modeling and estimation, however. One way is to adopt the functional form of the Power Function model, while allowing the proportional yield volatility to follow a GARCH process. For example:

EXHIBIT 8.10 Estimation of Power Function—GARCH(1,1) Models

	3-Month Treasury Bill	10-Year Treasury Zero	30-Year Treasury Zero
a_0	8.6802×10^{-7}	3.6185×10^{-7}	3.8821×10^{-7}
	(1.59)	(1.23)	(1.37)
a_1	0.1836	0.0556	0.0717
	(12.73)	(11.07)	(14.20)
a_2	0.6424	0.8920	0.8015
	(34.53)	(48.52)	(5.40)
γ	0.2094	0.3578	0.3331
	(10.33)	(28.20)	(6.94)

$$y_t - y_{t-1} = \varepsilon_t$$

$$\sigma_t = \sigma_{0,t} y_{t-1}^{\gamma} \tag{12}$$

$$\sigma_{0,t}^2 = a_0 + a_1 \varepsilon_{t-1}^2 + a_2 \sigma_{0,t-1}^2$$

With the above specification, yield volatility still depends on the level of yield, while past shocks and volatility affect current and future volatility through the proportional yield volatility, σ_0, which is now time varying instead of being a constant.[17] The estimation results are reported in Exhibit 8.10.

A noticeable difference between Exhibit 8.6 and Exhibit 8.10 is the fact that once the proportional yield volatility is modeled as a GARCH(1,1), γ assumes a smaller value than when yield volatility is only modeled as a power function of yield. In fact, γ for all maturities are all below 0.5, as assumed by the CIR model. This suggests that it is important to incorporate the dependence of current yield volatility on past information, or the sensitivity of yield volatility on level of yield may be overstated. For comparison purposes, Exhibit 8.11 plots the 250-day annualized yield volatility of the 30-year spot rate based on the estimated model in Exhibit 8.10.

[17] See Robin J. Brenner, Richard H. Harjes, and Kenneth F. Kroner, "Another Look at Models of the Short-Term Interest Rate," *Journal of Financial and Quantitative Analysis* (March 1996), pp. 85–107, for a similar treatment and extensions.

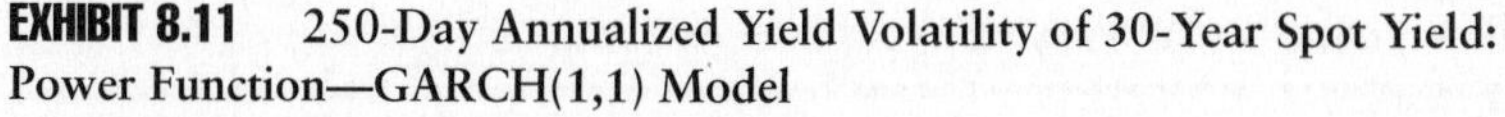

EXHIBIT 8.11 250-Day Annualized Yield Volatility of 30-Year Spot Yield: Power Function—GARCH(1,1) Model

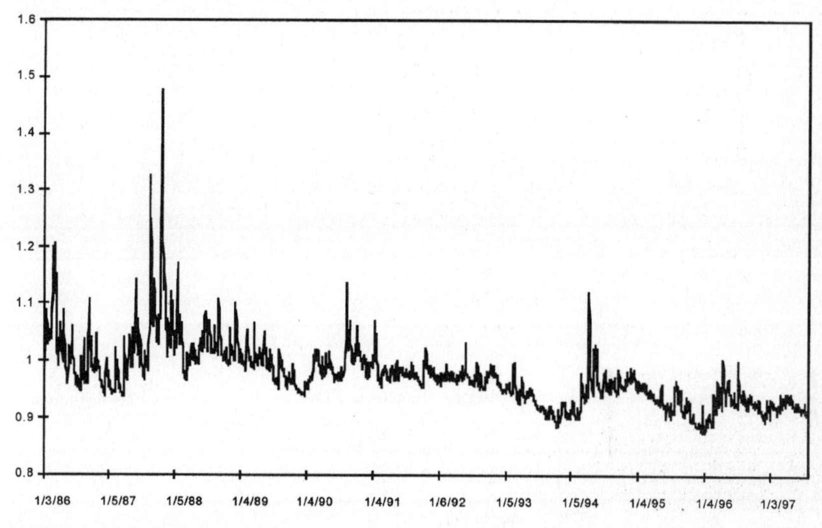

Implied Volatility

The second way to estimate yield volatility is based on the observed prices of interest rate derivatives, such as options on bond futures, or interest rate caps and floors. Yield volatility calculated using this approach is called *implied volatility.*

The implied volatility is based on some option pricing model. One of the inputs to any option pricing model in which the underlying is a Treasury security or Treasury futures contract is expected yield volatility. If the observed price of an option is assumed to be the fair price and the option pricing model is assumed to be the model that would generate that fair price, then the implied yield volatility is the yield volatility that when used as an input into the option pricing model would produce the observed option price. Because of their liquidity, options on Treasury futures, Eurodollar futures, and caps and floors on LIBOR are typically used to extract implied volatilities.

Computing implied volatilities of yield from interest rate derivatives is not as straight forward as from derivatives of, say, stock. Later in this section, we will explain that these implied volatilities are not only model-dependent, but on some occasions they are also difficult to interpret, and can be misleading as well. For the time being, we follow the common practice in the industry of using the Black option pricing model for futures.[18]

Although the Black model has many limitations and inconsistent assumptions, it has been widely adopted. Traders often quote the exchange-traded options on Treasury or Eurodollar futures in terms of implied volatilities based on the Black model. These implied volatilities are also published by some investment houses, and are available through data vendors. For illustration purposes, we use the data of CBOT traded call options on 30-year Treasury bond futures as of April 30, 1997. The contract details, as well as the extracted implied volatilities based on the Black model, are listed in Exhibit 8.12.

EXHIBIT 8.12 Call Options on 30-Year Treasury Bond Futures on April 30, 1997

Delivery Month	Futures Price	Strike Price	Option Price	Implied Price Volatility	Duration	Implied Yield Volatility
1997:6	109.281	105	4.297	9.334	9.57	0.975
1997:6	109.281	106	3.328	9.072	9.57	0.948
1997:6	109.281	107	2.406	8.811	9.57	0.921
1997:6	109.281	108	1.594	8.742	9.57	0.913
1997:6	109.281	109	0.938	8.665	9.57	0.905
1997:6	109.281	110	0.469	8.462	9.57	0.884
1997:6	109.281	111	0.188	8.205	9.57	0.857
1997:6	109.281	112	0.062	8.129	9.57	0.849
1997:6	109.281	113	0.016	7.993	9.57	0.835
1997:6	109.281	114	0.016	9.726	9.57	1.016
1997:6	109.281	116	0.016	13.047	9.57	1.363
1997:6	109.281	118	0.016	16.239	9.57	1.697
1997:6	109.281	120	0.016	19.235	9.57	2.010
1997:6	109.281	122	0.016	22.168	9.57	2.316
1997:6	109.281	124	0.016	25.033	9.57	2.616
1997:6	109.281	126	0.016	27.734	9.57	2.898
1997:6	109.281	128	0.016	30.392	9.57	3.176
1997:6	109.281	130	0.016	33.01	9.57	3.449
1997:9	108.844	100	8.922	8.617	9.54	0.903
1997:9	108.844	102	7.062	8.750	9.54	0.917
1997:9	108.844	104	5.375	8.999	9.54	0.943
1997:9	108.844	106	3.875	9.039	9.54	0.947

[18] Black, "The Pricing of Commodity Contracts."

EXHIBIT 8.12 (Continued)

Delivery Month	Futures Price	Strike Price	Option Price	Implied Price Volatility	Duration	Implied Yield Volatility
1997:9	108.844	108	2.625	9.008	9.54	0.944
1997:9	108.844	110	1.656	8.953	9.54	0.938
1997:9	108.844	112	0.969	8.913	9.54	0.934
1997:9	108.844	114	0.516	8.844	9.54	0.927
1997:9	108.844	116	0.250	8.763	9.54	0.919
1997:9	108.844	118	0.109	8.679	9.54	0.910
1997:9	108.844	120	0.047	8.733	9.54	0.915
1997:9	108.844	122	0.016	8.581	9.54	0.899
1997:9	108.844	124	0.016	9.625	9.54	1.009
1997:9	108.844	126	0.016	10.646	9.54	1.116
1997:9	108.844	128	0.016	11.65	9.54	1.221
1997:12	108.469	98	10.562	7.861	9.51	0.827
1997:12	108.469	106	4.250	9.036	9.51	0.950
1997:12	108.469	108	3.125	9.070	9.51	0.954
1997:12	108.469	110	2.188	9.006	9.51	0.947
1997:12	108.469	112	1.469	8.953	9.51	0.941
1997:12	108.469	114	0.938	8.881	9.51	0.934
1997:12	108.469	116	0.594	8.949	9.51	0.941
1997:12	108.469	118	0.359	8.973	9.51	0.944
1997:12	108.469	120	0.234	9.232	9.51	0.971
1997:12	108.469	122	0.141	9.340	9.51	0.982
1997:12	108.469	128	0.031	9.793	9.51	1.030

Since the options are written on futures prices, the implied volatilities computed directly from the Black model are thus the implied price volatilities of the underlying futures contract. To convert the implied price volatilities to implied yield volatilities, we need the duration of the corresponding cheapest-to-deliver Treasury bond. The conversion is based on the simple standard relationship between percentage change in bond price and change in yield:

$$\frac{\Delta P}{P} \approx -\text{Duration} \times \Delta y \tag{13}$$

which implies that the same relationship also holds for price volatility and yield volatility.

Looking at the implied yield volatilities of the options with the same delivery month, one can immediately notice the "volatility smile." For example, for the options with a delivery month in June 1997, the implied yield volatility starts at a value of 0.98% for the deep in-the-money option with a strike price of 105, steadily drops to a minimum of 0.84% for the out-of-money option with a strike price of 113, and rises back to a maximum of 3.45% for the deep out-of-money option with a strike price of 130. Since all the options with the same delivery month are written on the same underlying bond futures, the only difference is their strike prices. The question is, which implied volatility is correct? While the answer to this question largely depends on how we accommodate the volatility smile,[19] standard practice suggests that we use the implied volatility of the at-the-money, or the nearest-the money option. In this case, the implied yield volatility of 0.91% of the option with a strike price of 109 should be used

What is the meaning of an "implied yield volatility of 0.91%"? To interpret this number, one needs to be aware that this number is extracted from the observed option price based on the Black model. As a result, the meaning of this number not only depends on the assumption that the market correctly prices the option, but also the fact that the market prices the option in accordance with the Black model. Neither of these assumptions need to hold. In fact, most probably, both assumptions are unrealistic. Given these assumptions, one may interpret that the option market expects a *constant* annualized yield volatility of 0.91% for 30-year Treasury from April 30, 1997 to the maturity date of the option. Caps and floors can also be priced by the Black model, when they are interpreted as portfolios of options written on forward interest rates. Accordingly, implied volatilities can be extracted from cap prices and floor prices, but subjected to the same limitations of the Black model.

Limitations of the Black Model

There are two major assumptions of the Black model that makes it unrealistic. First, interest rates are assumed to be constant. Yet, the assumption is used to derive the pricing formula for the option which derives its payoff precisely from the fact that future interest rates (forward rates) are stochastic. It has been shown that the Black model implies a time evolution path for the term structure that leads to arbitrage opportunities. In other words, the model itself implicitly violates the no-arbitrage spirit in derivatives pricing.

[19] Current research typically uses either a jump diffusion process, a stochastic volatility model, or a combination of both to explain volatility smile. The details are beyond the scope of this chapter.

Second, volatilities of futures prices, or forward interest rates, are assumed to be constant over the life of the contract. This assumption is in sharp contrary to empirical evidence as well as intuition. It is well understood that a forward contract with one month to maturity is more sensitive to changes in the current term structure than a forward contract with one year to maturity. Thus, the volatility of the forward rate is inversely related to the time to maturity.

Finally, on the average, implied volatilities from the Black model are found to be higher than the realized volatilities during the same period of time.[20] A plausible explanation is that the difference in the two volatilities represents the fee for the financial service provided by the option writers, while the exact dynamics of the relationship between implied and realized volatilities remains unclear.

Practical Uses of Implied Volatilities from the Black Model

Typically, implied volatilities from exchange-traded options with sufficient liquidity are used to price over-the-counter interest rate derivatives such as caps, floors, and swaptions. Apart from the limitations as discussed above, another difficulty in practice is the fact that only options with some fixed maturities are traded. For example, in Exhibit 8.12, the *constant* implied volatilities only apply to the time periods from April 30, 1997 to the delivery dates in June, September, and December 1997, respectively. For instance, on May 1, 1997, we need a volatility input to price a 3-month cap on LIBOR. In this case, traders will either use the implied volatility from options with maturities closest to three months, or make an adjustment/judgment based on the implied volatilities of options with maturities just shorter than three months, and options with maturities just longer than three months.

Recent Development in Implied Volatilities

The finance industry is not unaware of the limitations of the Black model and its implied volatilities. Due to its simplicity and its early introduction to the market, it has become the standard in computing implied volatilities. However, there has been a tremendous amount of rigorous research going on in interest rate and interest rate derivatives models, especially since the mid 1980s. While a comprehensive review of this research is not provided here, it is useful to highlight the broad classes of models, which can help us understand where implied volatilities related research is going.

[20] See Laurie Goodman and Jeffrey Ho, "Are Investors Rewarded for Shorting Volatility?" *Journal of Fixed Income* (June 1997), pp. 38–42, for a comparison of implied versus realized volatility.

Broadly speaking, there are two classes of models. The first class is known as the *Equilibrium Model.* Some noticeable examples include the Vasciek model, CIR model, Brennan-Schwartz model, and Longstaff-Schwartz model, as mentioned earlier in this chapter. This class of models attempts to specify the equilibrium conditions by assuming that some state variables drive the evolution of the term structure. By imposing other structure and restrictions, closed-form solutions for equilibrium prices of bonds and other interest rate derivatives are then derived. Many of these models impose a functional form to interest rate volatility, such as the power function as discussed and estimated earlier, or assume that volatility follows certain dynamics. In addition, the models also specify a particular dynamics on how interest rate drifts up or down over time. To implement these models, one needs to estimate the parameters of the interest rate process, including the parameters of the volatility function, based on some advanced econometric technique applied to historical data.

There are two major shortcomings of this class of models. First, these models are not preference-free, which means that we need to specify the utility function in dictating how investors make choices. Second, since only historical data are used in calibrating the models, these models do not rule out arbitrage opportunities in the current term structure. Due to the nature of the models, volatility is an important input to these models rather than an output that we can extract from observed prices. In addition, it has been shown that the term structure of spot yield volatilities can differ across one-factor versions of these models despite the fact that all produce the same term structure of cap prices.[21]

The second class of models is known as the *No-Arbitrage Model.* The *Ho-Lee Model* is considered as the first model of this class. Other examples include the *Black-Derman-Toy Model,*[22] *Black-Karasinski Model,*[23] and the *Heath-Jarrow-Morton Model* (*HJM*).[24] In contrast to the equilibrium models which attempt to model equilibrium, these no-arbitrage models are less ambitious. They take the current term structure as given, and assume that no arbitrage opportunities are allowed during the evolution of the entire term structure. All interest rate sensi-

[21] Eduardo Canabarro, "Where Do One-Factor Interest Rate Models Fail?" *Journal of Fixed Income* (September 1995), pp. 31–52.

[22] Fischer Black, Emanuel Derman, and William Toy, "A One-Factor Model of Interest Rates and its Applications to Treasury Bond Options," *Financial Analysts Journal* (January–February 1990), pp. 33–39.

[23] Fischer Black and Piotr Karasinski, "Bond and Option Pricing when Short Rates are Lognormal," *Financial Analysts Journal* (1991), pp. 52–59.

[24] David Heath, Robert Jarrow, and Andrew Morton, "Bond Pricing and the Term-Structure of Interest Rates: A New Methodology," *Econometrica* (1992), pp. 77–105.

tive securities are assumed to be correctly priced at the time of calibrating the model. In this way, the models, together with the current term structure and the no-arbitrage assumption, impose some restrictions on how interest rates of different maturities will evolve over time. Some restrictions on the volatility structure may be imposed in order to allow interest rates to mean-revert, or to restrict interest rates to be positive under all circumstances. However, since these models take the current bond prices as given, more frequent recalibration of the models is required once bond prices change.

The HJM model, in particular, has received considerable attention in the industry as well as in the finance literature. Many other no-arbitrage models are shown to be special cases of HJM. In spirit, the HJM model is similar to the well-celebrated Black-Scholes model in the sense that the model does not require assumptions about investor preferences.[25] Much like the Black-Scholes model that requires volatility instead of expected stock return as an input to price a stock option, the HJM model only requires a description of the volatility structure of forward interest rates, instead of the expected interest rate movements in pricing interest rate derivatives. It is this feature of the model that, given current prices of interest rate derivatives, make extraction of implied volatilities possible.

Amin and Morton[26] and Amin and Ng[27] use this approach to extract a term structure of implied volatilities. Several points are noteworthy. Since the no-arbitrage assumption is incorporated into the model, the extracted implied volatilities are more meaningful than those from the Black model. Moreover, interest rates are all stochastic instead of being assumed constant. On the other hand, these implied volatilities are those of forward interest rates, instead of spot interest rates. Furthermore, interest rate derivatives with different maturities and sufficient liquidity are required to calibrate the model. Finally, the HJM model is often criticized as too complicated for practitioners, and is too slow for real-time practical applications.[28]

---

[25] This by no means implies that the Black-Scholes model is a no-arbitrage model. Although no-arbitrage condition is enforced, the Black-Scholes model does require equilibrium settings and market clearing conditions. Further details are beyond the scope of this chapter.

[26] Kaushik I. Amin and Andrew J. Morton, "Implied Volatility Functions in Arbitrage-Free Term Structure Models," *Journal of Financial Economics* (1994), pp. 141–180.

[27] Kaushik I. Amin and Victor K. Ng, "Inferring Future Volatility from the Information in Implied Volatility in Eurodollar Options: A New Approach," *Review of Financial Studies* (1997), pp 333–367.

[28] See David Heath, Robert Jarrow, Andrew Morton, and Mark Spindel, "Easier Done than Said," *Risk* (October 1992), pp. 77–80 for a response to this critique.

SUMMARY

Yield volatility estimates play a critical role in the measurement and control of interest rate risk. In this chapter we have discussed how historical yield volatility is calculated and the issues that are associated with its estimate. These issues include the number of observations and the time period to be used, the number of days that should be used to annualize the daily standard deviation, the expected value that should be used, and the weighting of observations. We then looked at modeling and forecasting yield volatility. The two approaches we discussed are historical volatility and implied volatility. For the historical volatility approach, we discussed various models, their underlying assumptions, and their limitations. These models include the Power Function Models and GARCH Models. While many market participants talk about implied volatility, we explained that unlike the derivation of this measure in equity markets, deriving this volatility estimate from interest rate derivatives is not as simple and straightforward. The implied volatility estimate depends not only on the particular option pricing model employed, but also on a model of the time evolution of the complete term structure and volatilities of yields of different maturities.

SECTION two

Modeling Factor Risk

CHAPTER 9

Term Structure Factor Models

Robert C. Kuberek
Senior Managing Director
Wilshire Associates Incorporated

Quantitative models of risk provide portfolio managers with valuable tools in the construction and maintenance of investment portfolios that meet specific performance objectives. Fixed-income portfolio management is especially amenable to quantitative risk modeling because so much structure is present in the pricing of fixed-income securities and because the returns of investment grade fixed-income securities are so highly correlated with one another. Factor models provide a particularly powerful technique for modeling fixed-income portfolio risk. Moreover, because the main sources of risk (and correlation) in the returns of investment grade fixed-income portfolios relate to the shape and position of the yield curve, *term structure* factor models represent the most important of these models.

The purpose of this chapter is to review some of the leading approaches to term structure factor modeling. However, to understand how term structure factor models work and how they fit into the risk management landscape, it is useful first to define this important class of risk models and to put their development in historical perspective. This is the objective of the next section. Succeeding sections discuss the application of factor models to risk management, identify the major types of term structure factor models, describe leading examples of each type of term structure model, and discuss the advantages and disadvantages of each.

FACTOR MODELS DEFINED AND HISTORICAL BACKGROUND

Whether risk is measured in terms of standard deviation of return, standard deviation of tracking error relative to a benchmark, value-at-risk or probability of underperforming some target, a useful first step in building a factor model is to develop a quantitative description of returns that relates returns meaningfully to other quantities and that has statistical moments that can be estimated easily and reliably. One of the simplest descriptions of return that meets these requirements is the market model for common stocks.[1] In this model, asset returns are generated by the process

$$\tilde{R}_i = a_i + b_i\tilde{R}_m + \tilde{e}_i \tag{1}$$

where

R_i = the total return of asset i
R_m = the total return of the market portfolio
e_i = a random error term that is uncorrelated with the market return

and the tilde (~) denotes a random variable.

If it is further assumed that the residual error terms in equation (1) are uncorrelated *across* assets after taking out the influence of the single index return R_m, then this model is an example of a simple "factor" model where the single factor is the return of the market portfolio. It is also a *linear* factor model because it is linear in the factor return R_m. The particular description of the return-generating process in (1) is closely identified with the Capital Asset Pricing Model (CAPM) of William Sharpe[2] and John Lintner.[3]

Another well-known example of a linear factor model for risky assets underlies the Arbitrage Pricing Theory (the APT) of Stephen Ross.[4] This type of return model, which is very general, assumes that it is not possible to completely eliminate the correlations of residuals across assets

[1] The market model follows from the assumption that stock returns are multi-variate normal. See Eugene F. Fama, *Foundations of Finance* (New York: Basic Books, 1976).

[2] William F. Sharpe, "Capital Asset Prices: A Theory of Market Equilibrium under Conditions of Risk," *Journal of Finance* (September 1964), pp. 425–442.

[3] John Lintner, "The Valuation of Risk Assets and the Selection of Risk Investments in Stock Portfolios and Capital Budgets," *Review of Economics and Statistics* (February 1965), pp. 13–37.

[4] Stephen A. Ross, "The Arbitrage Theory of Capital Asset Pricing," *Journal of Economic Theory* (December 1976), pp. 341–360.

with a single index. In this more general model, returns are generated by the following process:

$$\tilde{r}_i = a_i + b_{i1}\tilde{f}_1 + b_{i2}\tilde{f}_2 + \ldots + b_{ik}\tilde{f}_k + \tilde{e}_i \tag{2}$$

where

r_i = the excess return of asset i over the risk-free rate
f_j = the return to risk factor j
e_i = a mean-zero random residual error term that is uncorrelated with the factor returns and uncorrelated across assets

In the APT model, excess returns are generated by a linear process which is the sum of a risk premium a, a set of random factor effects bf, and a random, asset-specific residual. Examples of factors include index returns, unexpected changes in GNP, changes in corporate bond yield spreads, beta, and the ratio of earnings to price. It often simplifies matters further to assume that the factor returns and the residuals are normally distributed.

USING FACTOR MODELS TO MEASURE RISK

The moments of a linear factor model are the means, variances and covariances of the factor returns, and the variances of the residuals (one for each asset).[5] The usefulness and power of factor models in risk management lie in the fact that once the values of the moments are determined together with the exposures of the risky assets to the factors, it becomes possible to compute portfolio risk using any one of a number of definitions.

For example, suppose that the k factors f in equation (2) have $k \times k$ covariance matrix Ψ. Furthermore, suppose that a particular portfolio holds n ($>k$) assets with the $n \times 1$ weight vector **x**. The portfolio excess return can be written in matrix form as

$$\tilde{r}_p = x'a + x'\mathbf{B}\tilde{f} + x'\tilde{e} \tag{3}$$

[5] Factor models have moments and parameters. Moments are the means, variances, and covariances of the factor returns. Parameters are used in defining and measuring the factors. For example, the *variance* of a factor is a moment, while the *weights* of the stocks in the index that represents the factor are parameters. The number of moments (means, variances, and covariances) in a factor model is a function of the number of factors. The number of parameters in the model, on the other hand, depends on the specification of the model.

where **B** is an $n \times k$ matrix of exposures in which the ith row consists of the b's in equation (2).

Equation (3) gives the portfolio return for a portfolio of assets whose returns are generated by equation (2). The first term in equation (3) is the average risk premium in the portfolio, which is a weighted average of the risk premiums of the individual holdings. The second term is the part of the return that is explained by the k common factors f, and the third term is the aggregate residual return, the unexpected return or noise in the portfolio return that is not explained by the risk factors.

The variance, or total risk, of the portfolio return then is

$$\text{var}(\tilde{r}_p) = x'\mathbf{B}\Psi\mathbf{B}'x + x'\mathbf{D}x \tag{4}$$

where **D** is an $n \times n$ diagonal matrix whose non-zero elements are the variances of the residuals in equation (2).[6] Decomposition of return variance in this way has important computational benefits. By reducing the size of the non-diagonal covariance matrix from $n \times n$ to $k \times k$, for example, portfolio optimization can be performed using significantly less cpu time and computer memory.[7]

Equation (4) decomposes portfolio risk into two components. The first component represents the contribution to total risk from the exposures to the common risk factors while the second represents the contribution from residuals. The contributions to return variance can be separated in this way because of the assumption in equation (2) that the factor returns are uncorrelated with the residual returns. Moreover, the residual variance matrix **D** has the especially simple diagonal form because of the assumption in equation (2) that the residuals are uncorrelated *across* assets. An important feature of this measure of risk is that the second term, the residual variance, tends to shrink with the number of assets in the portfolio. Thus, portfolio managers can diversify away the residual risk in their portfolios but not the systematic, factor risk.

[6] The decomposition of return variance in this manner is traceable to William F. Sharpe, "A Simplified Model for Portfolio Analysis," *Management Science* (January 1963), pp. 277–293.

[7] In their original paper, which studied single and multiple index portfolios in portfolio selection, Kalman J. Cohen and Jerry A. Pogue ("An Empirical Evaluation of Alternative Portfolio Selection Models," *Journal of Business* 40 (1967), pp. 166–193), reported that a single optimization involving only 150 securities required 90 minutes of processing time on an IBM 7090 computer using the full $n \times n$ covariance matrix. While computers presumably have gotten faster in the years since Cohen and Pogue did their work, the relative advantage of equation (4) in computational time surely remains.

Furthermore, since equation (3) applies to any portfolio, including a benchmark portfolio, the variance of the tracking error of a portfolio relative to a benchmark can be written as

$$\text{var}(\tilde{r}_p - \tilde{r}_b) = [x_p - x_b]'\mathbf{B}\Psi\mathbf{B}'[x_p - x_b] + [x_p - x_b]'\mathbf{D}[x_p - x_b] \qquad (5)$$

where the weighting vectors x are now subscripted to denote whether they relate to the portfolio or to the benchmark. The reader will notice that in equation (5) the variance of the tracking error goes to zero as the weight differences from the benchmark go to zero—if one holds the index, the tracking error variance is zero.

TYPES OF FACTOR MODELS

In terms of equation (2), factor models can be categorized according to how the factor exposures and factor returns are measured. In this regard, it is customary to classify factor models as macroeconomic, statistical, or fundamental.

Macroeconomic Factor Models

In macroeconomic factor models, the factor returns in equation (2) represent unexpected changes in quantities that are observable. Quantities that are commonly employed as macroeconomic factors include the returns of specified indexes of common stocks, such as capital goods or materials and services indexes, as well as unexpected changes in measures of aggregate economic activity, such as industrial production, personal income, or employment. Since the factor returns are directly observable, the moments of the factor model (the means, variances, and covariances of the factor returns) can be estimated directly from the *time series* of factor returns. Assets are differentiated by their exposures to these variables, which are the b's in equation (2). These exposures can be estimated by regressing time series of individual stock returns (or of portfolios of similar stocks) on the observed factor returns, using equation (2), with the stock returns as the dependent variable and the observed factor returns f as the independent variables. Examples of macroeconomic factor models include the single and multiple index models of Cohen and Pogue[8] and the APT model of Chen, Roll, and Ross.[9]

[8] Cohen and Pogue, "An Empirical Evaluation of Alternative Portfolio Selection Models."

[9] Nai-Fu Chen, Richard Roll, and Stephen A. Ross, "Economic Forces and the Stock Market," *Journal of Business* (1986), pp. 383–404.

Macroeconomic factor models have the great advantage that because the factors are observable, they are easy to relate to the performance of individual stocks in an intuitive way. One can imagine (whether it is true or not), for example, that airline stocks would tend to do well in an economic upturn, while drug stocks might be relatively insensitive to general economic conditions. A disadvantage of this approach is that with only a small number of factors it may be difficult to eliminate correlation of residuals across assets. A second disadvantage of this type of factor model is that it may be difficult to measure either the exposures of the assets to the macroeconomic variables or the returns to these variables using data of arbitrary frequency. For example, one could identify a factor with the Federal Reserve's Industrial Production index, but this statistic is published only monthly, making it impossible to estimate and use the model in this form with daily returns data.

Statistical Factor Models

The second traditional type of factor model is the statistical model. In this type of model a statistical procedure, such as factor analysis or principal components analysis, is used both to identify the factors and to measure the factor returns. In principal components analysis, for example, a factor model is constructed using a multivariate time series of individual stock returns. The covariance (or correlation) matrix of stock returns is factored by identifying some small number of linear combinations (the principal components) of stock returns that account for most of the return variance in the sample. Thus the factor returns end up being linear combinations of individual stock returns and the factor exposures are the multiple regression coefficients of individual stock returns with these principal components.[10]

An advantage of this method relative to pure macroeconomic factor models is that one can remove as much of the correlation in residuals as one likes by including as many principal components as desired, all the way up to the number of stocks (or stock portfolios) in the original sample. A second advantage relative to macroeconomic factor models is that returns are the only inputs and thus frequency is not an issue: The model can be estimated with any frequency for which the individual stock returns are available.

A disadvantage of the statistical approach is that the factors are not observable in the sense that one cannot make measurements of the factor returns independently of the stock returns themselves and in the

[10] For an early application of this approach, see Benjamin King, "Market and Industry Factors in Stock Price Behavior," *Journal of Business* 39 (1966), pp. 139–190.

sense that the factors do not always correspond to quantities that can be related easily to stock returns.

A disadvantage of both the pure macroeconomic factor models (when the factor returns are observed and the exposures are estimated) and the statistical approaches is that the exposure of a given stock to a factor can, and probably does, change over time as the company's business mix and capital structure change. Because of their reliance on *time series* estimates of factor exposure, neither of these approaches handles this problem gracefully. A related disadvantage of both pure macroeconomic factor models and statistical factor models is that new securities are difficult to fit in a portfolio because there is no history with which to estimate the exposures.

Fundamental Factor Models

The fundamental approach combines some of the advantages of macroeconomic factor models and statistical factor models while avoiding certain of their difficulties.[11] The fundamental approach identifies the factors with a stock's exposures to a set of attributes, which can include the stock's beta, its ratio of earnings-to-price (e/p), its economic sector (e.g., capital goods), and its industry classification (e.g., automotive). In this type of factor model, the factor exposures are the exposures to the economic variables, the actual (or normalized) values of the fundamentals (e.g., the actual e/p ratio), and, in the case of a classification factor, simply a dummy variable that has a value of one if the stock falls into the category or zero otherwise. Factor returns are not observed directly but are inferred by regressing *cross-sections* of stock returns against their exposures to the set of factors.[12]

An important advantage of the fundamental approach relative to the macroeconomic and statistical approaches is that as the exposure of a stock to a given factor changes over time, these exposure changes can be tracked immediately so that measures of portfolio risk correctly reflect the current condition of the portfolio's underlying assets. By the same token it is easy to include new securities in a portfolio because no history is required to estimate their factor exposures.

---

[11] Examples of this approach include, Eugene F. Fama and James MacBeth, "Risk, Return and Equilibrium: Empirical Tests," *Journal of Political Economy* (1973), pp. 607–636, and Eugene F. Fama and Kenneth R. French, "The Cross-Section of Expected Stock Returns," *Journal of Finance* (June 1992), pp. 427–465.

[12] In this case the beta, if it is included as a factor, is estimated or modeled using *a prior* time series.

TYPES OF TERM STRUCTURE FACTOR MODELS

The general framework of equation (2) can be applied to fixed-income securities easily. However, for investment grade fixed-income securities, the main sources of risk relate to the level and shape of the yield curve. Thus, the appropriate factor models are term structure factor models, where the factors in equation (2) are defined specifically to explain the returns of default-free bonds, such as Treasuries or stripped Treasuries, and thus describe changes in yield curve level and shape.[13]

An important feature of term structure factor models is that, because the factors mainly explain the risk of yield changes, in each model there is a characteristic yield curve shift associated with each factor. Still, as will be seen, each of the models described here bears a resemblance to one or another of the common stock models already described. Along these lines, term structure factor models can be classified in three types, as follows:

1. Arbitrage models
2. Principal components models
3. Spot rate models and functional models

Term structure factor models that use equilibrium or arbitrage methods, especially Cox, Ingersoll, and Ross[14] and Richard[15] are analogous to macroeconomic factor models for common stocks. These models work by postulating dynamics for a set of observable state variables that are assumed to underlie interest rates and deriving (in the case of equilibrium models) or assuming (in the case of arbitrage models) some equilibrium condition for expected returns, then *deriving* the term structure. Examples of state variables underlying these models include the short-term nominal interest rate, the short-term "real" rate of interest, the rate of inflation, and the unexpected component of the change in the Consumer Price Index. A unique feature of the equilibrium/arbitrage approach, relative to other types of term structure factor models, is that the equilibrium/arbitrage approach produces term structure factor models that are rigorously consistent with security valuation. In other words, these models provide both bond prices and dynamics.

---

[13] For non-Treasury securities additional factors can be important in determining portfolio risk. See, for example, Robert C. Kuberek, "Common Factors in Bond Portfolio Returns," Wilshire Associates Incorporated (1989).

[14] John C. Cox, Jonathan E. Ingersoll, and Stephen A. Ross, "A Theory of the Term Structure of Interest Rates," Working Paper (August 1978) and John C. Cox, Jonathan E. Ingersoll, and Stephen A. Ross, "A Theory of the Term Structure of Interest Rates," *Econometrica* (1985), pp. 385–407.

[15] Scott F. Richard, "An Arbitrage Model of the Term Structure of Interest Rates," *Journal of Financial Economics* (1978), pp.33–57.

Term structure factor models based on principal components or factor analysis, such as Gultekin and Rogalski[16] and Litterman and Scheinkman,[17] are analogous to the statistical factor models for common stocks described previously. In this type of model, factor analysis or principal components analysis is used to identify the factors underlying the returns of bonds of different maturities or, almost equivalently, to identify the factors underlying the movements of yields at different maturities. As with the common stock return models, the factor returns typically are linear combinations of the returns of zero-coupon bonds and the factor exposures are the multiple regression coefficients of individual bond returns with these principal components.

Two other approaches, spot rate models and functional models, bear some resemblance to fundamental models for common stocks in that the factors are most naturally identified with different measures of exposure. Spot rate models identify the term structure factors directly with the durations of zero-coupon bonds at specified points along the term structure. An important example of this type of model is the RiskMetrics™ model,[18] which identifies factors with the durations of zero-coupon bonds at ten points along the yield curve, 3-months, 1-year, 2-years, 3-years, 5-years, 7-years, 10-years, 15-years, 20-years, and 30-years. Duration for coupon bonds can be calculated either directly from the cash flows, if the cash flows are well defined, using so-called cash-flow mapping techniques, or with the aid of a yield-curve-based valuation model (e.g., an option-adjusted-spread, or OAS, model), in the case of bonds with embedded options and payment contingencies.[19] The RiskMetrics™ model and approach are in wide use in a variety of risk management applications, but especially in applications focusing on value-at-risk.

[16] N. Bulent Gultekin and Richard J. Rogalski, "Government Bond Returns, Measurement of Interest Rate Risk and the Arbitrage Pricing Theory," *Journal of Finance* (1985), pp. 43–61.

[17] Robert Litterman and José Scheinkman, "Common Factors Affecting Bond Returns," *Journal of Fixed Income* (June 1991), pp. 54–61.

[18] For a comprehensive description of this approach, see "RiskMetrics—Technical Document," J.P. Morgan/Reuters, 1996.

[19] See, for example, Robert C. Kuberek and Prescott C. Cogswell, "On the Pricing of Interest Rate Contingent Claims in a Binomial Lattice," Wilshire Associates Incorporated (May 1990). These term structure-based OAS models are prerequisite for measuring exposures to term structure factors for any but the simplest fixed-income securities. The general approach is to fit the model to the quoted price of a bond by iterating on a spread over the initial term structure, then numerically to compute the factor exposure by shifting the starting term structure and recalculating the model value of the bond at the same spread.

Functional models, for example Kuberek[20] and Wilner,[21] seek to represent yield curve risk using approximating functions that are based on, or related, to polynomials. These models fit smooth curves to actual yield curve movements, where the fitted shifts represent a composite of a basic set of yield curve shift components, reflecting, for example, change in yield curve level, change in slope, and change in curvature. Factors are identified with the durations of zero-coupon Treasuries with respect to these prespecified shift components. Superficially, the basic yield curve shift components resemble principal components shifts, but are generated not by a historical data sample but by some underlying mathematical reasoning.

In fact, as will be seen, all of the term structure factor models described here can be represented as a form of equation (2). Moreover, all of the term structure factor models described here share the property that the factor returns in the model represent the amounts and direction of each characteristic yield curve shift allowed in the model, and the exposures, the *b*'s in equation (2), are the durations of the bonds with respect to these yield curve shifts. From this perspective, a useful way to distinguish the models is in the number of characteristic yield curve movements that each model implies and in the forms of these characteristic yield curve movements.

The remainder of this chapter will explore a leading example of each of the term structure factor models described above. The examples that will be used are (1) for arbitrage models, the one-factor equilibrium term structure model of Cox, Ingersoll, and Ross; (2) for principal components models, Litterman and Scheinkman; (3) for spot rate models, the RiskMetrics™ model; and, (4) for functional models, Kuberek. To facilitate the comparison of the different models, each of the models is recast to describe yield curve risk at the same 12 points along the yield curve—9 months, 1 year, 1.5 years, 2 years, 3 years, 4 years, 5 years, 7 years, 10 years, 15 years, 20 years, and 30 years.

ARBITRAGE MODELS

The Cox, Ingersoll, and Ross equilibrium term structure model (CIR) is developed fully within the context of a single-good production economy

[20] Robert C. Kuberek, "An Approximate Factor Model for U.S. Treasuries," *Proceedings of the Seminar on the Analysis of Security Prices* (November 1990), The University of Chicago Center for Research in Securities Prices, pp. 71–106.

[21] Ram Willner, "A New Tool for Portfolio Managers: Level, Slope and Curvature Durations," *Journal of Fixed Income* (June 1996), pp. 48–59.

with stochastic production possibilities and uncertain technological change.[22] However, the model can be developed using arbitrage arguments, providing that the specification of the equilibrium condition for expected bond returns is consistent with their general equilibrium formulation.[23]

Assume that there is one factor, which is represented by the short-term interest rate *r*. Further, assume that this rate evolves according to the process

$$dr = \kappa(\mu - r)dt + \sigma\sqrt{r}dz \tag{6}$$

where

μ = long-term average value of the short-term interest rate *r*
κ = rate of reversion of the short-term interest rate *r* toward its long-term average value
$\sigma r^{1/2}$ = standard deviation of unexpected changes in the short-term interest rate
dz = a standard Brownian motion

Equation (6) says that the change in the short-term interest rate *r* over the period *dt* is the sum of two components, a drift component, which represents the expected reversion of the short-term rate toward the mean, and a surprise term that reflects unexpected changes in interest rates. This description of interest rate dynamics has several important properties. These include mean reversion, volatility of interest rates that increases with the level of interest rates, and the fact that the future

[22] The CIR model is constructed for an economy where money does not play a role and therefore the short-term interest rate in the model is a "real" rate. Nevertheless, by convention the one-factor CIR model is applied to the nominal term structure, where the short-term rate in the model is regarded as a nominal rate.

[23] In distinguishing the arbitrage approach from their own equilibrium approach, Cox, Ingersoll, and Ross write, "An alternative to the equilibrium approach taken here is based purely on arbitrage considerations. Here is a brief summary of this argument. Assume that all uncertainty is described by some set of state variables. If there are no pure arbitrage opportunities in the economy, then there exists a (not necessarily unique) set of state-space prices which support current contingent claim values... By assuming that the state variables follow an *exogenously* specified diffusion process, one obtains a valuation equation of the same general form as [CIR (1978) eq.] (25). However, the resulting equation contains *undetermined* coefficients which depend on both preferences and production opportunities and *can be identified only in a general equilibrium setting*" (italics supplied). Notwithstanding this criticism, however, as Richard and others have shown, arbitrage models are powerful, easy to develop, and, provided one is willing and has the means to solve them numerically, reasonably practical.

behavior of the interest rate depends only on its current value and not on the history of its movements.

If the price $P(r,T)$ of a zero-coupon bond paying \$1 in T years depends only on the short-term interest rate r and the maturity T, it follows from Ito's lemma[24] that the return over a period dt of a zero-coupon bond with maturity T is

$$\tilde{r}_T = \left\{ (P_r/P)k(\mu - r) + P_t/P + \frac{1}{2}(P_{rr}/P)\sigma^2 r - r \right\} dt + (P_r/P)\sigma\sqrt{r}dz \tag{7}$$

The first term on the right-hand side of equation (7) is the expected excess return of the T-year maturity zero-coupon bond. It consists of four components. The first is that part of the return due to the expected movement of the short-term rate r toward its long-term average value μ. The second component is due to accretion toward par. The third component is a volatility premium that is proportional to convexity. The fourth component is the current value of the short-term rate, subtracted to obtain the expected excess return.

The second term on the right-hand side of equation (7) is the effect of the unexpected component of the change in the short-term interest rate.

If it is assumed that the expected excess return of the T-year zero-coupon bond in equilibrium is proportional to the bond's "duration" with respect to the short-term interest rate by a risk premium λr, that represents the price of interest rate risk per unit of duration, then equation (7) becomes

$$\tilde{r}_T = (P_r/P)\lambda r dt + (P_r/P)\sigma\sqrt{r}dz \tag{8}$$

Equation (8) says that the excess return on a zero-coupon bond of maturity T is the sum of two components, a risk premium that is proportional to the product of the bond's duration with respect to r and the risk premium λr, and a surprise that is the product of the bond's duration and the unexpected change in the interest rate r.

Inspection of equation (8) shows that it has exactly the form of equation (2) where

$$a = (P_r/P)\lambda r dt \tag{9a}$$

---

[24] For a discussion of the application of Ito's lemma to the pricing of bonds, see S. Fischer, "The Demand for Index Bonds," *Journal of Political Economy* (1975), pp. 509–534.

EXHIBIT 9.1 Characteristic Yield Shifts: CIR Model

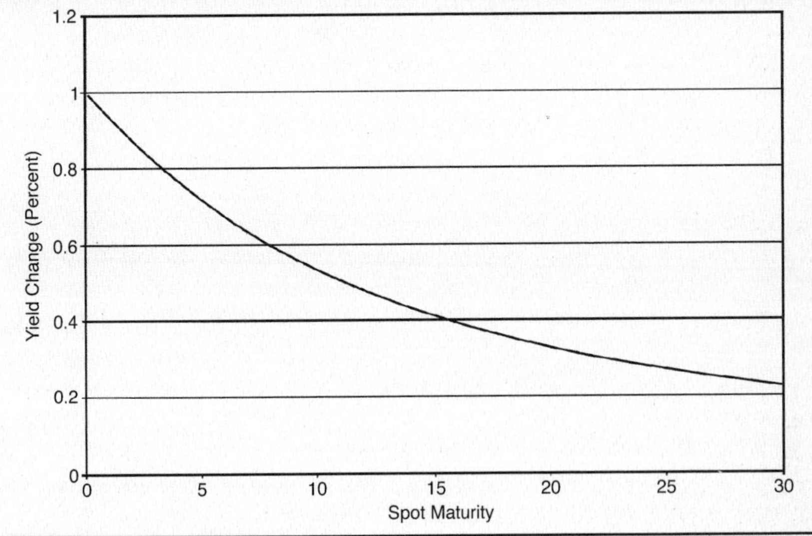

and

$$b = (P_r/P) \tag{9b}$$

Under these conditions CIR provide a closed-form expression for the duration P_r/P of a zero-coupon bond maturity T. This is given by the following formula:

$$\frac{P_r(r, T)}{P} = -\frac{2(e^{\gamma T} - 1)}{(\gamma + k + \lambda)(e^{\gamma T} - 1) + 2\gamma} \tag{10}$$

where

$$\gamma = \sqrt{(\kappa + \lambda)^2 + 2\sigma^2}$$

The CIR model produces a single characteristic yield shift as illustrated in Exhibit 9.1. The shift, which resembles a twist at the short end of the curve, describes yield curve behavior when yield changes are perfectly correlated and when short-term yields tend to move more than long-term yields. This tendency for short-term interest rates to be more volatile than long rates is a result of the mean reversion in the short rate assumed for the model and described in equation (6). For example, suppose that the values of the parameters in equation (10) for this example are as follows: $\kappa = 0.1$, $\lambda = -0.04$ (a negative value corresponds to a positive term premium), and $\sigma = 0.03578$. These parameter values are consistent with a 10-year mean reversion time, a term premium of 20 basis points per year of duration, and an annual standard deviation of short-term interest rate changes of 80 basis points. Given these values for the parameters, if the short rate increases by 100 basis points, the 30-year zero-coupon rate will increase by just over 20 basis points.

As can be seen in Exhibit 9.2, for this combination of parameter values the CIR durations of zero-coupon bonds do not increase as rapidly as their ordinary durations, which are just the times-to-maturity of the bonds. This is a reflection of the tendency for long rates to rise by less than short rates, when short rates rise, and for long rates to fall by less than short rates, when short rates fall. Thus, CIR durations suggest that ordinary durations overstate the risk of long maturity bonds relative to short maturity bonds.

The CIR model has several advantages over other approaches. First, it is rigorously consistent with the valuation of fixed-income securities. In other words, the model produces both prices and returns. A second advantage is that the model is defined continuously in maturity: Exposures can be calculated for zero-coupon bonds of any maturity without recourse to approximation or interpolation. A third advantage, which has already been mentioned, is that the moments—the mean and variance of the (single) factor return—can be estimated directly by observing the time series of factor returns, in this case the time series of changes in the short-term interest rate.

EXHIBIT 9.2 Bond Durations: CIR Model

Time to Maturity	b_1
0.75	−0.71
1.00	−0.93
1.50	−1.35
2.00	−1.74
3.00	−2.45
4.00	−3.05
5.00	−3.58
7.00	−4.43
10.00	−5.32
15.00	−6.16
20.00	−6.56
30.00	−6.84

A disadvantage of this model is that it allows only one type of yield curve shift and is thus very limited in the variety of actual yield curve behaviors that it can describe. This is not a shortcoming of the general approach, however. CIR also present a two-factor model, with uncertain short-term interest rates and uncertain inflation, within the context of their general equilibrium model, and Richard and others have proposed other two-factor and multi-factor models based on arbitrage arguments. However, for the variety of interest rate dynamics that have known solutions like equation (10), the models tend to have a large number of parameters and very complicated forms.

A second minor disadvantage of the one-factor CIR model as a factor model is evident from inspection of equation (8), namely, that the coefficients in the factor model depend on the level of interest rates. This dependence of the coefficients on the level of interest rates is plausible on the grounds that it is consistent with the presumption that interest rates tend to be more volatile when interest rate levels are higher. However, it means that this model cannot be implemented by regressing cross sections of bond returns on their durations, then averaging over time to obtain the moments, without first normalizing the exposures for the level of interest rates.

PRINCIPAL COMPONENTS MODELS

A second major category of term structure factor models is based on principal components analysis. In this approach, the returns of zero-coupon bonds of different maturities are factor analyzed to extract a (hopefully small) set of characteristic yield curve shifts, defined at discreet maturities, that together explain a large proportion of the total variance of returns in the sample. The factors are thus the amounts and direction of each type of characteristic yield curve shift that combine to explain the returns of a cross section of bond returns for a given performance period. Gultekin and Rogalski use this technique on coupon Treasuries, while Litterman and Scheinkman use the method to factor analyze the returns of Treasury implied zero-coupon bonds.[25] Because

[25] Implied zero-coupon bonds, or implied zeros, are hypothetical bonds that are priced using discount factors that are consistent with the discount factors that the market uses to price actual coupon Treasuries. While these bond prices cannot be observed directly, their existence is somewhat validated by the possibility of creating them synthetically by constructing a hedge portfolio of coupon Treasuries. Also, a closely related security, the Treasury strip, does actually exist. The reason for using implied zeros in preference to actual Treasury strips to build a factor model is the availability of more history for backtesting: Treasury strips did not exist before the early 1980s, whereas Treasury prices are widely available back to 1974 and implied zero curves are available back even further.

the use of implied zeros is more consistent with generalizations of equation (2) for any bond, the focus here will be on the approach of Litterman and Scheinkman (LS).

To illustrate the LS model, suppose that returns are available for implied zeros at twelve maturities, as follows: 9 months, 1 year, 1.5 years, 2 years, 3 years, 4 years, 5 years, 7 years, 10 years, 15 years, 20 years, and 30 years. With principal components one can specify any number of factors up to the number of securities in the data sample—in this case 12. Typically, a number is chosen such that most of the variance in the sample is explained by the factors selected. For the example here, the first three principal components typically explain more than 98% of the variance in the data sample, so three is chosen as the number of factors. The characteristic yield curve shifts that correspond to the first three yield curve factors are shown in Exhibit 9.3.

The first yield curve factor is the relatively flat curve near the top of Exhibit 9.3. This corresponds to a yield shift that is roughly, but not exactly, uniform. The second shift is a pivoting shift for which short rates fall and long rates rise. This shift is almost uniform for maturities greater than 15 years. The third shift is a change in curvature, with short rates rising, intermediate rates falling, and long rates rising. Actual yield curve shifts are represented as composites of these three characteristic yield shifts. The principal components procedure works in such a way that the factors are uncorrelated in the data sample that was used to generate them. This "uncorrelatedness" of the factors is a consequence of the property of principal components referred to as orthogonality.

EXHIBIT 9.3 Characteristic Yield Curve Shifts: Principal Components Model

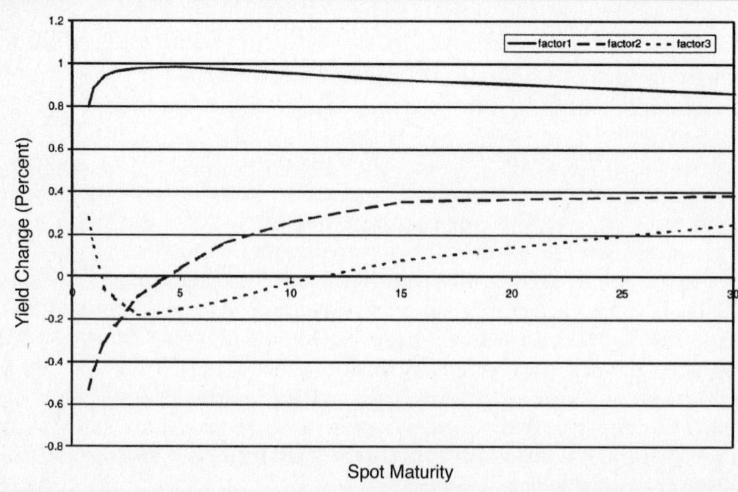

EXHIBIT 9.4 Bond Durations: Principal Components Model

Time to Maturity	b_1	b_2	b_3
0.75	−0.60	0.40	−0.21
1.00	−0.88	0.44	−0.14
1.50	−1.41	0.46	0.08
2.00	−1.93	0.46	0.20
3.00	−2.93	0.29	0.53
4.00	−3.93	0.10	0.67
5.00	−4.92	−0.20	0.75
7.00	−6.83	−1.13	0.77
10.00	−9.56	−2.60	0.24
15.00	−13.84	−5.33	−1.17
20.00	−18.10	−7.35	−2.81
30.00	−25.89	−11.58	−7.51

The exposures or "durations" of the implied zeros with respect to each of these factors, the *b*'s in equation (2), are shown in Exhibit 9.4. As with the analogous common stock models, factor returns are produced by the principal components procedure itself but, alternatively, can be estimated by regressing the returns of cross sections of zero-coupon bonds on the durations implied by the characteristic yield shifts that are produced by the principal components analysis (Exhibit 9.4). The durations are scaled to the characteristic yield shifts themselves, so that, for example, one unit of return for the second factor corresponds to a yield shift of 0.38% at 30 years. Thus, to obtain the return of the 5-year zero-coupon bond resulting from one half unit of return for the second factor, assuming the factor returns for the other factors are zero for a given period, it is only necessary to multiply the duration (−0.20) by the factor return (0.50) to get −0.10%. In practice, the realized factor returns will all be non-zero, but then the effects are computed in the same way for each factor and the results added together to get the total excess return predicted for that security, as in equation (2).[26]

[26] The scaling of principal components models is pretty arbitrary. Thus, for example, the model here could have been scaled so that the characteristic yield shift of the second factor was 1.00% at 30 years instead of 0.38% (see Exhibit 9.2). In this case the duration of the 30-year bond with respect to the second factor would have had to have been scaled up accordingly. The content and explanatory power of the complete factor model would remain the same, however. In particular, the returns predicted for a bond, given its exposures and given the realized factor returns estimated for the performance period, would be identical.

An advantage of the principal components approach in term structure factor modeling is that the actual data provide guidance in defining the factors. A disadvantage of the principal components model, which is inherent in the approach, is the large number of parameters required. In the example here with three principal components, 36 parameters are required. These are the parameters required to describe the characteristic yield curve shift for each of the three factors at each of 12 maturities. A second disadvantage is that the exact definition of the factors, and therefore of the exposures, depends on the data sample used to extract the principal components. As experience is accumulated, the data change and the definition of the factors, and thus the durations of bonds, change.

A third disadvantage of this approach is that the model is not defined continuously on maturity. Thus, to calculate factor exposures for bonds with maturity or cash flow dates different from the maturities of the zeros used to define the factors, some interpolation of the characteristic yield curve shifts must be performed. The larger the number of maturities used to define the factors, the less interpolation is needed, but the more parameters are required. Of course, there is no guarantee that once the factors are defined, using a particular historical data sample, the factor returns still will be uncorrelated out of sample.

SPOT RATE MODELS

Spot rate models identify factors with the durations of zero-coupon bonds at each of a number of points along the yield curve. The factors thus can be interpreted as changes in the yields of these hypothetical zero-coupon bonds. Moreover, any number of yield curve points can be used to define the model, so the portfolio manager has wide latitude in defining the model to suit the specific application. Spot rate models have the least content in terms of economic assumptions and, correspondingly, the fewest parameters.

One of the leading examples of spot rate models is J. P. Morgan's RiskMetrics™ model.[27] This model defines ten points along the yield curve and provides the variance-covariance matrix, the Ψ in equation (4), of spot rate changes for 13 countries including the United States. The RiskMetrics™ model is widely applied in measuring value-at-risk. The portfolio's "value-at-risk" is the largest *dollar* loss (or loss in terms

---

[27] For a discussion this approach as compared with the principal components approach, see Bennett W. Golub and Leo M. Tilman, "Measuring Yield Curve Risk Using Principal Components Analysis, Value at Risk and Key Rate Durations," *Journal of Portfolio Management* (Summer 1997), pp. 72–84.

of some other reference currency) that a portfolio will suffer "ordinarily." For example, if a portfolio will lose not more than \$100, 95% of the time, then the value-at-risk is said to be \$100. Value-at-risk can be computed from equation (4), as follows:

$$\text{Value-at-Risk} = 1.65\ (\text{Portfolio Value})\ [\text{var}(r_p)]^{1/2}$$

As with all the term structure factor models described here, however, spot rate models can be estimated in at least two ways. The time series of factor returns can be estimated by measuring the yield changes at each yield curve point in the model, as with a macroeconomic factor model for common stocks. Alternatively, one may calculate the durations of the bonds with respect to the spot rate changes and regress bond returns cross-sectionally on these durations to create a time-series of factor returns. Typically, the second method is more direct because, by using this method, the yield curve itself does not need to be estimated.

Exhibit 9.5 shows the characteristic yield curve shifts for the first four spot rate factors in the 12-factor formulation. As the exhibit makes clear, the characteristic yield curve movements of spot rate models have a very extreme appearance. A yield change is either zero, off a given yield curve point, or 100 basis points, on the yield curve point. Yield changes are interpolated between adjacent points. In other words, if one of the bond's cash flows falls between the stipulated yield curve points, that cash flow has *some* duration with respect to both the adjacent points. Spot rate factors can be scaled, as in the example here, so that the duration of a zero-coupon bond to a given spot rate change is just equal to that bond's time to maturity.

EXHIBIT 9.5 Characteristic Yield Shifts: Spot Rate Model

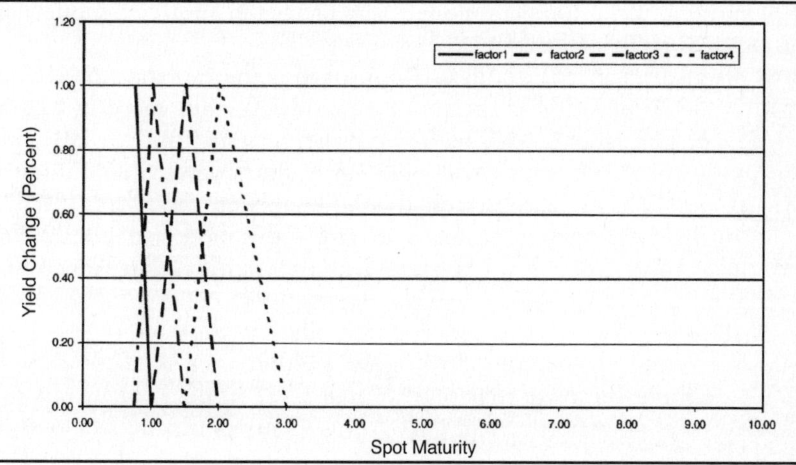

EXHIBIT 9.6 Bond Durations: Spot Rate Model

Time to Maturity	b_1	b_2	b_3	b_4
0.75	–0.75	0.00	0.00	0.00
1.00	0.00	–1.00	0.00	0.00
1.50	0.00	0.00	–1.50	0.00
2.00	0.00	0.00	0.00	–2.00
3.00	0.00	0.00	0.00	0.00
4.00	0.00	0.00	0.00	0.00
5.00	0.00	0.00	0.00	0.00
7.00	0.00	0.00	0.00	0.00
10.00	0.00	0.00	0.00	0.00
15.00	0.00	0.00	0.00	0.00
20.00	0.00	0.00	0.00	0.00
30.00	0.00	0.00	0.00	0.00

Exhibit 9.6 shows durations for the first four factors in the 12-factor spot rate model. A feature of spot rate models is that because of the way the models are defined, the spot rate durations of a bond, if scaled this way, add up approximately to the ordinary duration of the bond.

A major advantage of spot rate models over principal components models is that fewer parameters are required. Where principal components models imply that spot rate changes at various maturities can combine only in the ways implied by the principal components, in spot rate models spot rate changes can combine in any way that is possible using the number of spot rates in the model. Like arbitrage models and unlike principal components models, the factors in spot rate models are not required to be orthogonal.

A disadvantage of the spot rate approach is the fact that the characteristic yield curve shifts in the spot rate model, as illustrated in Exhibit 9.3, do not correspond with yield curve movements that actually take place. Nor are the characteristic yield curve shifts defined continuously on maturity. Thus, as with principal components models, some interpolation of yield changes is required to apply the model to bonds with cash flows (or yield curve exposures) at times other than the points defined in the model.

A third disadvantage of spot rate models is the fact that a large number of factors are required to model yield curve risk accurately. To use an example, suppose that one wanted to reproduce with spot rate changes the characteristic yield curve movements of a principal components model as described in Exhibit 9.3. To accomplish this, it would be necessary to combine 12 spot rate shifts in the appropriate proportions to recover the information in just one principal components shift. As a consequence, portfolio managers need to use a large number of durations to manage interest rate risk effectively using this approach.

FUNCTIONAL MODELS

Functional models combine the advantages of arbitrage models, continuity and consistency with equilibrium pricing, with the parsimony of principal components models. Functional models assume that zero-coupon yield changes are defined continuously in maturity, for example with a shift function $f(T)$:

$$f(T) = \Delta y(T) \tag{11}$$

where $\Delta y(T)$ is the change in the zero-coupon yield at maturity T. Then, a Taylor series or some other approximating function can be applied to the function $f(T)$, retaining the number of terms that are sufficient to describe actual yield curve movements adequately. Durations are computed from the approximating function directly. For example, the yield shift function $f(T)$ can be approximated by a Taylor series, as follows:

$$f(T) = c_0 + c_1 T + c_2 T^2 + \dots \tag{12}$$

The factors are identified with the resulting durations, which can be derived easily from equation (12).

Chambers, Carleton, and McEnally employ this idea to devolop risk measures for use in immunization and hedging, but do not explore the implications of this approach for developing term structure factor models.[28] Similarly, Nelson and Siegel use exponentials to fit yield levels at the short end of the yield curve, but do not extend their approach to the long end of the curve, except to test extrapolations of the model as fitted to Treasury bills, nor to the identification of a factor model.[29]

[28] D. R. Chambers, W. T. Carleton, and R. W. McEnally, "Immunizing Default free Bond Portfolios with a Duration Vector," *Journal of Financial and Quantitative Analysis* (1988), pp. 89–104. See also, D. R. Chambers and W. T. Carleton, "A More General Duration Approach," Unpublished Manuscript (1981).

[29] Charles R. Nelson and Andrew F. Siegel, "A Parsimonious Modeling of Yield Curves," *Journal of Business* (October 1987), pp. 473–489.

Kuberek uses the functions that are proposed by Nelson and Siegel, to model the short-end of the forward rate curve, for the purpose of approximating the shift function given by equation (11) for zero-coupon yields. This three-factor model has the following form:

$$f(T) \approx c_0 + c_1 e^{-T/q} + c_2 (T/q) e^{1 - T/q} \tag{13}$$

where q is a parameter.[30] The model given by equation (13) resembles equation (12) except that the second and third terms contain an exponential decay. This exponential form has the benefit that, in contrast to equation (12), changes in yield curve level and shape will not become unbounded in maturity.

With this formulation, the zero-coupon bond durations, the b's in equation (2), take the very simple form

$$b_{ij} = w_j(T_i)T_i \tag{14}$$

where

$$w_1 = -1$$
$$w_2 = -e^{-T/q}$$
$$w_3 = -T/qe^{1-T/q}$$

and where the b_{ij} are the exposures of the ith zero-coupon bond to the jth factor.

Thus, the first factor in this three-factor model represents the effect of a precisely uniform change in the level of interest rates, the second factor represents the effect of a change in slope of the yield curve, and the third factor represents the effect of a change in curvature of the yield curve. Factor returns can be estimated by regressing cross sections of zero-coupon bond returns on these durations.

Exhibit 9.7 shows these characteristic yield curve movements for the three-factor functional model in equation (13). In this exponential form, the characteristic yield shifts represent changes in level (factor 1), slope (factor 2), and curvature (factor 3). The model is specified so that changes in slope affect short rates more than long rates. This is consistent with the behavior of the yield curve at certain times, where short

[30] The value of the single parameters q, which represents the location of the maximum in the third shift component and simultaneously determines the rate of decay in the second, can be chosen in any convenient way. Kuberek ("An Approximate Factor Model for U.S. Treasuries") uses the value of q that maximizes the ability of the three-factor model to describe a wide variety of yield curve shifts under diffuse priors.

rates are more volatile than long rates. To reproduce yield curve movements where long rates change by more than short rates, factors 1 and 2 can be combined. For example, an upward shift of one unit of factor 2 (100 basis points at the short end) combined with a downward shift of one unit of factor 1 (100 basis points uniformly) produces a flattening of 100 basis points at the long end, with short rates unchanged. Additional complexity in yield curve movements, including various combinations of change in slope and curvature, can be achieved by including factor 3.

The zero-coupon bond durations are given in Exhibit 9.8. As can be seen, the durations at various maturities with respect to the first factor are equivalent to the ordinary (effective) duration of the bonds. The durations with respect to the second factor, which represents a change in slope, increase in magnitude with maturity to seven years, then decrease. The third factor's durations increase in magnitude to 14 years, then decrease.

The model described here, which is based on approximating functions, has several significant advantages. Most usefully, ordinary (effective) duration, as conventionally defined, is the first factor. Second, unlike the principal components models and spot rate models, the model is inherently consistent with rigorous equilibrium or arbitrage term structure models that imply yield changes that are continuous in maturity, including the CIR model already described. Third, it has only one parameter (and it has no more *moments* than any other three-factor model). Finally, the yield shifts implied by this model correspond with yield curve movements that portfolio managers can easily imagine occurring, namely, changes in level, slope, and curvature.

EXHIBIT 9.7 Characteristic Yield Curve Shifts: Functional Model

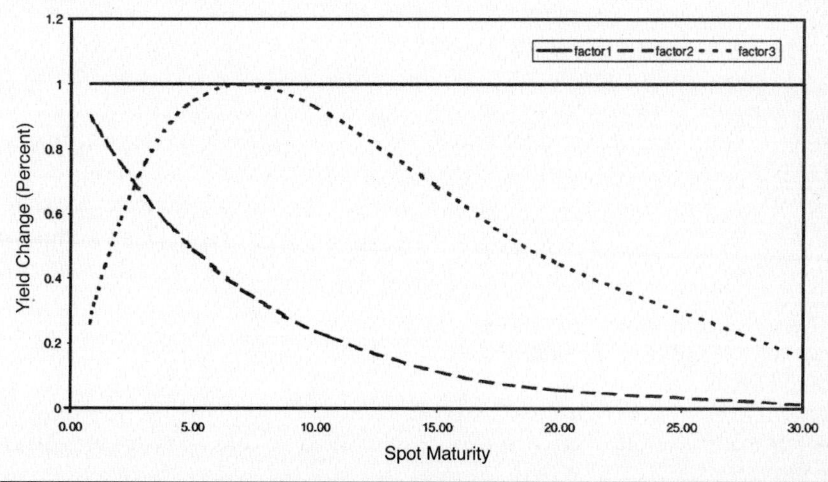

EXHIBIT 9.8 Bond Durations: Functional Model

Time to Maturity	b_1	b_2	b_3
0.75	−0.75	−0.67	−0.20
1.00	−1.00	−0.87	−0.34
1.50	−1.50	−1.21	−0.71
2.00	−2.00	−1.50	−1.17
3.00	−3.00	−1.95	−2.28
4.00	−4.00	−2.26	−3.51
5.00	−5.00	−2.45	−4.75
7.00	−7.00	−2.58	−7.00
10.00	−10.00	−2.40	−9.31
15.00	−15.00	−1.76	−10.25
20.00	−20.00	−1.15	−8.92
30.00	−30.00	−0.41	−4.81

Because of the particularly simple form of equation (14), the durations of coupon bonds also have a very simple form, as follows:

$$b_j = \sum_h w_j(T_h)s_h T_h / \sum_h s_h \tag{15}$$

where s_h is the present value of the hth cash flow and where the w's are as given in equation (14). Equation (15) is simply the formula for ordinary duration, with an added weighting term $w(T)$. For the first factor, w has a value of unity for all maturities T equation (14), so the associated duration is simply the ordinary (effective) duration. More generally, bond durations in this model are calculated in the same way as ordinary (effective) duration, except that cash flows are weighted differently to reflect the differential exposure to various alternative yield curve shifts.

Like the arbitrage and spot rate models, the factors in functional models are not required to be orthogonal. However, if uncorrelatedness of factor returns is desired, the three factors in equation (14) can easily be rotated to have this property, for example, by estimating the factor returns and extracting the principal components.

CONCLUSION

Term structure factor models can be classified in one of four categories: arbitrage models, principal components models, spot rate models, and functional models. Examples of those reviewed here are the models of Cox, Ingersoll and Ross (arbitrage), Litterman and Scheinkman (principal components), J. P. Morgan's RiskMetrics™ (spot rate), and Kuberek (functional). Each approach resembles, in some important way, one or another of the traditional types of factor models for common stocks, macroeconomic, statistical, and fundamental.

As with common stock models, the approaches to term structure factor models reviewed here differ primarily in the identification of the factors and in how the factor exposures and factor returns are measured. Arbitrage models assume some underlying set of state variables, then derive the term structure and its dynamics. Principal components models extract factor returns from the excess returns of zero-coupon bonds at specified maturities using statistical techniques. Spot rate models associate factors with yield changes at every point (of a specified set) along the yield curve, and functional models use prespecified yield curve shifts to fit actual yield curve movements, where the shift components are motivated by equilibrium considerations.

At the extremes, the one-factor model of Cox, Ingersoll, and Ross is most rigorously consistent with equilibrium pricing, but is also the most restrictive in describing actual yield curve movements, while spot rate models are most descriptive, but have the most factors (and thus, the most durations) of any approach. Principal components and functional models find a middle ground, compromising between the structure and rigorousness of arbitrage models, with few factors, and the explanatory power of spot rate models, with many. Principal components models have the advantage that actual data guide in the identification of the factors, but suffer from the defect that the durations are sample dependent. Functional models have the advantage that the factors can be prespecified in a manner that is convenient to the portfolio manager, for example by defining the factors in such a way that ordinary duration, as conventionally defined, is the first factor.

An important common feature of the models reviewed here relates to the fact that each one associates factors with characteristic yield curve movements. Specifically, factor exposures can be estimated in these models by subjecting a bond to each of the characteristic yield shifts, using a term structure-based valuation model, or OAS model, to see how much return results. Indeed, the application of term structure factor models crucially depends on the availability and usability of these ancillary valuation models.

The power and usefulness of term structure factor models lie in their application to risk management. Once the moments of the model are determined together with the exposures of the portfolio to each of the factors, it becomes possible to measure portfolio risk in any number of ways, including return variance, tracking error relative to a benchmark, and value-at-risk. By further assuming that the factor returns are normally distributed, it becomes possible to characterize the distribution of portfolio return fully, regardless of its composition.

CHAPTER 10

Multi-Factor Risk Models and Their Applications*

Lev Dynkin
Managing Director
Lehman Brothers

Jay Hyman
Senior Vice President
Lehman Brothers

The classical definition of investment risk is uncertainty of returns, measured by their volatility. Investments with greater risk are expected to earn greater returns than less risky alternatives. Asset allocation models help investors choose the asset mix with the highest expected return given their risk constraints (for example, avoid a loss of more than 2% per year in a given portfolio).

Once investors have selected a desired asset mix, they often enlist specialized asset managers to implement their investment goals. The performance of the portfolio is usually compared with a benchmark that reflects the investor's asset selection decision. From the perspective of most asset managers, risk is defined by performance relative to the benchmark rather than by absolute return. In this sense, the least-risky investment portfolio is one that replicates the benchmark. Any portfolio

* Wei Wu coauthored the original version of the paper from which this chapter is derived. The authors would like to thank Jack Malvey for his substantial contribution to this paper and Ravi Mattu, George Williams, Ivan Gruhl, Amitabh Arora, Vadim Konstantinovsky, Peter Lindner, and Jonathan Carmel for their valuable comments.

deviation from the benchmark entails some risk. For example, to the manager of a bond fund benchmarked against the High Yield Index, investing 100% in U.S. Treasuries would involve a much greater long-term risk than investing 100% in high yield corporate bonds. In other words, benchmark risk belongs to the plan sponsor, while the asset manager bears the risk of deviating from the benchmark.

In this chapter we discuss a risk model developed at Lehman Brothers that focuses on portfolio risk relative to a benchmark. The risk model is designed for use by fixed-income portfolio managers benchmarked against broad market indices.

QUANTIFYING RISK

Given our premise that the least-risky portfolio is the one that exactly replicates the benchmark, we proceed to compare the composition of a fixed-income portfolio to that of its benchmark. Are they similar in exposures to changes in the term structure of interest rates, in allocations to different asset classes within the benchmark, and in allocations to different quality ratings? Such portfolio versus benchmark comparisons form the foundation for modern fixed-income portfolio management. Techniques such as "stratified sampling" or "cell-matching" have been used to construct portfolios that are similar to their benchmarks in many components (i.e., duration, quality, etc.). However, these techniques can not answer quantitative questions concerning portfolio risk. How much risk is there? Is portfolio A more or less risky than portfolio B? Will a given transaction increase or decrease risk? To best decrease risk relative to the benchmark, should the focus be on better aligning term structure exposures or sector allocations? How do we weigh these different types of risk against each other? What actions can be taken to mitigate the overall risk exposure? Any quantitative model of risk must account for the magnitude of a particular event as well as its likelihood. When multiple risks are modeled simultaneously, the issue of correlation also must be addressed.

The risk model we present in this article provides quantitative answers to such questions. This multi-factor model compares portfolio and benchmark exposures along all dimensions of risk, such as yield curve movement, changes in sector spreads, and changes in implied volatility. Exposures to each *risk factor* are calculated on a bond-by-bond basis and aggregated to obtain the exposures of the portfolio and the benchmark.

Tracking error, which quantifies the risk of performance difference (projected standard deviation of the return difference) between the portfolio and the benchmark, is projected based on the differences in risk factor exposures. This calculation of overall risk incorporates historical information about the volatility of each risk factor and the correlations among them. The volatilities and correlations of all the risk factors are stored in a covariance matrix, which is calibrated based on monthly returns of individual bonds in the Lehman Brothers Aggregate Index dating back to 1987. The model is updated monthly with historical information. The choice of risk factors has been reviewed periodically since the model's introduction in 1990. The model covers U.S. dollar-denominated securities in most Lehman Brothers domestic fixed-rate bond indices (Aggregate, High Yield, Eurobond). The effect of non-index securities on portfolio risk is measured by mapping onto index risk categories. The net effect of all risk factors is known as systematic risk.

The model is based on historical returns of individual securities and its risk projections are a function of portfolio and benchmark positions in individual securities. Instead of deriving risk factor realizations from changes in market averages (such as a Treasury curve spline, sector spread changes, etc.) the model derives them from historical returns of securities in Lehman Indices. While this approach is much more data and labor intensive, it allows us to quantify residual return volatility of each security after all systematic risk factors have been applied. As a result, we can measure nonsystematic risk of a portfolio relative to the benchmark based on differences in their diversification. This form of risk, also known as concentration risk or security-specific risk, is the result of a portfolio's exposure to individual bonds or issuers. Nonsystematic risk can represent a significant portion of the overall risk, particularly for portfolios containing relatively few securities, even for assets without any credit risk.

PORTFOLIO MANAGEMENT WITH THE RISK MODEL

Passive portfolio managers, or "indexers," seek to replicate the returns of a broad market index. They can use the risk model to help keep the portfolio closely aligned with the index along all risk dimensions. Active portfolio managers attempt to outperform the benchmark by positioning the portfolio to capitalize on market views. They can use the risk model to quantify the risk entailed in a particular portfolio position relative to the market. This information is often incorporated into the performance review process, where returns achieved by a particular strategy are weighed against the risk taken. Enhanced indexers express views against the index, but limit the amount of risk assumed. They can use the model to keep risk within acceptable limits and to highlight unanticipated market exposures that might arise as the portfolio and index change over time. These management styles can be associated with approximate ranges of tracking errors. Passive managers typically seek tracking errors of 5 to 25 basis points per year. Tracking errors for enhanced indexers range from 25 to 75 bp, and those of active managers are even higher.

WHY A MULTI-FACTOR MODEL?

With the abundance of data available in today's marketplace, an asset manager might be tempted to build a risk model directly from the historical return characteristics of individual securities. The standard deviation of a security's return in the upcoming period can be projected to match its past volatility; the correlation between any two securities can be determined from their historical performance. Despite the simplicity of this scheme, the multi-factor approach has several important advantages. First of all, the number of risk factors in the model is much smaller than the number of securities in a typical investment universe. This greatly reduces the matrix operations needed to calculate portfolio risk. This increases the speed of computation (which is becoming less important with gains in processing power) and, more importantly, improves the numerical stability of the calculations. A large covariance matrix of individual security volatilities and correlations is likely to cause numerical instability. This is especially true in the fixed-income world, where returns of many securities are very highly correlated. Risk factors may also exhibit moderately high correlations with each other, but much less so than for individual securities.[1]

A more fundamental problem with relying on individual security data is that not all securities can be modeled adequately in this way. For illiquid securities, pricing histories are either unavailable or unreliable; for new securities, histories do not exist. For still other securities, there may be plenty of reliable historical data, but changes in security characteristics make this data irrelevant to future results. For instance, a ratings upgrade of an issuer would make future returns less volatile than those of the past. A change in interest rates can significantly alter the effective duration of a callable bond. As any bond ages, its duration

[1] Some practitioners insist on a set of risk factors that are uncorrelated to each other. We have found it more useful to select risk factors that are intuitively clear to investors, even at the expense of allowing positive correlations among the factors.

shortens, making its price less sensitive to interest rates. A multi-factor model estimates the risk from owning a particular bond based not on the historical performance of that bond, but on historical returns of all bonds with characteristics similar to those currently pertaining to the bond.

In this article, we present the risk model by way of example. In each of the following sections, a numerical example of the model's application motivates the discussion of a particular feature.

THE RISK REPORT

For illustration, we apply the risk model to a sample portfolio of 57 bonds benchmarked against the Lehman Brothers Aggregate Index. The model produces two important outputs: a tracking error summary report and a set of risk sensitivities reports that compare the portfolio composition to that of the benchmark. These various comparative reports form the basis of our risk analysis, by identifying structural differences between the two. Of themselves, however, they fail to quantify the risk due to these mismatches. The model's anchor is therefore the tracking error report, which quantifies the risks associated with each cross-sectional comparison. Taken together, the various reports produced by the model provide a complete understanding of the risk of this portfolio versus its benchmark.

From the overall statistical summary shown in Exhibit 10.1, it can be seen that the portfolio has a significant term structure exposure, as its duration (4.82) is longer than that of the benchmark (4.29). In addition, the portfolio is overexposed to corporate bonds and underexposed to Treasuries. We will see this explicitly in the sector report later; it is reflected in the statistics in Exhibit 10.1 by a higher average yield and coupon. The overall annualized tracking error, shown at the bottom of the statistics report, is 52 bp. Tracking error is defined as one standard deviation of the difference between the portfolio and benchmark annualized returns. In simple terms, this means that with a probability of about 68%, the portfolio return over the next year will be within ±52 bp of the benchmark return.[2]

[2] This interpretation requires several simplifying assumptions. The 68% confidence interval assumes that returns are normally distributed, which may not be the case. Second, this presentation ignores differences in the expected returns of portfolio and benchmark (due, for example, to a higher portfolio yield). Strictly speaking, the confidence interval should be drawn around the expected outperformance.

EXHIBIT 10.1 Top-Level Statistics Comparison
Sample Portfolio versus Aggregate Index, 9/30/98

	Portfolio	Benchmark
Number of Issues	57	6,932
Average Maturity/Average Life (years)	9.57	8.47
Internal Rate of Return (%)	5.76	5.54
Average Yield to Maturity (%)	5.59	5.46
Average Yield to Worst (%)	5.53	5.37
Average Option-Adjusted Convexity	0.04	−0.22
Average OAS to Maturity (bp)	74	61
Average OAS to Worst (bp)	74	61
Portfolio Mod. Adjusted Duration	4.82	4.29
Portfolio Average Price	108.45	107.70
Portfolio Average Coupon (%)	7.33	6.98
Risk Characteristics		
Estimated Total Tracking Error (bp/year)	52	
Portfolio Beta	1.05	

Sources of Systematic Tracking Error

What are the main sources of this tracking error? The model identifies market forces influencing all securities in a certain category as *systematic risk factors*. Exhibit 10.2 divides the tracking error into components corresponding to different categories of risk. Looking down the first column, we see that the largest sources of systematic tracking error between this portfolio and its benchmark are the differences in sensitivity to term structure movements (36.3 bp) and to changes in credit spreads by sector (32 bp) and quality (14.7 bp). The components of systematic tracking error correspond directly to the groups of risk factors. A detailed report of the differences in portfolio and benchmark exposures (sensitivities) to the relevant set of risk factors illustrates the origin of each component of systematic risk.

Sensitivities to risk factors are called *factor loadings*. They are expressed in units that depend on the definition of each particular risk factor. For example, for risk factors representing volatility of corporate spreads, factor loadings are given by spread durations; for risk factors measuring volatility of prepayment speed (in units of PSA), factor loadings are given by "PSA Duration." The factor loadings of a portfolio or an index are calculated as a market-value weighted average over all constituent securities. Differences between portfolio and benchmark factor loadings form a vector of *active portfolio exposures*. A quick comparison of the magnitudes of the different components of tracking error highlights the most significant mismatches.

EXHIBIT 10.2 Tracking Error Breakdown for Sample Portfolio
Sample Portfolio versus Aggregate Index, 9/30/98

	Tracking Error (bp/Year)		
	Isolated	Cumulative	Change in Cumulative*
Tracking Error Term Structure	36.3	36.3	36.3
Non-Term Structure	39.5		
Tracking Error Sector	32.0	38.3	2.0
Tracking Error Quality	14.7	44.1	5.8
Tracking Error Optionality	1.6	44.0	–0.1
Tracking Error Coupon	3.2	45.5	1.5
Tracking Error MBS Sector	4.9	43.8	–1.7
Tracking Error MBS Volatility	7.2	44.5	0.7
Tracking Error MBS Prepayment	2.5	45.0	0.4
Total Systematic Tracking Error			45.0
Nonsystematic Tracking Error			
Issuer-specific	25.9		
Issue-specific	26.4		
Total	26.1		
Total Tracking Error			52

	Systematic	Nonsystematic	Total
Benchmark Return Standard Deviation	417	4	417
Portfolio Return Standard Deviation	440	27	440

* Isolated Tracking Error is the projected deviation between the portfolio and benchmark return due to a single category of systematic risk. Cumulative Tracking Error shows the combined effect of all risk categories from the first one in the table to the current one.

EXHIBIT 10.3 Term Structure Report
Sample Portfolio versus Aggregate Index, 9/30/98

	Cash Flows		
Year	Portfolio	Benchmark	Difference
0.00	1.45%	1.85%	−0.40%
0.25	3.89	4.25	−0.36
0.50	4.69	4.25	0.45
0.75	4.34	3.76	0.58
1.00	8.90	7.37	1.53
1.50	7.47	10.29	−2.82
2.00	10.43	8.09	2.34
2.50	8.63	6.42	2.20
3.00	4.28	5.50	−1.23
3.50	3.90	4.81	−0.92
4.00	6.74	7.19	−0.46
5.00	6.13	6.96	−0.83
6.00	3.63	4.67	−1.04
7.00	5.77	7.84	−2.07
10.00	7.16	7.37	−0.21
15.00	4.63	3.88	0.75
20.00	3.52	3.04	0.48
25.00	3.18	1.73	1.45
30.00	1.22	0.68	0.54
40.00	0.08	0.07	0.01

Because the largest component of tracking error is due to term structure, let us examine the term structure risk in our example. Risk factors associated with term structure movements are represented by the fixed set of points on the theoretical Treasury spot curve shown in Exhibit 10.3. Each of these risk factors exhibits a certain historical return volatility. The extent to which the portfolio and the benchmark returns are affected by this volatility is measured by factor loadings (exposures). These exposures are computed as percentages of the total present value of the portfolio and benchmark cash flows allocated to each point on the curve. The risk of the portfolio performing differently from the benchmark due to term structure movements is due to the differences in the portfolio and benchmark exposures to these risk factors and to their volatilities and correlations. Exhibit 10.3 compares the term structure exposures of the portfolio and benchmark for our example. The Difference column shows the portfolio to be overweighted in the 2-year section of the curve, underweighted in the 3- to 10-year range, and overweighted at the long end. This makes the portfolio longer than the benchmark and more barbelled.

The tracking error is calculated from this vector of differences between portfolio and benchmark exposures. However, mismatches at different points are not treated equally. Exposures to factors with higher volatilities have a larger effect on tracking error. In this example, the risk exposure with the largest contribution to tracking error is the overweight of 1.45% to the 25-year point on the curve. While other vertices have larger mismatches (e.g., –2.07% at 7 years), their overall effect on risk is not as strong because the longer duration of a 25-year zero causes it to have a higher return volatility. It should also be noted that the risk caused by overweighting one segment of the yield curve can sometimes be offset by underweighting another. Exhibit 10.3 shows the portfolio to be underexposed to the 1.50-year point on the yield curve by –2.82% and overexposed to the 2.00-year point on the curve by +2.34%. Those are largely offsetting positions in terms of risk because these two adjacent points on the curve are highly correlated and almost always move together. To eliminate completely the tracking error due to term structure, differences in exposures to each term structure risk factor need to be reduced to zero. To lower term structure risk, it is most important to focus first on reducing exposures at the long end of the curve, particularly those that are not offset by opposing positions in nearby points.

The tracking error due to sector exposures is explained by the detailed sector report shown in Exhibit 10.4. This report shows the sector allocations of the portfolio and the benchmark in two ways. In addition to reporting the percentage of market value allocated to each sector, it shows the contribution of each sector to the overall spread duration.[3] These contributions are computed as the product of the percentage allocations to a sector and the market-weighted average spread duration of the holdings in that sector. Contributions to spread duration (factor loadings) measure the sensitivity of return to systematic changes in particular sector spreads (risk factors) and are a better measure of risk than simple market allocations. The rightmost column in this report, the difference between portfolio and benchmark contributions to spread duration in each sector, is the exposure vector that is used to

[3] Just as traditional duration can be defined as the sensitivity of bond price to a change in yield, spread duration is defined as the sensitivity of bond price to a change in spread. While this distinction is largely academic for bullet bonds, it can be significant for other securities, such as bonds with embedded options and floating-rate securities. The sensitivity to spread change is the correct measure of sector risk.

compute tracking error due to sector. A quick look down this column shows that the largest exposures in our example are an underweight of 0.77 years to Treasuries and an overweight of 1.00 years to consumer non-cyclicals in the industrial sector. (The fine-grained breakdown of the corporate market into industry groups corresponds to the second tier of the Lehman Brothers hierarchical industry classification scheme.) Note that the units of risk factors and factor loadings for sector risk differ from those used to model the term structure risk.

EXHIBIT 10.4 Detailed Sector Report
Sample Portfolio versus Aggregate Index, 9/30/98

	Portfolio			Benchmark			Difference	
Detailed Sector	% of Portf.	Adj. Dur.	Contrib. to Adj. Dur.	% of Portf.	Adj. Dur.	Contrib. to Adj. Dur.	% of Portf.	Contrib. to Adj. Dur.
Treasury								
Coupon	27.09	5.37	1.45	39.82	5.58	2.22	−12.73	−0.77
Strip	0.00	0.00	0.00	0.00	0.00	0.00	0.00	0.00
Agencies								
FNMA	4.13	3.40	0.14	3.56	3.44	0.12	0.57	0.02
FHLB	0.00	0.00	0.00	1.21	2.32	0.03	−1.21	−0.03
FHLMC	0.00	0.00	0.00	0.91	3.24	0.03	−0.91	−0.03
REFCORP	3.51	11.22	0.39	0.83	12.18	0.10	2.68	0.29
Other Agencies	0.00	0.00	0.00	1.31	5.58	0.07	−1.31	−0.07
Financial Inst.								
Banking	1.91	5.31	0.10	2.02	5.55	0.11	−0.11	−0.01
Brokerage	1.35	3.52	0.05	0.81	4.14	0.03	0.53	0.01
Financial Cos.	1.88	2.92	0.06	2.11	3.78	0.08	−0.23	−0.02
Insurance	0.00	0.00	0.00	0.52	7.47	0.04	−0.52	−0.04
Other	0.00	0.00	0.00	0.28	5.76	0.02	−0.28	−0.02
Industrials								
Basic	0.63	6.68	0.04	0.89	6.39	0.06	−0.26	−0.01
Capital Goods	4.43	5.35	0.24	1.16	6.94	0.08	3.26	0.16
Consumer Cycl.	2.01	8.37	0.17	2.28	7.10	0.16	−0.27	0.01
Consum. Non-cycl.	8.88	12.54	1.11	1.66	6.84	0.11	7.22	1.00
Energy	1.50	6.82	0.10	0.69	6.89	0.05	0.81	0.05
Technology	1.55	1.58	0.02	0.42	7.39	0.03	1.13	−0.01
Transportation	0.71	12.22	0.09	0.57	7.41	0.04	0.14	0.04
Utilities								
Electric	0.47	3.36	0.02	1.39	5.02	0.07	−0.93	−0.05
Telephone	9.18	2.08	0.19	1.54	6.58	0.10	7.64	0.09
Natural Gas	0.80	5.53	0.04	0.49	6.50	0.03	0.31	0.01
Water	0.00	0.00	0.00	0.00	0.00	0.00	0.00	0.00

EXHIBIT 10.4 (Continued)

Detailed Sector	Portfolio % of Portf.	Portfolio Adj. Dur.	Portfolio Contrib. to Adj. Dur.	Benchmark % of Portf.	Benchmark Adj. Dur.	Benchmark Contrib. to Adj. Dur.	Difference % of Portf.	Difference Contrib. to Adj. Dur.
Yankee								
Canadians	1.45	7.87	0.11	1.06	6.67	0.07	0.38	0.04
Corporates	0.49	3.34	0.02	1.79	6.06	0.11	−1.30	−0.09
Supranational	1.00	6.76	0.07	0.38	6.33	0.02	0.62	0.04
Sovereigns	0.00	0.00	0.00	0.66	5.95	0.04	−0.66	−0.04
Hypothetical	0.00	0.00	0.00	0.00	0.00	0.00	0.00	0.00
Cash	0.00	0.00	0.00	0.00	0.00	0.00	0.00	0.00
Mortgage								
Conventnl. 30-yr.	12.96	1.52	0.20	16.60	1.42	0.24	−3.64	−0.04
GNMA 30-yr.	7.53	1.23	0.09	7.70	1.12	0.09	−0.16	0.01
MBS 15-yr.	3.52	1.95	0.07	5.59	1.63	0.09	−2.06	−0.02
Balloons	3.03	1.69	0.05	0.78	1.02	0.01	2.25	0.04
OTM	0.00	0.00	0.00	0.00	0.00	0.00	0.00	0.00
European & International								
Eurobonds	0.00	0.00	0.00	0.00	0.00	0.00	0.00	0.00
International	0.00	0.00	0.00	0.00	0.00	0.00	0.00	0.00
Asset Backed	0.00	0.00	0.00	0.96	3.14	0.03	−0.96	−0.03
CMO	0.00	0.00	0.00	0.00	0.00	0.00	0.00	0.00
Other	0.00	0.00	0.00	0.00	0.00	0.00	0.00	0.00
Totals	100.00		4.82	100.00		4.29	0.00	0.54

The analysis of credit quality risk shown in Exhibit 10.5 follows the same approach. Portfolio and benchmark allocations to different credit rating levels are compared in terms of contributions to spread duration. Once again we see the effect of the overweighting of corporates: There is an overweight of 0.80 years to single As and an underweight of −0.57 years in AAAs (U.S. government debt). The risk represented by tracking error due to quality corresponds to a systematic widening or tightening of spreads for a particular credit rating, uniformly across all industry groups.

As we saw in Exhibit 10.2, the largest sources of systematic risk in our sample portfolio are term structure, sector, and quality. We have therefore directed our attention first to the reports that address these risk components; we will return to them later. Next we examine the reports explaining optionality risk and mortgage risk, even though these risks do not contribute significantly to the risk of this particular portfolio.

EXHIBIT 10.5 Quality Report
Sample Portfolio versus Aggregate Index, 9/30/98

	Portfolio			Benchmark			Difference	
Quality	% of Portf.	Adj. Dur.	Cntrb. to Adj. Dur.	% of Portf.	Adj. Dur.	Cntrb. to Adj. Dur.	% of Portf.	Cntrb. to Adj. Dur.
Aaa+	34.72	5.72	1.99	47.32	5.41	2.56	−12.60	−0.57
MBS	27.04	1.51	0.41	30.67	1.37	0.42	−3.62	−0.01
Aaa	1.00	6.76	0.07	2.33	4.84	0.11	−1.33	−0.05
Aa	5.54	5.67	0.31	4.19	5.32	0.22	1.35	0.09
A	17.82	7.65	1.36	9.09	6.23	0.57	8.73	0.80
Baa	13.89	4.92	0.68	6.42	6.28	0.40	7.47	0.28
Ba	0.00	0.00	0.00	0.00	0.00	0.00	0.00	0.00
B	0.00	0.00	0.00	0.00	0.00	0.00	0.00	0.00
Caa	0.00	0.00	0.00	0.00	0.00	0.00	0.00	0.00
Ca or lower	0.00	0.00	0.00	0.00	0.00	0.00	0.00	0.00
NR	0.00	0.00	0.00	0.00	0.00	0.00	0.00	0.00
Totals	100.00		4.82	100.00		4.29	0.00	0.54

Exhibit 10.6 shows the optionality report. Several different measures are used to analyze portfolio and benchmark exposures to changes in the value of embedded options. For callable and putable bonds, the difference between a bond's static duration[4] and its option-adjusted duration, known as "reduction due to call," gives one measure of the effect of optionality on pricing. This "reduction" is positive for bonds trading to maturity and negative for bonds trading to a call. These two categories of bonds are represented by separate risk factors. The exposures of the portfolio and benchmark to this "reduction," divided into option categories, constitute one set of factor loadings due to optionality. The model also looks at option delta and gamma, the first and second derivatives of option price with respect to security price.

[4] "Static duration" refers to the traditional duration of the bond assuming a fixed set of cash flows. Depending on how the bond is trading, these will be the bond's natural cash flows either to maturity or to the most likely option redemption date.

EXHIBIT 10.6 Optionality Report: Sample Portfolio versus Aggregate Index, 9/30/98

Optionality	% of Portfolio	Duration	Contrib. to Duration	Adjusted Duration	Contrib. to Adj. Dur.	Reduction Due to Call
PORTFOLIO						
Bullet	63.95	5.76	3.68	5.76	3.68	0.00
Callable Traded to Matur.	4.74	10.96	0.52	10.96	0.52	0.00
Callable Traded to Call	4.26	8.43	0.36	4.97	0.21	0.15
Putable Traded to Matur.	0.00	0.00	0.00	0.00	0.00	0.00
Putable Traded to Put	0.00	0.00	0.00	0.00	0.00	0.00
MBS	27.04	3.28	0.89	1.51	0.41	0.48
ABS	0.00	0.00	0.00	0.00	0.00	0.00
CMO	0.00	0.00	0.00	0.00	0.00	0.00
Others	0.00	0.00	0.00	0.00	0.00	0.00
Totals	100.00		5.45		4.82	0.63
BENCHMARK						
Bullet	57.53	5.70	3.28	5.70	3.28	0.00
Callable Traded to Matur.	2.66	9.06	0.24	8.50	0.23	0.01
Callable Traded to Call	7.06	6.93	0.49	3.56	0.25	0.24
Putable Traded to Matur.	0.35	11.27	0.04	9.64	0.03	0.01
Putable Traded to Put	0.78	11.59	0.09	5.77	0.04	0.05
MBS	30.67	3.25	1.00	1.37	0.42	0.58
ABS	0.96	3.14	0.03	3.14	0.03	0.00
CMO	0.00	0.00	0.00	0.00	0.00	0.00
Others	0.00	0.00	0.00	0.00	0.00	0.00
Totals	100.00		5.17		4.29	0.88

EXHIBIT 10.6 (Continued)

Option Delta Analysis

Option Delta	Portfolio			Benchmark			Difference	
	% of Portf.	Delta	Cntrb. to Delta	% of Portf.	Delta	Cntrb. to Delta	% of Portf.	Cntrb. to Delta
Bullet	63.95	0.000	0.000	57.53	0.000	0.000	6.43	0.000
Callable Traded to Matur.	4.74	0.000	0.000	2.66	0.057	0.002	2.08	−0.002
Callable Traded to Call	4.26	0.474	0.020	7.06	0.584	0.041	−2.80	−0.021
Putable Traded to Matur.	0.00	0.000	0.000	0.35	0.129	0.001	−0.35	−0.001
Putable Traded to Put	0.00	0.000	0.000	0.78	0.507	0.004	−0.78	−0.004
Totals	72.96		0.020	68.38		0.047	4.58	−0.027

Option Gamma Analysis

Option Gamma	Portfolio			Benchmark			Difference	
	% of Portf.	Delta	Cntrb. to Delta	% of Portf.	Delta	Cntrb. to Delta	% of Portf.	Cntrb. to Delta
Bullet	63.95	0.0000	0.0000	57.53	0.0000	0.0000	6.43	0.0000
Callable Traded to Matur.	4.74	0.0000	0.0000	2.66	0.0024	0.0001	2.08	−0.0001
Callable Traded to Call	4.26	0.0059	0.0002	7.06	0.0125	0.0009	−2.80	−0.0006
Putable Traded to Matur.	0.00	0.0000	0.0000	0.35	−0.0029	−0.0000	−0.35	0.0000
Putable Traded to Put	0.00	0.0000	0.0000	0.78	−0.0008	−0.0000	−0.78	0.0000
Totals	72.96		0.0002	68.38		0.0009	4.58	−0.0007

The risks particular to mortgage-backed securities consist of spread risk, prepayment risk, and convexity risk. The underpinnings for MBS sector spread risk, like those for corporate sectors, are found in the detailed sector report shown in Exhibit 10.4. Mortgage-backed securities are divided into four broad sectors based on a combination of originating agency and product: conventional 30-year; GNMA 30-year; all 15-year; and all balloons. The contributions of these four sectors to the portfolio and benchmark spread durations form the factor loadings for mortgage sector risk. Exposures to prepayments are shown in Exhibit 10.7. This group of risk factors corresponds to systematic changes in prepayment speeds by sector. Thus, the factor loadings represent the sensitivities of mortgage prices to changes in prepayment speeds (PSA durations). Premium mortgages will show negative prepayment sensitivities (i.e., prices will decrease with increasing prepayment speed), while those of discount mortgages will be positive. To curtail the exposure to sudden changes in prepayment rates, the portfolio should match the benchmark contributions to prepayment sensitivity in each mortgage sector. The third mortgage-specific component of tracking error is due to MBS volatility. Convexity is used as a measure of volatility sensitivity because volatility shocks will have the strongest impact on prices of those mortgages whose prepayment options are at the money (current coupons). These securities tend to have the most negative convexity. Exhibit 10.8 shows the comparison of portfolio and benchmark contributions to convexity in each mortgage sector, which forms the basis for this component of tracking error.

Sources of Nonsystematic Tracking Error

In addition to the various sources of systematic risk, Exhibit 10.2 indicates that the sample portfolio has 26 bp of nonsystematic tracking error, or special risk. This risk stems from portfolio concentrations in individual securities or issuers. The portfolio report in Exhibit 10.9 helps elucidate this risk. The rightmost column of the exhibit shows the percentage of the portfolio's market value invested in each security. As the portfolio is relatively small, each bond makes up a noticeable fraction. In particular, there are two extremely large positions in corporate bonds, issued by GTE Corp. and Coca-Cola. With $50 million a piece, each of these two bonds represents more than 8% of the portfolio. A negative credit event associated with either of these firms (i.e., a downgrade) would cause large losses in the portfolio, while hardly affecting the highly diversified benchmark. The Aggregate Index consisted of almost 7,000 securities as of September 30, 1998, so that the largest U.S. Treasury issue accounts for less than 1%, and most corporate issues contribute less than 0.01% of the index market value. Thus, any large position in a corporate issue represents a material difference between portfolio and benchmark exposures that must be considered in a full treatment of risk.

EXHIBIT 10.7 MBS Prepayment Sensitivity Report
Sample Portfolio versus Aggregate Index, 9/30/98

	Portfolio			Benchmark			Difference	
MBS Sector	% of Portfolio	PSA Sens.	Cntrb. to PSA Sens.	% of Portfolio	PSA Sens.	Cntrb. to PSA Sens.	% of Portfolio	Cntrb. to PSA Sens.
COUPON < 6.0%								
Conventional	0.00	0.00	0.00	0.00	1.28	0.00	0.00	0.00
GNMA 30-yr.	0.00	0.00	0.00	0.00	1.03	0.00	0.00	0.00
15-year MBS	0.00	0.00	0.00	0.14	0.01	0.00	−0.14	0.00
Balloon	0.00	0.00	0.00	0.05	−0.08	0.00	−0.05	0.00
6.0% ≤ COUPON < 7.0%								
Conventional	2.90	−1.14	−0.03	5.37	−1.05	−0.06	−2.48	0.02
GNMA 30-yr.	0.76	−1.19	−0.01	1.30	−1.11	−0.01	−0.53	0.01
15-year MBS	3.52	−0.86	−0.03	3.26	−0.88	−0.03	0.26	0.00
Balloon	3.03	−0.54	−0.02	0.48	−0.73	0.00	2.55	−0.01
7.0% ≤ COUPON < 8.0%								
Conventional	4.93	−2.10	−0.10	8.32	−2.79	−0.23	−3.39	0.13
GNMA 30-yr.	4.66	−3.20	−0.15	3.90	−2.82	−0.11	0.76	−0.04
15-year MBS	0.00	0.00	0.00	1.83	−1.92	−0.04	−1.83	0.04
Balloon	0.00	0.00	0.00	0.25	−1.98	−0.01	−0.25	0.01
8.0% ≤ COUPON < 9.0%								
Conventional	5.14	−3.91	−0.20	2.26	−4.27	−0.10	2.87	−0.10
GNMA 30-yr.	0.00	0.00	0.00	1.71	−4.71	−0.08	−1.71	0.08
15-year MBS	0.00	0.00	0.00	0.31	−2.16	−0.01	−0.31	0.01
Balloon	0.00	0.00	0.00	0.00	−2.38	0.00	0.00	0.00
9.0% ≤ COUPON < 10.0%								
Conventional	0.00	0.00	0.00	0.54	−6.64	−0.04	−0.54	0.04
GNMA 30-yr.	2.11	−7.24	−0.15	0.62	−6.05	−0.04	1.49	−0.12
15-year MBS	0.00	0.00	0.00	0.04	−1.61	0.00	−0.04	0.00
Balloon	0.00	0.00	0.00	0.00	0.00	0.00	0.00	0.00
COUPON ≥ 10.0%								
Conventional	0.00	0.00	0.00	0.10	−8.14	−0.01	−0.10	0.01
GNMA 30-yr.	0.00	0.00	0.00	0.17	−7.49	−0.01	−0.17	0.01
15-year MBS	0.00	0.00	0.00	0.00	0.00	0.00	0.00	0.00
Balloon	0.00	0.00	0.00	0.00	0.00	0.00	0.00	0.00
Subtotals								
Conventional	12.96		−0.34	16.6		−0.43	−3.64	0.09
GNMA 30-yr.	7.53		−0.31	7.70		−0.26	−0.16	−0.06
15-year MBS	3.52		−0.03	5.59		−0.07	−2.06	0.04
Balloon	3.03		−0.02	0.78		−0.01	2.25	−0.01
Totals	27.04		−0.70	30.67		−0.76	−3.62	0.07

EXHIBIT 10.8 MBS Convexity Analysis
Sample Portfolio versus Aggregate Index, 9/30/98

	Portfolio			Benchmark			Difference	
MBS Sector	% of Portfolio	Convexity	Cntrb. to Convexity	% of Portfolio	Convexity	Cntrb. to Convexity	% of Portfolio	Cntrb. to Convexity
COUPON < 6.0%								
Conventional	0.00	0.00	0.00	0.00	−0.56	0.00	0.00	0.00
GNMA 30-yr.	0.00	0.00	0.00	0.00	−0.85	0.00	0.00	0.00
15-year MBS	0.00	0.00	0.00	0.14	−0.88	0.00	−0.14	0.00
Balloon	0.00	0.00	0.00	0.05	−0.48	0.00	−0.05	0.00
6.0% ≤ COUPON < 7.0%								
Conventional	2.90	−3.52	−0.10	5.37	−3.19	−0.17	−2.48	0.07
GNMA 30-yr.	0.76	−3.65	−0.03	1.30	−3.13	−0.04	−0.53	0.01
15-year MBS	3.52	−1.78	−0.06	3.26	−2.06	−0.07	0.26	0.00
Balloon	3.03	−1.50	−0.05	0.48	−1.11	−0.01	2.55	−0.04
7.0% ≤ COUPON < 8.0%								
Conventional	4.93	−3.39	−0.17	8.32	−2.60	−0.22	−3.39	0.05
GNMA 30-yr.	4.66	−2.40	−0.11	3.90	−2.88	−0.11	0.76	0.00
15-year MBS	0.00	0.00	0.00	1.83	−1.56	−0.03	−1.83	0.03
Balloon	0.00	0.00	0.00	0.25	−0.97	0.00	−0.25	0.00
8.0% ≤ COUPON < 9.0%								
Conventional	5.14	−1.27	−0.07	2.26	−1.01	−0.02	2.87	−0.04
GNMA 30-yr.	0.00	0.00	0.00	1.71	−0.56	−0.01	−1.71	0.01
15-year MBS	0.00	0.00	0.00	0.31	−0.93	0.00	−0.31	0.00
Balloon	0.00	0.00	0.00	0.00	−0.96	0.00	0.00	0.00
9.0% ≤ COUPON < 10.0%								
Conventional	0.00	0.00	0.00	0.54	−0.80	0.00	−0.54	0.00
GNMA 30-yr.	2.11	−0.34	−0.01	0.62	−0.36	0.00	1.49	−0.01
15-year MBS	0.00	0.00	0.00	0.04	−0.52	0.00	−0.04	0.00
Balloon	0.00	0.00	0.00	0.00	0.00	0.00	0.00	0.00
COUPON ≥ 10.0%								
Conventional	0.00	0.00	0.00	0.10	−0.61	0.00	−0.10	0.00
GNMA 30-yr.	0.00	0.00	0.00	0.17	−0.21	0.00	−0.17	0.00
15-year MBS	0.00	0.00	0.00	0.00	0.00	0.00	0.00	0.00
Balloon	0.00	0.00	0.00	0.00	0.00	0.00	0.00	0.00
Subtotals								
Conventional	12.96		−0.33	16.6		−0.42	−3.64	0.08
GNMA 30-yr.	7.53		−0.15	7.70		−0.16	−0.16	0.02
15-year MBS	3.52		−0.06	5.59		−0.10	−2.06	0.04
Balloon	3.03		−0.05	0.78		−0.01	2.25	−0.04
Totals	27.04		−0.59	30.67		−0.69	−3.62	0.10

EXHIBIT 10.9 Portfolio Report: Composition of Sample Portfolio, 9/30/98

#	CUSIP	Issuer Name	Coup.	Maturity	Moody	S&P	Sect.	Dur. W	Dur. A	Par Val.	%
1	057224AF	BAKER HUGHES	8.000	05/15/04	A2	A	IND	4.47	4.47	5,000	0.87
2	097023AL	BOEING CO.	6.350	06/15/03	Aa3	AA	IND	3.98	3.98	10,000	1.58
3	191219AY	COCA-COLA ENTERPRISES I.	6.950	11/15/26	A3	A+	IND	12.37	12.37	50,000	8.06
4	532457AP	ELI LILLY CO.	6.770	01/01/36	Aa3	AA	IND	14.18	14.18	5,000	0.83
5	293561BS	ENRON CORP.	6.625	11/15/05	Baa2	BBB+	UTL	5.53	5.53	5,000	0.80
6	31359MDN	FEDERAL NATL MTG ASSN.	5.625	03/15/01	Aaa+	AAA+	USA	2.27	2.27	10,000	1.53
7	31359CAT	FEDERAL NATL MTG ASSN.-G	7.400	07/01/04	Aaa+	AAA+	USA	4.66	4.66	8,000	1.37
8	FGG06096	FHLM Gold 7-Years Balloon	6.000	04/01/26	Aaa+	AAA+	FHg	2.55	1.69	20,000	3.03
9	FGD06494	FHLM Gold Guar. Single Fam.	6.500	08/01/08	Aaa+	AAA+	FHd	3.13	1.95	23,000	3.52
10	FGB07098	FHLM Gold Guar. Single Fam.	7.000	01/01/28	Aaa+	AAA+	FHb	3.68	1.33	32,000	4.93
11	FGB06498	FHLM Gold Guar. Single Fam.	6.500	02/01/28	Aaa+	AAA+	FHb	5.00	2.83	19,000	2.90
12	319279BP	FIRST BANK SYSTEM	6.875	09/15/07	A2	A–	FIN	6.73	6.73	4,000	0.65
13	339012AB	FLEET MORTGAGE GROUP	6.500	09/15/99	A2	A+	FIN	0.92	0.92	4,000	0.60
14	FNA08092	FNMA Conventional Long T.	8.000	05/01/21	Aaa+	AAA+	FNa	2.56	0.96	33,000	5.14
15	31364FSK	FNMA MTN	6.420	02/12/08	Aaa+	AAA+	USA	2.16	3.40	8,000	1.23
16	345397GS	FORD MOTOR CREDIT	7.500	01/15/03	A1	A	FIN	3.62	3.62	4,000	0.65
17	347471AR	FORT JAMES CORP.	6.875	09/15/07	Baa2	BBB–	IND	6.68	6.68	4,000	0.63
18	GNA09490	GNMA I Single Family	9.500	10/01/19	Aaa+	AAA+	GNa	2.69	1.60	13,000	2.11
19	GNA07493	GNMA I Single Family	7.500	07/01/22	Aaa+	AAA+	GNa	3.13	0.75	30,000	4.66
20	GNA06498	GNMA I Single Family	6.500	02/01/28	Aaa+	AAA+	GNa	5.34	3.14	5,000	0.76
21	362320AQ	GTE CORP.	9.375	12/01/00	Baa1	A	TEL	1.91	1.91	50,000	8.32

EXHIBIT 10.9 (Continued)

#	CUSIP	Issuer Name	Coup.	Maturity	Moody	S&P	Sect.	Dur. W	Dur. A	Par Val.	%
22	458182CB	INT.-AMERICAN DEV. BANK-G	6.375	10/22/07	Aaa	AAA	SUP	6.76	6.76	6,000	1.00
23	459200AK	INTL. BUSINESS MACHINES	6.375	06/15/00	A1	A+	IND	1.58	1.58	10,000	1.55
24	524909AS	LEHMAN BROTHERS INC.	7.125	07/15/02	Baa1	A	FIN	3.20	3.20	4,000	0.59
25	539830AA	LOCKHEED MARTIN	6.550	05/15/99	A3	BBB+	IND	0.59	0.59	10,000	1.53
26	563469CZ	MANITOBA PROV. CANADA	8.875	09/15/21	A1	AA–	CAN	11.34	11.34	4,000	0.79
27	58013MDE	MCDONALDS CORP.	5.950	01/15/08	Aa2	AA	IND	7.05	7.05	4,000	0.63
28	590188HZ	MERRILL LYNCH & CO.-GLO	6.000	02/12/03	Aa3	AA–	FIN	3.77	3.77	5,000	0.76
29	638585BE	NATIONSBANK CORP.	5.750	03/15/01	Aa2	A+	FIN	2.26	2.26	3,000	0.45
30	650094BM	NEW YORK TELEPHONE	9.375	07/15/31	A2	A+	TEL	2.43	3.66	5,000	0.86
31	654106AA	NIKE INC.	6.375	12/01/03	A1	A+	IND	4.30	4.30	3,000	0.48
32	655844AJ	NORFOLK SOUTHERN CORP.	7.800	05/15/27	Baa1	BBB+	IND	12.22	12.22	4,000	0.71
33	669383CN	NORWEST FINANCIAL INC.	6.125	08/01/03	Aa3	AA–	FIN	4.12	4.12	4,000	0.62
34	683234HG	ONT PROV CANADA-GLOBAL	7.375	01/27/03	Aa3	AA–	CAN	3.67	3.67	4,000	0.65
35	744567DN	PUB. SVC. ELECTRIC + GAS	6.125	08/01/02	A3	A–	ELU	3.36	3.36	3,000	0.47
36	755111AF	RAYTHEON CO.	7.200	08/15/27	Baa1	BBB	IND	12.61	12.61	8,000	1.31
37	761157AA	RESOLUTION FUNDING CORP.	8.125	10/15/19	Aaa+	AAA+	USA	11.22	11.22	17,000	3.51
38	88731EAF	TIME WARNER ENT.	8.375	03/15/23	Baa2	BBB–	IND	11.45	11.45	5,000	0.90
39	904000AA	ULTRAMAR DIAMOND SHAM.	7.200	10/15/17	Baa2	BBB	IND	10.06	10.06	4,000	0.63
40	912810DB	U.S. TREASURY BONDS	10.375	11/15/12	Aaa+	AAA+	UST	6.30	6.38	10,000	2.17
41	912810DS	U.S. TREASURY BONDS	10.625	08/15/15	Aaa+	AAA+	UST	9.68	9.68	14,000	3.43

EXHIBIT 10.9 (Continued)

#	CUSIP	Issuer Name	Coup.	Maturity	Moody	S&P	Sect.	Dur. W	Dur. A	Par Val.	%
42	912810EQ	U.S. TREASURY BONDS	6.250	08/15/23	Aaa+	AAA+	UST	13.26	13.26	30,000	5.14
43	912827XE	U.S. TREASURY NOTES	8.875	02/15/99	Aaa+	AAA+	UST	0.37	0.37	9,000	1.38
44	912827F9	U.S. TREASURY NOTES	6.375	07/15/99	Aaa+	AAA+	UST	0.76	0.76	4,000	0.61
45	912827R4	U.S. TREASURY NOTES	7.125	09/30/99	Aaa+	AAA+	UST	0.96	0.96	17,000	2.59
46	912827Z9	U.S. TREASURY NOTES	5.875	11/15/99	Aaa+	AAA+	UST	1.06	1.06	17,000	2.62
47	912827T4	U.S. TREASURY NOTES	6.875	03/31/00	Aaa+	AAA+	UST	1.42	1.42	8,000	1.23
48	9128273D	U.S. TREASURY NOTES	6.000	08/15/00	Aaa+	AAA+	UST	1.75	1.75	11,000	1.70
49	912827A8	U.S. TREASURY NOTES	8.000	05/15/01	Aaa+	AAA+	UST	2.31	2.31	9,000	1.50
50	912827D2	U.S. TREASURY NOTES	7.500	11/15/01	Aaa+	AAA+	UST	2.72	2.72	10,000	1.67
51	9128272P	U.S. TREASURY NOTES	6.625	03/31/02	Aaa+	AAA+	UST	3.12	3.12	6,000	0.96
52	9128273G	U.S. TREASURY NOTES	6.250	08/31/02	Aaa+	AAA+	UST	3.45	3.45	10,000	1.60
53	912827L8	U.S. TREASURY NOTES	5.750	08/15/03	Aaa+	AAA+	UST	4.22	4.22	1,000	0.16
54	912827T8	U.S. TREASURY NOTES	6.500	05/15/05	Aaa+	AAA+	UST	5.33	5.33	1,000	0.17
55	9128273E	U.S. TREASURY NOTES	6.125	08/15/07	Aaa+	AAA+	UST	6.90	6.90	1,000	0.17
56	949740BZ	WELLS FARGO + CO.	6.875	04/01/06	A2	A–	FIN	5.89	5.89	5,000	0.80
57	961214AD	WESTPAC BANKING CORP.	7.875	10/15/02	A1	A+	FOC	3.34	3.34	3,000	0.49

EXHIBIT 10.10 Calculation of Variance Due to Special Risk (Issue-Specific Model)*

	Portfolio Weights	Benchmark Weights	Contribution to Issue-Specific Risk
Issue 1	w_{P_1}	w_{B_1}	$(w_{P_1} - w_{B_1})^2 \sigma_{\varepsilon_1}^2$
Issue 2	w_{P_2}	w_{B_2}	$(w_{P_2} - w_{B_2})^2 \sigma_{\varepsilon_2}^2$
. . .			
Issue $N - 1$	$w_{P_{N-1}}$	$w_{B_{N-1}}$	$(w_{P_{N-1}} - w_{B_{N-1}})^2 \sigma_{\varepsilon_{N-1}}^2$
Issue N	w_{P_N}	w_{B_N}	$(w_{P_N} - w_{B_N})^2 \sigma_{\varepsilon_N}^2$
Total Issue-Specific Risk			$\sum_{i=1}^{N} (w_{P_i} - w_{B_i})^2 \sigma_{\varepsilon_i}^2$

* w_{P_i} and w_{B_i} are weights of security i in the portfolio and in the benchmark as a percentage of total market value. $\sigma_{\varepsilon_i}^2$ is the variance of residual returns for security i. It is obtained from historical volatility of security-specific residual returns unexplained by the combination of all systematic risk factors.

The magnitude of the return variance that the risk model associates with a mismatch in allocations to a particular issue is proportional to the square of the allocation difference and to the residual return variance estimated for the issue. This calculation is shown in schematic form in Exhibit 10.10 and illustrated numerically for our sample portfolio in Exhibit 10.11. With the return variance based on the square of the market weight, it is dominated by the largest positions in the portfolio. The set of bonds shown includes those with the greatest allocations in the portfolio and in the benchmark. The large position in the Coca-Cola bond contributes 21 bp of the total nonsystematic risk of 26 bp. This is due to the 8.05% overweighting of this bond relative to its position in the index and the 77 bp monthly volatility of nonsystematic return that the model has estimated for this bond. (This estimate is based on bond characteristics such as sector, quality, duration, age, and amount outstanding.) The contribution to the annualized tracking error is then given by

$$\sqrt{12 \times (0.0805 \times 77)^2} = 21$$

EXHIBIT 10.11 Illustration of the Calculation of Nonsystematic Tracking Error

CUSIP	Issuer	Coupon	Maturity	Spec. Risk Vol. (bp/Mo.)	% of Portf.	% of Bnchmrk.	Diff.	Contrib. Tracking Error (bp/Mo.)
097023AL	BOEING CO.	6.350	06/15/03	44	1.58	0.01	1.58	2
191219AY	COCA-COLA ENTERPRISES INC.	6.950	11/15/26	77	8.06	0.01	8.05	21
362320AQ	GTE CORP.	9.375	12/01/00	37	8.32	0.01	8.31	11
532457AP	ELI LILLY CO.	6.770	01/01/36	78	0.83	0.01	0.82	2
563469CZ	MANITOBA PROV. CANADA	8.875	09/15/21	73	0.79	0.01	0.79	2
655844AJ	NORFOLK SOUTHERN CORP.	7.800	05/15/27	84	0.71	0.02	0.70	2
755111AF	RAYTHEON CO.	7.200	08/15/27	85	1.31	0.01	1.30	4
761157AA	RESOLUTION FUNDING CORP.	8.125	10/15/19	19	3.51	0.12	3.39	2
88731EAF	TIME WARNER ENT.	8.375	03/15/23	80	0.90	0.02	0.88	2
912810DS	U.S. TREASURY BONDS	10.625	08/15/15	17	3.43	0.18	3.25	2
912810EC	U.S. TREASURY BONDS	8.875	02/15/19	18	0.00	0.49	−0.49	0
912810ED	U.S. TREASURY BONDS	8.125	08/15/19	18	0.00	0.47	−0.47	0
912810EG	U.S. TREASURY BONDS	8.750	08/15/20	18	0.00	0.54	−0.54	0
912810EL	U.S. TREASURY BONDS	8.000	11/15/21	17	0.00	0.81	−0.81	0
912810EQ	U.S. TREASURY BONDS	6.250	08/15/23	19	5.14	0.46	4.68	3
912810FB	U.S. TREASURY BONDS	6.125	11/15/27	20	0.00	0.44	−0.44	0
FGB07097	FHLM Gold Guar. Single Fam. 30-yr.	7.000	04/01/27	16	0.00	0.56	−0.56	0
FGB07098	FHLM Gold Guar. Single Fam. 30-yr.	7.000	01/01/28	15	4.93	0.46	4.47	2
FNA06498	FNMA Conventional Long T. 30-yr.	6.500	03/01/28	15	0.00	1.16	−1.16	1
FNA07093	FNMA Conventional Long T. 30-yr.	7.000	07/01/22	16	0.00	0.65	−0.65	0
FNA07097	FNMA Conventional Long T. 30-yr.	7.000	05/01/27	16	0.00	0.69	−0.69	0
FNA08092	FNMA Conventional Long T. 30-yr.	8.000	05/01/21	17	5.14	0.24	4.90	3
GNA07493	GNMA I Single Fam. 30-yr.	7.500	07/01/22	16	4.66	0.30	4.36	2

While the overweighting to GTE is larger in terms of percentage of market value, the estimated risk is lower due to the much smaller nonsystematic return volatility (37 bp). This is mainly because the GTE issue has a much shorter maturity (12/2000) than the Coca-Cola issue (11/2026). For bonds of similar maturities, the model tends to assign higher special risk volatilities to lower-rated issues. Thus, mismatches in low-quality bonds with long duration will be the biggest contributors to nonsystematic tracking error. We assume independence of the risk from individual bonds, so the overall nonsystematic risk is computed as the sum of the contributions to variance from each security. Note that mismatches also arise due to bonds that are underweighted in the portfolio. Most bonds in the index do not appear in the portfolio, and each missing bond contributes to tracking error. However, the percentage of the index each bond represents is usually very small. Besides, their contributions to return variance are squared in the calculation of tracking error. Thus, the impact of bonds not included in the portfolio is usually insignificant. The largest contribution to tracking error stemming from an underweighting to a security is due to the 1998 issuance of FNMA 30-year 6.5% pass-throughs, which represents 1.16% of the benchmark. Even this relatively large mismatch contributes only a scant 1 bp to tracking error.

This nonsystematic risk calculation is carried out twice, using two different methods. In the issuer-specific calculation, the holdings of the portfolio and benchmark are not compared on a bond-by-bond basis, as in Exhibits 10.10 and 10.11, but are first aggregated into concentrations in individual issuers. This calculation is based on the assumption that spreads of bonds of the same issuer tend to move together. Therefore, matching the benchmark issuer allocations is sufficient. In the issue-specific calculation, each bond is considered an independent source of risk. This model recognizes that large exposures to a single bond can incur more risk than a portfolio of all of an issuer's debt. In addition to credit events that affect an issuer as a whole, individual issues can be subject to various technical effects. For most portfolios, these two calculations produce very similar results. In certain circumstances, however, there can be significant differences. For instance, some large issuers use an index of all their outstanding debt as an internal performance benchmark. In the case of a single-issuer portfolio and benchmark, the issue-specific risk calculation will provide a much better measure of nonsystematic risk. The reported nonsystematic tracking error of 26.1 bp for this portfolio, which contributes to the total tracking error, is the average of the results from the issuer-specific and issue-specific calculations.

Combining Components of Tracking Error

Given the origins of each component of tracking error shown in Exhibit 10.2, we can address the question of how these components combine to form the overall tracking error. Of the 52 bp of overall tracking error (TE), 45 bp correspond to systematic TE and 26 bp to nonsystematic TE. The net result of these two sources of tracking error does not equal their sum. Rather, the squares of these two numbers (which represent variances) sum to the variance of the result. Next we take its square root to obtain the overall TE ($[45.0^2 + 26.1^2]^{0.5} = 52.0$). This illustrates the risk-reducing benefits of diversification from combining independent (zero correlation) sources of risk.

When components of risk are not assumed to be independent, correlations must be considered. At the top of Exhibit 10.2, we see that the systematic risk is composed of 36.3 bp of term structure risk and 39.5 bp from all other forms of systematic risk combined (non-term structure risk). If these two were independent, they would combine to a systematic tracking error of 53.6 bp ($[36.3^2 + 39.5^2]^{0.5} = 53.6$). The combined systematic tracking error of only 45 bp reflects negative correlations among certain risk factors in the two groups.

The tracking error breakdown report in Exhibit 10.2 shows the sub-components of tracking error due to sector, quality, and so forth. These sub-components are calculated in two different ways. In the first column, we estimate the isolated tracking error due to the effect of each group of related risk factors considered alone. The tracking error due to term structure, for example, reflects only the portfolio/benchmark mismatches in exposures along the yield curve, as well as the volatilities of each of these risk factors and the correlations among them.

Similarly, the tracking error due to sector reflects only the mismatches in sector exposures, the volatilities of these risk factors, and the correlations among them. However, the correlations between the risk factors due to term structure and those due to sector do not participate in either of these calculations. Exhibit 10.12 depicts an idealized covariance matrix containing just three groups of risk factors relating to the yield curve (Y), sector spreads (S), and quality spreads (Q). Exhibit 10.12a illustrates how the covariance matrix is used to calculate the subcomponents of tracking error in the isolated mode. The three shaded blocks represent the parts of the matrix that pertain to: movements of the various points along the yield curve and the correlations among them ($Y \times Y$); movements of sector spreads and the correlations among them ($S \times S$); and movements of quality spreads and the correlations among them ($Q \times Q$). The unshaded portions of the matrix, which deal with the correlations among different sets of risk factors, do not contribute to any of the partial tracking errors.

EXHIBIT 10.12 Illustration of "Isolated" and "Cumulative" Calculations of Tracking Error Subcomponents*

a. Isolated Calculation of Tracking Error Components

$Y \times Y$	$Y \times S$	$Y \times Q$
$S \times Y$	$S \times S$	$S \times Q$
$Q \times Y$	$Q \times S$	$Q \times Q$

b. Cumulative Calculation of Tracking Error Components

$Y \times Y$	$Y \times S$	$Y \times Q$
$S \times Y$	$S \times S$	$S \times Q$
$Q \times Y$	$Q \times S$	$Q \times Q$

* Y – Yield curve risk factors; S – Sector spread risk factors; Q – Credit Quality spread risk factors.

The next two columns of Exhibit 10.2 represent a different way of subdividing tracking error. The middle column shows the *cumulative tracking error*, which incrementally introduces one group of risk factors at a time to the tracking error calculation. In the first row, we find 36.3 bp of tracking error due to term structure. In the second, we see that if term structure and sector risk are considered together, while all other risks are ignored, the tracking error increases to 38.3 bp. The rightmost column shows that the resulting "change in tracking error" due to the incremental inclusion of sector risk is 2.0 bp. As additional groups of risk factors are included, the calculation converges toward the total systematic tracking error, which is obtained with the use of the entire matrix. Exhibit 10.12b illustrates the rectangular section of the covariance matrix that is used at each stage of the calculation. The incremental tracking error due to sector reflects not only the effect of the $S \times S$ box in the diagram, but the $S \times Y$ and $Y \times S$ cross terms as well. That is, the partial tracking error due to sector takes into account the correlations between sector risk and yield curve risk. It answers the question, "Given the exposure to yield curve risk, how much more risk is introduced by the exposure to sector risk?"

The incremental approach is intuitively pleasing because the partial tracking errors (the "Change in Tracking Error" column of Exhibit 10.2) add up to the total systematic tracking error. Of course, the order in which the various partial tracking errors are considered will affect the magnitude of the corresponding terms. Also, note that some of the partial tracking errors computed in this way are negative. This reflects negative correlations among certain groups of risk factors. For example, in Exhibit 10.2, the incremental risk due to the MBS Sector is –1.7 bp.

The two methods used to subdivide tracking error into different components are complementary and serve different purposes. The isolated calculation is ideal for comparing the magnitudes of different types of risk to highlight the most significant exposures. The cumulative approach produces a set of tracking error subcomponents that sum to the total systematic tracking error and reflect the effect of correlations among different groups of risk factors. The major drawback of the cumulative approach is that results are highly dependent on the order in which they are computed. The order currently used by the model was selected based on the significance of each type of risk; it may not be optimal for every portfolio/benchmark combination.

Other Risk Model Outputs

The model's analysis of portfolio and benchmark risk is not limited to the calculation of tracking error. The model also calculates the absolute return volatilities (sigmas) of portfolio and benchmark. *Portfolio sigma* is calculated in the same fashion as tracking error, but is based on the factor loadings (sensitivities to market factors) of the portfolio, rather than on the differences from the benchmark. Sigma represents the volatility of portfolio returns, just as tracking error represents the volatility of the return difference between portfolio and benchmark. Also like tracking error, sigma consists of systematic and nonsystematic components, and the volatility of the benchmark return is calculated in the same way. Both portfolio and benchmark sigmas appear at the bottom of the tracking error report (Exhibit 10.2). Note that the tracking error of 52 bp (the annualized volatility of return difference) is greater than the difference between the return volatilities (sigmas) of the portfolio and the benchmark (440 bp – 417 bp = 23 bp). It is easy to see why this should be so. Assume a benchmark of Treasury bonds, whose entire risk is due to term structure. A portfolio of short-term, high-yield corporate bonds could be constructed such that the overall return volatility would match that of the Treasury benchmark. The magnitude of the credit risk in this portfolio might match the magnitude of the term structure risk in the benchmark, but the two would certainly not cancel each other out. The tracking error in this case might be larger than the sigma of either the portfolio or the benchmark.

In our example, the portfolio sigma is greater than that of the benchmark. Thus, we can say that the portfolio is "more risky" than the benchmark—its longer duration makes it more susceptible to a rise in interest rates. What if the portfolio was shorter than the benchmark and had a lower sigma? In this sense, we could consider the portfolio to be less risky. However, tracking error could be just as big given its capture of the risk of a yield curve rally in which the portfolio would lag. To reduce the risk of underperformance (tracking error), it is necessary to match the risk exposures of portfolio and benchmark. Thus, the reduction of tracking error will typically result in bringing portfolio sigma nearer to that of the benchmark; but sigma can be changed in many ways that will not necessarily improve the tracking error.

It is interesting to compare the nonsystematic components of portfolio and benchmark risk. The first thing to notice is that, when viewed in the context of the overall return volatility, the effect of nonsystematic risk is negligible. To the precision shown, for both the portfolio and benchmark, the overall sigma is equal to its systematic part. The portfolio-level risk due to individual credit events is very small when compared to the total volatility of returns, which includes the entire exposure to all systematic risks, notably yield changes. The portfolio also has significantly more nonsystematic risk (27 bp) than does the benchmark (4 bp), because the latter is much more diversified. In fact, because the benchmark exposures to any individual issuer are so close to zero, the nonsystematic tracking error (26 bp) is almost the same as the nonsystematic part of portfolio sigma. Notice that the nonsystematic risk can form a significant component of the tracking error (26.1 bp out of a total of 52 bp) even as it is a negligible part of the absolute return volatility.

Another quantity calculated by the model is beta, which measures the risk of the portfolio relative to that of the benchmark. The beta for our sample portfolio is 1.05, as shown at the bottom of Exhibit 10.1. This means that the portfolio is more risky (volatile) than the benchmark. For every 100 bp of benchmark return (positive or negative), we would expect to see 105 bp for the portfolio. It is common to compare the beta produced by the risk model with the ratio of portfolio and benchmark durations. In this case, the duration ratio is 4.82/4.29 = 1.12, which is somewhat larger than the risk model beta. This is because the duration-based approach considers only term structure risk (and only parallel shift risk at that), while the risk model includes the combined effects of all relevant forms of risk, along with the correlations among them.

RISK MODEL APPLICATIONS

In this section we explore several applications of the model to portfolio management.

Quantifying Risk Associated with a View

The risk model is primarily a diagnostic tool. Whatever position a portfolio manager has taken relative to the benchmark, the risk model will quantify how much risk has been assumed. This helps measure the risk of the exposures taken to express a market view. It also points out the potential unintended risks in the portfolio.

Many firms use risk-adjusted measures to evaluate portfolio performance. A high return achieved by a series of successful but risky market plays may not please a conservative pension plan sponsor. A more modest return, achieved while maintaining much lower risk versus the benchmark, might be seen as a healthier approach over the long term. This point of view can be reflected either by adjusting performance by the amount of risk taken or by specifying in advance the acceptable level of risk for the portfolio. In any case, the portfolio manager should be cognizant of the risk inherent in a particular market view and weigh it against the anticipated gain. The increasing popularity of risk-adjusted performance evaluation is evident in the frequent use of the concept of an *information ratio*—portfolio outperformance of the benchmark per unit of standard deviation of observed outperformance. Plan sponsors often diversify among asset managers with different styles, looking for some of them to take more risk and for others to stay conservative, but always looking for high information ratios.

Risk Budgeting

To limit the amount of risk that may be taken by its portfolio managers, a plan sponsor can prescribe a maximum allowable tracking error. In the past, an asset management mandate might have put explicit constraints on deviation from the benchmark duration, differences in sector allocations, concentration in a given issuer, and total percentage invested outside the benchmark. Currently, we observe a tendency to constrain the overall risk versus the benchmark and leave the choice of the form of risk to the portfolio manager based on current risk premia offered by the market. By expressing various types of risk in the same units of tracking error, the model makes it possible to introduce the concept of opportunistic risk budget allocation. To constrain specific types of risk, limits can be applied to the different components of tracking error produced by the model. As described above, the overall tracking error represents the best way to quantify the net effect of multiple dimensions of risk in a single number.

With the model-specific nature of tracking error, there may be situations where the formal limits to be placed on the portfolio manager must be expressed in more objective terms. Constraints commonly found in investment policies include limits on the deviation between the portfolio and the benchmark, both in terms of Treasury duration and in spread duration contributions from various fixed-income asset classes. Because term structure risk tends to be best understood, many organizations have firm limits only for the amount of duration deviation allowed. For example, a portfolio manager may be limited to ±1 around benchmark duration. How can this limit be applied to risks along a different dimension?

The risk model can help establish relationships among risks of different types by comparing their tracking errors. Exhibit 10.13 shows the tracking errors achieved by several different blends of Treasury and spread product indices relative to the Treasury Index. A pure Treasury composite (Strategy 1) with duration one year longer than the benchmark has a tracking error of 85 bp per year. Strategies 2 and 3 are created by combining the investment-grade Corporate Index with both intermediate and long Treasury Indices to achieve desired exposures to spread duration while remaining neutral to the benchmark in Treasury duration. Similar strategies are engaged to generate desired exposures to spread duration in the MBS and high-yield markets. As can be seen in Exhibit 10.13, an increase in pure Treasury duration by 1 (Strategy 1) is equivalent to an extension in corporate spread duration by 2.5, or an extension in high-yield spread duration by about 0.75. Our results with MBS spreads show that an MBS spread duration of 1 causes a tracking error of 58 bp, while a duration of 1.5 gives a tracking error of 87 bp. A simple linear interpolation would suggest that a tracking error of 85 bp (the magnitude of the risk of an extension of duration by 1) thus corresponds to an extension in MBS spread duration of approximately 1.47.

Of course, these are idealized examples in which spread exposure to one type of product is changed while holding Treasury duration constant. A real portfolio is likely to take risks in all dimensions simultaneously. To calculate the tracking error, the risk model considers the correlations among the different risk factors. As long as two risks along different dimensions are not perfectly correlated, the net risk is less than the sum of the two risks. For example, we have established that a corporate spread duration of 2.5 produces roughly the same risk as a Treasury duration of 1, each causing a tracking error of about 85 bp. For a portfolio able to take both types of risk, an investor might allocate half of the risk budget to each, setting limits on Treasury duration of 0.5 and on corporate spread duration of 1.25. This should keep the risk within the desired range of tracking error. As shown in Exhibit 10.13, this combination of risks produces a tracking error of only 51 bp. This method of allocating risk under a total risk budget (in terms of equivalent duration mismatches) can provide investors with a method of controlling risk that is easier to implement and more conservative than a direct limit on tracking error. This macro view of risk facilitates the capablity to set separate but uniformly expressed limits on portfolio managers responsible for different kinds of portfolio exposures.

EXHIBIT 10.13 "Risk Budget": An Example Using Components of Treasury and Spread Indices Relative to a Treasury Benchmark

Index	Treasury	Intermediate Treasury	Long Treasury	Corporate	MBS	High-Yield
Duration	5.48	3.05	10.74	5.99	3.04	4.68
Spread Duration	0.00	0.00	0.00	6.04	3.46	4.58

Strategy No.	Risk Strategy	Tsy. Dur. Diff.	Spread Dur. Diff.	% Interm. Treasury	% Long Treasury	% Sprd. Sector	Tracking Error versus Tsy. Index (bp/Yr.)
	Treasury Index			68.40	31.60	0.00	0
1	Treasury Duration	1.0	0.00	55.40	44.60	0.00	85
2	Corp. Spread Duration	0.0	1.00	58.17	25.27	16.56	34
3		0.0	2.50	42.83	15.78	41.39	85
4	Tsy. Dur. & Corp. Sprd. Dur.	0.5	1.25	49.12	30.19	20.70	51
5	MBS Spread Duration	0.0	1.00	39.46	31.64	28.90	58
6		0.0	1.47	25.99	31.65	42.36	85
7		0.0	1.50	24.99	31.66	43.35	87
8	High-Yield Spread Duration	0.0	0.75	55.50	28.13	16.38	84
9		0.0	1.00	51.19	26.97	21.83	119

EXHIBIT 10.14 A Simple Diversification Trade: Cut the Size of the Largest Position in Half

Issuer	Coupon	Maturity	Par Value ($000s)	MV ($000s)	Sector	Quality	Dur Adj.
Sell: Coca-Cola Enterprises Inc.	6.95	11/15/2026	25000	27053	IND	A3	12.37
Buy: Anheuser-Busch Co., Inc.	6.75	12/15/2027	25000	26941	IND	A1	12.86

Projecting the Effect of Proposed Transactions on Tracking Error

Proposed trades are often analyzed in the context of a 1-for-1 (substitution) swap. Selling a security and using the proceeds to buy another may earn a few additional basis points of yield. The risk model allows analysis of such a trade in the context of the portfolio and its benchmark. By comparing the current portfolio versus benchmark risk and the pro forma risk after the proposed trade, an asset manager can evaluate how well the trade fits the portfolio. Our portfolio analytics platform offers an interactive mode to allow portfolio modifications and immediately see the effect on tracking error.

For example, having noticed that our sample portfolio has an extremely large position in the Coca-Cola issue, we might decide to cut the size of this position in half. To avoid making any significant changes to the systematic risk profile of the portfolio, we might look for a bond with similar maturity, credit rating, and sector. Exhibit 10.14 shows an example of such a swap. Half the position in the Coca-Cola 30-year bond is replaced by a 30-year issue from Anheuser-Busch, another single-A rated issuer in the beverage sector. As shown later, this transaction reduces nonsystematic tracking error from 26 bp to 22 bp. While we have unwittingly produced a 1 bp increase in the systematic risk (the durations of the two bonds were not identical), the overall effect was a decrease in tracking error from 52 bp to 51 bp.

Optimization

For many portfolio managers, the risk model acts not only as a measurement tool but plays a major role in the portfolio construction process. The model has a unique optimization feature that guides investors to transactions that reduce portfolio risk. The types of questions it addresses are: What single transaction can reduce the risk of the portfolio relative to the benchmark the most? How could the tracking error be reduced with minimum turnover? The portfolio manager is given an opportunity to intervene at each step in the optimization process and select transactions that lead to the desired changes in the risk profile of the portfolio and are practical at the same time.

As in any portfolio optimization procedure, the first step is to choose the set of assets that may be purchased. The composition of this investable universe, or bond swap pool, is critical. This universe should be large enough to provide flexibility in matching all benchmark risk exposures, yet it should contain only securities that are acceptable candidates for purchase. This universe may be created by querying a bond database (selecting, for instance, all corporate bonds with more than $500 million outstanding that were issued in the last three years) or by providing a list of securities available for purchase.

Once the investable universe has been selected, the optimizer begins an iterative process (known as *gradient descent*), searching for 1-for-1 bond swap transactions that will achieve the investor's objective. In the simplest case, the objective is to minimize the tracking error. The bonds in the swap pool are ranked in terms of reduction in tracking error per unit of each bond purchased. The system indicates which bond, if purchased, will lead to the steepest decline in tracking error, but leaves the ultimate choice of the security to the investor. Once a bond has been selected for purchase, the optimizer offers a list of possible market-value-neutral swaps of this security against various issues in the portfolio (with the optimal transaction size for each pair of bonds), sorted in order of possible reduction in tracking error. Investors are free to adjust the model's recommendations, either selecting different bonds to sell or adjusting (e.g., rounding off) recommended trade amounts.

Exhibit 10.15 shows how this optimization process is used to minimize the tracking error of the sample portfolio. A close look at the sequence of trades suggested by the optimizer reveals that several types of risk are reduced simultaneously. In the first trade, the majority of the large position in the Coca-Cola 30-year bond is swapped for a 3-year Treasury. This trade simultaneously changes systematic exposures to term structure, sector, and quality; it also cuts one of the largest issuer exposures, reducing nonsystematic risk. This one trade brings the overall tracking error down from 52 bp to 29 bp. As risk declines and the portfolio risk profile approaches the benchmark, there is less room for such drastic improvements. Transaction sizes become smaller, and the improvement in tracking error with each trade slows. The second and third transactions continue to adjust the sector and quality exposures and fine-tune the risk exposures along the curve. The fourth transaction addresses the other large corporate exposure, cutting the position in GTE by two-thirds. The first five trades reduce the tracking error to 16 bp, creating an essentially passive portfolio.

EXHIBIT 10.15 Sequence of Transactions Selected by Optimizer Showing Progressively Smaller Tracking Error, $000s
Initial Tracking Error: 52.0 bp

Transaction # 1		
Sold:	31000 of COCA-COLA ENTERPRISES	6.950 2026/11/15
Bought:	30000 of U.S. TREASURY NOTES	8.000 2001/05/15
Cash Left Over:	−17.10	
New Tracking Error:	29.4 bp	
Cost of this Transaction:	152.500	
Cumulative Cost:	152.500	
Transaction # 2		
Sold:	10000 of LOCKHEED MARTIN	6.550 1999/05/15
Bought:	9000 of U.S. TREASURY NOTES	6.125 2007/08/15
Cash Left Over:	132.84	
New Tracking Error:	25.5 bp	
Cost of this Transaction:	47.500	
Cumulative Cost:	200.000	
Transaction # 3		
Sold:	4000 of NORFOLK SOUTHERN CORP.	7.800 2027/05/15
Bought:	3000 of U.S. TREASURY BONDS	10.625 2015/08/15
Cash Left Over:	−8.12	
New Tracking Error:	23.1 bp	
Cost of this Transaction:	17.500	
Cumulative Cost:	217.500	
Transaction # 4		
Sold:	33000 of GTE CORP.	9.375 2000/12/01
Bought:	34000 of U.S. TREASURY NOTES	6.625 2002/03/31
Cash Left Over:	412.18	
New Tracking Error:	19.8 bp	
Cost of this Transaction:	167.500	
Cumulative Cost:	385.000	
Transaction # 5		
Sold:	7000 of COCA-COLA ENTERPRISES	6.950 2026/11/15
Bought:	8000 of U.S. TREASURY NOTES	6.000 2000/08/15
Cash Left Over:	−304.17	
New Tracking Error:	16.4 bp	
Cost of this Transaction:	37.500	
Cumulative Cost:	422.500	

EXHIBIT 10.16 Tracking Error Summary
Passive Portfolio versus Aggregate Index, 9/30/98

	Tracking Error (bp/Year)		
	Isolated	Cumulative	Change
Tracking Error Term Structure	7.0	7.0	7.0
Non-Term Structure	9.6		
Tracking Error Sector	7.4	10.5	3.5
Tracking Error Quality	2.1	11.2	0.7
Tracking Error Optionality	1.6	11.5	0.3
Tracking Error Coupon	2.0	12.3	0.8
Tracking Error MBS Sector	4.9	10.2	−2.1
Tracking Error MBS Volatility	7.2	11.1	0.9
Tracking Error MBS Prepayment	2.5	10.3	−0.8
Total Systematic Tracking Error		10.3	
Nonsystematic Tracking Error			
Issuer-specific	12.4		
Issue-specific	3.0		
Total	12.7		
Total Tracking Error Return		16	

	Systematic	Nonsystematic	Total
Benchmark Sigma	417	4	417
Portfolio Sigma	413	13	413

An analysis of the tracking error for this passive portfolio is shown in Exhibit 10.16. The systematic tracking error has been reduced to just 10 bp and the nonsystematic risk to 13 bp. Once systematic risk drops below nonsystematic risk, the latter becomes the limiting factor. In turn, further tracking error reduction by just a few transactions becomes much less likely. When there are exceptionally large positions, like the two mentioned in the above example, nonsystematic risk can be reduced quickly. Upon completion of such risk reduction transactions, further reduction of tracking error requires a major diversification effort. The critical factor that determines nonsystematic risk is the percentage of the portfolio in any single issue. On average, a portfolio of 50 bonds has 2% allocated to each position. To reduce this average allocation to 1%, the number of bonds would need to be doubled.

EXHIBIT 10.17 Term Structure Risk Report for Passive Portfolio, 9/30/98

	Cash Flows		
Year	Portfolio	Benchmark	Difference
0.00	1.33%	1.85%	−0.52%
0.25	3.75	4.25	−0.50
0.50	4.05	4.25	−0.19
0.75	3.50	3.76	−0.27
1.00	8.96	7.37	1.59
1.50	7.75	10.29	−2.54
2.00	8.30	8.09	0.21
2.50	10.30	6.42	3.87
3.00	5.32	5.50	−0.19
3.50	8.24	4.81	3.43
4.00	6.56	7.19	−0.63
5.00	5.91	6.96	−1.05
6.00	3.42	4.67	−1.24
7.00	5.75	7.84	−2.10
10.00	6.99	7.37	−0.38
15.00	4.00	3.88	0.12
20.00	2.98	3.04	−0.05
25.00	2.37	1.73	0.64
30.00	0.47	0.68	−0.21
40.00	0.08	0.07	0.01

The risk exposures of the resulting passive portfolio match the benchmark much better than the initial portfolio. Exhibit 10.17 details the term structure risk of the passive portfolio. Compared with Exhibit 10.3, the overweight at the long end is reduced significantly. The overweight at the 25-year vertex has gone down from 1.45% to 0.64%, and (perhaps more importantly) it is now offset partially by underweights at the adjacent 20- and 30-year vertices. Exhibit 10.18 presents the sector risk report for the passive portfolio. The underweight to Treasuries (in contribution to duration) has been reduced from −0.77% to −0.29% relative to the initial portfolio (Exhibit 10.4), and the largest corporate overweight, to consumer non-cyclicals, has come down from +1.00% to +0.24%.

EXHIBIT 10.18 Sector Risk Report for Passive Portfolio, 9/30/98

Detailed Sector	Portfolio			Benchmark			Difference	
	% of Portfolio	Adj. Dur.	Contrib. to Adj. Dur.	% of Portfolio	Adj. Dur.	Contrib. to Adj. Dur.	% of Portfolio	Contrib. to Adj. Dur.
Treasury								
Coupon	40.98	4.72	1.94	39.82	5.58	2.22	1.16	−0.29
Strip	0.00	0.00	0.00	0.00	0.00	0.00	0.00	0.00
Agencies								
FNMA	4.12	3.40	0.14	3.56	3.44	0.12	0.56	0.02
FHLB	0.00	0.00	0.00	1.21	2.32	0.03	−1.21	−0.03
FHLMC	0.00	0.00	0.00	0.91	3.24	0.03	−0.91	−0.03
REFCORP	3.50	11.22	0.39	0.83	12.18	0.10	2.68	0.29
Other Agencies	0.00	0.00	0.00	1.31	5.58	0.07	−1.31	−0.07
Financial Institutions								
Banking	1.91	5.31	0.10	2.02	5.55	0.11	−0.11	−0.01
Brokerage	1.35	3.52	0.05	0.81	4.14	0.03	0.53	0.01
Financial Cos.	1.88	2.92	0.05	2.11	3.78	0.08	−0.23	−0.02
Insurance	0.00	0.00	0.00	0.52	7.47	0.04	−0.52	−0.04
Other	0.00	0.00	0.00	0.28	5.76	0.02	−0.28	−0.02
Industrials								
Basic	0.63	6.68	0.04	0.89	6.39	0.06	−0.26	−0.01
Capital Goods	2.89	7.88	0.23	1.16	6.94	0.08	1.73	0.15
Consumer Cycl.	2.01	8.37	0.17	2.28	7.10	0.16	−0.27	0.01
Consum. Non-cycl.	2.76	12.91	0.36	1.66	6.84	0.11	1.10	0.24
Energy	1.50	6.82	0.10	0.69	6.89	0.05	0.81	0.05
Technology	1.55	1.58	0.02	0.42	7.39	0.03	1.13	−0.01
Transportation	0.00	0.00	0.00	0.57	7.41	0.04	−0.57	−0.04
Utilities								
Electric	0.47	3.36	0.02	1.39	5.02	0.07	−0.93	−0.05
Telephone	3.69	2.32	0.09	1.54	6.58	0.10	2.15	−0.02
Natural Gas	0.80	5.53	0.04	0.49	6.50	0.03	0.31	0.01
Water	0.00	0.00	0.00	0.00	0.00	0.00	0.00	0.00
Yankee								
Canadians	1.45	7.87	0.11	1.06	6.67	0.07	0.38	0.04
Corporates	0.49	3.34	0.02	1.79	6.06	0.11	−1.30	−0.09
Supranational	1.00	6.76	0.07	0.38	6.33	0.02	0.62	0.04
Sovereigns	0.00	0.00	0.00	0.66	5.95	0.04	−0.66	−0.04
Hypothetical	0.00	0.00	0.00	0.00	0.00	0.00	0.00	0.00
Cash	0.00	0.00	0.00	0.00	0.00	0.00	0.00	0.00
Mortgage								
Conventional 30-yr.	12.96	1.52	0.20	16.60	1.42	0.24	−3.64	−0.04
GNMA 30-yr.	7.53	1.23	0.09	7.70	1.12	0.09	−0.17	0.01
MBS 15-yr.	3.52	1.95	0.07	5.59	1.63	0.09	−2.07	−0.02
Balloons	3.02	1.69	0.05	0.78	1.02	0.01	2.24	0.04
OTM	0.00	0.00	0.00	0.00	0.00	0.00	0.00	0.00
European & International								
Eurobonds	0.00	0.00	0.00	0.00	0.00	0.00	0.00	0.00
International	0.00	0.00	0.00	0.00	0.00	0.00	0.00	0.00
Asset Backed	0.00	0.00	0.00	0.96	3.14	0.03	−0.96	−0.03
CMO	0.00	0.00	0.00	0.00	0.00	0.00	0.00	0.00
Other	0.00	0.00	0.00	0.00	0.00	0.00	0.00	0.00
Totals	100.00		4.35	100.00		4.29	0.00	0.00

Minimization of tracking error, illustrated above, is the most basic application of the optimizer. This is ideal for passive investors who want their portfolios to track the benchmark as closely as possible. This method also aids investors who hope to outperform the benchmark mainly on the basis of security selection, without expressing views on sector or yield curve. Given a carefully selected universe of securities from a set of favored issuers, the optimizer can help build security picks into a portfolio with no significant systematic exposures relative to the benchmark.

For more active portfolios, the objective is no longer minimization of tracking error. When minimizing tracking error, the optimizer tries to reduce the largest differences between the portfolio and benchmark. But what if the portfolio is meant to be long duration or overweighted in a particular sector to express a market view? These views certainly should not be "optimized" away. However, unintended exposures need to be minimized, while keeping the intentional ones.

For instance, assume in the original sample portfolio that the sector exposure is intentional but the portfolio should be neutral to the benchmark for all other sources of risk, especially term structure. The risk model allows the investor to keep exposures to one or more sets of risk factors (in this case, sector) and optimize to reduce the components of tracking error due to all other risk factors. This is equivalent to reducing all components of tracking error but the ones to be preserved. The model introduces a significant penalty for changing the risk profile of the portfolio in the risk categories designated for preservation.

Exhibit 10.19 shows the transactions suggested by the optimizer in this case.[5] At first glance, the logic behind the selection of the proposed transactions is not as clear as before. We see a sequence of fairly small transactions, mostly trading up in coupon. Although this is one way to change the term structure exposure of a portfolio, it is usually not the most obvious or effective method. The reason for this lies in the very limited choices we offered the optimizer for this illustration. As in the example of tracking error minimization, the investable universe was limited to securities already in the portfolio. That is, only rebalancing trades were permitted. Because the most needed cash flows are at vertices where the portfolio has no maturing securities, the only way to increase those flows is through higher coupon payments. In a more realistic optimization exercise, we would include a wider range of maturity

[5] Tracking error does not decrease with each transaction. This is possible because the optimizer does not minimize the tracking error itself in this case, but rather a function that includes the tracking error due to all factors but sector, as well as a penalty term for changing sector exposures.

dates (and possibly a set of zero-coupon securities as well) in the investable universe to give the optimizer more flexibility in adjusting portfolio cash flows. Despite these self-imposed limitations, the optimizer succeeds in bringing down the term structure risk while leaving the sector risk almost unchanged. Exhibit 10.20 shows the tracking error breakdown for the resulting portfolio. The term structure risk has been reduced from 36 bp to 12 bp, while the sector risk remains almost unchanged at 30 bp.

EXHIBIT 10.19 Sequence of Transactions Selected by Optimizer, Keeping Exposures to Sector, $000s
Initial Tracking Error: 52.0 bp

Transaction # 1		
Sold:	2000 of COCA-COLA ENTERPRISES	6.950 2026/11/15
Bought:	2000 of NORFOLK SOUTHERN CORP.	7.800 2027/05/15
Cash Left Over:	−235.19	
New Tracking Error:	52.1 bp	
Cost of this Transaction:	10.000	
Cumulative Cost:	10.000	
Transaction # 2		
Sold:	2000 of COCA-COLA ENTERPRISES	6.950 2026/11/15
Bought:	2000 of NEW YORK TELEPHONE	9.375 2031/07/15
Cash Left Over:	−389.36	
New Tracking Error:	50.1 bp	
Cost of this Transaction:	10.000	
Cumulative Cost:	20.000	
Transaction # 3		
Sold:	10000 of U.S. TREASURY BONDS	6.250 2023/08/15
Bought:	10000 of NEW YORK TELEPHONE	9.375 2031/07/15
Cash Left Over:	−468.14	
New Tracking Error:	47.4 bp	
Cost of this Transaction:	50.000	
Cumulative Cost:	70.000	
Transaction # 4		
Sold:	2000 of COCA-COLA ENTERPRISES	6.950 2026/11/15
Bought:	2000 of FHLM Gold Guar. Single Fam.	7.000 2028/01/01
Cash Left Over:	−373.47	
New Tracking Error:	46.0 bp	
Cost of this Transaction:	10.000	
Cumulative Cost:	80.000	

EXHIBIT 10.19 (Continued)

Transaction # 5		
Sold:	6000 of U.S. TREASURY BONDS	6.250 2023/08/15
Bought:	6000 of GNMA I Single Fam.	7.500 2022/07/01
Cash Left Over:	272.43	
New Tracking Error:	47.2 bp	
Cost of this Transaction:	30.000	
Cumulative Cost:	110.000	
Transaction # 6		
Sold:	1000 of NORFOLK SOUTHERN CORP.	7.800 2027/05/15
Bought:	1000 of U.S. TREASURY NOTES	6.125 2007/08/15
Cash Left Over:	343.44	
New Tracking Error:	46.4 bp	
Cost of this Transaction:	5.000	
Cumulative Cost:	115.000	
Transaction # 7		
Sold:	2000 of NORFOLK SOUTHERN CORP.	7.800 2027/05/15
Bought:	2000 of ANHEUSER-BUSCH CO., INC.	6.750 2027/12/15
Cash Left Over:	587.60	
New Tracking Error:	45.7 bp	
Cost of this Transaction:	10.000	
Cumulative Cost:	125.000	

EXHIBIT 10.20 Summary of Tracking Error Breakdown for Sample Portfolios

Tracking Error Due to:	Original Portfolio	Swapped Coca-Cola	Passive	Keep Sector Exposures
Term Structure	36	37	7	12
Sector	32	32	7	30
Systematic Risk	45	46	10	39
Nonsystematic Risk	26	22	13	24
Total	52	51	16	46

Proxy Portfolios

How many securities does it take to replicate the Lehman Corporate Index (containing about 4,500 bonds) to within 25 bp/year? How close could a portfolio of $50 million invested in 10 MBS securities get to the MBS index return? How many high-yield securities does a portfolio need to hold to get sufficient diversification relative to the High Yield Index? How could one define "sufficient diversification" quantitatively? Investors asking any of these questions are looking for "index proxies"—portfolios with a small number of securities that nevertheless closely match their target indices.

Proxies are used for two distinct purposes: passive investment and index analysis. Both passive portfolio managers and active managers with no particular view on the market at a given time might be interested in insights from index proxies. These proxy portfolios represent a practical method of matching index returns while containing transaction costs. In addition, the large number of securities in an index can pose difficulties in the application of computationally intensive quantitative techniques. A portfolio can be analyzed against an index proxy of a few securities using methods that would be impractical to apply to an index of several thousand securities. As long as the proxy matches the index along relevant risk dimensions, this approach can speed up many forms of analysis with only a small sacrifice in accuracy.

There are several approaches to the creation of index proxies. Quantitative techniques include stratified sampling or cell-matching, tracking error minimization, and matching index scenario results. (With limitations, replication of index returns can also be achieved using securities outside of indices, such as Treasury futures contracts.[6] An alternative way of getting index returns is entering into an index swap or buying an appropriately structured note.) Regardless of the means used to build a proxy portfolio, the risk model can measure how well the proxy is likely to track the index.

In a simple cell-matching technique, a benchmark is profiled on an arbitrary grid that reflects the risk dimensions along which a portfolio manager's allocation decisions are made. The index contribution to each cell is then matched by one or more representative liquid securities. Duration (and convexity) of each cell within the benchmark can be targeted when purchasing securities to fill the cell. We have used this technique to produce proxy portfolios of 20-25 MBS passthroughs to track the Lehman Brothers MBS Index. These portfolios have tracked the index of about 600 MBS generics to within 3 bp per month.[7]

To create or fine-tune a proxy portfolio using the risk model, we can start by selecting a seed portfolio and an investable universe. The tracking error minimization process described above then recommends a sequence of transactions. As more bonds are added to the portfolio, risk decreases. The level of tracking achieved by a proxy portfolio depends on the number of bonds included. Exhibit 10.21a shows the annualized tracking errors achieved using this procedure, as a function of the number of bonds, in a proxy for the Lehman Brothers Corporate Bond Index. At first, adding more securities to the portfolio reduces tracking error rap-

[6] *Replicating Index Returns with Treasury Futures*, Lehman Brothers, November 1997.

[7] *Replicating the MBS Index Risk and Return Characteristics Using Proxy Portfolios*, Lehman Brothers, March 1997.

idly. But as the number of bonds grows, the improvement levels off. The breakdown between systematic and nonsystematic risk explains this phenomenon. As securities are added to the portfolio, systematic risk is reduced rapidly. Once the corporate portfolio is sufficiently diverse to match index exposures to all industries and credit qualities, nonsystematic risk dominates, and the rate of tracking error reduction decreases.

Exhibit 10.21b illustrates the same process applied to the Lehman Brothers High-Yield Index. A similar pattern is observed: Tracking error declines steeply at first as securities are added; tracking error reduction falls with later portfolio additions. The overall risk of the high-yield proxy remains above the investment-grade proxy. This reflects the effect of quality on our estimate of nonsystematic risk. Similar exposures to lower-rated securities carry more risk. As a result, a proxy of about 30 investment-grade corporates tracks the Corporate Index within about 50 bp/year. Achieving the same tracking error for the High-Yield Index requires a proxy of 50 high-yield bonds.

To demonstrate that proxy portfolios track their underlying indices, we analyze the performance of three proxies over time. The described methodology was used to create a corporate proxy portfolio of about 30 securities from a universe of liquid corporate bonds (minimum $350 million outstanding). Exhibit 10.22 shows the tracking errors projected at the start of each month from January 1997 through September 1998, together with the performance achieved by portfolio and benchmark. The return difference is sometimes larger than the tracking error. (Note that the monthly return difference must be compared to the monthly tracking error, which is obtained by scaling down the annualized tracking error by $\sqrt{12}$.) This is to be expected. Tracking error does not constitute an upper bound of return difference, but rather one standard deviation. If the return difference is normally distributed with the standard deviation given by the tracking error, then the return difference should be expected to be within ±1 tracking error about 68% of the time, and within ±2 tracking errors about 95% of the time. For the corporate proxy shown here, the standard deviation of the return difference over the observed time period is 13 bp, almost identical to the projected monthly tracking error. Furthermore, the result is within ±1 tracking error in 17 months out of 24, or about 71% of the time.

Exhibit 10.23 summarizes the performance of our Treasury, corporate, and mortgage index proxies. The MBS Index was tracked with a proxy portfolio of 20–25 generics. The Treasury index was matched using a simple cell-matching scheme. The index was divided into three maturity cells, and two highly liquid bonds were selected from each cell to match the index duration. For each of the three proxy portfolios, the observed standard deviation of return difference is less than the tracking error. The corporate portfolio tracks as predicted by the risk model, while the Treasury and mortgage proxies track better than predicted. The corporate index proxy was generated by minimizing the tracking error relative to the Corporate Index using 50–60 securities. Being much less diversified than the index of about 4,700 securities, the corporate proxy is most exposed to nonsystematic risk. In the difficult month of September 1998, when liquidity in the credit markets was severely stemmed, this resulted in a realized return difference three times the projected tracking error.

EXHIBIT 10.21 Corporate Proxy—Tracking Error as a Function of Number of Bonds (Effect of Diversification)
a. Proxy for Corporate Bond Index

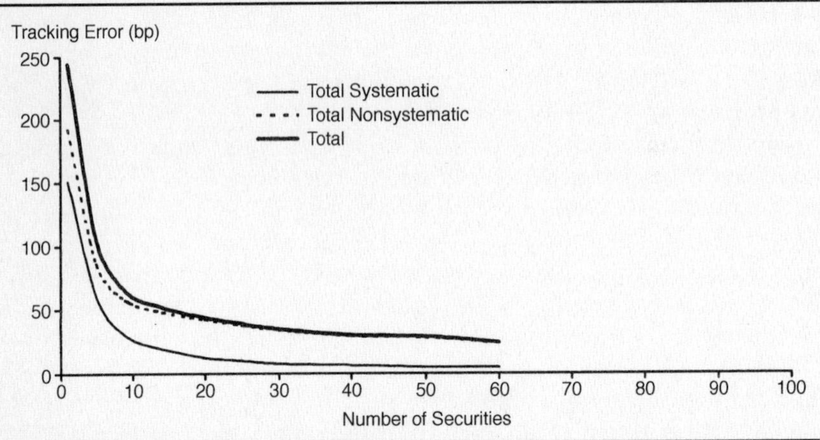

b. Proxy for High-Yield Index

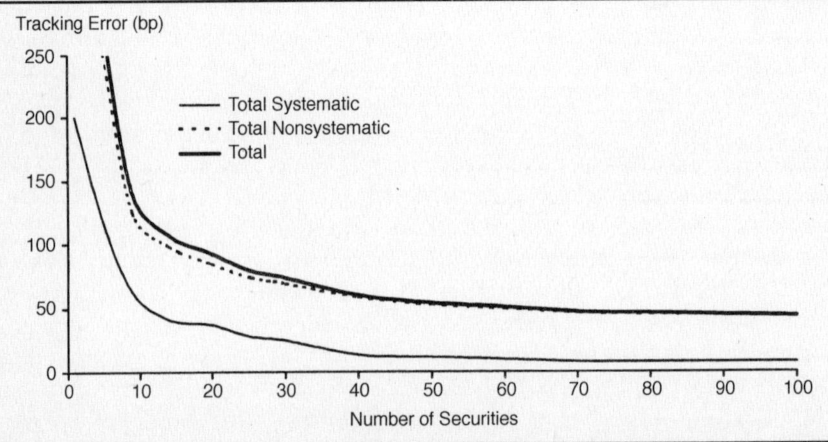

EXHIBIT 10.22 Corporate Proxy Portfolio: Comparison of Achieved Results with Projected Tracking Errors

Date	Annual Tracking Error (bp)	Monthly Tracking Error (bp)	Return (%/mo.) Proxy	Return (%/mo.) Index	Return Difference (bp/Mo.)	Ret. Diff./ Monthly Tracking Error
Jan-97	48	14	0.15	0.14	0	0.03
Feb-97	48	14	0.37	0.42	−5	−0.34
Mar-97	48	14	−1.60	−1.56	−4	−0.30
Apr-97	47	14	1.60	1.52	8	0.60
May-97	48	14	1.14	1.13	1	0.04
Jun-97	48	14	1.42	1.42	0	0.03
Jul-97	47	14	3.62	3.66	−4	−0.27
Aug-97	48	14	−1.48	−1.48	0	−0.01
Sep-97	47	14	1.65	1.75	−10	−0.72
Oct-97	48	14	1.43	1.27	16	1.13
Nov-97	49	14	0.60	0.57	4	0.25
Dec-97	49	14	1.33	1.06	27	1.88
Jan-98	49	14	1.36	1.19	17	1.19
Feb-98	46	13	0.05	−0.03	8	0.59
Mar-98	46	13	0.39	0.37	2	0.16
Apr-98	45	13	0.75	0.63	12	0.93
May-98	44	13	1.22	1.19	3	0.24
Jun-98	45	13	0.79	0.74	6	0.42
Jul-98	45	13	−0.18	−0.10	−8	−0.63
Aug-98	44	13	0.76	0.47	29	2.26
Sep-98	44	13	3.62	3.24	38	2.99
Oct-98	46	13	−1.40	−1.54	15	1.11
Nov-98	45	13	2.04	1.88	16	1.20
Dec-98	47	14	0.17	0.29	−12	−0.87
Std. Dev.:					13	

	Number	Percentage
Observations within +/– 1 × tracking error	17	71%
Observations within +/– 2 × tracking error	22	92%
Total number of observations	24	

EXHIBIT 10.23 Summary of Historical Results of Proxy Portfolios for Treasury, Corporate, and MBS Indices, in bp per Month

	Treasury		Corporate		MBS	
	Tracking Error	Return Difference	Tracking Error	Return Difference	Tracking Error	Return Difference
Jan-97	5.5	−1.7	13.9	0.4	4.3	0.8
Feb-97	5.2	−0.6	13.9	−4.7	4.3	−0.3
Mar-97	5.5	−1.8	13.9	−4.2	4.0	2.9
Apr-97	5.5	1.7	13.6	8.2	4.3	−3.3
May-97	5.8	−0.3	13.9	0.6	4.0	1.6
Jun-97	6.6	3.5	13.9	0.4	4.0	−0.5
Jul-97	6.6	3.8	13.6	−3.7	4.0	−2.5
Aug-97	6.9	−3.8	13.9	−0.1	4.3	1.5
Sep-97	6.4	1.5	13.6	−9.8	4.3	−1.2
Oct-97	6.4	3.2	13.9	15.7	4.0	−0.6
Nov-97	6.1	−2.3	14.1	3.5	4.0	0.8
Dec-97	6.6	6.0	14.1	26.6	4.0	−2.4
Jan-98	6.6	1.0	14.1	16.9	4.3	1.8
Feb-98	6.6	−1.8	13.3	7.8	4.9	2.2
Mar-98	6.6	1.8	13.3	2.1	4.0	−1.9
Apr-98	6.6	−1.8	13.0	12.1	4.6	−0.9
May-98	6.6	3.8	12.7	3.1	4.6	−0.3
Jun-98	7.8	−1.4	13.0	5.5	4.9	0.4
Jul-98	7.5	−1.7	13.0	−8.2	4.3	−1.3
Aug-98	7.5	−0.6	12.7	28.7	4.3	−3.4
Sep-98	8.1	−6.1	12.7	38.0	4.0	−1.7
Oct-98	7.8	5.4	13.3	14.7	4.0	3.4
Nov-98	7.8	−4.9	13.0	15.6	4.6	−1.8
Dec-98	6.1	−2.7	13.6	−11.8	4.3	−1.6
Mean	6.6	0.0	13.5	6.6	4.3	−0.3
Std. Dev.		3.2		12.5		1.9
Min		−6.1		−11.8		−3.4
Max		6.0		38.0		3.4

A proxy portfolio for the Lehman Brothers Aggregate Index can be constructed by building proxies to track each of its major components and combining them with the proper weightings. This exercise clearly illustrates the benefits of diversification. The aggregate proxy in Exhibit 10.24 is obtained by combining the government, corporate, and mortgage proxies shown in the same exhibit. The tracking error achieved by the combination is smaller than that of any of its constituents. This is because the risks of the proxy portfolios are largely independent.

EXHIBIT 10.24 Effect of Diversification—Tracking Error versus Treasury, Corporate, MBS, and Aggregate

Index	No. of Bonds in Proxy	No. of Bonds in Index	Tracking Error (bp/Year)
Treasury	6	165	13
Government	39	1,843	11
Corporate	51	4,380	26
Mortgage	19	606	15
Aggregate	109	6,928	10

When using tracking error minimization to design proxy portfolios, the choice of the "seed" portfolio and the investable universe should be considered carefully. The seed portfolio is the initial portfolio presented to the optimizer. Due to the nature of the gradient search procedure, the path followed by the optimizer will depend on the initial portfolio. The seed portfolio will produce the best results when it is closest in nature to the benchmark. At the very least, asset managers should choose a seed portfolio with duration near that of the benchmark. The investable universe, or bond swap pool, should be wide enough to offer the optimizer the freedom to match all risk factors. But if the intention is to actually purchase the proxy, the investable universe should be limited to liquid securities.

These methods for building proxy portfolios are not mutually exclusive, but can be used in conjunction with each other. A portfolio manager who seeks to build an investment portfolio that is largely passive to the index can use a combination of security picking, cell matching, and tracking error minimization. By dividing the market into cells and choosing one or more preferred securities in each cell, the manager can create an investable universe of candidate bonds in which all sectors and credit qualities are represented. The tracking error minimization procedure can then match index exposures to all risk factors while choosing only securities that the manager would like to purchase.

Benchmark Selection: Broad versus Narrow Indices

Lehman Brothers' development has been guided by the principle that benchmarks should be broad-based, market-weighted averages. This leads to indices that give a stable, objective, and comprehensive representation of the selected market. On occasion, some investors have expressed a preference for indices composed of fewer securities. Among the rationales, transparency of pricing associated with smaller indices and a presumption that smaller indices are easier to replicate have been most commonly cited.

We have shown that it is possible to construct proxy portfolios with small numbers of securities that adequately track broad-based benchmarks. Furthermore, broad benchmarks offer more opportunities for outperformance by low-risk security selection strategies.[8] When a benchmark is too narrow, each security represents a significant percentage, and a risk-conscious manager might be forced to own nearly every issue in the benchmark. Ideally, a benchmark should be diverse enough to reduce its nonsystematic risk close to zero. As seen in Exhibit 10.2, the nonsystematic part of sigma for the Aggregate Index is only 4 bp.

Defining Spread and Curve Scenarios Consistent with History

The tracking error produced by the risk model is an average expected performance deviation due to possible changes in all risk factors. In addition to this method of measuring risk, many investors perform "stress tests" on their portfolios. Here scenario analysis is used to project performance under various market conditions. The scenarios considered typically include a standard set of movements in the yield curve (parallel shift, steepening, and flattening) and possibly more specific scenarios based on market views. Often, though, practitioners neglect to consider spread changes, possibly due to the difficulties in generating reasonable scenarios of this type. (Is it realistic to assume that industrial spreads will tighten by 10 bp while utilities remain unchanged?) One way to generate spread scenarios consistent with the historical experience of spreads in the marketplace is to utilize the statistical information contained within the risk model.

For each sector/quality cell of the corporate bond market shown in Exhibit 10.25, we create a corporate sub-index confined to a particular cell and use it as a portfolio. We then create a hypothetical Treasury bond for each security in this sub-index. Other than being labeled as belonging to the Treasury sector and having Aaa quality, these hypothetical bonds are identical to their corresponding real corporate bonds. We run a risk model comparison between the portfolio of corporate bonds versus their hypothetical Treasury counterparts as the benchmark. This artificially forces the portfolio and benchmark sensitivity to term structure, optionality and any other risks to be neutralized, leaving only sector and quality risk. Exhibit 10.25 shows the tracking error components due to sector and quality, as well as their combined effect. Dividing these tracking errors (standard deviations of return differences) by the average durations of the cells produces approximations for the standard deviation of spread changes. The standard deviation of the overall spread change, converted to a monthly number, can form the basis for a set of spread change scenarios. For instance, a scenario of "spreads widen by one standard deviation" would imply a widening of 6 bp for Aaa utilities, and 13 bp for Baa financials. This is a more realistic scenario than an across-the-board parallel shift, such as "corporates widen by 10 bp."

[8] *Value of Security Selection versus Asset Allocation in Credit Markets: A "Perfect Foresight" Study*, Lehman Brothers, March 1999.

EXHIBIT 10.25 Using the Risk Model to Define Spread Scenarios Consistent with History

		Dur.	Annual Tracking Error (%)			Spread Volatility (bp)			
		(Years)	Sector	Quality	Both	Sector	Quality	Both	Monthly
U.S. Agencies	Aaa	4.54	0.26	0.00	0.26	6	0	6	2
Industrials	Aaa	8.42	2.36	0.00	2.36	28	0	28	8
	Aa	6.37	1.72	0.57	2.03	27	9	32	9
	A	6.97	1.89	0.82	2.43	27	12	35	10
	Baa	6.80	1.87	1.36	2.96	27	20	43	13
Utilities	Aaa	7.34	1.62	0.13	1.65	22	2	22	6
	Aa	5.67	1.21	0.45	1.39	21	8	25	7
	A	6.03	1.33	0.63	1.67	22	10	28	8
	Baa	5.68	1.36	1.01	2.07	24	18	36	11
Financials	Aaa	4.89	1.41	0.00	1.41	29	0	29	8
	Aa	4.29	1.31	0.34	1.50	30	8	35	10
	A	4.49	1.31	0.49	1.65	29	11	37	11
	Baa	4.86	1.58	0.86	2.14	32	18	44	13
Banking	Aa	4.87	1.23	0.44	1.40	25	9	29	8
	A	5.68	1.43	0.62	1.72	25	11	30	9
	Baa	5.06	1.27	1.13	2.11	25	22	42	12
Yankees	Aaa	6.16	1.23	0.06	1.26	20	1	20	6
	Aa	5.45	1.05	0.49	1.27	19	9	23	7
	A	7.03	1.62	0.89	2.17	23	13	31	9
	Baa	6.17	1.51	1.36	2.60	24	22	42	12

Hedging

Since the covariance matrix used by the risk model is based on monthly observations of security returns, the model cannot compute daily hedges. However, it can help create long-term positions that over time perform better than a naïve hedge. This point is illustrated by a historical simulation of a simple barbell versus bullet strategy in Exhibit 10.26, in which a combination of the 2- and 10-year on-the-run Treasuries is used to hedge the on-the-run 5-year. We compare two methods of calculating the relative weights of the two bonds in the hedge. In the first method, the hedge is rebalanced at the start of each month to match the duration of the 5-year Treasury. In the second, the model is engaged on a monthly basis to minimize the tracking error between the portfolio of 2- and 10-year securities and the 5-year benchmark. As shown in

Exhibit 10.26, the risk model hedge tracks the performance of the 5-year bullet more closely than the duration hedge, with an observed tracking error of 19 bp/month compared with 20 bp/month for the duration hedge.

The duration of the 2- and 10-year portfolio built with the minimal tracking error hedging technique is consistently longer than that of the 5-year. Over the study period (1/94–2/99), the duration difference averaged 0.1 years. This duration extension proved very stable (standard deviation of 0.02) and is rooted in the shape of the historically most likely movement of the yield curve. It can be shown that the shape of the first principal component of yield curve movements is not quite a parallel shift.[9] Rather, the 2-year will typically experience less yield change then the 5- or 10-year. To the extent that the 5- and 10-year securities experience historically similar yield changes, a barbell hedge could benefit from an underweighting of the 2-year and an overweighting of the 10-year security. Over the 62 months analyzed in this study, the risk-based hedge performed closer to the 5-year than the duration-based hedge 59% of the time.

A similar study conducted using a 2- and 30-year barbell versus a 5-year bullet over the same study period (1/94–2/99) produced slightly more convincing evidence. Here, the risk-based hedge tracked better than the duration hedge by about 3 bp/month (33 bp/month tracking error versus 36 bp/month) and improved upon the duration hedge in 60% of the months studied. Interestingly, the duration extension in the hedge was even more pronounced in this case, with the risk-based hedge longer than the 5-year by an average of 0.36 years.

EXHIBIT 10.26 **Historical Performance of a Two-Security Barbell versus the 5-Year On-the-Run Treasury Bullet; Duration-Based Hedge versus a Tracking Error-Based Hedge, January 1994–February 1999**

		Difference				% of Months
		Duration Hedge		Tracking Error Hedge		Tracking
		Return	Duration	Return	Duration	Improved
2–10 vs. 5	Mean	0.03	0.00	0.03	0.10	59%
	Std. Dev.	0.20	0.00	0.19	0.02	
2–30 vs. 5	Mean	0.04	0.00	0.04	0.36	62%
	Std. Dev.	0.36	0.00	0.33	0.03	

[9] *Managing the Yield Curve with Principal Component Analysis*, Lehman Brothers, November 1998.

EXHIBIT 10.27 Projected Distribution of Total Return Difference (in bp/Year) between Portfolio and Benchmark, Based on Yield Advantage of 16 bp and Tracking Error of 52 bp, Assuming Normal Distribution

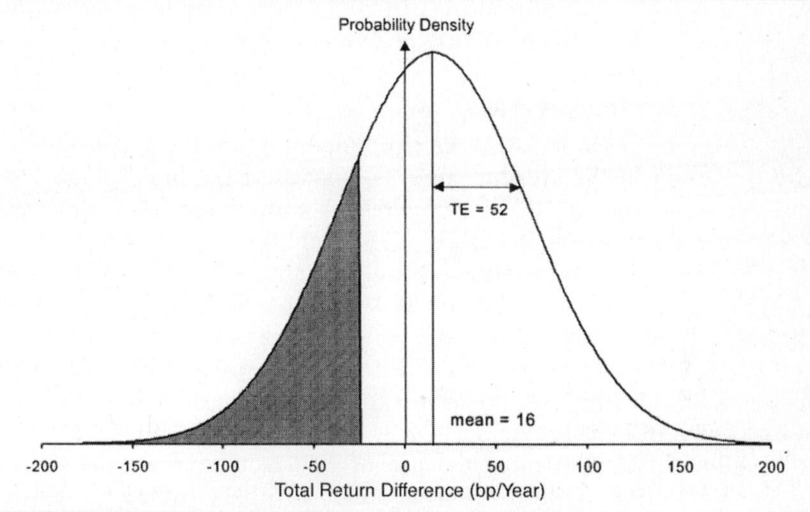

Estimating the Probability of Portfolio Underperformance

What is the probability that a portfolio will underperform the benchmark by 25 basis points or more over the coming year? To answer such questions, we need to make some assumptions about the distribution of the performance difference. We assume this difference to be distributed normally, with the standard deviation given by the tracking error calculated by the risk model. However, the risk model does not provide an estimate of the mean outperformance. Such an estimate may be obtained by a horizon total return analysis under an expected scenario (e.g., yield curve and spreads unchanged), or by simply using the yield differential as a rough guide. In the example of Exhibit 10.1, the portfolio yield exceeds that of the benchmark by 16 bp, and the tracking error is calculated as 52 bp. Exhibit 10.27 depicts the normal distribution with a mean of 16 bp and a standard deviation of 52 bp. The area of the shaded region, which represents the probability of underperforming by 25 bp or more, may be calculated as

$$N[(-25) - 16)/52] = 0.215 = 21.5\%$$

where $N(x)$ is the standard normal cumulative distribution function. As the true distribution of the return difference may not be normal, this approach must be used with care. It may not be accurate in estimating the probability of rare events such as the "great spread sector crash" in August 1998. For example, this calculation would assign a probability of only 0.0033 or 0.33% to an underperformance of −125 bp or worse. Admittedly, if the tails of the true distribution are slightly different than normal, the true probability could be much higher.

Measuring Sources of Market Risk

As illustrated in Exhibit 10.2, the risk model reports the projected standard deviation of the absolute returns (sigma) of the portfolio and the benchmark as well as that of the return difference (tracking error). However, the detailed breakdown of risk due to different groups of risk factors is reported only for the tracking error. To obtain such a breakdown of the absolute risk (sigma) of a given portfolio or index, we can measure the risk of our portfolio against a riskless asset, such as a cash security. In this case, the relative risk is equal to the absolute risk of the portfolio, and the tracking error breakdown report can be interpreted as a breakdown of market sigma.

Exhibit 10.28 illustrates the use of this technique to analyze the sources of market risk in four Lehman Brothers indices: Treasury, (investment grade) Corporate, High-Yield Corporate, and MBS. The results provide a clear picture of the role played by the different sources of risk in each of these markets. In the Treasury Index, term structure risk represents the only significant form of risk. In the Corporate Index, sector and quality risk add to term structure risk, but the effect of a negative correlation between spread risk and term structure risk is clearly visible. The overall risk of the Corporate Index (5.47%) is less than the term structure component alone (5.81%). This reflects the fact that when Treasury interest rates undergo large shocks, corporate yields often lag, moving more slowly in the same direction. The High-Yield Index shows a marked increase in quality risk and in nonsystematic risk relative to the Corporate Index. But, the negative correlation between term structure risk and quality risk is large as well, and the overall risk (4.76%) is less than the term structure risk (4.98%) by even more than it is for corporates. The effect of negative correlations among risk factors is also very strong in the MBS Index, where the MBS-specific risk factors bring the term structure risk of 3.25% down to an overall risk of 2.69%.

MODELING THE RISK OF NON-INDEX SECURITIES

The risk model calculates risk factor exposures for every security in the portfolio and the benchmark. As the model supports all securities in the

Lehman Brothers Aggregate Index, the risk of the benchmark usually is fully modeled. Portfolios, however, often contain securities (and even asset classes) not found in the Aggregate Index. Our portfolio analytics platform has several features designed to represent out-of-index portfolio holdings. In addition, modeling techniques can be used to synthesize the risk characteristics of non-index securities through a combination of two or more securities.

Bonds

The analytics platform supports the modeling of all types of government and corporate bonds. User-defined bonds may contain calls, puts, sinking fund provisions, step-up coupon schedules, inflation linkage, and more. Perpetual-coupon bonds (and preferred stock) can be modeled as bonds with very distant maturity dates. Floating-rate bonds are represented by a short exposure to term structure risk (as though the bond would mature on the next coupon reset date) and a long exposure to spread risk (the relevant spread factors are loaded by the bond's spread duration, which is based on the full set of projected cash flows through maturity).

EXHIBIT 10.28 Risk Model Breakdown of Market Risk (Sigma) to Different Categories of Risk Factors (Isolated Mode) for Four Lehman Brothers Indices, as of 9/30/98, in Percent per Year

Index:	Treasury	Corporate	High-Yield	MBS
Duration (years)	5.58	6.08	4.74	1.37
Convexity	0.69	0.68	0.20	−2.19
Term Structure Risk	5.25	5.81	4.98	3.25
Non-term Structure Risk	0.17	2.14	5.20	2.28
Risk Due to:				
Corp. Sector	0.00	1.50	1.21	0.00
Quality	0.00	0.84	4.67	0.00
Optionality	0.01	0.08	0.15	0.00
Coupon	0.17	0.01	0.19	0.00
MBS Sector	0.00	0.00	0.00	1.15
MBS Volatility	0.00	0.00	0.00	1.27
MBS Prepayment	0.00	0.00	0.00	0.73
Total Systematic Risk	5.26	5.47	4.75	2.69
Nonsystematic Risk	0.04	0.08	0.17	0.09
Total Risk (std. dev. of annual return)	5.26	5.47	4.76	2.69

Mortgage Passthroughs

The Lehman Brothers MBS Index is composed of several hundred "generic" securities. Each generic is created by combining all outstanding pools of a given program, passthrough coupon, and origination year (e.g., FNMA conventional 30-year 8.0% of 1993).[10] The index database contains over 3000 such generics, offering comprehensive coverage of the agency passthrough market, even though only about 600 meet the liquidity requirements for index inclusion. In addition to this database of MBS generics and their risk factor loadings, the analytics platform contains a lookup table of individual pools. This allows portfolios that contain mortgage pools to be bulk loaded based on either the pool CUSIP or the agency and pool number. For portfolio analytics, the characteristics of the appropriate generic are used as a proxy for the pool. This can lead to some inaccuracy for esoteric pools that differ considerably from the generic to which they are mapped, but adequately represents most mortgage portfolios in our experience.

CMOs

CMOs are not included in the Lehman Brothers MBS Index because their collateral has already been included as passthroughs. At present, the portfolio analytics recognize and process structured securities as individual tranches, but do not possess deal-level logic to project tranche cash flows under different assumptions. Thus, each tranche is represented in the system by a fixed set of cash flows, projected using the Lehman Brothers prepayment model for the zero-volatility interest rate path calibrated to the forward curve. Risk factor loadings for these securities are calculated as a hybrid between the characteristics of the tranche and the underlying collateral. Term structure risk is assumed to follow the cash flows of the tranche.

For PAC securities with less than 3 years to maturity (WAM), the model assigns no mortgage sector risk. For PACs with WAM greater than 10 years and for other types of tranches, the mortgage sector risk is assumed to be equal to that of a position in the underlying collateral with the same dollar duration. For PACs with WAM between 3 and 10 years, we use a prorated portion of the mortgage risk exposure of the collateral. This set of assumptions well represents tranches with stable cash flows, such as PACs trading within their bands. Tranches with extremely volatile cash flows, such as IOs and inverse floaters, cannot be represented adequately in the current system. The mechanism of defin-

[10] For a discussion of MBS Index composition and the relationship between pools and generics, see the Lehman Brothers report, "MBS Index Returns: A Detailed Look," August 1998.

ing a "cash flow bond" (with an arbitrary fixed cash flow stream), with or without the additional treatment of mortgage risk, can be used to model many kinds of structured transactions.

Futures

A bond futures contract may be represented as a combination of a long position in the Treasury security that is the cheapest-to-deliver issue (CDI) and a short position in a cash instrument. To match the dollar duration of a Treasury futures position with a notional market value of N_f, the size of the position N_t in the CDI Treasury bond should satisfy

$$(P_t + A_t)N_tD_t = P_fN_fD_f$$

where D_f is the option-adjusted duration of the futures contract. The negative holding N_c in the cash instrument has to offset the market value of the CDI:

$$(P_c + A_c)N_c + (P_t + A_t)N_t = 0$$

If the cash instrument is priced at par and has no accrued interest, the amount needed is simply

$$N_c = -(P_t + A_t)N_t$$

If the option-adjusted duration of the futures contract is not known, one could approximate N_t for a given CDI using the conversion factor CF_t:

$$N_t = N_f / CF_t$$

The disadvantage of a representation using a single CDI is that the notional values N_t and N_c need to be regularly maintained in order to properly reflect the risk of an unchanged position in futures. As yields change, the resulting changes in the delivery probabilities of different bonds will change the futures duration. A failure to update the portfolio frequently enough can lead to a discontinuity, especially around a switch in the CDI. A more sophisticated synthetic representation of a futures contract may involve more than one deliverable instrument weighted by the probability of delivery.

Index Swaps

The analytics platform provides a mechanism for including index swaps in portfolios. An individual security can be defined as paying the total return of a particular index, and a specific face amount of such a security can be included in a portfolio, corresponding to the notional value of the swap. These special securities have been created for all widely used Lehman Indices and are stored in the standard security database. Swaps written on other custom indices or portfolios can be modeled in a similar fashion. These capabilities, in conjunction with the dollar-based risk reporting described below, allow a comprehensive risk analysis of a portfolio of index swaps versus a hedge portfolio.

SUMMARY

In this chapter, we described a risk model for dollar-denominated government, corporate, and mortgage-backed securities. The model quantifies expected deviation in performance ("tracking error") between a portfolio of fixed-income securities and an index representing the market, such as the Lehman Brothers Aggregate, Corporate, or High-Yield Index.

The forecast of the return deviation is based on specific mismatches between the sensitivities of the portfolio and the benchmark to major market forces ("risk factors") that drive security returns. The model uses historical variances and correlations of the risk factors to translate the structural differences of the portfolio and the index into an expected tracking error. The model quantifies not only this systematic market risk, but security-specific (nonsystematic) risk as well.

Using an illustrative portfolio, we demonstrated the implementation of the model. We showed how each component of tracking error can be traced back to the corresponding difference between the portfolio and benchmark risk exposures. We described the methodology for the minimization of tracking error and discussed a variety of portfolio management applications.

CHAPTER 11

Measuring Plausibility of Hypothetical Interest Rate Shocks*

Bennett W. Golub, Ph.D.
Managing Director
Risk Management and Analytics Group
BlackRock Financial Management, Inc.

Leo M. Tilman
Head of Institutional Investment Strategies
Managing Director
Bear, Stearns & Co., Inc.

Many areas of modern portfolio and risk management are based on portfolio managers' view on the way the U.S. yield curve will evolve in the future. These predictions are often formulated as hypothetical *shocks* to the spot curve that portfolio managers expect to occur over the specified *horizon*. Via key rate durations as defined by Thomas Ho[1] or as

[1] T.S.Y. Ho, "Key Rate Durations: Measures of Interest Rate Risks," *Journal of Fixed Income* (September 1992), pp. 29–44

* The authors would like to thank Yury Geyman, Lawrence Polhman, Ehud Ronn, Michael Salm, Irwin Sheer, Pavan Wadhwa, and Adam Wizon for their helpful comments and feedback.

implied by principal component durations,[2] these shocks can be used to assess the impact of implicit duration and yield curve bets on a portfolio's return. Other common uses of hypothetical interest rate shocks include various what-if analyses and stress tests, numerous [duration] measures of portfolios' sensitivity to the slope of the yield curve, and so forth.

The human mind can imagine all sorts of unusual interest rate shocks, and considerable time and resources may be spent on investigating the sensitivity of portfolios to these interest rate shocks without questioning their *historical plausibility.* Our goal in this chapter is to define what historical plausibility is and how to measure it quantitatively. In order to achieve that, we will employ the approaches suggested by principal component analysis. We will introduce the framework which derives statistical distributions and measures historical plausibility of hypothetical interest rate shocks, thus providing historical validity to the corresponding yield curve bets.

We start with a brief overview of the principal component analysis and then utilize its methods to directly compute the probabilistic distribution of hypothetical interest rate shocks. The same section also introduces the notions of *magnitude plausibility* and *explanatory power* of interest rate shocks. Then we take the analysis one step further and introduce the notion of *shape plausibility.* We conclude by establishing a relationship between the shape of the first principal component and the term structure of volatility and verify the obtained results on the historical steepeners and flatteners of U.S. Treasury spot and on-the-run curves.

PROBABILISTIC DISTRIBUTION OF HYPOTHETICAL INTEREST RATE SHOCKS

The U.S. Treasury spot curve is continuous. This fact complicates the analysis and prediction of spot curve movements, especially using statistical methods. Therefore, practitioners usually *discretize* the spot curve, presenting its movements as changes of key rates—selected points on the spot curve.[3] Changes in spot key rates are assumed to be random variables which follow a multivariate normal distribution with zero mean and the covariance matrix computed from the historical data. There exist different ways to estimate the parameters of the distribution of key rates: equally-weighted, exponentially-weighted, fractional exponentially-

[2] B.W. Golub and L.M. Tilman, "Measuring Yield Curve Risk Using Principal Component Analysis, Value-at-Risk, and Key Rate Durations," *Journal of Portfolio Management* (Summer 1997).

[3] See Ho, "Key Rate Durations: Measures of Interest Rate Risks."

weighted, and so on. Although extensive research is being conducted on the connection between the appropriate estimation procedures and different styles of money management, this issue is beyond the scope of this chapter. Ideas presented below are invariant over the methodology used to create the covariance matrix ($\Im$) of key rate changes. We assume that the covariance matrix $\Im$ is given.

Principal component analysis is a statistical procedure which significantly simplifies the analysis of the covariance structure of complex systems such as interest rate movements. Instead of key rates, it creates a new set of random variables called principal components. The latter are the special linear combinations of key rates designed to explain the variability of the system as parsimoniously as possible. The output of the principal component analysis of the RiskMetrics™ monthly dataset is presented in Exhibit 11.1.

The data in Exhibit 11.1 can be interpreted as follows: Over 92% of the historical interest rate shocks are "explained" by the first principal component, over 97% by the first two, and over 98% by the first three. Also note that the "humped" shape of the first principal component is similar to that of the term structure of volatility of changes in spot rates. Later in this chapter we will demonstrate that this is a direct implication of the high correlation between U.S. spot key rates.[4]

Since key rates and principal components are random variables, any hypothetical (and, for that matter, historical) interest rate shock is a particular realization of these variables. We will use the subscripts "*KR*" and "*PC*" to indicate whether we are referring to a key rate or principal component representation of interest rate shocks. For instance,

$$\vec{X} = (x_1, \ldots, x_n)^T_{KR} \tag{1}$$

is an interest rate shock formulated in terms of changes in key rates. As mentioned earlier, our goal in this chapter is to analyze the shape and magnitude plausibility of hypothetical interest rate shocks and derive statistical distribution of interest rate shocks of a *given shape*. We start with the following definition.

Let

$$\vec{X} = (x_1, \ldots, x_n)^T_{KR} \tag{2}$$

[4] For a detailed discussion of principal components and their use in portfolio and risk management, see Golub and Tilman, "Measuring Yield Curve Risk Using Principal Component Analysis, Value-at-Risk, and Key Rate Durations."

EXHIBIT 11.1 Principal Components Implied by JP Morgan RiskMetrics^{TM} Monthly Dataset (9/30/96)

		3-Mo.	1-Yr.	2-Yr.	3-Yr.	5-Yr.	7-Yr.	10-Yr.	15-Yr.	20-Yr.	30-Yr.
Annualized ZCB Yield Vol (%)		9.63	16.55	18.33	17.82	17.30	16.62	15.27	14.25	13.26	12.09
One Std. Dev. of ZCB Yields (bps)		52	96	113	112	113	111	104	101	97	83
Correlation Matrix	3-Mo.	1.00	0.80	0.72	0.68	0.65	0.61	0.58	0.54	0.51	0.46
	1-Yr.	0.80	1.00	0.91	0.91	0.89	0.87	0.85	0.81	0.78	0.76
	2-Yr.	0.72	0.91	1.00	0.99	0.97	0.95	0.93	0.89	0.85	0.84
	3-Yr.	0.68	0.91	0.99	1.00	0.99	0.97	0.96	0.92	0.90	0.88
	5-Yr.	0.65	0.89	0.97	0.99	1.00	0.99	0.98	0.96	0.93	0.92
	7-Yr.	0.61	0.87	0.95	0.97	0.99	1.00	0.99	0.98	0.96	0.95
	10-Yr.	0.58	0.85	0.93	0.96	0.98	0.99	1.00	0.99	0.98	0.97
	15-Yr.	0.54	0.81	0.89	0.92	0.96	0.98	0.99	1.00	0.99	0.98
	20-Yr.	0.51	0.78	0.85	0.90	0.93	0.96	0.98	0.99	1.00	0.99
	30-Yr.	0.46	0.76	0.84	0.88	0.92	0.95	0.97	0.98	0.99	1.00

EXHIBIT 11.1 (Continued)

PC No.	Eig. Val.	Vol. PC	Var. Expl.	CVar. Expl.	Principal Components 3-Mo.	1-Yr.	2-Yr.	3-Yr.	5-Yr.	7-Yr.	10-Yr.	15-Yr.	20-Yr.	30-Yr.
1	9.24	3.04	92.80	92.80	11.09	28.46	35.69	36.37	36.94	36.30	34.02	32.40	30.33	25.71
2	0.48	0.69	4.80	97.60	43.93	48.66	34.19	20.37	5.23	−9.32	−18.63	−30.09	−37.24	−36.94
3	0.13	0.36	1.27	98.87	42.43	54.93	−44.61	−35.28	−21.02	−8.43	0.31	19.59	27.12	17.76
4	0.06	0.25	0.62	99.49	76.77	−61.47	9.21	−0.18	−0.01	−2.08	−0.65	10.46	11.30	−0.31
5	0.02	0.14	0.20	99.69	12.33	−4.93	−55.03	−3.84	38.06	47.35	33.64	−21.36	−35.74	−14.98
6	0.01	0.10	0.11	99.79	8.94	0.33	18.59	−11.83	−15.02	−2.14	19.64	−44.15	−30.58	77.03
7	0.01	0.09	0.09	99.88	3.02	−0.79	−38.42	49.35	45.01	−48.00	−28.08	−10.93	7.76	27.93
8	0.00	0.07	0.06	99.94	3.26	−1.14	−24.96	66.51	−66.82	17.27	13.02	−0.70	−2.46	−1.38
9	0.00	0.06	0.03	99.97	0.76	−0.46	−1.46	−0.97	0.21	60.38	−72.73	−20.12	19.52	16.59
10	0.00	0.05	0.03	100.00	0.54	0.00	−2.53	1.32	−0.42	5.15	−27.03	67.98	−64.58	21.03

ZCB = Zero-coupon bond
Eig. Val. = Eigenvalues (i.e., principal component variances) × 10,000
Vol. PC = Volatility of principal components × 100
Var. Expl. = Percentage of variance explained
CVar. Expl. = Cumulative percentage of variance explained

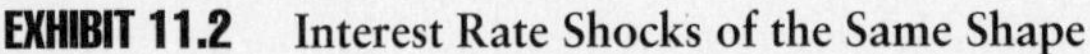

EXHIBIT 11.2 Interest Rate Shocks of the Same Shape

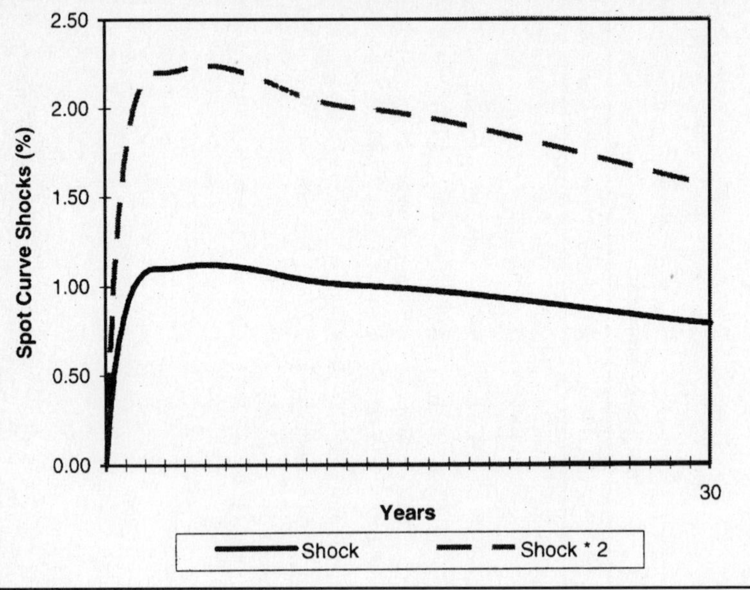

and

$$\vec{Y} = (y_1, \ldots, y_n)^T_{KR}$$

be spot curve shocks represented as vectors of key rate changes. We will say that $\vec{X}$ and $\vec{Y}$ have the *same shape* if they differ only by a factor, as in,

$$(y_1, \ldots, y_n)^T = (c \times x_1, \ldots, c \times x_n)^T$$

where c is a real number. (See Exhibit 11.2.)

As this section will show, it turns out that all interest rate shocks of a given *shape* correspond to the realizations of an underlying standard normal random variable. Once we know that, we can talk about the probability associated with a given shock (i.e., given realization). For instance, if a given interest rate shock corresponds to a three standard deviation realization of this underlying standard normal random variable, we will conclude that it is improbable. While deriving the probabilistic distribution of hypothetical interest rate shocks, we will utilize approaches used while constructing principal components. Namely, we will start with the discussion of how to compute *one standard deviation principal component shocks* used in a variety of instances including principal component durations. Relationships discussed below apply to random variables and their realizations alike.

Let

$$\vec{X} = (x_1, ..., x_n)^T_{KR}$$

be a spot curve shock formulated in terms of changes in key rates. Let

$$\vec{X} = (p_1, ..., p_n)^T_{PC}$$

be a representation of the *same* interest rate shock $\vec{X}$ corresponding to the coordinate system of principal components (x_i and p_i are the particular realizations of key rates and principal components respectively). Then the relationship between the two representations of the same vector $\vec{X}$ is given by

$$\begin{bmatrix} p_1 \\ ... \\ p_n \end{bmatrix} = \begin{bmatrix} pc_{1,1} & ... & pc_{1,n} \\ ... & ... & ... \\ pc_{n,1} & ... & pc_{n,n} \end{bmatrix} \times \begin{bmatrix} x_1 \\ ... \\ x_n \end{bmatrix} \tag{3}$$

where $\Omega = \{pc_{i,j}\}$ is a matrix whose rows are principal component coefficients. They are the unit vectors of the form

$$\begin{bmatrix} pc_{i,1} & ... & pc_{i,n} \end{bmatrix}$$

If K_i are [random] changes in key rates, then the principal components are defined as the following linear combinations

$$pc_{i,1} \times K_1 + ... + pc_{i,n} \times K_n$$

of key rate changes. From the linear algebra viewpoint, the matrix Ω allows us to translate the representation of an interest rate shock in one coordinate system (key rates) into another (principal components). The matrix Ω is orthogonal by construction, for example, $\Omega^{-1} = \Omega^T$. Therefore, we can rewrite equation (1) as follows:

$$\begin{bmatrix} x_1 \\ ... \\ x_n \end{bmatrix} = \begin{bmatrix} pc_{1,1} & ... & pc_{n,1} \\ ... & ... & ... \\ pc_{1,n} & ... & pc_{n,n} \end{bmatrix} \times \begin{bmatrix} p_1 \\ ... \\ p_n \end{bmatrix} \tag{4}$$

or simply

$$\begin{bmatrix} x_1 \\ \dots \\ x_n \end{bmatrix} = \sum_{i=1}^{n} \begin{bmatrix} pc_{i,1} \\ \dots \\ pc_{i,n} \end{bmatrix} \times p_i \tag{5}$$

Equation (3) allows us to interpret an arbitrary interest rate shock $\vec{X}$ as a *sum of principal component coefficients which are multiplied by a realization of the appropriate principal component.*

For example, consider a one standard deviation shock corresponding to the first principal component (PC_1). The realization of such an event in terms of principal components is given by

$$(\sqrt{\lambda_1}, 0, \dots, 0)_{PC}^T$$

where $\sqrt{\lambda_1}$ is the one standard deviation of PC_1. In terms of key rate changes, however, via equation (3) this shock has the following familiar representation

$$(\sqrt{\lambda_1} \times pc_{1,1}, \dots, \sqrt{\lambda_1} \times pc_{1,n})_{KR}$$

The splined shapes of the first three principal components are presented in Exhibit 11.3.

Principal components constitute an orthogonal basis PC in the space of spot curve movements. By definition, the i-th principal component is obtained from the covariance matrix $\Im$ of key rate changes via the following optimization problem:

- Compute the remaining variability in the system not explained by the first $i - 1$ principal components;
- Find a linear combination of key rates which explains as much of the remaining variability as possible;
- The i-th principal component should be orthogonal to all the previously selected $i - 1$ principal components.

Clearly, in an n-dimensional linear space of spot curve movements, there exist orthogonal *bases other than the one consisting of principal components*. Surprisingly, this fact will help us derive the distribution of interest rate shocks of a given shape.

EXHIBIT 11.3 Principal Component Shocks to Spot Curve Smoothed Via Cubic Splines

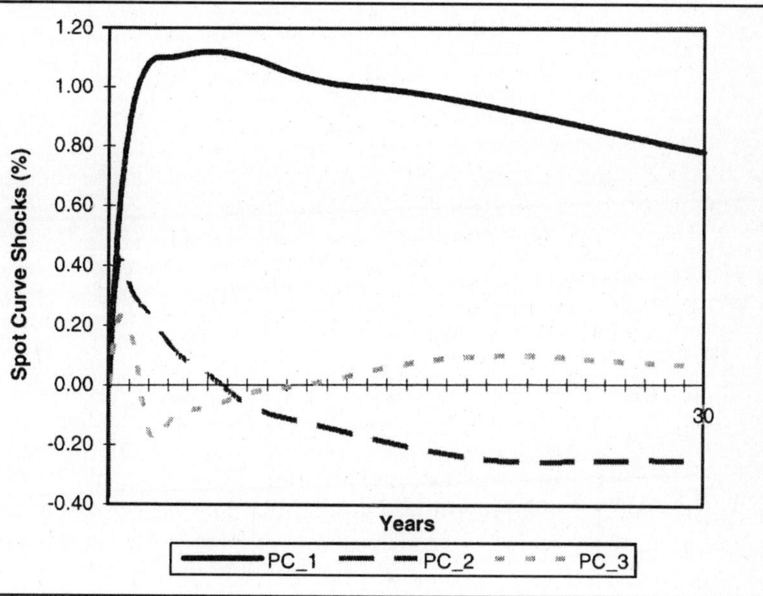

Suppose

$$\vec{Y} = (y_1, \ldots, y_n)_{KR}$$

is a hypothetical interest rate shock defined in terms of key rate changes. We claim that $\vec{Y}$ corresponds to a particular realization of some standard normal random variable y. In other words, all interest rate shocks of a given shape are in one-to-one correspondence with the set of realizations of y. Therefore, we can speak about the probability of $\vec{Y}$ occurring. We will now construct y and establish its relationship with $\vec{Y}$.

Let

$$\vec{y} = (\hat{y}_1, \ldots, \hat{y}_n)_{KR}$$

be a unit vector whose shape is the same as that of $\vec{Y}$, in other words,

$$\hat{y}_i = y_i / \sqrt{\sum_{i=1}^{n} y_i^2}$$

Similarly to the way we define principal components, define a new random variable Y to be the linear combination

$$Y = \sum_{i=1}^{n} \hat{y}_i \times K_i$$

where $\hat{y}_i$ are real numbers and K_i are changes in key rates (random variables). Then the variance of Y is given by

$$\sigma^2(Y) = (\hat{y}_1, \ldots, \hat{y}_n) \times \Im \times (\hat{y}_1, \ldots, \hat{y}_n)^T \tag{6}$$

We will now construct a new coordinate system in the space of spot curve changes. It will correspond to the new orthogonal basis B (different from principal components) such that Y is the first element in B. We modify the principal component optimization problem as follows:

- In the first step, instead of selecting a linear combination of changes in key rates which explains the maximum amount of variance, select Y.
- In each following step, find a linear combination of key rates which explains the maximum of the remaining variability in the system.
- Every newly selected element of the basis B should be orthogonal to all previously selected elements of B.

As a result, we have selected a set of n orthogonal variables which explain the total historical variability of interest rate movements. Moreover, Y is the first element in this basis. Define $y = Y/\sigma(Y)$, then y is a standard normal variable. The analog of equation (3) in this new coordinate system is given by

$$\begin{bmatrix} x_1 \\ \ldots \\ x_n \end{bmatrix} = \begin{bmatrix} \hat{y}_1 \\ \ldots \\ \hat{y}_n \end{bmatrix} \times Y + \ldots \tag{7}$$

or simply

$$\begin{bmatrix} x_1 \\ \ldots \\ x_n \end{bmatrix} = \begin{bmatrix} \sigma(Y) \times \hat{y}_1 \\ \ldots \\ \sigma(Y) \times \hat{y}_n \end{bmatrix} \times y + \ldots \tag{8}$$

where

$$(\sigma(Y) \times \hat{y}_1, \ldots, \sigma(Y) \times \hat{y}_n)_{KR}^T$$

is the one standard deviation shock corresponding to Y. Therefore, due to orthogonality, *every interest rate shock whose shape is the same as that of* $\vec{Y}$ *(and* $\vec{y}$*) corresponds to a particular realization of the standard normal variable* y*.*

For example, consider 10 key rates ($n = 10$) and suppose $\vec{Y}$ is a 200 bps parallel spot curve shock:

$$\vec{Y} = (200, \ldots, 200)_{KR}$$

Then

$$\vec{y} = (1/\sqrt{10}, \ldots, 1/\sqrt{10})_{KR}$$

is the corresponding unit vector which has the same shape as $\vec{Y}$. Using the RiskMetrics™ dataset, we can compute the standard deviation of the corresponding random variable Y. It can be shown that the "one standard deviation parallel shock" on 9/30/96 was 92 bps. Therefore, since we started with a parallel 200 bps spot curve shock, it implies a 200/92 = 2.17 standard deviation realization in the underlying standard normal variable. Then the probability of an annualized parallel shock over 200 bps is 0.015.

The magnitude of a one standard deviation parallel shock varies with the total variability in the market. Thus, on 2/4/97 the one standard deviation parallel shock was 73 bps and the probability of a parallel shock being over 200 bps was 0.003.

Ability to derive the distribution of interest rate shocks of a given shape leads us to the following important concepts.

Parallel First Principal Component

Many practitioners believe that it is convenient and intuitive to force the first principal component duration to equal effective duration.[5] To achieve this, we need to assume that the first principal component is a parallel spot curve shock. However, unlike the first principal component, a parallel spot curve shock is correlated with steepness and curva-

[5] Ram Wilner, "A New Tool for Portfolio Managers: Level, Slope, and Curvature Durations," *Journal of Fixed Income* (June 1996), pp. 48–59.

ture (second and third principal components, respectively). Therefore, immunization and simulation techniques involving principal components become more complicated. Via the method introduced above, we can create a new coordinate system which has a parallel shock as the first basis vector. In this case, since we need to maintain orthogonality in the new coordinate system, the shapes of steepness and curvature will change. Nevertheless, the first three factors will still explain a vast majority of the total variability in the system. We believe, however, that the humped shape of the first principal component should not be ignored. As discussed below, it is meaningful and can be used as a tool while placing yield curve bets.

Explanatory Power of a Given Curve Shock

Among all interest rate shocks, the first principal component has the maximum explanatory power by construction. For instance, Exhibit 11.1 indicates that the first principal component "explains" 92% of the recent historical spot curve movements. The number 92% is the ratio of the variance of the first principal component to the total variance in the system (sum of all principal components' variances). We now know how to compute a "one standard deviation shock" of a given shape as well as its variance via equation (4). The ratio of the variance of the parallel shock to the total variance in the system in the above example is 87%. This means that on 9/30/96 a parallel spot curve shock "explained" 87% of the historical spot curve movements. We will call the ratio of the percentage of total variability explained by a given shock to the percentage of total variability explained by the first principal component the *explanatory power* of the given shock. The explanatory power of the first principal component is 1; that of a parallel spot shock in the given example is 95%.

Magnitude Plausibility of a Given Curve Shock

Once we know how many standard deviations k of the underlying standard normal variable a given interest rate shock Y implies, we can talk about the historical magnitude plausibility $mpl(Y)$ of this shock. Let Ψ denote the event "we guessed the direction of change in rates." We define the magnitude plausibility of a given interest rate shock $\vec{Y}$ as

$$mpl(\vec{Y}) = Prob(y > |k| \mid \Psi) \tag{9}$$

We can simplify equation (7) as follows:

$$mpl(\vec{Y}) = 2 \times Prob(y > |k|) \tag{10}$$

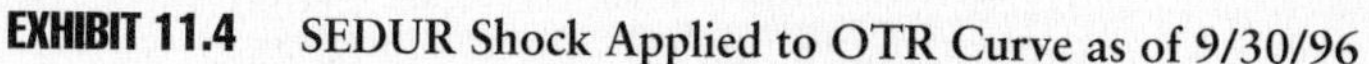

EXHIBIT 11.4 SEDUR Shock Applied to OTR Curve as of 9/30/96

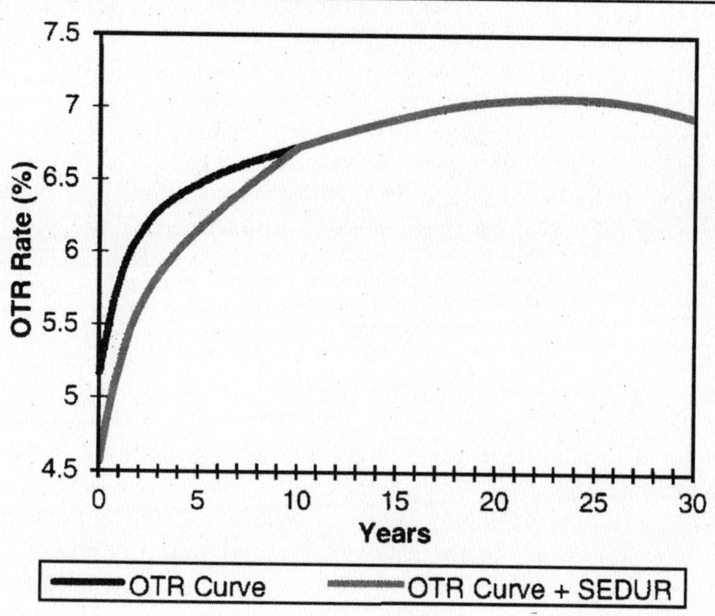

For example, the magnitude plausibility of a 200 bps spot curve shock is 3% whereas the magnitude plausibility of a 25 bps parallel spot curve shock is 78%.

The interest rate shock used by Klaffky, Ma, and Nozari to compute what they call short-end duration (SEDUR) is defined as a 50-basis point steepener at the short end.[6] (See Exhibit 11.4.) It can be shown that the explanatory power of SEDUR is 38% and the magnitude plausibility is 54%.

SHAPE PLAUSIBILITY

The previous section deals with the quantitative measurement of the *magnitude plausibility* of a given spot curve shock. Thus we start with an interest rate shock of a *given shape* and then derive its distribution

[6] T.E. Klaffky, Y.Y. Ma, and A. Nozari, "Managing Yield Curve Exposure: Introducing Reshaping Durations," *Journal of Fixed Income* (December 1992), pp. 5–15. Note that SEDUR shock is applied to the OTR curve. To perform principal component decomposition, we first need to analytically transform it into a shock to the spot curve.

which is used to determine if the magnitude of the given shock is reasonable given the recent covariance of interest rates. However, the issue of whether the shape of the shock is plausible from the historical perspective is never considered. This section deals with an independent assessment of the *shape plausibility* of interest rate shocks.

Principal components are the latent factors which depict the historical dynamics of interest rates. Therefore, we have a specific notion of plausibility at hand. The "most plausible" or "ideal" shock is the one whose "decomposition" into principal components is exactly that of the system (Exhibit 11.1):

$$\lambda = \{92.80, 4.80, 1.27, \ldots 0.03\}$$

In other words, the first principal component should "contribute" 92.8% to the "ideal" shock, the second should contribute 4.8%, the third 1.3%, and so on. The measure of plausibility should be defined in a way that the plausibility of an "ideal" shock is 1. On the other hand, it is natural to consider "the least plausible" shock to be the last principal component which has the least explanatory power and therefore is the least probable one. Clearly, the decomposition of the least plausible shock into principal components is $\gamma = \{0, \ldots 0, 100\}$. Thus, the measure of plausibility should be defined in a way that the plausibility of the least plausible shock is 0. Any other shock $\vec{X}$ will be somewhere in between the "ideal" and "the least plausible" shocks, and will have plausibility $spl(\vec{X})$ between 0 and 1. Below we present one such measure of plausibility.[7]

Write a hypothetical interest rate shock $\vec{X}$ in terms of principal components:

$$\vec{X} = (p_1, \ldots, p_n)_{PC}$$

Since $\vec{X}$ is a vector, it is reasonable to define the "contribution" of the *i*-th principal component in $\vec{X}$ based on the percentage of the squared length of $\vec{X}$ due to p_i, for example,

$$\hat{p}_i = p_i^2 / \sum_{i=1}^{n} p_i^2$$

[7] For alternative approaches, see "measures of consistency" introduced by P.M. Brusilovsky and L.M. Tilman ("Incorporating Expert Judgement into Multivariate Polynomial Modeling," *Decision Support Systems* (October 1996), pp. 199–214). One may also think of the explanatory power of a shock as an alternative measure of shape plausibility.

Hence, to measure the shape plausibility of $\vec{X}$ is equivalent to measuring *how different the vector* $\hat{p} = \{\hat{p}_i\}$ *is from the "ideal" shock*. Let $D(\hat{p}, \lambda)$ be the "distance" between $\vec{X}$ and the ideal shock. Since the maximum distance between any two vectors is the distance $D(\lambda, \gamma)$ between an "ideal" and "the least plausible" shocks, there is a way to normalize the measure of plausibility and present it as a number between 0 and 1.

We define the shape plausibility of $\vec{X}$ as

$$spl(\vec{X}) = 1 - \frac{D(\hat{p}, \lambda)}{D(\gamma, \lambda)} \tag{11}$$

where

$$D(\hat{a}, \lambda) = D(\{\hat{a}_i\}, \{\lambda_i\}) = \sum \left|\hat{a}_i - \lambda_i\right| \tag{12}$$

The functional form of the "distance" measure in equation (10) is not unique. We have experimented with several other functional representations only to discover that they fail to effectively differentiate between shapes of interest rate shocks, thus making the mapping spl: $\vec{X} \to [0, 1]$ almost a step function.

For example, to measure the shape plausibility of SEDUR, write its decomposition into principal components along with that of the "ideal" and "least plausible" shocks (Exhibit 11.5). It can be shown via equations (9) and (10) that $spl(SEDUR) = 0.41$. This means that from the historical perspective, the shape of SEDUR shock is not very plausible. Therefore, one may question the meaningfulness of the corresponding duration.

It should be noted that all characteristics of a given interest rate shock, such as "explanatory power," "magnitude plausibility," and "shape plausibility" depend on historical data and may vary dramatically over time.

EXHIBIT 11.5 Shape Plausibility and Principal Component Decomposition

		Principal Component Decomposition (%)									
Shock	Spl (.)	1	2	3	4	5	6	7	8	9	10
Ideal	1.00	92.80	4.80	1.27	0.62	0.20	0.11	0.09	0.06	0.03	0.03
Least Plausible	0.00	0.00	0.00	0.00	0.00	0.00	0.00	0.00	0.00	0.00	100.00
SEDUR	0.41	34.67	59.58	0.67	1.87	0.17	0.30	1.08	0.02	1.62	0.02

FIRST PRINCIPAL COMPONENT AND THE TERM STRUCTURE OF VOLATILITY

Changes in U.S. Treasury spot rates are generally highly correlated. This fact has significant implications in interpreting the shape of the first principal component. This section deals with this issue. We claim that when spot rates are highly correlated, the shape of the first principal component resembles the shape of the term structure of volatility (TSOV) of changes in spot rates. The above statement provides the intuition behind the reason why, according to Ehud Ronn, "large-move days reflect more of a level [first principal component] shift in interest rates."[8] It also enables us to conclude that on days when the market moves substantially (e.g., more than two standard deviations) the relative changes in spot rates are almost solely a function of their historical volatilities. We now provide the informal proof of this claim.

Let r_i and r_j be spot rates of maturities i and j, respectively. Let σ_i and σ_j be the volatilities of *changes* of r_i and r_j, respectively, while $pc_{1,i}$ and $pc_{1,j}$ be the coefficients of the first principal component corresponding to r_i and r_j. The statement "*the shape of the first principal component resembles that of TSOV of spot rate changes*" is equivalent to the following identity:

$$\frac{\sigma_i}{\sigma_j} \approx \frac{pc_{1,i}}{pc_{1,j}} \tag{13}$$

Our argument is based on the following representation of the principal component coefficients:[9]

$$pc_{1,i} = \frac{\rho_{1,i} \times \sigma_i}{\sqrt{\lambda_1}}; \qquad pc_{1,j} = \frac{\rho_{1,j} \times \sigma_j}{\sqrt{\lambda_1}} \tag{14}$$

where $\rho_{1,i}$ and $\rho_{1,j}$ are the correlations between the first principal component and the rates r_i and r_j, respectively. Note that since all spot key rates are highly correlated, they will be also highly correlated with the principal components, $\rho_{1,i} \approx \rho_{1,j}$, and then equation (11) yields

[8] E.I. Ronn, "The Impact of Large Changes in Asset Prices on Intra-Market Correlations in the Stock and Bond Markets," Working Paper, University of Texas in Austin, 1996.

[9] See R.A. Johnson and D.W. Wichern, *Applied Multivariate Statistical Analysis* (Englewood Cliffs: Prentice-Hall, 1982).

$$\frac{pc_{1,i}}{pc_{1,j}} = \frac{\rho_{1,i}\times\sigma_i}{\sqrt{\lambda_1}} \Big/ \frac{\rho_{1,j}\times\sigma_j}{\sqrt{\lambda_1}} = \frac{\rho_{1,i}}{\rho_{1,j}} \times \frac{\sigma_i}{\sigma_j} \approx \frac{\sigma_i}{\sigma_j} \tag{15}$$

There are a number of interesting implications of the above result. For instance, *when the market rallies, the long end of the spot curve steepens, and when the market sells off, the long end of the spot curve flattens.* To see that, just notice that since the historical volatility of the 10-year rate is higher than the historical volatility of the 30-year rate, the changes in the former are generally larger than those in the latter. Therefore when the market rallies, according to the shape of the first principal component, the 10-year rate should decrease more than the 30-year rate; hence the spot curve should steepen.

U.S. Treasury bond market data seems to support this result:[10] over the 4-year period November 1992–November 1996, the ratio of bull steepenings to bull flattenings of the spot curve was 2.5:1, and the ratio of bear flattenings to bear steepenings was 2.75:1. If we study the steepeners/flatteners of the OTR Treasury curve instead, we will notice that while bull steepening and bear flattening patterns dominate, the proportions are different: Over the same time period, the ratio of bull steepenings to bull flattenings of the OTR Treasury curve was 1.6:1, and the ratio of bear flattenings to bear steepenings was 6.5:1.

CONCLUSION

One of the advantages of key rate durations is the ability to estimate the instantaneous return on a portfolio given a hypothetical curve shift. The latter does not require us to do any additional simulations. Until now, sensitivity analysis was never concerned with the issue of whether the utilized hypothetical shocks were plausible from a historical perspective. The measures of plausibility of interest rate shocks introduced in this chapter constrain interest rate shocks used in sensitivity analysis and portfolio optimization. They provide discipline to the scenario analysis by excluding historically implausible interest rate shocks from consideration. The framework which allows us to compute the distribution of

[10] Monthly changes in the level and steepness of the U.S. spot and OTR curves were considered. We define the market as "bull" if the 10-year spot (OTR) key rate fell more that 5 bps, "bear" if it rose more that 5 bps, and "neutral" otherwise. Likewise, a change in the slope of the spot (OTR) curve is defined as a "steepening" if the spread between the 2-year and 30-year increased by more than 5 bps, "flattening" if it decreased by more than 5 bps, and "neutral" otherwise.

interest rate shocks of a given shape is important by itself. In another study,[11] we utilize the knowledge about these distributions to simulate interest rate shocks and make conscious tradeoffs between the value surface and the yield curve dynamics while computing value-at-risk.

[11] Chapter 5 in B. Golub and L. Tilman, *Risk Management: Approaches for Fixed Income Markets* (New York: J. Wiley & Sons, 2000).

SECTION
three

Valuation Models

CHAPTER 12

Understanding the Building Blocks for OAS Models

Philip O. Obazee*
Vice President
Delaware Investments

Investors and analysts continue to wrestle with the differences in option-adjusted-spread (OAS) values for securities they see from competing dealers and vendors. And portfolio managers continue to pose fundamental questions about OAS with which we all struggle in the financial industry. Some of the frequently asked questions are

- How can we interpret the difference in dealers' OAS values for a specific security?
- What is responsible for the differences?
- Is there really a correct OAS value for a given security?

In this chapter, we examine some of the questions about OAS analysis, particularly the basic building block issues about OAS implementation. Because some of these issues determine "good or bad" OAS results, we believe there is a need to discuss them. To get at these fundamental issues, we hope to avoid sounding pedantic by relegating most of the notations and expressions to the footnotes.

Clearly, it could be argued that portfolio managers do not need to understand the OAS engine to use it but that they need to know how to

---

* This chapter was written while Philip Obazee was Vice President, Quantitative Research, First Union Securities, Inc.

apply it in relative value decisions. This argument would be correct if there were market standards for representing and generating interest rates and prepayments. In the absence of a market standard, investors need to be familiar with the economic intuitions and basic assumptions made by the underlying models. More important, investors need to understand what works for their situation and possibly identify those situations in which one model incorrectly values a bond. Exhibit 12.1 shows a sample of OAS analysis for passthrough securities. Although passthroughs are commoditized securities, the variance in OAS results is still wide. This variance is attributable to differences in the implementation of the respective OAS models.

Unlike other market measures, for example, yield to maturity and the weighted average life of a bond, which have market standards for calculating their values, OAS calculations suffer from the lack of a standard and a black-box mentality. The lack of a standard stems from the required inputs in the form of interest rate and prepayment models that go into an OAS calculation. Although there are many different interest rate models available, there is little agreement on which one to use. Moreover, there is no agreement on how to model prepayments. The black-box mentality comes from the fact that heavy mathematical machinery and computational algorithms are involved in the development and implementation of an OAS model. This machinery is often so cryptic that only a few initiated members of the intellectual tribe can decipher it. In addition, dealers invest large sums in the development of their term structures and prepayment models and, consequently, they are reluctant to share it.

EXHIBIT 12.1 Selected Sample of OAS Analysis Results*

Security Name	FUSI OAS	Major Vendor Espiel OAS	Major Street Firm OAS
FNCL600	122	118	119
FNCL650	115	113	113
FNCL700	113	117	112
GN600	106	114	100
GN650	101	111	101
GN700	100	116	103
FNCI600	95	98	103
FNCI650	94	99	103
FNCI700	92	101	103

OAS: Option-adjusted spread.
* As of July 12, 2000, close.
Source: First Union Securities, Inc. (FUSI).

In this chapter, we review some of the proposed term structures and prepayments. Many of the term structure models describe "what is" and only suggest that the models could be used. Which model to use perhaps depends on the problem at hand and the resources available. In this chapter, we review some of the popular term structure models and provide some general suggestions on which ones should *not* be used.

Investors in asset-backed securities (ABS) and mortgage-backed securities (MBS) hold long positions in noncallable bonds and short positions in call (prepayment) options. The noncallable bond is a bundle of zero-coupon bonds (e.g., Treasury strips), and the call option gives the borrower the right to prepay the mortgage at any time prior to the maturity of the loan. In this framework, the value of MBS is the difference between the value of the noncallable bond and the value of the call (prepayment) option. Suppose a theoretical model is developed to value the components of ABS/MBS. The model would value the noncallable component, which we loosely label the *zero volatility component*, and the *call option component*. If interest rate and prepayment risks are well accounted for, and if those are the only risks for which investors demand compensation, one would expect the theoretical value of the bond to be equal to its market value. If these values are not equal, then market participants demand compensation for the unmodeled risks. One of these unmodeled risks is the forecast error associated with the prepayments. By this, we mean the actual prepayment may be faster or slower than projected by the model. Other unmodeled risks are attributable to the structure and liquidity of the bond. In this case, OAS is the market price for the unmodeled risks.

To many market participants, however, OAS indicates whether a bond is mispriced. All else being equal, given that interest rate and prepayment risks have been accounted for, one would expect the theoretical price of a bond to be equal to its market price. If these two values are not equal, a profitable opportunity may exist in a given security or a sector. Moreover, OAS is viewed as a tool that helps identify which securities are cheap or rich when the securities are relatively priced.

The zero volatility component of ABS/MBS valuation is attributable to the pure interest rate risk of a known cash flow—a noncallable bond. The forward interest rate is the main value driver of a noncallable bond. Indeed, the value driver of a noncallable bond is the sum of the rolling yield and the value of the convexity. The rolling yield is the return earned if the yield curve and the expected volatility are unchanged. Convexity refers to the curvature of the price-yield curve. A noncallable bond exhibits varying degrees of positive convexity. Positive convexity means a bond's price rises more for a given yield decline than it falls for the same yield. By unbundling the noncallable bond components in ABS/MBS to their zero-coupon bond components, the rolling yield becomes dominant. Hence, it is called the *zero volatility component*—that is, the component of the yield spread that is attributable to no change in the expected volatility.

The call option component in ABS/MBS valuation consists of intrinsic and time values. To the extent the option embedded in ABS/MBS is the delayed American exercise style—in other words, the option is not exercised immediately but becomes exercisable any time afterward—the time value component dominates. Thus, in valuing ABS/MBS, the time value of the option associated with the prepayment volatility needs to be evaluated. To evaluate this option, OAS analysis uses an option-based technique to evaluate ABS/MBS prices under different interest rate scenarios. OAS is the spread differential between the zero volatility and option value components of MBS. These values are expressed as spreads measured in basis points. Exhibit 12.2 shows the FNMA 30-year current-coupon OAS over a 3-year period.

The option component is the premium paid (earned) from going long (shorting) a prepayment option embedded in the bond. The bondholders are short the option, and they earn the premium in the form of an enhanced coupon. Mortgage holders are long the prepayment option, and they pay the premium in spread above the comparable Treasury. The option component is the cost associated with the variability in cash flow that results from prepayments over time.

The two main inputs into the determination of an OAS of a bond are as follows:

- Generate the cash flow as a function of the principal (scheduled and unscheduled) and coupon payments.
- Generate interest rate paths under an assumed term structure model.

EXHIBIT 12.2 FNMA 30-Year Current-Coupon OAS

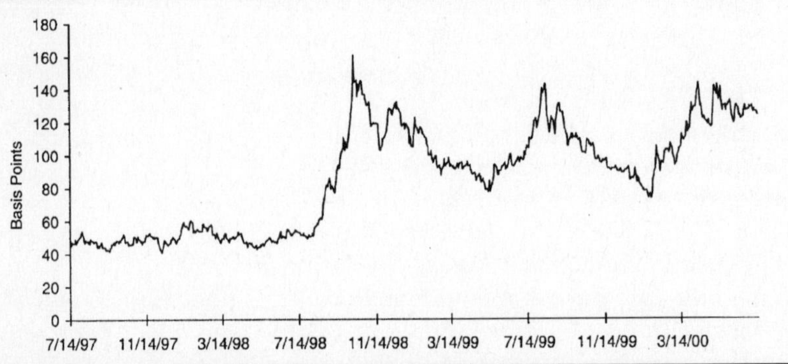

FNMA: Fannie Mae; OAS: Option-adjusted spread.
Source: First UnSecurities, Inc.

At each cash flow date, a spot rate determines the discount factor for each cash flow. The present value of the cash flow is equal to the sum of the product of the cash flow and the discount factors.[1] When dealing with a case in which uncertainty about future prospects is important, the cash flow and the spot rate need to be specified to account for the uncertainty.[2] The cash flow and spot rate become a function of time and the state of the economy. The time consideration is that a dollar received now is worth more than one received tomorrow. The state of the economy consideration accounts for the fact that a dollar received in a good economy may be perceived as worth less than a dollar earned in a bad economy. For OAS analysis, the cash flow is run through different economic environments represented by interest rates and prepayment scenarios. The spot rate, which is used to discount the cash flow, is run through time steps and interest rate scenarios. The spot rate represents the instantaneous rate of risk-free return at any time, so that \$1 invested now will have grown by a later time to \$1 multiplied by a continuously compounded rollover rate during the time period.[3] Arbitrage pricing theory

---

[1] In the world of certainty, the present value is

$$PV = \sum_{i=1}^{n} \frac{cf_i}{(1+r_i)^i}$$

where, r_i is the spot rate applicable to cash flow cf_i. In terms of forward rates, the equation becomes

$$PV = \sum_{i=1}^{n} \frac{cf_i}{(1+f_1)(1+f_2)\ldots(1+f_n)}$$

where f_i is the forward rate applicable to cash flow cf_i.

[2] The present value formula becomes more complicated and could be represented as

$$PV_\Omega = \sum_{\omega_i}^{\Omega}\sum_{t_i}^{T} \frac{cf(t_i, \omega_i)}{(1+r(t_i, \omega_i))} \qquad \forall\, i = 1, 2, \ldots N$$

where,

PV_Ω = the present value of uncertain cash flow

$cf(t_i, \omega_i)$ = the cash flow received at time t_i and state ω_i

$r(t_i, \omega_i)$ = the spot rate applicable at time t_i and state ω_i

For OAS analysis, a stylized version of the previous equation is given by

$$PV_\Omega = \lim_{N\to\infty} \frac{1}{N} \frac{cf(t_i, \omega_i)}{(1+r(t_i, \omega_i))} \qquad \forall\, i = 1, 2, \ldots N$$

[3]

$$\$1\left[\exp\left(\int_t^T r(u)du\right)\right]$$

stipulates the price one should pay now to receive \$1 at later time is the expected discount of the payoff.[4] So by appealing to the arbitrage pricing theory, we are prompted to introduce an integral representation for the value equation; in other words, the arbitrage pricing theory allows us to use the value additivity principle across all interest rate scenarios.

IS IT EQUILIBRIUM OR AN ARBITRAGE MODEL?

Market participants are guided in their investment decision making by received economic philosophy or intuition. Investors, in general, look at value from either an absolute or relative value basis. Absolute value basis proceeds from the economic notion that the market clears at an exogenously determined price that equates supply-and-demand forces. Absolute valuation models are usually supported by general or partial equilibrium arguments. In implementing market measure models that depend on equilibrium analysis, the role of an investor's preference for risky prospects is directly introduced. The formidable task encountered with respect to preference modeling and the related aggregation problem has rendered these types of models useless for most practical considerations. One main exception is the present value rule that explicitly assumes investors have a time preference for today's dollar. Where the present value function is a monotonically decreasing function of time, today's dollar is worth more than a dollar earned tomorrow. Earlier term structure models were supported by equilibrium arguments, for example, the Cox, Ingersoll, and Ross (CIR) model.[5] In particular, CIR provides an equilibrium foundation for a class of yield curves by specifying the endowments and preferences of traders, which, through the clearing of competitive markets, generates the proposed term structure model.

Relative valuation models rely on arbitrage and dominance principles and characterize asset prices in terms of other asset prices. A well-known example of this class is the Black-Scholes[6] and Merton[7] option pricing model. Modern term structure models, for example, Hull and White,[8]

---

[4] $p(t, T) = E\left[\exp\left(-\int_t^T r(u)du\right)\middle|F_t\right]$

[5] J. Cox, J. Ingersoll, and S. Ross, "A Theory of the Term Structure of Interest Rates," *Econometrica,* 53 (1985), pp. 385–408.

[6] F. Black and M. Scholes, "The Pricing of Options and Corporate Liabilities," *Journal of Political Economy*, 81 (1973), pp. 637–654.

[7] R. Merton, "The Theory of Rational Option Pricing," *Bell Journal of Economics and Management Science*, 4 (1974), pp. 141–183.

[8] J. Hull and A. White, "Pricing Interest Rate Derivatives Securities," *Review of Financial Studies*, 3 (1990), pp. 573–592.

Black-Derman-Toy (BDT),[9] and Heath, Jarrow, and Morton (HJM),[10] are based on arbitrage arguments. Although relative valuation models based on arbitrage principles do not directly make assumptions about investors' preferences, there remains a vestige of the continuity of preference, for example, the notion that investors prefer more wealth to less. Thus, whereas modelers are quick in attributing "arbitrage-freeness" to their models, assuming there are no arbitrage opportunities implies a continuity of preference that can be supported in equilibrium. So, if there are no arbitrage opportunities, the model is in equilibrium for some specification of endowments and preferences. The upshot is that the distinction between equilibrium models and arbitrage models is a stylized fetish among analysts to demarcate models that explicitly specify endowment and preference sets (equilibrium) and those models that are outwardly silent about the preference set (arbitrage). Moreover, analysts usually distinguish equilibrium models as those that use today's term structure as an output and no-arbitrage models as those that use today's term structure as an input.

Arbitrage opportunity exists in a market model if there is a strategy that guarantees a positive payoff in some state of the world with no possibility of negative payoff and no initial net investment. The presence of arbitrage opportunity is inconsistent with economic equilibrium populated by market participants that have increasing and continuous preferences. Moreover, the presence of arbitrage opportunity is inconsistent with the existence of an optimal portfolio strategy for market participants with nonsatiated preferences (prefer more to less) because there would be no limit to the scale at which they want to hold an arbitrage position. The economic hypothesis that maintains two perfect substitutes (two bonds with the same credit quality and structural characteristics issued by the same firm) must trade at the same price is an implication of no arbitrage. This idea is commonly referred to as the *law of one price*. Technically speaking, the fundamental theorem of asset pricing is a collection of canonical equivalent statements that implies the absence of arbitrage in a market model. The theorem provides for weak equivalence between the absence of arbitrage, the existence of a linear pricing rule, and the existence of optimal demand from some market participants who prefer more to less. The direct consequence of these canonical statements is the pricing rule: the existence of a positive linear pricing rule, the existence of positive risk-neutral probabilities, and associated riskless rate or the existence of a positive state price density.

[9] F. Black, E. Derman, and W. Toy, "A One Factor Model of Interest Rates and Its Application to Treasury Bond Options," *Financial Analysts Journal* (1990), pp. 33–39.

[10] D. Heath, R. Jarrow, and A. Morton, "Bond Pricing and the Term Structure of Interest Rates: A New Methodology for Contingent Claims Valuation," *Econometrica*, 60 (1992), pp. 77–105.

In essence, the pricing rule representation provides a way of correctly valuing a security when the arbitrage opportunity is eliminated. A fair price for a security is the arbitrage-free price. The arbitrage-free price is used as a benchmark in relative value analysis to the extent that it is compared with the price observed in actual trading. A significant difference between the observed and arbitrage-free values may indicate the following profit opportunities:

- If the arbitrage price is above the observed price, all else being equal, the security is *cheap* and a *long position* may be called for.
- If the arbitrage price is below the observed price, all else being equal, the security is *rich* and a *short position* may be called for.

In practice, the basic steps in determining the arbitrage-free value of the security are as follows:

- Specify a model for the evolution of the underlying security price.
- Obtain a risk-neutral probability.
- Calculate the expected value at expiration using the risk-neutral probability.
- Discount this expectation using the risk-free rates.

In studying the solution to the security valuation problem in the arbitrage pricing framework, analysts usually use one of the following:

- Partial differential equation (PDE) framework
- Equivalent martingale measure framework

The PDE framework is a direct approach and involves constructing a risk-free portfolio, then deriving a PDE implied by the lack of arbitrage opportunity. The PDE is solved analytically or evaluated numerically.[11]

---

[11] For example, the PDE for a zero-coupon bond price is

$$\frac{\partial p}{\partial t} + \frac{1}{2}\sigma^2\frac{\partial^2 p}{\partial r^2} + (\mu - \lambda\sigma)\frac{\partial p}{\partial r} - rp = 0$$

where

p = zero-coupon price
r = instantaneous risk-free rate
μ = the drift rate
σ = volatility
λ = market price of risk

To solve the zero-coupon price PDE, we must state the final and boundary conditions. The final condition that corresponds to payoff at maturity is $p(r, T) = k$.

Although there are few analytical solutions for pricing PDEs, most of them are evaluated using numerical methods such as lattice, finite difference, and Monte Carlo. The equivalent martingale measure framework uses the notion of arbitrage to determine a probability measure under which security prices are martingales once discounted. The new probability measure is used to calculate the expected value of the security at expiration and discounting with the risk-free rate.

WHICH IS THE RIGHT MODEL OF THE INTEREST RATE PROCESS?

The bare essential of the bond market is a collection of zero-coupon bonds for each date, for example, now, that mature later. A zero-coupon bond with a given maturity date is a contract that guarantees the investor \$1 to be paid at maturity. The price of a zero-coupon bond at time t with a maturity date of T is denoted by $P(t, T)$. In general, analysts make the following simplifying assumptions about the bond market:

- There exists a frictionless and competitive market for a zero-coupon bond for every maturity date. By a frictionless market, we mean there is no transaction cost in buying and selling securities and there is no restriction on trades such as a short sale.
- For every fixed date, the price of a zero-coupon bond, $\{P(t, T); 0 \le t \le T\}$, is a stochastic process with $P(t, t) = 1$ for all t. By stochastic process, we mean the price of a zero-coupon bond moves in an unpredictable fashion from the date it was bought until it matures. The present value of a zero-coupon bond when it was bought is known for certain and it is normalized to equal one.
- For every fixed date, the price for a zero-coupon bond is continuous in that at every trading date the market is well bid for the zero-coupon bond.

In addition to zero-coupon bonds, the bond market has a money market (bank account) initialized with a unit of money.[12] The bank account serves as an accumulator factor for rolling over the bond.

A term structure model establishes a mathematical relationship that determines the price of a zero-coupon bond, $\{P(t, T); 0 \le t \le T\}$, for all

[12] The bank account is denoted by

$$B(t) = \exp\left[\int_0^t r(u)du\right]$$

and $B(0) = 1$.

dates t between the time the bond is bought (time 0) and when it matures (time T). Alternatively, the term structure shows the relationship between the yield to maturity and the time to maturity of the bond. To compute the value of a security dependent on the term structure, one needs to specify the dynamic of the interest rate process and apply an arbitrage restriction. A term structure model satisfies the arbitrage restriction if there is no opportunity to invest risk-free and be guaranteed a positive return.[13]

To specify the dynamic of the interest rate process, analysts have always considered a dynamic that is mathematically tractable and anchored in sound economic reasoning. The basic tenet is that the dynamic of interest rates is governed by time and the uncertain state of the world. Modeling time and uncertainty are the hallmarks of modern financial theory. The uncertainty problem has been modeled with the aid of the probabilistic theory of the stochastic process. The stochastic process models the occurrence of random phenomena; in other words, the process is used to describe unpredictable movements. The stochastic process is a collection of random variables that take values in the state space. The basic elements distinguishing a stochastic process are state space[14] and index parameter,[15] and the dependent relationship among the random variables (e.g., X_t).[16] The Poisson process and Brownian motion are two fundamental examples of continuous time stochastic

[13] Technically, the term structure model is said to be arbitrage-free if and only if there is a probability measure **Q** on Ω (**Q** ~ **P**) with the same null

$$Z(t, T) = \frac{P(t, T)}{B(t)}, 0 \le t \le T$$

set as **P**, such that for each t, the process is a martingale under **Q**.

[14] State space is the space in which the possible values of X_t lie. Let S be the state space. If $S = (0, 1, 2...)$, the process is called the discrete state process. If $S = \Re(-\infty, \infty)$ that is the real line, and the process is called the real-valued stochastic process. If S is Euclidean d-space, then the process is called the d-dimensional process.

[15] Index parameter: If $T = (0, 1...)$, then X_t is called the discrete-time stochastic process. If $T = \Re_+[0, \infty)$, then X_t is called a continuous time stochastic process.

[16] Formally, a stochastic process is a family of random variables $X = \{x_t; t \in T\}$, where T is an ordered subset of the positive real line $\Re_+$. A stochastic process X with a time set $[0, T]$ can be viewed as a mapping from $\Omega \times [0, T]$ to $\Re$ with $x(\omega, t)$ denoting the value of the process at time t and state ω. For each $\omega \in \Omega$, $\{x(\omega, t); t \in [0,T]\}$ is a sample path of X sometimes denoted as $x(\omega, \bullet)$. A stochastic process $X = \{x_t; t \in [0, T]\}$ is said to be adapted to filtration F if x_t is measurable with respect to F_t for all $t \in [0, T]$. The adaptedness of a process is an informational constraint: The value of the process at any time t cannot depend on the information yet to be revealed strictly after t.

processes. Exhibits 12.3 and 12.4 show the schematics of the Poisson process and Brownian motion.

In everyday financial market experiences, one may observe, at a given instant, three possible states of the world: Prices may go up a tick, decrease a tick, or do not change. The ordinary market condition characterizes most trading days; however, security prices may from time to time exhibit extreme behavior. In financial modeling, there is the need to distinguish between rare and normal events. Rare events usually bring about discontinuity in prices. The Poisson process is used to model jumps caused by rare events and is a discontinuous process. Brownian motion is used to model ordinary market events for which extremes occur only infrequently according to the probabilities in the tail areas of normal distribution.[17]

EXHIBIT 12.3 Poisson Process

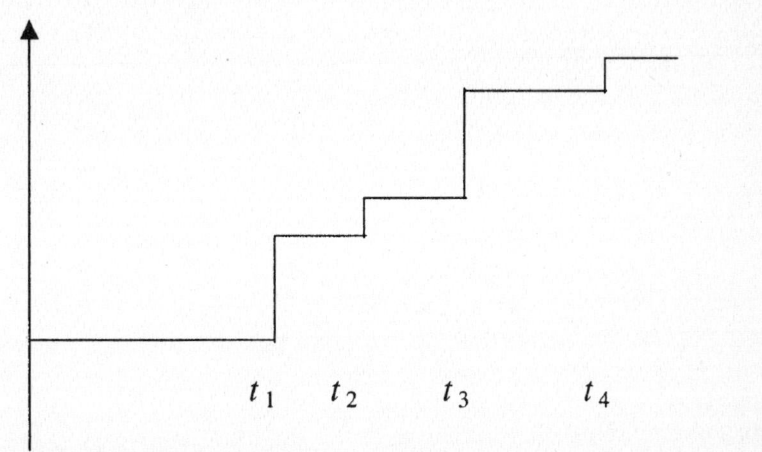

Source: First Union Securities, Inc.

[17] A process X is said to have an independent increment if the random variables $x(t_1) - x(t_0)$, $x(t_2) - x(t_1)$ ... and $x(t_n) - x(t_{n-1})$ are independent for any $n \geq 1$ and $0 \leq t_0 < t_1 < \ldots < t_n \leq T$. A process X is said to have a stationary independent increment if, moreover, the distribution of $x(t) - x(s)$ depends only on $t - s$. We write $z \sim N(\mu, \sigma^2)$ to mean the random variable z has normal distribution with mean μ and variance σ^2. A standard Brownian motion W is a process having continuous sample paths, stationary independent increments and $W(t) \sim N(\mu, t)$ (under probability measure P). Note that if X is a continuous process with stationary and independent increments, then X is a Brownian motion. A strong Markov property is a memoryless property of a Brownian motion. Given X as a Markov process, the past and future are statistically independent when the present is known.

EXHIBIT 12.4 Brownian Motion Path

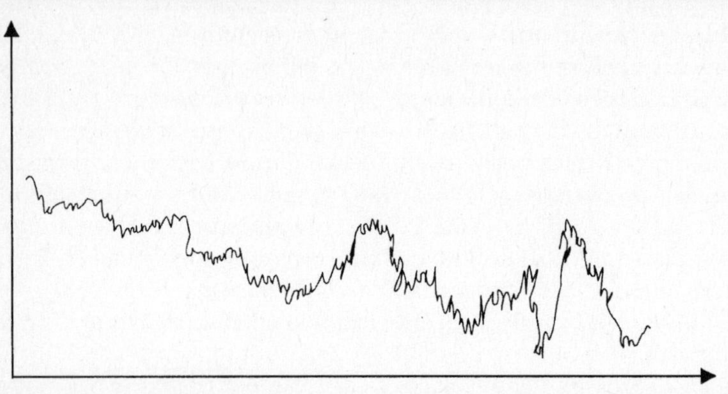

Source: First Union Securities, Inc.

Brownian motion is a continuous martingale. Martingale theory describes the trend of an observed time series. A stochastic process behaves like a martingale if its trajectories display no discernible trends.

- A stochastic process that, on average, increases is called a submartingale.
- A stochastic process that, on average, declines is called a supermartingale.

Suppose one has an interest in generating a forecast of a process (e.g., R_t – interest rate) by expressing the forecast based on what has been observed about R based on the information available (e.g., F_t) at time t.[18] This type of forecast, which is based on conditioning on information observed up to a time, has a role in financial modeling. This role is encapsulated in a martingale property.[19] A martingale is a process, the expectation for which future values conditional on current information are equal

[18] We write

$$E_t[R_t] = E[R_T|F_t],\ t < T$$

[19] More concretely, given a probability space, a process $\{R_t\ t \in (0, \infty)\}$ is a martingale with respect to information sets F_t, if for all $t > 0$,

1. R_t is known, given F_t, that is, R_t is F_t adapted
2. Unconditional forecast is finite; $E|R_t| < \infty$
3. And if

$$E_t[R_t] = R_T, \quad \forall\, t < T$$

with a probability of 1. The best forecast of unobserved future value is the last observation on R_t.

to the value of the process at present. A martingale embodies the notion of a fair gamble: The expected gain from participating in a family of fair gambles is always zero and, thus, the accumulated wealth does not change in expectation over time. Note the actual price of a zero-coupon bond does not move like a martingale. Asset prices move more like submartingales or supermartingales. The usefulness of martingales in financial modeling stems from the fact one can find a probability measure that is absolutely continuous with objective probability such that bond prices discounted by a risk-free rate become martingales. The probability measures that convert discounted asset prices into martingales are called equivalent martingale measures. The basic idea is that, in the absence of an arbitrage opportunity, one can find a synthetic probability measure Q absolutely continuous with respect to the original measure P so that all properly discounted asset prices behave as martingales. A fundamental theorem that allows one to transform R_t into a martingale by switching the probability measure from P to Q is called the Girsanov Theorem.

The powerful assertion of the Girsanov Theorem provides the ammunition for solving a stochastic differential equation driven by Brownian motion in the following sense: By changing the underlying probability measure, the process that was driving the Brownian motion becomes, under the equivalent measure, the solution to the differential equation. In financial modeling, the analog to this technical result says that in a risk-neutral economy assets should earn a risk-free rate. In particular, in the option valuation, assuming the existence of a risk-neutral probability measure allows one to dispense with the drift term, which makes the diffusion term (volatility) the dominant value driver.

To model the dynamic of interest rates, it is generally assumed the change in rates over instantaneous time is the sum of the drift and diffusion terms (see Exhibit 12.5).[20] The drift term could be seen as the average movement of the process over the next instants of time, and the diffusion is the amplitude (width) of the movement. If the first two moments are sufficient to describe the distribution of the asset return, the drift term accounts for the mean rate of return and the diffusion accounts for the standard deviation (volatility). Empirical evidence has suggested

[20] In particular, assume

$$dX(t) = \alpha(t, X(t))dt + \beta(t, X(t))dW(t)$$

for which the solution $X(t)$ is the factor. Depending on the application, one can have n-factors, in which case we let X be an n-dimensional process and W an n-dimensional Brownian motion. Assume the stochastic differential equation for $X(t)$ describes the interest process $r(t)$, (i.e., $r(t)$ is a function of $X(t)$). A one-factor model of interest rate is

$$dr(t) = \alpha(t)dt + \beta(t)dW(t)$$

that interest rates tend to move back to some long-term average, a phenomenon known as mean reverting that corresponds to the Ornstein-Ulhenbeck process (see Exhibit 12.6).[21] When rates are high, mean reversion tends to cause interest rates to have a negative drift; when rates are low, mean reversion tends to cause interest rates to have a positive drift.

EXHIBIT 12.5 Drift and Diffusion

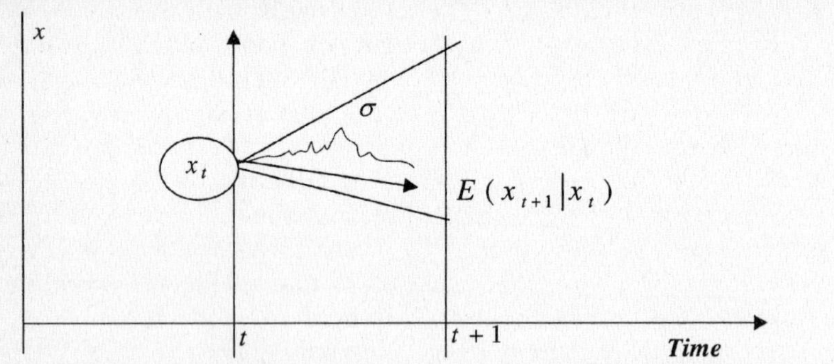

Source: First Union Securities, Inc.

EXHIBIT 12.6 Process with Mean Reversion (Ornstein-Uhlenbeck Process)

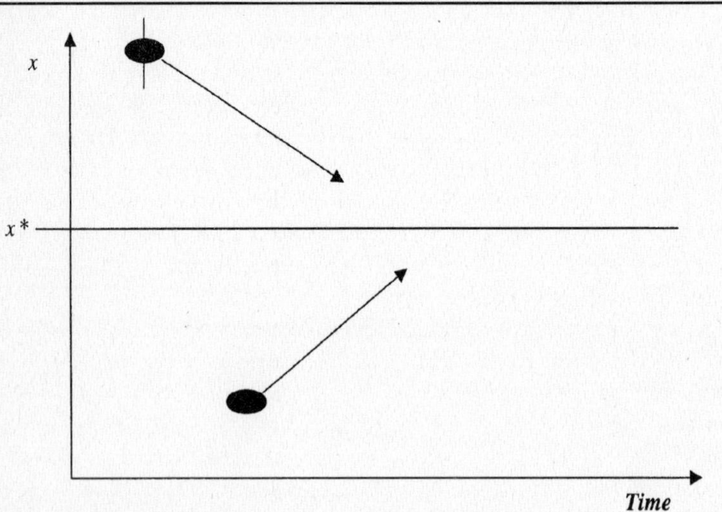

Source: First Union Securities, Inc.

[21] This process is represented as

$$dr = a(b - r)dt + \sigma r^{\beta} dW$$

where, a and b are called the reversion speed and level, respectively.

The highlights of the preceding discussion are as follows:

- The modeler begins by decomposing bonds to their bare essentials, which are zero-coupon bonds.
- To model a bond market that consists of zero-coupon bonds, the modeler makes some simplifying assumptions about the structure of the market and the price behaviors.
- A term structure model establishes a mathematical relationship that determines the price of a zero-coupon bond and, to compute the value of a security dependent on the term structure, the modeler needs to specify the dynamic of the interest rate process and apply arbitrage restriction.
- The stochastic process is used to describe the time and uncertainty components of the price of zero-coupon bonds.
- There are two basic types of stochastic processes used in financial modeling: The Poisson process is used to model jumps caused by rare events, and Brownian motion is used to model ordinary market events for which extremes occur only infrequently.
- We assume the market for zero-coupon bonds is well bid, that is, the zero-coupon price is continuous. Brownian motion is the suitable stochastic process to describe the evolution of interest rates over time. In particular, Brownian motion is a continuous martingale. Martingale theory describes the trend of the observed time series.
- Once we specify the evolution of interest rate movements, we need an arbitrage pricing theory that tells us the price one should pay now to receive $1 later is an expected discounted payoff. The issue to be resolved is, What are the correct expected discount factors to use? The discount must be determined by the market and based on risk-adjusted probabilities. In particular, when all bonds are properly risk-adjusted, they should earn risk-free rates; if not, arbitrage opportunity exists to earn riskless profit.
- The risk-adjusted probability consistent with the no-arbitrage condition is the equivalent martingale measure; it is the probability measure that converts the discounted bond price to a martingale (fair price). The elegance of the martingale theory is the "roughs and tumbles" one finds in the world of partial differentiation are to some extent avoided and the integral representation it allows fits nicely with Monte Carlo simulations.

Several term structure models have been proposed with subtle differences. However, the basic differences amount to how the dynamic of the interest rate is specified, the number of factors that generate the rate process, and whether the model is closed by equilibrium or arbitrage arguments. Some of the most popular term structure models can be summarized in Exhibit 12.7.

EXHIBIT 12.7 Summary of Popular Term Structure Models

Hull and White (1990)/Extended Vasicek (1977)

Assumptions

- Evolution of interest rates is driven by the short rate (one factor).
- Short rates are normally distributed.
- Instantaneous standard deviation of the short rate is constant.
- Short rates are mean reverting with a constant reversion rate.

Model

- Extended Vasicek model.
- The two volatility parameters are a and θ.
- a determines the relative volatilities of long and short rates, and the high value of a causes short-term rate movement to dampen such that long-term volatility is reduced.
- θ determines the overall volatility.
- The short-rate dynamic is

$$dr = [\theta(t) - ar] + \sigma dW$$

Issues

- Computational advantages (speed and convergence).
- Analytical solution exists for pricing some European-style derivatives.
- Normally distributed interest rates imply a finite probability of rates becoming zero or negative.

Ho and Lee (HL, 1986)

Assumptions

- Evolution of interest rates is driven by the short rate (one factor).
- Short rates are normally distributed.
- Instantaneous standard deviation of the short rate is constant.
- Short rates are not mean reverting.

Model

- The short-rate process is assumed to be an arithmetic process.
- In continuous time, the short-rate dynamic of HL is

$$dr = \theta(t) + \sigma dW$$

- $\theta(t)$ makes the model consistent with the initial term structure, and it can be seen approximately as the slope of the forward curve.

EXHIBIT 12.7 (Continued)

Issues

- Computational advantages (speed and convergence)
- Closed-form solution exists for pricing European-style derivatives.
- Nonexistence of a mean-reverting parameter on the model simplifies the calibration of the model to market data.
- Normally distributed interest rates imply a finite probability of rates becoming zero or negative.
- Nonexistence of mean reversion in the model implies all interest rates have the same constant rate, which is different from market observations (the short rate is more volatile than the long rate).

Cox, Ingersoll and Ross (CIR, 1985)

Assumptions

- Evolution of interest rates is driven by the short rate (one factor).
- Short rates are normally distributed.
- Instantaneous standard deviation of the short rate is constant times the square root of the interest rate.
- Short rates are mean reverting with a constant reversion rate.

Model

- The short-rate process is assumed to be a square root process.
- In continuous time, the short-rate dynamic of CIR is

$$dr = a[\theta - r] + \sigma r^{1/2} dW$$

Issues

- Eliminating the possibility of negative interest rates
- Analytical solution is difficult to implement, if you find one
- Popular among academics because of its general equilibrium overtone

Black-Derman-Toy (BDT, 1990)

Assumptions

- Evolution of interest rates is driven by the short rate (one factor).
- Short rates are log normally distributed, and short rates cannot become negative.
- Instantaneous standard deviation of the logarithmic short rate is constant.
- The reversion rate is a function of the short-rate volatility.

Model

- In continuous time, the short-rate dynamic of BDT is

$$d\mathrm{Log}(r) = [\theta(t) + (\sigma'(t)/\sigma(t))\mathrm{Log}(r)]dt + \sigma(t)dW$$

where $\sigma'(t)/\sigma(t)$ is the reversion rate that is a function of the short-rate volatility, $\sigma'(t)$ and its derivative with respect to time, $\sigma'(t)$.

EXHIBIT 12.7 (Continued)

Issues

- Eliminating the possibility of negative interest rates
- No closed-form solution

Black and Karasinski (BK, 1991)

Assumptions

- Separates the reversion rate and volatility in BDT
- Provides a procedure for implementing the model using a binomial lattice with time steps of varying lengths

Model

- In continuous time, the short-rate dynamic of BK is

$$d\mathrm{Log}(r) = [\theta(t) + a(t)\mathrm{Log}(r)]dt + \sigma(t)dW$$

Issues

- Whether mean reversion and volatility parameter should be functions of time; by making them a function of time, the volatility can be fitted at time zero correctly, however, the volatility structure in the future may be dramatically different from today

Heath, Jarrow, and Morton (HJM, 1992)

Assumptions

- Evolution of interest rates is driven by the forward rates (one factor or multifactor).
- Involves specifying the volatilities of all forward rates at all times
- Non-Markovian
- Expected drift of forward rate in risk-neutral world is calculated from its volatilities

Model

- The HJM model characterizes the fundamental stochastic process for the evolution of forward rates across time. The model takes as a given the initial forward rate curve and imposes a fairly general stochastic structure on it. By using the equivalent martingale technique, the model shows the condition that the evolution of forward rates must satisfy to be arbitrage-free. The basic condition is the existence of a unique equivalent martingale measure under which the prices of all bonds, risk-adjusted in terms of money market account, are martingales. HJM describes the evolution of forward curves as follows:

$$df(t, T) = \mu(t, T, \omega)dt + \sum_{i=1}^{n} \sigma_i(t, T, \omega)dW_i(t)$$

or,

$$f(t, T) = f(0, T) + \int_0^t \mu(v, T, \omega)dv + \int_0^t \sum_{i=1}^{n} \sigma_i(v, T, \omega)dW_i(v)$$

EXHIBIT 12.7 (Continued)

where $\mu(t, T, \omega)$ is the random drift term of the forward rate curve, $\sigma(t, T, \omega)$ is the stochastic volatility function of the forward rate curve and the initial forward rate curve $f(0, t)$ is taken as a given. Taking the spot rate at time t to be the instantaneous forward rate at time t that is

$$r(t) \equiv \lim_{T \to t} f(t, T)$$

we can write

$$r(t) = f(0, t) + \int_0^t \mu(v, t, \omega)dv + \int_0^t \sum_{i=1}^{n} \sigma_i(v, t, \omega)dW_i(v)$$

Notice the spot rate equation is similar to the forward-rate process with explicit differences in time and maturity arguments.

Issues

- Difficult to implement
- Instantaneous forward rate is not a market observable
- Useful in valuing path-dependent securities such as mortgages

Which of these models to use in OAS analysis depends on the available resources. Where resource availability is not an issue, we favor models that account for the path-dependent nature of mortgage cash flows. Good rules-of-thumb in deciding which model to use are as follows:

- *Flexibility:* How flexible is the model?
- *Simplicity:* Is the model easy to understand?
- *Specification:* Is the specification of the interest rate process reasonable?
- *Realism:* How real is the model?
- *Good fit:* How well does the result fit the market data?
- *Internal consistency rule:* A necessary condition for the existence of market equilibrium is the absence of arbitrage, and the external consistency rule requires models to be calibrated to market data.

First Union Securities, Inc.'s (FUSI) proprietary interest rate model is based on the HJM framework.

TERM STRUCTURE MODELS: WHICH IS THE RIGHT APPROACH FOR OAS?

Numerical schemes are constructive or algorithmic methods for obtaining practical solutions to mathematical problems. They provide methods for effectively finding practical solutions to asset pricing PDEs.

The first issue in a numerical approach is discretization. The main objective for discretizing a problem is to reduce it from continuous parameters formulation to an equivalent discrete parameterization in a way that makes it amenable to practical solution. In financial valuation, one generally speaks of a continuous time process in an attempt to find an analytical solution to a problem; however, nearly all the practical solutions are garnered by discretizing space and time. Discretization involves finding numerical approximatizations to the solution at some given points rather than on a continuous domain.

Numerical approximation may involve the use of a pattern, lattice, network, or mesh of discrete points in place of the (continuous) whole domain, so that only approximate solutions are obtained for the domain in the isolated points, and other values such as integrals and derivatives can be obtained from the discrete solution by the means of interpolation and extrapolation.

With the discretization of the continuous domain come the issues of adequacy, accuracy, convergence, and stability. Perhaps how these issues are faithfully addressed in the implementation of OAS models speaks directly to the type of results achieved. Although these numerical techniques—lattice methods, finite difference methods, and Monte Carlo methods—have been used to solve asset pricing PDEs, the lattice and Monte Carlo methods are more in vogue in OAS implementations.

Lattice Method

The most popular numerical scheme used by financial modelers is the lattice (or tree) method. A lattice is a nonempty collection of vertices and edges that represent some prescribed mathematical structures or properties. The node (vertex) of the lattice carries particular information about the evolution of a process that generates the lattice up to that point. An edge connects the vertices of a lattice. A lattice is initialized at its root, and the root is the primal node that records the beginning history of the process.

The lattice model works in a discrete framework and calculates expected values on a discrete space of paths. A node in a given path of a nonrecombining lattice distinguishes not only the value of the underlying claim there but also the history of the path up to the node. A bushy tree represents every path in the state space and can numerically value path-dependent claims. A node in a given path of a bushy tree distinguishes not only the value of the underlying claim there but also the history of the path to the node. There is a great cost in constructing a bushy tree model. For example, modeling a 10-year Treasury rate in a binary bushy tree with each time period equal to one coupon payment would require a tree with 2^{20} (1,048,576) paths. Exhibit 12.8 shows a schematic of a bushy tree.

In a lattice construction, it is usually assumed the time to maturity of the security, *T*, can be divided into discrete (finite and equal) time-steps *M*, $\Delta t = T/M$. The price of the underlying security is assumed to have a finite number of "jumps" (or up-and-down movements) *N* between the time-steps Δt. In a recombining lattice, the price or yield of the underlying security is assumed to be affected by *N* and not the sequences of the jumps. For computational ease, *N* is usually set to be two or three; the case where $N = 2$ is called *binomial lattice* (or tree), and $N = 3$ is the *trinomial lattice*. Exhibits 12.9 and 12.10 show the binomial and trinomial lattices, respectively, for the price of a zero-coupon bond.

Monte Carlo Method

The Monte Carlo method is a numerical scheme for solving mathematical models that involve random sampling. This scheme has been used to solve problems that are either deterministic or probabilistic in nature. In the most common application, the Monte Carlo method uses random or pseudo-random numbers to simulate random variables. Although the Monte Carlo method provides flexibilities in dealing with a probabilistic problem, it is not precise especially when one desires the highest level of accuracy at a reasonable cost and time.

EXHIBIT 12.8 Bushy or Nonrecombining Tree

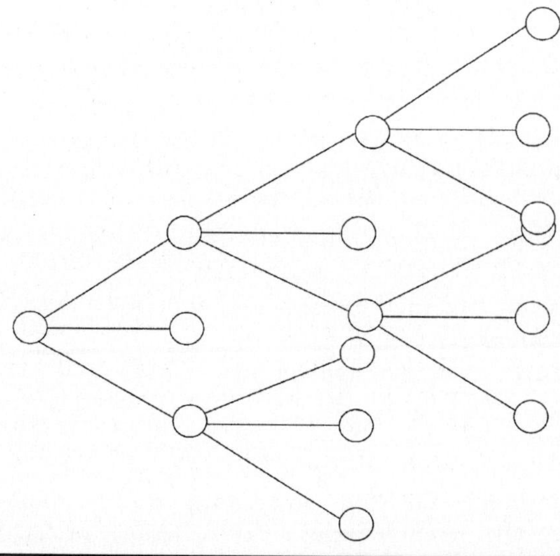

Source: First Union Securities, Inc.

EXHIBIT 12.9 Binomial Lattice for the Price of a Zero-Coupon Bond

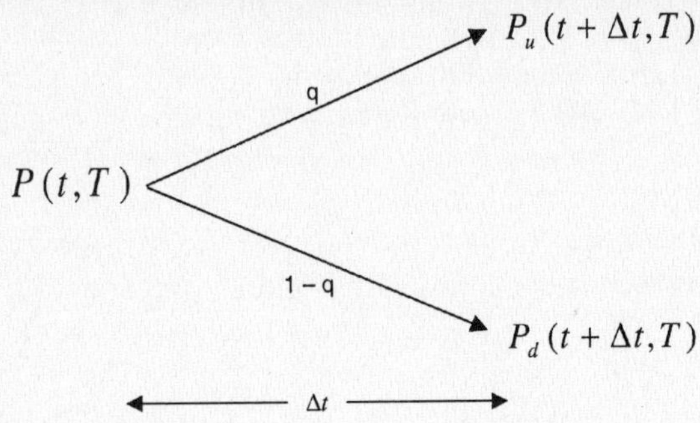

Source: First Union Securities, Inc.

EXHIBIT 12.10 Trinomial Lattice for the Price of a Zero-Coupon Bond

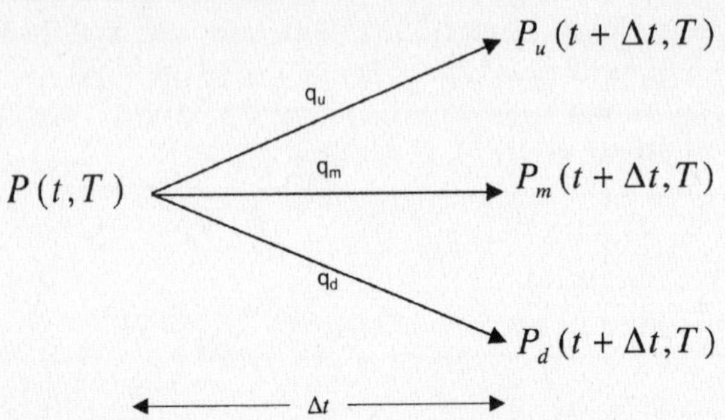

Source: First Union Securities, Inc.

Aside from this drawback, the Monte Carlo method has been shown to offer the following advantages:

- It is useful in dealing with multidimensional problems and boundary value problems with complicated boundaries.
- Problems with random coefficients, random boundary values, and stochastic parameters can be solved.
- Solving problems with discontinuous boundary functions, nonsmooth boundaries, and complicated right-hand sides of equations can be achieved.

The application of the Monte Carlo method in computational finance is predicated on the integral representation of security prices. The approach taken consists of the following:

- Simulating in a manner consistent with a risk-neutral probability (equivalent martingale) measure the sample path of the underlying state variables
- Evaluating the discounted payoff of the security on each sample path
- Taking the expected value of the discounted payoff over the entire sample paths

The Monte Carlo method computes a multidimensional integral—the expected value of discounted cash flows over the space of sample paths. For example, let $f(x)$ be an integral function over d-dimensional unit hypercube, then a simple (or crude) estimate of the integral is equal to the average value of the function f over n points selected at random (more appropriately, pseudorandom) from the unit hypercube. By the law of large numbers,[22] the Monte Carlo estimate converges to the value as n tends to infinity. Moreover, we know from the central limit theorem that the standard error of estimate tends toward zero as $1/(\sqrt{n})$. To improve on the computational efficiency of the crude Monte Carlo method, there are several variance-reduction techniques available. These techniques are discussed in the Appendix. Exhibit 12.11 shows a crude Monte Carlo simulation of the short-rate process.

EXHIBIT 12.11 A Hypothetical Crude Monte Carlo Simulation of the Short-Rate Process

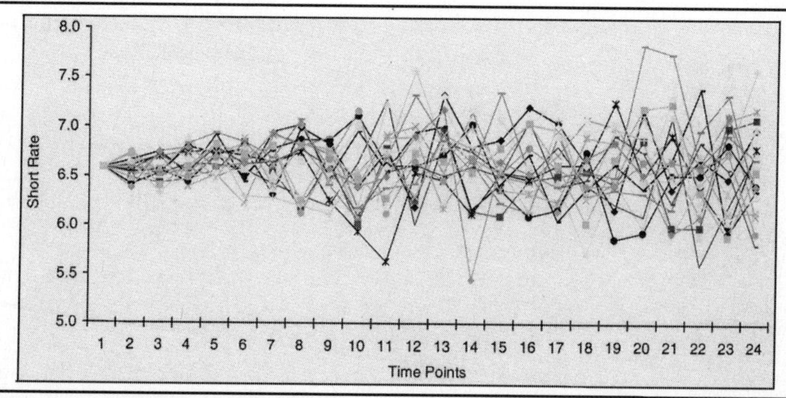

Source: First Union Securities, Inc.

[22] *Strong Law of Large Numbers.* Let $X = X_1, X_2$ ... be an independent identically distributed random variable with $E(X^2) < \infty$ then the mean of the sequence up to the nth term, though itself a random variable, tends as n get larger and larger, to the expectation of X with probability 1. That is

$$P\left(\lim_{n \to \infty}\left(\frac{1}{n}\sum_{i=1}^{n} X_i\right) = E(X)\right) = 1$$

IS THERE A RIGHT WAY TO MODEL PREPAYMENTS?

Because cash flows are one of the most important inputs in determining the value of a security, there has to be a model for cash flow. The cash flow model consists of a model for distributing the coupon and scheduled principal payments to the bondholders, as contained in the deal prospectus, and a prepayment model that projects unscheduled principal payments. The basic types of prepayment models are as follows:

- *Rational prepayment models.* These models apply an option-theoretic approach and link prepayment and valuation in a single unified framework.
- *Econometric prepayment models.* This class of models is based on econometric and statistical analysis.
- *Reduced-form prepayment models.* This type of model uses past prepayment rates and other endogenous variables to explain current prepayment. It fits the observed prepayment data, unrestricted by theoretical consideration.

The reduced-form prepayment model is the most widely used approach among dealers and prepayment vendors because of its flexibility and unrestricted calibration techniques. The basic determinants of the voluntary and involuntary components of total prepayments are collateral and market factors. Collateral factors are the origination date, weighted average coupon (WAC) and weighted average maturity, and the market-related factors are benchmark rates and spreads. A simple generalized version of such a model defines total prepayment (voluntary and involuntary) as follows:

$$TP_{\text{CPR}} = \text{turnover} + \text{rate-refi} + \text{curing} + \text{default}$$

This expression is not necessarily a linear function and could get complicated quickly. It is usually easier to identify a set of model parameters and fit its relationship to observed historical prepayment data. For example, in FUSI proprietary model for a particular category of collateral is defined by specifying the values of numerous parameters that control the projected effects of various contributions to total prepayments. The control parameters that we identify are

- *Seasoning period.* The number of months over which base voluntary prepayments (housing turnover, cash-out refinancing and credit upgrades but not rate refinancing or defaults) are assumed to increase to long-term levels.

- *Housing turnover.* Turnover is the long-term rate at which borrowers in a pool prepay their mortgages because they sell their homes.
- *Default.* Default is expressed as a percentage of the PSA Standard Default Assumption (SDA) or a loss curve.
- *Credit curing.* This is the long-term rate at which borrowers prepay their mortgages because improved credit and/or increased home prices enable them to get better rates and/or larger loans. As the pool burns out, the rate of curing declines.
- *Maximum rate-related conditional prepayment rate (CPR).* This occurs when rates fall below the saturation point for rate-related financing.
- *Maximum rate-related CPR for burnout.* The CPR is lower for a pool that has experienced no prior rate-related refinancing. The lower the ratio, the faster the pool burns out.
- *Refinancing threshold.* This is the amount by which the current market loan rate must fall below the collateral WAC to trigger rate-related financing.
- *Curing threshold.* This is the amount by which the current market loan rate must increase above the collateral WAC to eliminate curing-related financing.
- *Yield curve sensitivity.* This sensitivity is the maximum yield curve correction of rate-related CPR that occurs when the yield curve slope rises above/falls below the historical average.
- *Half-life burnout.* This is the time frame in years that a collateral pool must be fully refinancable to reduce interest rate sensitivity 50% of the way from maximum rate-related CPR to maximum rate-related CPR for burnout.

To calibrate these parameters, we developed a database of mortgage loan groups. The collateral groups backing each deal are assigned a prepayment model based on the percentile ranking of their initial credit spread. We define this spread as the collateral WAC minus the Treasury yield at the time of origination. The rationale for our approach is that borrowers who pay a higher credit spread tend to be less creditworthy. Moreover, these borrowers tend to have more opportunities to lower their rate by curing their credit problem, but they are less able to refinance in response to declining rates. Exhibit 12.12 details the specific parameter values assigned to each FUSI prepayment model. Exhibit 12.13 shows the aggregate historical CPR versus FUSI's model projection for EQCC Home Equity Loan Trust.

EXHIBIT 12.12 Agency, Whole, and Home Equity Loan Collateral Parameters

Agency and Whole Loan Collateral

Name	FN30yr	FN15yr	FN7yr	FN5yr	GN30yr	GN15yr	JUMBO	JUMBO15	JUMBO7	ALTER	ALTER15	ALTER7	ARM_ AGY	ARM_ JUMBO	ARM_ ALTER
Seas. Prd.	24	22	20	15	26	22	22	20	18	16	15	14	20	16	14
Turnover CPR	6.5%	7.5%	7.0%	9.0%	6.5%	7.0%	5.5%	5.5%	7.0%	5.5%	6.0%	7.0%	9.0%	8.0%	8.0%
%SDA	0%	0%	0%	0%	0%	0%	75%	75%	75%	125%	125%	125%	0%	75%	125%
Max. Curing CPR	2.5%	2.0%	6.0%	6.5%	2.0%	3.5%	2.0%	2.5%	7.0%	14.0%	15.0%	15.0%	2.5%	8.0%	16.0%
Curing CPR (BO)	2.5%	2.0%	2.0%	3.0%	2.0%	1.0%	2.0%	2.5%	2.0%	6.0%	7.0%	8.0%	1.0%	3.0%	8.0%
Max. Refi. CPR	52.0%	50.0%	53.0%	45.0%	50.0%	48.0%	62.0%	55.0%	60.0%	50.0%	35.0%	35.0%	35.0%	40.0%	30.0%
Max. Refi .CPR (BO)	14.0%	11.0%	20.0%	15.0%	12.0%	8.0%	14.0%	12.0%	20.0%	10.0%	10.0%	12.0%	8.0%	8.0%	8.0%
Refi. Threshold	0.50%	0.70%	0.50%	0.75%	0.60%	1.00%	0.20%	0.25%	0.50%	0.10%	0.75%	0.75%	1.00%	0.50%	1.00%
Curing Threshold	2.50%	2.50%	2.50%	2.50%	2.50%	2.50%	2.50%	2.00%	1.50%	1.50%	1.50%	1.50%	1.50%	1.50%	2.00%
Yield Curve CPR	10.0%	15.0%	0.0%	–5.0%	10.0%	8.0%	15.0%	20.0%	0.0%	8.0%	10.0%	0.0%	–35.0%	–35.0%	–30.0%
Half-Life (BO)	1.25	1.00	1.00	1.00	1.25	1.00	1.25	1.00	1.00	1.00	1.00	1.00	1.00	1.00	1.00
Ref. Category	AGY	AGY	AGY	AGY	AGY	AGY	A+	A+	A+	A–	A–	A–	AGY	A+	A–

Home Equity Loan Collateral

Name	FIX_ LO	FIX_ MID	FIX_ HI	ARM_ LO	ARM_ MID	ARM_ HI	LTV 125	Home Impr.	CRA	Vendee	FIX_ RASC	ARM_ HELOC	FIX_ MANHS	FIX_ HI	ARM_ MANHS
Seas. Prd.	14	15	16	12	13	14	26	14	30	20	14	10	26	18	12
Turnover CPR	5.0%	4.0%	3.0%	8.0%	6.0%	5.0%	6.0%	4.0%	3.5%	4.0%	4.0%	3.0%	4.0%	4.0%	5.0%
%SDA	325.00%	750.00%	1,200.00%	500.00%	1,000.00%	1,500.00%	1,000.00%	750.00%	150.00%	400.00%	325.0%	1,350.00%	600.00%	900.00%	900.00%
Max. Curing CPR	20.0%	26.0%	24.0%	28.0%	38.0%	45.0%	14.0%	18.0%	1.0%	2.0%	24.0%	38.0%	6.5%	8.5%	8.0%
Curing CPR (BO)	12.0%	14.0%	16.0%	10.0%	12.0%	14.0%	14.0%	10.0%	1.0%	1.0%	12.0%	20.0%	5.0%	6.0%	4.0%
Max. Refi .CPR	14.0%	10.0%	8.0%	18.0%	12.0%	8.0%	20.0%	15.0%	20.0%	24.0%	24.0%	2.0%	5.0%	3.0%	3.0%
Max. Refi. CPR (BO)	10.0%	6.0%	4.0%	8.0%	5.0%	4.0%	16.0%	8.0%	10.0%	8.0%	10.0%	1.0%	2.0%	1.0%	1.0%
Refi. Threshold	0.75%	1.00%	1.50%	0.75%	1.00%	1.00%	1.50%	1.38%	0.50%	1.50%	0.75%	2.00%	1.00%	1.00%	0.75%
Curing Threshold	2.50%	3.25%	3.75%	2.50%	2.75%	3.50%	3.50%	2.50%	1.00%	1.00%	1.50%	3.75%	2.00%	2.00%	2.00%
Yield Curve CPR	4.0%	3.0%	2.0%	–20.0%	–10.0%	–5.0%	1.0%	3.0%	5.0%	5.0%	8.0%	–1.0%	1.0%	1.0%	–2.0%
Half-Life (BO)	1.00	1.00	1.20	0.90	0.90	0.90	3.00	2.00	1.00	1.00	1.40	1.00	0.80	0.80	0.80
Ref. Category	LO	MID	HI	LO	MID	HI	HI	HI	A+	LO	LO	HI	MID	HI	HI

BO: Burnout; CPR: Constant prepayment rate; Refi: Refinancing; SDA: Standard default assumption; Seas Prd: Seasoning period.

Source: First Union Securities, Inc.

EXHIBIT 12.13 Aggregrate Historical CPR versus FUSI Model for EQCC Home Equity Loan Trust

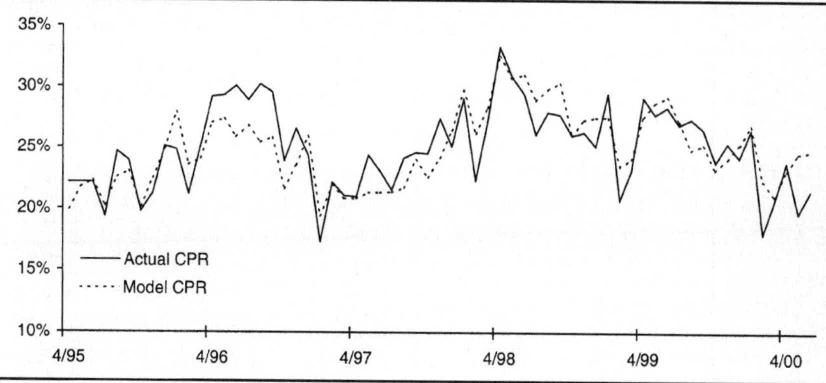

CPR: Conditional prepayment rate.
Source: First Union Securities, Inc. (FUSI).

CONCLUSION

In this chapter, we examine some of the foundational issues that explain (1) why there is a difference in dealers' OAS values for a specific bond, (2) what may be responsible for the differences, and (3) why one OAS value may be more correct than another. As a general guideline, we urge portfolio managers to get familiar with the economic intuitions and basic assumptions made by the models. We believe the reasonableness of the OAS values produced by different models should be considered. Moreover, because prepayment options are not traded in the market, calibrating OAS values using the prices of these options is not possible. With respect to the basic building block issues, the key points that we made in this report are as follows:

- Interest rate models, which are closed by precluding arbitrage opportunities, are more tractable and realistic.
- Interest rate models that account for the path-dependent natures of ABS and MBS cash flows are more robust.
- With the path-dependent natures of ABS and MBS cash flows come the difficulties of implementation, in particular, the speed of calculation; the toss-up here is between the lattice and Monte Carlo schemes. There is a tendency for market participants to believe that because we are talking about interest rate scenarios, the ideal candidate for the job would be Monte Carlo techniques, but this should not necessarily

be the case. Although lattice implementation could do a good job, the success of this scheme depends highly on ad hoc techniques that have not been time-tested. Hence, whereas the OAS implementation scheme is at the crux of what distinguishes good or bad results, the preferred scheme is an open question that critically depends on available resources.

- We favor reduced-form prepayment models because of their flexibility and unrestricted calibration techniques. In particular, a model that explicitly identifies its control parameters and is amenable to the perturbation of these parameters is more robust and transparent.

As a final thought, we rehash two of the questions we asked at the beginning of this chapter. How do we interpret the differences in dealers' OAS value for a specific security? On this question, we paraphrase John Maynard Keynes who said that when news in the market is interpreted differently by market participants, then we have a viable market. In our case, we believe decisions by dealers, vendors, and portfolio managers to choose one interest rate and prepayment model over others and the different approaches they take in implementing these models largely account for the wide variance in OAS results, which precipitates a hunt-for-value mentality that augurs well for the market. Moreover, to complicate the issue, the lack of a market for tradable prepayment options makes calibrating the resulting OAS values dicey at best. On the question of whether there is a correct OAS value for a given security, we say it is a state of nirvana that we would all treasure. However, we believe examining the change in OAS value over time, the sensitivity of OAS parameters, and their implications to relative value analysis are some of the important indicators of the reasonableness of OAS value.

APPENDIX: VARIANCE-REDUCTION TECHNIQUES

Antithetic Variates

The most widely used variance-reduction technique in financial modeling is the antithetic variates. Suppose f has a standard normal distribution, then by symmetrical property of normal distribution so does $-\phi$. Antithetic variates involve taking the same set of random numbers but changing their sign, that is, replacing ϕ by $-\phi$ and simulating the rate paths using ϕ and $-\phi$. The antithetic variates technique increases efficiency in pricing options that depend monotonically on inputs (e.g., average options).

Control Variates

Loosely speaking, the principle behind the control variates technique is "use what you know." The idea is to replace the evaluation of unknown expectations with the evaluation of the difference between the unknown quantity and another expectation whose value is known. Suppose there is a known analytical solution to value a security that is similar to the one we want to simulate. Let the values estimated by Monte Carlo simulation be ξ'_1 and ξ'_2, respectively. If the accurate value of the known security is ξ_2, then an improved estimate for the value of the simulated security is $\xi'_1 - \xi'_2 + \xi_2$. The notion here is that the error in ξ'_1 will be the same as error in ξ'_2, and the latter is known.

Moment Matching

Let X_i, $i = 1, 2,..., n$, be independent standard normals used in a simulation. The sample moment of n X's will not exactly match those of the standard normal. The idea of moment matching is to transform the X's to match a finite moment of the underlying population. One drawback of moment matching is that a confidence interval is not easy to obtain.

Stratified and Latin Hypercube Sampling

Stratified sampling seeks to make the inputs to simulation more regular than random inputs. It forces certain empirical probabilities to match theoretical probabilities. The idea is, suppose we want to generate 250 normal random variates as inputs to a simulation. The empirical distribution of an independent sample X_1, X_2, ..., X_{250} will look roughly like the normal density. The tails of the distribution—often the most important part—are underrepresented. Stratified sampling can be used to force exactly one observation to lie between the $(i-1)$th and the ith percentile, $j = 1, 2, ..., 250$, thus producing a better match to normal distribution. X_1,

$X_2, \ldots, X_{250}$ are highly dependent, thus complicating the estimation of standard error. Latin hypercube sampling is a way of randomly sampling n points of a stratified sample while preserving some of the regularity property of stratification.

Importance Sampling

The key observation that an expectation under one probability measure can be expressed as an expectation under another by appealing to the Radon Nikodym theorem is the foundation for this method. In a Monte Carlo simulation, the change of measure is used to try to obtain a more efficient estimator.

Conditional Monte Carlo

A direct consequence of Jensen inequality for condition expectation says that for any random variables X and Y, $\mathrm{Var}[E(X|Y) \leq \mathrm{Var}[X]]$. In replacing an estimator with its conditional expectation, we reduce variance essentially because we are doing a part of the integration analytically and leaving less for Monte Carlo simulation.

Low-Discrepancy Sequences

These sequences use preselected deterministic points for simulation. Discrepancy measures the extent to which the points are evenly dispersed throughout a region: The more evenly dispersed the points are, the lower the discrepancy. Low-discrepancy sequences are sometimes called quasi-random even though they are not random.

CHAPTER 13

Yield Curves and Valuation Lattices: A Primer

Frank J. Fabozzi, Ph.D., CFA
Adjunct Professor of Finance
School of Management
Yale University

Andrew Kalotay, Ph.D.
President
Andrew Kalotay Associates

Michael Dorigan, Ph.D.
Senior Associate
Andrew Kalotay Associates

The complication in building a model to value bonds with embedded options and option-type derivatives is that cash flows will depend on interest rates in the future. Academicians and practitioners have attempted to capture this interest rate uncertainty through various models, often designed as one- or two-factor models. These models attempt to capture the stochastic behavior of rates.

In practice, these elegant mathematical models must be converted to numeric applications. Here we focus on one such model—a single factor model that assumes a stationary variance, or, as it is more often called, volatility. We demonstrate how to move from the yield curve to a valuation lattice. Effectively, the lattice is a representation of the model, capturing the distribution of rates over time. In our illustration, we will reduce the lattice to a binomial tree, the most simple lattice form.

The lattice holds all the information required to perform the valuation of certain option-like interest rate products. First, the lattice is used to generate the cash flows across the life of the security. Next, the interest rates on the lattice are used to compute the present value of those cash flows.

There are several interest rate models that have been used in practice to construct an interest rate lattice. These are described in other chapters. In each case, interest rates can realize one of several possible rates when we move from one period to the next. A lattice model where it is assumed that only two rates are possible in the next period is called a binomial model. A lattice model where it is assumed that interest rates can take on three possible rates in the next period is called a trinomial model. There are even more complex models that assume more than three possible rates in the next period can be realized.

Regardless of the underlying assumptions, each model shares a common restriction. The interest rate tree generated must produce a value for an on-the-run optionless issue that is consistent with the current par yield curve. In effect, the value output from the model must be equal to the observed market price for the optionless instrument. Under these conditions the model is said to be "arbitrage-free." A lattice that produces an arbitrage-free valuation is said to be "fair." The lattice is used for valuation only when it has been calibrated to be fair. More on calibration below.

In this chapter we will demonstrate how a lattice is constructed. In Chapter 14, we will use the model to value bonds with an embedded option and floating-rate securities with option-type derivatives. Later, the application of the lattice model to value swaptions and forward start swaps will be demonstrated.

THE INTEREST RATE LATTICE

Exhibit 13.1 provides an example of a binomial interest rate tree, which consists of a number of "nodes" and "legs." Each leg represents a one-year interval over time. A simplifying assumption of one-year intervals is made to illustrate the key principles. The methodology is the same for smaller time periods. In fact, in practice the selection of the length of the time period is critical, but we need not be concerned with this nuance here.

EXHIBIT 13.1 Four-Year Binomial Interest Rate Tree

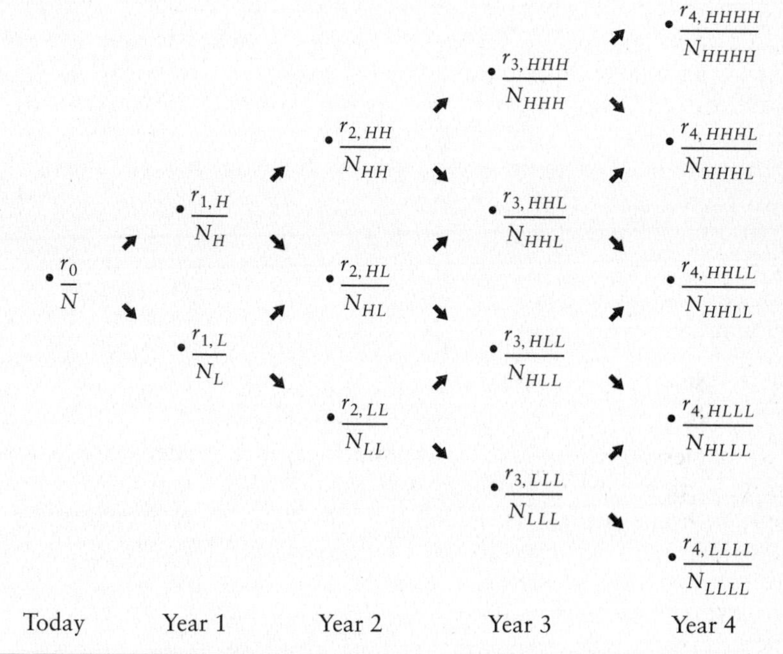

The distribution of future interest rates is represented on the tree by the nodes at each point in time. Each node is labeled as "*N*" and has a subscript, a combination of *L*'s and *H*'s. The subscripts indicate whether the node is lower or higher on the tree, respectively, relative to the other nodes. Thus, node N_{HH} is reached when the 1-year rate realized in the first year is the higher of the two rates for that period, then the highest of the rates in the second year.

The root of the tree is *N*, the only point in time at which we know the interest rate with certainty. The 1-year rate today (i.e., at *N*) is the current 1-year spot rate, which we denote by r_0.

We must make an assumption concerning the probability of reaching one rate at a point in time. For ease of illustration, we have assumed that rates at any point in time have the same probability of occurring, in other words, the probability is 50% on each leg.

The interest rate model we will use to construct the binomial tree assumes that the 1-year rate evolves over time based on a lognormal random walk with a known (stationary) volatility. Technically, the tree represents a one-factor model. Under the distributional assumption, the relationship between any two adjacent rates at a point in time is calculated via the following equation:

$$r_{1,H} = r_{1,L}e^{2\sigma\sqrt{t}}$$

where σ is the assumed volatility of the 1-year rate, t is time in years, and e is the base of the natural logarithm. Since we assume a 1-year interval, i.e., $t = 1$, we can disregard the calculation of the square root of t in the exponent.

For example, suppose that $r_{1,L}$ is 4.4448% and σ is 10% per year, then:

$$r_{1,H} = 4.4448\%(e^{2 \times 0.10}) = 5.4289\%$$

In the second year, there are three possible values for the 1-year rate. The relationship between $r_{2,LL}$ and the other two 1-year rates is as follows:

$$r_{2,HH} = r_{2,LL}(e^{4\sigma}) \quad \text{and} \quad r_{2,HL} = r_{2,LL}(e^{2\sigma})$$

So, for example, if $r_{2,LL}$ is 4.6958%, and assuming once again that σ is 10%, then

$$r_{2,HH} = 4.6958\%(e^{4 \times 0.10}) = 7.0053\%$$

and

$$r_{2,HL} = 4.6958\%(e^{2 \times 0.10}) = 5.7354\%$$

This relationship between rates holds for each point in time. Exhibit 13.2 shows the interest rate tree using this new notation.

Determining the Value at a Node

In general, to get a security's value at a node we follow the fundamental rule for valuation: The value is the present value of the expected cash flows. The appropriate discount rate to use for cash flows one year forward is the 1-year rate at the node where we are computing the value. Now there are two present values in this case: the present value of the cash flows in the state where the 1-year rate is the higher rate, and one where it is the lower rate state. We have assumed that the probability of both outcomes is equal. Exhibit 13.3 provides an illustration for a node assuming that the 1-year rate is r^* at the node where the valuation is sought and letting:

V_H = the bond's value for the higher 1-year rate state
V_L = the bond's value for the lower 1-year rate state
C = coupon payment

EXHIBIT 13.2 Four-Year Binomial Interest Rate Tree with 1-Year Rates*

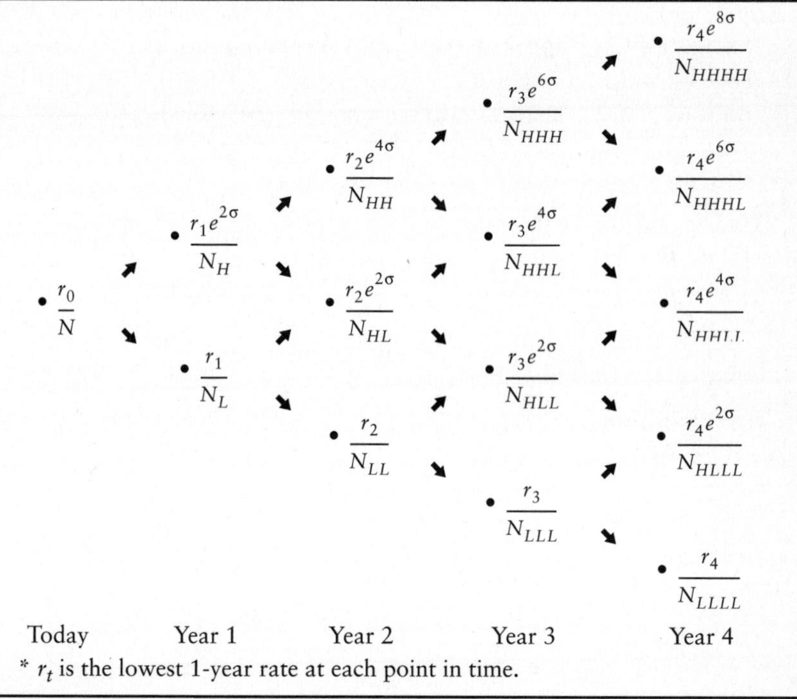

* r_t is the lowest 1-year rate at each point in time.

EXHIBIT 13.3 Calculating a Value at a Node

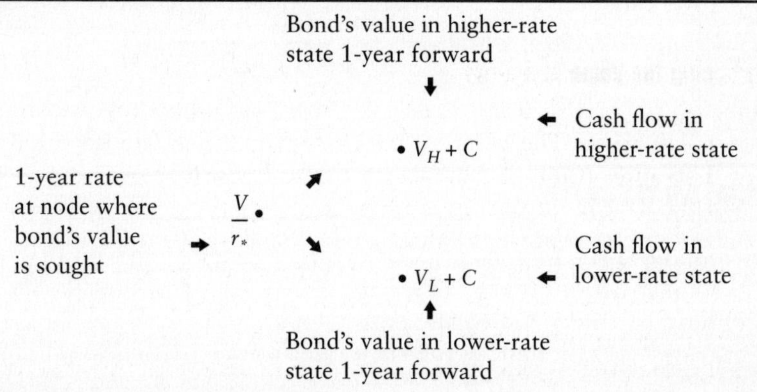

From where do the future values come? Effectively, the value at any node depends on the future cash flows. The future cash flows include (1) the coupon payment one year from now and (2) the bond's value one year from now, both of which may be uncertain. Starting the process from the last year in the tree and working backwards to get the final valuation resolves the uncertainty. At maturity, the instrument's value is known with certainty—par. The final coupon payment can be determined from the coupon rate, or from prevailing rates to which it is indexed. Working back through the tree, we realize that the value at each node is quickly calculated. This process of working backward is often referred to as *recursive valuation*.

Using our notation, the cash flow at a node is either:

$V_H + C$ for the higher 1-year rate

$V_L + C$ for the lower 1-year rate

The present value of these two cash flows using the 1-year rate at the node, r^*, is:

$$\frac{V_H + C}{(1 + r_*)} = \text{present value for the higher 1-year rate}$$

$$\frac{V_L + C}{(1 + r_*)} = \text{present value for the lower 1-year rate}$$

Then, the value of the bond at the node is found as follows:

$$\text{Value at a node} = \frac{1}{2}\left[\frac{V_H + C}{(1 + r_*)} + \frac{V_L + C}{(1 + r_*)}\right]$$

CALIBRATING THE LATTICE

We noted above the importance of the no-arbitrage condition that governs the construction of the lattice. To assure this condition holds, the lattice must be calibrated to the current par yield curve, a process we demonstrate here. Ultimately, the lattice must price optionless par bonds at par.

EXHIBIT 13.4 Issuer Par Yield Curve

Maturity	Par Rate	Market Price
1 year	3.50%	100
2 years	4.20%	100
3 years	4.70%	100
4 years	5.20%	100

EXHIBIT 13.5 The 1-Year Rates for Year 1 Using the 2-Year 4.2% On-the-Run Issue: First Trial

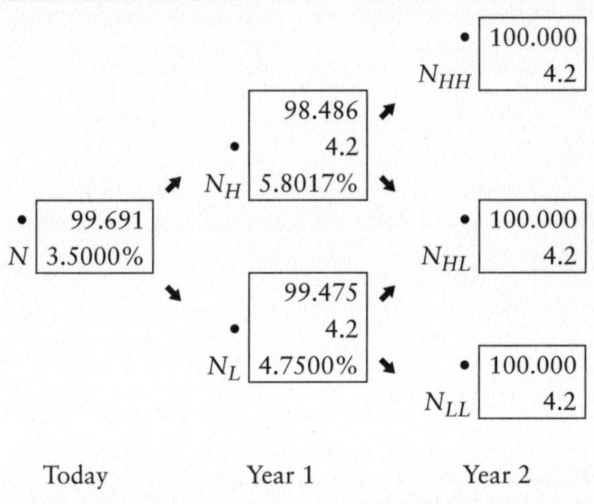

Assume the on-the-run par yield curve for a hypothetical issuer as it appears in Exhibit 13.4. The current 1-year rate is known, 3.50%. Hence, the next step is to find the appropriate 1-year rates one year forward. As before, we assume that volatility, σ, is 10% and construct a 2-year tree using the 2-year bond with a coupon rate of 4.2%, the par rate for a 2-year security.

Exhibit 13.5 shows a more detailed binomial tree with the cash flow shown at each node. The root rate for the tree, r_0, is simply the current 1-year rate, 3.5%. At the beginning of Year 2 there are two possible 1-year rates, the higher rate and the lower rate. We already know the relationship between the two. A rate of 4.75% rate at N_L has been arbitrarily chosen as a starting point. An iterative process determines the proper rate (i.e., trial-and-error). The steps are described and illustrated below. Again, the goal is a rate that, when applied in the tree, provides a value of par for the 2-year, 4.2% bond.

Step 1: Select a value for r_1. Recall that r_1 is the lower 1-year rate. In this first trial, we arbitrarily selected a value of 4.75%.

Step 2: Determine the corresponding value for the higher 1-year rate. As explained earlier, this rate is related to the lower 1-year rate as follows: $r_1e^{2\sigma}$. Since r_1 is 4.75%, the higher 1-year rate is 5.8017% (= 4.75% $e^{2\times0.10}$). This value is reported in Exhibit 13.5 at node N_H.

Step 3: Compute the bond value's one year from now. This value is determined as follows:

a. Determine the bond's value two years from now. In our example, this is simple. Since we are using a 2-year bond, the bond's value is its maturity value ($100) plus its final coupon payment ($4.2). Thus, it is $104.2.
b. Calculate V_H. Cash flows are known. The appropriate discount rate is the higher 1-year rate, 5.8017% in our example. The present value is $98.486 (= $104.2/ 1.058017).
c. Calculate V_L. Again, cash flows are known—the same as those in Step 3b. The discount rate assumed for the lower 1-year rate is 4.75%. The present value is $99.475 (= $104.2/1.0475).

Step 4: Calculate V.

a. Add the coupon to both V_H and V_L to get the cash flow at N_H and N_L, respectively. In our example we have $102.686 for the higher rate and $103.675 for the lower rate.
b. Calculate V. The 1-year rate is 3.50%. (Note: At this point in the valuation, r^* is the root rate, 3.50%). Therefore, $99.691 = ½($99.214 + $100.169)

Step 5: Compare the value in Step 4 to the bond's market value. If the two values are the same, then the r_1 used in this trial is the one we seek. If, instead, the value found in Step 4 is not equal to the market value of the bond, this means that the value r_1 in this trial is not the 1-year rate that is consistent with the current yield curve. In this case, the five steps are repeated with a different value for r_1.

EXHIBIT 13.6 The 1-Year Rates for Year 1 Using the 2-Year 4.2% On-the-Run Issue

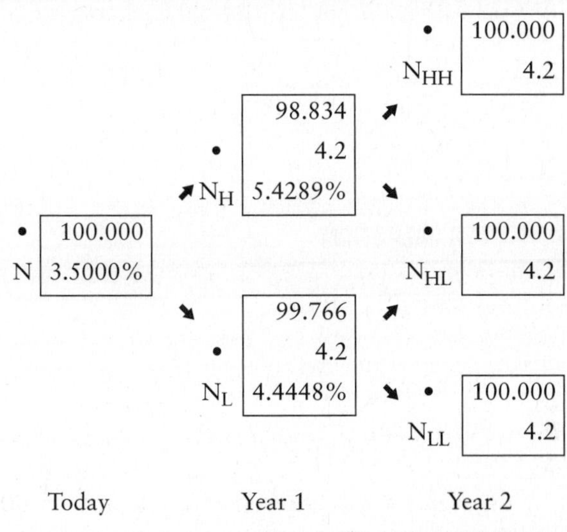

When r_1 is 4.75%, a value of \$99.691 results in Step 4, which is less than the observed market price of \$100. Therefore, 4.75% is too large and the five steps must be repeated trying a lower rate for r_1.

Let's jump right to the correct rate for r_1 in this example and rework steps 1 through 5. This occurs when r_1 is 4.4448%. The corresponding binomial tree is shown in Exhibit 13.6. The value at the root is equal to the market value of the 2-year issue (par).

We can "grow" this tree for one more year by determining r_2. Now we will use the 3-year on-the-run issue, the 4.7% coupon bond, to get r_2. The same five steps are used in an iterative process to find the 1-year rates in the tree two years from now. Our objective is now to find the value of r_2 that will produce a bond value of \$100. Note that the two rates one year from now of 4.4448% (the lower rate) and 5.4289% (the higher rate) do not change. These are the fair rates for the tree 1-year forward.

The problem is illustrated in Exhibit 13.7. The cash flows from the 3-year, 4.7% bond are in place. All we need to perform a valuation are the rates at the start of Year 3. In effect, we need to find r_2 such that the bond prices at par. Again, an arbitrary starting point is selected, and an iterative process produces the correct rate.

The completed version of Exhibit 13.7 is found in Exhibit 13.8. The value of r_2, or equivalently $r_{2,LL}$, which will produce the desired result is 4.6958%. The corresponding rates $r_{2,HL}$ and $r_{2,HH}$ would be 5.7354% and 7.0053%, respectively. To verify that these are the correct 1-year rates two years from now, work backwards from the four nodes at the right of the tree in Exhibit 13.8. For example, the value in the box at N_{HH} is found by taking the value of \$104.7 at the two nodes to its right and discounting at 7.0053%. The value is \$97.846. Similarly, the value in the box at N_{HL} is found by discounting \$104.70 by 5.7354% and at N_{LL} by discounting at 4.6958%.

USING THE LATTICE FOR VALUATION

To illustrate how to use the lattice for valuation purposes, consider a 6.5% option-free bond with four years remaining to maturity. Since this bond is option-free, it is not necessary to use the lattice model to value it. All that is necessary to obtain an arbitrage-free value for this bond is to discount the cash flows using the spot rates obtained from bootstrapping the yield curve shown in Exhibit 13.4. The spot rates are as follows:

1-year	3.5000%
2-year	4.2147%
3-year	4.7345%
4-year	5.2707%

EXHIBIT 13.7 **Information for Deriving the 1-Year Rates for Year 2 Using the 3-Year 4.7% On-the-Run Issue**

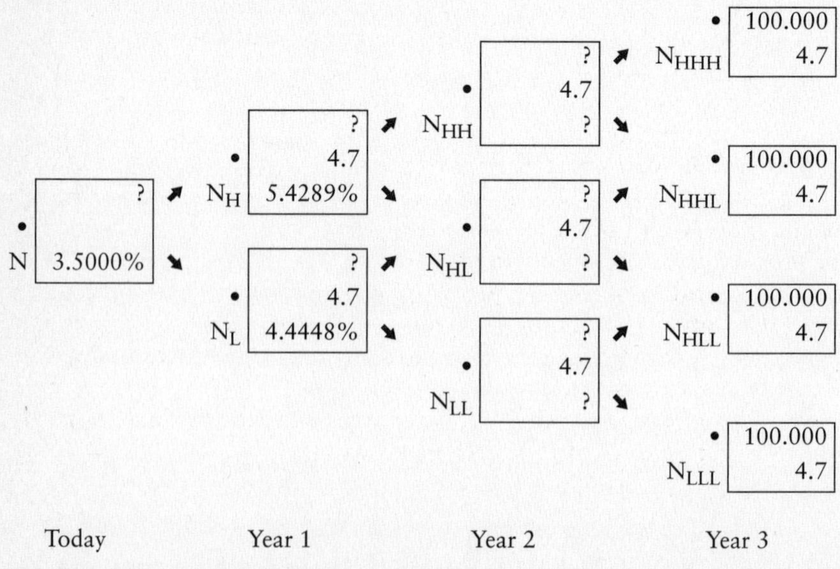

EXHIBIT 13.8 The 1-Year Rates for Year 2 Using the 3-Year 4.7% On-the-Run Issue

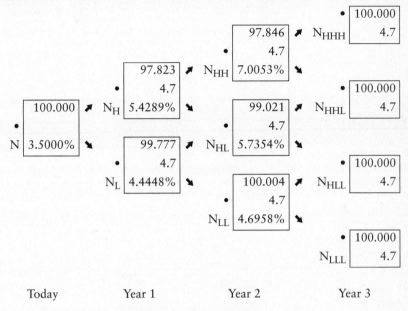

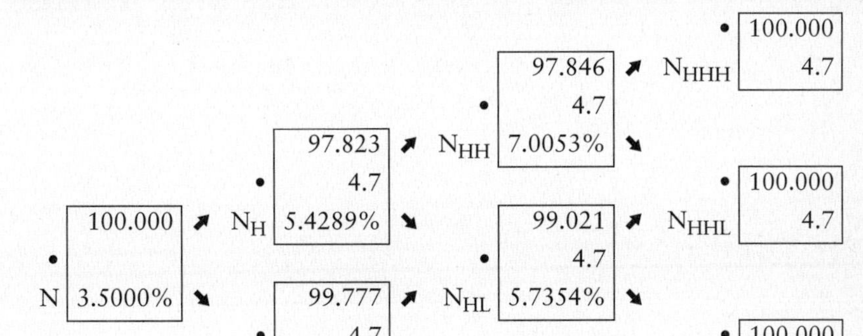

Discounting the 6.5% 4-year option-free bond with a par value of $100 at the above spot rates would give a bond value of $104.643.

Exhibit 13.9 contains the fair tree for a four-year valuation. Exhibit 13.10 shows the various values in the discounting process using the lattice in Exhibit 13.9. The root of the tree shows the bond value of $104.643, the same value found by discounting at the spot rate. This demonstrates that the lattice model is consistent with the valuation of an option-free bond when using spot rates.

In Chapter 14, we apply the lesson here to more complex instruments, those with option features that require the lattice-based process for proper valuation. The methodology is applied to swaptions in Chapter 15. Regardless of the security or derivative to be valued, the generation of the lattice follows the same no-arbitrage principles outlined here. Subsequently, cash flows are determined at each node, the recursive valuation process undertaken to arrive at fair values. Hence, a single lattice and a valuation process prove to be robust means for obtaining fair values for a wide variety of fixed-income instruments.

EXHIBIT 13.9 Binomial Interest Rate Tree for Valuing Up to a 4-Year Bond for Issuer (10% Volatility Assumed)

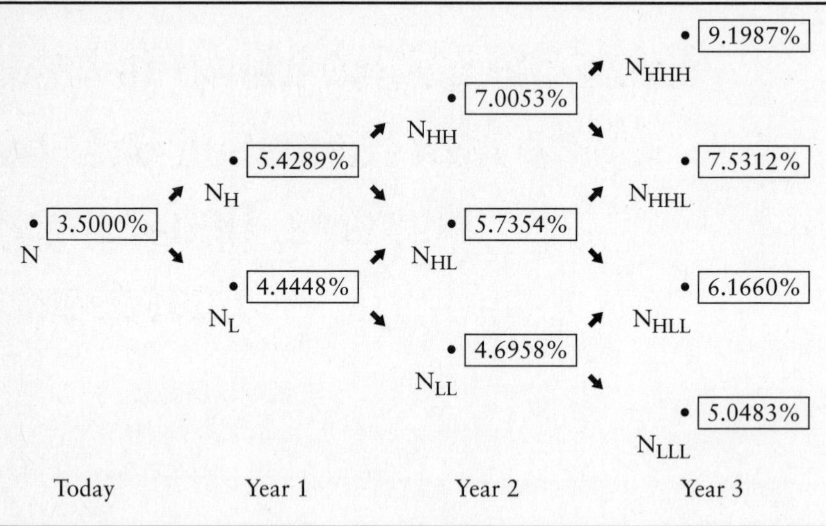

EXHIBIT 13.10 Valuing an Option-Free Bond with Four Years to Maturity and a Coupon Rate of 6.5% (10% Volatility Assumed)

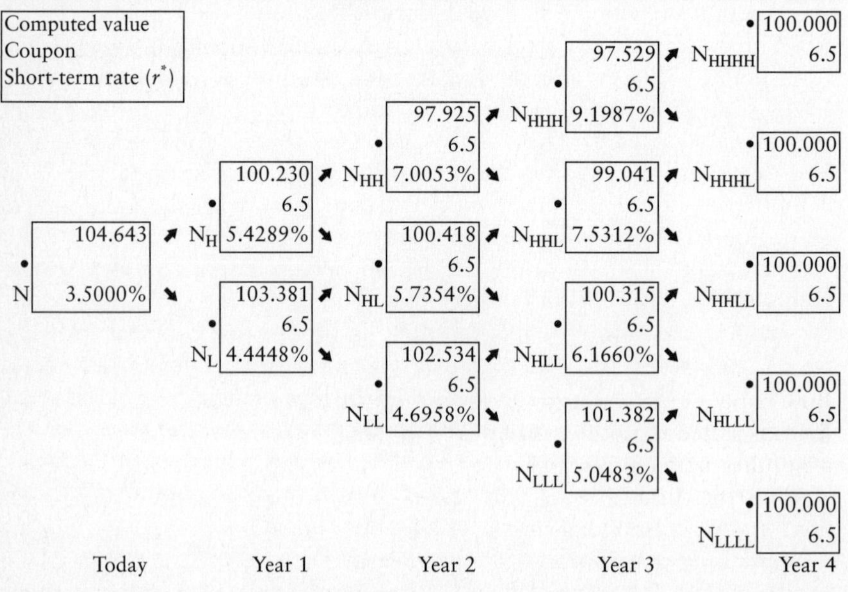

CHAPTER 14

Using the Lattice Model to Value Bonds with Embedded Options, Floaters, Options, and Caps/Floors

Frank J. Fabozzi, Ph.D., CFA
Adjunct Professor of Finance
School of Management
Yale University

Andrew Kalotay, Ph.D.
President
Andrew Kalotay Associates

Michael Dorigan, Ph.D.
Senior Associate
Andrew Kalotay Associates

In Chapter 13 it was explained how a lattice can be constructed. Further, it was stated that the lattice provides a robust means for the valuation of a number of fixed-income securities and derivatives. In this chapter, we demonstrate how a lattice can be used to value a variety of fixed- and floating-rate coupon instruments and interest rate derivatives. In addition, we extend the application of the interest rate tree to the calculation of the option adjusted spread (OAS), as well as the effective duration and convexity of a fixed-income instrument. We begin with fixed-coupon bonds.

FIXED-COUPON BONDS WITH EMBEDDED OPTIONS

The valuation of bonds with embedded options proceeds in the same fashion as in the case of an option-free bond. However, the added complexity of an embedded option requires an adjustment to the cash flows on the tree depending on the structure of the option. A decision on whether to call or put must be made at nodes on the tree where the option is eligible for exercise. Examples for both callable and putable bonds follow.

Valuing a Callable Bond

In the case of a call option, the call will be made when the present value (PV) of the future cash flows is greater than the call price at the node where the decision to exercise is being made. Effectively, the following calculation is made:

$$V_t = \text{Min [Call Price, PV(Future Cash Flows)]}$$

where V_t represents the PV of future cash flows at the node, notation analogous to that in Chapter 13. This operation is performed at each node where the bond is eligible for call.

For example, consider a 6.5% bond with four years remaining to maturity that is callable in one year at $100. We will value this bond, as well as the other instruments in this chapter, using a binomial tree. Exhibit 14.1 is the binomial interest rate tree that was derived in Chapter 13 and then used to value an option-free bond. In constructing the binomial tree in Exhibit 14.1, it is assumed that interest rate volatility is 10%. This binomial tree will be used throughout this chapter.

Exhibit 14.2 shows two values are now present at each node of the binomial tree. The discounting process (explained in Chapter 13) is used to calculate the first of the two values at each node. The second value is the value based on whether the issue will be called. Again, the issuer calls the issue if the PV of future cash flows exceeds the call price. This second value is incorporated into the subsequent calculations.

In Exhibit 14.3, certain nodes from Exhibit 14.2 are highlighted. Panel (a) of the exhibit shows nodes where the issue is not called (based on the simple call rule used in the illustration) in year 2 and year 3.[1] The values reported in this case are the same as in the valuation of an option-free bond. Panel (b) of the exhibit shows some nodes where the issue is called in year 2 and year 3. Notice how the methodology changes the cash flows. In year 3, for example, at node N_{HLL} the recursive valuation process produces a PV of 100.315. However, given the call rule, this issue would be

[1] We assume cash flows occur at the end of the year.

called. Therefore, 100 is shown as the second value at the node and it is this value that is then used as the valuation process continues. Taking the process to its end, the value for this callable bond is 102.899.

The value of the call option is computed as the difference between the value of an optionless bond and the value of a callable bond. In our illustration, the value of the option-free bond is 104.643 (Calculated in Chapter 13.). The value of the callable bond is 102.899. Hence, value of the call option is 1.744 (= 104.634 – 102.899).

Valuing a Putable Bond

A putable bond is one in which the bondholder has the right to force the issuer to pay off the bond prior to the maturity date. The analysis of the putable bond follows closely that of the callable bond. In the case of the putable, we must establish the rule by which the decision to put is made. The reasoning is similar to that for the callable bond. If the PV of the future cash flows is less than the put price (i.e., par), then the bond will be put. In equation form,

$$V_t = \text{Max (Put Price, PV(Future Cash Flows)]}$$

Exhibit 14.4 is analogous to Exhibit 13.3. It shows the binomial tree with the values based on whether or not the investor exercises the put option at each node. The bond is putable any time after the first year at par. The value of the bond is 105.327. Note that the value is greater than the value of the corresponding option-free bond.

EXHIBIT 14.1 Binomial Interest Rate Tree for Valuing Up to a 4-Year Bond for Issuer (10% Volatility Assumed)

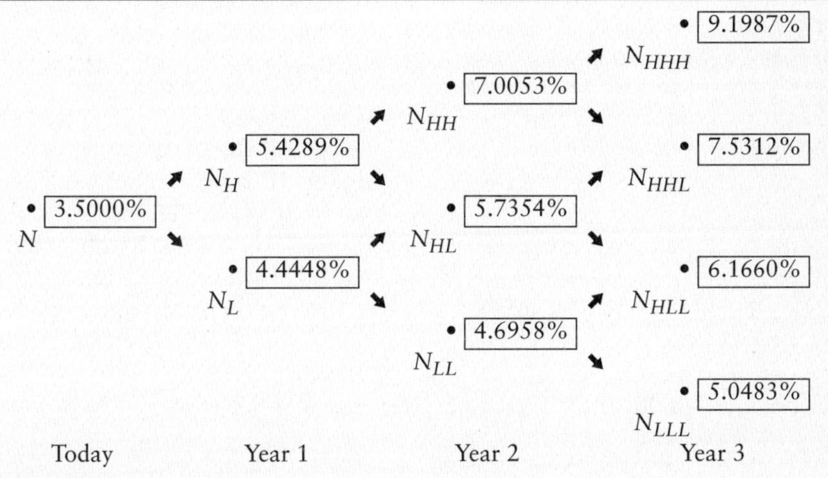

EXHIBIT 14.2 Valuing a Callable Bond with Four Years to Maturity, a Coupon Rate of 6.5%, and Callable after the First Year at 100 (10% Volatility Assumed)

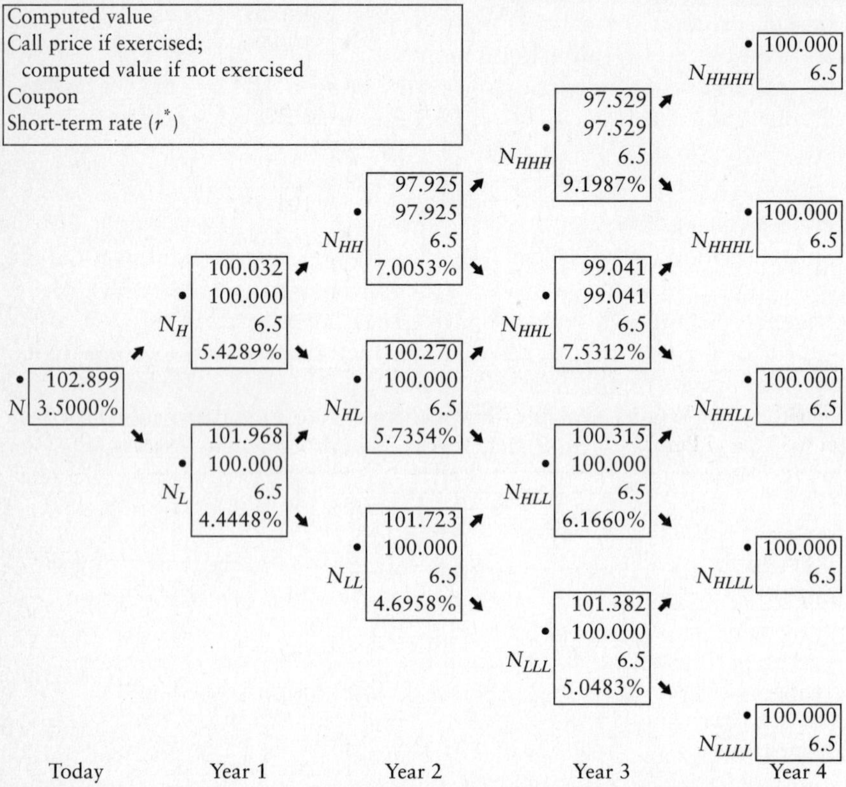

Legend: Computed value / Call price if exercised; computed value if not exercised / Coupon / Short-term rate (r^*)

		Computed value	Call price if exercised; computed value if not exercised	Coupon	Short-term rate (r^*)
Today	N	102.899			3.5000%
Year 1	N_H	100.032	100.000	6.5	5.4289%
Year 1	N_L	101.968	100.000	6.5	4.4448%
Year 2	N_{HH}	97.925	97.925	6.5	7.0053%
Year 2	N_{HL}	100.270	100.000	6.5	5.7354%
Year 2	N_{LL}	101.723	100.000	6.5	4.6958%
Year 3	N_{HHH}	97.529	97.529	6.5	9.1987%
Year 3	N_{HHL}	99.041	99.041	6.5	7.5312%
Year 3	N_{HLL}	100.315	100.000	6.5	6.1660%
Year 3	N_{LLL}	101.382	100.000	6.5	5.0483%
Year 4	N_{HHHH}	100.000		6.5	
Year 4	N_{HHHL}	100.000		6.5	
Year 4	N_{HHLL}	100.000		6.5	
Year 4	N_{HLLL}	100.000		6.5	
Year 4	N_{LLLL}	100.000		6.5	

EXHIBIT 14.3 Highlighting Nodes in Years 2 and 3 for a Callable Bond
a. Nodes Where Call Option is Not Exercised

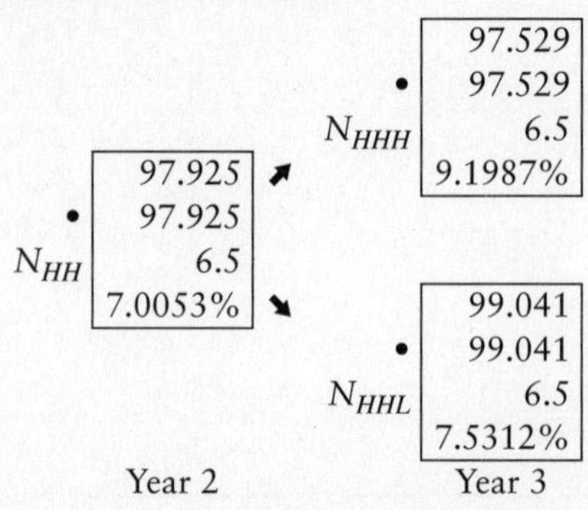

EXHIBIT 14.3 (Continued)
b. Selected Nodes Where the Call Option is Exercised

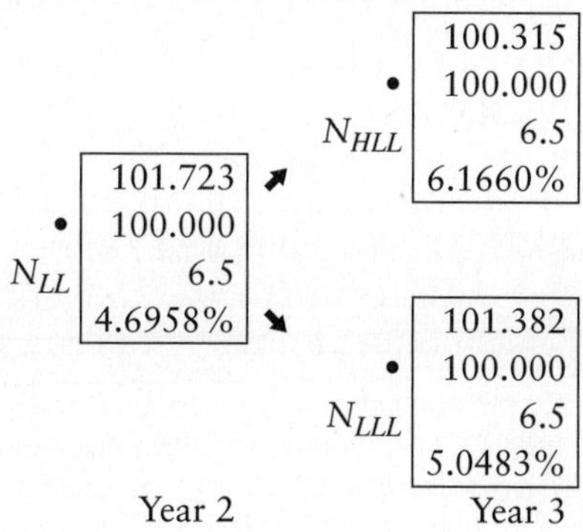

EXHIBIT 14.4 Valuing a Putable Bond with Four Years to Maturity, a Coupon Rate of 6.5%, and Putable after the First Year at 100 (10% Volatility Assumed)

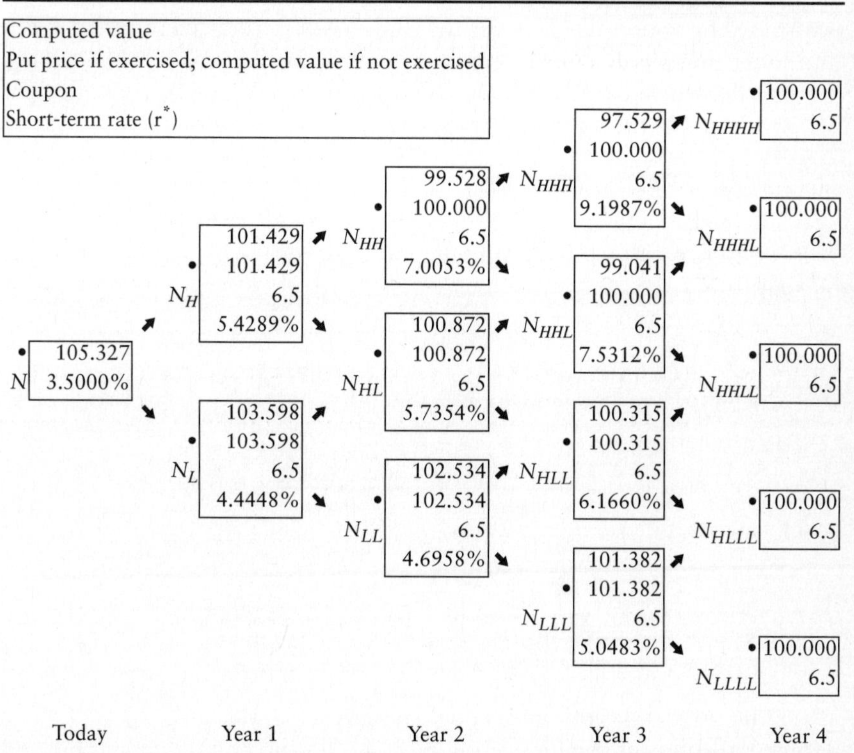

With the two values in hand, we can calculate the value of the put option. Since the value of the putable bond is 105.327 and the value of the corresponding option-free bond is 104.643, the value of the embedded put option purchased by the investor is effectively 0.684.

Suppose that a bond is both putable and callable. The procedure for valuing such a structure is to adjust the value at each node to reflect whether the issue would be put or called. Specifically, at each node there are two decisions about the exercising of an option that must be made. If it is called, the value at the node is replaced by the call price. The valuation procedure then continues using the call price at that node. If the call option is not exercised at a node, it must be determined whether or not the put option will be exercised. If it is exercised, then the put price is substituted at that node and is used in subsequent calculations.

FLOATING-COUPON BONDS WITH EMBEDDED OPTIONS

Simple discounted cash flow methods of analysis fail to handle floaters with embedded or option-like features that have been introduced in recent years. In this section we demonstrate how to use the lattice model to value (1) a capped floater, and (2) a callable capped floater. We will streamline the notation used in the binomial tree for the exhibits in this section.

Valuing Capped Floating-Rate Bonds

Consider a floating-rate bond with a coupon indexed to the 1-year rate (the reference rate) plus a spread. For our purposes, assume a 25 bp spread to the reference rate. The coupon adjusts at each node to reflect the level of the reference rate plus the spread.

Using the same valuation method as before, we can find the value at each node. Recall the value of the bond is 100 (par) at the end of year 4. Consider N_{HLL}.

$$N_{HLL} = \frac{1}{2}\left[\frac{100 + 6.416}{1.06166} + \frac{100 + 6.416}{1.06166}\right] = 100.235$$

Stepping back one period

$$N_{LL} = \frac{1}{2}\left[\frac{100.235 + 4.9458}{1.046958} + \frac{100.238 + 4.9458}{1.046958}\right] = 100.465$$

Following this same procedure, we arrive at the price of 100.893.[2] How would this change if the interest rate on the bond were capped?

[2] We leave this calculation to the reader.

EXHIBIT 14.5 Valuation of a Capped Floating-Rate Bond

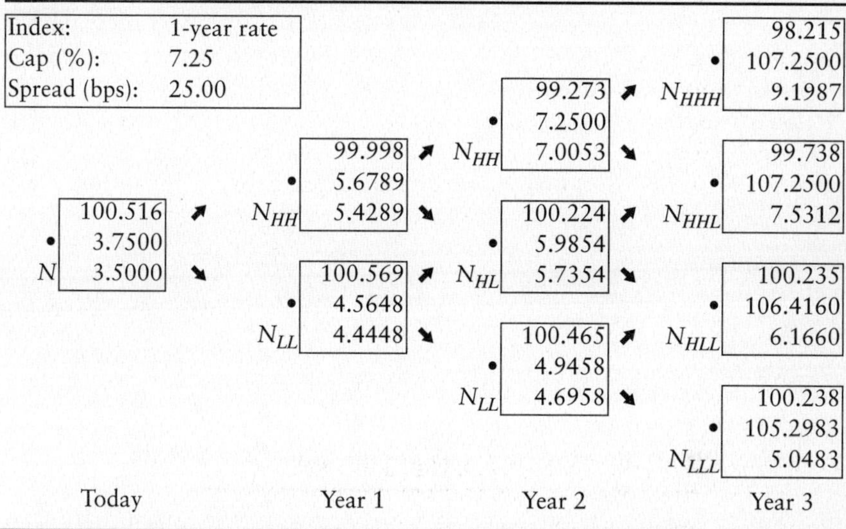

EXHIBIT 14.6 Spread to Index to Price Cap at Par

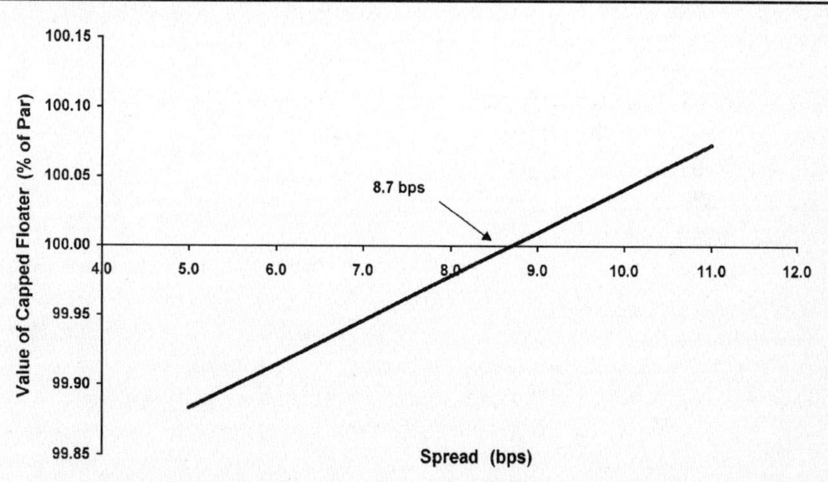

Assume that the cap is 7.25%. In Exhibit 14.5, we've taken the tree from Exhibit 14.1 and, as was the case with the optionless fixed-coupon bond, at each node we've entered the cash flow expected at the end of each period based on the reset formula. As rates move higher there is a possibility that the current reference rate exceeds the cap. Such is the case at N_{HHH} and N_{HHL}. The coupon is subject to the following constraint:

$$C_t = \text{Min}\ [r_t, 7.25\%]$$

As a result of the cap, the value of the bond in the upper nodes at $t = 3$ falls below par. For example,

$$N_{HHH} = \frac{1}{2}\left[\frac{100 + 7.25}{1.091987} + \frac{100 + 7.25}{1.09198}\right] = 98.215$$

Valuing recursively through the tree, we arrive at the current value of the capped floater, 100.516 a value lower than the plain-vanilla floater. This last calculation gives us a means for pricing the embedded option. Without a cap, the bond is priced at 100.893. The difference between these two prices is the value of the cap, 0.377. It is important to note that the price of the cap is volatility dependent. Any change in the volatility would result in a different valuation for the cap. The greater the volatility, the higher the price of the option, and vice versa.

We can extend the application of the lattice to the initial pricing of securities. What if an issuer wanted to offer this bond at par? In such a case, an adjustment has to be made to the coupon. To lower the price from 100.516 to par, a lower spread over the reference rate is offered to investors. It turns out that this is not enough. Exhibit 14.6 shows the relationship between the spread over the 1-year reference rate and the bond price. At a spread of 8.70 bps over the 1-year reference rate, the capped floater in Exhibit 14.5 will be priced at par. Again, the spread of 8.7 bps is volatility dependent.

Callable Capped Floating-Rate Bonds

Now consider a call option on the capped floater. As was the case for a fixed-coupon bond, we must be careful to specify the appropriate rules for calling the bond on the valuation tree. It turns out that the rule is the same for floaters and fixed-coupon bonds. Any time the bond has a PV above par at a node where the bond is callable, the bond will be called. (Here we assume a par call to simplify the illustration.)

Before we get into the details, it is important to motivate the need for a call on a floating-rate bond. The value of a cap to the issuer increases as market rates near the cap and there is the potential for rates to exceed the cap prior to maturity. As rates decline, so does the value of the cap. The problem for the issuer in the event of low rates is the additional basis-point spread it is paying for a cap that now has little or no value. Thus, when rates decline, a call has value to the issuer because it can call and reissue at a different spread.

Suppose that the capped floater is callable at par anytime after the first year. Exhibit 14.7 provides details on the effect of the call option on valuation of the capped floater. Again, for a callable bond, when the PV exceeds par in a recursive valuation model, the bond is called. In the case of our 4-year bond, you can see that the value of the bond at nodes N_{LL}, N_{LLH}, and N_{LLL} is now 100, the call price. The full effect of the call option on price is evident with today's price for the bond moving to 99.9140.

The byproduct of this analysis is the value of the call option on a capped floater. We now have the fair value of the capped floater versus the callable capped floater. So, the call option has a value of 100.516 – 100.189 = 0.327.

How would one structure the issue so that it is priced at par? We have to offer a lower spread over the floating rate than the holder is already receiving for accepting the cap. In this case, we need to move the total spread over the one-year floating rate to 13.37 bps. Exhibit 14.8 shows the relationship between spread and value.

VALUING CAPS AND FLOORS

An interest rate cap is nothing more than a package or strip of options. More specifically, a cap is a strip of European options on interest rates. Thus, to value a cap, the value of each period's cap, called a *caplet*, is found and all the caplets are then summed.

To illustrate how this is done, we will once again use the binomial tree given in Exhibit 14.1 to value a cap. Consider a 5.2% 3-year cap with a notional amount of $10 million. The reference rate is the 1-year rate. The payoff for the cap is annual.

The three panels in Exhibit 14.9 show how this cap is valued by valuing the three caplets. The value for the caplet for any year, say Year X, is found as follows. First, calculate the payoff in Year X at each node as either:

1. zero if the 1-year rate at the node is less than or equal to 5.2%, or
2. the notional amount of $10 million times the difference between the 1-year rate at the node and 5.2% if the 1-year rate at the node is greater than 5.2%.

Then, the recursive valuation process is used to determine the value of the Year X caplet.

EXHIBIT 14.7 Valuation of a Capped Floating-Rate Bond

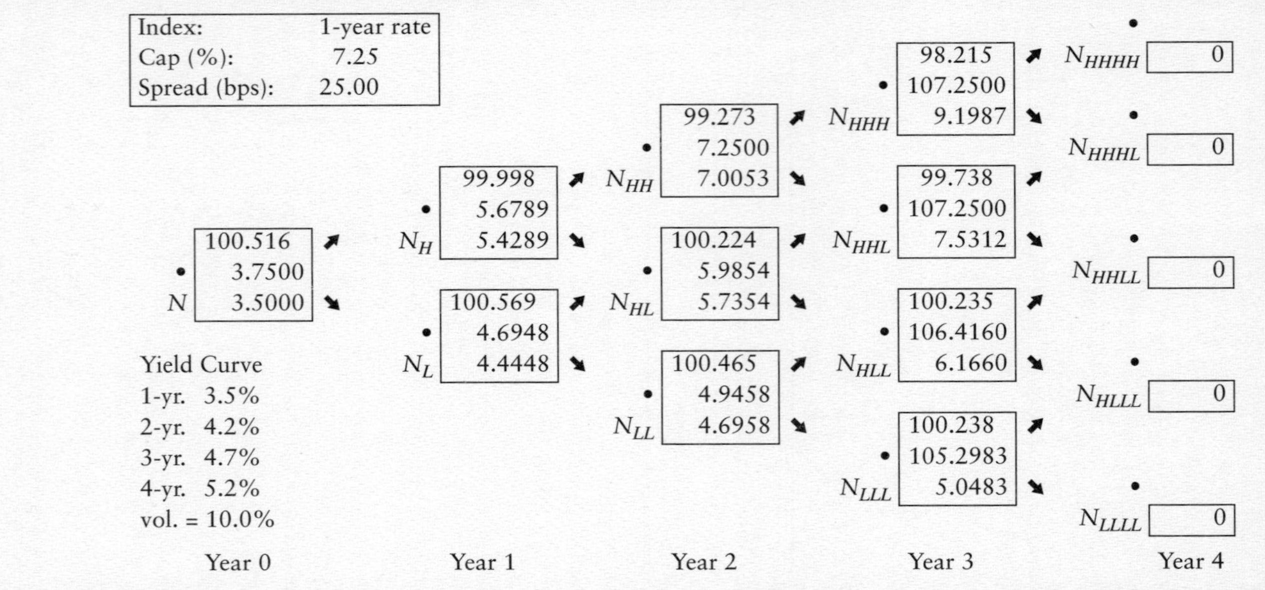

EXHIBIT 14.8 Spread to Index to Price Callable Cap at Par

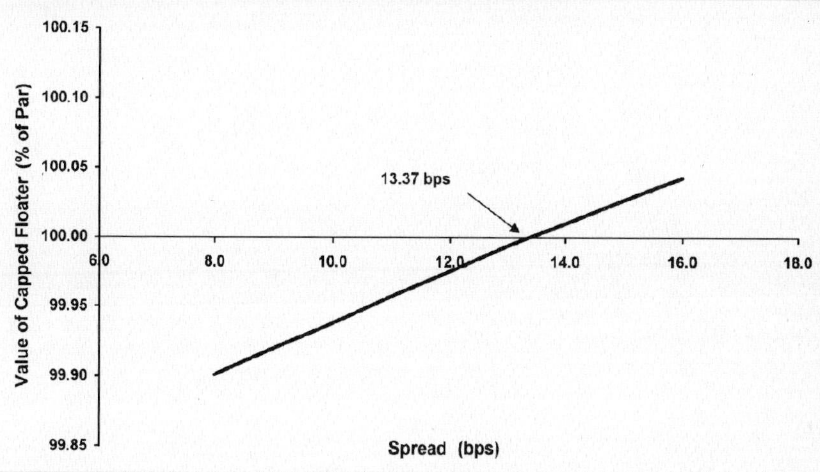

EXHIBIT 14.9 Valuation of a 3-Year 5.2% Cap (10% Volatility Assumed)

Assumptions
Cap rate: 5.2%
Notional amount: $10,000,000
Payment frequency: Annual

Panel A: The Value of the Year 1 Caplet

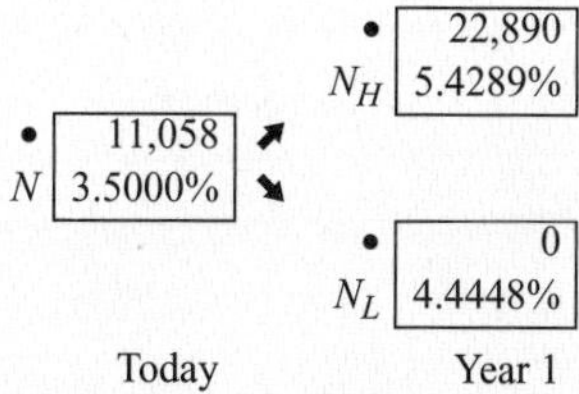

Value of Year 1 caplet = $11,058

Panel B: The Value of the Year 2 Caplet

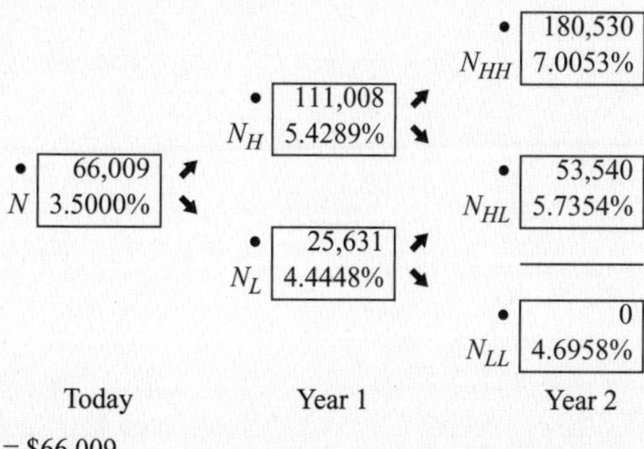

Value of Year 2 caplet = $66,009

EXHIBIT 14.9 (Continued)

Panel C: The Value of the Year 3 Caplet

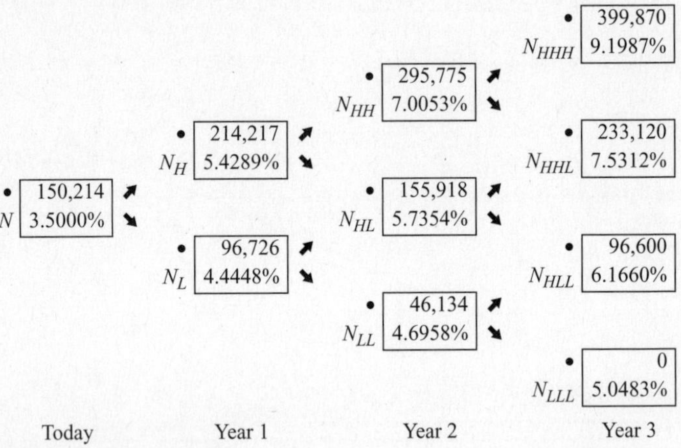

Value of Year 3 caplet = $150,214

Summary: Value of 3-Year Cap = $11,058 + $66,009 + $150,214 = $227,281

Note on calculations: Payoff in last box of each exhibit is

$\$10,000,000 \times \text{Maximum}[(\text{Rate at node} - 5.2\%, 0)]$

For example, consider the Year 3 caplet. At the top node in Year 3 of Panel (c) of Exhibit 14.9, the 1-year rate is 9.1987%. Since the 1-year rate at this node exceeds 5.2%, the payoff in Year 3 is:

$$\$10,000,000 \times (0.091987 - 0.052) = \$399,870$$

For node N_{HH} we look at the value for the cap at the two nodes to its right, N_{HHH} and N_{HHL}. Discounting the values at these nodes, $399,870 and $233,120, by the interest rate from the binomial tree at node N_{HH}, 7.0053%, we arrive at a value of $295,755. That is,

$$\begin{aligned}\text{Value at } N_{HH} &= [\$399,870/(1.070053) + \$233,120(1.070053)]/2 \\ &= \$295,775\end{aligned}$$

The values at nodes N_{HH} and N_{HL} are discounted at the interest rate from the binomial tree at node N_H, 5.4289%, and then the value is computed. That is,

$$\begin{aligned}\text{Value at } N_H &= [\$295,775/(1.054289) + \$155,918/(1.054289)]/2 \\ &= \$214,217\end{aligned}$$

Finally, we get the value at the root, node N, which is the value of the Year 3 caplet found by discounting the value at N_H and N_L by 3.5% (the interest rate at node N). Doing so gives:

$$\text{Value at } N = [\$214{,}217/(1.035) + \$96{,}726/(1.035)]/2 = \$150{,}214$$

Following the same procedure, the value of the Year 2 caplet is \$66,009 and the value of the Year 1 caplet is \$11,058. The value of the cap is then the sum of the three caplets.

Thus, the value of the cap is \$227,281, found by adding \$11,058, \$66,009, and \$150,214.

The valuation of an interest rate floor is done in the same way.

VALUATION OF TWO MORE EXOTIC STRUCTURES

The lattice-based recursive valuation methodology is robust. To further support this claim, we address the valuation of two more exotic structures—the step-up callable note and the range floater.

Valuing a Step-Up Callable Note

Step-up callable notes are callable instruments whose coupon rate is increased (i.e., "stepped up") at designated times. When the coupon rate is increased only once over the security's life, it is said to be a single step-up callable note. A multiple step-up callable note is a step-up callable note whose coupon is increased more than one time over the life of the security. Valuation using the lattice model is similar to that for valuing a callable bond described above except that the cash flows are altered at each node to reflect the coupon characteristics of a step-up note.

Suppose that a 4-year step-up callable note pays 4.25% for two years and then 7.5% for two more years. Assume that this note is callable at par at the end of Year 2 and Year 3. We will use the binomial tree given in Exhibit 14.1 to value this note.

Exhibit 14.10 shows the value of the note if it were not callable. The valuation procedure is the now familiar recursive valuation from Exhibit 14.2. The coupon in the box at each node reflects the step-up terms. The value is 102.082. Exhibit 14.11 shows that the value of the single step-up callable note is 100.031. The value of the embedded call option is equal to the difference in the optionless step-up note value and the step-up callable note value, 2.051.

EXHIBIT 14.10 Valuing a Single Step-Up Noncallable Note with Four Years to Maturity (10% Volatility Assumed)

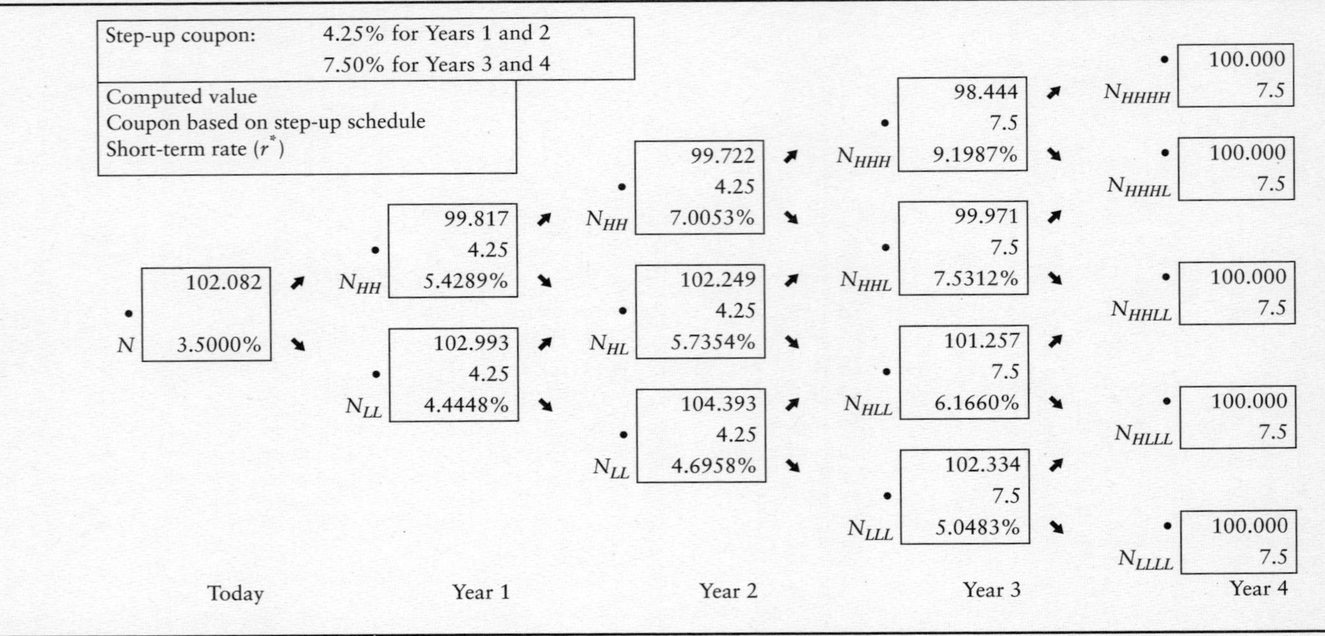

EXHIBIT 14.11 Valuing a Single Step-Up Callable Note with Four Years to Maturity, Callable in Two Years at 100 (10% Volatility Assumed)

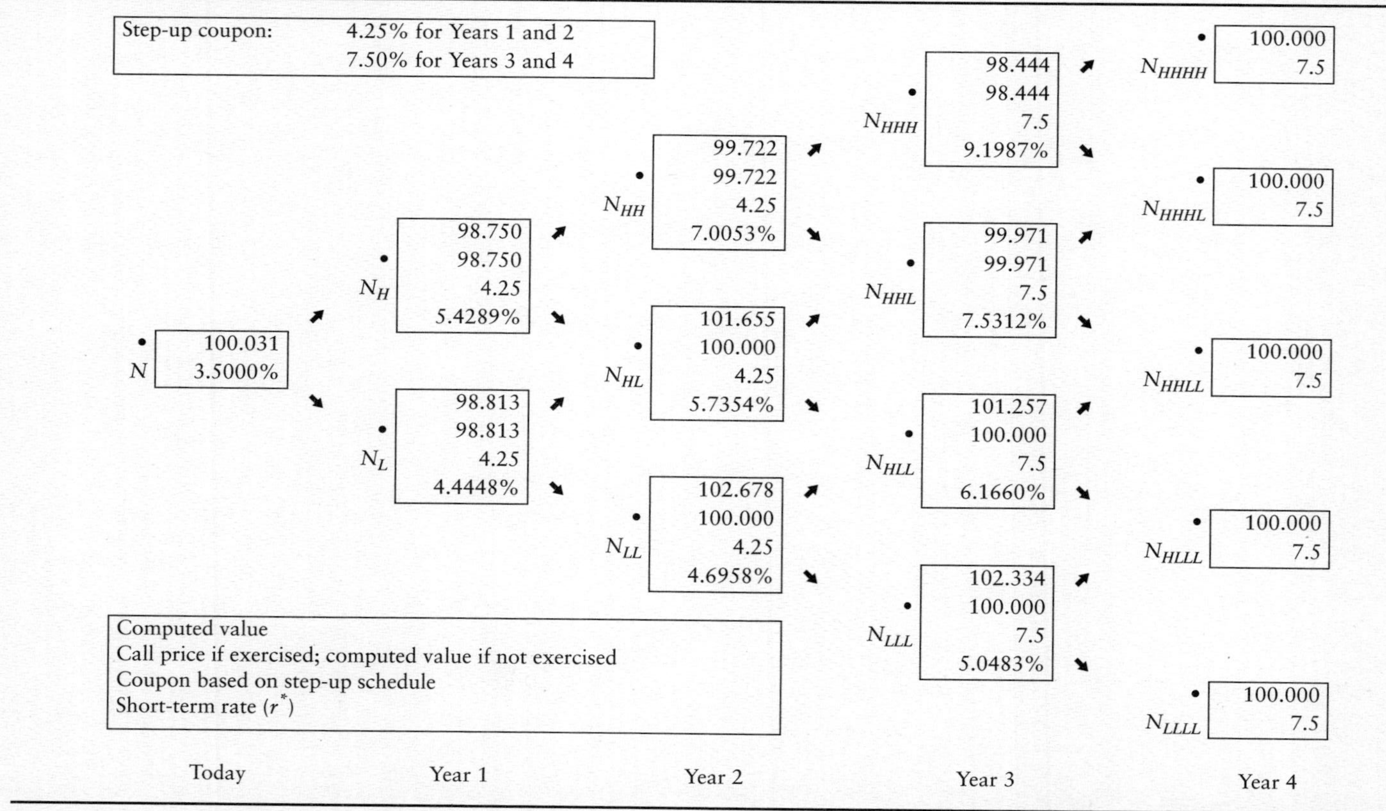

EXHIBIT 14.12 Coupon Schedule (Bands) for a Range Note

	Year 1	Year 2	Year 3
Lower Limit	3.00%	4.00%	5.00%
Upper Limit	5.00%	6.25%	8.00%

EXHIBIT 14.13 Valuation of a 3-Year Range Floater

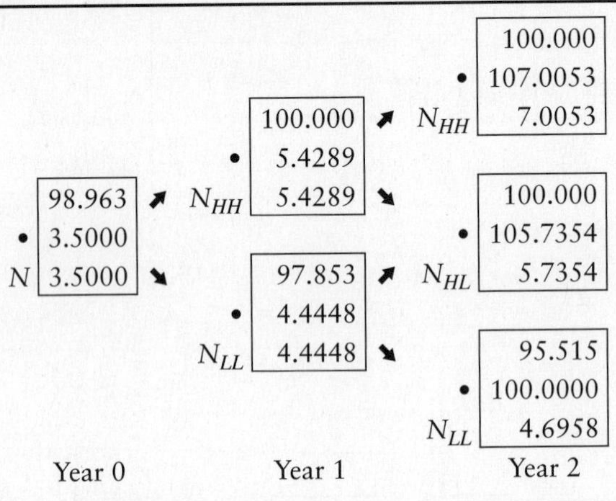

Now we move to another structure where the coupon floats with a reference rate, but is restricted. In this next case, a range is set in which the bond pays the reference rate when the rate falls within a specifed range, but outside the range no coupon is paid.

Valuing a Range Note

A range note is a security that pays the reference rate only if the rate falls within a band. If the reference rate falls outside the band, whether the lower or upper boundary, no coupon is paid. Typically, the band increases over time.

To illustrate, suppose that the reference rate is, again, the 1-year rate and the note has 3 years to maturity. Suppose further that the band (or coupon schedule) is defined as in Exhibit 14.12. Exhibit 14.13 holds our tree and the cash flows expected at the end of each year. Either the 1-year reference rate is paid, or nothing. In the case of this 3-year note, there is only one state in which no coupon is paid. Using our recursive valuation method, we can work back through the tree to the current value, 98.963.

EXHIBIT 14.14 Issuer Par Yield Curve

Maturity	Par Rate	Market Price
1 year	3.50%	100
2 years	4.20%	100
3 years	4.70%	100
4 years	5.20%	100

VALUING AN OPTION ON A BOND

Thus far we have seen how the lattice can be used to value bonds with embedded options. The same tree can be used to value a stand-alone option on a bond.

To illustrate how this is done, consider a 2-year American call option on a 6.5% 2-year Treasury bond with a strike price of 100.25 which will be issued two years from now. We will assume that the on-the-run Treasury yields are those represented in Exhibit 14.14. Within the binomial tree we find the value of the Treasury bond at each node. Exhibit 14.15 shows the value of our hypothetical Treasury bond (excluding coupon interest) at each node at the end of Year 2.

The decision rule at a node for determining the value of an option on a bond depends on whether or not the call or put option being valued is in the money. Moreover, the exercise decision is only applied at the expiration date. That is, a call option will be exercised at the option's expiration date if the bond's value at a node is greater than the strike price. In the case of a put option, the option will be exercised if the strike price at a node is greater than the bond's value (i.e., if the put option is in the money).

Three values for the underlying 2-year bond are shown in Exhibit 14.15: 97.925, 100.418, and 102.534. Given these three values, the value of a call option with a strike price of 100.25 can be determined at each node. For example, if in Year 2 the price of this Treasury bond is 97.925, then the value of the call option would be zero. In the other two cases, since the value at the end of Year 2 is greater than the strike price, the value of the call option is the difference between the price of the bond at the node and 100.25.

Given these values, the binomial tree is used to find the present value of the call option using recursive valuation. The discount rates are the now familiar one-year forward rates from the binomial tree. The expected value at each node for Year 1 is found by discounting the call option value from Year 2 using the rate at the node. Move back one more year to "Today." The value of the option is $0.6056.

The same procedure is used to value a put option.

EXHIBIT 14.15 Using the Arbitrage-Free Binomial Method

Expiration: 2 years; Strike price: 100.25; Current price: 104.643; Volatility assumption: 10%

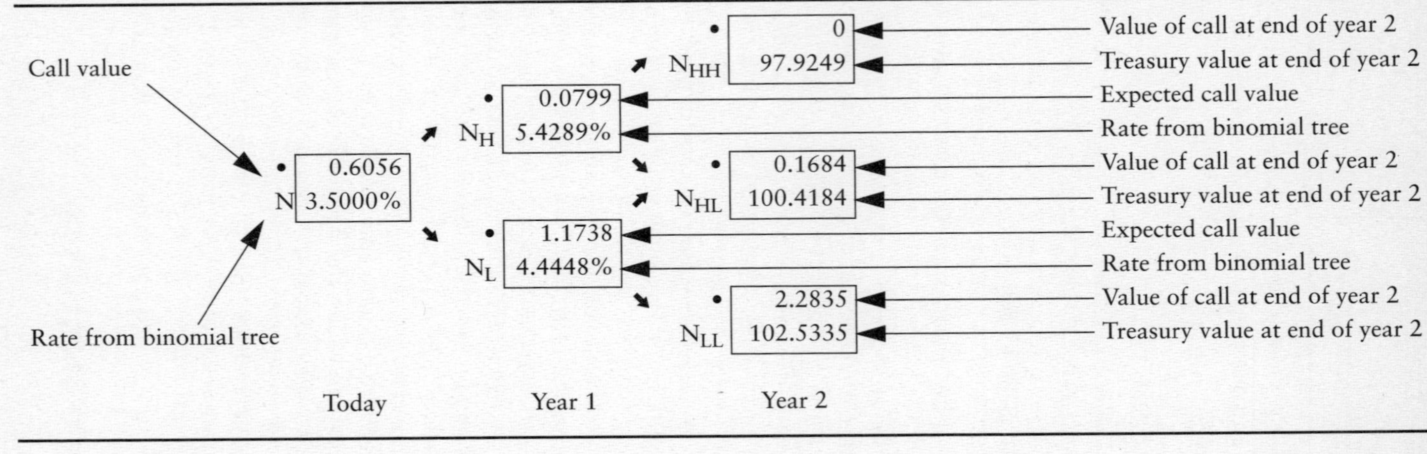

EXTENSIONS

We next demonstrate how to compute the option-adjusted spread, effective duration, and the convexity for a fixed-income instrument with an embedded option.

Option-Adjusted Spread

We have concerned ourselves with valuation to this point. However, financial market transactions determine the actual price for a fixed-income instrument, not a series of calculations on an interest rate lattice. If markets are able to provide a meaningful price (usually a function of the liquidity of the market in which the instrument trades), this price can be translated into an alternative measure of value, the option-adjusted spread (OAS).

The OAS for a security is the fixed spread (usually measured in basis points) over the benchmark rates that equates the output from the valuation process with the actual market price of the security. For an optionless security, the calculation of OAS is a relatively simple, iterative process. The process is much more analytically challenging with the added complexity of optionality. And, just as the value of the option is volatility dependent, the OAS for a fixed-income security with embedded options or an option-like interest rate product is volatility dependent.

Recall our illustration in Exhibit 14.2, where the value of a callable bond was calculated as 102.899. Suppose that we had information from the market that the price is actually 102.218. We need the OAS that equates the value from the lattice with the market price. Since the market price is lower than the valuation, the OAS is a positive spread to the rates in the exhibit, rates which we assume to be benchmark rates.

The solution in this case is 35 basis points, which is incorporated into Exhibit 14.16 that shows the value of the callable bond after adding 35 basis points to each rate. The simple, binomial tree provides evidence of the complex calculation required to determine the OAS for a callable bond. In Exhibit 14.2, the bond is called at N_{HLL}. However, once the tree is shifted 35 bps in Exhibit 14.16, the PV of future cash flows at N_{HLL} falls below the call price to 99.985, so the bond is not called at this node. Hence, as the lattice structure grows in size and complexity, the need for computer analytics becomes obvious.

Effective Duration and Effective Convexity

Duration and convexity provide a measure of the interest rate risk inherent in a fixed-income security. We rely on the lattice model to calculate the effective duration and effective convexity of a bond with an embedded option and other option-like securities. The formula for these two risk measures are given below:

$$\text{Effective duration} = \frac{V_- - V_+}{2V_0(\Delta r)}$$

$$\text{Effective convexity} = \frac{V_+ + V_- - 2V_0}{2V_0(\Delta r)^2}$$

EXHIBIT 14.16 **Demonstration that the Option-Adjusted Spread is 35 Basis Points for a 6.5% Callable Bond Selling at 102.218 (Assuming 10% Volatility)**

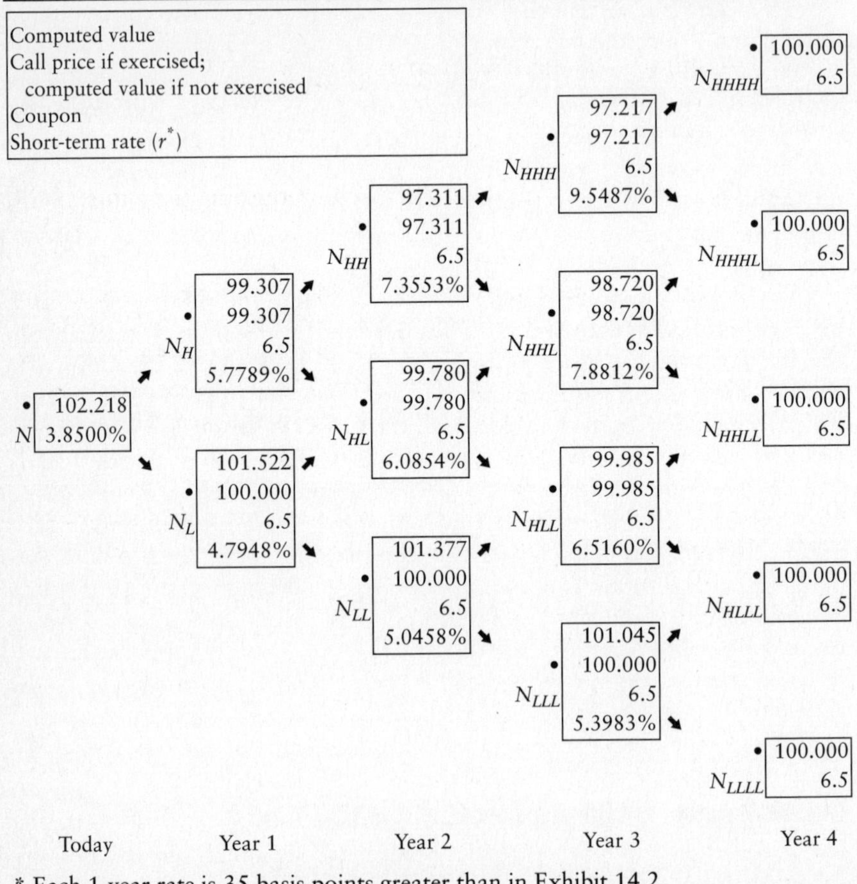

* Each 1-year rate is 35 basis points greater than in Exhibit 14.2.

where V_- and V_+ are the values derived following a parallel shift in the yield curve down and up, respectively, by a fixed spread. The model adjusts for the changes in the value of the embedded call option that result from the shift in the curve in the calculation of V_- and V_+.

Note that the calculations must account for the OAS of the security. Below we provide the steps for the proper calculation of V_+. The calculation for V_- is analogous.

Step 1: Given the market price of the issue, calculate its OAS.

Step 2: Shift the on-the-run yield curve up by a small number of basis points (Δr).

Step 3: Construct a binomial interest rate tree based on the new yield curve from Step 2.

Step 4: Shift the binomial interest rate tree by the OAS to obtain an "adjusted tree." That is, the calculation of the effective duration and convexity assumes a constant OAS.

Step 5: Use the adjusted tree in Step 4 to determine the value of the bond, V_+.

We can perform this calculation for our 4-year callable bond with a coupon rate of 6.5%, callable at par selling at 102.218. We computed the OAS for this issue as 35 basis points. Exhibit 14.17 holds the adjusted tree following a shift in the yield curve up by 25 basis points, and then adding 35 basis points (the OAS) across the tree. The adjusted tree is then used to value the bond. The resulting value, V_+ is 101.621.

To determine the value of V_-, the same five steps are followed except that in Step 2, the on-the-run yield curve is shifted down by a small number of basis points (Δr). It can be demonstrated that for our callable bond, the value for V_- is 102.765.

The results are summarized below:

$$\Delta r = 0.0025$$
$$V_+ = 101.621$$
$$V_- = 102.765$$
$$V_0 = 102.218$$

Therefore,

$$\text{effective duration} = \frac{102.765 - 101.621}{2(102.218)(0.0025)} = 2.24$$

EXHIBIT 14.17 Determination of V_+ for Calculating Effective Duration and Convexity*

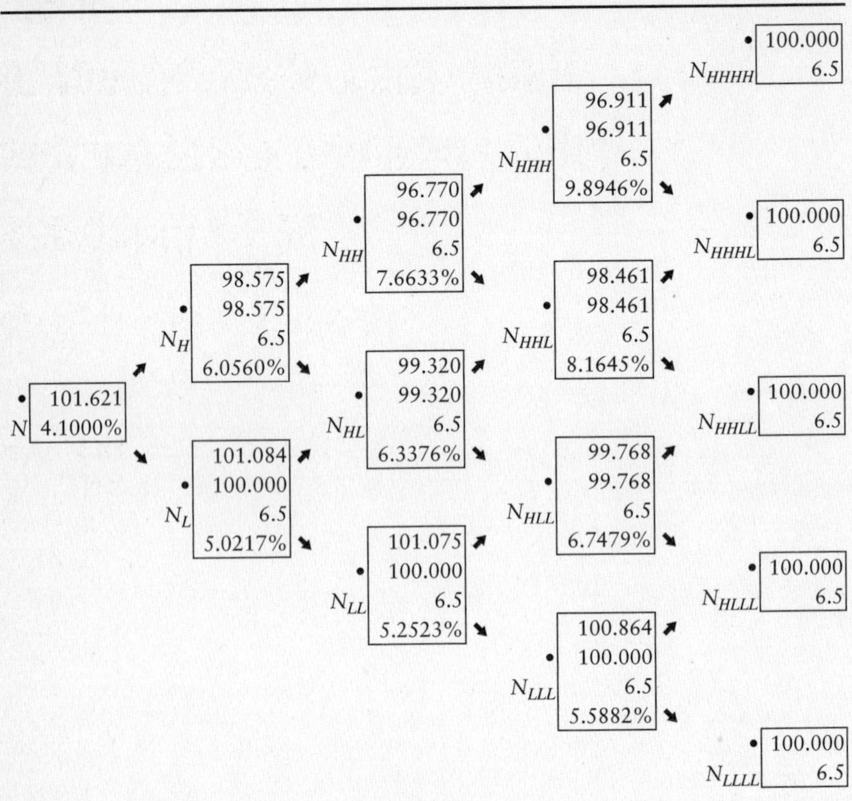

* +25 basis point shift in on-the-run yield curve.

$$\text{Effective convexity} = \frac{101.621 + 102.765 - 2(102.218)}{2(102.218)(0.0025)^2} = -39.1321$$

Notice that this callable bond exhibits negative convexity.

CHAPTER 15

Using the Lattice Model to Value Forward Start Swaps and Swaptions

Gerald W. Buetow, Jr., Ph.D., CFA
President
BFRC Services, LLC

Frank J. Fabozzi, Ph.D., CFA
Adjunct Professor of Finance
School of Management
Yale University

In this chapter we will demonstrate how to value forward start swaps and swaptions using the lattice model described in the previous chapters.[1] We begin with a description of interest rate swaps and how they are valued.

BASICS OF AN INTEREST RATE SWAP

In an interest rate swap, two parties agree to exchange interest payments at specified future dates. The dollar amount of the interest payments exchanged is based on the notional principal or notional amount. The payment each party pays to the other is the agreed-upon periodic interest

[1] A more comprehensive treatment of the subject is provided in Gerald W. Buetow, Jr. and Frank J. Fabozzi, *Valuation of Interest Rate Swaps and Swaptions* (New York, NY: John Wiley & Sons, 2001).

rate times the notional principal. The only dollars that are exchanged between the parties are the interest payments, not the notional principal.

In the most common type of swap, one party agrees to pay the other party fixed interest payments at designated dates for the life of the contract. This party is referred to as the *fixed-rate payer.* The fixed rate that the fixed-rate payer must make is called the *swap fixed rate* or *swap rate.* The other party, who agrees to make payments that float with some reference rate (for example, LIBOR), is referred to as the *fixed-rate receiver.* The fixed-rate payer is also referred to as the floating-rate receiver and the fixed-rate receiver is also called the floating-rate payer. The type of swap that we have just described is called a *plain vanilla swap*.

The payments between the parties are usually netted. We shall refer to this netted payment between the two parties as the *cash flow for the swap* for the period. We note that throughout the literature the terms "swap payments" and "cash flows" are used interchangeably. However, in this chapter we will use the term *swap payments* to mean the payment made by a counterparty before any netting and cash flow to mean the netted amount.

The convention that has evolved for quoting a swap fixed rate is that a dealer sets the floating rate equal to the reference rate and then quotes the swap fixed rate that will apply. The swap fixed rate is some "spread" above the Treasury yield curve with the same term to maturity as the swap. This spread is called the *swap spread.*

There are swaps where the notional principal changes in a predetermined manner over time. A swap in which the notional principal declines over the life of the swap is called an *amortizing swap*. A swap in which the notional principal increases over the life of the swap is called an *accreting swap*. A *roller coaster swap* is a swap where the notional principal can increase or decrease from the previous period. While the illustrations presented throughout this chapter assume a constant notional principal, the valuation framework is equally applicable to swaps with a changing notional principal.

Risk/Return Profile of the Swap Counterparties

The value of an interest rate swap will fluctuate with market interest rates. How the value of a swap changes for each party to a swap is summarized below:

	Change in Swap Value if Rates	
Party	Increase	Decrease
Fixed-rate payer	Increases	Decreases
Floating-rate receiver	Decreases	Increases

Interpreting a Swap

A swap can be viewed in terms of more basic interest rate derivatives: forward rate agreements. Specifically, a swap can be viewed as a package of forward contracts. Let's contrast the position of the counterparties in an interest rate swap to the position of a long and short interest rate forward position. The short forward position gains if interest rates decline and loses if interest rates rise. This is similar to the risk/return profile for a fixed-rate receiver. The risk/return profile for a fixed-rate payer is similar to that of a long forward position: There is a gain if interest rates increase and a loss if interest rates decrease. By taking a closer look at an interest rate swap we can understand why the risk/return profiles are similar.

Consider a swap in which the swap fixed rate is 6%, the payments are swapped quarterly, the notional principal is $100 million, and the reference rate is 3-month LIBOR. The fixed-rate payer has agreed to buy a commodity called "3-month LIBOR" for $1.5 million each quarter (6% times $100 million divided by 4). This is effectively a 3-month forward contract where the fixed-rate payer agrees to pay $1.5 million in exchange for delivery of 3-month LIBOR. If interest rates increase to 7%, the price of that commodity (3-month LIBOR) in the market is higher, resulting in a gain for the fixed-rate payer, who is effectively long a 3-month forward contract on 3-month LIBOR. The fixed-rate receiver is effectively short a 3-month forward contract on 3-month LIBOR. There is therefore an implicit forward contract corresponding to each exchange date.

Now we can see why there is a similarity between the risk/return profile for an interest rate swap and a forward contract. If interest rates increase to, say, 7%, the price of that commodity (3-month LIBOR) increases to $1.75 million (7% times $100 million divided by 4). The long forward position (the fixed-rate payer) gains, and the short forward position (the fixed-rate receiver) loses. If interest rates decline to, say, 5%, the price of our commodity decreases to $1.25 million (5% times $100 million divided by 4). The short forward position (the fixed-rate receiver) gains, and the long forward position (the fixed-rate payer) loses.

This is an important interpretation of a swap because the pricing of a swap will then depend on the price of a package of forward contracts with the same settlement dates in which the underlying for the forward contract is the same reference rate. We will make use of this principle below.

VALUING AN INTEREST RATE SWAP

In order to be able to value swap products such as a forward start swap and a swaption, it is first necessary to understand how the value of a plain vanilla swap is determined. To value a swap it is necessary to determine the present value of the fixed payments and the present value of the floating payments. The difference between these two present values is the value of a swap. Whether the value is positive (i.e., an asset) or negative (i.e., a liability) will depend on whether the party is the fixed-rate payer or the fixed-rate receiver.

Calculating the Swap's Floating Payments

Since the floating rate is set at the beginning of the period, the first floating payment is known. For all subsequent payments, the floating payments depend on the value of the reference rate when the floating rate is determined. To illustrate the issues associated with calculating the floating payment, we will assume that

- A swap starts today, January 1 of year 1 (swap settlement date).
- The floating payments are made quarterly based on "actual/360."
- The reference rate is 3-month LIBOR.
- The notional principal of the swap is $100.
- The term of the swap is five years (20 payments).

The quarterly floating payments are based on an "actual/360" day count convention.[2] The floating payment is set at the beginning of the quarter but paid at the end of the quarter—that is, the floating payments are made in arrears. In general, the floating payment is determined as follows:

$$\text{notional principal} \times (\text{3-month LIBOR}) \times \frac{\text{number of days in period}}{360}$$

There is no uncertainty about the floating payment that will be received by the fixed-rate payer in the first quarter. The difficulty is in determining the floating payments after the first quarterly payment. That is, for the 3-year swap there will be 12 quarterly floating payments. So, while the first quarterly payment is known, the next 11 are not. However, there is a way to hedge the next 11 floating payments by using a futures contract. Specifically, the futures contract used to hedge the future floating payments in a swap whose reference rate is 3-month LIBOR is the Eurodollar CD futures contract.

The 3-month Eurodollar CD is the underlying instrument for the Eurodollar CD futures contract. The contract is for $1 million of face value and is traded on an index price basis. The index price basis in which

[2] This convention means that 360 days are assumed in a year and that in computing the interest for the quarter, the actual number of days in the quarter are used.

the contract is quoted is equal to 100 minus the annualized LIBOR futures rate. For example, a Eurodollar CD futures price of 93.00 means a 3-month LIBOR futures rate of 7% (100 minus 93.00 divided by 100). The Eurodollar CD futures contract is a cash settlement contract. That is, the parties settle in cash for the value of a Eurodollar CD based on LIBOR at the settlement date.

The Eurodollar CD futures contract allows the buyer of the contract to lock in the rate on 3-month LIBOR today for a future 3-month period. For example, suppose that on February 1 an investor purchases a Eurodollar CD futures contract that settles in March of the same year. Assume that the LIBOR futures rate for this contract is 7%. This means that the investor has agreed to invest in a 3-month Eurodollar CD that pays a rate of 7%. Specifically, the investor has locked in a rate for a 3-month investment of 7% beginning in March. If the investor on February 1 purchased a contract that settles in September of the following year and the LIBOR futures rate is 7.4%, the investor has locked in the rate on a 3-month investment beginning September of the following year.

From the perspective of the seller of a Eurodollar CD futures contract, the seller is agreeing to lend funds for three months at some future date at the LIBOR futures rate. For example, suppose on February 1 a bank sells a Eurodollar CD futures contract that settles in March of the same year and the LIBOR futures rate is 7%. The bank locks in a borrowing rate of 7% for three months beginning in March of that year. If the settlement date is September of the following year and the LIBOR futures rate is 7.4%, the bank is locking in a borrowing rate of 7.4% for the 3-month period beginning September of the following year.

The key point here is that the Eurodollar CD futures contract allows a hedge to lock in a 3-month rate on an investment or a 3-month borrowing rate. The 3-month period begins in the month that the contract settles.

Now let's return to our objective of determining the future floating payments. These payments can be locked in over the life of the swap using the Eurodollar CD futures contract. We will show how these floating payments are computed using this contract.

We will begin with the next quarterly payment—from April 1 of year 1 to June 30 of year 1. This quarter has 91 days. The floating payment will be determined by 3-month LIBOR on April 1 of year 1 and paid on June 30 of year 1. There is a 3-month Eurodollar CD futures contract for settlement on June 30 of year 1. That futures contract will have the market's expectation of what 3-month LIBOR on April 1 of year 1 is. For example, if the futures price for the 3-month Eurodollar CD futures contract that settles on June 30 of year 1 is 93.055, then as explained above, the 3-month Eurodollar futures rate is 6.945%. We will refer to that rate for 3-month LIBOR as the "forward rate." Therefore, if the fixed-rate payer bought one of these 3-month Eurodollar CD futures contracts on January 1 of year 1 (the inception of the swap) that settles on June 30 of year 1, then the payment that will be locked in for the quarter (April 1 to June 30 of year 1) is

$$\$100 \times 0.06945 \times \frac{91}{360}$$

Similarly, the Eurodollar CD futures contract can be used to lock in a floating payment for each of the next 10 quarters. It is important to remember that the reference rate at the beginning of period t determines the floating-rate that will be paid for the period. However, the floating payment is not made until the end of period t, denoted $t + 1$.

Exhibit 15.1 shows this for the 5-year swap. Shown in Column (1) is when the quarter begins and in Column (2) when the quarter ends. The payment will be received at the end of the first quarter (March 31 of year 1) and is \$1.74625. That is the known floating payment as explained earlier. It is the only payment that is known. The information used to compute the first payment is in Column (4) which shows the current 3-month LIBOR (6.99%). The payment is shown in the last column, Column (8).

Notice that Column (7) numbers the quarters from 1 through 20. Look at the heading for Column (7). It identifies each quarter in terms of the end of the quarter. This is important because we will eventually be discounting the payments. We must take care to understand when each payment is to be exchanged in order to properly discount. So, the first payment of \$1.74625 it is going to be received at the end of quarter 1. When we refer to the time period for any payment, the reference is to the end of quarter. So, the fifth payment of \$1.7367 would be identified as the payment for period 5, where period 5 means that it will be exchanged at the end of the fifth quarter.

Computing the Present Value of the Floating Payments

At the initiation of an interest rate swap, the counterparties are agreeing to exchange future payment and no upfront payment by either party is made. This means that the swap terms must be such that the present value of the payments to be made by the counterparties must be at least equal to the present value of the payments that will be received. In fact, to eliminate arbitrage opportunities, the present value of the payments made by a party must be equal to the present value of the payments received by that same party. The equivalence (or no arbitrage) of the present value of the payments is the key principle in calculating the swap rate. Here we will demonstrate how to compute the present value of the fixed and floating payments for a swap.

EXHIBIT 15.1 Floating Payments Based on Initial LIBOR and Eurodollar CD Futures

(1)	(2)	(3)	(4)	(5)	(6)	(7)	(8)
Quarter Starts	Quarter Ends	Number of Days in Quarter	Current 3-Month LIBOR	Eurodollar CD Futures Price	Forward Rate	End of Quarter	Floating Payment at End of Quarter
1/1/YR1	3/31/YR1	90	6.99%			1	1.74625
4/1/YR1	6/30/YR1	90		93.055	6.945%	2	1.73625
7/1/YR1	9/30/YR1	91		93.035	6.965%	3	1.76059
10/1/YR1	12/31/YR1	91		93.030	6.970%	4	1.76186
1/1/YR2	3/31/YR2	89		92.975	7.025%	5	1.73673
4/1/YR2	6/30/YR2	90		93.025	6.975%	6	1.74375
7/1/YR2	9/30/YR2	91		93.015	6.985%	7	1.76565
10/1/YR2	12/31/YR2	91		93.015	6.985%	8	1.76565
1/1/YR3	3/31/YR3	89		92.950	7.050%	9	1.74291
4/1/YR3	6/30/YR3	90		92.995	7.005%	10	1.75125
7/1/YR3	9/30/YR3	91		92.975	7.025%	11	1.77576
10/1/YR3	12/31/YR3	91		92.965	7.035%	12	1.77829
1/1/YR4	3/31/YR4	89		92.895	7.105%	13	1.75651
4/1/YR4	6/30/YR4	90		92.930	7.070%	14	1.76750
7/1/YR4	9/30/YR4	91		92.900	7.100%	15	1.79472
10/1/YR4	12/31/YR4	91		92.875	7.125%	16	1.80104
1/1/YR5	3/31/YR5	90		92.790	7.210%	17	1.80250
4/1/YR5	6/30/YR5	90		92.825	7.175%	18	1.79375
7/1/YR5	9/30/YR5	91		92.790	7.210%	19	1.82252
10/1/YR5	12/31/YR5	91		92.755	7.245%	20	1.83137

We must be careful about how we compute the present value of the swap payments. In particular, we must carefully specify (1) the timing of the payment and (2) the interest rates that should be used to discount the payments. We addressed the first issue earlier. In constructing the exhibit for the payments, we indicated that the payments are at the end of the quarter. So, we denoted the timing of the payments with respect to the end of the quarter.

Let's look at the interest rates that should be used for discounting. To do so we draw on two important principles from financial theory. First, every cash flow should be discounted at its own discount rate using a spot rate. So, if we discounted a cash flow of \$1 using the spot rate for period t, the present value would be:

$$\text{present value of \$1 to be received in period } t = \frac{\$1}{(1+\text{spot rate for period } t)^t}$$

The second principle is that forward rates are derived from spot rates so that if we discounted a cash flow using forward rates rather than a spot rate, we would come up with the same value. That is, the present value of \$1 to be received in period t can be rewritten as:

$$\text{present value of \$1 to be received in period } t = \frac{\$1}{(1+f_1)(1+f_2)\ldots(1+f_t)}$$

where f_i = forward rate for period i.

We will refer to the present value of \$1 to be received in period t as the *forward discount factor.* In our calculations involving swaps, we will compute the forward discount factor for a period using the forward rates. These are the same forward rates that are used to compute the floating payments—those obtained from the Eurodollar CD futures contract.

We must make just one more adjustment. We must adjust the forward rates used in the formula for the number of days in the period (i.e., the quarter in our illustrations) in the same way that we made this adjustment to obtain the payments. Specifically, the forward rate for a period, which we will refer to as the *period forward rate*, is computed using the following equation:

$$\text{period forward rate} = \text{annual forward rate} \times \left(\frac{\text{number of days in period}}{360}\right)$$

EXHIBIT 15.2 Calculating the Forward Discount Factor

(1)	(2)	(3)	(4)	(5)	(6)	(7)
Quarter Starts	Quarter Ends	Number of Days in Quarter	End of Quarter	Forward Rate	Period Forward Rate	Forward Discount Factor
1/1/YR1	3/31/YR1	90	1	6.99%	1.7463%	0.98284
4/1/YR1	6/30/YR1	90	2	6.94%	1.7363%	0.96606
7/1/YR1	9/30/YR1	91	3	6.97%	1.7606%	0.94935
10/1/YR1	12/31/YR1	91	4	6.97%	1.7619%	0.93291
1/1/YR2	3/31/YR2	89	5	7.03%	1.7367%	0.91699
4/1/YR2	6/30/YR2	90	6	6.97%	1.7438%	0.90127
7/1/YR2	9/30/YR2	91	7	6.99%	1.7657%	0.88563
10/1/YR2	12/31/YR2	91	8	6.99%	1.7657%	0.87027
1/1/YR3	3/31/YR3	89	9	7.05%	1.7429%	0.85536
4/1/YR3	6/30/YR3	90	10	7.01%	1.7513%	0.84064
7/1/YR3	9/30/YR3	91	11	7.03%	1.7758%	0.82597
10/1/YR3	12/31/YR3	91	12	7.04%	1.7783%	0.81154
1/1/YR4	3/31/YR4	89	13	7.11%	1.7565%	0.79753
4/1/YR4	6/30/YR4	90	14	7.07%	1.7675%	0.78368
7/1/YR4	9/30/YR4	91	15	7.10%	1.7947%	0.76986
10/1/YR4	12/31/YR4	91	16	7.13%	1.8010%	0.75624
1/1/YR5	3/31/YR5	90	17	7.21%	1.8025%	0.74285
4/1/YR5	6/30/YR5	90	18	7.18%	1.7938%	0.72976
7/1/YR5	9/30/YR5	91	19	7.21%	1.8225%	0.71670
10/1/YR5	12/31/YR5	91	20	7.25%	1.8314%	0.70381

Column (5) in Exhibit 15.2 shows the annual forward rate for all 20 periods and Column (6) shows the period forward rate for all 20 periods. (Note that the period forward rate for period 1 is 90/360 of 6.99%, which is 90/360 of the known rate for 3-month LIBOR.) Also shown in Exhibit 15.2 is the forward discount factor for all 20 periods. These values are shown in the last column.

Given the floating payment for a period and the forward discount factor for the period, the present value of the payment can be computed. Exhibit 15.3 shows the present value for each payment. The total present value of the 20 floating payments is $29.61893. Thus, the present value of the payments that the fixed-rate payer will receive is $29.61893 and the present value of the payments that the fixed-rate receiver will make is $29.61893.

EXHIBIT 15.3 Present Value of the Floating Payments

(1) Quarter Starts	(2) Quarter Ends	(3) End of Quarter	(4) Forward Discount Factor	(5) Floating Payment at End of Quarter	(6) PV of Floating Payments
1/1/YR1	3/31/YR1	1	0.982837	1.746250	1.716279
4/1/YR1	6/30/YR1	2	0.966064	1.736250	1.677328
7/1/YR1	9/30/YR1	3	0.949350	1.760597	1.671422
10/1/YR1	12/31/YR1	4	0.932913	1.761861	1.643663
1/1/YR2	3/31/YR2	5	0.916987	1.736736	1.592565
4/1/YR2	6/30/YR2	6	0.901271	1.743750	1.571592
7/1/YR2	9/30/YR2	7	0.885634	1.765653	1.563723
10/1/YR2	12/31/YR2	8	0.870268	1.765653	1.536592
1/1/YR3	3/31/YR3	9	0.855360	1.742917	1.490821
4/1/YR3	6/30/YR3	10	0.840638	1.751250	1.472168
7/1/YR3	9/30/YR3	11	0.825971	1.775764	1.466730
10/1/YR3	12/31/YR3	12	0.811540	1.778292	1.443154
1/1/YR4	3/31/YR4	13	0.797531	1.756514	1.400874
4/1/YR4	6/30/YR4	14	0.783679	1.767500	1.385153
7/1/YR4	9/30/YR4	15	0.769862	1.794722	1.381689
10/1/YR4	12/31/YR4	16	0.756242	1.801042	1.362024
1/1/YR5	3/31/YR5	17	0.742852	1.802500	1.338991
4/1/YR5	6/30/YR5	18	0.729762	1.793750	1.309011
7/1/YR5	9/30/YR5	19	0.716700	1.822528	1.306206
10/1/YR5	12/31/YR5	20	0.703811	1.831375	1.288941
				Total	29.61893

Present Value of the Fixed Payments

In our illustration we will assume that the frequency of settlement is quarterly for the fixed payments, the same as with the floating payments. The day count convention is the same as for the floating payment, "actual/360." The equation for determining the dollar amount of the fixed payment for the period is:

$$\text{notional principal} \times (\text{swap fixed rate}) \times \frac{\text{number of days in period}}{360}$$

It is the same equation as for determining the floating payment except that the swap fixed rate is used instead of the reference rate (3-month LIBOR in our illustration).

EXHIBIT 15.4 Fixed Payments Assuming a Swap Fixed Rate of 7.0513%

(1) Quarter Starts	(2) Quarter Ends	(3) Number of Days in Quarter	(4) End of Quarter	(5) Fixed Payment
1/1/YR1	3/31/YR1	90	1	1.762825
4/1/YR1	6/30/YR1	90	2	1.762825
7/1/YR1	9/30/YR1	91	3	1.782412
10/1/YR1	12/31/YR1	91	4	1.782412
1/1/YR2	3/31/YR2	89	5	1.743238
4/1/YR2	6/30/YR2	90	6	1.762825
7/1/YR2	9/30/YR2	91	7	1.782412
10/1/YR2	12/31/YR2	91	8	1.782412
1/1/YR3	3/31/YR3	89	9	1.743238
4/1/YR3	6/30/YR3	90	10	1.762825
7/1/YR3	9/30/YR3	91	11	1.782412
10/1/YR3	12/31/YR3	91	12	1.782412
1/1/YR4	3/31/YR4	89	13	1.743238
4/1/YR4	6/30/YR4	90	14	1.762825
7/1/YR4	9/30/YR4	91	15	1.782412
10/1/YR4	12/31/YR4	91	16	1.782412
1/1/YR5	3/31/YR5	90	17	1.762825
4/1/YR5	6/30/YR5	90	18	1.762825
7/1/YR5	9/30/YR5	91	19	1.782412
10/1/YR5	12/31/YR5	91	20	1.782412

Exhibit 15.4 shows the fixed payments based on the swap fixed rate (SFR) of 7.0513%. The first three columns of the exhibit show the same information as in Exhibit 15.1—the beginning and end of the quarter and the number of days in the quarter. Column (4) simply uses the notation for the period. That is, period 1 means the end of the first quarter, period 2 means the end of the second quarter, and so on. Column (5) shows the fixed payments for each period based on a swap fixed rate of 7.0513%.

The present value of the fixed payments can be computed. To be consistent with the computing of the present value of the floating payments, the same discount rates are used. It can be demonstrated that if the fixed payments shown in the last column of Exhibit 15.4 are computed using the period forward rates (and therefore forward discount rates) shown in Exhibit 15.3, the present value of the fixed payments will be \$29.61893.

The swap value is the difference between the present value of the floating payment and the present value of the fixed payments. In our swap, at the inception of the swap, the two values are equal ($29.61893) so the swap value is zero as it should be, so that neither party compensates the other in order to enter into the swap. In fact, the swap rate is determined by finding the interest rate that would produce fixed payments whose present value is equal to the present value of the floating payments.

Changes in Swap Value after Inception

After the inception date, market interest rates change and it is therefore necessary to determine how the value of the swap changes. Changes in market interest rates will change the payments of the floating-rate leg of the swap. The value of an interest rate swap is the difference between the present value of the payments of the two legs of the swap. The 3-month LIBOR forward rates from the current Eurodollar CD futures contracts are used to:

- calculate the floating payments and
- determine the discount factors at which to calculate the present value of the payments

To illustrate this, consider the hypothetical 5-year swap. Suppose that two years later, interest rates change as shown in Columns (4) and (6) in Exhibit 15.5. Column (4) shows the current 3-month LIBOR. In Column (5) are the Eurodollar CD futures prices for each period. These rates are used to compute the forward rates in Column (6). Note that the interest rates have increased two years later since the rates in Exhibit 15.5 are greater than those in Exhibit 15.1. The current 3-month LIBOR and the forward rates are used to compute the floating-rate payments.

In addition to using the new forward rates to obtain the floating payments, the new forward rates in Exhibit 15.5 are used to compute the period forward rates and new forward discount factors. Column (3) of Exhibit 15.6 shows the new forward discount factors.

We now have all the information needed to calculate the value of the swap. In Exhibit 15.6 the forward discount factors and the floating payments (from Exhibit 15.5) are shown. The fixed payments need not be recomputed. They are the payments shown in Column (8) of Exhibit 15.4. These are the fixed payments based on the initial swap rate of 7.0513%. Now the two payment streams must be discounted using the new forward discount factors. As shown at the bottom of Exhibit 15.6, the two present values are as follows:

Present value of floating payments	$19.12716
Present value of fixed payments	$18.97279

EXHIBIT 15.5 Rates and Floating Payments Two Years Later

(1)	(2)	(3)	(4)	(5)	(6)	(7)	(8)
Quarter Starts	Quarter Ends	Number of Days in Quarter	Current 3-Month LIBOR	Eurodollar CD Futures Price	Forward Rate	End of Quarter	Floating Payment at End of Quarter
1/1/YR3	3/31/YR3	89	7.05%	92.950		1	1.7429
4/1/YR3	6/30/YR3	90		92.995	7.01%	2	1.7512
7/1/YR3	9/30/YR3	91		92.975	7.03%	3	1.7757
10/1/YR3	12/31/YR3	91		92.965	7.04%	4	1.7782
1/1/YR4	3/31/YR4	89		92.895	7.11%	5	1.7565
4/1/YR4	6/30/YR4	90		92.930	7.07%	6	1.7675
7/1/YR4	9/30/YR4	91		92.900	7.10%	7	1.7947
10/1/YR4	12/31/YR4	91		92.875	7.13%	8	1.8010
1/1/YR5	3/31/YR5	90		92.790	7.21%	9	1.8025
4/1/YR5	6/30/YR5	90		92.825	7.18%	10	1.7937
7/1/YR5	9/30/YR5	91		92.790	7.21%	11	1.8225
10/1/YR5	12/31/YR5	91		92.755	7.25%	12	1.8313

EXHIBIT 15.6 Valuing the Swap Two Years Later

(1) Quarter Starts	(2) Quarter Ends	(3) Forward Discount Factor	(4) Floating Payment at End of Quarter	(5) PV of Floating Payment	(6) Fixed Payment at End of Quarter	(7) PV of Fixed Payment
1/1/YR3	3/31/YR3	0.9829	1.742916667	1.713059	1.743226	1.713363
4/1/YR3	6/30/YR3	0.9660	1.751250000	1.691625	1.762813	1.702794
7/1/YR3	9/30/YR3	0.9491	1.775763889	1.685376	1.782399	1.691674
10/1/YR3	12/31/YR3	0.9325	1.778291667	1.658286	1.782399	1.662117
1/1/YR4	3/31/YR4	0.9164	1.756513889	1.609704	1.743226	1.597526
4/1/YR4	6/30/YR4	0.9005	1.767500000	1.591639	1.762813	1.587418
7/1/YR4	9/30/YR4	0.8846	1.794722222	1.587659	1.782399	1.576758
10/1/YR4	12/31/YR4	0.8690	1.801041667	1.565062	1.782399	1.548862
1/1/YR5	3/31/YR5	0.8536	1.802500000	1.538596	1.762813	1.504719
4/1/YR5	6/30/YR5	0.8385	1.793750000	1.504146	1.762813	1.478204
7/1/YR5	9/30/YR5	0.8235	1.822527778	1.500923	1.782399	1.467876
10/1/YR5	12/31/YR5	0.8087	1.831375000	1.481085	1.782399	1.441477
			Total	19.12716	Total	18.97279

Summary	Fixed-Rate Payer	Fixed-Rate Receiver
PV of payments received	$19.12716	$18.97279
PV of payments made	18.97279	19.12716
Value of swap	$0.15437	–$0.15437

The two present values are not equal and therefore for one party the value of the swap increased and for the other party the value of the swap decreased. The fixed-rate payer will receive the floating payments. These payments have a present value of $19.12716. The present value of the payments that must be made by the fixed-rate payer is $18.97279. Thus, the swap has a positive value for the fixed-rate payer equal to the difference in the two present values of $0.15437. This is the value of the swap to the fixed-rate payer. In contrast, the fixed-rate receiver must make payments with a present value of $19.12716 but will only receive fixed payments with a present value equal to $18.97279 Thus, the value of the swap for the fixed-rate receiver is –$0.15437.

USING THE LATTICE MODEL TO VALUE A PLAIN VANILLA SWAP

The lattice model is needed to value more complex swaps such as forward start swaps and swaptions. Before we show how, let's see how the lattice model can be used to value a plain vanilla swap. We will use the binomial model for this purpose.

As explained earlier, in valuing the cash flows of a swap (i.e., the difference between the payments received and payments paid for each period) an arbitrage value for these cash flows is obtained by discounting at the forward rates implied from the Eurodollar CD futures contracts, or equivalently, the spot rates implied from the Eurodollar CD futures contracts. The first complication in building a model to value more complex swaps is that the future cash flows will depend on what happens to interest rates in the future. This means that future interest rate movements must be considered. This is incorporated into a valuation model by considering how interest rates can change based on some assumed interest rate volatility. Given the assumed interest rate volatility, an interest rate lattice representing possible future interest rates consistent with the volatility assumption can be constructed. It is from the interest rate lattice that two important elements in the valuation process are obtained. First, the interest rates in the lattice are used to generate the cash flows for the swap given the swap terms. Second, the interest rates in the lattice are used to compute the present value of the cash flows.

The Binomial Interest Rate Lattice

In valuing more complex swaps, we will see that consideration must be given to interest rate volatility. This can be done by introducing an interest rate lattice. This lattice is nothing more than a graphical depiction of the one-period or short-term interest rates over time based on some assumption about interest rate volatility. How this lattice is constructed is described in Chapter 13.

To demonstrate swap valuation using the lattice model, we will use the following swap:

swap term: 5 years
cash flows for fixed and floating: semiannual
notional principal: $100
swap fixed rate (SFR) = 7.0513%

Notice that a swap with semiannual payments is used. This is done just to simplify the illustration. Another simplifying assumption is that each semiannual period has the same number of days.

We will assume the forward rates shown in Exhibit 15.7 in our illustration. Following the procedure explained in Chapter 13, Exhibit 15.8 shows the binomial interest rate lattice for valuing any swap using the forward rates in Exhibit 15.7 and assuming annual interest rate volatility is 10%.

From the interest rate lattice, the cash flow at each node is computed. Let's use the semiannual pay swap to illustrate how to get each cash flow. From the perspective of the fixed-rate payer, the cash flow at a node is found using the following formula:

$$(F_{i,j-1} - \text{SFR}) \times NP_j \times 0.5$$

EXHIBIT 15.7 Assumed Forward Rates for 5-Year Swap

(1)	(2)	(3)	(4)	(5)
Period Starts	Period Ends	Forward Rate	Floating Payment at End of Period	Forward Discount Factors
1/1 YR1	6/30 YR1	6.96%	3.482499754	0.966346969
7/1 YR1	12/31 YR1	6.97%	3.483749998	0.933815183
1/1 YR2	6/30 YR2	7.00%	3.500000067	0.902236891
7/1 YR2	12/31 YR2	6.99%	3.492500025	0.871789638
1/1 YR3	6/30 YR3	7.03%	3.513750789	0.842196936
7/1 YR3	12/31 YR3	7.03%	3.515000816	0.813598927
1/1 YR4	6/30 YR4	7.09%	3.543754086	0.785753747
7/1 YR4	12/31 YR4	7.11%	3.556255474	0.758769949
1/1 YR5	6/30 YR5	7.19%	3.596265167	0.732429830
7/1 YR5	12/31 YR5	7.23%	3.613768418	0.706884656
			Total	8.313822725

EXHIBIT 15.8 Semiannual No-Arbitrage Interest Rate Lattice from Eurodollar Futures Prices

									13.4584%
								12.4902%	
							11.5207%		11.6836%
						10.7102%		10.8431%	
					9.9125%		10.0013%		10.1428%
				9.2477%		9.2977%		9.4131%	
			8.5798%		8.6053%		8.6824%		8.8052%
		8.0272%		8.0282%		8.0716%		8.1717%	
	7.4606%		7.4484%		7.4705%		7.5374%		7.6440%
6.9650%		6.9686%		6.9694%		7.0071%		7.0941%	
	6.4767%		6.4661%		6.4853%		6.5434%		6.6359%
		6.0496%		6.0503%		6.0831%		6.1585%	
			5.6134%		5.6300%		5.6805%		5.7608%
				5.2524%		5.2808%		5.3464%	
					4.8876%		4.9314%		5.0011%
						4.5844%		4.6413%	
							4.2810%		4.3416%
								4.0292%	
									3.7690%
Time in Years	0.5	1.0	1.5	2.0	2.5	3.0	3.5	4.0	4.5

where

$F_{i,j\text{-}1}$ = the rate corresponding to the floating rate at node (i, j–1) that dictates the arrears cash flow at j. j – 1 means that the cash flow at j is determined by the forward rate at j – 1. (For example, $F_{3,7}$ is the forward rate that corresponds to period 7 (3.5 in years) and fourth from the top node (i = 0, 1, 2, 3) or 7.5374%.)

NP_j = the notional principal at j. The notional principal can change to whatever value is necessary (they are all constant for this plain vanilla swap).

In the above expression 0.5 is the daycount (semiannual in this case, 0.25 for quarterly, and so on) approximation.

For the fixed-rate receiver, the cash flow is:

$$(\text{SFR} - F_{i,j\text{-}1}) \times NP_j \times 0.5$$

Exhibit 15.9 shows the cash flows for the fixed-rate payer in our swap using the rates in Exhibit 15.8. For example, let's see how we get the cash flow in year 5 (CF5) for the node where rates increase each period. We know from Exhibit 15.9:

$$F_{i,j\text{-}1} = F_{0,9} = F_{0,4.5 \text{ years}} = 13.4584\%$$

Then

$$(13.4584\% - 7.0513\%) \times 100 \times 0.5 = 3.2036$$

This is the value shown in Exhibit 15.9.

The valuation of this swap is shown in Exhibit 15.10. We will refer to this lattice as the *cumulative swap valuation lattice*. Using the cash flow lattice given by Exhibit 15.9, each node shows the present value of all the nodes that take place after it. For example, take the middle node at year 3.0 in Exhibit 15.10 (i = 3, j = 6) where the value of 0.0576 is shown. This represents the cumulative present value of all the cash flows that feed into that node plus the cash flow that corresponds to that node at the 3-year point. To see how this is done, let's perform the following backward induction exercise to see how we arrive at 0.0576.

The values at year 4.5 are simply the discounted value of the cash flows at year 5.0 (CF5):

$$0.8769/(1+8.8052\%/2) = 0.8400$$
$$0.2964/(1+7.6440\%/2) = 0.2854$$

EXHIBIT 15.9 Swap Cash Flow Lattice

	CF .5	CF 1	CF 1.5	CF 2	CF 2.5	CF 3.0	CF 3.5	CF 4	CF 4.5	CF 5
Notional==>	100.00	100.00	100.00	100.00	100.00	100.00	100.00	100.00	100.00	100.00
										3.2036
									2.7195	
								2.2347		2.3161
							1.8294		1.8959	
						1.4306		1.4750		1.5457
					1.0982		1.1232		1.1809	
				0.7643		0.7770		0.8156		0.8769
			0.4880		0.4884		0.5102		0.5602	
		0.2047		0.1985		0.2096		0.2431		0.2964
	–0.0431		–0.0413		–0.0409		–0.0221		0.0214	
		–0.2873		–0.2926		–0.2830		–0.2539		–0.2077
			–0.5008		–0.5005		–0.4841		–0.4464	
				–0.7190		–0.7106		–0.6854		–0.6452
					–0.8994		–0.8852		–0.8525	
						–1.0819		–1.0600		–1.0251
							–1.2334		–1.2050	
								–1.3851		–1.3549
									–1.5110	
										–1.6411
Time in Years	0.5	1.0	1.5	2.0	2.5	3.0	3.5	4.0	4.5	5.0

EXHIBIT 15.10 Cumulative Swap Valuation Lattice

									3.0016
								5.0020	
							6.1485		2.1883
						6.6241		3.5340	
					6.5137		4.1502		1.4711
				5.9373		4.1876		2.2314	
			4.9360		3.7136		2.3679		0.8400
		3.5961		2.8297		2.0050		1.0789	
	1.9335		1.5689		1.1962		0.7837		0.2854
0.0000		0.0057		0.0278		0.0576		0.0614	
	−1.8472		−1.4743		−1.0569		−0.6203		−0.2010
		−3.2452		−2.4866		−1.6740		−0.8348	
			−4.2108		−3.0658		−1.8613		−0.6272
				−4.7334		−3.2089		−1.6227	
					−4.8508		−2.9556		−1.0001
						−4.5659		−2.3144	
							−3.9187		−1.3261
								−2.9206	
									−1.6108
Time in Years	0.5	1.0	1.5	2.0	2.5	3.0	3.5	4.0	4.5

$$-0.2077/(1+6.6359\%/2) = -0.2010$$
$$-0.6452/(1+5.7608\%/2) = -0.6272$$

The values at year 4.0 are going to be the discounted values of the values at year 4.5 plus the discounted value of arrears cash flows that take place at year 4.5 (CF4.5). In other words, these are the cumulative swap values at year 4.0:

$$(0.5 \times 0.8400 + 0.5 \times 0.2854 + 0.5602)/(1 + 8.1717\%/2) = 1.0789$$

$$(0.5 \times 0.2854 + 0.5 \times -0.2010 + 0.0214)/(1 + 7.0941\%/2) = 0.0614$$

$$(0.5 \times (-0.2010) + 0.5 \times (-0.6272) + (-0.4464))/(1 + 6.1585\%/2)$$
$$= -0.8348$$

The values at year 3.5 are going to be the discounted values of the values at year 4.0 plus the discounted value of arrears cash flows that take place at year 4.0 (CF4.0). In other words, these are the cumulative swap values at year 3.5:

$$(0.5 \times 1.0789 + 0.5 \times 0.0614 + 0.2431)/(1 + 7.5374\%/2) = 0.7837$$

$$(0.5 \times 0.0614 + 0.5 \times (-0.8348) + (-0.2539))/(1 + 6.5434\%/2) = -0.6203$$

Finally, to arrive at the middle node at year 3.0, we perform the analogous computation:

$$(0.5 \times 0.7837 + 0.5 \times (-0.6203) + (-0.0221))/(1 + 7.0071\%/2) = 0.0576$$

One important feature of the above process should be noted. The discount rate is the floating rate that is used to compute the arrears cash flow. For example the 7.0071% is the rate that computes the –0.0221 (= (7.0071% – 7.0513%) × 100 × 0.5). This will always be the case—this approach allows us not to have to show 10 different lattices to value the swap (and later to value a swaption). The alternative would be to present a separate lattice for each cash flow and discount it back using backward induction and then add them all together at the point where valuation is desired. Using this approach combines all the lattices into one and is easy to follow. We will also see later that this approach enables tremendous versatility in the valuation of forward start swaps and swaptions, as well as swaps that do not pay in arrears.

While in our illustration we valued a swap at inception that has a value of zero, the procedure for valuing a swap after rates change (i.e., valuing an off market swap) is the same. First, given the new Eurodollar CD futures prices, new forward rates are determined. Given the forward rates, a new interest rate lattice is generated. Then the swap (given its remaining term) is valued using the new interest rate lattice.

To illustrate this, let's look at our hypothetical swap two years later. Exhibit 15.11 shows the valuation of this swap two years later assuming the forward rates in Columns (3) and (6) in panel a. The balance of the exhibit shows how to value the swap without a lattice using the procedure described earlier. The value of the swap is shown in panel d. The lattice approach should provide the same value for the swap.

EXHIBIT 15.11 Valuing a Swap Two Years Later after Rates Rise (Semiannual Payments and Rounded Day Count)

a. Semiannual Forward Rates and Floating Payments

(1)	(2)	(3)	(4)	(5)	(6)
Beginning Period	End of Period	Current 6-Month LIBOR	Forward Rate	End of Period	Floating Payments at End of Period
1/1/YR1	6/30/YR1	7.0275%		1	3.513751
7/1/YR1	12/31/YR1		7.0300%	2	3.515001
1/1/YR2	6/30/YR2		7.0875%	3	3.543754
7/1/YR2	12/31/YR2		7.1125%	4	3.556255
1/1/YR3	6/30/YR3		7.1925%	5	3.596265
7/1/YR3	12/31/YR3		7.2275%	6	3.613768

b. Period Forward Rates and Forward Discount Factors

(1)	(2)	(3)	(4)	(5)	(6)
Beginning Period	End of Period	End of Period	Forward Rate	Period Forward Rate	Forward Discount Factor
1/1/YR2	6/30/YR2	1	7.0275%	3.5138%	0.966055
7/1/YR2	12/31/YR2	2	7.0300%	3.5150%	0.933251
1/1/YR3	6/30/YR3	3	7.0875%	3.5438%	0.901311
7/1/YR3	12/31/YR3	4	7.1125%	3.5563%	0.870359
1/1/YR4	6/30/YR4	5	7.1925%	3.5963%	0.840145
7/1/YR4	12/31/YR4	6	7.2275%	3.6138%	0.810843

EXHIBIT 15.11 (Continued)
c. Valuing the Swap Two Years Later if Interest Rates Increase

(1)	(2)	(3)	(4)	(5)	(6)	(7)
Beginning Period	End of Period	Forward Discount Factor	Floating Cash Flow at End of Period	PV of Floating Payment	Fixed Payment at End of Period	PV of Fixed Payment
1/1/YR2	6/30/YR2	0.966055	3.513751	3.394477	3.525635	3.405958
7/1/YR2	12/31/YR2	0.933251	3.515001	3.280380	3.525635	3.290304
1/1/YR3	6/30/YR3	0.901311	3.543754	3.194025	3.525635	3.177694
7/1/YR3	12/31/YR3	0.870359	3.556255	3.095219	3.525635	3.068568
1/1/YR4	6/30/YR4	0.840145	3.596265	3.021385	3.525635	2.962045
7/1/YR4	12/31/YR4	0.810843	3.613768	2.930199	3.525635	2.858737
			Total	18.91569		18.76331

d. Value of the Swap

Summary	Fixed-Rate Payer	Floating-Rate Receiver
PV of payments received	$18.91569	$18.76331
PV of payments made	18.76331	18.91569
Value of swap	$0.15238	–$0.15238

To use the lattice approach to value a swap after rates change, the new rates are used to construct a new lattice. Panel b of Exhibit 15.12 shows the binomial interest rate lattice based on these rates. Based on this binomial interest rate lattice, panel b shows the cash flows for the pay-fixed swap. In panel c, the pay-fixed swap value at each node is computed. The value of the swap two years later is shown at the root of the lattice in panel c. For a pay-fixed swap it is $0.1524 per $100 of notional principal. This is the same value as computed in Exhibit 15.11.

VALUING A FORWARD START SWAP

A *forward start swap* is a swap structure wherein the swap does not begin until some future date that is specified in the swap agreement. Thus, there is a beginning date for the swap at some time in the future and a maturity date. We use the notation "(y_s, y_e) forward start swap" to denote a forward start swap that starts y_s years from now and ends (matures) in y_e years after the start date. Notice that we use years in the notation, not periods.

A forward start swap will also specify the swap fixed rate at which the counterparties agree to exchange payments commencing at the start date. We refer to this rate as the *forward swap fixed rate* for the forward start swap.

EXHIBIT 15.12 Valuing a Swap after Rates Rise Using the Binomial Interest Rates Rise (Semiannual Pay and Rounded Day Count)

Panel a. Interest Rate Lattice Two Years Later

					10.19%
				9.47%	
			8.74%		8.85%
		8.13%		8.22%	
	7.53%		7.58%		7.68%
7.03%		7.06%		7.13%	
	6.53%		6.58%		6.67%
		6.13%		6.19%	
			5.72%		5.79%
				5.38%	
					5.03%
Time in Years	0.5	1	1.5	2	2.5

Panel b. Pay Fixed Swap Cash Flows Two Years Later

					1.5702
				1.2069	
			0.8427		0.8981
		0.5382		0.5828	
	0.2381		0.2666		0.3147
−0.0119		0.0023		0.0410	
	−0.2582		−0.2335		−0.1917
		−0.4630		−0.4293	
			−0.6677		−0.6314
				−0.8377	
					−1.0131
CF0.5	CF1	CF1.5	CF2	CF2.5	CF3

EXHIBIT 15.12 (Continued)
Panel c. Pay Fixed Swap Values Two Years Later

					1.4940
				2.2763	
			2.4337		0.8601
		2.0911		1.1185	
	1.3018		0.8421		0.3031
0.1524		0.1342		0.0964	
	−0.9626		−0.5686		−0.1855
		−1.6059		−0.8040	
			−1.8156		−0.6136
				−1.5957	
					−0.9882
Time in Years	0.5	1	1.5	2	2.5

Shortly, we will look at swaptions. In a swaption, one of the counterparties (the buyer of the swaption) has the right, but not the obligation, to initiate a swap at some future date. In the case of a forward start swap, both counterparties must perform; that is, both counterparties parties are committing to make the designated payments in the future.

To illustrate the valuation of a forward start swap we will assume that the swap starts in two years and the swap then has a tenor of three years. Using our notation, this is a (2,3) forward start swap. We will assume that the forward swap fixed rate is 7.1157%. In this illustration, we will use a 5-year swap based on a semiannual pay and a rounded day count.

Using the Cumulative Swap Valuation Lattice

To value a forward start swap, it is necessary to first determine the possible values of the swap at the start date. The cumulative swap valuation lattice can be used to obtain the possible swap values at the start date of the forward start swap. The values in the lattice are in terms of present value.

Exhibit 15.13 shows the cumulative swap valuation lattice for the 5-year swap for which the swap fixed rate is 7.1157%. For example, if the swap starts in year 2, then there are five possible values: 5.7720, 2.6611, −0.1438, −2.6608, and −4.9100. It might seem that the value of a forward start swap is the average value of the swap values for that period. In our illustration it would be $0.1437 for the pay fixed swap and –$0.1437 for the receive fixed swap if the swap starts in year 2.0. The problem with using a simple average is that the possible swap values for a given period may not have the same probability of occurrence. Instead of a simple averaging of the values at the period where the swap begins, the value at each node in Exhibit 15.13 should be weighted by the probability of realizing its value.

Obtaining the Weights at a Node

When there are only two movements for the rate in the next period from a given node (i.e., in the binomial interest rate lattice), the number of paths that arrive at a given node can be calculated using the following relationship:

$$\frac{n!}{j!(n-j)!}$$

where n is the number of periods and j is the number of down states.

Exhibit 15.14 shows the number of paths that arrive at each node for a 5-year swap with semiannual payments. Let's illustrate the above formula using the exhibit to explain the notation and then to demonstrate how to calculate the number of paths leading to each node in Exhibit 15.14. Look at year 2. Start at the top of year 2. At that node, there are no down states. Thus, j in the formula is 0. Since we are looking at year 2, the number of periods is 4. Thus, n is equal to 4. Substituting these values into the formula we have:

$$\begin{aligned}\frac{4!}{0!(4-0)!} &= \frac{4\times3\times2\times1}{1(4\times3\times2\times1)}\\ &= \frac{24}{1(24)} = 1\end{aligned}$$

This is a simple case since there is only 1 path that arrives at the top of the lattice. For the second node from the top at year 2, there is one down state so j is equal to 1. Since n is still 4 (as it is for all the nodes at year 2), then

$$\begin{aligned}\frac{4!}{1!(4-1)!} &= \frac{4\times3\times2\times1}{1(3\times2\times1)}\\ &= \frac{24}{1(6)} = 4\end{aligned}$$

EXHIBIT 15.13 Cumulative Swap Valuation Lattice for Forward Start Swaps at a Forward Swap Fixed Rate of 7.1157%

									2.9714
								4.9432	
							6.0621		2.1579
						6.5109		3.4745	
					6.3742		4.0625		1.4405
				5.7720		4.0725		2.1713	
			4.7450		3.5715		2.2791		0.8091
		3.3795		2.6611		1.8883		1.0182	
	1.6913		1.3738		1.0519		0.6939		0.2544
−0.2678		−0.2157		−0.1438		−0.0607		0.0003	
	−2.0949		−1.6731		−1.2033		−0.7109		−0.2322
		−3.4709		−2.6608		−1.7936		−0.8963	
			−4.4127		−3.2140		−1.9526		−0.6585
				−4.9100		−3.3297		−1.6846	
					−5.0006		−3.0477		−1.0315
						−4.6877		−2.3766	
							−4.0114		−1.3576
								−2.9831	
									−1.6424
Time in Years	0.5	1	1.5	2	2.5	3	3.5	4	4.5

EXHIBIT 15.14 Lattice Showing the Number of Paths that Arrive at a Node

										1
									1	
								1		9
							1		8	
						1		7		36
					1		6		28	
				1		5		21		84
			1		4		15		56	
		1		3		10		35		126
	0		2		6		20		70	
		1		3		10		35		126
			1		4		15		56	
				1		5		21		84
					1		6		28	
						1		7		36
							1		8	
								1		9
									1	
										1
Time in Years		0.5	1	1.5	2	2.5	3	3.5	4	4.5

We'll do one more. Let's compute the number of paths to arrive at the node that is the third one down for year 2. In this case j is 2 and therefore,

$$\frac{4!}{2!(4-2)!} = \frac{4 \times 3 \times 2 \times 1}{(2 \times 1)(2 \times 1)}$$
$$= \frac{24}{2(2)} = 6$$

Given the lattice that shows the number of paths to arrive at a node, the probability of reaching a node can be computed. This is done by first adding up the total number of possible paths for a period and then for a given node dividing the number of paths that arrive at that node by the total number of possible paths for that period.

To illustrate this calculation, we will again use year 2. The total number of paths is 16 (= 1 + 4 + 6 + 4 + 1). For the top node at year 2, the probability is 1⁄16 or 6.25%. For the second node from the top of the lattice at year 2, the probability is 4⁄16 or 25.0%. Exhibit 15.15 shows in tabular form the number of paths that arrive at a node and the associated probability.

Computing the Forward Start Swap Value

Given the cumulative swap valuation lattice and the probability associated for each value of that lattice, the value of a forward start swap can be computed. This is done at a starting period for the forward rate swap as follows. Calculate at each node for the starting period the product of the cumulative swap value at the node and the corresponding probability. Then, sum up these products. The summation is the value of the forward start swap.

The calculations are shown in Exhibit 15.15 for a (2,3) forward start swap. For year 2, Column (1) shows the five swap values from the cumulative swap valuation lattice (Exhibit 15.13). Column (3) shows the probability corresponding to each of the five swap values. The last column shows the product of the swap value in Column (1) and the corresponding probability in Column (3). The last row of the last column is the sum of these products and is the value of our (2,3) forward start swap. The value is zero for the forward start swap party that pays fixed and therefore zero for the party that receives fixed.

Exhibit 15.16 shows the probability weighted cumulative swap valuation lattice. The two rows at the bottom of the lattice show for each counterparty the value of a forward start swap for each period. Notice that for year 2.0, the value agrees with what was computed in Exhibit 15.15.

EXHIBIT 15.15 Calculating the Probability Weighted Value for Year 2

(1)	(2)	(3)	(4)
Cumulative Swap Value at Node	No. of Paths that Arrive at Node	Probability of Realizing Node Value	Probability Weighted Value at Node
5.7720	1	6.25%	0.3608
2.6611	4	25.00%	0.6653
–0.1438	6	37.50%	–0.0539
–2.6608	4	25.00%	–0.6652
–4.9100	1	6.25%	–0.3069
Total	16	100.00%	0.0000

EXHIBIT 15.16 Probability Weighted Cumulative Swap Values with an SFR of 7.1157% and Value of Forward Start Swaps

										0.005804
									0.019309	
								0.04736		0.037931
							0.101733		0.108577	
						0.199194		0.222171		0.101283
					0.360748		0.3818		0.237486	
				0.593131		0.55805		0.373921		0.132745
			0.844887		0.665276		0.442561		0.222725	
		0.845652		0.515174		0.328713		0.189743		0.062609
	−0.2678		−0.107826		−0.05394		−0.018958		7.71E–05	
		−1.047472		−0.627396		−0.376034		−0.194393		−0.057141
			−0.867734		−0.665211		−0.420365		−0.196072	
				−0.55159		−0.502185		−0.320356		−0.108034
					−0.306873		−0.312157		−0.184258	
						−0.156268		−0.166669		−0.072529
							−0.073245		−0.074269	
								−0.031339		−0.023864
									−0.011653	
										−0.003208
Time in Years		0.5	1	1.5	2	2.5	3	3.5	4	4.5
FWD Start Pay Fixed Swaps==>		−0.2018	−0.1307	−0.0707	0.0000	0.0515	0.1014	0.1204	0.1219	0.0756
FWD Start Receive Fixed Swaps==>		0.2018	0.1307	0.0707	0.0000	−0.0515	−0.1014	−0.1204	−0.1219	−0.0756

Forward Start Swaps and Interest Rate Volatility

The following table shows the effect of the assumed interest rate volatility on several pay fixed forward start swap values (recall that the assumed interest rate volatility is 10% in our illustrations):

Volatility	(1, 4)	(2, 3)	(3, 2)
0.00%	–0.0041	–0.0191	–0.0333
5.00%	–0.0032	–0.0143	–0.0250
10.00%	0	0	0
15.00%	0.0049	0.0238	0.0418
20.00%	0.0118	0.0567	0.1003

Notice that the higher the interest rate volatility assumed, the higher the value of the forward rate swap.

So why is there a difference as volatility increases? This is due to the fact that the term structure model used in our illustration has an implied drift rate that is an increasing function of interest rate volatility. As volatility increases, so will the implied drift rate; the drift rate implies that the rates are rising on average so as volatility increases and the drift rate increases, so do the implied forward rates. As the implied forward rates increase so will the swap fixed rate that produces a zero net present value. This is seen as we move down any column in the table.

SWAPTION VALUATION

Options on interest rate swaps, called *swaptions*, grant the option buyer the right to enter into an interest rate swap at a future date. The time until expiration of the swap, the term of the swap, and the swap fixed rate are specified. The swap fixed rate is the *strike rate* for the option.

There are two types of swaptions. A *pay fixed swaption* (also called a *payer's swaption*) entitles the option buyer to enter into an interest rate swap in which the buyer of the option pays a fixed rate and receives a floating rate. If the option buyer has the right to enter into the swap at the expiration date of the option, the option is referred to as a European style swaption. In contrast, if the option buyer has the right to enter into the swap at any time until the expiration date, the option is referred to as an American style swaption. In our discussion, when we refer to a swaption, we will mean a European style swaption. For example, suppose that a pay fixed swaption has a strike rate equal to 7%, a term of three years, and expires in two years. This means that at the end of two years the buyer of this pay fixed swaption has the right to enter into a 3-year interest rate swap in which the buyer pays 7% (the swap fixed rate which is equal to the strike rate) and receives the reference rate.

In a *receive fixed swaption* (also called a *receiver's swaption*), the buyer of the swaption has the right to enter into an interest rate swap that requires paying a floating rate and receiving a fixed rate. For example, if the strike rate is 6.75%, the swap term is four years, and the option expires in one year, the buyer of this receiver fixed swaption has the right at the end of the next year to enter into a 4-year interest rate swap in which the buyer receives a swap fixed rate of 6.75% (i.e., the strike rate) and pays the reference rate.

We will let "(y_e, y_t) swaption" denote a swaption that expires in year y_e on a swap with a tenor of y_t years. So, a (2,3) swaption is one that expires in 2 years for a swap that has a tenor of 3 years.

The Role of the Cumulative Swap Valuation Lattice

In our illustration we will use the 5-year interest rate lattice based on semiannual rates and rounded day count shown in Exhibit 15.8. Since we will be valuing a pay fixed swaption with a strike rate of 7% in our illustration later, Exhibit 15.17 shows the pay fixed swap cash flow lattice for a plain vanilla swap with a notional principal of \$100 based on a swap fixed rate of 7%. As described earlier, the cumulative swap valuation lattice can be constructed.

Just to repeat how the values in Exhibit 15.17 are determined, let's look at year 1.5. We know that the cash flow at a node in the lattice is found as follows:

$$(F_{i,j\text{-}1} - \text{Strike rate}) \times NP_j \times 0.5$$

where $F_{i,j\text{-}1}$ is the floating rate at node $(i,j–1)$ that dictates the arrears cash flow at j, strike rate is the strike rate of the pay fixed swaption, and NP_j is the notional principal at j. For our semiannual pay swap and rounded day count, the formula for the cash flow for a \$100 notional principal is:

$$(\text{LIBOR at node} - \text{Strike rate}) \times \$100 \times 0.5$$

For a swap fixed rate of 7%, the formula is then:

$$(\text{LIBOR at node} - 0.07) \times \$100 \times 0.5$$

Let's use the three LIBOR values shown at year 1.5 to illustrate the calculation. The three values are 8.0272%, 6.9686%, and 6.0496%. The corresponding cash flow at each node is:

EXHIBIT 15.17 Pay Fixed Swap Cash Flow Lattice for Plain Vanilla Swap with a Strike Rate of 7%

	CF 0.5	CF 1	CF 1.5	CF 2	CF 2.5	CF 3.0	CF 3.5	CF 4	CF 4.5	CF 5
Notional==>	100.00	100.00	100.00	100.00	100.00	100.00	100.00	100.00	100.00	100.00
CF Lattice										3.2292
									2.7451	
								2.2603		2.3418
							1.8551		1.9215	
						1.4563		1.5007		1.5714
					1.1239		1.1489		1.2066	
				0.7899		0.8026		0.8412		0.9026
			0.5136		0.5141		0.5358		0.5859	
		0.2303		0.2242		0.2352		0.2687		0.3220
	–0.0175		–0.0157		–0.0153		0.0036		0.0470	
		–0.2616		–0.2669		–0.2574		–0.2283		–0.1820
			–0.4752		–0.4748		–0.4585		–0.4207	
				–0.6933		–0.6850		–0.6598		–0.6196
					–0.8738		–0.8596		–0.8268	
						–1.0562		–1.0343		–0.9995
							–1.2078		–1.1793	
								–1.3595		–1.3292
									–1.4854	
										–1.6155
Time in Years	0.50	1.00	1.50	2.00	2.50	3.00	3.50	4.00	4.50	5.00

$$(0.080272 - 0.07) \times \$100 \times 0.5 = \$0.5136$$
$$(0.069686 - 0.07) \times \$100 \times 0.5 = -\$0.0157$$
$$(0.060496 - 0.07) \times \$100 \times 0.5 = -\$0.4752$$

For the cash flow lattice shown in Exhibit 15.17, the corresponding cumulative swap valuation lattice is shown in Exhibit 15.18. From the root of Exhibit 15.18 it can be seen that the value of the 5-year pay fixed swap is 0.2132. This lattice will be the basis for all pay fixed swaption valuations with a strike rate of 7%. We will see that all permutations of pay fixed swaptions are simply an exercise of the backward induction methodology.

Expiration Values and the Swaption Valuation Lattice

We will use the cumulative swap valuation lattice as shown in Exhibit 15.18 to produce corresponding pay fixed swaption valuation lattices. We will value a (4,1) and a (2,3) pay fixed swaption.

Exhibit 15.19 presents the results of the procedure for valuing the (4,1) pay fixed swaption. Here is how we get the values in this lattice. Look at year 4.0, the year when the option expires. The values for that year shown in Exhibit 15.19 are called the expiration values. The expiration value at the expiration date will be either:

- zero if the value at the corresponding node in Exhibit 15.18 is negative, or
- the cumulative swap value at the corresponding node in Exhibit 15.18, if the value is positive.

The reason the expiration value is zero if the swap value at the node in Exhibit 15.18 is negative is that the owner of a swaption does not have to exercise the option. That is, the swaption owner will allow the swaption to expire unexercised.

The expiration value at a node can be expressed as follows:

$$\max(\text{cumulative swap value}, 0)$$

Look at Exhibit 15.19. The five expiration values starting from the top of year 4.0 are the same as in Exhibit 15.18 because the corresponding swap value is positive. (They do differ in terms of the number of decimal places.) For the lower four expiration values in year 4.0 in Exhibit 15.19, the value is zero because the corresponding swap value in Exhibit 15.18 is negative.

EXHIBIT 15.18 Pay Fixed Cumulative Swap Valuation Lattice for a Plain Vanilla Swap with a Strike Rate of 7%

Value Lattice									
									3.0256
								5.0489	
							6.2173		2.2125
						6.7142		3.5814	
					6.6246		4.2200		1.4955
				6.0689		4.2792		2.2793	
			5.0880		3.8266		2.4386		0.8645
		3.7684		2.9639		2.0980		1.1271	
	2.1262		1.7241		1.3111		0.8551		0.3101
0.2132		0.1819		0.1643		0.1517		0.1101	
	−1.6500		−1.3162		−0.9404		−0.5482		−0.1762
		−3.0656		−2.3479		−1.5788		−0.7858	
			−4.0500		−2.9478		−1.7886		−0.6023
				−4.5929		−3.1128		−1.5734	
					−4.7315		−2.8824		−0.9751
						−4.4690		−2.2648	
							−3.8450		−1.3010
								−2.8708	
									−1.5856
Time in Years	0.50	1.00	1.50	2.00	2.50	3.00	3.50	4.00	4.50

EXHIBIT 15.19 (4,1) Pay Fixed Swaption with a Strike Rate of 7%

								5.048867
							4.080103	
						3.260828		3.581393
					2.56019		2.790793	
				1.953041		2.113332		2.27931
			1.441984		1.526504		1.632364	
		1.0307		1.054647		1.071036		1.127147
	0.715378		0.702152		0.667458		0.596158	
0.483679033		0.453428		0.401957		0.313741		0.110104
	0.285668		0.236302		0.164471		0.053308	
		0.13641		0.085926		0.025867		0
			0.044771		0.01258		0	
				0.006129		0		0
					0		0	
						0		0
							0	
								0
Time in Years	0.50	1.00	1.50	2.00	2.50	3.00	3.50	4.00

EXHIBIT 15.20 (2,3) Pay Fixed Swaption with a Strike Rate of 7%

				6.068853
			4.330618	
		2.806647		2.963943
	1.722592		1.507972	
1.020846477		0.767053		0.16432
	0.390203		0.079587	
		0.038625		0
			0	
				0
Time in Years	0.5	1	1.5	2

Applying the Backward Induction Methodology to Obtain a Swaption's Value

Once the expiration values are computed at the swaption's expiration date, year 4.0 in our (4,1) swaption, it is simply an exercise of backward induction thereafter, using the interest rate lattice to compute the discount factors. For example, the top value at year 3.5 in Exhibit 15.19 is computed as follows:

$$0.5(5.048867 + 3.581393)/(1 + 0.115207/2) = 4.080103$$

For the lower value at year 1.5, the value in Exhibit 15.19 is found as follows:

$$0.044771 = 0.5(0.085926 + 0.006129)/(1 + 0.056134/2)$$

Repeating this process throughout the lattice in Exhibit 15.19 results in a (4,1) pay fixed swaption value of $0.48368 per $100 of notional principal.

The swaption lattice shown in Exhibit 15.20 corresponds to the (2,3) pay fixed swaption. The lattices are computed in the same manner as the lattice for the (4,1) pay fixed swaption except that the expiration values take place at different times within the swap value lattice.

We will repeat the approach above for a receive fixed swaption. We will use a swap fixed rate (i.e., strike rate) of 6.75% instead of 7% which was used for the pay fixed swaption. Exhibit 15.21 is the cash flow lattice for a receive fixed swap with a swap fixed rate of 6.75%. In general the cash flow lattice is found as follows:

$$(\text{strike rate} - F_{i,j-1}) \times NP_j \times 0.5$$

EXHIBIT 15.21 Receive Fixed Swap Cash Flow Lattice for a Swap Fixed Rate of 6.75%

	CF 0.5	CF 1	CF 1.5	CF 2	CF 2.5	CF 3.0	CF 3.5	CF 4	CF 4.5	CF 5
Notional==>	100.00	100.00	100.00	100.00	100.00	100.00	100.00	100.00	100.00	100.00
CF Lattice										–3.3542
									–2.8701	
								–2.3853		–2.4668
							–1.9801		–2.0465	
						–1.5813		–1.6257		–1.6964
					–1.2489		–1.2739		–1.3316	
				–0.9149		–0.9276		–0.9662		–1.0276
			–0.6386		–0.6391		–0.6608		–0.7109	
		–0.3553		–0.3492		–0.3602		–0.3937		–0.4470
	–0.1075		–0.1093		–0.1097		–0.1286		–0.1720	
		0.1366		0.1419		0.1324		0.1033		0.0570
			0.3502		0.3498		0.3335		0.2957	
				0.5683		0.5600		0.5348		0.4946
					0.7488		0.7346		0.7018	
						0.9312		0.9093		0.8745
							1.0828		1.0543	
								1.2345		1.2042
									1.3604	
										1.4905

Therefore, given LIBOR at a node, the cash flow is determined as follows:

$$(\text{strike rate} - \text{LIBOR at node}) \times \$100 \times 0.5$$

For a swap fixed rate of 6.75%, the formula is then:

$$(0.0675 - \text{LIBOR at node}) \times \$100 \times 0.5$$

Again, we will use the three LIBOR values shown at year 1.5 to illustrate the calculation. The three values are 8.0272%, 6.9686%, and 6.0496%. The corresponding value for the cash flow at each node at year 1.5 is:

$$(0.0675 - 0.080272) \times \$100 \times 0.5 = -\$0.6386$$
$$(0.0675 - 0.069686) \times \$100 \times 0.5 = -\$0.1093$$
$$(0.0675 - 0.060496) \times \$100 \times 0.5 = \$0.3502$$

Exhibit 15.22 shows the corresponding receive fixed swap values for a plain vanilla swap with a strike rate of 6.75%. Notice that the value of the swap is negative. This is due to the fact that the swap is worth zero when the swap fixed rate is 7.0513%; since we have decreased the swap fixed rate, the receive fixed counterparty has lost value relative to the higher swap fixed rate, therefore, the swap becomes negative.

We follow the same process as in a pay fixed swaption to value a (4,1) receive fixed swaption. Exhibit 15.23 shows the valuation lattice. The value of the (4,1) receive fixed swap with a strike of 6.75% is $0.26503 per $100 of notional principal. The other receive fixed swaptions are computed in the same manner.

The Effect on Interest Rate Volatility on a Swaption's Value

It is important to understand that a critical factor in the value of a swaption is the assumed interest rate volatility. Regardless of the type of swaption, increasing volatility will increase a swaption's value. In other words, as with all options, volatility increases the value of a swaption. The exhibits show that regardless of the level of the strike rate, volatility will increase a swaption's value. This can be seen in Exhibit 15.24 which shows the effects of volatility on a (2,3) pay fixed swaption (PFS) and a (2,3) receiver fixed swaption (RFS) with a strike rate of 6.75%. The graphs clearly demonstrate that increasing volatility increases the value of both types of swaptions.

EXHIBIT 15.22 Receive Fixed Swap Values for a Plain Vanilla Swap with a Strike Rate of 6.75%

Value Lattice										
										−3.1427
									−5.2772	
								−6.5527		−2.3306
							−7.1534		−3.8124	
						−7.1657		−4.5602		−1.6145
					−6.7103		−4.7258		−2.5127	
				−5.8291		−4.3777		−2.7830		−0.9843
			−4.6087		−3.6182		−2.5510		−1.3626	
		−3.0658		−2.4810		−1.8711		−1.2033		−0.4305
	−1.2524		−1.0409		−0.8301		−0.6105		−0.3474	
		0.6888		0.5452		0.3725		0.1966		0.0552
			2.1898		1.6719		1.1149		0.5469	
				3.2665		2.3728		1.4340		0.4808
					3.9077		2.6444		1.3331	
						4.1503		2.5253		0.8531
							3.9966		2.0233	
								3.4856		1.1786
									2.6282	
										1.4629
Time in Years		0.5	1	1.5	2	2.5	3	3.5	4	4.5

EXHIBIT 15.23 (4,1) Receive Fixed Swaption with a Strike Rate of 6.75%

								0
							0	
						0		0
					0		0	
				0		0		0
			0.014208		0		0	
		0.05855		0.029636		0		0
	0.141993		0.107592		0.06165		0	
0.26506334		0.23603		0.193563		0.127906		0
	0.406595		0.380916		0.338965		0.264775	
		0.603494		0.5929		0.572008		0.546874
			0.862581		0.882706		0.914036	
				1.180683		1.243102		1.333119
					1.540674		1.637813	
						1.913548		2.023274
							2.277007	
								2.628219
Time in Years	0.5	1	1.5	2	2.5	3	3.5	4

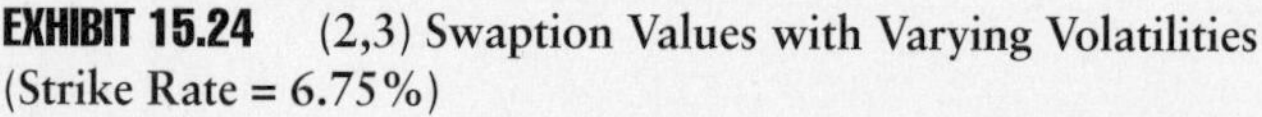

EXHIBIT 15.24 (2,3) Swaption Values with Varying Volatilities (Strike Rate = 6.75%)

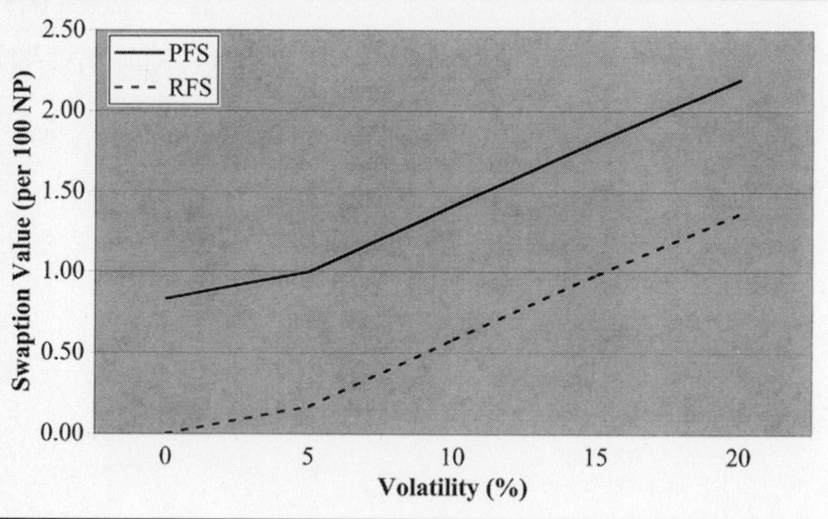

CONCLUSION

We have introduced an interest rate lattice-based approach to value swaps, forward start swaps, and swaptions. The method is extraordinarily flexible and easy to use. It is also easily extended to other types of interest rate lattice structures like the trinomial or tetranomial. The lattice structure can incorporate volatility structures as well. Moreover, it is also easily extended to Monte Carlo-based interest rate models. We believe that the approach offers advantages over other more popular methodologies.

CHAPTER 16

Valuing Path-Dependent Securities*

C. Douglas Howard, Ph.D.
Associate Professor of Mathemetics
Baruch College, CUNY

Lattice-based valuation techniques are today commonly used to value a host of financial instruments. The procedure typically involves modeling the random behavior of a relevant market observable (often called the "factor"). If the application involved valuing a stock option, for example, the factor would be the underlying stock price. To value a collateralized mortgage obligation (CMO), some proxy for the general level of interest rates would be more relevant. The underlying lattice usually represents a discrete version of a continuous stochastic process that the factor is presumed to follow over time. With some securities, the stock option for example, the procedure is quite straightforward. With other securities, however, the methodology becomes quite cumbersome. The CMO is an extreme example of this latter category.

A major source of complexity arises from "path dependence." This occurs when knowing the value $F(t^*)$ of the factor at some time $t^*>0$ (our convention is that time 0 corresponds to today) does not provide sufficient information to calculate the cash flow generated by the security at time t^*. Rather, in the case of path dependence, the time t^* cash flow also depends in some manner on $F(t)$ for all or some of $0 \leq t < t^*$, that is, how the value of F got to $F(t^*)$ is important.

* Research for this chapter was supported by Andrew Kalotay Associates, Inc. The author thanks Lee Bittengle for surveying the literature on this topic.

Consider again a stock option, a European call to be precise. Path dependence is not present in this example. Let $F(t)$ denote the underlying stock price at time t. Suppose the option is exercisable at time T at a strike of K. At any time prior to T, a European option generates no cash flow regardless of what happens to F, thus exhibiting path independence for times $t^* < T$. At time T, the cash flow generated is given by max $(0, F(T) - K)$—how F got to $F(T)$ is again irrelevant. Note that path dependence *does not* mean simply that the security's cash flow depends on the factor's path. Indeed, the stock option's time T payoff depends on the path of the underlying stock—but *only* through the underlying's value at time T.

A CMO, on the other hand, is heavily path-dependent. Among many other things, we must certainly know the amount of the underlying mortgage pool still outstanding at time t^* to calculate the time t^* cash flow of the CMO. This, unfortunately, is a function of the prepayment experience from time 0 to time t^* which, in turn, is a function of the path of interest rates over this entire period—not just the rate environment at time t^*.

In this chapter we examine closely two fixed-income securities exhibiting intermediate degrees of path dependence. The first, an indexed amortizing note (IAN), is simply a bond that makes principal payments prior to its stated maturity that are a prescribed function of the prevailing level of interest rates: Principal payments are structured to accelerate in low rate environments. As with the much more complicated CMO, path dependence arises because the amount of the IAN outstanding at any point in time (and hence the IAN's cash flow at that time) depends on prior interest rates. The second example, an interest rate derivative, is a periodic cap on a short-term rate. Specifically we study a floating-rate note (FRN) with the feature that its coupon rate, which adjusts yearly, is permitted to increase only a limited amount from one year to the next. If market rates decrease from one year to the next, the FRN's coupon rate decreases accordingly, unaffected by the periodic cap. Periodic caps are commonly found embedded along with a host of other option-like features in adjustable-rate mortgages. In this chapter, a one-factor model is used because it is simpler to illustrate the concept of path-dependent securities and their valuation. The principles also apply when a two-factor model is used, where payments are tied to one factor (and its evolution) and valuation is performed using the short-rate factor.

This chapter is organized as follows: In the next section we review the basic methodology of lattice-based arbitrage-free pricing, first abstractly and then with a concrete example. We outline the difference between recursive and Monte Carlo (path sampling) methodologies. This section also develops the notation we use in subsequent sections. Following this, we value a simple IAN first via Monte Carlo and then, with the introduction of a necessary non-stochastic "state" variable, via a recursive procedure. In the last section we subject the periodic cap to the same analysis and discuss some numerical procedures that make problems of this sort more tractable. In this second example, a different state variable is called for.

In this chapter, a one-factor model (i.e., a model with one stochastic variable) is used because it is simpler to illustrate the concept of path-dependent securities and their valuation. In some applications, two or more factors may be needed to determine a security's cash flow. The principles illustrated here work equally well in this setting. Note that, for purposes of discounting, the short-term interest rate must always be one of the factors present.

To the author's knowledge, recursive techniques using coupled non-stochastic state variables first appeared in practice in the late 1980s to value sinking fund bonds[1] whose complicated package of embedded options exhibit substantial path-dependence. Hull and White[2] describe the use of this procedure in a different context. Prior to the advent of the state variable technique, less efficient Monte Carlo procedures were commonly used to value path-dependent securities.[3]

ARBITRAGE-FREE PRICING

The Single-Period Case

Consider the following single-period setup. At some future time $\Delta t > 0$, m different "states of the world" are possible. We label these possible outcomes 1, 2, ..., m. For the moment we leave the notion of what exactly a state of the world is as an abstraction. However, let's suppose that this notion contains sufficient information to know the payoff of any security C at time Δt once the outcome is specified. We denote these state-dependent (future) payoffs by $C(1)$, $C(2)$, ..., $C(m)$ and we presume there is no cash flow prior, nor subsequent, to time Δt . Let $aC + bC'$ denote the security that pays $aC(j)+bC'(j)$ in state j (i.e., $aC+bC'$ is a

[1] Salomon Brothers Inc. developed such a model.

[2] See J. Hull and A. White, "Efficient Procedures for Valuing European and American Path-Dependent Options," *Journal of Derivatives* (Fall 1993), pp. 21–31. For other numerical examples and a good list of further references, see Chapter 18 in J. Hull, *Options, Futures, and Other Derivatives* (Englewood Cliffs, NJ: Prentice Hall, 1997).

[3] See, for example, W.C. Hunter and D.W. Stowe, "Path-Dependent Options: Valuation and Applications," *Economic Review*, Federal Reserve Bank of Atlanta, 77:2 (1992), pp. 29–34.

portfolio comprising a units of security C and b units of security C'). Any reasonable method $V(\cdot)$ of ascribing value to securities based on these future payoffs should satisfy:

$$V(aC + bC') = aV(C) + bV(C') \tag{1}$$

$$\text{if } C(j) > 0 \text{ for } 1 \le j \le m \text{ then } V(C) > 0 \tag{2}$$

Condition (1) says that a portfolio may be valued by summing the values of its constituent securities weighted by amounts held in the portfolio, while condition (2) is the "arbitrage-free" condition that any security generating positive payoff in every future outcome has positive value today. One can show that any such $V(\cdot)$ must be of the form:

$$V(C) = e^{-r\Delta t}(p_1 C(1) + p_2 C(2) + \ldots + p_m C(m)) \tag{3}$$

where $p_1, p_2, \ldots, p_m$ satisfy

$$\text{each } p_j \ge 0 \text{ and } \sum_{j=1}^{m} p_j = 1 \tag{4}$$

Note, in particular, that the p_j behave like probabilities (they are referred to as *arbitrage probabilities*). For any security C, this calculation represents the expected payoff of C at time Δt discounted back to today at the continuously compounding annual risk-free rate r.

The Multi-Period Case

Most securities generate a sequence of cash flow over time—not just one future payoff. The single-period model generalizes to accommodate this fact. Suppose our security C generates cash flow at a sequence of times $0 = t < t_1 < t_2 < \ldots < t_n = T$. Between the t_i and after T there is no possibility of cash flow. At the i-th period there are $m(i)$ possible states of the world which, again, we label $1, 2, \ldots, m(i)$. When $i=0$, of course, there is only one state so $m(0)=1$. We assume that the description of the states at period i contains any information necessary to calculate the state-dependent period i cash flow $CF_i(j)$ for each state $1 \le j \le m(i)$. In the multi-period model, an "outcome" corresponds to a sequence of states

$$\omega = (j_1, \ldots, j_n) \text{ where } 1 \le j_i \le m(i)$$

representing how the world unfolds over time. We let Ω represent the space of all such outcomes.

We shall refer to a pair (i,j), where i is a time period $(0 \le i < n)$ and j is a state $(1 \le j \le m(i))$, as a "node." Assume that at each node there resides a single-period arbitrage-free pricing (AFP) model specified by the node-dependent risk-free rate r_{ij} and arbitrage probabilities $p_i(j \to j')$ for each j' with $1 \le j' \le m(i+1)$. This latter expression represents the probability of a transition from state j in period i to state j' in period i+1.

Suppose that at time t_i we are in state j. The aggregate payoff of C one period forward (at time t_{i+1}) comes from two sources: (1) the cash flow $CF_{i+1}(j')$ generated by C at time t_{i+1} (which depends on the period i+1 state j'); and (2) the value, which we denote $V_{i+1}(j')$, assigned at node $(i+1,j')$ to the *subsequent* cash flow that C may generate at times $t_{i+2}, \ldots, t_n$. Using equation (3), we deduce that we must have

$$V_i(j) = e^{-r_{ij}(t_{i+1}-t_i)} \sum_{j'=1}^{m(i+1)} p_i(j \to j')[CF_{i+1}(j') + V_{i+1}(j')] \qquad (5)$$

if our model is to satisfy conditions (1) and (2) at each node. Since we know the state dependent cash flow $CF_{i+1}(j')$, this procedure makes sense if we know the $V_{i+1}(j')$'s. But we know that $V_n(j') = 0$ for $1 \le j' \le m(n)$: this is merely the statement that there *is no* cash flow subsequent to time t_n. This allows us to apply equation (5) when $i=n-1$ to calculate the $V_{n-1}(j)$'s. But then we can apply equation (5) to $i=n-2$ and so forth, backwards (recursively) through the lattice, until we have calculated $V_0(1)$. But $V_0(1)$ represents the value today of all future cash flow—precisely what we are interested in.

A Simple Example

We make this concrete with a simple example. In the subsequent sections, we will expand upon this same example for purposes of valuing the IAN and periodic cap. Suppose each $t_i = i$ (so cash flow can occur only annually) and consider the lattice shown in Exhibit 16.1. The arbitrage probabilities are prescribed as follows:

$$p_i(j \to j') = \begin{cases} 0.5 \text{ if } j' = j \text{ or } j' = j+1 \\ 0 \quad \text{otherwise} \end{cases}$$

and only those transitions with positive probability are shown in Exhibit 16.1. The numbers at each node correspond to the r_{ij} stated as rates compounded *annually* so as to correspond, for convenience, to the time increments. With the r_{ij} quoted in this manner and noting that $t_{i+1} - t_i = 1$, equation (5) must be rewritten as

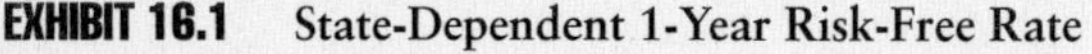

EXHIBIT 16.1 State-Dependent 1-Year Risk-Free Rate

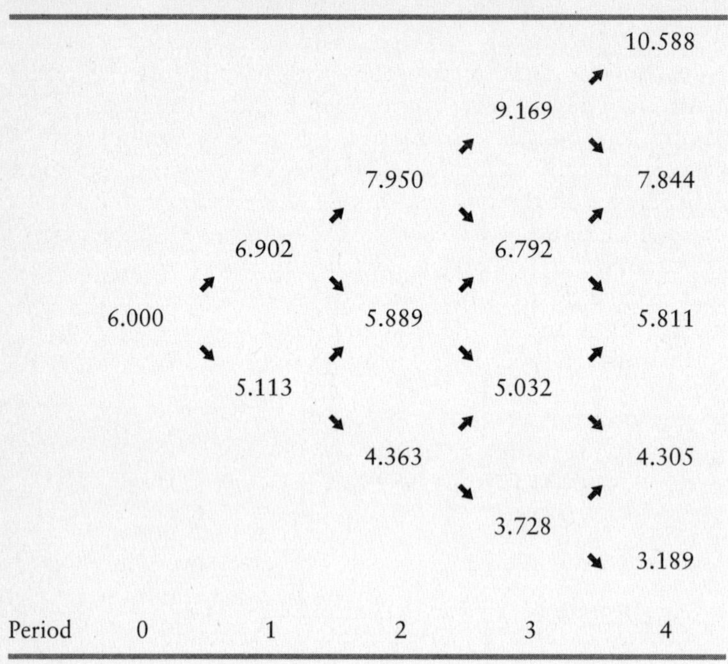

$$V_i(j) = \frac{1}{1 + r_{ij}} \sum_{j'=1}^{m(i+1)} p_i(j \rightarrow j')[CF_{i+1}(j') + V_{i+1}(j')] \tag{6}$$

and setting into this the values for our arbitrage probabilities yields

$$V_i(j) = \frac{1}{1 + r_{ij}}\{0.5[CF_{i+1}(j) + V_{i+1}(j)] + 0.5[CF_{i+1}(j+1) + V_{i+1}(j+1)]\} \tag{7}$$

We use this setup to value a (risk-free) bond that pays \$6 in years 1, 2, and 3, and \$106 in year 4, irrespective of the states in those periods. Exhibit 16.2 shows the values of $C_i(j)$ and $V_i(j)$ that equation (7) produces in this setting. For example, letting ⟨6.902⟩ denote the state (in period 1) in which the 1-year rate is 6.902%, the calculation of V_1 (⟨6.902⟩) is

$$V_1(\langle 6.902 \rangle) = \frac{1}{1.06902}[0.5(6.0 + 100.190) + 0.5(6.0 + 96.505)] = 97.610$$

We note that this bond is valued today at 100.0. In fact, the four bonds paying a 6% annual coupon maturing in 1, 2, 3, and 4 years are all valued at 100.0. This lattice was *constructed* to explain a flat 6% term structure. One can also confirm that the local volatility of the 1-year rate is 15% throughout the lattice (e.g., ½ log(6.902/5.113) = 0.15).

There is another algorithm that arrives at the 100.0 value of the 4 year 6% bond. Specifically: (1) Calculate the period-by-period cash flow corresponding to each of the (sixteen) 4-year paths through the lattice; (2) discount each of those flows back to today using the earlier path-dependent r_{ij} to arrive at a "path-dependent present value" $PV(\omega)$; (3) calculate the expected PV over the sixteen paths ω. We represent a path ω by a sequence of +'s and –'s, depending on whether at each juncture we move up or down, respectively. Then, for this 4-year 6% bond, we have, for example:

$$
\begin{aligned}
PV(++++) &= 106.0/1.09169/1.0795/1.06902/1.0 \\
&\quad + 6.0/1.0795/1.06902/1.06 + 6.0/1.06902/1.06 \\
&\quad + 6.0/1.06 \\
&= 95.237
\end{aligned}
$$

EXHIBIT 16.2 State-Dependent $C_i(\cdot)$ and $V_i(\cdot)$ for the 3-Year Note

					106.000
					0.000
				6.000	
				97.097	
			6.000		106.000
			96.505		0.000
		6.000		6.000	
		97.610		99.258	
			6.000		106.000
	100.000		100.190		0.000
		6.000		6.000	
		102.390		100.922	
			6.000		106.000
			103.060		0.000
				6.000	
				102.190	
					106.000
					0.000
Period	0	1	2	3	4

Note also that $PV(+++-) = 95.237$ also. This is because neither the year 4 cash flow nor the discounting process depend on the year 4 interest rate. This holds in this case for all paths ω: $PV(\omega)$ is independent of the last + or – step. Notationally, we write this as $PV(+++\pm) = 95.237$. Calculating an expected value over the eight equally likely pairs of paths $(+++\pm)$, $(++-\pm)$, $(+-+\pm)$, $(+--\pm)$, $(-++\pm)$, $(-+-\pm)$, $(--+\pm)$, and $(---\pm)$ (respectively) gives:

$$\begin{aligned} V_0(1) &= (95.237 + 97.004 + 98.678 + 100.064 \\ &\quad + 100.261 + 101.671 + 102.997 + 104.088)/8 \\ &= 100.000 \end{aligned} \tag{8}$$

This procedure works for general securities in the setting of equation (6). In fact, letting

$$p(\omega) = \prod_{i=0}^{n-1} p_i(j_i \to j_{i+1})$$

denote the probability of observing the path $\omega = (j_1, \ldots, j_n)$, (where $j_0=1$—today's state) we have in general that

$$V_0(1) = \sum_{\omega \in \Omega} PV(\omega)p(\omega) = \sum_{\omega \in \Omega} \left[\sum_{i=1}^{n} CF_i(j_i)d_i(\omega) \right] p(\omega) \tag{9}$$

where

$$d_i(\omega) = \prod_{k=0}^{i-1} \frac{1}{1 + r_{kj_k}}$$

is the path-dependent discount factor that discounts a period i cash flow to today. (Equation (9) can be proved by induction on the length of the lattice and partitioning Ω on the value of j_1.)

We refer to equation (9) as the Monte Carlo approach. This is somewhat of a misnomer since equation (9) samples *every* path ω through the lattice and calculates the average of $PV(\omega)$ weighted by the probability of observing each path ω. In practice, the scale of the problem will be much larger and there will be too many paths through the lattice to perform an exhaustive sampling. Usually, therefore, Monte Carlo simulation involves *estimating* $V_0(1)$ by randomly sampling paths through the lattice in a manner such that the probability of selecting any particular path ω is precisely $p(\omega)$. In general (and depending on the variance of

$PV(\omega)$ across paths), accurate estimates require a large number of sample paths making the method computationally inefficient.

INDEXED AMORTIZING NOTES

Presently we apply these two approaches to the IAN—our first example of a path-dependent security. The stochastic factor is the one-year risk-free rate, which follows the stochastic process in the previous example (Exhibit 16.1). Recall that this means 6% is a market yield for risk-free bonds maturing in 1, 2, 3, and 4 years. The security is a 4-year IAN paying interest annually at a fixed rate of 6% per year. Regardless of what happens to interest rates, there is no principal payment the first year (the "lock-out" period). In years 2 and 3, the amount of principal paid depends on the level of the 1-year rate via the "amortization schedule": if the 1-year rate is below 5%, 75% of the remaining balance is repaid; if the rate is between 5% and 6%, 50% of the balance is repaid; if the rate exceeds 6%, there is no principal payment. If a principal payment made in accordance with this formula brings the outstanding balance below 20% of the amount originally issued (which we take to be 100.0), the entire bond is retired immediately (the "clean-up" provision). At maturity, in year 4, any remaining principal is amortized. Instruments with these qualitative features are quite common, both as stand-alone notes and, more frequently, as the fixed-pay side of interest rate swaps. We observe that the amortization schedule accelerates principal payment in low rate environments and thus behaves like a partial par call. We expect, therefore, that this note will be valued below 100.0 since a note with the same coupon but no principal acceleration is valued at 100.0.

Valuation Via Monte Carlo

First we value the IAN via Monte Carlo, where it is again feasible to sample every path and calculate exactly the expected value of $PV(\omega)$. Again, we describe paths by a sequence of + or – signs, so, for example $\omega = (- - - -)$ corresponds to the following progression of the 1-year yield:

		year 1		year 2		year 3		year 4
6.000%	→	5.113%	→	4.363%	→	3.728%	→	3.189%

producing the following sequence of principal payments:

year 1	year 2	year 3	year 4
0.0	75.0	25.0	0.0

EXHIBIT 16.3 Path-by-Path Analysis of the IAN

ω	Year 1	Year 2	Year 3	Year 4	$PV(\omega)$
(+ + + +)	6.000	6.000	6.000	106.000	95.237
(+ + + −)	6.000	6.000	6.000	106.000	95.237
(+ + − +)	6.000	6.000	6.000	106.000	97.004
(+ + − −)	6.000	6.000	6.000	106.000	97.004
(+ − + +)	6.000	56.000	3.000	53.000	98.941
(+ − + −)	6.000	56.000	3.000	53.000	98.941
(+ − − +)	6.000	56.000	28.000	26.500	99.442
(+ − − −)	6.000	56.000	28.000	26.500	99.442
(− + + +)	6.000	56.000	3.000	53.000	100.528
(− + + −)	6.000	56.000	3.000	53.000	100.528
(− + − +)	6.000	56.000	28.000	26.500	101.038
(− + − −)	6.000	56.000	28.000	26.500	101.038
(− − + +)	6.000	81.000	26.500	0.000	101.148
(− − + −)	6.000	81.000	26.500	0.000	101.148
(− − − +)	6.000	81.000	26.500	0.000	101.148
(− − − −)	6.000	81.000	26.500	0.000	101.148

This particular path illustrates the lock-out period (year 1: There is no amortization even though 5.113 < 6.0), the amortization schedule (year 2: The payment is 75.0 because 4.363 < 5.0), and the clean-up provision (year 3: The payment *would be* 0.75 × 25.0 but this would leave only 6.25 outstanding, which is less than the clean-up provision). When interest payments on the outstanding principal are added, the following sequence of cash flow results:

year 1	year 2	year 3	year 4
6.0	81.0	26.5	0.0

The resulting *PV* is calculated as

$$\begin{aligned} PV(----) &= 26.5/1.04363/1.05113/1.06 \\ &\quad + 81.0/1.05113/1.06 + 6.0/1.06 \\ &= 101.148 \end{aligned}$$

Repeating this exercise for each of the 16 paths through the lattice yields the table of cash flow and *PV* shown in Exhibit 16.3. Since each path through this lattice has equal probability, we may calculate the expected value of $PV(\omega)$ by simply averaging the final column in this table. This yields 99.311. Any recursive procedure, of course, must agree with this calculation of value.

The path dependence of the IAN can be observed in this table. For example, consider the paths (+ + – –), (+ – + –), (– + – +), and (– – + +). In each case, the state in year 4 corresponds to a 1-year rate of 5.811%, that is, each of these paths ends up in state ⟨5.811⟩. However, the year 4 cash flow corresponding to these paths is 106.0, 53.0, 26.5, and 0.0, respectively. Hence the cash flow in year 4 cannot be deduced from the state in year 4—it is influenced also by how one gets to that state.

Recursive Valuation

To value the IAN recursively, we partition the interest rate states (like ⟨5.811⟩) by further specifying how much of the IAN is outstanding *before* the principal payment of that year. The state ⟨5.811⟩, for example, is partitioned into ⟨5.811, 100⟩, ⟨5.811, 50⟩, ⟨5.811, 25⟩, and ⟨5.811, 0⟩. This additional variable, whose values partition the state as specified by the value of the stochastic variable, is referred to as a non-stochastic state variable and its range of attainable values is referred to as the state space. (It is easy in this example to verify that the state space is {0, 25, 50, 100}, i.e., at all times one of these amounts must be outstanding. More about this later.) Notice that some states, ⟨3.189, 100⟩ for example, are impossible to reach. This phenomenon will not make our calculations incorrect, it just means that we will do some unnecessary calculations.

Once the time t 1-year rate and amount outstanding (prior to current-period amortization) are *both* specified as, say, $\langle r, P\rangle$, the time t cash flow can easily be calculated: The interest component is just $0.06P$; the principal component is deduced from the value of P, the lock-out period, the amortization table, and the clean-up provision by the formula

$$\text{time } t \text{ principal payment} = \begin{cases} 0 & \text{if } t = 1 \\ 0.75P & \text{if } t = 2 \text{ or } 3,\ r < 5\%, \text{ and } 0.25P > 20 \\ 0.5P & \text{if } t = 2 \text{ or } 3,\ 5\% \le r < 6\%, \text{ and } 0.5P > 20 \\ 0 & \text{if } t = 2 \text{ or } 3, \text{ and } r \ge 6\% \\ P & \text{otherwise} \end{cases}$$

and the state-dependent cash flow is the sum of interest and principal. We begin our recursive calculations at the end of the lattice, just as we do when there is no path dependence. Exhibit 16.4 shows for periods 1 through 4 the cash flow $CF_i(\langle r, P\rangle)$ calculated as just described (and shown as principal and interest combined) as well as the value of subsequent cash flow $V_i(\langle r, P\rangle)$ (shown just below the cash flow) for each combination of r and P.

EXHIBIT 16.4 $CF_i(\cdot)$ and $V_i(\cdot)$ for the IAN

		Amount Outstanding			
		0	25	50	100
Period 1	6.902%	0.000	1.500	3.000	6.000
		0.000	24.381	48.732	97.515
	5.113	0.000	1.500	3.000	6.000
		0.000	25.211	50.393	101.024
Period 2	7.950	0.000	1.500	3.000	6.000
		0.000	24.127	48.253	96.506
	5.889	0.000	26.500	28.000	56.000
		0.000	0.000	24.939	49.986
	4.363	0.000	26.500	53.000	81.000
		0.000	0.000	0.000	25.392
Period 3	9.169	0.000	1.500	3.000	6.000
		0.000	24.274	48.549	97.097
	6.792	0.000	1.500	3.000	6.000
		0.000	24.815	49.629	99.258
	5.032	0.000	26.500	28.000	56.000
		0.000	0.000	25.230	50.461
	3.728	0.000	26.500	53.000	81.000
		0.000	0.000	0.000	25.548
Period 4	10.588	0.000	26.500	53.000	106.000
		0.000	0.000	0.000	0.000
	7.844	0.000	26.500	53.000	106.000
		0.000	0.000	0.000	0.000
	5.811	0.000	26.500	53.000	106.000
		0.000	0.000	0.000	0.000
	4.305	0.000	26.500	53.000	106.000
		0.000	0.000	0.000	0.000
	3.189	0.000	26.500	53.000	106.000
		0.000	0.000	0.000	0.000

We reiterate that $V_4(\langle r, P\rangle)=0$ for all r and P since there is no cash flow after year 4. Since the IAN matures in period 4, the cash flow is simply the sum of the amount outstanding and interest on that amount—a calculation that is independent of the 1-year rate at period 4. For example, the period 4 cash flow corresponding to state $\langle 4.305, 25\rangle$ is 25.0 + 1.5 = 26.5.

The situation is more complicated in period 3. Here the amortization schedule and the amount outstanding interact to determine the cash flow. Consider, for example, the calculations corresponding to state ⟨5.032,50⟩. The interest payment of 3 is calculated as 0.06×50.0. Also, since $5.0 \leq 5.032 < 6.0$, 50% of the outstanding amount is prepaid in period 3. This principal payment of 25.0 leaves 25.0 still outstanding—an amount which exceeds the clean-up provision. The state ⟨5.032,50⟩ cash flow is therefore 25.0+3.0=28.0. Next we calculate $V_3(\langle 5.032,50\rangle)$. From a rate of 5.032% in year 3, the stochastic interest rate process moves to either 4.305% or 5.811% in year 4—each possibility with probability ½ (see Exhibit 16.1). Since 50.0 of principal was outstanding (before the period 3 payment) and 25.0 is paid off in period 3, the amount outstanding changes to 25.0. Thus, from state ⟨5.032,50⟩ in period 3, one moves to either ⟨4.305,25⟩ or ⟨5.811,25⟩ in year 4 with each possibility having probability ½. We therefore have, using equation (6) and the period 4 results in Exhibit 16.4,

$$V_3(\langle 5.032, 50\rangle) = \frac{1}{1.05032}[0.5(26.5 + 0.0) + 0.5(26.5 + 0.0)] = 25.230$$

Compare this with the analogous calculations for state ⟨5.032,25⟩ in period 3. The interest cash flow is $0.06 \times 25.0 = 1.5$. The principal payment specified by the amortization schedule is again 50% of the amount outstanding which results in a payment of $12.5 = 0.5 \times 25.0$. This would leave only 12.5 remaining outstanding, however, so the clean-up provision requires that the entire amount of 25.0 be retired leaving nothing outstanding. Thus, from state ⟨5.032,25⟩ in period 3, one moves to either ⟨4.305,0⟩ or ⟨5.811,0⟩ in period 4, with probability ½. Hence

$$V_3(\langle 5.032, 25\rangle) = \frac{1}{1.05032}[0.5(0.0 + 0.0) + 0.5(0.0 + 0.0)] = 0.0$$

The calculations in period 2 are analogous. For example, in state ⟨5.889,100⟩, the principal payment is 50.0 generating a cash flow of 6.0+50.0=56.0 and leaving 50.0 remaining outstanding. Hence one moves from state ⟨5.889,100⟩ in period 2 to either ⟨5.032,50⟩ or ⟨6.792,50⟩ in period 3, each with equal likelihood. Thus

$$\begin{aligned} V_2(\langle 5.889, 100\rangle) &= \frac{1}{1.05889}[0.5(28.0 + 25.230) + 0.5(3.0 + 49.629)] \\ &= 49.986 \end{aligned}$$

Similarly, in period 1, one moves from state ⟨5.113,100⟩ to either ⟨4.363,100⟩ or ⟨5.889,100⟩ in period 2, each with equal likelihood. Thus, $CF_1(\langle 5.113,100\rangle) = 0.06 \times 100.0$ (plus 0 principal) and

$$\begin{aligned} V_1(\langle 5.113, 100\rangle) &= \frac{1}{1.05113}[0.5(81.0 + 25.392) + 0.5(56.0 + 49.986)] \\ &= 101.024 \end{aligned}$$

Finally, at time 0 (not shown in Exhibit 16.4), there is only today's state ⟨6.000, 100⟩ to calculate. From this state we move to either ⟨5.113,100⟩ or ⟨6.902,100⟩, each with probability ½. We therefore have

$$\begin{aligned} V_0(1) = V_0(\langle 6.000, 100\rangle) &= \frac{1}{1.06}[0.5(6.0 + 101.024) + 0.5(6.0 + 97.515)] \\ &= 99.311 \end{aligned}$$

This agrees, as required, with the result obtained via the Monte Carlo analysis.

Selecting the Necessary State Space

As we previously observed, only the amounts in the list {0,25,50,100} can be outstanding at any point in time. This is because the IAN starts with 100.0 outstanding and this list is closed under the rules of principal amortization (the amortization schedule and the clean-up provision). (For example, if we amortize 50% of 50.0 we get 25.0 outstanding, another number in the list.) In general, it may not be so easy to construct an exhaustive list of possible states or, commonly, the list of possible states may be very large. A very effective numerical procedure is to partition the range of the state space (in this case, the range is from 0 to 100 outstanding) into a manageable number of "buckets," for example: 0, 20–30, 30–40, ..., 90–100. Sometimes a surprisingly small number of buckets can lead to a very good approximation of the precise answer. We illustrate this technique with the periodic cap in the next section.

Notice also that not all the states in each period can be reached. For example, in periods 1 and 2 only those states with 100.0 outstanding are reached. This is because the lock-out provision prevents any amortization until year 2. Thus, even in year 2, the amount outstanding prior to that year's amortization must be 100.0. In Exhibit 16.4 we have highlighted the region of each period's state space that is actually reachable.

From the standpoint of computational efficiency, it may be better to first pass *forward* through the lattice to determine which states are actually reachable. Then, during the recursive process described above, it is only necessary to calculate the CF_i and V_i values for those states that are flagged as reachable in the first pass. In our IAN example, this would result in substantial savings. On the other hand, in some situations, this forward pass may take more time than it saves. It may be better to compromise and avoid only some of the unused state space by (non-time-consuming) ad hoc reasoning. In the case of the IAN, for example, the unnecessary states in periods 1 and 2 could be avoided simply by recognizing the effects of the lock-out provision. The best computational strategy will certainly depend on the application.

PERIODIC CAPS

In this final section we subject a floating-rate note with an embedded periodic cap to similar analyses. We illustrate with this application both the bucketing and forward pass numerical procedures described above. Specifically, consider a 4-year FRN that, for ease of exposition, pays interest annually. Its initial rate of interest is 6%—today's 1-year risk-free rate. Each year, the note's rate of interest resets to the new 1-year risk-free rate subject to the constraint that the rate is not permitted to increase (a very strong periodic cap!). In year 4, the note makes a final interest rate payment (of at most 6% due to the periodic cap) and returns the original principal (which we again take to be 100.0). We study this instrument in the same yield environment as before: a flat 6% term structure with a 15% volatility. Exhibit 16.1 again represents the underlying interest rate process.

Valuation via Monte Carlo

Consider again the interest rate path $\omega = (- - - -)$ through the lattice in Exhibit 16.1:

		year 1		year 2		year 3		year 4
6.000%	→	5.113%	→	4.363%	→	3.728%	→	3.189%

Since the 1-year yield decreases steadily along this path, the periodic cap has no impact. The capped FRN behaves just as an uncapped FRN producing the following sequence of cash flow:

year 1	year 2	year 3	year 4
6.000	5.113	4.363	103.728

resulting in the PV calculation:

$$\begin{aligned} PV(----) &= 103.728/1.03728/1.04363/1.05113/1.06 \\ &\quad + 4.363/1.04363/1.05113/1.06 \\ &\quad + 5.113/1.05113/1.06 + 6.0/1.06 \\ &= 100.000 \end{aligned}$$

It is not surprising that for this choice of ω we have a path-dependent present value of exactly 100.000, since the security is always paying a rate of interest equal to the discount rate.

In the scenario corresponding to ω = (+ + + +), which unfolds as follows:

		year 1		year 2		year 3		year 4
6.000%	→	6.902%	→	7.950%	→	9.169%	→	10.588%

the situation is very different. In each year, the periodic cap is binding, preventing the interest rate from increasing. The resulting sequence of cash flow is therefore:

year 1		year 2		year 3		year 4
6.000	→	6.000	→	6.000	→	106.000

which produces the result $PV(\omega) = 95.237$.

Exhibit 16.5 shows the same analysis for all 16 paths through the lattice. Since the paths are all equally likely, the arithmetic average of the path-dependent present values yields the value of the capped FRN. This number is 98.343. Noting that the value of the uncapped FRN is 100.000 (this follows since, in every path, the uncapped FRN is always paying an interest rate equal to the discount rate), we deduce that the value of the periodic cap (to the issuer) is 100.000 – 98.343 = 1.657. As with the IAN, this is an exact calculation representing an exhaustive sampling of the 16 paths through the lattice. In practice, of course, an exhaustive sampling would be impossible and valuing a periodic cap with this approach would require true Monte Carlo path sampling.

Exhibit 16.5 reveals the path-dependent nature of the capped FRN. In particular, the six paths that end in year 4 at the interest rate state ⟨5.881⟩ (i.e., paths with two +'s and two –'s) produce five different cash flow amounts corresponding to that state. Notice also that the periodic cap behaves very differently from a straight cap at 6% (see, for example, the path ω = (– + – +)).

Recursive Valuation

Finally, we use a recursive procedure to value the capped FRN and hence the periodic cap itself. In this example, the non-stochastic state variable that we couple with the stochastic process governing the 1-year risk-free rate is simply the current interest rate that the capped FRN is paying, a number which we call *C*. At any period a state is denoted by $\langle r, C \rangle$, where *C* takes on values in

$$C = \{3.728, 4.363, 5.032, 5.113, 5.889, 6.000\}$$

and *r* is the state-dependent 1-year risk-free rate. We remark that only in year 4 are all six possibilities for C attainable. In our simple example, C is quickly obtained from a glance at Exhibit 16.5. As previously mentioned, in general it may be impractical to explicitly calculate the state space or its size may render the calculations intractable. A numerical shortcut is necessary.

Bucketing and the Forward Pass

We illustrate the bucketing procedure described above by crudely *assuming* that C takes on one of the four values in

$$C = \{3.000, 4.000, 5.000, 6.000\}$$

EXHIBIT 16.5 Path-by-Path Analysis of the Capped FRN

ω	Year 1	Year 2	Year 3	Year 4	*PV*(ω)
(++++)	6.000	6.000	6.000	106.000	95.237
(+++−)	6.000	6.000	6.000	106.000	95.237
(++−+)	6.000	6.000	6.000	106.000	97.004
(++−−)	6.000	6.000	6.000	106.000	97.004
(+−++)	6.000	6.000	5.889	105.889	98.499
(+−+−)	6.000	6.000	5.889	105.889	98.499
(+−−+)	6.000	6.000	5.889	105.032	99.204
(+−−−)	6.000	6.000	5.889	105.032	99.204
(−+++)	6.000	5.113	5.113	105.113	98.010
(−++−)	6.000	5.113	5.113	105.113	98.010
(−+−+)	6.000	5.113	5.113	105.032	99.342
(−+−−)	6.000	5.113	5.113	105.032	99.342
(−−++)	6.000	5.113	4.363	104.363	99.452
(−−+−)	6.000	5.113	4.363	104.363	99.452
(−−−+)	6.000	5.113	4.363	103.728	100.000
(−−−−)	6.000	5.113	4.363	103.728	100.000

a numerical simplification that will result in obtaining only an approximate solution. (We think of these numbers as buckets into which intermediate values are placed.) In period 4, for example, r assumes one of five possible values each of which is partitioned by the four states of C, yielding 20 states of the world.

Exhibit 16.6 shows the forward pass analysis that is used to flag the subset of states in each period that are actually reachable. The period 0 analysis is straightforward. Referring to today's state simply as ⟨6.000⟩ (today's value of r), the value of r moves from 6.000 to either 5.113 or 6.902 (refer again to Exhibit 16.1) and in either case the period 1 value of C will be 6.000 (the capped FRN's initial interest rate). Hence only the states ⟨5.113, 6.000⟩ and ⟨6.902,6.000⟩ are reachable in period 1. The period 1 analysis illustrates a ramification of the bucketing approximation. From state ⟨5.113, 6.000⟩ the value of r moves to either 4.363 or 5.889. The value of C, however, should change to 5.113 (because the FRN is permitted to reset downward) which is a number not present in $\hat{C}$. Numerically, we will interpolate between what happens when C=5.000 and C=6.000 in period 2. Therefore, to calculate values in state ⟨5.113, 6.000⟩ in period 1 we must have already calculated values in states ⟨4.363,5.000⟩, ⟨4.363,6.000⟩, ⟨5.889,5.000⟩, and ⟨5.889,6.000⟩ in period 2. We therefore flag these four states as reachable. From state ⟨6.902,6.000⟩ in period 1, in contrast, the value of C is not permitted to reset upward to 6.902 and only states ⟨5.889,6.000⟩ and ⟨7.950,6.000⟩ are reachable in period 2. We collect the (five) states in period 2 that it is possible to reach from the reachable states in period 1 and repeat the analysis at each of these states. Moving forward period-by-period confirms that we need only calculate values for the portion of the state space in Exhibit 16.7 where numbers are displayed.

The Recursive Valuation Pass

Finally, we move backward through the lattice calculating the relevant values of $CF_i(\cdot)$ and $V_i(\cdot)$ (see Exhibit 16.7—calculations start at the bottom).

In period 4 (at maturity), $V_4(\cdot)=0$ as usual. The cash flow at maturity is just 100.000 (the return of principal) plus C (the current interest rate that the FRN is paying). This produces the period 4 results. For example: $CF_4(\langle 7.844,\ 5.000\rangle) = 100.0 + 5.0 = 105.0$. In periods 1 through 3, $CF_i(\langle r, C\rangle)=C$ since the FRN repays principal only at maturity.

We verify three calculations of $V_i(\cdot)$. First, from state ⟨5.032, 5.000⟩ in period 3, the value of r moves to either 4.305 or 5.811 with equal likelihood. The value of C does not change in this case since 5.032 > 5.000. So from state ⟨5.032, 5.000⟩ in period 3, we branch to either ⟨4.305, 5.000⟩ or ⟨5.811, 5.000⟩ in period 4 with equal likelihood and we have

EXHIBIT 16.6 State Transitions for the Capped FRN

Period	From	To
Today	⟨6.000⟩	⟨5.113, 6.000⟩, ⟨6.902, 6.000⟩
1	⟨5.113, 6.000⟩	⟨4.363, 5.000⟩, ⟨4.363, 6.000⟩, ⟨5.889, 5.000⟩, ⟨5.889, 6.000⟩
	⟨6.902, 6.000⟩	⟨5.889, 6.000⟩, ⟨7.950, 6.000⟩
2	⟨4.363, 5.000⟩	⟨3.728, 4.000⟩, ⟨3.728, 5.000⟩, ⟨5.032, 4.000⟩, ⟨5.032, 5.000⟩
	⟨4.363, 6.000⟩	⟨3.728, 4.000⟩, ⟨3.728, 5.000⟩, ⟨5.032, 4.000⟩, ⟨5.032, 5.000⟩
	⟨5.889, 5.000⟩	⟨5.032, 5.000⟩, ⟨6.792, 5.000⟩
	⟨5.889, 6.000⟩	⟨5.032, 5.000⟩, ⟨5.032, 6.000⟩, ⟨6.792, 5.000⟩, ⟨6.792, 6.000⟩
	⟨7.950, 6.000⟩	⟨6.792, 6.000⟩, ⟨9.169, 6.000⟩
3	⟨3.728, 4.000⟩	⟨3.189, 3.000⟩, ⟨3.189, 4.000⟩, ⟨4.305, 3.000⟩, ⟨4.305, 4.000⟩
	⟨3.728, 5.000⟩	⟨3.189, 3.000⟩, ⟨3.189, 4.000⟩, ⟨4.305, 3.000⟩, ⟨4.305, 4.000⟩
	⟨5.032, 4.000⟩	⟨4.305, 4.000⟩, ⟨5.811, 4.000⟩
	⟨5.032, 5.000⟩	⟨4.305, 5.000⟩, ⟨5.811, 5.000⟩
	⟨5.032, 6.000⟩	⟨4.305, 5.000⟩, ⟨4.305, 6.000⟩, ⟨5.811, 5.000⟩, ⟨5.811, 6.000⟩
	⟨6.792, 5.000⟩	⟨5.811, 5.000⟩, ⟨ 7.844, 5.000⟩
	⟨6.792, 6.000⟩	⟨5.811, 6.000⟩, ⟨7.844, 6.000⟩
	⟨9.169, 6.000⟩	⟨7.844, 6.000⟩, ⟨10.588, 6.000⟩

EXHIBIT 16.7 $CF_i(\cdot)$ and $V_i(\cdot)$ for the Capped FRN

		Current Coupon Rate			
		3.000	4.000	5.000	6.000
Period 1	6.902%				6.000
					97.334
	5.113				6.000
					99.139
Period 2	7.950				6.000
					96.505
	5.889			5.000	6.000
				98.354	99.599
	4.363			5.000	6.000
				99.695	99.695

EXHIBIT 16.7 (Continued)

		Current Coupon Rate			
		3.000	4.000	5.000	6.000
Period 3	9.169				6.000
					97.097
	6.792			5.000	6.000
				98.322	99.258
	5.032		4.000	5.000	6.000
			99.017	99.970	100.000
	3.728		4.000	5.000	
			100.000	100.000	
Period 4	10.588				106.000
					0.000
	7.844			105.000	106.000
				0.000	0.000
	5.811		104.000	105.000	106.000
			0.000	0.000	0.000
	4.305	103.000	104.000	105.000	106.000
		0.000	0.000	0.000	0.000
	3.189	103.000	104.000		
		0.000	0.000		

$$
\begin{aligned}
&V_3(\langle 5.032, 5.000\rangle) \\
&= \frac{1}{1.05032}[0.5(CF_4(\langle 4.305, 5.000\rangle) + V_4(\langle 4.305, 5.000\rangle)) \\
&\quad + 0.5(CF_4(\langle 5.881, 5.000\rangle) + V_4(\langle 5.881, 5.000\rangle))] \\
&= \frac{1}{1.05032}[0.5(105.000 + 0.0) + 0.5(105.000 + 0.0)] \\
&= 99.970
\end{aligned}
$$

Next, from state $\langle 4.363, 5.000\rangle$ in period 2, the value of r moves to either 3.728 or 5.032, each with probability ½. The value of C should change to 4.363 since 4.363 < 5.000, but this number is not in $\hat{C}$. If it *were*, we would calculate

$$
\begin{aligned}
&V_2(\langle 4.363, 5.000\rangle) \\
&= \frac{1}{1.04363}[0.5(CF_3(\langle 3.728, 4.363\rangle) + V_3(\langle 3.728, 4.363\rangle)) \\
&\quad + 0.5(CF_3(\langle 5.032, 4.363\rangle) + V_3(\langle 5.032, 4.363\rangle))]
\end{aligned} \tag{10}
$$

However, we have calculated neither $V_3(\langle 3.728, 4.363\rangle)$ nor $V_3(\langle 5.032, 4.363\rangle)$ nor the corresponding values for $CF_3(\langle \cdot, 4.363\rangle)$, so we estimate them by interpolating between values that we have calculated. In particular,

$$
\begin{aligned}
&V_3(\langle 3.728, 4.363\rangle) \\
&\quad \approx 0.637 V_3(\langle 3.728, 4.000\rangle) + 0.363 V_3(\langle 3.728, 5.000\rangle) \\
&\quad = 100.000
\end{aligned}
$$

and

$$
\begin{aligned}
&V_3(\langle 5.032, 4.363\rangle) \\
&\quad \approx 0.637 V_3(\langle 5.032, 4.000\rangle) + 0.363 V_3(\langle 5.032, 5.000\rangle) \\
&\quad = 99.363
\end{aligned}
$$

while both interpolated values for $CF_3(\langle \cdot, 4.363\rangle)$ are, not surprisingly, 4.363. Setting these estimates into equation (10) gives $V_2(\langle 4.363, 5.000\rangle) = 99.695$.

Finally, today's value of the capped FRN is calculated from the period 1 values by

$$
V_0(\langle 6.000\rangle) = \frac{1}{1.06}[0.5(6.0 + 99.139) + 0.5(6.0 + 97.334)] = 98.336
$$

which puts the value of the periodic cap at 100.000 – 98.336 = 1.664. As predicted, this is not in precise agreement with the exhaustive path-by-path analysis that produced the value of 98.343 for the capped FRN and 1.657 for the periodic cap. This is because we bucketed the state space of C into the four quantities in $\hat{C}$. By increasing the number of states (using more, and smaller, buckets), the degree of error is reduced. For example, when we take

$$
\hat{C} = \{3.000, 3.500, 4.000, 4.500, 5.000, 5.500, 6.000\}
$$

the recursive process yields 98.341 (1.659 for the periodic cap).

CONCLUSION

We have worked through two simple numerical examples that illustrate how non-stochastic state variables may be coupled with a stochastic interest rate process to value path-dependent fixed-income securities using recursive techniques. In our 4-period examples, of course, this technique offers little, if any, improvement over exhaustive path sampling. In more realistic settings, however, recursion is generally much more efficient than Monte Carlo path sampling.

Path dependence occurs in many forms and with varying degrees of complexity. Sometimes it is necessary to couple more than one state variable to the stochastic process. Consider, for example, a hybrid of the IAN and capped FRN. Such a note would pay down principal in accordance with a rate sensitive amortization schedule, while paying a rate of interest that resets periodically but that is permitted to increase only a limited amount with each reset. Generalizing the notation of our previous sections, a state would be described as $\langle r, P, C\rangle$ where r is the stochastic risk-free rate, P is the amount of the note currently outstanding, and C is its current coupon rate.

CHAPTER 17

Monte Carlo Simulation/OAS Approach to Valuing Residential Real Estate-Backed Securities

Frank J. Fabozzi, Ph.D., CFA
Adjunct Professor of Finance
School of Management
Yale University

Scott F. Richard, DBA
Portfolio Manager
Miller, Anderson & Sherrerd

David S. Horowitz
Portfolio Manager
Miller, Anderson & Sherrerd

The traditional approach to the valuation of fixed-income securities is to calculate yield—the yield to maturity, the yield to call for a callable bond, and the cash flow yield for a real estate-backed security—and them determine a nominal spread relative to a benchmark Treasury security. A superior approach employs the option-adjusted spread (OAS) methodology. Our objective in this chapter is to describe the Monte Carlo simulation/OAS approach to valuation and apply it to real estate-backed securities—agency mortgage-backed securities and credit sensitive mortgage-backed securities (i.e., nonagency mortgage-backed securities and real estate-backed asset-backed securities).

In this chapter, we describe the theoretical foundations of this approach to valuation, the inputs and assumptions that go into the development of a Monte Carlo simulation/OAS model, and the output of the model, which in addition to the theoretical value/OAS, also includes the option-adjusted duration and option-adjusted convexity. Because the user of a Monte Carlo simulation/OAS model is exposed to modeling risk, it is necessary to test the sensitivity of these numbers to changes in the assumptions.

Valuation modeling for multi-class structures such as agency collateralized mortgage obligations (CMOs) and agency mortgage strips (interest only and principal only securities) is similar to valuation modeling for passthroughs, although the difficulties are amplified because the issuer has sliced and diced both the prepayment risk and the interest rate risk into smaller pieces called *tranches*. The sensitivity of the passthrough securities from which a multi-class structure backed by agency collateral is created to these two risks is not transmitted equally to every tranche. Some of the tranches wind up more sensitive to prepayment risk and interest rate risk than the collateral, while some of them are much less sensitive.

Credit sensitive mortgage-backed securities include a senior tranche and one or more junior or subordinated tranches. For such securities, the tranches are exposed to different degrees of credit risk. If the senior tranches are carved up, they are exposed to different degrees of prepayment risk. Even in the absence of the tranching of prepayment risk for the senior tranche, prepayment risk exists because in the typical structure there is a shifting interest mechanism. While the purpose of this mechanism is to prevent the senior interest in the structure to grow by shifting a larger share of the prepayments to the senior tranche in the early years, the net effect is that this form of credit enhancement increases prepayment risk to the senior tranches.

The objective of the money manager is to figure out how the OAS of the collateral, or, equivalently, the value of the collateral, gets transmitted to the tranches. More specifically, the objective is to find out where the value goes and where the risk goes so that the money manager can identify the tranches with low risk and high value: the ones he or she wants to buy. The good news is that this combination usually exists in every deal. The bad news is that in every deal there are usually tranches with low OAS, low value, and high risk.

STATIC VALUATION

Using OAS to value mortgages is a dynamic technique in that many scenarios for future interest rates are analyzed. Static valuation analyzes only a single interest rate scenario, usually assuming that the yield curve remains unchanged. Static valuation results in two measures, average life and static spread, which we review below.

Average Life

The *average life* of a mortgage-backed security is the weighted average time to receipt of principal payments (scheduled payments and projected prepayments). The formula for the average life is:

$$\frac{1(\text{Principal at time 1}) + \ldots + T(\text{Principal at time } T)}{12(\text{Total principal received})}$$

where T is the number of months.

In order to calculate average life, an investor must either assume a prepayment rate for the mortgage security being analyzed or use a prepayment model. By calculating the average life at various prepayment rates, the investor can gain some feeling for the stability of the security's cash flows. For example, a planned amortization class (PAC) bond's average life will not change within the PAC bands, but may shorten significantly if the prepayment rate exceeds the upper band. By examining the average life at prepayment rates greater than the upper band, an investor can judge some of the PAC's risks. With a prepayment model available, the average life of a mortgage security can be calculated by changing the mortgage refinancing rate. As the refinancing rate rises, the prepayment model will slow the prepayment rate and thus cause the bond's average life to extend. Conversely, if the refinancing rate is lowered, the model will cause prepayments to rise and shorten the average life.

Static Spread

One of the standard measures in evaluating any mortgage-backed security is the cash flow yield, or simply "yield." The yield spread, sometimes referred to as the *nominal spread*, is found by spreading the yield to the average life on the interpolated Treasury yield curve. This practice is improper for an amortizing bond even in the absence of interest rate volatility.

What should be done instead is to calculate what is called the *static spread*. This is the yield spread in a static scenario (i.e., no volatility of interest rates) of the bond over the entire theoretical Treasury spot rate curve, not a single point on the Treasury yield curve. The magnitude of the difference between the nominal spread and the static yield depends on the steepness of the yield curve: The steeper the curve, the greater the difference between the two values. In a relatively flat interest rate environment, the difference between the nominal spread and the static spread will be small.

There are two ways to compute the static spread. One way is to use today's yield curve to discount future cash flows and keep the mortgage refinancing rate fixed at today's mortgage rate. Since the mortgage refinancing rate is fixed, the investor can usually specify a reasonable prepayment rate for the life of the security. Using this prepayment rate, the bond's future cash flow can be estimated. Use of this approach to calculate the static spread recognizes different prices today of dollars to be delivered at future dates. This results in the proper discounting of cash flows while keeping the mortgage rate fixed. Effectively, today's prices indicate what the future discount rates will be, but the best estimates of future rates are today's rates.

The second way to calculate the static spread allows the mortgage rate to go up the curve as implied by the forward interest rates. This procedure is sometimes called the *zero volatility OAS*. In this case, a prepayment model is needed to determine the vector of future prepayment rates implied by the vector of future refinancing rates. A money manager using static spread should determine which approach is used in the calculation.

DYNAMIC VALUATION MODELING

A technique known as simulation is used to value complex securities such as passthroughs and CMOs. Simulation is used because the monthly cash flows are path-dependent. This means that the cash flows received this month are determined not only by the current and future interest rate levels, but also by the path that interest rates took to get to the current level.

For a passthrough security, prepayments are path-dependent because this month's prepayment rate depends on whether there have been prior opportunities to refinance since the underlying mortgages were issued. For a CMO tranche, there are two sources of path dependency. The first is the source just described for passthroughs (i.e., the collateral backing an agency structure). The second is that cash flow to be received this month by a CMO tranche depends on the outstanding balances of the other tranches in the deal. We need the history of prepayments to calculate these balances.

Conceptually, the valuation of passthrough securities using the simulation method is simple. In practice, however, it is very complex. The simulation involves generating a set of cash flows based on simulated future mortgage refinancing rates, which in turn imply simulated prepayment rates.

The typical model that Wall Street firms and commercial vendors use to generate these random interest rate paths takes as input today's term structure of interest rates and a volatility assumption. The term structure of interest rates is the theoretical spot rate (or zero coupon) curve implied by today's Treasury securities. The volatility assumption determines the dispersion of future interest rates in the simulation. The simulations should be normalized so that the average simulated price of a zero coupon Treasury bond equals today's actual price.

Each Monte Carlo simulation/OAS model has its own model of the evolution of future interest rates and its own volatility assumptions. Until recently, there have been few significant differences in the interest rate models of dealer firms and vendors of analytical systems, although their volatility assumptions can be significantly different.

The random paths of interest rates should be generated from an arbitrage-free model of the future term structure of interest rates. By arbitrage-free it is meant that the model replicates today's term structure of interest rates, an input of the model, and that for all future dates there is no possible arbitrage within the model.

The simulation works by generating many scenarios of future interest rate paths. In each month of the scenario, a monthly interest rate and a mortgage refinancing rate are generated. The monthly interest rates are used to discount the projected cash flows in the scenario. The mortgage refinancing rate is needed to determine the cash flow because it represents the opportunity cost the mortgagor is facing at that time.

If the refinancing rates are high relative to the mortgagor's original coupon rate, the mortgagor will have less incentive to refinance, or even a disincentive (i.e., the homeowner will avoid moving in order to avoid refinancing). If the refinancing rate is low relative to the mortgagor's original coupon rate, the mortgagor has an incentive to refinance.

For agency collateral, prepayments are projected by feeding the refinancing rate and loan characteristics, such as age, into a prepayment model. Given the projected prepayments, the cash flow along an interest rate path can be determined. For credit-sensitive products, the prepayment model includes both voluntary and involuntary prepayments (i.e., defaults). The prepayment model for collateral backing credit-sensitive products takes into account default rates, recovery rates, and the time it takes to recover principal from defaulted mortgages.

To make this more concrete, consider a newly issued mortgage passthrough security with a maturity of 360 months. Exhibit 17.1 shows N simulated interest rate path scenarios. Each scenario consists of a path of 360 simulated 1-month future interest rates. Just how many paths should be generated is explained later. Exhibit 17.2 shows the paths of simulated mortgage refinancing rates corresponding to the scenarios shown in Exhibit 17.1. Assuming these mortgage refinancing rates, the cash flow for each scenario path is shown in Exhibit 17.3.

EXHIBIT 17.1 Simulated Paths of 1-Month Future Interest Rates

	Interest Rate Path Number						
Month	1	2	3	...	n		N
1	$f_1(1)$	$f_1(2)$	$f_1(3)$	...	$f_1(n)$	...	$f_1(N)$
2	$f_2(1)$	$f_2(2)$	$f_2(3)$	...	$f_2(n)$	...	$f_2(N)$
3	$f_3(1)$	$f_3(2)$	$f_3(3)$	...	$f_3(n)$	...	$f_3(N)$
t	$f_t(1)$	$f_t(2)$	$f_t(3)$	...	$f_t(n)$	...	$f_t(N)$
358	$f_{358}(1)$	$f_{358}(2)$	$f_{358}(3)$	...	$f_{358}(n)$	...	$f_{358}(N)$
359	$f_{359}(1)$	$f_{359}(2)$	$f_{359}(3)$	...	$f_{359}(n)$	...	$f_{359}(N)$
360	$f_{360}(1)$	$f_{360}(2)$	$f_{360}(3)$	...	$f_{360}(n)$	...	$f_{360}(N)$

Notation:

$f_t(n)$ = one-month future interest rate for month t on path n
N = total number of interest rate paths

EXHIBIT 17.2 Simulated Paths of Mortgage Refinancing Rates

	Interest Rate Path Number						
Month	1	2	3	...	n	...	N
1	$r_1(1)$	$r_1(2)$	$r_1(3)$	...	$r_1(n)$	...	$r_1(N)$
2	$r_2(1)$	$r_2(2)$	$r_2(3)$	...	$r_2(n)$	...	$r_2(N)$
3	$r_3(1)$	$r_3(2)$	$r_3(3)$	...	$r_3(n)$	...	$r_3(N)$
t	$r_t(1)$	$r_t(2)$	$r_t(3)$	...	$r_t(n)$	...	$r_t(N)$
358	$r_{358}(1)$	$r_{358}(2)$	$r_{358}(3)$	...	$r_{358}(n)$	...	$r_{358}(N)$
359	$r_{359}(1)$	$r_{359}(2)$	$r_{359}(3)$	...	$r_{359}(n)$	...	$r_{359}(N)$
360	$r_{360}(1)$	$r_{360}(2)$	$r_{360}(3)$	...	$r_{360}(n)$	...	$r_{360}(N)$

Notation:

$r_t(n)$ = mortgage refinancing rate for month t on path n
N = total number of interest rate paths

EXHIBIT 17.3 Simulated Cash Flow on Each of the Interest Rate Paths

	Interest Rate Path Number						
Month	1	2	3	...	n	...	N
1	$C_1(1)$	$C_1(2)$	$C_1(3)$	...	$C_1(n)$	...	$C_1(N)$
2	$C_2(1)$	$C_2(2)$	$C_2(3)$	...	$C_2(n)$	...	$C_2(N)$
3	$C_3(1)$	$C_3(2)$	$C_3(3)$	...	$C_3(n)$	...	$C_3(N)$
t	$C_t(1)$	$C_t(2)$	$C_t(3)$	...	$C_t(n)$	...	$C_t(N)$
358	$C_{358}(1)$	$C_{358}(2)$	$C_{358}(3)$	...	$C_{358}(n)$	...	$C_{358}(N)$
359	$C_{359}(1)$	$C_{359}(2)$	$C_{359}(3)$	...	$C_{359}(n)$	...	$C_{359}(N)$
360	$C_{360}(1)$	$C_{360}(2)$	$C_{360}(3)$	...	$C_{360}(n)$	...	$C_{360}(N)$

Notation:

$C_t(n)$ = cash flow for month t on path n

N = total number of interest rate paths

Calculating the Present Value for a Scenario Interest Rate Path

Given the cash flow on an interest rate path, its present value can be calculated. The discount rate for determining the present value is the simulated spot rate for each month on the interest rate path plus an appropriate spread. The spot rate on a path can be determined from the simulated future monthly rates. The relationship that holds between the simulated spot rate for month T on path n and the simulated future 1-month rates is:

$$z_T(n) = \{[1 + f_1(n)][1 + f_2(n)]...[1 + f_{2T}(n)]\}^{1/T} - 1$$

where

$z_T(n)$ = simulated spot rate for month T on path n

$f_j(n)$ = simulated future 1-month rate for month j on path n

Consequently, the interest rate path for the simulated future 1-month rates can be converted to the interest rate path for the simulated monthly spot rates as shown in Exhibit 17.4. Therefore, the present value of the cash flow for month T on interest rate path n discounted at the simulated spot rate for month T plus some spread is:

$$PV[C_T(n)] = \frac{C_T(n)}{[1 + z_T(n) + K]^{1/T}}$$

where

$PV[C_T(n)]$ = present value of cash flow for month T on path n
$C_T(n)$ = cash flow for month T on path n
$z_T(n)$ = spot rate for month T on path n
K = spread

The present value for path n is the sum of the present value of the cash flow for each month on path n. That is,

$$PV[Path(n)] = PV[C_1(n)] + PV[C_2(n)] + \ldots + PV[C_{360}(n)]$$

where PV[Path(n)] is the present value of interest rate path n.

The option-adjusted spread is the spread, K, that when added to all the spot rates on all interest rate paths will make the average present value of the paths equal to the observed market price (plus accrued interest). Mathematically, OAS is the spread K that will satisfy the following condition:

EXHIBIT 17.4 Simulated Paths of Monthly Spot Rates

	Interest Rate Path Number						
Month	1	2	3	...	n	...	N
1	$z_1(1)$	$z_1(2)$	$z_1(3)$	...	$z_1(n)$	...	$z_1(N)$
2	$z_2(1)$	$z_2(2)$	$z_2(3)$	...	$z_2(n)$	...	$z_2(N)$
3	$z_3(1)$	$z_3(2)$	$z_3(3)$	...	$z_3(n)$	...	$z_3(N)$
t	$z_t(1)$	$z_t(2)$	$z_t(3)$	...	$z_t(n)$	...	$z_t(N)$
358	$z_{358}(1)$	$z_{358}(2)$	$z_{358}(3)$	...	$z_{358}(n)$	...	$z_{358}(N)$
359	$z_{359}(1)$	$z_{359}(2)$	$z_{359}(3)$	...	$z_{359}(n)$	...	$z_{359}(N)$
360	$z_{360}(1)$	$z_{360}(2)$	$z_{360}(3)$	...	$z_{360}(n)$	...	$z_{360}(N)$

Notation:

$z_t(n)$ = spot rate for month t on path n
N = total number of interest rate paths

$$\text{Market Price} = \frac{PV[Path(1)] + PV[Path(2)] + \ldots + PV[Path(N)]}{N}$$

where N is the number of interest rate paths.

This procedure for valuing a passthrough is also followed for a tranche of interest within a multi-class structure. The cash flow for each month on each interest rate path is found according to the principal repayment and interest distribution rules of the deal. In order to do this, a structuring model is needed. In any analysis of a tranche within a multi-class structure, one of the major stumbling blocks is getting a good structuring model.

Selecting the Number of Interest Rate Paths

Let's now address the question of the number of scenario paths or repetitions, N, needed to value a security. A typical run will be done for 512 to 1,024 interest rate paths. The scenarios generated using the simulation method look very realistic, and furthermore reproduce today's Treasury curve. By employing this technique, the money manager is effectively saying that Treasuries are fairly priced today and that the objective is to determine whether a specific tranche is rich or cheap relative to Treasuries.

The number of interest rate paths determines how "good" the estimate is, not relative to the truth but relative to the model used. The more paths, the more average spread tends to settle down. It is a statistical sampling problem.

Most models employ some form of *variance reduction* to cut down on the number of sample paths necessary to get a good statistical sample.[1] Variance reduction techniques allow us to obtain price estimates within a tick. By this we mean that if the model is used to generate more scenarios, price estimates from the model will not change by more than a tick. So, for example, if 1,024 paths are used to obtain the estimated price for a tranche, there is little more information to be had from the model by generating more than that number of paths. (For some very sensitive complex tranches, more paths may be needed to estimate prices within one tick.)

To reduce computational time, a statistical methodology has been used by vendors that involves the analysis of a small number of interest rate paths. Basically, the methodology is as follows. A large number of paths of interest rates are generated. These paths can be reduced to a

---

[1] For a discussion of variance reduction, see Phelim P. Boyle, "Options: A Monte Carlo Approach," *Journal of Financial Economics* 4 (1977), pp. 323–338.

small representative number of interest rate paths. These interest rate paths are called *representative paths*. The money manager is typically given the choice of the number of representative paths. The security is then valued on each representative path. The value of the security is then the weighted average of the representative path values. The weight used for a representative path is determined by the percentage of the interest rate paths it represents. This approach is called the *representative path method*.

Interpretation of the OAS

The procedure for determining the OAS is straightforward, although time-consuming. The next question, then, is how to interpret the OAS. Basically, the OAS is used to reconcile value with market price. On the left-hand side of the last equation is the market's statement: the price of a mortgage-backed security or mortgage derivative. The average present value over all the paths on the right-hand side of the equation is the model's output, which we refer to as value.

What a money manager seeks to do is to buy securities whose value is greater than their price. A valuation model such as the one described above allows a money manager to estimate the value of a security, which at this point would be sufficient to determine whether to buy a security. That is, the money manager can say that this bond is 1 point cheap or 2 points cheap, and so on. The model does not stop here, however. Instead, it converts the divergence between price and value into a yield spread measure, as most market participants find it more convenient to think about yield spread than about price differences.

The OAS was developed as a measure of the yield spread that can be used to reconcile dollar differences between value and price. But what is it a "spread" over? In describing the model above, we can see that the OAS is measuring the average spread over the Treasury spot rate curve, not the Treasury yield curve. It is an average spread because the OAS is found by averaging over the interest rate paths for the possible spot rate curves.

While in our illustrations we have used the on-the-run Treasury rates as the benchmark, many funded investors will use LIBOR as the benchmark. To see the impact of the benchmark on the computed OAS, the table below shows the OAS computed in November 1999 for a 15-year 6.5% FNMA TBA passthrough (seasoned and unseasoned) and a 30-year 6.5% FNMA TBA using the on-the-run Treasuries and LIBOR:[2]

[2] This table was reported in the November 16, 1999 issue of PaineWebber's *Mortgage Strategist*, p. 10. The values reported were computed on Bloomberg.

Issue: 6.5% Coupon FNMA TBA	OAS (bps) Benchmark		
	Average Life	Treasuries	LIBOR
15-year unseasoned	5.9 years	70	–10
15-year seasoned (1994 production)	4.0 years	75	1
30-year	9.5 years	87	–2

As can be seen from the table, the selection of the benchmark has a dramatic impact on the computed OAS. It cannot be overemphasized that the user of an OAS number should make sure that the benchmark is known, as well as the volatility assumption.

Option Cost

The implied cost of the option embedded in any mortgage-backed security can be obtained by calculating the difference between the OAS at the assumed volatility of interest rates and the static spread. That is,

$$\text{Option cost} = \text{Static spread} - \text{Option-adjusted spread}$$

The reason that the option cost is measured in this way is as follows. In an environment of no interest rate changes, the investor would earn the static spread. When future interest rates are uncertain, the spread is less, however, because of the homeowner's option to prepay; the OAS reflects the spread after adjusting for this option. Therefore, the option cost is the difference between the spread that would be earned in a static interest rate environment (the static spread) and the spread after adjusting for the homeowner's option.

In general, a tranche's option cost is more stable than its OAS in the face of market movements. This interesting feature is useful in reducing the computational expensive costs of calculating the OAS as the market moves. For small market moves, the OAS of a tranche may be approximated by recalculating the static spread (which is relatively cheap and easy to calculate) and subtracting its option cost.

Other Products of the Model

Other products of the valuation model are option-adjusted duration, option-adjusted convexity, and simulated average life.

Option-Adjusted Duration

In general, duration measures the price sensitivity of a bond to a small change in interest rates. Duration can be interpreted as the approximate percentage change in price for a 100-basis point parallel shift in the yield curve. For example, if a bond's duration is 4, this means a 100-basis point increase in interest rates will result in a price decrease of approximately 4%. A 50-basis point increase in yields will decrease the price by approximately 2%. The smaller the change in basis points, the better the approximated change in price will be.

The duration for any security can be approximated as follows:

$$Duration = \frac{V_{-} - V_{+}}{2V_0\Delta r}$$

where

V_{-} = price if yield is decreased (per \$100 of par value) by Δr
V_{+} = price if yield is increased (per \$100 of par value) by Δr
V_0 = initial price (per \$100 of par value)
Δr = number of basis points change in rates used to calculate V_{-} and V_{+}

The standard measure of duration is modified duration. The limitation of modified duration is that it assumes that if interest rates change, the cash flow does not change. While modified duration is fine for option-free securities such as Treasury bonds, it is inappropriate for mortgage-backed securities, because projected cash flows change as interest rates and prepayments change. When prices in the duration formula are calculated assuming that the cash flow changes when interest rates change, the resulting duration is called *effective duration*.

Effective duration can be computed using an OAS model as follows. First the bond's OAS is found using the current term structure of interest rates. Next the bond is repriced holding OAS constant, but shifting the term structure. Two shifts are used; in one yields are increased, and in the second they are decreased. This produces the two prices, V_{-} and V_{+}, used in the above formula. Effective duration calculated in this way is often referred to as *option-adjusted duration* or *OAS duration*.

The assumption in using modified or effective duration to project the percentage price change is that all interest rates change by the same number of basis points; that is, there is a parallel shift in the yield curve. If the term structure does not change by a parallel shift, then effective duration will not correctly predict the change in a bond's price.

Option-Adjusted Convexity

The convexity measure of a security is the approximate change in price that is not explained by duration. *Positive convexity* means that if yields change by a given number of basis points, the percentage increase in price will be greater than the percentage decrease in price. *Negative convexity* means that if yield changes by a given number of basis points, the percentage increase in price will be less than the percentage decrease in price. That is, for a 100-basis point change in yield:

Type of Convexity	Increase in Price	Decrease in Price
Positive convexity	X%	less than X%
Negative convexity	X%	more than X%

Obviously, positive convexity is a desirable property of a bond. A passthrough security can exhibit either positive or negative convexity, depending on the prevailing mortgage rate relative to the rate on the underlying mortgage loans. When the prevailing mortgage rate is much higher than the mortgage rate on the underlying mortgage loans, the passthrough usually exhibits positive convexity. It usually exhibits negative convexity when the underlying coupon rate is near or above prevailing mortgage refinancing rates.

The convexity of any bond can be approximated using the formula:

$$\frac{V_{+} + V_{-} - 2(V_0)}{2V_0(\Delta r)^2}$$

When the prices used in this formula assume that the cash flows do not change when yields change, the resulting convexity is a good approximation of the standard convexity for an option-free bond. When the prices used in the formula are derived by changing the cash flows (by changing prepayment rates) when yields change, the resulting convexity is called *effective convexity*. Once again, when a Monte Carlo simulation/OAS model is used to obtain the prices, the resulting value is referred to as the *option-adjusted convexity* or *OAS convexity*.

Simulated Average Life

The average life reported in a Monte Carlo simulation/OAS model is the average of the average lives along the interest rate paths. That is, for each interest rate path, there is an average life. The average of these average lives is the average life reported for the model.

Additional information is conveyed by the distribution of the average life. The greater the range and standard deviation of the average life, the more the uncertainty about the tranche's average life.

EXHIBIT 17.5 Diagram of Principal Allocation Structure of FHLMC 1915

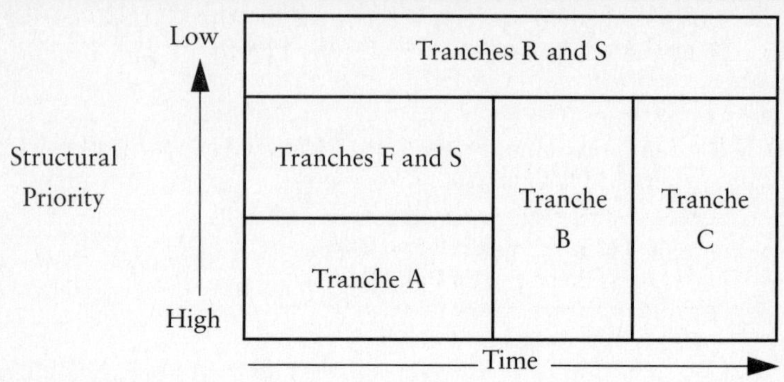

ILLUSTRATIONS

We conclude this chapter by illustrating how to apply the Monte Carlo simulation/OAS model using four actual deals: a plain vanilla structure, a PAC/support structure, and credit sensitive products (a home equity loan deal and a manufactured housing loan deal).[3]

Plain Vanilla Structure

The plain vanilla sequential-pay CMO bond structure in our illustration is FHLMC 1915. A diagram of the principal allocation structure is given in Exhibit 17.5 for six of the tranches. The structure actually includes eight tranches, A, B, C, D, E, F, G, and S, and two residual classes. Tranche F is a floating-rate tranche, and tranche S is an inverse floating rate IO. Tranches D, E, and G are special "exchangeable bonds" which allow for the combination of tranches F and S. The focus of our analysis is on tranches A, B, and C.

The top panel of Exhibit 17.6 shows the OAS and the option cost for the collateral and the five classes in the CMO structure. The OAS for the collateral is 51 basis points. Since the option cost is 67 basis points, the static spread is 118 basis points (51 basis points plus 67 basis points). The weighted-average OAS of all the classes (including the residual) is equal to the OAS of the collateral.

At the time this analysis was performed, March 10, 1998, the Treasury yield curve was not steep. As we noted earlier, in such a yield curve

[3] For a description of the various types of tranches referred to in the illustrations, see Frank J. Fabozzi and Chuck Ramsey, *Collateralized Mortgage Obligations: Structures and Analysis, Third Edition* (New Hope, PA: Frank J. Fabozzi Associates, 1999).

environment the static spread will not differ significantly from the traditionally computed yield spread. Thus, for the three tranches shown in Exhibit 17.6, the static spread is 83 for A, 115 for B, and 116 for C.

EXHIBIT 17.6 OAS Analysis of FHLMC 1915 Classes A, B, and C (As of 3/10/98)
Base Case (Assumes 13% Interest Rate Volatility)

	OAS (in Basis Points)	Option Cost (in Basis Points)
Collateral	51	67
Class		
A	32	51
B	33	82
C	46	70

Prepayments at 80% and 120% of Prepayment Model
(Assumes 13% Interest Rate Volatility)

	New OAS (in Basis Points)		Change in Price per $100 Par (Holding OAS Constant)	
	80%	120%	80%	120%
Collateral	63	40	$0.45	–$0.32
Class				
A	40	23	0.17	–0.13
B	43	22	0.54	–0.43
C	58	36	0.97	–0.63

Interest Rate Volatility of 9% and 17%

	New OAS (in Basis Points)		Change in Price per $100 Par (Holding OAS Constant)	
	9%	17%	9%	17%
Collateral	79	21	$1.03	–$0.94
Class				
A	52	10	0.37	–0.37
B	66	–3	1.63	–1.50
C	77	15	2.44	–2.08

Notice that the classes did not share the OAS equally. The same is true for the option cost. The value tended to go toward the longer bonds, something that occurs in the typical deal. Both the static spread and the option cost increase as the maturity increases. The only tranche where there appears to be a bit of a bargain is tranche C. A money manager contemplating the purchase of this last cash flow tranche can see that C offers a higher OAS than B and appears to bear less of the risk, as measured by the option cost. The problem money managers may face is that they might not be able to go out as long on the yield curve as the C tranche because of duration, maturity, and average life constraints.

Now let's look at modeling risk. Examination of the sensitivity of the tranches to changes in prepayments and interest rate volatility will help us to understand the interaction of the tranches in the structure and who is bearing the risk.

We begin with prepayments. Specifically, we keep the same interest rate paths as those used to get the OAS in the base case (the top panel of Exhibit 17.6), but reduce the prepayment rate on each interest rate path to 80% of the projected rate.

As can be seen in the second panel of Exhibit 17.6, slowing down prepayments increases the OAS and price for the collateral. This is because the collateral is trading above par. Tranches created by this collateral will typically behave the same way. However, if a tranche was created with a lower coupon, allowing it to trade below par, then it may behave in the opposite fashion. The exhibit reports two results of the sensitivity analysis. First, it indicates the change in the OAS. Second, it indicates the change in the price, holding the OAS constant at the base case.

To see how a money manager can use the information in the second panel, consider tranche A. At 80% of the prepayment speed, the OAS for this class increases from 32 basis points to 40 basis points. If the OAS is held constant, the panel indicates that the buyer of tranche A would gain $0.17 per $100 par value.

Notice that for all of the tranches reported in Exhibit 17.6, there is a gain from a slowdown in prepayments. This is because all of the sequential tranches in this deal are priced over par. If the F and S tranches were larger, then the coupon on tranche A would have been smaller. This coupon could have been made small enough for tranche A to trade at a discount to par, which would have caused the bond to lose in a prepayment slowdown. Also notice that, while the changes in OAS are about the same for the different tranches, the changes in price are quite different. This arises because the shorter tranches have less duration. Therefore, their prices do not move as much from a change in OAS as a longer tranche. A money manager who is willing to go to the long end of the curve, such as tranche C, would realize the most benefit from the slowdown in prepayments.

Also shown in the second panel of the exhibit is the second part of our experiment to test the sensitivity of prepayments: The prepayment rate is assumed to be 120% of the base case. The collateral loses money in this scenario because it is trading above par. This is reflected in the OAS of the collateral which declines from 51 basis points to 40 basis points.

Now look at the four tranches. They all lost money. Additionally, the S tranche, which is not shown in the exhibit, loses in a faster prepayment scenario. The S tranche is an IO tranche, and, in general, IO types of tranches will be adversely affected by an increase in prepayments.

Now let's look at the sensitivity to the interest rate volatility assumption, 13% in the base case. Two experiments are performed: reducing the volatility assumption to 9% and increasing it to 17%. These results are reported in the third panel of Exhibit 17.6.

Reducing the volatility to 9% increases the dollar price of the collateral by $1.03 and increases the OAS from 51 in the base case to 79 basis points. This $1.03 increase in the price of the collateral is not equally distributed, however, among the four tranches. Most of the increase in value is realized by the longer tranches. The OAS gain for each of the tranches follows more or less the OAS durations of those tranches. This makes sense, because the longer the duration, the greater the risk, and when volatility declines, the reward is greater for the accepted risk.

At the higher level of assumed interest rate volatility of 17%, the collateral is severely affected. The collateral's loss is distributed among the tranches in the expected manner: The longer the duration, the greater the loss. In this case tranche F and the residual are less affected.

Using the Monte Carlo simulation/OAS methodology, a fair conclusion that can be made about this simple plain vanilla structure is: What you see is what you get. The only surprise in this structure is the lower option cost in tranche C. In general, however, a money manager willing to extend duration gets paid for that risk in a plain vanilla structure.

PAC/Support Bond Structure

Now let's look at how to apply the Monte Carlo simulation/OAS methodology to a more complicated CMO structure, FHLMC Series 1706. The collateral for this structure is Freddie Mac 7s. A summary of the deal is provided in Exhibit 17.7. A diagram of the principal allocation is given in Exhibit 17.8.

While this deal is more complicated than the previous one, it is still relatively simple compared to some deals that have been recently printed. Nonetheless, it brings out all the key points about application of OAS analysis, specifically, the fact that most deals include cheap bonds, expensive bonds, and fairly priced bonds. The OAS analysis helps a money manager identify how a tranche should be classified.

EXHIBIT 17.7 Summary of Federal Home Loan Mortgage Corporation—Multiclass Mortgage Participation Certificates (Guaranteed), Series 1706

Total Issue:	$300,000,000	Original Settlement Date:	3/30/94
Issue Date:	2/18/94		
Structure Type:	REMIC CMO	Days Delay:	30
Issuer Class:	Agency	Payment Frequency:	Monthly; 15th day of month
Dated Date:	3/1/94		

Tranche	Original Balance ($)	Coupon (%)	Stated Maturity	Original Issue Pricing (225% PSA Assumed) Average Life (Yrs.)	Expected Maturity
A (PAC Bond)	24,600,000	4.50	10/15/06	1.3	6/15/96 *
B (PAC Bond)	11,100,000	5.00	9/15/09	2.5	1/15/97 *
C (PAC Bond)	25,500,000	5.25	4/15/14	3.5	6/15/98
D (PAC Bond)	9,150,000	5.65	8/15/15	4.5	1/15/99
E (PAC Bond)	31,650,000	6.00	1/15/19	5.8	1/15/01
G (PAC Bond)	30,750,000	6.25	8/15/21	7.9	5/15/03
H (PAC Bond)	27,450,000	6.50	6/15/23	10.9	10/15/07
J (PAC Bond)	5,220,000	6.50	10/15/23	14.4	9/15/09
K (PAC Bond)	7,612,000	7.00	3/15/24	18.8	5/15/19
LA (SCH Bond)	26,673,000	7.00	11/15/21	3.5	3/15/02
LB (SCH Bond)	36,087,000	7.00	6/15/23	3.5	9/15/02
M (SCH Bond)	18,738,000	7.00	3/15/24	11.2	10/15/08
O (TAC Bond)	13,348,000	7.00	2/15/24	2.5	1/15/08
OA (TAC Bond)	3,600,000	7.00	3/15/24	7.2	4/15/09
IA (IO, PAC Bond)	30,246,000	7.00	10/15/23	7.1	9/15/09
PF (FLTR, Support Bond)	21,016,000	6.75	3/15/24	17.5	5/15/19
PS (INV FLTR, Support Bond)	7,506,000	7.70	3/15/24	17.5	5/15/19
R (Residual)	—	0.00	3/15/24		
RS (Residual)	—	0.00	3/15/24		

Structural Features	
Prepayment Guarantee:	None
Assumed Reinvestment Rate:	0%

EXHIBIT 17.7 (Continued)

Structural Features	
Cash Flow Allocation:	Excess cash flow is not anticipated; in the event that there are proceeds remaining after the payment of the bonds, however, the Class R and RS Bonds will receive them. Commencing on the first principal payment date of the Class A Bonds, principal equal to the amount specified in the Prospectus will be applied to the Class A, B, C, D, E, G, H, J, K, LA, LB, M, O, OA, PF, and PS Bonds. After all other Classes have been retired, any remaining principal will be used to retire the Class O, OA, LA, LB, M, A, B, C, D, E, G, H, J, and K Bonds. The Notional Class IA Bond will have its notional principal amount retired along with the PAC Bonds.
Redemption Provisions:	Nuisance provision for all Classes: Issuer may redeem the Bonds, in whole but not in part, on any Payment Date when the outstanding principal balance declines to less than 1% of the original amount.
Other:	The PAC Range is 95% to 300% PSA for the A–K Bonds, 190% to 250% PSA for the LA, LB, and M Bonds, and 225% PSA for the O and OA Bonds.

EXHIBIT 17.8 Diagram of Principal Allocation Structure of FHLMC 1706 (as of 3/10/98)

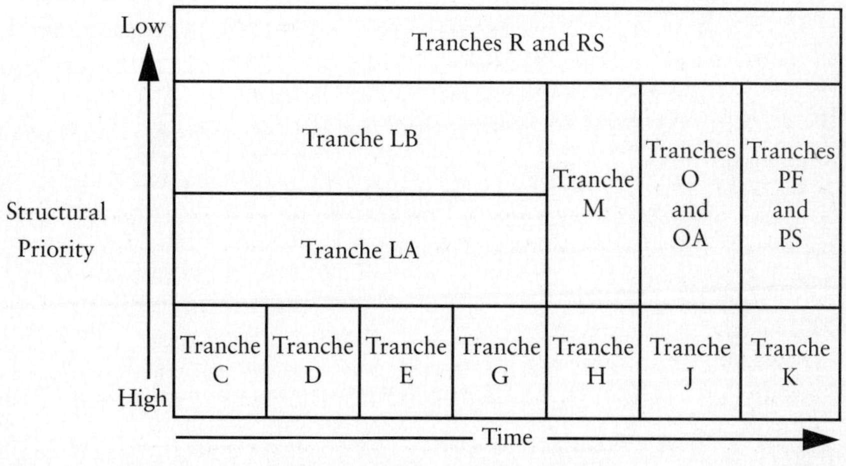

There are 19 classes in this structure: ten PAC bonds (including one PAC IO bond), three scheduled bonds, two TAC support bonds, a floating-rate support bond, an inverse floating-rate support bond, and two residual bonds. This deal contains no principal-only (PO) tranches.

The deal also includes an IO tranche, IA, which is structured such that the underlying collateral's interest not allocated to the PAC bonds is paid to the IO bond, which causes the PAC bonds to have discount coupons (as shown by the lower coupons of the front PACs in Exhibit 17.7). Unlike a typical mortgage-backed security backed by deep discount collateral, prepayments for the front tranches will be faster because the underlying collateral is Freddie Mac 7s, which was premium collateral at the time this analysis was computed. Thus, with PAC C the investor realizes a low coupon rate but a much higher prepayment rate than would be experienced by such a low coupon mortgage bond.

Tranches A and B had already paid off all of their principal when this analysis was performed. The other PAC bonds are still available. Tranche IA is a PAC IO. The prepayment protection for the PAC bonds is provided by the support or companion bonds. The support bonds in this deal are tranches LA, LB, M, O, OA, PF, and PS. LA is the shortest tranche (a scheduled [SCH] bond), while the floating-rate bonds, PF and PS, are the longest. SCH bonds, as represented by tranches LA and LB, have PSA bands similar to a PAC bond, but they typically have a narrower window of speeds. Also, they are often much less protected from prepayment surprises when the bands are exceeded. The LB tranche, for example, is essentially a support bond, once the PSA bands are broken.

The top panel of Exhibit 17.9 shows the base case OAS and the option cost for the collateral and all but the residual classes. The collateral OAS is 60 basis points, and the option cost is 44 basis points. The static spread of the collateral to the Treasury spot curve is 104 basis points.

The 60 basis points of OAS did not get equally distributed among the tranches—as was the case with the plain vanilla structure. Tranche LB, the scheduled support, did not realize a good OAS allocation, only 29 basis points, and had an extremely high option cost. Given the prepayment uncertainty associated with this bond, its OAS would be expected to be higher. The reason for the low OAS is that this tranche was priced so that its cash flow yield is high. Using the static spread as a proxy for the spread over the Treasury yield curve, the 103-basis point spread for tranche LB is high given that this appears to be a short-term tranche. Consequently, "yield buyers" probably bid aggressively for this tranche and thereby drove down its OAS, trading off "yield" for OAS. From a total return perspective, however, tranche LB should be avoided. It is a rich, or expensive, bond. The three longer supports did not get treated as badly as tranche LB; the OAS for tranches M, O, and OA are 72, 70, and 68 basis points, respectively.

EXHIBIT 17.9 OAS Analysis of FHLMC 1706 (As of 3/10/98)
Base Case (Assumes 13% Interest Rate Volatility)

	OAS (in Basis Points)	Option Cost (in Basis Points)
Collateral	60	44
Class		
C (PAC)	15	0
D (PAC)	16	4
E (PAC)	26	4
G (PAC)	42	8
H (PAC)	50	12
J (PAC)	56	14
K (PAC)	57	11
LA (SCH)	39	12
LB (SCH)	29	74
M (SCH)	72	53
O (TAC)	70	72
OA (TAC)	68	68
PF (Support Fltr.)	17	58
PS (Support Inverse Fltr.)	54	137
IA (PAC IO)	50	131

Prepayments at 80% and 120% of Prepayment Model (Assumes 13% Interest Rate Volatility)

	Base Case OAS	New OAS (in Basis Points)		Change in Price per $100 Par (Holding OAS Constant)	
		80%	120%	80%	120%
Collateral	60	63	57	$0.17	–$0.11
Class					
C (PAC)	15	15	15	0.00	0.00
D (PAC)	16	16	16	0.00	0.00
E (PAC)	26	27	26	0.01	–0.01
G (PAC)	42	44	40	0.08	–0.08
H (PAC)	50	55	44	0.29	–0.27
J (PAC)	56	63	50	0.50	–0.47
K (PAC)	57	65	49	0.77	–0.76
LA (SCH)	39	31	39	–0.12	0.00
LB (SCH)	29	39	18	0.38	–0.19
M (SCH)	72	71	76	–0.07	0.18
O (TAC)	70	69	72	–0.06	0.10
OA (TAC)	68	69	71	0.07	0.15
PF (Support Fltr.)	17	26	7	0.75	–0.69
PS (Support Inverse Fltr.)	54	75	49	1.37	–0.27
IA (PAC IO)	50	144	–32	0.39	–0.32

EXHIBIT 17.9 (Continued)
Interest Rate Volatility of 9% and 17%

	Base Case OAS	New OAS (in Basis Points)		Change in Price per $100 Par (Holding OAS Constant)	
		9%	17%	9%	17%
Collateral	60	81	35	$0.96	–$0.94
Class					
C (PAC)	15	15	15	0.00	0.00
D (PAC)	16	16	16	0.00	0.00
E (PAC)	26	27	24	0.02	–0.04
G (PAC)	42	48	34	0.21	–0.27
H (PAC)	50	58	35	0.48	–0.72
J (PAC)	56	66	41	0.70	–1.05
K (PAC)	57	66	44	0.82	–1.19
LA (SCH)	39	47	24	0.09	–0.18
LB (SCH)	29	58	–4	0.80	–0.82
M (SCH)	72	100	41	1.80	–1.72
O (TAC)	70	103	30	2.03	–1.74
OA (TAC)	68	103	30	2.40	–1.98
PF (Support Fltr.)	17	51	–27	3.11	–2.92
PS (Support Inverse Fltr.)	54	123	–5	4.85	–2.85
IA (PAC IO)	50	158	–70	0.45	–0.48

It should be apparent from the results of the base case OAS analysis reported in the top panel of Exhibit 17.9 where the cheap bonds in the deal are. They are the long PACs, which have a high OAS, a low option cost, and can be positively convex. These are well-protected cash flows.

Notice that the option cost for tranches IA and PS are extremely high. These two tranches are primarily IOs. An investor who purchases an IO has effectively sold an option, and this explains the large option cost. As long as volatility is low, the owner of the IO will be able to collect the premium, because the realized option cost will be less than that implied by the model.

The next two panels in Exhibit 17.9 show the sensitivity of the OAS and the price (holding OAS constant at the base case) to changes in the prepayment speed (80% and 120% of the base case) and to changes in volatility (9% and 17%). This analysis shows that the change in the prepayment speed does not affect the collateral significantly, while the change in the OAS (holding the price constant) and price (holding OAS constant) for each tranche can be significant. For example, a faster prepayment speed, which decreases the time period over which a PAC IO bondholder is receiving a coupon, significantly reduces the OAS and price. The opposite effect results if prepayments are slower than the base case.

Tranche H, a premium priced medium-term PAC, benefits from a slowing in prepayments, as the bondholder will receive the coupon for a longer time. Faster prepayments represent an adverse scenario. The PAC bonds are quite well-protected. The long PACs will actually benefit from a reduced prepayment rate because they will be earning the higher coupon interest longer. So, on an OAS basis, our earlier conclusion that the long PACs were allocated a good part of the deal's value holds up under our first stress test.

A slowdown in prepayments helps the support tranche LB and a speedup hurts this tranche. A somewhat surprising result involves the effect that the change in prepayments has on the TAC bond OA. Notice that whether the prepayment speeds are slower or faster, the OAS and the price increases. This result arises from the structure of the bond. The prepayment risk of this bond is most prevalent when prepayments increase sharply, and then soon return to the base speed. This phenomenon, known as a "whipsaw," would adversely affect the OA tranche. Without the use of the framework presented in this chapter, this would not be intuitively obvious.

The sensitivity of the collateral and the tranches to changes in volatility are shown in the third panel of Exhibit 17.9. A lower volatility increases the value of the collateral, while a higher volatility reduces its value. Similarly, but in a more pronounced fashion, lower volatility increases the value of IO instruments, and higher volatility decreases their value. This effect can be seen on the PAC IO tranche IA in Exhibit 17.9.

The long PACs continue to be fairly well-protected, whether the volatility is lower or higher. In the two volatility scenarios, they continue to get a good OAS, although not as much as in the base case if volatility is higher (but the OAS still looks like a reasonable value in this scenario). This reinforces our earlier conclusion concerning the investment merit of the long PACs in this deal.

Home Equity Loan and Manufactured Housing Asset-Backed Securities

Finally, we will apply the Monte Carlo simulation/OAS model to a home equity loan ABS and a manufactured housing ABS.[4] Exhibits 17.10 and 17.11 provide information about these deals. The analysis was performed on April 14, 2000. Market implied volatility is assumed.

[4] This illustration is adapted from Frank J. Fabozzi, Shrikant Ramamurthy, and Laurent Gauthier, "Analysis of ABS," Chapter 28 in Frank J. Fabozzi (ed.), *Investing in Asset-Backed Securities* (New Hope, PA: Frank J. Fabozzi Associates, 2000).

EXHIBIT 17.10 Analysis of Home-Equity Loan

Issuer:	Residential Asset Securities Corp. (RASC)	Prepay. Assumption:[a]	25 HEP
Deal Date:	February 2000	Credit Support:	Wrapped by AMBAC
Type:	HEL REMIC	Volatility Assumption:	Market implied

Class	Size ($ mm)	Type	Coupon (%)	Maturity	Avg. Life	Price	Yield (%)	Spread to WAL (bps)	Zero-vol Spd. (bps)	OAS[b] (bps)	Option Cost[c] (bps)	Eff. Dur.	Eff. Conv.	St. Dev. of Avg. Life
A1	220	AAA Seq	7.615	1/15	0.9	100-11	6.585	40[d]	50	45	5	0.9	–0.3	0.10
A2	100	AAA Seq	7.700	6/21	2.0	100-00	7.525	110	113	93	20	2.1	–0.5	0.45
A3	105	AAA Seq	7.735	11/25	3.1	100-04	7.612	122	130	92	38	3.2	–0.7	0.98
A4	105	AAA Seq	8.040	11/28	5.1	100-16	7.915	163	175	127	48	4.7	–0.6	2.35
A5	55	AAA Seq	8.195	1/31	7.9	100-20	8.126	200	212	176	36	6.3	0.6	2.63
A6	65	AAA NAS	7.905	1/31	6.2	100-24	7.763	155	162	144	18	4.9	0.3	0.74
Weighted avg.			7.794		3.2	100.34	7.358				24	3.0		

Analysis as of 4/4/00

[a] Yields and spreads are computed relative to a constant prepayment assumption.

[b] OASs and durations are calculated by a Monte Carlo simulation of rates which utilizes Prudential Securities Inc.'s home equity loan prepayment model.

[c] Option cost is defined as the difference between the OAS at market volatility and at zero volatility.

[d] The spread to WAL for this class is lower than the OAS because the spread and OAS are computed at different prepayment speeds. The spread is computed at a constant prepayment speed assumption, while the OAS is computed assuming that prepayment speeds vary by time and interest-rate scenario.

EXHIBIT 17.11 Analysis of Manufactured Housing

Issuer:	Vanderbilt Mortgage and Finance	Prepay. Assumption:[a]	250 MHP
Deal Date:	February 2000	Credit Support:	Senior/sub structure
Type:	MH REMIC	Volatility Assumption:	Market implied

Class	Size ($ mm)	Type	Coupon (%)	Maturity	Avg. Life	Price	Yield (%)	Spread to WAL (bps)	Zero-vol Spd. (bps)	OAS[b] (bps)	Option Cost[c] (bps)	Eff. Dur.	Eff. Conv.	St. Dev. of Avg. Life
A2	33.0	AAA Seq	7.580	8/12	3.0	100-16	7.434	103	105	78	27	2.4	–0.3	0.73
A3	32.0	AAA Seq	7.820	11/17	5.1	101-00	7.639	133	145	127	18	3.8	–0.2	2.18
A4	27.2	AAA Seq	7.955	12/24	9.2	101-20	7.877	169	190	175	15	5.8	–0.2	3.76
A5	9.1	AA Seq	8.195	11/32	12.0	102-12	7.989	200	220	212	8	7.9	0.2	3.18
M1	7.3	A Seq	8.635	11/32	8.7	101-16	8.502	240	254	239	15	6.3	0.3	1.53
B1	7.3	BBB Seq	9.250	9/15	6.1	100-09	9.330	310	314	292	22	4.7	0.0	0.54
B2	12.8	BBB Seq	9.250	11/32	10.2	99-02+	9.536	355	363	353	10	6.9	0.4	2.12
Weighted avg.			8.083		6.7	100.90	7.995				18	4.6		

Analysis as of 4/4/00

[a] Yields and spreads are computed relative to a constant prepayment assumption.

[b] OASs and durations are calculated by a Monte Carlo simulation of rates which utilizes Prudential Securities Inc.'s manufactured housing prepayment model.

[c] Option cost is defined as the difference between the OAS at market volatility and at zero volatility.

Exhibit 17.10 shows the information for the home equity loan ABS—the Residential Asset Securities Corp. (RASC) issued in February 2000. The deal has six tranches. The weighted average life of the tranches is 3.2 years and the average option cost is 24 basis points per tranche. Exhibit 17.11 shows the information for the Vanderbilt Mortgage and Finance manufactured housing loan deal issued in February 2000. The deal has six tranches with a weighted average life of 6.7 years. The average option cost is 18 basis points per tranche.

Notice that the average option cost is lower than in the home equity loan deal. Also note that comparable tranches have lower option costs and a lower standard deviation for the average life in the manufactured housing deal versus the home equity loan deal as summarized below:

	Option Cost		Average Life Std. Dev.	
Average Life	HEL	MH	HEL	MH
3 Years	38	27	0.98	0.73
5 Years	48	18	2.35	2.18

Manufactured housing prepayments are typically insensitive to interest rates, while agency mortgage borrowers are much more able to benefit from refinancing opportunities. Home equity loan borrowers—first-lien mortgages for subprime borrowers—are less able to profit from decreasing interest rates to refinance their loans.

Unlike the home equity loan deal shown here, this manufactured housing structure does not have an outside insurance company guaranteeing the payments. Instead, the AAA rating on the senior tranches is obtained through a schedule of default losses. The lower rated bonds suffer losses of principal before the senior tranches, thereby allowing for a AAA rating. Therefore, a complete analysis of the relative value of these bonds would have to include an opinion of the credit risk of the underlying loans, in addition to the prepayment analysis described in detail in this chapter. For the home equity loan deal shown here, the credit work should focus on the ability and willingness of the outside insurer to honor its obligations. Conversely, the credit analysis of this unwrapped manufactured housing deal should center on the strength of the structure to withstand difficult credit events.

CHAPTER 18

Mortgage Pricing on Low-Dimensional Grids*

Alexander Levin, Ph.D.
Senior Developer/Consultant
Andrew Davidson and Co.

The theory and practice of option pricing suggest that the most time-efficient pricing structures (trees and grids) should be favored, avoiding the brute-force Monte Carlo simulation whenever possible. However, it has also become a common and trivial argument that mortgage pricing does necessitate time-consuming Monte Carlo simulations, and most mortgage valuation systems employ this method. Otherwise, the valuation scheme would call for additional dimensions caused by different sources of path-dependence.[1] Many also believe that mortgage valuation under two- or even three-factor term structure models reveals value hidden by simple single-factor models.

We noticed in the past that the major shortcoming of the Monte Carlo method is not in its speed only, but in the fact it is not structurally tailored for the goals of one- and multi-factor risk measurement and management.[2] Indeed, all simulations (possibly thousands) are solely

[1] See, for example, Chapter 17.

[2] A. Levin, "A New Approach to Option-Adjusted Valuation of MBS on a Multi-Scenario Grid," in Frank J. Fabozzi (ed.) *Advances in the Valuation and Management of Mortgage-Backed Securities* (New Hope, PA: Frank J. Fabozzi Associates, 1998).

* This study is a part of a long-term collaborative work with Jim Daras and Ken Schmidt at the Dime Bancorp.

intended to compute one value. This may satisfy the needs of a trader seeking *one accurate price*, but is reasonably deemed a waste of time by risk managers who need many (possibly, approximate) prices to assess, hedge, and report on each of the risk dimensions. The entire Monte Carlo scheme has to be rerun for each new pricing point (such as a yield curve shock)—in sharp contrast to the finite difference methods where all prices are sought simultaneously.

The purpose of this chapter is to demonstrate that some sources of mortgage path-dependence are spurious and can be avoided via a simple problem transformation; others can be "cured" by proper model selection. Finally, for a "non-curable" path-dependence, we consider using the Expected Instantaneous Return Method (EIRS)[3] complemented by control variate correction. This idea will lead to a rather accurate approximation, retaining all structural and computational advantages of finite difference schemes. The results of our study suggest that most non-CMO mortgage instruments and even some CMOs can be efficiently priced on finite difference grids.

INSTANTANEOUS RETURN PDE AND THE PROBLEM OF PATH-DEPENDENCE

Let us consider a hypothetical dynamic asset market price of which $P(t,x)$ depends on time t and one generalized market factor x. The latter can be formally anything and does not necessarily have to be the short market rate or the yield on the security analyzed. We treat $x(t)$ as a random process having a (generally, variable) drift rate μ and a volatility rate σ, and being disturbed by a standard Brownian motion $z(t)$—that is,

$$dx = \mu dt + \sigma dz \tag{1}$$

Instantaneous Return is a random return measured over an infinitesimal investment horizon and annualized. The essential statement in the Instantaneous Return concept is a partial differential equation (PDE) that is traditionally derived by applying the following mathematical operations:

- Ito's Lemma (a stochastic differential equation) written for the random dynamics of price $P(t,x)$ given process (1) for $x(t)$

[3] See Levin, "A New Approach to Option-Adjusted Valuation of MBS on a Multi-Scenario Grid."

- Collecting all the cash flow-related components of Instantaneous Return
- Finding the mathematical expectation of both sides
- Equating the obtained expectation to the risk-free rate $r(t,x)$ prevailing on the market plus a return spread (OAS) that investors expect from this type of risky financial instruments

We assume that the asset continuously pays a $c(t,x)$ coupon rate and its balance B gets amortized at a $\lambda(t,x)$ rate. Then one can prove that the price function $P(t,x)$ should solve the following PDE[4]

$$\underbrace{r + \text{OAS}}_{\text{expected return}} = \underbrace{\frac{1}{P}\frac{\partial P}{\partial t} + \frac{1}{P}(c + \lambda) - \lambda}_{\text{time return}} + \underbrace{\frac{1}{P}\frac{\partial P}{\partial x}\mu}_{\text{drift return}} + \underbrace{\frac{1}{2P}\frac{\partial^2 P}{\partial x^2}\sigma^2}_{\text{diffusion return}} \quad (2)$$

Note that this PDE can be derived following the above listed steps for the total market value, that is, P times B, and computing all needed partial derivatives. In particular,

$$\dot{B} = -\lambda B$$

due to the definition of λ, whereas

$$\frac{\partial B}{\partial x} \text{ and } \frac{\partial^2 B}{\partial x^2}$$

are replaced by zeros because the balance is not an "immediate" function of the factor. Another way to arrive at equation (2) is to integrate by parts the expected present value of the principal cash flow and map thus obtained pricing formula onto the PDE using the "inverse" Feynman-Kac theorem.[5] A notable feature of the above written PDE is that it does not contain the balance variable, B. The entire effect of possibly random prepayments is represented by the amortization rate function, $\lambda(t,x)$. Although the total cash flow observed for each accrual period does

[4] An introduction of pricing PDE for randomly amortizing instruments goes back at least to F. Fabozzi and G. Fong, *Advanced Fixed Income Portfolio Management* (Burr Ridge: Irwin Professional Publishing, 1994).

[5] A. Levin, "Deriving Closed-Form Solutions for Gaussian Pricing Models: A Systematic Time-Domain Approach," *International Journal of Theoretical and Applied Finance*, 1(3) (1998), pp. 348–376.

depend on the beginning-period balance, construction of a finite difference scheme and the backward induction will require the knowledge of $\lambda(t,x)$, not the balance. This observation agrees with a trivial practical rule stating that the relative price is generally independent of the investment size.

Another important observation is as follows. If we transform the economy having shifted all the rates, $r(t,x)$ and $c(t,x)$, by amortization rate $\lambda(t,x)$, then equation (2) will be reduced to the constant-par asset's pricing PDE. It means that a finite difference pricing grid built in the "λ-shifted" economy should, in principle, have as many dimensions as the total number of factors or state variables that affect r, c, and λ. In particular, even if $r(t,x)$ and $c(t,x)$ are functions of time and one factor x, but $\lambda(t,x,\xi)$ depends upon an additional state variable, ξ, the grid will necessarily have all three dimensions, for t, x, and ξ.

This "discount-rate-like" role of the λ-variable is in contrast to some other state variables that may affect the asset's value. We already mentioned that the balance variable drops from the PDE and therefore does not cause any path-dependence directly. Another class of financial instruments includes "linear" assets where additional state variables (such as ξ above) linearly affect the coupon rate only ("perfect" floaters, for example). For such instruments, a finite difference scheme can sometimes be built without additional axes as we explain later in this chapter. However, in most circumstances, mortgages are not "linear" in factors and state variables. This problem encourages us to look for a proper model selection that would enable mortgage pricing on a low-dimensional grid.

ACTIVE-PASSIVE DECOMPOSITION IN BURNOUT MODELING[6]

Prepayment burnout is a strong source of path-dependence because future refinancing activity is affected by past incentives. One can think of a mortgage pool as a heterogeneous population of participants having different refinancing propensities.[7] Once most active mortgagors leave the pool, future prepayment activity gradually declines. In modeling prepayment burnout, we propose decomposing a mortgage pool into two subpools (components). The "active" component, also known as the "fast"

[6] The presentation in this section follows, A. Levin, "Active-Passive Decomposition in Burnout Modelling," *The Journal of Fixed Income* (March 2001), pp. 27–40.

[7] See L. Hayre, "A Simple Statistical Framework for Modeling Burnout and Refinancing Behavior," *The Journal of Fixed Income* (December 1994), pp. 69–74, and "Anatomy of Prepayments," *The Journal of Fixed Income* (June 2000), pp. 19–49.

component, includes all ready-to-refinance mortgagors, whereas the "passive" ("slow") component prepays at a speed generally reflecting a typical housing turnover rate and loan curtailments. Any migration between these two components is prohibited.

It can be shown that this simple two-component model is not only powerful enough to replicate the burnout effect, but is also perfectly tractable for a much wider range of mortgage valuation and modeling problems than once thought possible.[8] In particular, it cures burnout as a source of path-dependence because, in complete absence of migration, each constituent component (active or passive) remains path-independent.

Forward Evolution

Let ψ denote the active portion of the pool; then its evolution satisfies the following ordinary differential equation,

$$\dot{\psi} = -(\lambda_a - \lambda_p)\psi(1-\psi)$$

which gets solved by

$$\frac{1-\psi(t)}{1-\psi_0} = \left[1 - \psi_0 + \psi_0 \exp\left\{-\int_0^t [\lambda_a(\tau) - \lambda_p(\tau)]d\tau\right\}\right]^{-1} \quad (3)$$

where indices a and p refer to the active and passive parts, correspondingly. Assuming that the active speed contains housing turnover and curtailment, we note that $\lambda_a - \lambda_p$ is simply the pure refinancing rate. Initial active part, ψ_0, is considered a parameter of prepayment model. The left-hand side of equation (3) is defined as *burnout factor,* that is, the relative growth of the passive component.

Initializing the Burnout Factor for Seasoned Mortgages

Let us consider a problem of valuation and modeling of a seasoned mortgage pool having an age of t years. What would it take to recover its current burnout stage? If we knew the model's key parameter ψ_0 and the entire prepayment history for the active and passive prepayment speeds, $\lambda_a(\tau)$ and $\lambda_p(\tau)$, $0 \le \tau \le t$, we could find the active part of the pool $\psi(t)$ from solution (3). Can we solve the same problem without this unreliable, and not always available, retrospective analysis? The following formula shows how easy it can be done:

[8] See Levin, "Active-Passive Decomposition in Burnout Modeling."

$$\frac{1-\psi(t)}{1-\psi_0} = \frac{F_p(t)}{F(t)} \tag{4}$$

where the overall current pool factor F is observable and the passive part's factor F_p can be easily computed using the scheduled amortization $F_{\text{sch}}(t)$ and the model's parameter, passive rate λ_p,

$$F_p(t) = F_{\text{sch}}(t)\exp\left[-\int_0^t \lambda_p(\tau)d\tau\right]$$

Interestingly enough, the current active part $\psi(t)$ defined by equation (4) appears to be an increasing function of each of its arguments: pool factor F, age t, initial value ψ_0, and the passive speed λ_p. It is easy to see that the important relationship in equation (4) is, in essence, almost a definitional one. Since the entire mortgage consists of only two components, knowledge of the total and the passive part uniquely determines the active part. In its derivation, we have not used any assumptions about the particular properties of the active prepayment speed, $\lambda_a(\tau)$—we simply do not have to know it. If the passive rate λ_p is not constant, equation (4) will still hold true, but, in order to reconstruct the current passive factor F_p, we will need to know the entire history of $\lambda_p(\tau)$, since issuance. In other words, *knowing only the factor and the age of the pool*, as well as the model's parameters, ψ_0 and λ_p [or historical $\lambda_p(\tau)$], one can reconstruct the current active part, $\psi(t)$. This result presents a serious practical advantage of the proposed analytical burnout model over any other approach that requires the retrospective analysis of the past prepayment incentives or ad-hoc judgments about the achieved degree of burnout.

Curing Burnout as a Source of Path-Dependence

Let us consider again equation (3). If $\psi_0 = 0$ or $\psi_0 = 1$, then $\psi(t)$ retains the initial value, for life (i.e., the mortgage prepayments never vary due to the burnout effect). This observation agrees with our underlying assumption that, in a complete absence of migration, initially active mortgagors will always remain active and passive mortgagors will always stay passive. Nevertheless, this simple underlying assumption results in some non-trivial pricing implications. Indeed, the mortgage is essentially modeled as a portfolio of two instruments. Whereas this portfolio is certainly path-dependent as its prepayments burn out, each of the constituent components is not. We therefore can employ low-dimensional finite-difference schemes when pricing two mortgages instead of one and just add up the values. The processing time doubles, but this is a relatively small cost to pay for getting around path-dependence. The decomposition works only for today's valuation, not in the future, because the active-passive mix becomes unknown at forward nodes. Furthermore, speaking of this simple, but important, opportunity, we have to make sure that the mortgage instrument in question has no other sources of path-dependence or structural provisions that would prevent decomposition. Counterexamples include CMO structures, senior/sub structures, and clean up calls (written for the entire mortgage, not for components).

Valuation Features of Mortgage Servicing Rights

Mortgage servicing rights (MSR) differ from IOs in that they carry some fixed (non-proportional) dollar income and cost components counted per loan. For example, a mortgage servicer may receive annually \$40 per loan in the form of ancillary income (insurance fees, etc.) and earns on escrow and floats regardless of the loan size. It is clear that the proportional rate c used in the pricing PDE (2) will now change gradually with the average loan balance even if the stated servicing spread is constant. Does the existence of non-proportional income or cost create path-dependence?

Consider the following simple transformation of the fixed dollar income (or cost):

$$\begin{aligned}\text{Income per \$1 of balance} &= \text{Income per loan} \times \frac{\text{Number of loans}}{\text{Total pool balance}} \\ &= \text{Income per loan/Average loan balance}\end{aligned}$$

Income per loan is fixed whereas the average loan balance gradually amortizes. The only two sources of a particular loan's amortization are the scheduled payments and curtailments (refinancing or turnover would eliminate the loan immediately). Considering assumptions that underpinned the active-passive decomposition method, we note that the curtailment process was included in the passive amortization. Since we assumed that the passive speed (λ_p) is interest-rate independent, the same would naturally apply to the curtailment. As the scheduled amortization is also market-independent, at least for fixed-rate mortgages, we arrive at the following practically important conclusion: *Average loan balance can be deemed as a function of time only.* This conjecture makes fixed dollar income or cost path-independent. The rest of the MSR valuation is not any different from regular unstructured passthroughs and can be carried over using finite difference methods employed for the active component and the passive component, as explained previously.

VALUATION MODELS FOR STRUCTURED MBS

Let us assume that the mortgage instrument in question has structural provisions or (other than burnout) sources of path-dependence that would prevent active-passive decomposition. For example, the issuer may have a right to clean up the entire pool, any time after the remaining pool factor falls below a predefined level (often 10% or 20%). Therefore, one can describe this feature as a knock-in American option. Another example of path-dependence met in non-agency passthroughs is the senior/sub credit enhancement structure. During the lockout period, all principal cash flow is directed to the senior class.[9] If the MBS in question is the senior class of such structure, its amortization rate, $\lambda(t)$ in PDE (2), becomes a direct function of the remaining senior factor, or, in the presence of only two classes, the pool factor. The lower the pool factor is within the lockout period, the larger is the relative principal distribution paid to the senior class.

Both the clean up knock-in condition and the senior/sub structure represent sources of path-dependence that would normally require complementing the state space with one additional variable, the pool factor.[10] We will describe here a method that yields a fairly accurate pricing without an additional dimension. Its idea employs the Expected Instantaneous Return Method (EIRS),[11] which is an ad-hoc surrogate for option-adjusted valuation—not particularly sensitive to path-dependence. Used as the base method, it is corrected with a specially constructed control variate stripped out of path-dependence and priced on the same low-dimensional grid.

The EIRS Method

The simplifying assumption, which underpins the EIRS method, relates to the time behavior of the *static discount spread(s)* over the forward curve. Each cash flow vector used by the method is computed along the corresponding average-rate path (i.e., convexity-adjusted forwards).

[9] In some structures, the sub-class receives the scheduled principal payments.

[10] See Dorigan, Fabozzi, and Kalotay, "Valuation of Floating-Rate Bonds."

[11] See Levin, "A New Approach to Option-Adjusted Valuation of MBS on a Multi-Grid Scenario," and "One- and Multi-factor Valuation of Mortgages: Computational Problems and Shortcuts," *International Journal of Theoretical and Applied Finance* (1999), pp. 441–469.

Note that the average path for the entire term structure is conditioned upon the observed market rates. The simplest ("first-order") hypothesis has a form of:

$$ds(t, x)/dt|_{t=0} = 0$$

therefore, s remains unchanged, at least for a short time horizon. This is to say that the same average-rate scenario's cash flow will be priced at the same static discount spread in the nearest future. Under the first-order assumption, PDE (2) reduces to the following approximate ordinary differential equation:

$$OAS \approx s(x) + \frac{\sigma^2}{2}\left[\frac{1}{P}\frac{\partial^2 P(0, x)}{\partial x^2} - C_x^{\text{static}}(x)\right] \equiv EIRS \qquad (5)$$

where C_x^{static} is the static (benchmark) convexity of the average-rate scenario cash flow measured with respect to the same factor x. The OAS approximated according to equation (5) was called EIRS. We therefore have transformed the instantaneous return linear PDE (2) to a nonlinear second-order ODE, in which $s(x)$ is a known function of price $P(0,x)$ uniquely defined by the average-rate scenario cash flow conditioned upon the initial value of the factor, $x(0)$. The time variable has disappeared from the model, therefore, the pricing grid need not be propagated along the t-axis.

Equation (5) can be viewed as an equation for $P(0,x)$ as well as equation for $s(x)$. To solve it, one needs to know either the base scenario price, $P(0,0)$, or OAS, and specify two boundary conditions. For an MBS, for example, one can consider two extreme scenarios for which the cash flow is practically insensitive to x. The interest rate sensitivity of the prepayment speed is typically ranged between the turnover rate and refinancing credit limitations; in addition, the ARM's coupon is bound by caps and floors. For these boundary scenarios, the convexity costs are assumed to be zero—that is,

$$\frac{1}{P}\frac{\partial^2 P(0, x)}{\partial x^2} = C_x^{\text{static}}(x)$$

To solve pricing equation (5) with two boundary conditions, we apply a finite difference method. Namely, along with the currently observed forward curve ("base case") we consider a grid of scenarios induced by initial shocks of the factor, $x(0) = -N_{dn}\Delta, \ldots, -\Delta, 0, \Delta, \ldots, N_{up}\Delta$, for sufficiently small step Δ and sufficiently large numbers of "down" shocks N_{dn} and "up" shocks N_{up}. Then, we replace

$$\frac{\partial^2 P(0, x)}{\partial x^2}$$

by its finite difference approximation, rewrite equation (5) for every scenario, employ boundary conditions, and solve the obtained system of $N = N_{dn} + N_{up} + 1$ algebraic equations using the multidimensional Newton-Raphson iterations.

Some features of the EIRS method make it valuable for pricing path-dependent MBS. First, the method's error is due to its underlying assumption about the static spread's time behavior, and not directly related to the problem of path-dependence. The EIRS computational scheme introduces a systematic error even when pricing instruments having no path-dependence. In fact, the finite difference scheme used to solve equation (5) has no time axis and operates with prices or spreads at time $t = 0$ where path-dependence simply "does not exist." All deterministic scenarios comprising the valuation grid are constructed forward in time with path-dependent state variables "naturally" simulated along those paths, starting with their actual initial values.

Second, although the method does not propagate the pricing equation beyond today's instance of time ($t = 0$), it actually employs the same grid of scenarios and cash flows that are used by more conventional, full-scale finite difference methods (Crank-Nicholson, for example). As we will see below, this feature naturally makes the EIRS method an excellent base method to be complemented with a control variate correction provided by other finite difference methods.

Third, the EIRS method can be applied to financial instruments having no dynamic prepayment model available at all. For example, a simple grid of PSA or CPR speeds can be used instead of a rigorous prepayment model. Certainly, such a "model" is path-independent, and one can compare pricing results obtained from the EIRS scheme with ones computed by the Crank-Nicholson method. This important advantage, as we show later, can be efficiently used for constructing and pricing a control variate.

Since the EIRS method is an ad-hoc approximation intended to value complex, path-dependent instruments, the method generally does not require splitting mortgages into active and passive components. As we explained above, such decomposition allows for a very accurate pricing by the Crank-Nicholson (or other conventional) finite difference method—provided there is no path-dependence other than the burnout.

Adding a Control Variate

"Control variate" is an auxiliary financial instrument, which (a) is "close" to the MBS in question and (b) allows for exact or very accurate valuation on its own. Leaving aside the question of finding mortgage prices in a closed form, we will assume that the control variate (CV) is valued with a standard backward inducting Crank-Nicholson method. Then, the MBS value obtained with the EIRS method is symbolically corrected as follows:[12]

$$MBS = MBS_{EIRS} + \underbrace{CV_{CN} - CV_{EIRS}}_{\text{correction}} \tag{6}$$

The valuation process starts with pricing actual MBS using the EIRS method. Then, the control variate is constructed and priced twice—using the EIRS method and the Crank-Nicholson method—and the difference is used to correct the original value. Both pricing methods employed in this chain along with equation (6) end up with a set of values computed for different factor points at $t = 0$.

A legitimate use of the Crank-Nicholson method assumes that the financial instrument used as control variate is stripped out of path-dependence (other than the burnout modeled and cured by active-passive decomposition). Constructing a control variate is a creative task, which takes into consideration existing path-dependencies and replaces them properly.

Example 1: Valuing MBS with a Clean-Up Call Provision

Clean-up call is an option that becomes exercisable once the pool factor drops below the clean-up threshold. Prevailing interest rates are not the only factor affecting the exercise decision. The clean-up feature is itself designed to reduce expenses of servicing a small pool of loans, not to take advantage of low interest rates. In addition, the "quality" of collateral may play an essential role in affecting the exercise decision. Everything being even, a pool of delinquent or otherwise credit-impaired loans will less likely be called. It makes sense to model the clean-up call exercise "probabilistically," as an accelerated prepayment option[13] (if interest rates are low, the pool will be more likely to be cleaned up than if they were high). These comments only explain how we suggest simu-

---

[12] The control variate method is clearly described in J. Hull, *Options, Futures, and Other Derivative Securities*, Second Edition (Englewood Cliffs, NJ: Prentice Hall, 1996).

[13] This approach was developed with Kenneth Schmidt.

lating the clean up exercise decision once the option is knocked in; in no way do they alter the path-dependent knock-in condition.

In order to construct the control variate, we use the original MBS subject to the clean up provision, and modify this feature as to eliminate the path-dependence. The first, most trivial, encouragement would be to eliminate the clean-up option altogether when constructing the control variate. For a new or moderately seasoned MBS having a remote clean-up event, this step could be well justified. However, if the clean-up is about to be knocked in, the brute elimination of this provision can drastically change the average life and violate condition (a) above. An idea we propose for constructing the control variate for very seasoned mortgages is to use the same ("synchronized") knock-in time for all scenarios of the finite difference grid, namely, the time corresponding to the *base scenario knock-in condition for the original MBS.*

Note that the traditional control variate technique uses the first step of valuation (in our case, the EIRS method for the original MBS) only to compute the first term (price) in equation (6). The practical novelty of our approach is to extract some information on cash flows and timing of events and apply them when constructing the control variate. Apparently, it becomes possible due to topological identity of the EIRS scheme and the Crank-Nicholson scheme as shown in Exhibit 18.1.

As an example, we consider an MBS with only an 11% remaining factor with a 10% stated clean-up threshold. If the rates evolve along the base path, the clean up is knocked-in four months from now. (After this option is knocked-in, the pool is not necessarily cleaned up; the exercise is modeled probabilistically as discussed previously.) For the "up" scenarios (factor levels 1 and 2 in Exhibit 18.1A), the clean up is knocked-in later, for the "down" scenarios (factor level –1 and –2)—sooner. When constructing the control variate, we synchronize the clean-up knock-in events as to have them all in four months regardless of the scenario. In such a setting, the clean up does not present a source of path-dependence. Moreover, when now employing the Crank-Nicholson scheme to price thus constructed control variate, we can legitimately apply the active-passive decomposition because both components, active and passive, are cleaned up synchronously.

Exhibit 18.2 compares the accuracy of three valuation models for the very seasoned MBS in our example, measured across the factor grid. A brute liquidation of the clean-up provision in control variate leaves us with a considerable pricing error, but the more delicate way of replacing the actual clean-up condition leads to an accuracy found suitable for trading and risk management.

EXHIBIT 18.1A Pricing Grid for a Very Seasoned MBS

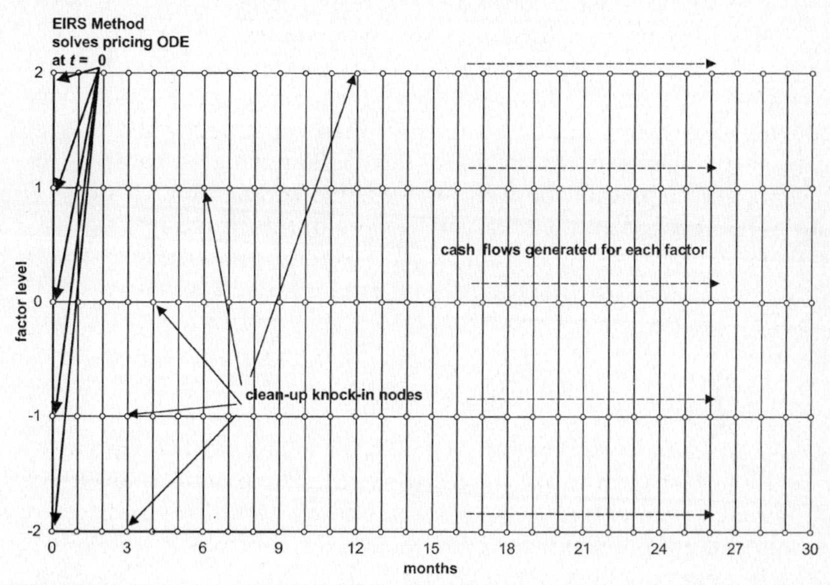

EXHIBIT 18.1B Pricing Grid for the Control Variate

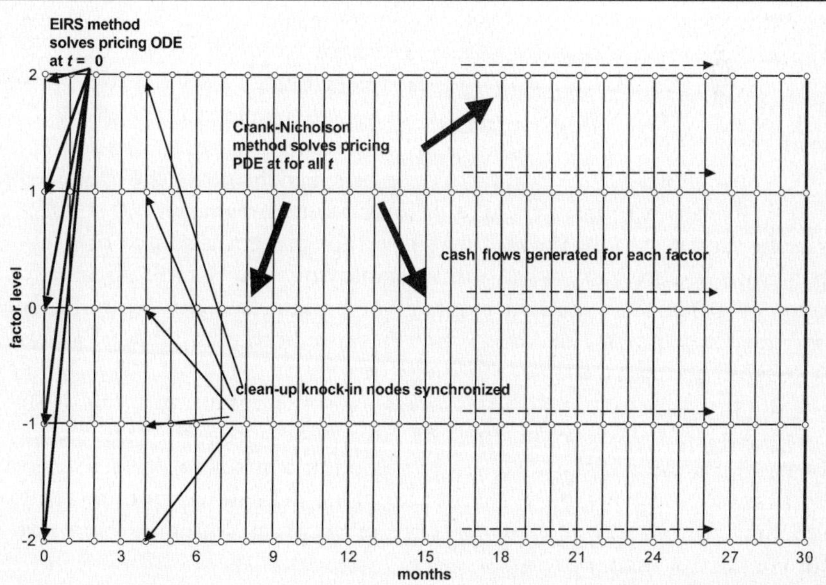

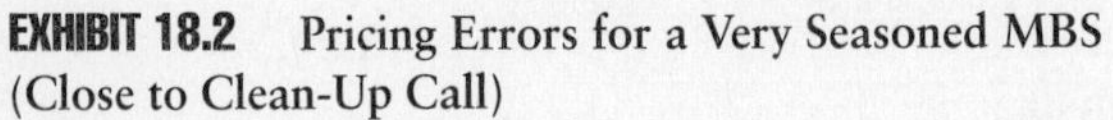

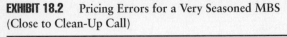

EXHIBIT 18.2 Pricing Errors for a Very Seasoned MBS (Close to Clean-Up Call)

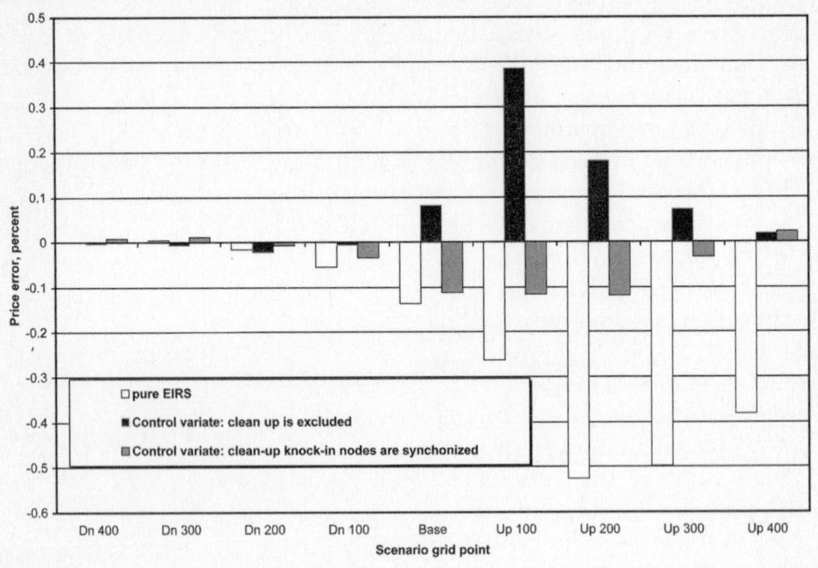

Example 2: Valuing MBS in Senior/Sub and Some CMO Structures

Many non-agency passthroughs (typically not classified as CMOs) are sliced into "senior" and "sub" pieces in order to enhance the senior piece's credit (losses are absorbed by the sub piece). Let us consider this structure from a senior-class-investor point. The senior class amortization is path-dependent because the sub piece is locked from getting prepaid principal[14] (60 months is a typical lockout period). Ignoring delinquencies and defaults, the prepaid rate of the entire pool is magnified when directed to the senior class, in the inverse relation to the senior portion of the pool. Therefore, the amortization rate, λ, in the pricing PDE appears to be a function of the remaining pool factor and the senior class factor.

Again, we start with the use of the EIRS method as described previously and correct its results with the help of a control variate. When constructing the control variate, we could simply set the sub class size to zero (i.e., to treat the senior class as a plain passthough). When the sub class is relatively small, this could be a decent idea, but, when it is large, such an assumption seems to be too rough. More rigor can be brought in by essentially drawing on the knowledge of the average life (WAL) for each of the

[14] This is referred to as a "shifting interest mechanism."

grid scenarios. Indeed, we can attempt to replace the actual senior/sub structure with a simple unstructured passthrough while selecting prepayment PSA or CPR speeds (one for each grid scenario) to match the actual average lives. In doing so we, in essence, replace the actual (path-dependent) principal amortization rules with a simple $\lambda = \lambda(t,x)$ model that carries no path-dependence, but results in the same grid of average lives.

Note that we again employ some non-trivial information (other than the price) delivered by the EIRS method implemented for the actual MBS. Exhibit 18.3 compares the accuracy of the pure EIRS method, and two EIRS methods with different methods of control variate construction. The accuracy is drastically improved when the control variate is designed with the WAL replication.

An anxious reader may immediately attempt to build a virtual bridge to a nirvana of pricing CMOs on finite difference grids. Indeed, a simple senior/sub structure prototypes some features of the CMO complexity. The difference between the senior class of a structured passthrough and the first class of a CMO is not very significant for the proposed valuation scheme. Our experiments with the first class of a sequential CMO confirms that, constructing the control variate as a passthrough with WALs matched on the scenario grid allows us to achieve fair pricing accuracy. We see an exciting research opportunity of pricing more complex CMO structures by employing the main EIRS scheme complemented by specially constructed control variates.

EXHIBIT 18.3 Pricing Errors for a Senior MBS Class in a 50/50 Senior/Sub Structure

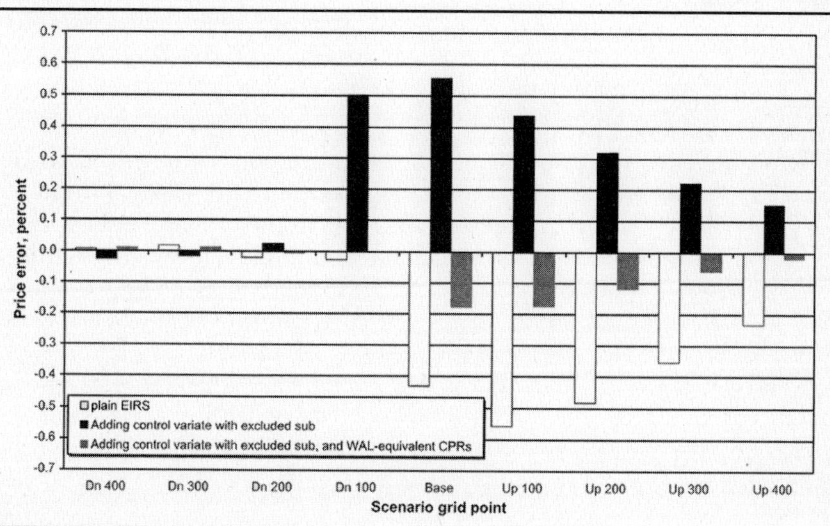

CONSIDERATION OF ARMS AND FLOATERS

So far, we have been concerned with sources of path-dependence that are caused by special provisions or mortgage features affecting the principal distribution. In other words, the principal amortization rate (λ) was considered "path-dependent" since it depended on some additional state variables such as the pool factor. Adjustable-rate mortgages (ARMs) present another case of path-dependence where the paid rate (c) depends on the path of the ARM index (such as 1-year Constant-Maturity-Treasury, CMT) and its value in the past. There are some interesting theoretical facts about "linear floaters" (i.e., floating-rate bonds resetting freely and proportionally to the market index). Namely, if

- the coupon rate $c(t,x,\xi)$ is linear in some additional state variable ξ,
- ξ is linear in factor x,
- variables x (the factor), r (the short rate), and λ (amortization rate) are ξ-independent,

then PDE solution $P(t,x,\xi)$ is also going to be linear in ξ, and the diffusion term in the PDE can be computed correctly even without a ξ-axis.[15]

These conditions suffice for a linear floater resetting discretely, proportionally to an index, possibly with a lookback, but without caps or floors. In this case, we can put $\xi \equiv c$. Although the coupon rate c seems to be a function of past rates, the above conditions guarantee that the price is linear in ξ, and the ξ-axis is not required. Therefore, discrete resets as well as lookbacks often found in floaters and ARMs would not call for additional pricing dimensions themselves—if they were not capped or floored, and the coupon did not affect prepayments.

Here is why this simplification is theoretically possible and how a single-dimension finite-difference grid can be used to price linear floaters. In the presence of additional state variable ξ, pricing PDE (2) should be modified to include the drift term for ξ (note that no new diffusion term arises since ξ is not a "factor"):

$$r + \text{OAS} = \frac{1}{P}\frac{\partial P}{\partial t} + \frac{1}{P}(c+\lambda) - \lambda + \frac{1}{P}\frac{\partial P}{\partial x}\mu + \frac{1}{2P}\frac{\partial^2 P}{\partial x^2}\sigma^2 + \frac{1}{P}\frac{\partial P}{\partial \xi}\mu_\xi \qquad (7)$$

Two following main statements justify valuation without an ξ-axis:

[15] All these conditions are listed for illustration only; some of them could be relaxed.

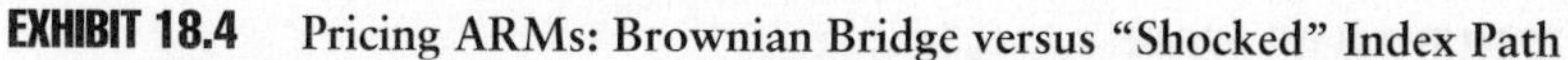

EXHIBIT 18.4 Pricing ARMs: Brownian Bridge versus "Shocked" Index Path

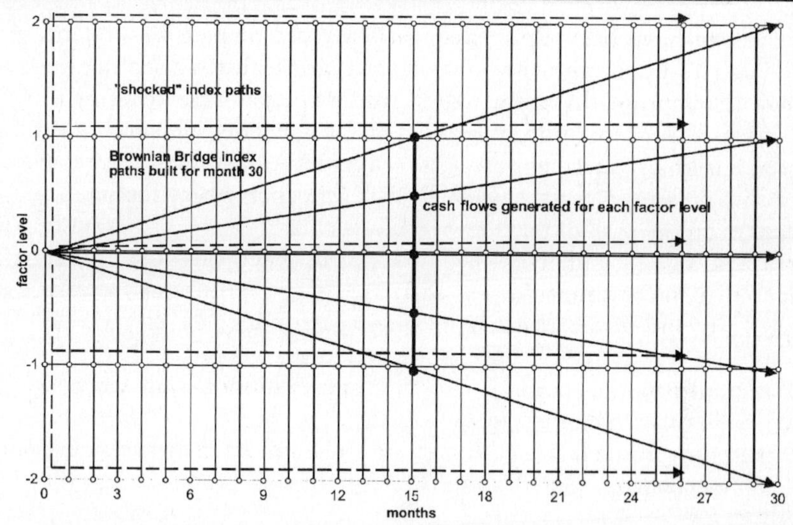

1. The diffusion term in PDE (7) can be correctly computed on a factor-only grid even if the pricing nodes have differing values of ξ: The linearity conditions exclude any price convexity with respect to ξ.
2. If ξ is centered (i.e., set to its conditional mean path), then the drift term μ_ξ by definition is equal to zero.

Let us assume that the underlying term structure model is Gaussian. This means that we can find the mean rate of any maturity measured at any instance of time between the pricing date and the node date. This problem is known as constructing the *Brownian bridge* and is well covered in stochastic calculus.[16] In particular this concept helps us find the mean coupon by just looking at the index rate at two nodes, the initial and the current. For example, let us consider a floater indexed to a market rate and resetting in month 15 (counted from today). In order to meet condition 2 above, all pricing nodes of the finite-difference grid located, say, 30 months from now, employ the Brownian bridge's mean path for the floater's index built between now and month 30. This allows for the computation of the mean index rate for month 15 (the last reset, shown in bold on Exhibit 18.4[17]). Of course, nodes having different factor levels at

[16] See, for example, I. Karatsas and S. Shreve, *Brownian Motion and Stochastic Calculus*, Second Edition (New York: Springer, 1991).

[17] The exact shape of the mean index path may depend on the term structure specifications.

month 30 will get different expected index levels for month 15, and therefore different expected coupon rates (c). This coupon is then used to compute the interest cash flow at every pricing node. The factor-only grid will ultimately result in the same price as a two-dimensional grid built for both factor and coupon index—thanks to the linearity conditions. This method can be used for valuation of regular floaters, ARMs with rare uncapped resets or with prepayment penalties, rolling CDs, and similar instruments.

Unfortunately, most mortgage instruments are prepayable, and the redemption rate λ is a function of coupon rate c, clearly violating the linearity concept. Fortunately, most ARMs reset at least once a year with essential periodic caps and floors. These actual features reduce the coupon path-dependence as well as pricing errors when either the EIRS method or the Crank-Nicholson method is used directly. The cash flow for all grid points is constructed "naturally" forward: For each pricing node, the factor level is assumed to match one for the shocked initial term structure (see Exhibit 18.4). Exhibit 18.5 depicts a typical pricing error profile for G2AR6.5 ARM using three, single-dimension, finite-difference methods. As seen, the 1-year CMT coupon is not a strong source of path-dependence as the valuation errors for both the EIRS scheme and the Crank-Nicholson scheme are within the practical trading tolerance. Yet, more robust results and a slight accuracy improvement are achieved when complementing the EIRS method with a monthly-resetting control variate (i.e., formally eliminating any path-dependence).

EXHIBIT 18.5 Pricing Errors for G2AR6.5

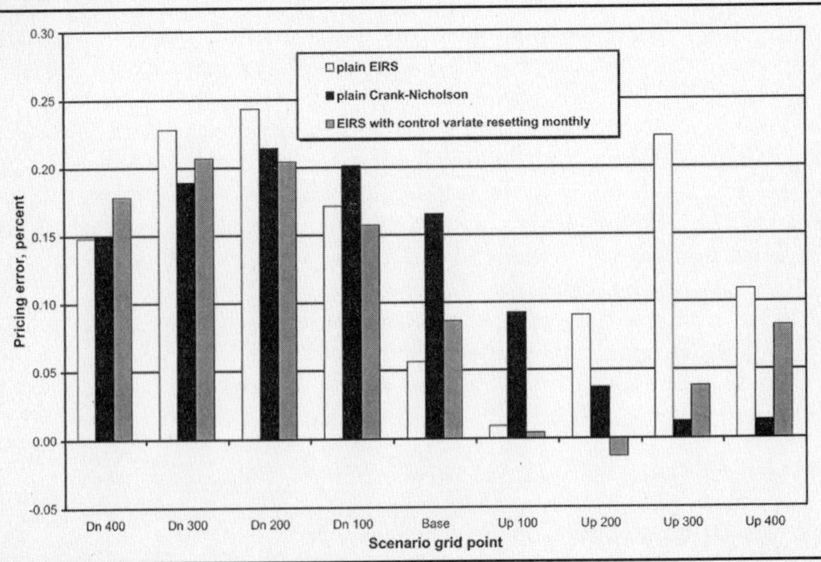

CONCLUSIONS

We have demonstrated that some sources of mortgage path-dependence are spurious and can be avoided via a simple problem transformation; others can be "cured" by a proper model selection. The most notable example is illustrated with the burnout modeling: Decomposing the mortgage pool into two path-independent components, "active" and "passive," properly simulates the burnout effect and enables using regular finite-difference pricing methods. Finally, for a "non-curable" path-dependencies, we have considered employing the EIRS method complemented by a specially constructed control variate correction and achieved a suitable trading approximation while retaining all structural and computational advantages of finite-difference schemes. We have also found that the coupon reset provisions found in typical ARMs do not cause strong path-dependence.

The results of our study suggest that most non-CMO mortgage instruments and even some CMOs can be efficiently priced on low-dimensional finite-difference grids.

CHAPTER 19

The Effect of Mean Reversion on the Valuation of Embedded Options and OAS*

David Audley
Consultant

Richard Chin
Consultant

Many bonds have embedded options. For example, many corporate and agency securities have embedded call options in which the investor effectively sells the right of early retirement to the issuer. Similarly, investors in mortgage-backed securities (MBSs) implicitly sell calls on the underlying collateral to home owners by granting the right to prepay their mortgages. In each case, for otherwise identical bonds, the investor expects to receive a higher yield on a callable bond as compensation for the short sale of the call option.

Option-adjusted spread (OAS) analysis assesses the value of such embedded options so as to provide investors with valuable insights concerning alternative securities. The OAS on a fairly priced bond is its average spread over the risk-free rate for a sample of possible interest rates. The risk-free rate is usually defined as the return on the on-the-run Treasury bonds. In simple terms, if a callable bond's OAS is lower

* This chapter is based on a research paper written by the authors while employed by Prudential Securities.

than its underlying credit and liquidity spread, it is rich and the investor is not being compensated for the risk of shorting the call. If the computed OAS is higher than the underlying credit spread, it is attractively priced. However, this simple rule is complicated by the fact that OASs are not the product of a fixed formula. Rather, OASs vary depending on the underlying assumptions made in a particular OAS model. One of the variables that affects these calculations is the interest rate model on which the OASs are based. The interest rate model itself is affected by the presence or absence of a mean-reversion feature.

In this chapter we demonstrate the effect that mean reversion has on the valuation of embedded options and, consequently, on the calculation of OASs.

WHAT IS MEAN REVERSION

The modeling of future possibilities for interest rates is central to OAS analysis. This is a process of simulating uncertain future events. The level of uncertainty is termed randomness and the key issue is specifying how random the future can be. As an example, Exhibit 19.1 shows three sets of random interest-rate paths (scenarios). Each starts at 5% and varies widely across 10 periods. In time periods 3 and 10, the interest rate path declines to 0% while other random paths lead to interest rates as high as 40%. Given what we know of American economic and political systems today, an average interest rate of 0%, 40%, or even 100% is possible, but the probability is so remote that it may be considered negligible.

EXHIBIT 19.1 Random Interest-Rate Paths without Mean Reversion

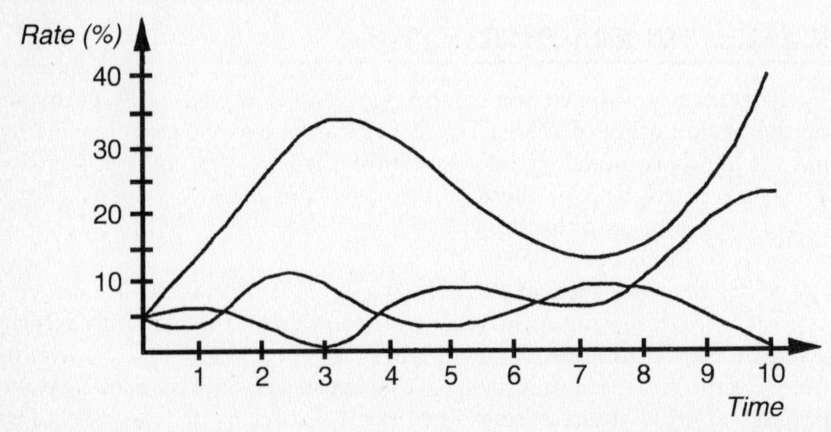

EXHIBIT 19.2 Interest-Rate Paths with Mean Reversion

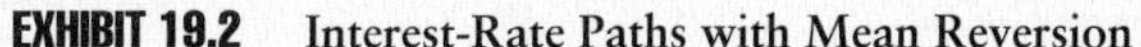

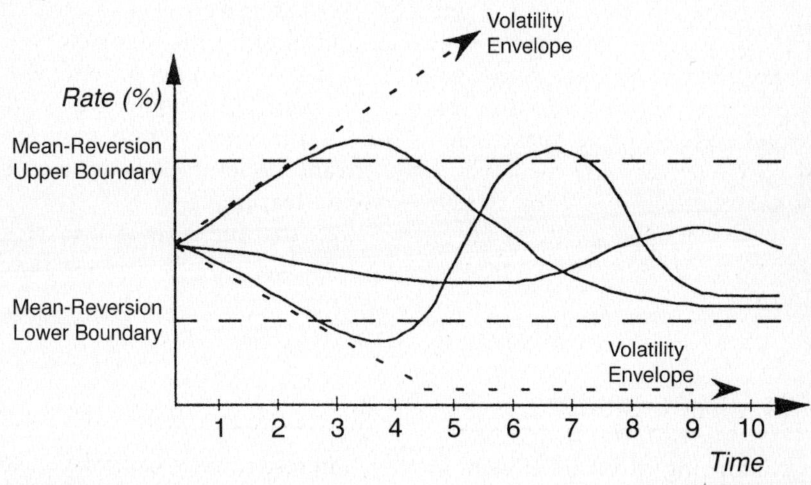

Guarding against possibly unrealistic levels of interest rates is the value and essence of mean reversion. As randomly generated interest-rate levels are produced, an interest rate model that includes mean reversion "bends" the scenarios back inside some reasonable range of rates. Thus, as the name implies, the results revert toward the mean interest rate. Exhibit 19.2 provides a graphic representation of this process. Note that rates fluctuate within a much narrower band than would exist within the envelope shown for a specified level of volatility.

HOW DOES MEAN REVERSION RELATE TO OAS?

The presence or absence of a mean-reversion feature has a direct impact on the computation of OASs. This is because one of the steps in generating the OASs is modeling interest rate paths over the life of a security. The characterization of these future rates can directly affect the projected cash flows and the value of any embedded put or call options. As an example, consider MBSs.

MBSs are one type of security whose cash flows are interest-rate contingent. Decreasing or increasing interest rates may result in accelerating or decelerating prepayment rates. As the first step in calculating the OAS of an MBS, interest rate paths are generated and used as proxies for monthly interest rates on new 30-year mortgages. With that information, a prepayment model can determine the likelihood that some portion of the home owners will pay off their outstanding mortgages. Each of these monthly prepayment evaluations then may be used to project the expected cash flows and resultant yields for MBSs.

A mean-reversion feature in the rate-process model affects the generation of random interest rate paths, which in turn are used to predict future cash flows and yields. The yields themselves are the building blocks of OAS calculations.

PROBLEMS IN MODELING INTEREST RATE BEHAVIOR

The objective of OAS analysis is to evaluate a security over the range of interest rate environments that may occur over the life of the security. This raises two issues: (1) how to model interest rate movements and (2) how to ensure that the resulting hypothetical interest rate paths are consistent with reality (i.e., with actual historical rate behavior).

Modeling Interest Rate Movement

The first question is the more straightforward of the two. We can assign a probability distribution to possible interest rate changes over a given period and then use statistical methods to examine resulting interest rate behavior. For example, a widely used approach is Monte Carlo simulation. This involves using sequences of computer-generated random numbers that have the characteristics of the specified probability distribution to determine the changes in interest rates from period to period. Typically, a large number of hypothetical interest rate paths are generated to evaluate the effects of embedded options.

Are These Interest Rates Realistic?

Care must be taken to ensure that the set of interest rate paths generated is consistent with historical interest rate behavior. Even if the period-to-period changes are reasonable, it does not follow necessarily that the interest rate path as a whole is realistic. This seemingly contradictory result is a consequence of the statistical properties of random paths as they evolve over time.

For example, suppose that relative monthly changes in rates have the bell-shaped probability distribution known in statistics as the normal distribution. Suppose recent annualized volatilities for Treasury bill rates are about 15%. We then generate paths for the 6-month Treasury bill rate using monthly changes that display an annualized volatility of 15%. Exhibit 19.3 shows the range of possible Treasury bill rates that are obtained after a number of years, given an initial value of 8%. These ranges are within three standard deviations of the mean Treasury bill rate and, therefore, may be expected statistically to contain 99.9% of the possible outcomes.

While the range after one year is reasonable (rates have moved several hundred basis points) the range for longer periods is at odds with interest rate behavior in the United States. The highest value ever for the 6-month Treasury rates was about 18%, in 1981. The discrepancy between reality and the statistically generated interest rates reported in Exhibit 19.3 arises from the fact that this method of generation does not incorporate the economic or social pressures that are likely to influence interest rates when they reach historical highs or lows. Instead, it assumes that interest rates follow a random walk regardless of their level.

It is clear that to model interest rates in a realistic way, the statistical process has to be modified to incorporate the reversion forces that rates are likely to experience when they change dramatically. Such modifications are usually labeled "mean reversion" and their effect is to exert a downward pressure when rates are too high and an upward pressure when rates are too low. Before describing these modifications, we first discuss how mean reversion influences prices and rates in practice.

MEAN REVERSION IN PRICES AND INTEREST RATES

The basic force behind mean reversion is simply that of supply and demand. If the price of a commodity increases substantially, supply is likely to increase and demand is likely to decrease, causing downward pressure on the price. A striking example is provided by the price of silver in the early 1980s when the Hunt brothers tried to corner the market. As they caused the price to increase to record levels, unanticipated events began to occur. People all over the world began selling silver heirlooms, silver mines that had been closed because they were uneconomical were reopened and so on. This eventually caused a flood of new supply, prices declined dramatically, and the Hunts lost several billion dollars.

EXHIBIT 19.3 Range of 6-Month Treasury Bill Rates Generated without Mean Reversion

After 1 Year	5.1% to 12.5%
After 10 Years	1.9% to 33.2%
After 25 Years	0.8% to 75.9%
After 40 Years	0.5% to 138.0%

The Federal Reserve Bank strongly influences interest rates and is unlikely to allow rates to follow a random walk if they are not within acceptable limits. However, even if an activist central bank did not exist, the natural business cycle would dictate that rates have some built-in mean reversion. For example, suppose interest rates rise, which typically indicates that the business cycle is in a late expansion phase. If rates keep rising, the higher cost of borrowing reduces the demand for credit as businesses postpone plans for expansion and consumer spending declines. The reduced demand for credit eventually forces down interest rates. Similarly, once rates have declined sufficiently, the lower cost of borrowing spurs business expansion and consumer spending which, in turn, causes interest rates to increase.

While this is obviously a very simplistic description of modern business cycles, it does describe the basic underlying trends within which random movements in interest rates are likely to occur. To model interest rate behavior realistically, any statistical model used to generate interest rate paths should incorporate these likely trends.

INCORPORATING MEAN REVERSION IN THE INTEREST RATE PROCESS

There are many ways to incorporate mean reversion in the rate generation process. In general, the objective is to apply a downward trend when rates are high and an upward trend when rates are low. Around these trends, interest rate movements are still random and recognize the myriad, unpredictable forces that affect them. In this section, we describe a modeling philosophy used in the interest rate process models found at one dealer firm.

For MBS, explicit generation of interest rate scenarios drives the prepayment model. The model assumes that month-to-month proportional changes in interest rates have a bell-shaped frequency distribution with a specified volatility. More precisely, the rates are lognormally distributed. Within a specified range, rates are allowed to follow a true random walk in which there are no obvious upward or downward trends caused by business cycles or other economic or social pressures. As illustrated in Exhibit 19.2, if rates go above this range, a downward trend is applied that is proportional to the square of the amount by which the rate exceeds the upper end of the range. There is a similar upward trend if rates go below the lower end of the range.

The rationale for this model is two-fold. First, interest rates do follow a random walk much of the time. It is only when they become too high or low that predetermined trends should be imposed. While it is not totally clear what is too high or too low, one can use historical data to set these bounds. Second, once rates do exceed these bounds, having mean reversion that is proportional to the square of the distance between the rate and boundary parallels many models of real-life phenomena. The end result of this process is an envelope of modeled interest rate paths that does not go below 2% to 3% at the lower end and does not exceed 22% to 25% at the upper end. The exact values for the lowest and highest possible values depend on the specified volatility of monthly changes in rates.

The case for corporate securities is slightly different. The contingency for the cash flows depends on the value of the security (e.g., the bond may be called at par after a certain date and the attractiveness of the issuer's exercise of the option depends on the embedded option's market price and call structure). Accordingly, we concentrate on modeling rates so that the bond price conforms to reality. As such, an interest rate model with mean reversion is selected so that the daily proportional price changes have a bell-shaped frequency distribution with a specified volatility. More precisely, the prices are lognormally distributed, while the underlying rate process model is selected so that its mean-reverting effect translates into appropriate price and yield behavior across the term structure.

EFFECT OF MEAN REVERSION ON OAS

Incorporating mean reversion in an interest rate model that is then used to compute OASs has a pervasive effect on the calculations. The OASs on most types of securities differ depending on the presence or absence of mean reversion. This occurs because mean reversion reduces the long-term volatility displayed by the sample interest rate paths. While the month-to-month changes still have the specified volatility, the range of possible values that rates can take over time is reduced. For example, after 25 years, the range of possible values without mean reversion shown in Exhibit 19.3 is 1% to 76%. Using the model with mean reversion, the range is between 3% and about 25%.

Exhibit 19.4 shows OASs and option costs. The option cost measures the cost to the investor of interest rate volatility. It is approximately equal to the difference between the traditional spread to Treasuries and the OASs on three types of securities with embedded options: fixed-rate mortgage-backed passthroughs, adjustable-rate mortgage passthroughs (ARMS), and callable corporate bonds. Representative securities are chosen from each group. The two corporates are not actual issues but are typical of newly issued callable 10-year and 30-year bonds. The following are a few of the the specific effects shown:

- OASs on callable bonds usually are higher with mean reversion because the reduction in overall volatility tends to reduce the calculated values of embedded options. The stronger the mean reversion, the higher the OAS, all other things being equal.
- The impact of mean reversion largely depends on the average life or maturity of the security, since the difference between interest rate paths generated with and without mean reversion increases over time. Longer-term bonds exhibit the greatest differences in OAS with mean reversion. Another important factor is the degree and nature of the interest rate contingency of the security's cash flows.
- For fixed-rate mortgage passthroughs, OASs decrease between 5 and 12 basis points if mean reversion is removed from the interest rate process. For the three passthroughs shown in Exhibit 19.4, the FNMA 9 is affected most since it has the longest average life. Although the premium FNMA 12 has a shorter average life than the discount FNMA 8, it is affected slightly more by the lack of mean reversion due to its greater prepayment volatility.
- Because of their coupon caps, the OASs on ARMs are affected more than fixed-rate passthroughs. A wider dispersion of interest rate paths means that when the ARM is capped out, there is a greater loss of potential coupon interest relative to a similar but uncapped ARM.
- The OAS on the 10-year corporate bond changes by about the same amount as the fixed-rate passthroughs, reflecting their similar average lives. As expected, the longer corporate is affected more and the OAS declines by 23 basis points. The call premiums (with the call price starting at 106 in 1995 and declining to 100 over 15 years) mitigate the effect of not having mean reversion. If the call price is always par, then the lack of mean reversion reduces the OAS by 29 basis points.

The specified volatility also affects the impact of mean reversion. The higher the volatility, the greater the divergence between the interest rate paths generated with and without mean reversion. For example, for the 30-year callable corporate, the difference in OASs is 23 basis points at a 15% short-term rate volatility, as shown in Exhibit 19.4. At a 10% volatility, the difference is only 8 basis points, while at a 20% volatility the difference increases to 46 basis points.

These results are obviously for a particular type of interest rate process and form of mean reversion. However, the general conclusions hold for any rate or mean-reversion process. The lack of mean reversion leads to a wider dispersion of interest rate paths than may be realistically expected in the United States and this, in turn, tends to overstate the effect of embedded options in fixed-income securities.

EXHIBIT 19.4 OASs of Securities with and without Mean Reversion

			With Mean Reversion		Without Mean Reversion	
	Price	Rem. Term (Yrs.)	OAS (bps)	Opt. Cost (bps)	OAS (bps)	Opt. Cost (bps)
MBS Passthroughs						
FNMA 8%	90-06	22-00	95	13	89	19
FNMA 9%	93-26	29-08	91	26	81	36
FNMA 12%	105-28	21-10	100	32	92	40
ARM Passthroughs						
FHLMC 7.5, Resets 5/91, Caps 2/13.5	98-25	30-00	97	56	77	76
FHLMC 9.25, Reset 5/91, Caps 1/15.25	101-05	30-00	133	35	112	56
Callable Corporates						
AA, Mat. 5/00, Cpn. = 10% Callable @ 100 from 5/95	100	10-00	42	54	33	63
AAA, Mat. 5/20, Cpn. = 10% Callable @ 106 in 5/95, Call price declines to 100 in 5/10	100	30-00	38	62	15	85

Analysis assumes a 15% per annum short-rate volatility and is based on closing prices and Treasury yield curve of Thrusday May 3, 1990. The two ARM passthroughs shown have coupons that reset annually at 200 basis points over the one-year Treasury, subject to the periodic coupon-change cap and life cap shown.

CONCLUSIONS

The valuation of embedded options and option-adjusted spreads is a complex mathematical process whose results are strongly dependent on the fundamental assumptions on which the model is based. Before an investor can apply these results usefully, it is almost a prerequisite to have an understanding of the factors that can influence the values that a model produces. An investor needs to be aware of the subtle, or perhaps not so subtle, effects that particular interest rate models can have before making investment decisions based on any one specific value of OAS. In short, the investor needs to determine whether this broadly used valuation metric is generated with or without the mean reversion process. This provides a good deal of insight as to how much of the answer is explained by scenarios that are highly divergent from the expected course of future interest rates.

index